THE CARIBBEAN ENVIRONMENT

THE CARIBBEAN ENVIRONMENT

Geography for the CXC

MARK WILSON

Queen's College, Barbados

Editorial adviser:

Vena Jules, Faculty of Education, The University of the West Indies, St Augustine, Trinidad

OXFORD UNIVERSITY PRESS

CONTENTS

PREFACE

This book has been written for students taking the Caribbean Examinations Council Geography examination. It covers all aspects of the syllabus – landforms, climate, vegetation, soils, agriculture, industry, and settlement. Extensive use is made of examples and case studies from the Caribbean; there are also studies of contrasting areas in North America, Nigeria, Japan, Switzerland and India.

Throughout the book there is an emphasis on the interrelationships between human and physical geography and on the relevance of geography to problems of economic and social development, resource use, and conservation. Many of the case studies relate to practical problems in these areas.

The organisation of the text encourages students to learn from the interpretation of maps, statistical tables, photographs and diagrams. The questions and exercises emphasise the student's active role in the learning process.

ACKNOWLEDGEMENTS

In researching and writing this book I have received a tremendous amount of help from family, friends, colleagues, and professionals in many fields. I am very grateful for this help, and in particular I would like to thank:

Mr Michael Morrissey of the University of the West Indies, Mona, Jamaica, Miss Y. Burke, Mrs J. Foster, Mr J. Hopkin, Miss M. Hunte, Miss J. Ottley, Mrs R. Mauro, Mrs D. Pile, Dr R. Potter, Miss P. Ruddell, Miss K. Thompson, Mr H. Burton of the Caribbean Meteorological Institute, Mr B. Chakilall of the Caribbean Conservation Association, and Mr N. Sealy of Barbados Water Authority for reading and commenting on sections of the manuscript.

Paddy and Deirdre O'Callaghan, Edna Dawson, Carmen Latty, Vivalyn Latty-Scott and Robert Lee for providing help with accommodation and transport in Jamaica and Trinidad.

The librarians at Barbados Central Bank, the Canadian High Commissions in London and Bridgetown, the City Business Library in London, the FAO office in Bridgetown, the Planning Institute of Jamaica, the United States Information Service in Bridgetown and the University of the West Indies for help in tracking down statistical and other information.

Mapps College, Barbados for use of their photocopying machine.

Of the many people and organisations who gave advice and information, I would like to give special thanks to those listed below for their help with particular chapters:

Chapter 3: Seismic Research Unit, U.W.I.; Dr M. Hendry.

Chapter 5: Barbados Water Authority; Audio-visual aids department, Barbados.

Chapter 7: Caribbean Meteorological Institute; Barbados Meteorological Service.

Chapter 10: Forestry Division and Physical Planning Unit, St Lucia; Earthscan.

Chapter 11: Belize Fisheries Department.

Chapter 12: Dr S. Bennet; Mr V. Bissessar; Dixie Farms Ltd; Scott Fraser; French Agricultural Mission, St Lucia; Geest Industries (WI) Ltd; Pine Hill Dairy; Mr S. Ramoutar; Winban.

Chapter 13: BIDCO, Guyana; ISCOTT; Jamaica Bauxite Institute; Japanese Information Centre, London; Ministry of Energy and Natural Resources, Trinidad and Tobago; Plipdeco; Primo Catelli; St Vincent Children's Wear; Trintoc.

Chapter 14: Caribbean Tourism Research Centre; Swiss National Tourist Office.

Chapter 15: Ministry of Housing and Construction, Statistical Institute, Town and Country Planning Department, and Urban Development Corporation, Jamaica; Town Planning Department, St Vincent; Dr E. Kirby; Miss J. Semple; Japanese Information Centre, London.

Chapter 16: Mr L. Honychurch.

In a book of this sort it is not possible to list all the written sources of information used. However, the following were particularly useful in the preparation of certain sections:

Simon Fass, *The economics of survival: A study of poverty and planning in Haiti*, USAID, 1980.

Geological Society of Jamaica, *Proceedings of VI Bauxite Symposium*, March, 1985.

Kingston Harbour Research Project, *The Pollution Ecology of Kingston Harbour*, U.W.I., 1975.

Proceedings of Caribbean Geological Conferences.

The following textbooks provide useful background material, and are recommended for further reading:

J.A. Hocking and N.R. Thomson, *Land and Water Resources of West Africa*, Moray House, Edinburgh.

M.J. Selby, *Earth's Changing Surface*, Oxford University Press.

N. Sealey, *Tourism in the Caribbean*, Hodder & Stoughton.

C.C. Weir, *Caribbean Soils*, Heinemann.

The publishers and author would also like to thank the following for the use of photographs in the book (those not listed were taken by the author):

I should add that any errors, major or minor, are the sole responsibility of the author.

1 • THE CARIBBEAN ENVIRONMENT

1.1 A Caribbean landscape

The photograph on this page shows a Caribbean landscape.

In the landscape, there are:

- *Natural* features, like mountains, forests, and the sea.
- *Human* features, like buildings, roads, and cultivated crops.

1 List ten of the features in this landscape in your exercise book.

2 Which of the features on your list are natural, and which are human?

3 Are any of the features difficult to classify in this way?

4 Have you listed any features which have nothing to do with geography?

All the different features of the landscape affect each other. Each feature is influenced by its *environment.*

5 Make a list of the main features of the environment which affect:
(a) The growth of a tree.
(b) The site of the village.

6 How does each of these two features affect the rest of the landscape?

The people living in the village also depend on their environment.

7 In what way might they need to make use of:
(a) The forest?
(b) The road?
(c) The soil?
(d) The sea?

1.1 A Caribbean landscape.

1.2 Resources

Resources are features of the environment which can be used by human society. Figure 1.2 is a painting of an old Amerindian settlement.

1 In this settlement, what resources are used:
   (a) For food?
   (b) For building materials?
2 How many of these resources could be found within a few kilometres of the settlement?

The early inhabitants of the Caribbean had a very good understanding of some aspects of their environment, and of some of the resources around them. They knew a great deal about the wild plants which grow here, and about which ones were useful for food or as medicines. They were efficient cultivators who could grow cassava and sweet potato. As fishermen, they had a lot of practical knowlege about the winds and ocean currents, and about when and where to fish.

But there were other resources which they did not know how to use. They did not know how to refine or work metals. They might find a patch of red clay, but they would have no idea that it was bauxite, which could be used to make aluminium for cooking pots or window frames. As the Amerindians did not know how to use bauxite, it was not really a resource for them; nor were iron ore, petroleum, or natural gas.

3 List some other resources which the Amerindians would not have known how to use.

A present-day community uses a much wider range of different resources to meet its needs.

4 List the resources needed to build:
   (a) An Arawak house.
   (b) A modern house.
5 Is either of your lists complete, or could more items be added?
6 Classify the resources on each list into three groups:
   (a) Local resources, from within a few kilometres.
   (b) Regional resources, from elsewhere in the Caribbean.
   (c) World resources, from outside the Caribbean.
7 Write a few sentences explaining:
   (a) Why an Arawak settlement was an almost self-contained community.
   (b) Why a modern community depends on national, regional, and international trade.

We are able to make use of a wide range of different resources because modern society possesses these advantages:

- It is *organised* in a way which makes it possible for a large number of people to work together in many different places, so as to produce something useful and make sure that it is in the right place at the right time.
- It has the *technology* to use resources like bauxite and petroleum.

In most parts of the Caribbean, good use of a wide range of resources means that people have a higher *standard of living* than ever before.

But in some places, even though the technology is there to develop and make use of natural resources, ordinary people probably live less well than the Arawak villagers of several centuries ago.

Classifying resources

There are many different types of resource. These include:

- Mineral resources, like bauxite.
- Climatic resources, like rainfall.

1.2 An Amerindian settlement.

1.3 The effects of deforestation in Haiti.

- Water resources, such as rivers.
- Soil resources, for agriculture.
- Biotic resources, like fish and wild plants.
- Locational resources: a place which is well situated.

And there are many others.

If a group of people is *organised* so that they can work together to make good use of the resources available; and if they have a high level of *technology* and a good understanding of their environment – then they are sometimes said to have good *human resources*.

Renewable and non-renewable resources

Climatic resources are *renewable* resources.

If rain falls and provides moisture for crops to grow during one year, it does not mean that there will be less rain available the next year.

8 Which other resources are renewable?

Mineral resources are non-renewable resources. If oil is extracted from the ground, it will not be replaced. We are using up a reserve of oil that has been built up over several million years. Sooner or later, the oilfield will be *exhausted*.

9 Which other resources are non-renewable?

Non-renewable resources provide an opportunity for human society. But they must be used wisely and not wasted.

Oil is one of the world's most important resources. It was estimated in 1985 that:

- The world's total proven reserves of oil were 96,000 million tonnes.
- Oil production was 2,800 million tonnes per year.

10 If production continues at the present rate, how long will it be before today's proven reserves are used up?

Of course there are enormous 'probable' and 'possible' reserves of oil which have not been thoroughly investigated; there is a great deal of oil in the earth's crust waiting to be discovered. But think carefully about the following questions.

11 At the moment there is a 'glut' of oil. Too much is being produced, and prices are very low. Can this situation last?

12 If oil reserves start to run out, what effect will this have on:
(a) The transport system?
(b) Oil prices?
(c) Countries which produce oil for export?

Renewable resources will not run out, but they must also be used carefully.

A forest is a renewable resource. If a single tree is cut down, then another can be grown to replace it. But when all the trees are removed, then the other aspects of the environment are affected.

Figure 1.3 shows a landscape where most of the trees have been cut down. The area has been deforested.

13 How has the environment been damaged?

14 How might this affect people living in the area?

If renewable resources are used unwisely on a large scale, the results cannot be predicted in advance, and may be extremely serious. Figure 1.3 shows a small area, but we may now be damaging the environment on a much larger scale. Many scientists think that human activities have altered the world's climate, making droughts much more common in Africa and elsewhere, and causing the Sahara Desert to spread southwards.

If resources are misused, then the consequences for human society are disastrous. If they are used wisely, they provide us with the opportunities for economic and social development.

1.3 The Caribbean Nations

Figure 1.4 gives some information about the countries which are included in the Caribbean region for CXC Geography, and about some countries outside the region.

1 Take a blank outline map of the Caribbean, and use your atlas to mark in all the Caribbean countries.
2 Copy Figure 1.4 into your exercise book, and add extra columns to show:
   (a) The capital of each country.
   (b) Which countries are independent.
   (c) Which countries are in Caricom.
   (d) The main language of each Caribbean country.
3 Which Caribbean country has:
   (a) The largest area?
   (b) The largest population?
4 Add up the population of the countries in each language group. Which is the most widely spoken language in the Caribbean?

The countries of the Caribbean are very different in character; but they also have many points in common:

- Most of the population lives within a few kilometres of the sea. International trade, shipping, and tourism are all important for the Caribbean.
- They have all at some time been European possessions, and have also been strongly influenced by the USA.
- Their economies have in the past been based on exporting tropical crops like sugar and bananas to Europe and the USA.
- Many people are descended from African slaves or Indian indentured labourers who were brought in to grow these crops.

	Area (km^2)	Population (thousand)	Population density (persons per sq km)
Anguilla	88	9	102
Antigua and Barbuda	440	79	180
The Bahamas	13,935	226	16
Barbados	431	252	585
Belize	22,965	156	7
Cayman Islands	259	19	95
Cuba	110,861	9,992	90
Dominica	751	77	103
Dominican Republic	48,734	6,102	125
Grenada	344	112	326
Guadeloupe	1,779	331	186
Guyana	214,969	936	4
Haiti	27,750	5,185	186
Jamaica	10,991	2,290	208
Martinique	1,102	327	297
Montserrat	98	13	133
Netherlands Antilles	961	260	271
Puerto Rico	8,897	3,404	383
St Christopher and Nevis	306	44	144
St Lucia	616	126	205
St Vincent and the Grenadines	388	104	268
Trinidad and Tobago	5,130	1,105	215
Turks and Caicos Islands	430	8	19
Virgin Islands (UK)	153	13	85
Virgin Islands (US)	342	103	301

Source: UN Demographic Yearbook, 1984.

1.4 The countries of the Caribbean.

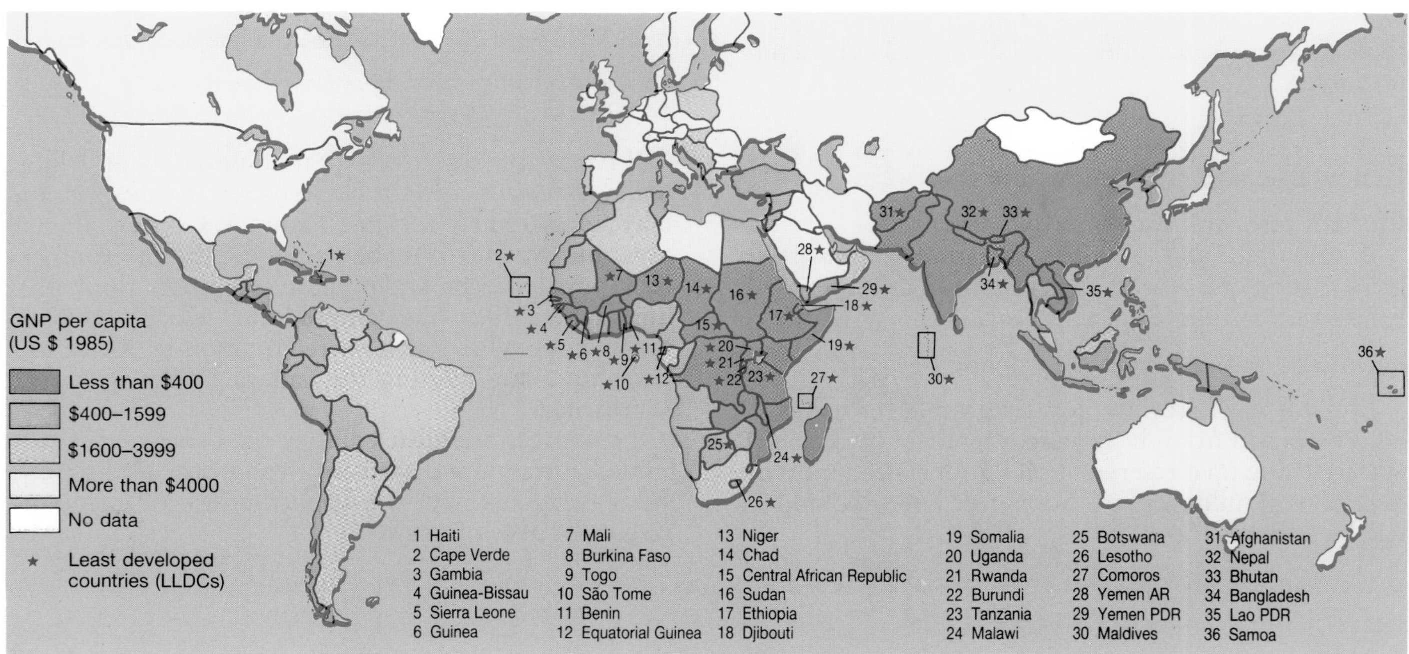

1.5 World patterns of economic development.

- Most countries are now politically independent, and there is a strong trend towards economic and cultural independence as well.

The Caribbean in the world

Look at Figure 1.4. Compared with most countries, even the larger Caribbean nations are small in *area* and in *population*, although there are also some very small nations in other parts of the world.

The Caribbean countries depend on international trade, and they are very strongly influenced by the world outside, particularly by events in the United States, Western Europe, and Japan. Many of the goods people buy, and the television programmes they watch, and much of the music they listen to, is from outside the region. Even the most successful Caribbean economies can get into trouble because of changes in the world price of oil, or of bauxite or sugar; or because of movements in the pound–dollar exchange rate, and so on. These changes are brought about by decisions and events in Washington, London, and Tokyo, rather than Kingston, Georgetown, or Port of Spain.

But although the Caribbean has a small population, it has also been a significant influence on the world outside:

- Caribbean nations play an important part in the UN and other international bodies.
- There are big communities of Caribbean origin in the UK, the USA, Canada, Europe, and Latin America. The Caribbean has influenced the culture and way of life of these countries.
- Many Caribbean musicians, sportsmen, economists, scientists, and writers now have an international reputation.

1.4 Economic development

The world is often divided into More Developed Countries and Less Developed Countries:

- In the More Developed Countries, industry, agriculture and social services are well established. Wages are relatively high, and most people have a reasonable income. These countries are sometimes called industrial countries.
- In the Less Developed Countries, there is less modern industry. Social services like health care and education are not available to many people. There are many small farmers, who earn a low income. The towns are growing rapidly, because people move there in search of a better life; but living conditions in the towns can be very bad indeed, because there are not enough jobs to go round. This group of countries is sometimes called the 'Third World'.

The 'Gross National Product per person' is a rough measure of how productive the economy of a country is. In a country with a high average GNP, the average person buys many goods and services; in a country with a low average GNP, most people have less money to spend. But it is important to remember that these figures may not give a very good idea of how most people live, because:

- In most 'rich' countries there are many people who do not have enough money, and who have to worry about basic necessities like food, health care, and housing.
- Even in the poorest countries, a few people are very wealthy indeed. This means that many of the others must have much less than the average to spend. But even in these countries, there are some modern industries and farms, which may be economically successful.

In reality, it is not always so easy to draw a line between the More Developed and Less Developed countries. There are many 'middle-income' countries which do not fit easily into either group.

In the Caribbean, there are:

- Some countries where the standard of living has increased rapidly, and which may soon be grouped with the More Developed countries.
- Many countries where there has been some development in industry and agriculture, but where unemployment is still high, and wages are much lower than in the More Developed countries.
- One country, Haiti, which is one of the world's poorest nations.

1 Figure 1.5 shows one way of grouping the economies of the world:
   (a) List five high-income countries.
   (b) List five 'least developed' countries.
   (c) List five middle-income countries.

There is no easy 'recipe' for economic, social and cultural development. In this book, you will learn a little about some of the approaches that have been taken in the Caribbean and elsewhere by people who are trying to promote development. But you should remember that this is a very complex topic, and one in which there are no simple answers.

2 · USING MAPS

2.1 Satellite photographs

Figure 2.1 is a satellite picture of an island in the Bahamas. It was made using information from a satellite called Landsat. Landsat takes in visible light and infra-red radiation, and transmits electronic messages about what it 'sees' back to earth. On earth, computers use these messages to produce a picture we can understand. Landsat orbits around the earth 14 times a day; every part of the earth's surface is covered by a Landsat picture once every nine days.

This is a *false-colour* picture. It has been processed so that:

- Vegetation looks red.
- Healthy vegetation which is growing well looks deep red. Less healthy plants have a paler colour.
- Clear, deep water looks very dark blue or black.
- Water containing sand or sediment, or which is very shallow, looks pale blue.
- Buildings and roads look blue-grey in colour.
- Beach sand looks white.
- Bare soil and rocks look blue, yellow, or brown, depending on what they are made of and how wet they are.

2.1 Satellite photograph of the Bahamas Platform.

1 Find a map of the Bahamas in your atlas:
   (a) What is the name of the island in the picture?
   (b) How long is the island?
   (c) What is the name of the island whose tip can be seen in the top right-hand corner of the picture?
2 Make a sketch map of the island and the sea around it. Do not show the clouds. Show:
   (a) The coastline.
   (b) An area of deep, clear water.
   (c) Areas where the water is shallow or contains sand and sediment.
   (d) The areas where there is most vegetation.
   (e) An approximate scale, to show the size of the island.
   (f) The names of any other places you can identify.
3 Make a list of what you have learnt about the island from:
   (a) The satellite picture.
   (b) Your atlas.
4 Say whether an atlas or satellite picture would be most useful for each of these purposes:
   (a) Finding out which country a town with a big sports competition is in.
   (b) Measuring the distance to a city overseas where you have friends or relatives.
   (c) Estimating the size of an area where crops have been damaged by a serious drought.
   (d) Finding out about a country where you have a pen-friend.
   (e) Finding out how much new construction has taken place around a large city over a two-year period.

Figure 7.32 on page 100 is another type of satellite picture. It shows weather conditions in the Caribbean, the Atlantic, and North America on 6 December 1986. Pictures like this can be seen on the television in many Caribbean countries every day. They are used to help in forecasting the weather.

The satellite photograph shows a larger area than the Landsat picture. The individual Caribbean islands look very small. A large area has to be included in a picture like this because it is used to watch the development of weather systems which are several hundred kilometres across. A Landsat picture would show only a small part of a big weather system.

2.2 Using an atlas

Map projections

If you compare the weather picture with a *small-scale* map of the Caribbean and North America in your atlas, you will see that the shapes of the countries near the edge of the photograph look different. This is because the earth is round. In a *flat* photograph of a *curved* surface, the shapes on the surface will be distorted because they are not being seen directly from above. Atlas maps are distorted, too, because they try to show a curved surface on a flat sheet of paper. All atlas maps use a projection which changes the shape and size of the countries they cover.

Figure 2.2 is drawn on Mercator's projection. Countries which are near the poles look larger than they really are. Figure 2.3 is on an *equal-area* projection. The shape of the countries near the poles is distorted, but they are all the right size.

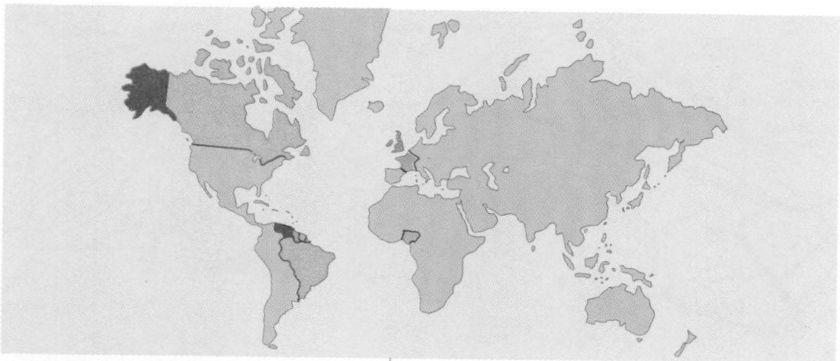

2.2 Mercator's projection.

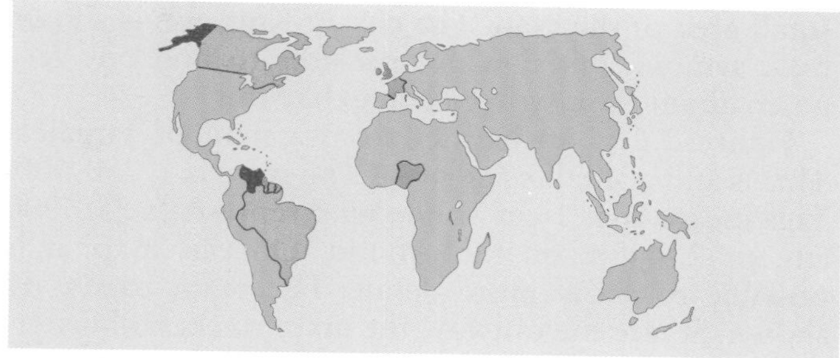

2.3 An equal area projection.

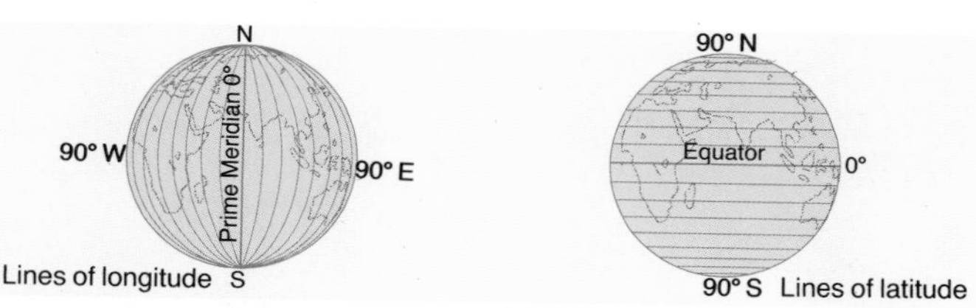

2.4 Lines of latitude and longitude.

1 Use the two maps to compare the size of:
   (a) Brazil and Canada.
   (b) Venezuela and Alaska.
   (c) Guyana and the UK.
   (d) Nigeria and France.

On large-scale maps, which cover only a small area, shapes are still distorted, but the distortions are very slight, and would not be noticed by most people.

Latitude and longitude

It is often difficult to pick out the coastline on a weather photograph like the one in Section 7.10. For this reason, dots have been added to show where the coast is. It is an American map, so there are also dots to show the boundaries of the states of the USA.

There are also dots to show the lines of latitude and longitude. These are imaginary lines which can be used to pinpoint the location of any place on the earth. Figure 2.4 shows how these lines run on the surface of the earth.

- The equator is a line of latitude. It is latitude 0°.
- The other lines of latitude are all parallel to the equator.
- The north pole is at latitude 90° north. The south pole is at latitude 90° south.
- The lines of longitude are not parallel to each other. They meet at the poles.
- The line of longitude which runs through the old Royal Observatory at Greenwich in England is referred to as the Prime Meridian. It is at longitude 0°. It was chosen for historical reasons.
- The other lines of longitude are measured off so many degrees east or west of this line.
- Each degree of latitude and longitude is divided into sixty *minutes* (60′); and each minute is divided into sixty *seconds* (60″).
- A degree of latitude measures 111 km. A minute measures 1.85 km; and a second measures 31 m.
- Degrees, minutes, and seconds of longitude vary in size, depending on the distance from the poles.

Atlases have an index at the back, in which you can look up a place if you want to find where it is. In most atlases, the index will tell you what page to look on, and will give you the location of the place you need in degrees and minutes of latitude and longitude.

2 Find the latitude and longitude of:
   (a) Kingston, Jamaica.
   (b) Port of Spain, Trinidad.
   (c) London, UK.
   (d) Lagos, Nigeria.
   (e) New Delhi, India.
   (f) Tokyo, Japan.

3 Remembering that 1° of longitude measures 111 km, work out the distances:
   (a) From Kingston, Jamaica to Washington DC, USA.
   (b) From London, UK to Accra, Ghana.

2.3 Large-scale maps

Figure 2.5 is an extract from a small-scale atlas map of the Caribbean. The island of Jamaica covers a very small area of the map. The city of Kingston is shown by a symbol, but it is not possible to find out very much about the city from a map like this.

Figure 2.6 is an extract from a map of Jamaica. This is still a small-scale map. The scale is 1:250,000. This means that 1 cm on the map represents 250,000 cm, or 2.5 km, on the ground. On this map, it is possible to show more detail. The main roads are shown. So are the railway, the main rivers and water-courses. But the city still covers a very small area.

Figure 2.10 is a large-scale map of Kingston. Figure 2.9 is the key to this map. The scale is 1:50,000. One cm on the map represents 50,000 cm, or 0.5 km, on the ground. Two cm represents 1 km. Maps like these are very useful for geographers, because they give a lot of information about the landscape. They show natural and man-made features very clearly.

Knowing how to use maps like these is an important skill.

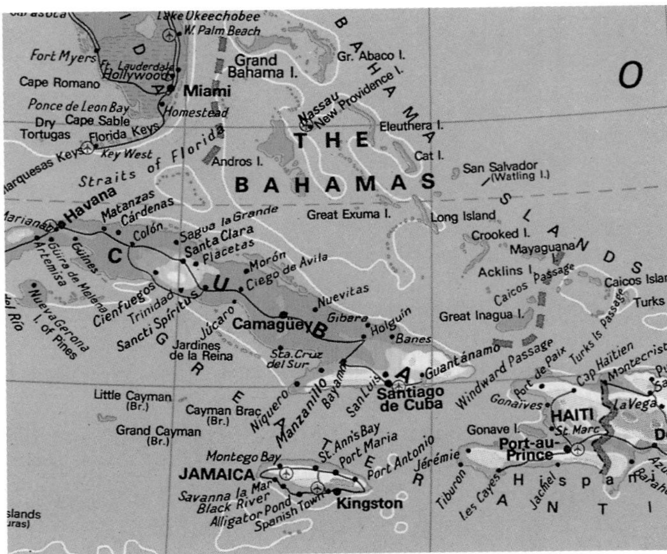

2.5 An atlas map showing Jamaica. 1:16 000 000

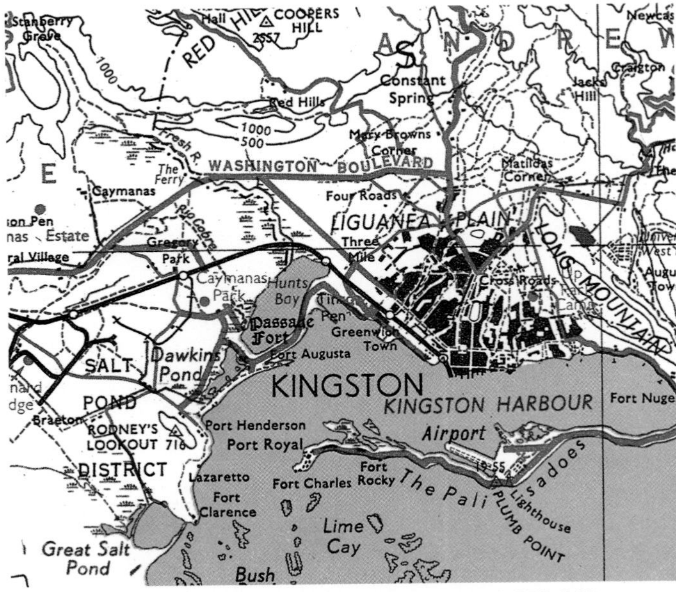

2.6 A small-scale map of Kingston, Jamaica. 1:250 000

2.4 Grid references and symbols

On a large scale map, lines of latitude and longitude are usually shown where they cross the margin; but it is much easier to use the *grid*.

The grid is made up of a series of blue lines which run north–south and east–west across the map. The distance between two grid lines is exactly 2 cm on the map and exactly 1 km on the ground. There is a two-figure number opposite the end of every grid line on the margin of the map.

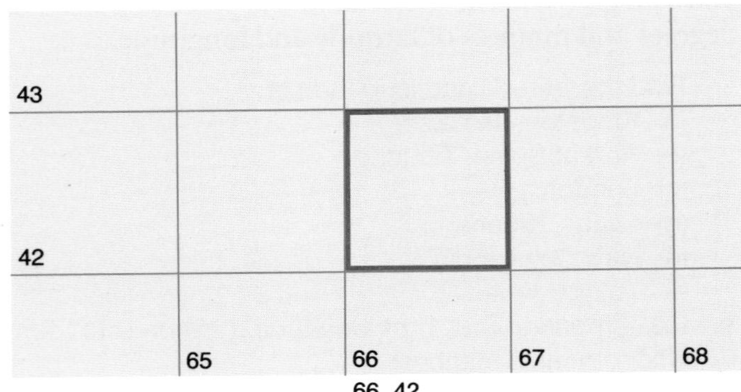

2.7 Using a four-figure reference to locate a kilometre square.

You can identify any 1 km square on the map by giving the number of the grid line to the *west*, and the number of the grid line to the *south* (see Figure 2.7). This is called a *four-figure* grid reference.

1 What places are in these grid squares on Figure 2.10?
   (a) 69 47.
   (b) 74 50.
   (c) 67 48.
   (d) 75 43.
   (e) What line of latitude is grid line 50 on?
   (f) What line of longitude is between grid line 67 and grid line 68?

You can give a more exact grid reference if you imagine that there is a smaller grid (see Figure 2.8) inside each 1-km grid square.

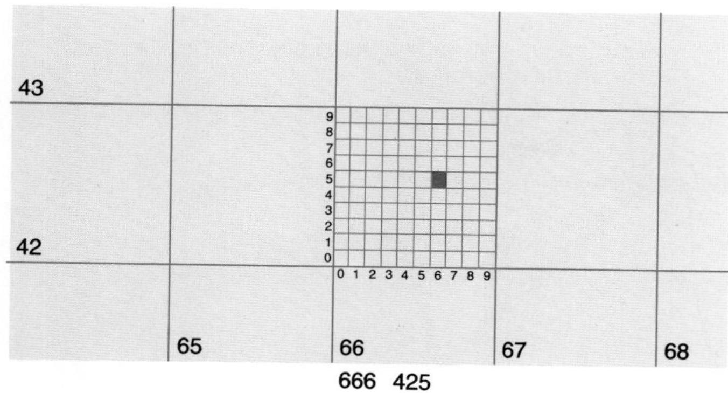

2.8 Using a six-figure reference to locate a 100 metre square.

The lines on the imaginary grid would be 2 mm apart on the map, or 100 m apart on the ground. Each of the imaginary small grid squares would measure 100 m × 100 m, and would have an area of exactly 1 ha. The square which has been shaded in has a *six-figure* grid reference, 666 425.

2 What letter of the alphabet is at each of these six-figure grid references on Figure 2.10?
   (a) 724 518.
   (b) 661 522.
   (c) 749 423.
   (d) 699 424.
   (e) 686 455.
   (f) 670 425.
   (g) 677 486.

- Grid lines which run north–south tell you how far east you have gone. They are called *eastings*.
- Grid lines which run east–west tell you how far north you have gone. They are called *northings*.

Symbols

The use of symbols and abbreviations is one way of packing as much information into a map as possible without making it hard to read:

- It takes up less space to write 'UC', instead of 'under construction'.
- Less room is needed to mark a Games Field or Playground like this ⍋ rather than write the words out in full.
- It is much easier to use a green background colour rather than write the word 'woodland' all over a forested area.

Figure 2.9 shows the symbols used in 1:50,000 maps of Jamaica. Maps at different scales, and maps of other islands, use different symbols. You will be given a key to help you answer a mapwork question in the CXC exam; but you will save time if you learn the most important symbols, which are the same for almost every island.

3 Look at the background colour or shading. What is the main land use in each of these grid squares on map 2.10?
   (a) 68 50.
   (b) 78 48.
   (c) 76 53.
   (d) 65 49.
   (e) 63 51.
   (f) 78 51.
   (g) 64 49 (2 land uses).

4 What would you find at these grid references?
   (a) 631 460.
   (b) 718 458.
   (c) 756 519.
   (d) 680 490.
   (e) 777 480.
   (f) 667 425.
   (g) 752 436.

5 What are the lines which run from:
   (a) 670 430 to 790 437?
   (b) 660 518 to 684 495?
   (c) 713 462 to 670 499?
   (d) 781 480 to 774 520?
   (e) 779 501 to 790 474?
   (f) 649 526 to 640 499?
   (g) 760 475 to 763 480?
   (h) 710 519 to 678 490?

LEGEND

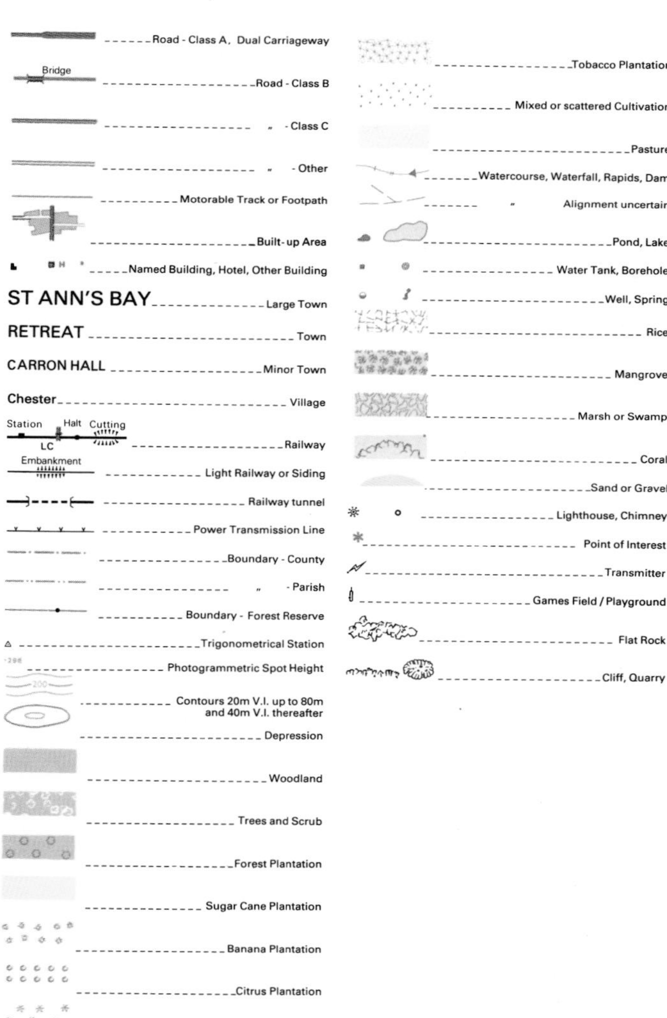

2.9 These are the symbols used on 1:50 000 maps of Jamaica.

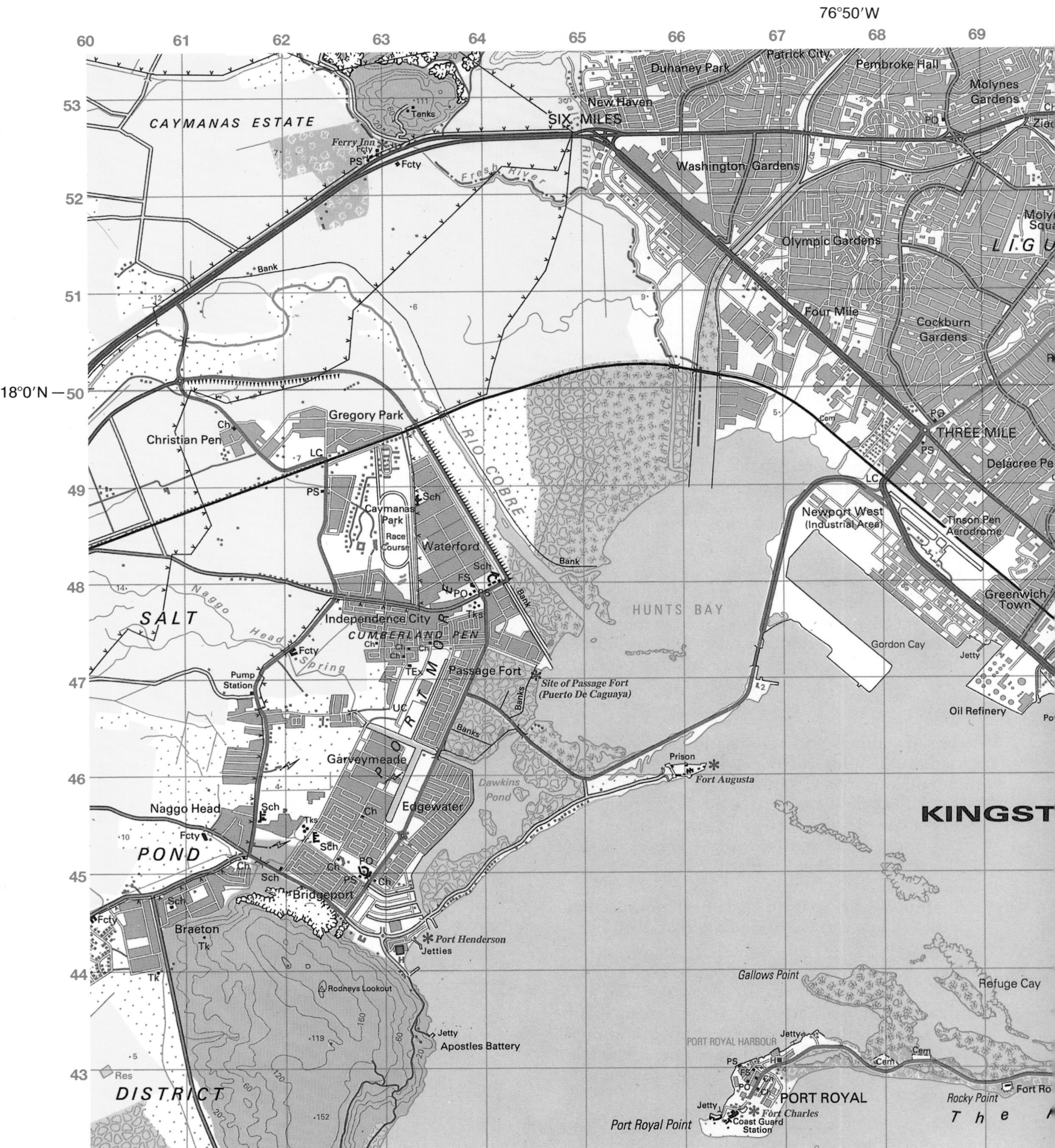

2.10 A 1:50 000 map of Kingston, Jamaica.

2.11 A 1:10 000 map of downtown Kingston.

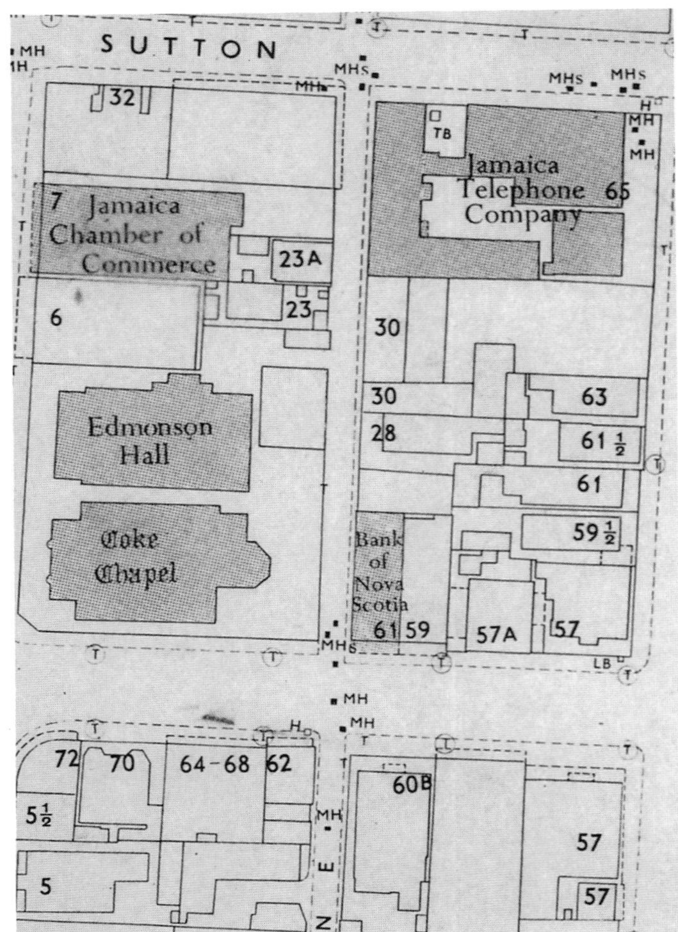

2.12 A 1:1250 map of part of downtown Kingston.

Figure 2.11 is a very large-scale map. It is drawn to a scale of 1:10,000. One cm on this map represents 10,000 cm, or 100 m, on the ground; so 10 cm represents 1 km. This map shows the downtown area of Kingston.

1 List five features which can be identified on this map but not on the 1:50,000 map.

Figure 2.12 is at an even larger scale, 1:1,250; so 1 cm on the map represents 1,250 cm, or 12.5 m, on the ground. At this scale, only a very small area can be shown; but it is possible to include a lot of detail which has to be left off the other maps. Even on the 1:10,000 map there would be no room to show every building separately.

2 List five features which can be identified on this map but not on the 1:10,000 map.

3 You have now seen five maps at very different scales. Which of these maps would be most suitable for
   (a) Deciding how to drive into Kingston?
   (b) Finding your way about the city on foot?
   (c) Identifying the site for a new office building?
   (d) Finding out how far it is from Kingston to Port au Prince, Haiti?
   (e) Showing how much woodland and agricultural land there is around Kingston?

4 Identify the area of the 1:1,250 map on:
   (a) The 1:10,000 map.
   (b) The 1:50,000 map.

5 The 1:10,000 map was printed in 1972, while the 1:50,000 map was surveyed in 1982. What changes were there in the plan of downtown Kingston between these two dates?

Measuring distances

Measuring distances in a straight line on a map is very easy:

- Check the scale of the map.
- Measure the staight-line distance in cm with a ruler.
- Now work out the distance on the ground in km like this:

- If it is a 1:50,000 map, divide the distance in cm by 2.
- If it is a 1:25,000 map, divide the distance in cm by 4.
- If it is a 1:10,000 map, divide the distance in cm by 10.

For example, to measure the distance along the new airport runway from 711 432 to 737 421 on Figure 2.10:

- Check the scale of the map 1:50,000.
- Measure the distance on the map 7.5 cm.
- Divide by 2 2.75.
- The distance is 2.75 km or 2,750 m.

6 On Figure 2.10, measure the straight-line distance from:
(a) 730 460 to 730 430.
(b) 730 430 to 690 430.
(c) 730 460 to 690 430.
(d) 710 464 to 681 490.
(e) 713 457 to 665 430.
(f) 757 478 to 763 480.

7 On Figure 2.11, measure the straight-line distance:
(a) Along Orange Street, from Harbour Street to South Parade.
(b) Along Barry Street from Hanover Street to Church Street.
(c) From the chapel on East Parade to the market on West Parade.

It is almost as easy to measure distance along a line which is not straight:

- Place the edge of a piece of scrap paper along the first section of the line.
- Mark it off as shown in Figure 2.13.
- Then place the paper against the second section of the line, and mark it off as shown in Figure 2.13.
- When you have marked off all the sections of the line, measure the total distance in cm.
- Check the scale of the map again.
- Divide the distance in cm:
  - By 2 for a 1:50,000 map.
  - By 4 for a 1:25,000 map.
  - By 10 for a 1:10,000 map.

8 On Figure 2.10, measure the distance along the road:
(a) From 680 490 to 700 467.
(b) From 730 420 to 790 437.
(c) From 720 465 to 745 490.
(d) From 700 517 to 697 483.
(e) From 713 460 to 665 430.
(f) From 757 478 to 763 480.

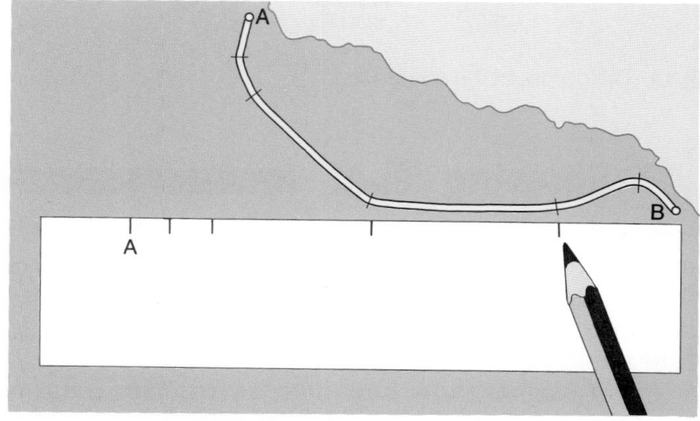

2.13 Measuring the distance along a road.

2.6 Direction

There are two ways of giving the *direction* from one place to another:

- You can use the *points of the compass.*
- You can use a *bearing.*

Figure 2.14 shows the sixteen points of the compass. Using compass points is accurate enough for most purposes, but when a ship or aircraft is plotting its exact course it is better to use a bearing. A bearing is more precise. Surveyors and engineers also use bearings when they are making measurements on the ground.

1 Look at Figure 2.14. What bearing corresponds to each of these compass points:
(a) North.
(b) South.
(c) East.
(d) West.
(e) North-East.
(f) North-North-East.
(g) West-North-West.

When a bearing does not correspond exactly to a compass point, then use the *nearest* compass point.

2 What compass point is nearest to:
(a) 46°.
(b) 185°.
(c) 280°.
(d) 35°.
(e) 358°.

Figure 2.15 shows how you can use a grid line to help you measure a bearing. Measuring bearings is much easier if you have a 360° circular protractor. When you are using your protractor, make sure that you measure in a clockwise direction from the 0° mark, which corresponds to North.

3 Using the Kingston map extract give the direction of travel using points of the compass and bearings for:
(a) A boat sailing from 690 450 to 760 450.
(b) A helicopter flying from 730 520 to 730 430.
(c) A train going from 670 499 towards 713 462.
(d) A car travelling from 771 514 to 744 520.

(e) An aeroplane travelling along the airport runway from 711 431 to 735 422.

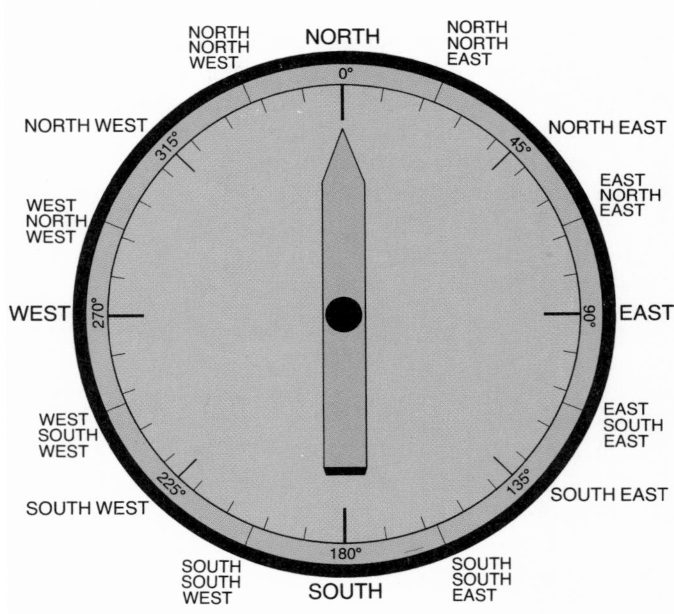

2.14 The points of the compass.

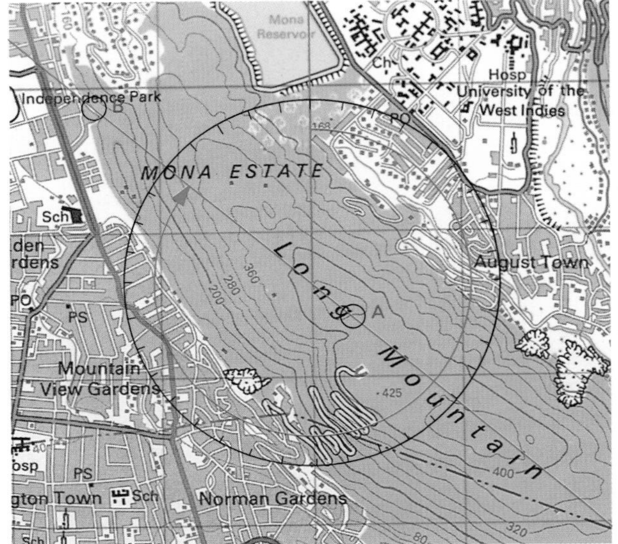

2.15 Using grid lines to help measure the bearing from A to B.

2.7 Showing relief

It is not easy to show hills and valleys on a flat sheet of paper. Old maps often used to have little pictures to show where the land was hilly. This is not a very accurate way of showing relief. Modern maps use four methods of showing relief:

- *Spot heights* show how high a particular point is above sea level.
- *Contours* are lines which join up all the places which are at the same height.
- Land above a certain height may be coloured in. This is called *layer colouring*.
- Slopes can be shaded, as if the land was being lit from the north-west. Slopes which face away from the north-west are shaded darker, as if they were in shadow. This is called *hill shading*.

1 Look at Figure 2.16. Which of the methods shown is good for:
 (a) Giving accurate information about the height of the hill, so that precise measurements can be made?
 (b) Giving a clear impression of what the land looks like to someone who is not used to reading maps?

2 Copy Figure 2.17a into your exercise book. Add:
 (a) Contours.
 (b) Layer colouring.
 (c) Hill shading.

3 In which direction is the river flowing in Figure 2.17a?

When you are used to reading contour maps, you will begin to recognise certain patterns. These include:

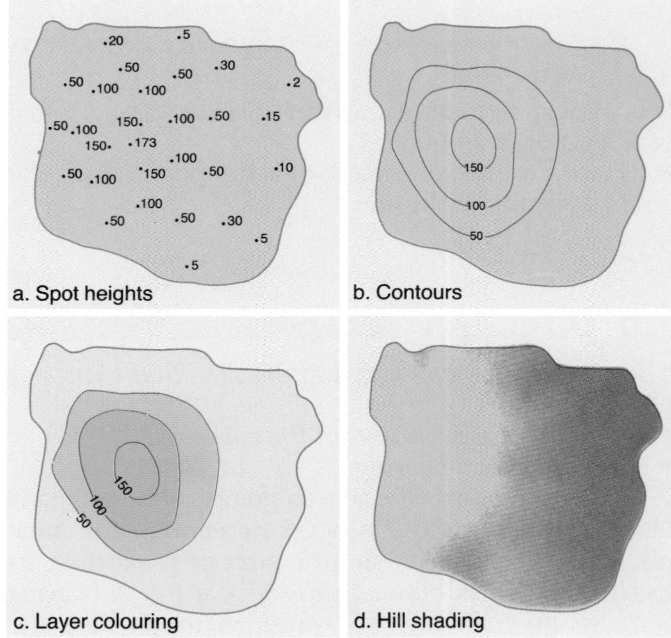

2.16 Ways of showing relief.

- Flat land (no contours).
- Gentle slopes (contours widely spaced).
- Steep slopes (contours close together).

The hill in Figure 2.17b is steeper on the west than on the east. The valley in Figure 2.17c has a flat floor; but the one in Figure 2.17d is narrow and steep-sided.

Figure 2.10 uses spot heights and contours. There

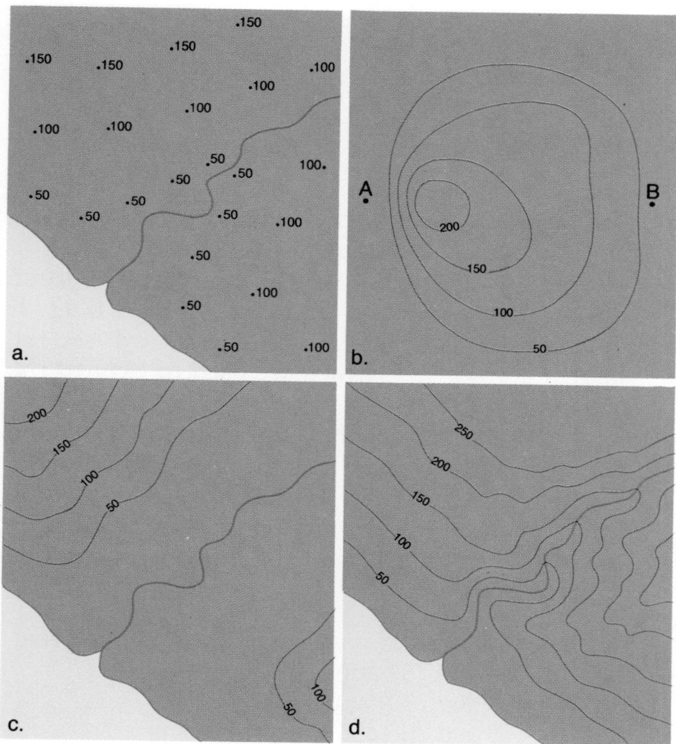

2.17 Spot heights and contour patterns.

are contours at 20, 40, 60, and 80 m above sea level; after that, there are contours at 40-m intervals. The contours at 200-m intervals are shown by thicker lines, so they are easy to pick out.

4 Look at the grid squares on Figure 2.10. Is the land steeply sloping, gently sloping, or flat?
(a) 68 48.
(b) 78 52.
(c) 62 43.
(d) 78 49.
(e) 75 50.

5 How far above sea level are the spot heights at these grid references?
(a) 713 432.
(b) 724 481.
(c) 764 479.
(d) 669 497.

Figure 2.11 is a large-scale map, so there is room for more information. There are contours every 10 feet (3.05 m) up to 60 feet (18.29 m). After that, there are contours at 20-feet (6.10 m) intervals.

The map of the St Vincent Soufrière (Fig 3.16 in section 3.5) uses hill shading and layer colouring as well as contours and spot heights to show relief. Many atlas maps use layer colouring with no hill shading.

6 What colours are used for high and low ground in your atlas?

Cross-sections

A cross-section shows what an area of land would look like if it were cut through, and we could look at all the hills and valleys from the side, in profile.

Figure 2.18 is a cross-section of Long Mountain. It starts at 750 460 and finishes at 780 490. This is how to draw a cross-section:

- Check the contour interval of the map you are using. On the 1:50,000 map of Jamaica, it is 40 m except near sea level.
- Choose a vertical scale that fits the contour interval. For this cross-section, the vertical scale is 2 mm to 40 m.
- Take a sheet of graph paper, and measure off the length of the cross-section.
- Make a frame and label it. You will have to look at the maximum and minimum height of the cross-section, to make sure it will fit into your frame.
- Place the edge of a strip of paper along the line of the cross-section. Mark off the places where the contours cross the line, and label the important ones.

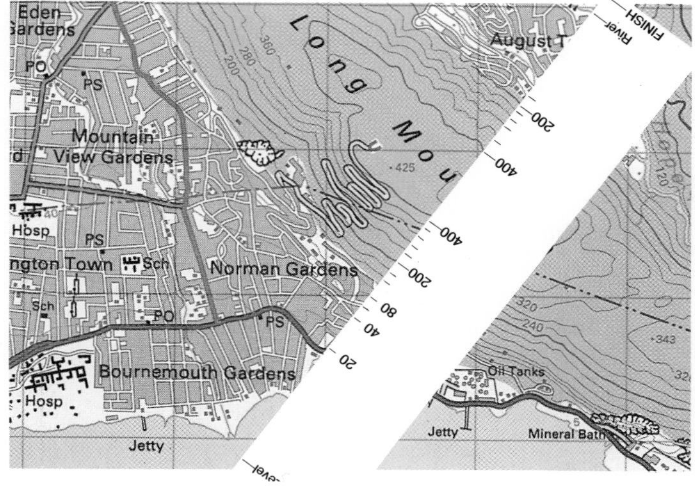

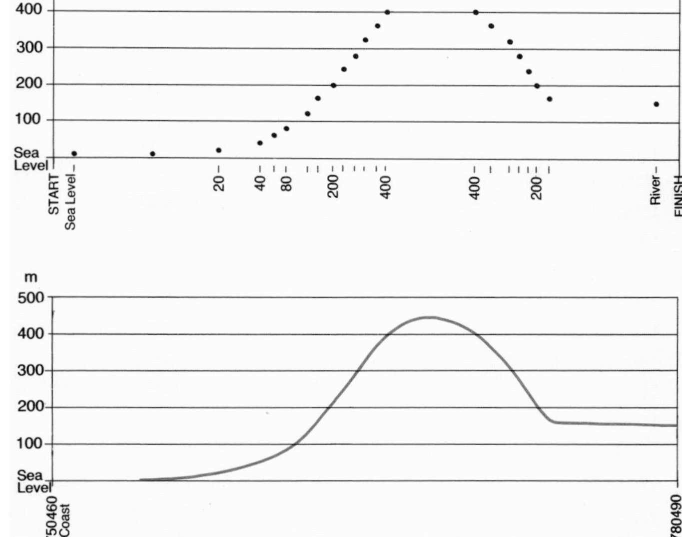

2.18 Drawing a cross-section of Long Mountain.

- Place the strip of paper next to your frame. Make a dot inside the frame at the right height for every mark on the paper.
- Join the dots up neatly with a smooth curve.
- Check your work, and make sure that it is properly labelled.

7 Draw a cross-section of the hill in Figure 2.17b from 'A' to 'B'.

8 Draw a cross-section from 730 500 to 780 500 on Figure 2.10. Use a vertical scale of 2 mm to 40 m.

Gradients

We can use the contours on a map to work out how steep a slope is, or measure its *gradient*. This is how to work out the gradient of the slope of Long Mountain between 770 475 and 770 465.

- To calculate the gradient of a slope, use this formula:

$$\frac{\text{difference in height}}{\text{horizontal distance}}$$

- Make sure that both parts of the fraction are expressed in the same units.
- Use the contours and spot heights to work out the height above sea level at the top of Long Mountain (770 475). This is 440 m.
- Then work out the height above sea level at the foot of the slope (770 465). This is 20 m.
- Now work out the difference in height. This is 440 m – 20 m, which equals 420 m.
- Now work out the horizontal distance. This is 2 cm on the map. The map has a scale of 1:50,000, so this represents 1 km or 1000 m on the ground.
- So the gradient is:

$$\frac{420\text{ m}}{1000\text{ m}}$$

- This works out as $\frac{1}{2.38}$ or approximately $\frac{1}{2.4}$
- Expressed as a ratio, the average gradient of the slope of Long Mountain at this point is 1:2.4.
- If you use a calculator, you will get the same answer expressed as a decimal, which is 0.42. If you use the reciprocal function, you will see the figures 2.38 or 2.4, which we used to express the answer as a ratio.
- You can use the decimal, 0.42, to work out the angle of the slope. The decimal is actually the Tangent of the slope angle. So if you use the Tan^{-1} or Inverse Tan function on your calculator, this will give you the angle of slope, which in this case is 22° 47′.

9 Work out the average gradient of the slope between:
(a) 790 480 and 781 480.
(b) 758 490 and 750 500.
(c) 757 478 and 763 480 *in a straight line.*
(d) 757 478 and 763 480 *along the road.*

On most Caribbean maps, contours and spot heights are still labelled in feet. This makes it slightly harder to calculate gradients. The vertical difference has to be converted from feet to metres. You can do this by either of these two methods:

- Using the conversion table which should be printed on the map you are using.
- Multiplying the difference in feet by 0.305.

2.8 Making maps

Figure 2.19 shows students in Barbados using surveying equipment to make a map of their school. In the past, atlas maps and large-scale maps were prepared entirely by *ground survey*. Teams of surveyors made careful measurements using instruments like these. First of all, sightings would be taken to fix the position of hilltops and islands. Then the detail would be filled in. It took an enormous amount of work to map all the streets and buildings in a town, or the contour lines in a mountainous area.

Today, ground survey is still important. In fact, it is more accurate than ever before, because surveying instruments which use lasers and radio micro-waves are available. But much of the detail on large-scale maps can be filled in by using air photographs.

2.19 Using a plane table to make a map.

Figure 2.20 was used to help prepare the 1:50,000 map of Kingston. Look at the photograph carefully.

1 Make a sketch from the photograph, showing:
   (a) The coastline.
   (b) The airport.
   (c) Waves approaching the shore.
   (d) Saint William Grant Park.
   (e) Three other features you can identify.
2 Which of these features would not be shown on the map? Why?
3 This photograph was taken from a high altitude. What features would you be able to see on a low-altitude photograph?
4 Now list three features which you can identify on the map, but which are not shown clearly on the air photograph.

When a set of air photographs is taken, they are always made to overlap, so that every piece of ground can be seen in at least two pictures. When two overlapping photographs are viewed through a *stereoscope*, you can see a three-dimensional picture. Hills and tall buildings seem to stand out from the surrounding land. This means that air photographs can be used to add contours to large-scale maps; though it is still necessary to use ground survey to check on the height of the most important features.

If you look at a map of an area you know well, you will probably notice that it is not completely up to date. New buildings, new roads, and other features which have been constructed since the map was made will not be shown.

5 Explain why it takes a long time to prepare a large-scale map.
6 Explain why air photographs are useful for bringing map information up to date.

2.20 An air photograph of Kingston Harbour.

2.9 Sketch maps

Figure 2.21 is a sketch map, showing transport facilities around Kingston Harbour.

A sketch map is not a copy of a printed map. It is prepared to draw attention to a few selected features. This is how to prepare a sketch map:

- If there is not a printed grid on the map you are working from, add one carefully in pencil. It is generally best to draw your grid lines 2 cm apart.
- Decide on the scale of the sketch map. Figure 2.21 is at a scale of 1:100,000. But a sketch map can be at the same scale as the printed map.
- Draw a grid on a piece of plain paper. Because the scale of this sketch map is twice as small as the main map, the grid lines are 1 cm apart.
- Use the grid to copy the features you want to show. It is often useful to start with the coastline. Show the main lines of these features. Do not worry about all the little details.
- Use appropriate colours to show the features you have selected. Make a key, and label your sketch map properly.
- Do not show features which are not relevant for the sketch, or it will become too cluttered.

1 Make a sketch of the area to the east of grid line 73, showing built-up areas, woodland, trees and scrub, and cultivation.

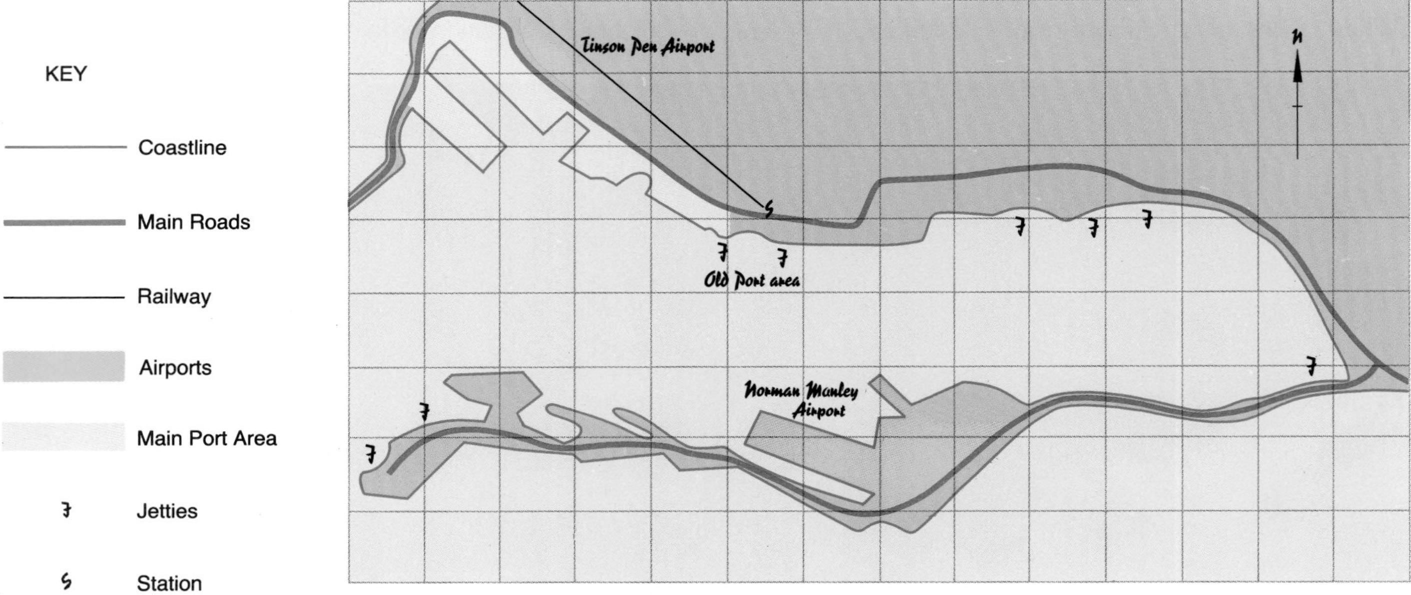

2.21 Sketch map to show transportation facilities around Kingston Harbour. Scale 1:100 000

3 • THE EARTH'S CRUST

3.1 Earthquakes

On 26 September 1985, Mexico City was shaken by a powerful earthquake. Cars swung across the road out of control; lamp-posts and buildings swayed from side to side; people ran out into the streets in panic. The electricity for many parts of the city was cut off, and most of the television and radio stations went off the air when the main television tower fell down.

In the city centre, 250 buildings collapsed, and many more were so badly damaged that they had to be demolished. Children were crushed to death in a four-storey school building, and when the maternity wing of the general hospital collapsed, over 200 people – mothers, staff and new-born babies – were killed.

3.1 The Mexico City earthquake.

Where earthquakes occur

Every year, there are several hundred earthquakes. Most of them are slight tremors which cause no damage. Only a few are really powerful and destructive. The most disastrous earthquake this century occurred in China in 1976 – over 240,000 people were killed. Some even more powerful earthquakes have disturbed regions like Alaska, where few people live and where the loss of life has been much less.

Figure 3.2 shows the location of major earthquakes in a typical five-year period. There are large areas where earthquakes occur very rarely, if at all. These areas are geologically *stable*. And there are a number of linear zones where earth movements are very frequent.

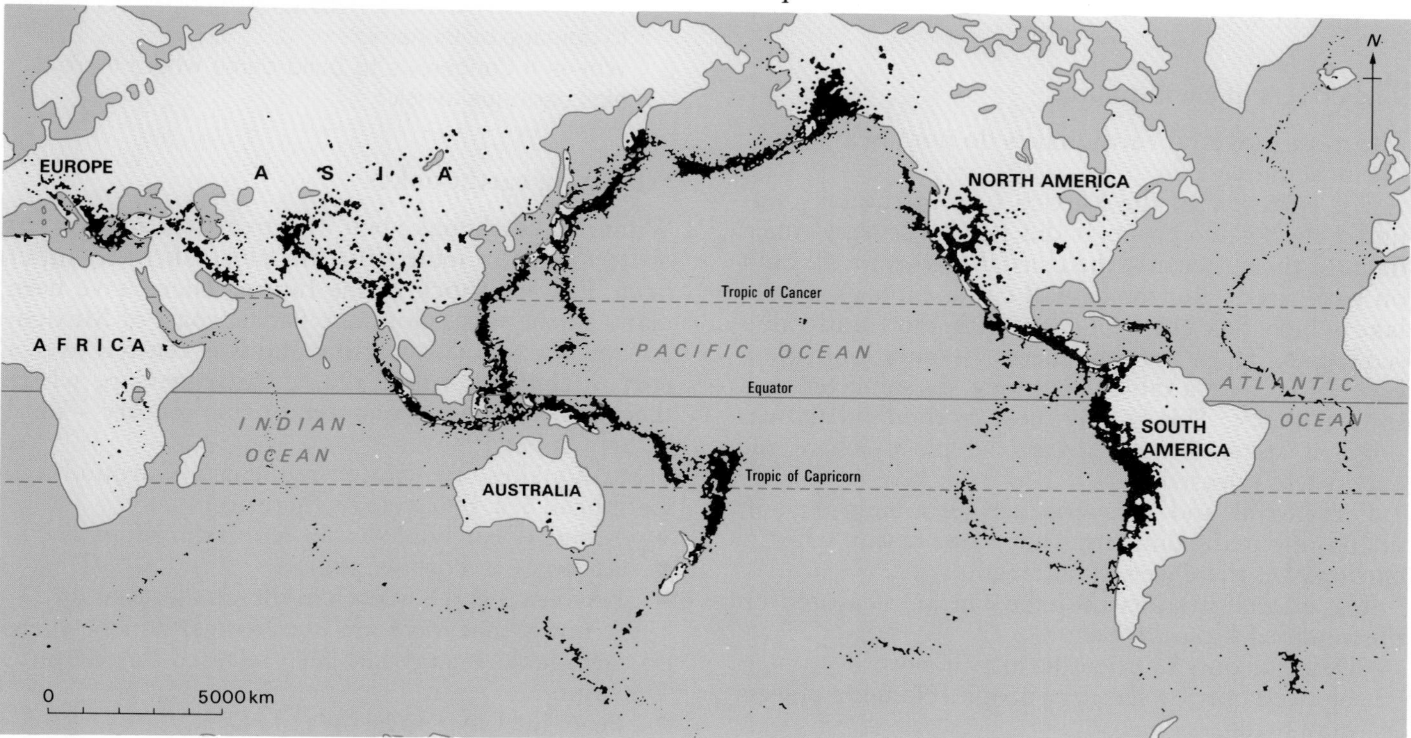

3.2 A world pattern of earthquakes. Each dot shows the epicentre of an earthquake – the point on the surface which is directly above the shock.

1 Which of these areas have frequent earthquakes?
   (a) Africa.
   (b) Japan.
   (c) California.
   (d) Australia.
   (e) Guyana.
   (f) The Eastern Caribbean.

Jamaica has been hit by two particularly damaging earthquakes:

- In 1692, the old city of Port Royal on the Palisadoes was virtually destroyed. More than 2,000 people were killed, and much of the land on which the town was built slumped into the sea.
- In 1907, Kingston was devastated by a powerful earthquake, and then by a fire which started in the ruins. More than 800 people were killed.

The Richter Scale

The amount of energy released during an earthquake can be measured on the Richter Scale. A one-point jump on the Richter Scale means that ten times as much energy has been released.

The Mexico City earthquake had a magnitude of 7.8:

- It was 10 times as powerful as the Baja California earthquake of 1956, which measured 6.8.
- It was about 630,000 times as powerful as the smallest tremors that can be detected with scientific instruments, which have a magnitude of 2.0.
- It released 1/13 as much energy as the most powerful earthquake this century, which shook the island of Sumba in Indonesia in 1977 and had a magnitude of 8.9.

The effects of earthquakes

The most powerful earthquakes do not always cause the most damage.

The *epicentre* of the Mexico City earthquake was under the Pacific coast. It did not cause very much damage there, because the coastal towns are all built on hard rocks. But the capital city is built on an old lake which has been filled in with mud and other sediments. These soft sediments shake about like a bowl of jelly on a table when they are subjected to a sudden shock. This is why most of the damage was done at some distance from the place where the energy was released.

Port Royal and Kingston are also built on soft unconsolidated sediments. That is one reason why the earthquakes there were so damaging.

The effects of an earthquake can be measured on the modified *Mercalli Scale*:

1 Detected only by scientific instruments.
2 Noticed only by sensitive people. Hanging objects may swing.
3 Parked cars may rock slightly. Like vibration from a passing truck.
4 Some people wake up. Walls may make cracking sound.
5 Dishes and windows may be broken.
6 Enough to frighten many people.
7 Badly built structures damaged.
8 Many buildings damaged. Heavy furniture overturned.
9 Ground cracked conspicuously. Pipes burst.
10 Most buildings destroyed. Many landslides.
11 Few buildings remain. Broad cracks in ground.
12 Total damage. Waves seen on ground surface.

2 Look at Figure 3.1, and estimate the effects of the Mexico City earthquake on the modified Mercalli Scale.

3 Explain why earthquake damage is often worse in modern industrial cities than in traditional village communities.

Tsunamis

Some of the worst earthquake damage is caused by *Tsunamis* – giant waves produced by earthquakes beneath the sea. Some tsunamis have travelled right across the Pacific Ocean; and the height of the wave may be as much as five, ten, or even thirty metres.

A tsunami may also be produced by an erupting volcano: the largest tsunami recorded was produced by the Krakatoa eruption in 1883, and drowned 30,000 people.

4 Why are the Caribbean islands particularly vulnerable to damage by tsunamis?

5 Why is it dangerous to build dams where there is a high earthquake risk?

Predicting earthquakes

Within an earthquake belt, the areas which have had no tremors for some time are most likely to suffer from a major shock in the future. There have been many earthquakes along the Pacific coast of Mexico; but the Mexico City earthquake was centred over a part of this belt called the Michoacan Gap, where there had been no major tremor this century – until 26 September 1985.

Earthquakes are quite frequent all around the Caribbean Sea. On average, there are:

- About 17 earthquakes per century in Kingston.
- About 14 in Port of Spain.
- Between 3 and 8 in each of the smaller islands.

We know that there are two 'danger zones' where no earthquake energy has been released this century. They run:

- From the Cayman Islands to Haiti.
- From Grenada to St Lucia.

It is very likely that there will be a major earthquake

in these two zones at some stage – but we cannot say when. It is almost impossible to say when an earthquake will happen.

The Chinese have had some success in predicting earth movements. All over China, part-time earthquake watchers look for signs which show that the ground is shifting slightly under stress. A report is made if any of these signs are noticed:

- Horses and dogs become restless.
- Wells start to bubble.
- Rats all disappear.
- Fish begin to behave in an unusual way.

If many reports come in, then an earthquake warning is issued. There were five major earthquakes in China in the period 1972–7.

- For all of them, a long-term warning was issued.
- In four cases, there was an 'alarm' a few hours beforehand, so that buildings could be evacuated.
- In the fifth earthquake, there was no alarm; and 240,000 people were killed.

It is also sometimes possible to predict an earthquake by monitoring slight changes in the ground with sensitive instruments, or by studying the way shock waves travel through the earth.

Taking precautions

Because earthquakes are impossible to predict, it is not easy to take precautions against them. In theory, it should be possible to avoid building on:

- Areas with a high earthquake risk.
- Low-lying areas which could easily be damaged by tsunamis.
- Unconsolidated rocks, which shake more violently during an earthquake.

But this sort of policy is not easy to follow.

However, it is possible to develop a plan to reduce the effects of earthquakes in a vulnerable area. Tokyo's earthquake protection plan is described in Section 15.6.

6 Where in the Caribbean is there no risk of earthquake damage?

7 Why do people live in low-lying areas near the coast?

8 Explain why it would not be possible to re-site cities like Kingston, Mexico City, or San Francisco which have a high risk of earthquake damage.

9 Look at Figure 2.10. What installations have been constructed on:
(a) The Palisadoes?
(b) Low-lying areas north of Kingston Harbour?

3.2 The structure of the earth

The solid crust of the earth is comparatively thin. It is about 5 kilometres deep below the oceans, and 20–65 kilometres thick under the continents. The crust looks stable and rigid to the ordinary observer; but it is being slowly warped or *deformed* in many places, and, as we have seen, it can move quite suddenly when there is an earthquake.

The crust is made up of two types of material. The oceanic crust, and the lower part of the crust under the continents, is a thin layer of dense material known as *sima*. The upper part of the continental crust is composed of lighter rocks, or *sial*, which float on the denser material beneath.

The mantle, which is below the crust, behaves like a solid in many ways – but the material in the mantle can flow very slowly, like an extremely sticky liquid. It is difficult to understand the way materials behave below the surface of the earth, however, because temperatures and pressures are so much greater than anything we experience on the surface.

Crustal plates

The earth's crust is divided into several large *plates*. Figure 3.4 shows the location of the major plates and their boundaries.

1 Compare Figure 3.4 with Figure 3.2. What do you notice about the location of the zones where earthquakes are common?

2 Make a copy of the section of Figure 3.4 inside the red box. Shade in the Caribbean plate, and name each of the other plates.

Plate margins

Look at Figure 3.5. The crustal plates are all moving very slowly. Where two plates touch, there is a *plate margin*. There are three types of plate margin:

- *Divergent* plate margins occur when two plates are being pushed apart. Molten rock is forced slowly upwards between the two plates, and when it hardens a strip of new crust has been formed. There are divergent or *constructive* plate margins beneath each of the world's oceans. The best known is the Mid-Atlantic Ridge.
- *Convergent* plate margins are found where two plates are being pushed together. When there is a convergent plate boundary under the oceans or at the edge of an ocean, there is a *subduction zone* or *destructive* plate margin. The oceanic crust, which is made up of heavy sima, is drawn down-

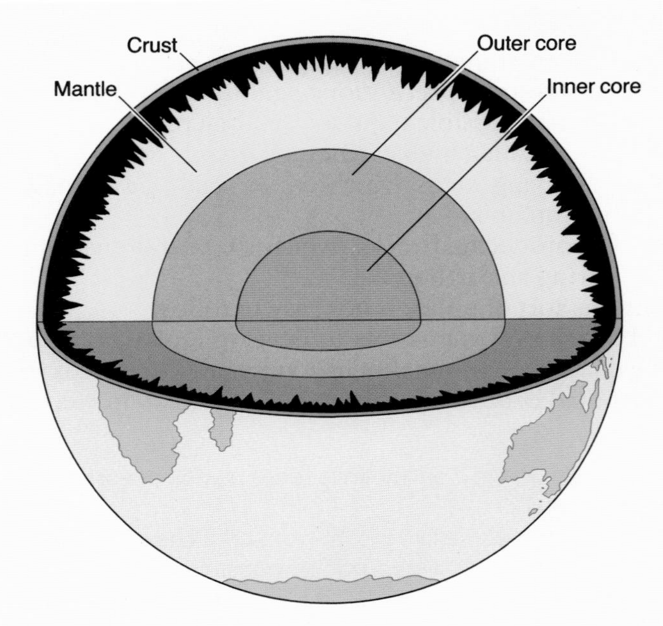

3.3 The structure of the earth.
The crust is a thin layer, made up of patches of sial 'floating' in a continuous layer of sima.
The mantle consists of iron and magnesium silicates. Temperatures within the mantle increase to 1600°.
The outer core is made up of iron and nickel. The temperature is 2000° to 5000°. The material in the outer core has the characteristics of a liquid.
The inner core is solid. The material making up the inner core is three times as dense as the rocks at the earth's surface.

wards beneath the adjoining plate and reabsorbed into the mantle.

- *Transform* plate margins are found when two plates are moving past each other without converging or diverging.

When two continents meet at a convergent plate margin, there is a *collision zone*. The continental crust, which is made of sial, is too light to be drawn downwards and reabsorbed into the mantle. One continent is forced forward under the other, and there is a double thickness of continental crust.

The world's highest mountains, the Himalayas, are in a collision zone where the Indian plate is being pushed northwards under the Eurasian plate.

Earthquakes and plate margins

Plates often move steadily or in a series of small jumps. When this happens, there will be a large number of small earth tremors which can be detected only by *seismographs*.

When two plates are locked tightly together by friction, these small movements cannot occur. The plates still move – but they are warped or deformed near this part of the boundary. Instead of being released gradually, energy is stored up over a period of many years. Eventually, the strain is too much, and the rocks along the plate margin snap suddenly into a new position.

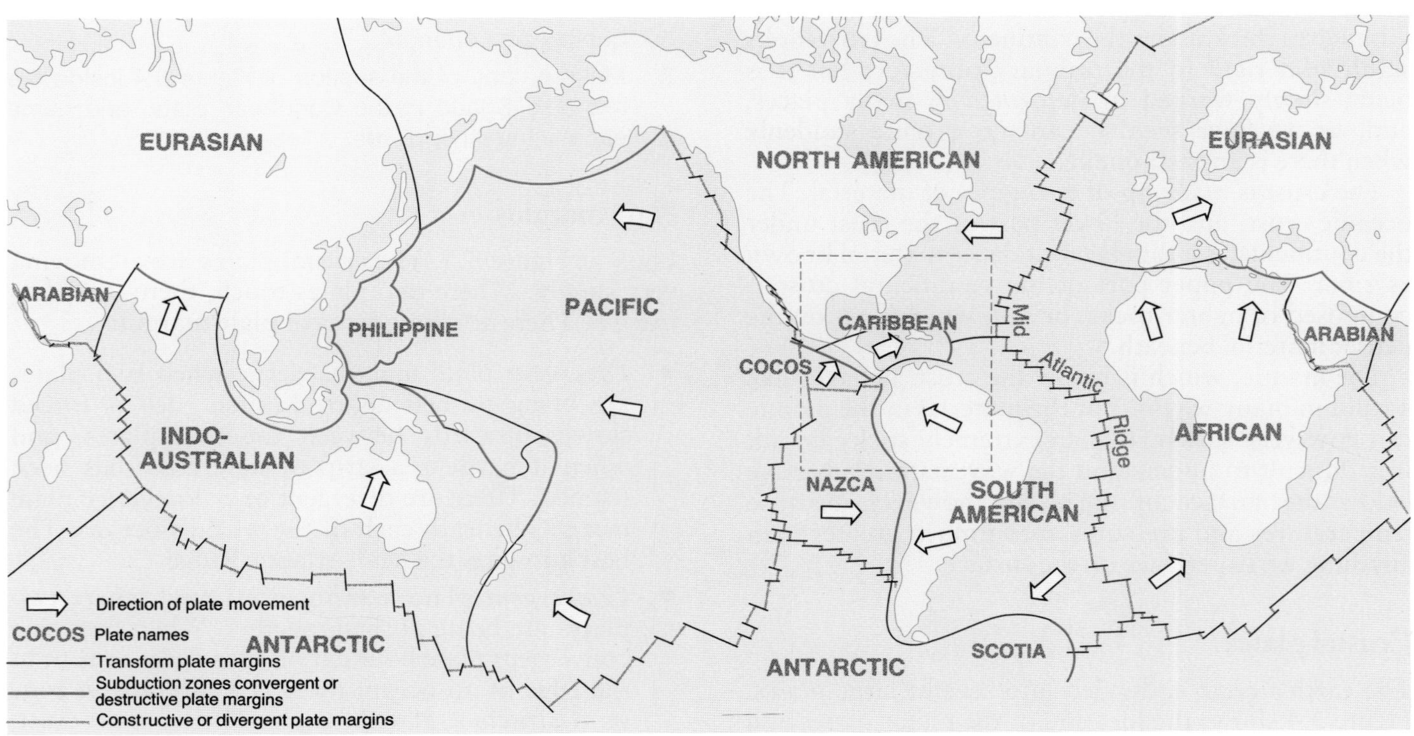

3.4 The earth's crust is made up of these plates. There is a more detailed map of the Caribbean Plate on page 35.

In the Mexico City earthquake, the Cocos Plate suddenly moved forward 3 metres under the North American plate.

3 What type of plate margin is located:
(a) To the north of the Caribbean plate?
(b) To the east of the Caribbean plate?
(c) Between the South American and African plates?
(d) Beneath the Nazca and South American plates?

Continental drift

The Mid-Atlantic Ridge is a divergent plate margin. New crustal material is being formed here, and the continents of South America and Africa are being pushed further apart.

This is happening at a rate of about 4 centimetres per year – which is about the rate at which human fingernails grow.

About 150 million years ago, the two continents were joined together. We know this because:

- It is possible to measure the rate at which the continents are now moving apart.
- There are no sediments older than this on the floor of the South Atlantic.
- Rocks which formed more than 150 million years ago in eastern South America are very similar to rocks which formed at the same period in western Africa.
- We have evidence that animals which lived in South America and Africa at this time were very similar.

4 How much has the distance between the two continents increased:
(a) Over the past century?
(b) Over the past million years?
(c) Over the past 150 million years?

5 Make a diagram in your exercise book to show how the two continents probably fitted together.

South America and Africa are not the only continents that have moved apart in this way. North America was once joined to Europe. And all the southern continents – Australia and Antarctica as well as Africa and South America – were once joined together. India also formed part of this huge land mass, and moved north to join onto Asia about 40 million years ago.

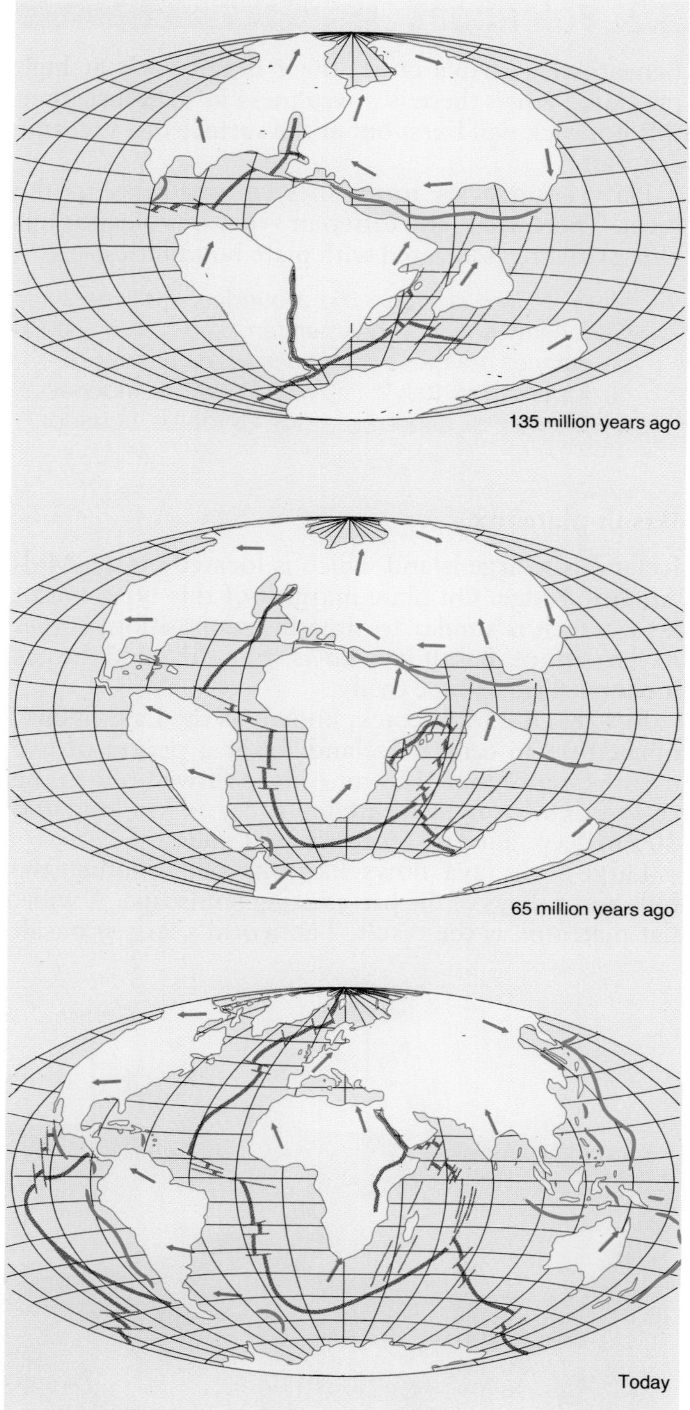

3.5 How the position of the continents has changed.

3.3 Volcanoes

Beneath the earth's crust, there is hot rock at high pressure. When there is a weakness in the crust, then this hot rock will burst out at the surface in a volcanic eruption.

Plate boundaries form lines of weakness in the crust. There are many different types of volcano; but almost all are associated with plate boundaries.

1 Mont Pelée is near the boundary between the Caribbean and South American plates. What plate boundaries are these volcanoes associated with:
(a) Mount Etna, Italy?
(b) Mount Fuji, Japan?
(c) Krakatoa, Indonesia?
(d) Cotopaxi, Ecuador?

Basalt plateaux

Iceland is a large island which is located on the Mid-Atlantic Ridge. On plate margins of this type, basalt lava, which is similar to sima in composition, comes to the surface. Basalt lava flows smoothly, and the gas it contains can escape easily.

In 1783, a 25-km crack, known as the Laki fissure, opened up in central Iceland. Over a period of five months, more than 12 km^3 of lava flowed out to the surface. One tongue of molten rock, 56 km long and 100 m deep, filled up an entire river valley.

Large-scale lava flows like this one smother the hills and valleys of the pre-existing landscape. A wide, flat plateaux, is the result. The world's largest basalt plateaux in India, South America, and Africa, each cover an area larger than Guyana. They were formed by a series of different eruptions – there are layers of lava with gravel and fossil soil trapped between them.

Shield volcanoes

The Hawaiian islands are an isolated group of volcanoes in the central Pacific which produce basalt lava. Repeated eruptions of smoothly flowing lava from a series of vents have formed *shield volcanoes* which rise gradually with a slope of between 2° and 10° from the ocean floor to as much as 4,000 m above sea level.

Destructive plate margins

Eruptions near destructive plate margins and subduction zones produce lava which is derived from many different types of material – not just from sima, but from the rocks of the continental crust and from the upper part of the mantle.

The lava from these eruptions is usually much more *viscous* than basalt lava – it does not flow nearly as easily. Most Caribbean eruptions have produced viscous lava.

There are many lava flows in St Vincent, Dominica, and elsewhere in the Caribbean; but because viscous lava does not spread out so rapidly as basalt, the

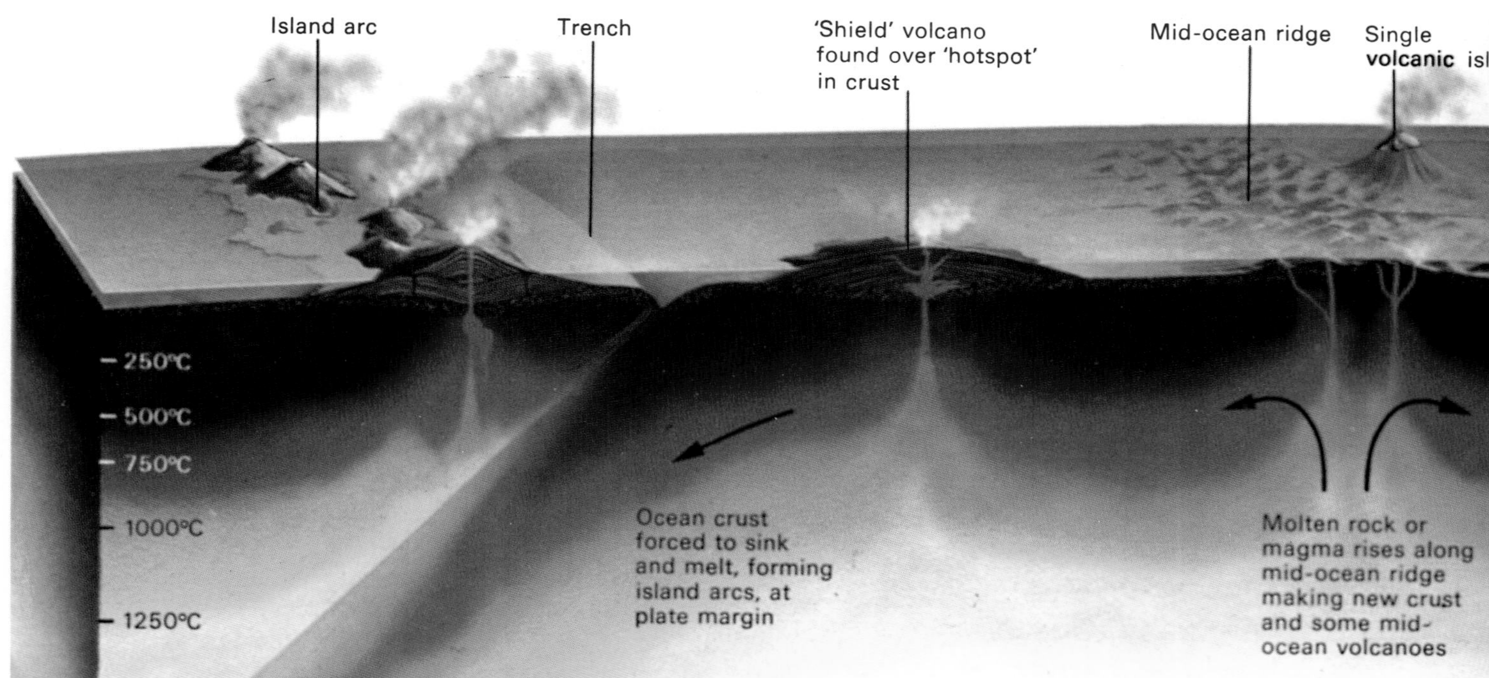

3.6 Some of the large scale landforms caused by movements of the crustal plates.

3.7 The Pitons, St Lucia. Two viscous lava domes.

3.8 A composite volcanic cone.

sheets of rock produced by each eruption are much thicker. There are no extensive lava plateaux, like those of India or Iceland.

Very viscous lava, or dacite, does not flow out in sheets at all. It is so 'sticky' that it is pushed upwards as a dome above the vent of the volcano. These steep-sided domes are very different from the gently sloping shield volcanoes which are produced by basalt lava.

Ash falls

Many volcanoes throw out molten material into the atmosphere, where it is cooled and solidified. This material, known as *tephra*, varies from fine 'ash' to large 'bombs' which may weigh as much as several tonnes. Most tephra is dark grey in colour, and contains tiny gas bubbles which were trapped when the boiling lava was cooled.

Most of the ash, and all the large particles, fall back to the ground quite close to the volcano. Several falls of tephra can build up a symmetrical ash cone; but *composite* volcanoes, which contain many different layers of ash and lava built up over a long period, are much more common.

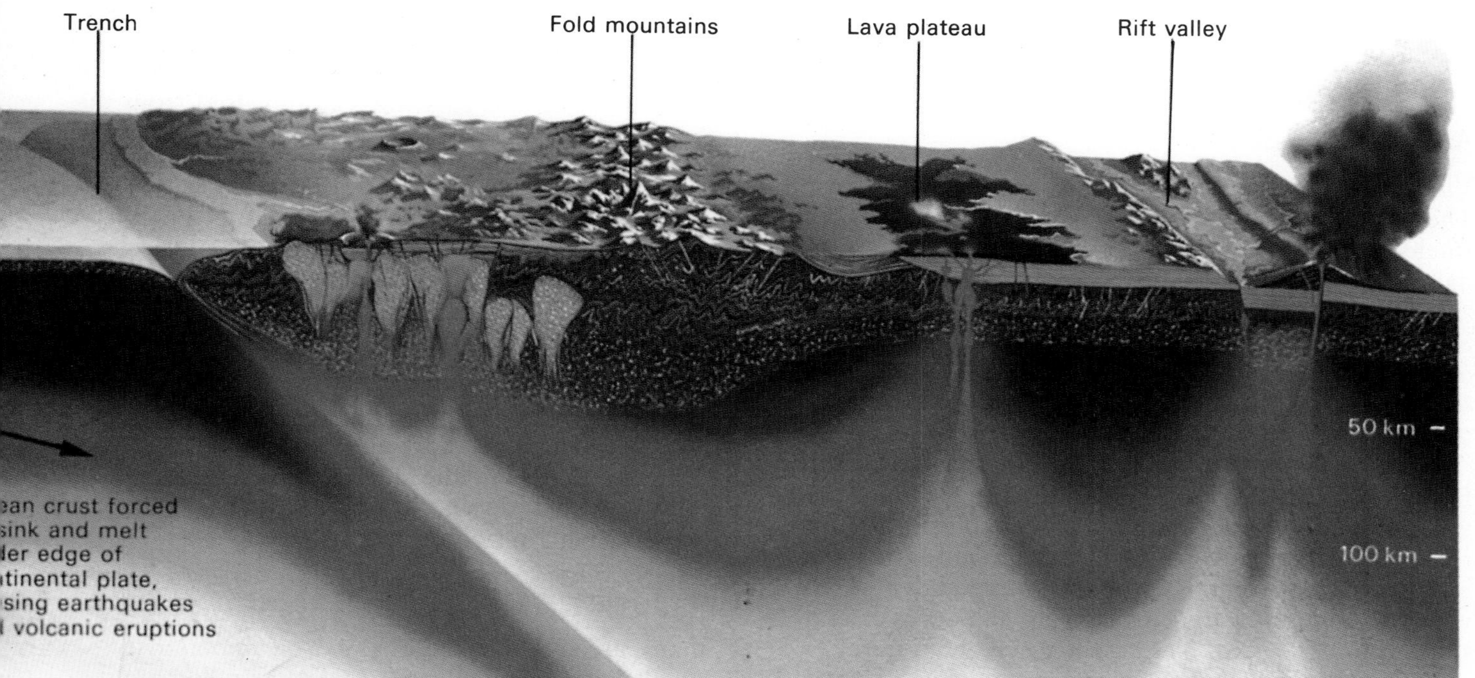

Fine ash particles are often carried a considerable distance by the wind. When the St Vincent Soufrière erupted in 1902, 3.6 million tonnes of volcanic ash fell on Barbados, 180 km away. After the Krakatoa eruption in Indonesia in 1883, the ash cloud rose to 80 km in height, and spread right round the world. There were spectacular red sunsets for several months, and particles of ash from Krakatoa were identified as far away as Europe.

Calderas

The most destructive volcanic events are *ignimbrite* eruptions. A huge mass of incandescent material bubbles out of a fissure or vent in the ground. When the ignimbrite cools, it has an ashy or sandy consistency. The only ignimbrite eruption known to have occurred in historic times was in an uninhabited region of Alaska around Mount Katmai in 1912. Ten km^3 of material flooded out of the volcano in only 20 hours, completely filling a river valley, and turning it into a flat plain 4 km across – and known as the Valley of Ten Thousand Smokes, because for several years after the eruption it was dotted with jets of steam which spurted out into the cold air.

When a volume of material like this is ejected by a volcano, a large cavity is opened up beneath the cone. The upper part of the mountain cannot be supported any more – and collapses inwards to form a big circular depression called a caldera.

Crater Lake in the state of Oregon in the USA was created about 6,000 years ago after a major ignimbrite eruption. A volcano 3,600 m high subsided to form a depression 9 km wide and 1,200 m deep. Wizard Island, in the centre of the lake, is a more recent volcanic cone.

A volcanic eruption

Viscous-lava volcanoes do not erupt very often. They do not release energy nearly as frequently as shield volcanoes; but their eruptions are much more damaging when they do occur.

St Pierre, at the foot of Mont Pelée in Martinique, is rather a quiet little town today; but at the beginning of the century it had a population of 20,000, and was one of the liveliest and most prosperous settlements in the Caribbean.

In April 1902, sulphur fumes were noticed in the Etang Sec, a small dried-up lake in the crater of the volcano. There were some minor explosions, and rock fragments were thrown into the air. Then the lake bed began to fill up with water, and a small volcanic cone appeared in it. Light falls of ash and sulphur fumes began to affect the town of St Pierre.

The wife of the American consul wrote: 'The smell of sulphur is so strong that horses in the street stop and snort, and some of them drop in their harness and die of suffocation. Many of the people are obliged to wear wet handkerchiefs to protect themselves from the fumes of sulphur.'

3.9 Crater Lake and Wizard Island.

A mass of lava was being forced up through the floor of the crater. It did not flow away as basalt lava would have done, but gradually pushed its way upwards. On 5 May, it was large enough to force out the water that had been collecting in the crater. This water had been heated almost to boiling-point, and picked up mud and stones as it poured down the mountainside. The flow of hot mud hit a sugar factory just north of St Pierre, and killed 30 people there.

No attempt was made to evacuate the town. In fact, the authorities did their best to discourage people who wanted to move away – partly because they did not want to disrupt an election which was due a few days later.

At 7.50 a.m. on 8 May, a dense violet-grey cloud of superheated gas and glowing ash appeared from the crater of the volcano. Within a few minutes, the town was on fire, and almost everyone in it had been suffocated by the blast of hot gas. The force of the moving cloud was enough to knock down walls a metre thick; and the heat was enough to melt glass and fuse piles of plates together. Only two people are known to have survived the disaster.

There were further eruptions over the next few months; then, in November 1902, a spine of solid lava was pushed up from the crater. It grew at a rate of over 10 metres per day, and by May 1903 it was 310 metres high; but the spine did not last long. As the lava cooled down, it began to crack, and it collapsed soon afterwards.

Hot springs

In many areas where there is no volcanic activity at present, there may still be a mass of hot or molten rock quite close to the surface.

Many Caribbean islands, such as Dominica and Montserrat, have hot springs, where water seeps down through the ground to a point where it is heated by the rock, and then flows back towards the surface. The water cools as it moves away from the underground heat source, but it may still reach the surface at boiling-point.

Most substances dissolve more easily in hot water than cold, particularly if the hot water has already picked up traces of acid. Hot springs often contain dissolved minerals. People used to believe that water containing dissolved minerals would help to cure certain diseases, but most would now think that the minerals simply make the water taste unpleasant.

Many hot springs contain a high concentration of sulphur. There are also *fumaroles*, where steam with sulphur in it rises out of the ground. Large quantities of sulphur are deposited around fumaroles, so no plants can grow. There is also a strange smell in the air. The Soufrière fumarole in St Lucia contains two hot springs. It occupies a small volcanic crater.

Intrusive features

Magma, or molten rock, forces its way to the surface through a line of weakness in the earth's crust. It pushes into a joint, and then widens it to anything from a few centimetres to tens of metres across; more magma flows in, and pushes further on towards the surface.

When the molten rock has cooled and hardened beneath the surface of the earth, it forms a sheet which runs through the surrounding rock:

- A vertical sheet of igneous rock is known as a *dyke*. It is formed by magma moving directly upwards towards the surface.
- When the magma flows horizontally between two rock layers and roughly parallel to the surface, then a *sill* is formed.
- A *plug* is a vertical pipe of rock which is formed when the molten material in the vent of a volcano cools and hardens. The plug may remain as an isolated feature long after the rest of the volcano has been eroded away.

Dykes, sills, and plugs are known as *intrusive* features because they are formed underground, by magma which cools and hardens before it reaches the surface. Features which form at the surface, like basalt plateaux and shield volcanoes, are called *extrusive* features. The main types of intrusive and extrusive features are shown in Figure 3.12.

There are other intrusive features – *laccoliths* and *batholiths* – which are formed when a large underground reservoir of molten rock cools and hardens below the surface. Batholiths are much larger than laccoliths, and are formed at a greater depth.

Predicting eruptions

Volcanic eruptions are easier to predict than earthquakes. All volcanoes in the eastern Caribbean are very carefully monitored. If it was threatened today, St Pierre would almost certainly be evacuated in time. Before the St Vincent Soufrière erupted in 1979, 20,000 people were evacuated from the north of the island; so there were no casualties, although there was damage to crops and livestock.

There are various warning signs before an eruption:

- Growth of an underground mass of molten rock will push the surface up slightly. A *tiltmeter* can be used to detect very slight changes in the slope of the ground. Movements as small as 1 mm per km can be picked up.

3.10 Mont Pelée and St Pierre after the 1902 eruption.

3.11 A fumarole near Soufrière, St Lucia.

- There will also be a slight increase in temperature, which can be detected by infra-red equipment; and there may be changes in the magnetic pattern of the rocks.
- Before the eruption, there will be a series of small earthquakes.

But this simply means that it is *usually* possible to predict *some* types of eruption:

- There are many volcanoes which are thought to be extinct, but we are never quite sure when they will erupt again. When Mount Lamington in New Guinea erupted in 1951, nobody had even known that it was a volcano.
- It is not usually possible to predict how devastating an eruption will be. When Mount St. Helens erupted in 1980, geologists had predicted a major event, but were still surprised by the extent of the damage.

When an eruption starts, nothing can be done about ash falls, but lava flows can sometimes be controlled:

- In 1935, and again in 1942, the city of Hilo in Hawaii was threatened by a lava flow. The lava was bombed – and this made it spread out on the slopes above the town where it caused little damage.
- In 1973, lava actually covered part of the town of Heimaey in Iceland; but it was brought under control when thousands of tonnes of sea water were pumped onto the molten rock to cool it down.

The effects of eruptions

Most volcanic eruptions are less damaging than the Mont Pelée disaster of 1902; but it is quite common for buildings, crops, and agricultural land to be destroyed by lava flows and either buried or severely damaged by heavy falls of volcanic ash.

The indirect effects of an eruption can be very serious. After the Laki fissure eruption in 1783, there was large-scale flooding when ice melted and rivers were dammed; and crops and farm animals were poisoned by ash and sulphur fumes. Over 20% of Iceland's population was drowned, or starved in the famine which followed the eruption.

But in the long term, volcanic activity can create some very useful resources:

- New material is brought to the surface of the earth, which will eventually produce a rich soil.
- Deposits of gold, copper, and other minerals are created in some volcanic areas.
- Masses of hot rock close to the surface can be used to generate electric power. There are large generating stations that work on this principle in Italy, New Zealand, and the United States, and there have been studies to investigate whether geothermal power would be a practical proposition in St Lucia and other Caribbean islands.

2 On a world map, mark in and name each of the volcanoes mentioned in Section 3.3.

3 Make a diagram in your book to illustrate:
(a) A shield volcano.
(b) A lava plateau.
(c) A composite cone.
(d) A viscous lava dome.
Give an example of each of these features, and write a few sentences to explain how each feature is formed.

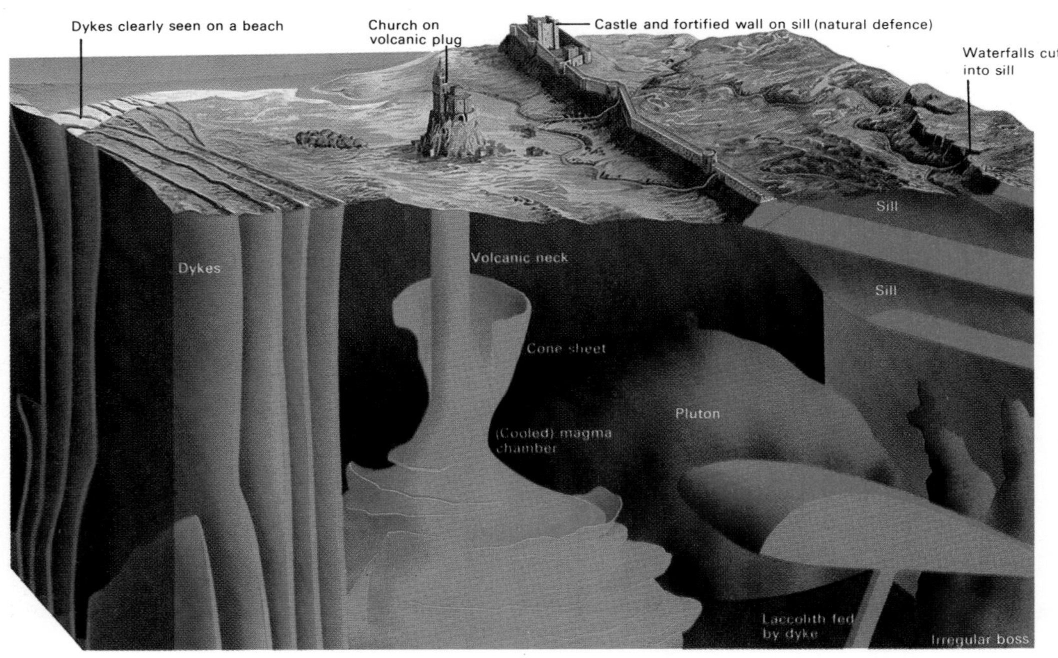

3.12 Intrusive volcanic features.

3.4 Rock types and landforms

Rock types

Igneous rocks are formed from 'new' molten material from below the surface of the earth. Most igneous rocks have a grainy structure, because they are made up of the crystals which different minerals form in the molten rock as it solidifies. The structure of an igneous rock can be seen clearly under a microscope. There are many different types of igneous rock, which can be distinguished by grain size, colour, and mineral composition.

Igneous rocks contain a small amount of radioactive material. This material decays as the rock gets older. By looking at the proportion of radioactive material which has decayed, it is possible to estimate the age of the rock.

Sedimentary rocks are formed at the earth's surface. Many of them are *clastic* sediments, formed when other rocks are broken up to produce loose material which is eroded and then deposited beneath the sea or elsewhere. A fresh deposit of sediment will still be loose and unconsolidated; but when it has been buried deeply for some time, the particles which make it up may be cemented together to form a hard, cohesive rock.

- Fine sediments form clay and silt; and then harder rocks like shale and mudstone.
- Coarser sediments form sand; this may be consolidated to form sandstone.
- Small stones form gravel. When this is cemented together by fine material, it becomes *breccia* or conglomerate.

There are also other types of sedimentary rocks, including:

- Limestone, which is made up of coral, shells, and other material of the same type.
- Evaporites, which are produced when water from the sea or a salt lake dries up, leaving a layer of salts and other material behind.

By studying sedimentary rocks, geologists can learn a great deal about the conditions in which they were formed – whether they were laid down on land or in a shallow sea; in a forest or a desert; what type of rocks were eroded to form a layer of clastic sediments; and so on.

Metamorphic rocks are formed where rocks from near the surface are being dragged down to much greater depths at a convergent plate boundary. These rocks are subjected to high temperatures and enormous pressures, so that their structure is completely altered and the minerals in them are recrystallised. Schist, gneiss, and marble are all metamorphic rocks.

Metamorphic rocks are also formed nearer the surface when smaller areas are heated by lava in a volcanic eruption.

Erosion

When rocks are exposed at the surface of the earth, they come into contact with air and water. Under these conditions, they are gradually broken down by *weathering* into smaller fragments – clay and silt particles, grains of sand, and small stones.

Loose material of this sort can be easily *eroded* or

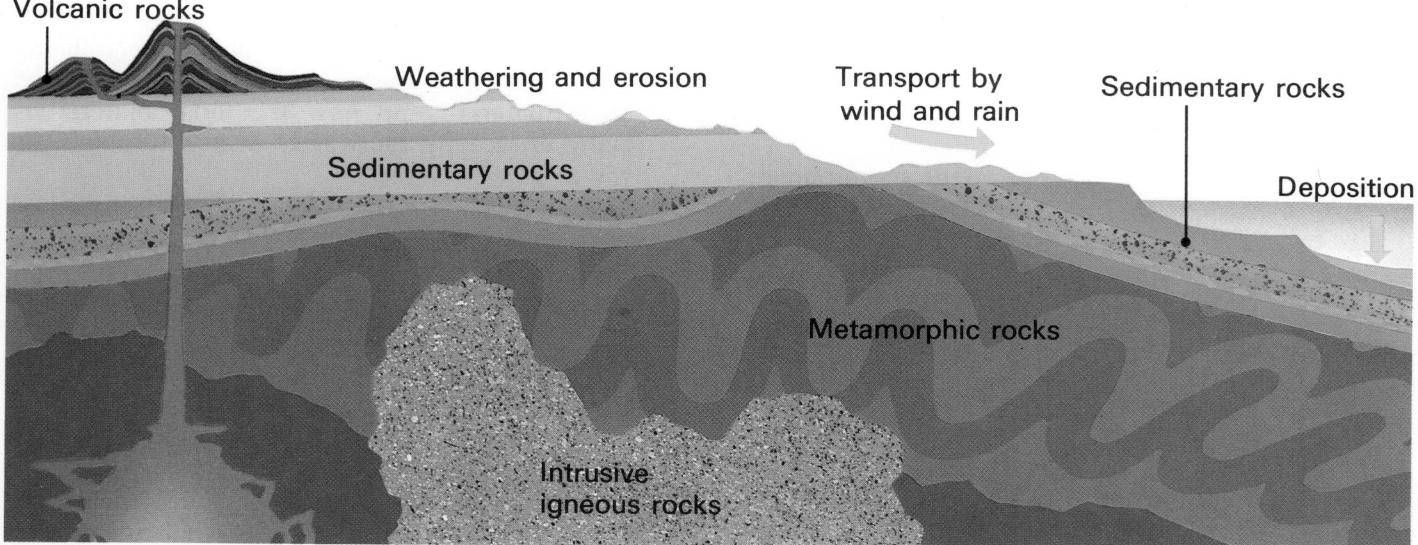

3.13 Different types of rock.

3.14 Rain action and small streams have eroded the summit of Mont Pelée.

worn away by rainwater, by rivers, by the wind, by ice, or by waves.

Near the summit of Mont Pelée, there is a network of gullies and small channels. The loose material near the peak has been:

1 *Eroded* by rainwater and small streams.
2 *Transported* down the side of the mountain by rivers and streams.
3 *Deposited* in the sea, where it will settle and form a layer of sediment on the sea bed.

Landforms

Hills, rivers, valleys, beaches, and cliffs are all *landforms*.

In order to understand landforms, it is necessary to know about:

- The *structure* of the area where they are found; what type of rocks there are; whether the rocks are easily broken up; how the rocks have been affected by earth movements; and so on.
- The *processes* by which the landscape is being altered; how the rocks are being weathered into loose material; and how the loose material is being eroded by rainwater, rivers, the wind, or waves.
- The amount of *time* that has passed since the last set of earth movements affecting the area.
- The *history* of the area; whether it has ever been flooded by the sea; or whether sea levels were once lower than they are now; whether there has been any major change in climate which has affected weathering and erosion.

The structure of the Caribbean

Figure 3.15 shows some of the ways in which large scale earth movements have affected the landforms of the Caribbean.

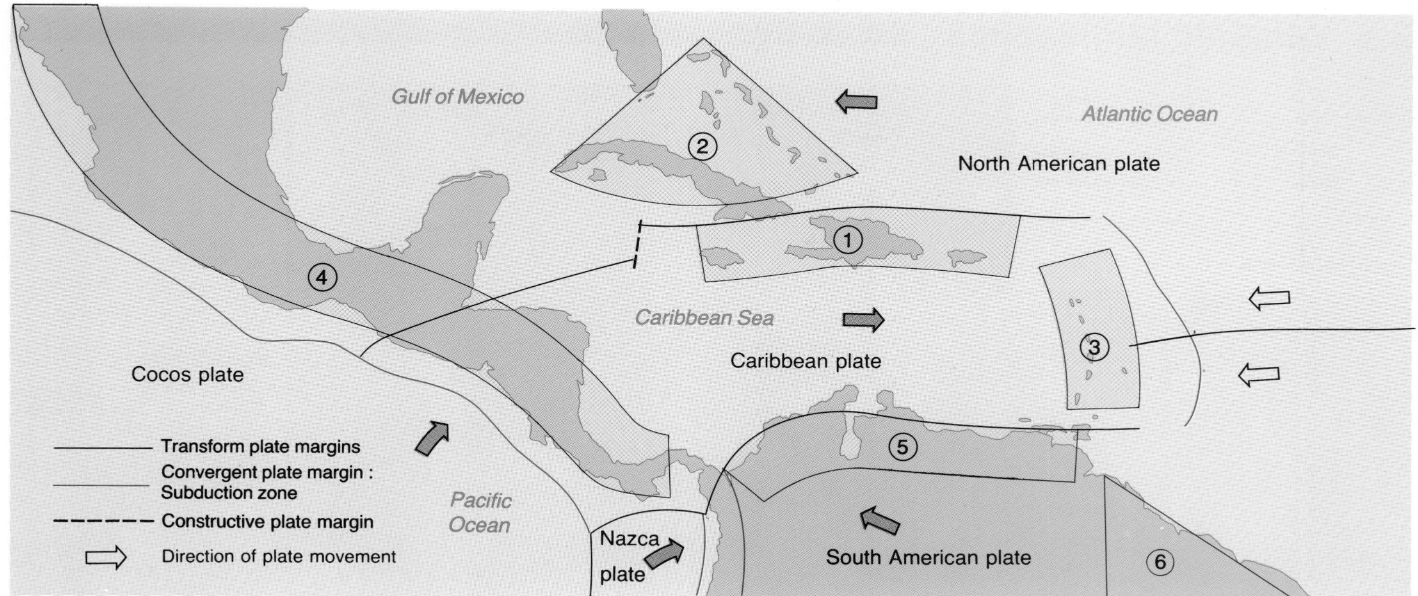

3.15 The structure of the Caribbean.

Zone 1 The oldest rocks in Jamaica, Hispaniola, and Puerto Rico were formed as part of an old island arc system about 100 million years ago. Since then, many newer igneous, metamorphic, and sedimentary rocks have been formed there.

This is no longer a subduction zone. It is a transform plate margin. There is no volcanic activity here now, but there are frequent earthquakes. The older rocks have been folded and distorted, and then uplifted and eroded.

Zone 2 The Bahamas and Cuba are part of the North American plate. The Bahamas are geologically stable, and consist of thick layers of limestone which rest on a firm foundation of older rocks. But because the Bahamas are very low-lying, they have been strongly affected by changes in sea level since the ice age.

Zone 3 The eastern Caribbean is an *island arc* which follows the line of the subduction zone along the edge of the Caribbean plate. Figure 3.6 shows how an island arc is formed along a convergent plate margin.

All the islands in the eastern Caribbean are geologically quite recent. In some, there are no rocks more than a million years old.

There are many *constructional* landforms, like coral reefs and active volcanoes, which are now being built up. Almost all the landforms are directly related to the structure, or to one of the processes by which the landscape is being shaped today.

Zone 4 Mexico and Central America is a very complex area. There is a destructive plate boundary along the Pacific coast. Earthquakes are very common here, and there are many active volcanoes.

Most of the rocks have been folded and distorted in the subduction zone at the plate boundary; then they have been lifted upwards by earth movements, and then they have been eroded. There are high mountain ranges, which form part of a chain stretching right down the west coast of North and South America, from Alaska to Chile.

Zone 5 There are more *fold mountains* along the southern edge of the Caribbean, in northern Venezuela and Trinidad.

Zone 6 Guyana is part of the South American plate. The southern part of the country consists of very old rocks, which were folded and distorted more than 1,600 million years ago, but are now very stable. These ancient rocks contain many valuable minerals, such as gold and diamonds.

In northern Guyana, these rocks have been covered by more recent sediments.

The landforms of southern Guyana were developed over a long period. Many large-scale features are no longer influenced directly by the structure of the rocks; but have been shaped by the way the land was eroded in the distant past.

1 Use Figures 3.6 and 3.15 to make a labelled cross-section of the east Caribbean island arc. Your cross-section should show:
   (a) The South American plate.
   (b) The Caribbean plate.
   (c) A deep ocean trench at the plate boundary.
   (d) The subduction zone.
   (e) Molten rock rising towards the surface.
   (f) A volcanic island, which is part of the island arc.

3.5 Volcanic landscapes

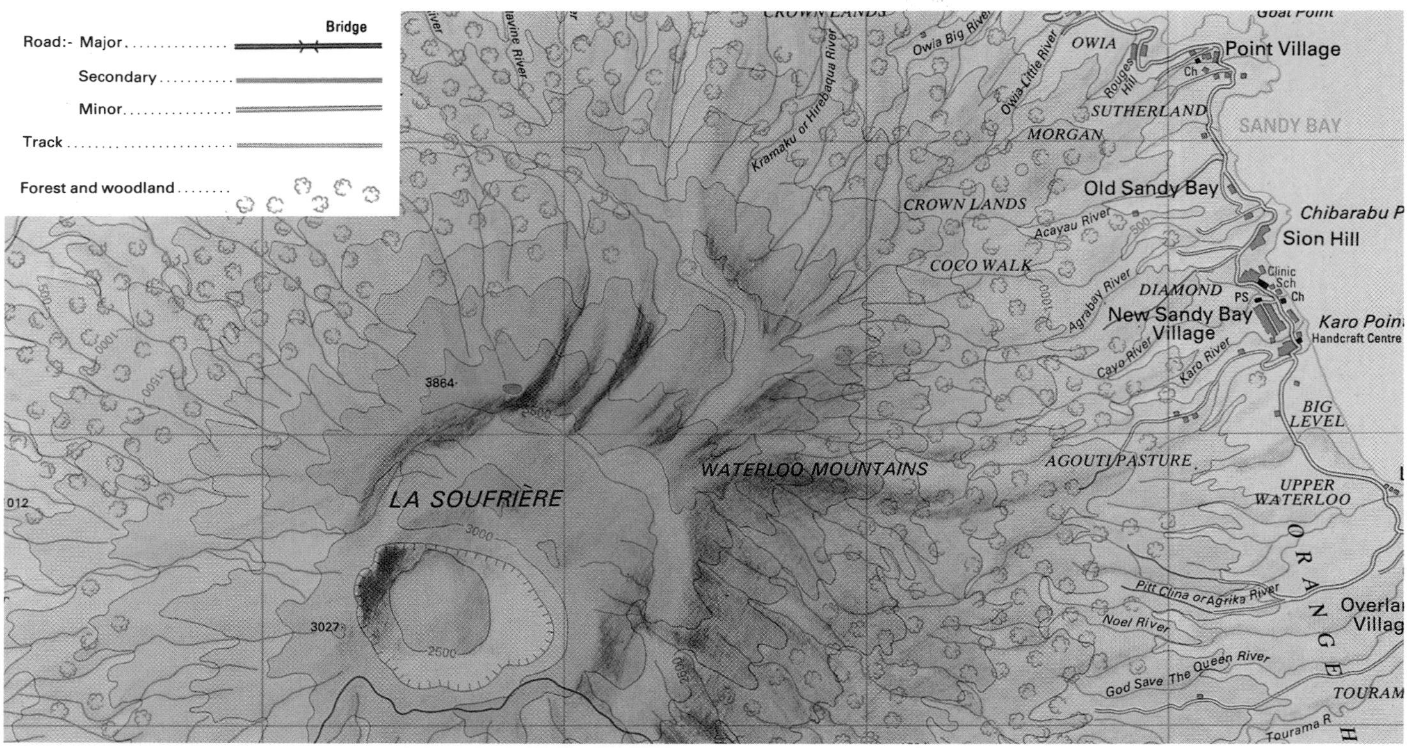

3.16 The St Vincent Soufrière – scale 1:50 000.

St Vincent

Figure 3.16 is a map of the Soufrière volcano in St Vincent which is a composite volcano, built up from layers of ash and lava over the last million years.

- Like many volcanoes, it has a roughly *conical* shape.
- There are ridges of high ground formed by tongues of lava flowing down the side of the volcano. Some of these lava flows form headlands when they reach the sea.
- There are many small rivers and streams flowing down the sides of the mountain. They have cut small valleys.
- At the top of the volcano, there is a *caldera*, which was formed when the top of the mountain collapsed in a gigantic eruption in prehistoric times; and a *crater* which has been formed by volcanic activity since then.
- Until the 1971 eruption, there was a lake within the crater, which was more than a kilometre across. Now, there is a small lava dome.

The Soufrière is an active volcano. There have been eruptions in 1718, 1812, 1902, 1971, and 1979. Some of these eruptions have altered the shape of the volcano in quite a dramatic way.

1 Figure 3.17 shows the cross-section of the summit of the volcano in 1968 and 1981. Describe the changes which were brought about by the eruptions of 1971 and 1979.

2 Make a sketch map of the coastline, showing a headland which was probably formed by a lava flow.

3 Make a sketch map of the volcano as it is today, which should show:
   (a) The caldera.
   (b) The crater.
   (c) The lava dome.

4 Use the map to calculate:
   (a) The maximum diameter of the crater and of the caldera.
   (b) The average gradient of the slope from the peak of the volcano to the coast of Sandy Bay.

Remember that the scale of the map is 1:50,000, and that heights are shown in feet.

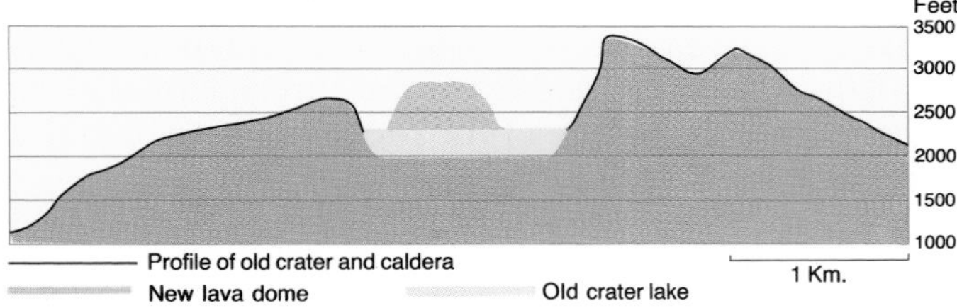

3.17 Changes to the summit of the St Vincent Soufrière, after the 1971 and 1979 eruptions.

St Lucia

St Lucia is also a volcanic island, but most of the activity there took place several million years ago, and there has not been a major eruption for 40,000 years.

This means that the landforms there have been very much altered by erosion. Most parts of the island do not 'look' volcanic in the way that the St Vincent Soufrière does. However, there are volcanic landforms which can still be recognised.

5 Figure 3.19 shows a view across Southern Lucia from the Moule à Chique. Make a sketch of the view, and label these features:
(a) The Pitons.
(b) Volcanic cones around Mount Gimie.
(c) Older volcanic hills.
(d) Gently sloping ignimbrite flow.
(e) Recent sand and alluvium.

1 Most of the rocks in this area were laid down in the first phase of volcanic activity, around 10 million years ago. The original volcanic landscape has been completely altered by erosion. There are no conical hills; but there are many ridges of high ground, formed by dykes which have resisted erosion.

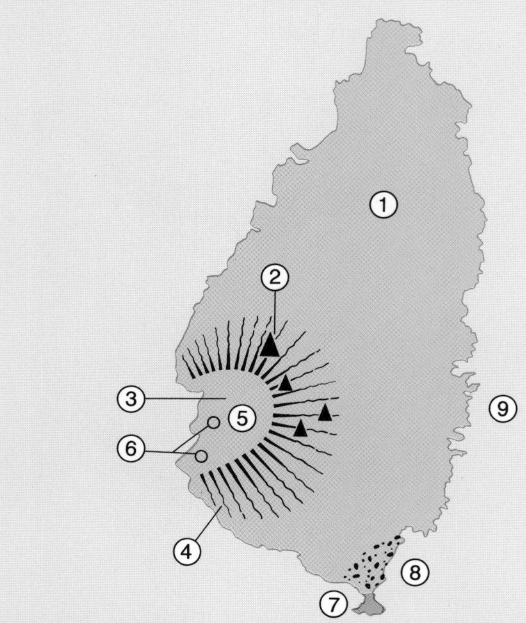

2 Mount Gimie is the largest of a group of volcanic cones which was formed about 1.7 million years ago. These cones have been altered by erosion, but they are still recognisable.
3 Several hundred thousand years ago, there was a very large volcano, centred near to the town of Soufrière.
4 About 40,000 years ago, there was a major ignimbrite eruption from this volcano. Thick sheets of soft ashy material were laid down here. This material is being rapidly eroded by rivers and the sea.
5 After the eruption, the centre of the volcano collapsed, leaving a large caldera. The western side of the caldera is missing, so it is not so easy to recognise as Crater Lake.
6 Inside the caldera are fifteen intruded viscous lava plugs. The largest of them are the two Pitons. There are also seven small craters formed by recent activity. One of these contains the Soufrière fumarole.
7 This headland, the Moule à Chique, is formed of layers of ash and lava which were laid down around ten million years ago. The steep cliff has been produced by wave erosion. It cuts across the original constructional landforms.
8 North of the town of Vieux Fort, there is a large flat area formed of recent sand and alluvium.
9 Many of the headlands of this stretch of coast are formed by old lava flows.

3.18 Volcanic landforms in St Lucia.

3.19 A view across southern St Lucia. The ridge in the foreground follows the line of a dyke.

3.6 Faulting

Faulting

In an earthquake, a fracture is created in the rocks as they snap into a new position as a result of large-scale movements, caused by forces of *tension* and *compression* in the earth's crust, which are often associated with plate margins.

When there have been many earthquakes in the same area, a *fault line* develops. This is a major fracture where the rocks have been displaced over a long period by anything from a few metres to several hundred kilometres.

- In a *normal fault*, the rocks have been pulled apart. The earth's crust is being stretched.
- In a *reverse fault*, the rocks have been pushed together. The earth's crust is being compressed.
- In a *transform fault*, two masses of rock are being pushed past each other. The earth's crust is being torn, but not stretched or compressed.

Faulting can produce:

- Continental-scale landforms, hundreds or even thousands of kilometres across.
- Regional-scale landforms, tens of kilometres across.
- Local-scale landforms, which are still impressive but are only a few kilometres across.

A block of rocks which has been moved downwards by faulting is called a *rift valley* or *graben*. A block of rocks which has been pushed upwards is a *horst* or *block mountain*. When the rocks have been pushed up on one side only, it is a *tilt block*.

Fault patterns in Jamaica

The oldest rocks in Jamaica were formed around 100 million years ago, when this part of the earth's crust was an island arc between the North American and Caribbean plates.

About 30 million years ago, earth movements pushed the island below sea level. Limestone was deposited on top of the older volcanic and sedimentary rocks. The island had already been broken up by major fault lines.

Over the last 10 million years, the island has been faulted upwards by as much as 2,000 m. It is a large-scale *horst*. It has also been broken up by many local faults, which mostly run east–west or NNW–SSE.

Many landforms in Jamaica have been influenced by local-scale faulting:

- Long Mountain, just east of Kingston on Figure 2.10, is a horst. It is a block of white limestone which has been faulted upwards above the surrounding rocks.
- Along a fault, the rocks are shattered. This means that they are more easily eroded. For this reason, many rivers follow fault lines. The upper course of the Yallahs river follows a major fault line.
- The John Crow Mountains are a tilt block. There is a steep escarpment on the south-west side of the range, and a gentle *dip slope* on the north-east.
- To the east of Mandeville, the Milk River flows through a wide valley, known as the Porus *graben*. There are steep slopes on each side of this valley.

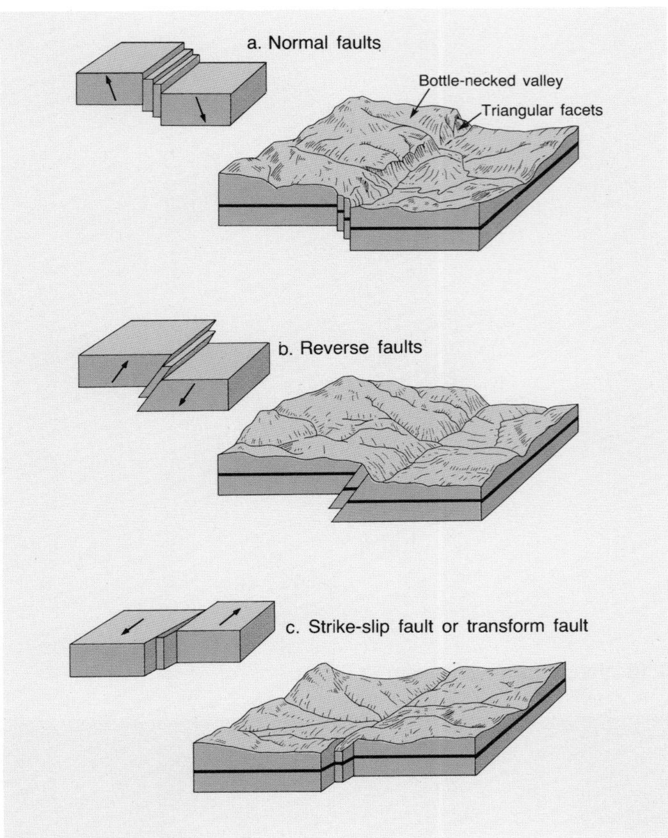

3.20 Types of faulting.

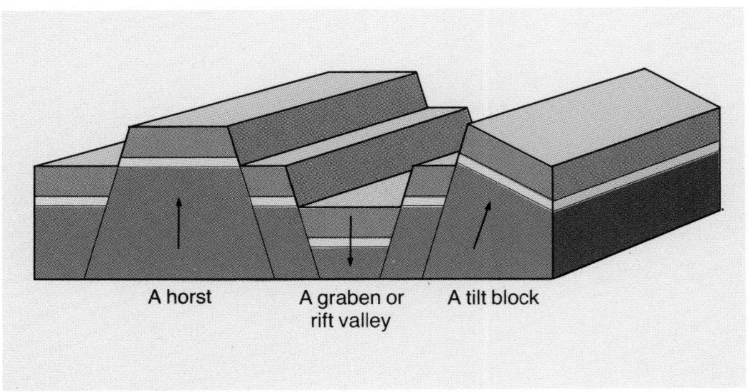

3.21 A fault system.

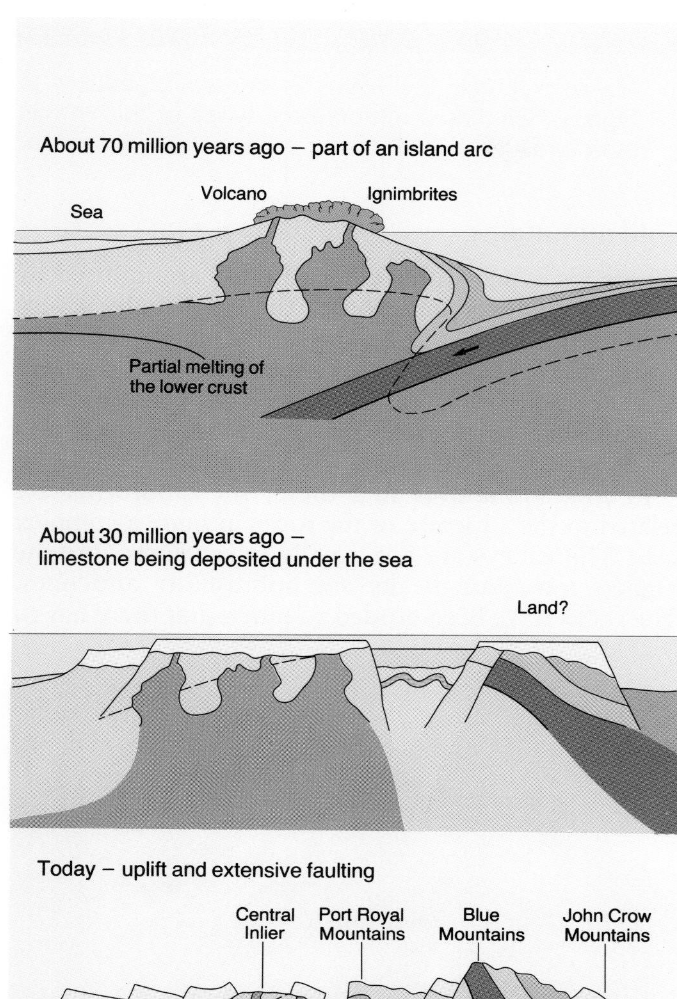

3.22 The development of the major landforms of Jamaica.

1 Figure 3.23 shows the major fault lines of Jamaica. The coastline has been simplified. How many stretches of coast are:
(a) Parallel to east–west faults?
(b) Parallel to NNW–SSE faults?
(c) Not parallel to major fault lines?
2 Look back to Figure 2.10, and make a sketch map of the Long Mountain horst.

The Great Rift Valley

Along plate boundaries, faulting can develop continental-scale landforms. Figure 3.24 shows the Great Rift Valley in Africa. The eastern part of the continent is being pulled away from the rest of the land mass along a divergent plate margin. A series of faults has formed a steep *scarp* 400 to 2,000 m high on each side of the valley floor. The valley is gradually getting wider. In 50 million years, it will probably be as wide and as deep as the Red Sea is now.

3 How long is the Great Rift Valley?
4 Find the Rift Valley in your atlas. Name three of the lakes which have formed in the valley floor.

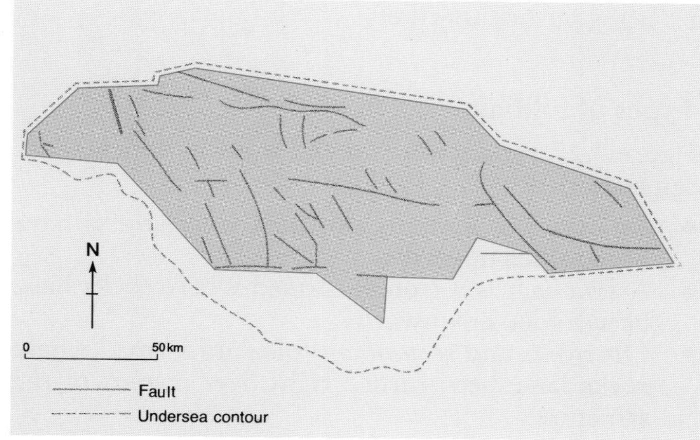

3.23 Fault lines in Jamaica.

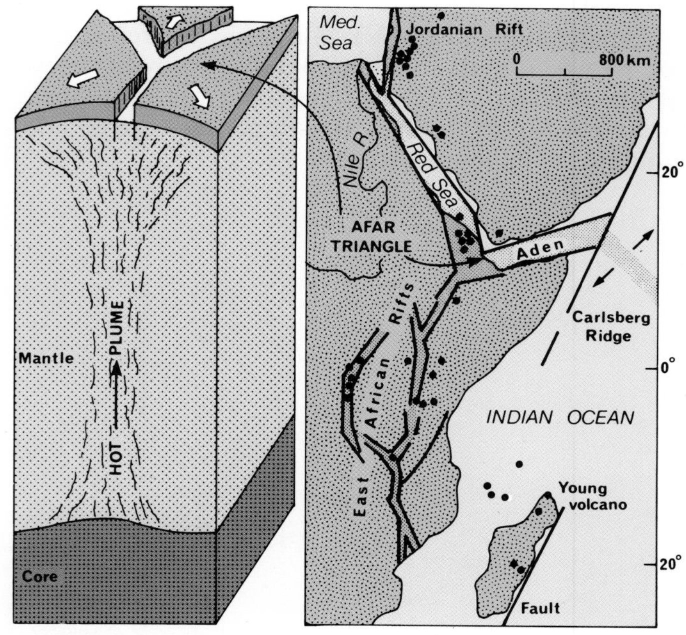

3.24 The East African Rifts.

3.7 Folding

Figure 3.25 shows layers of sedimentary rock in the Scotland District of Barbados. The rocks have been *folded* upwards to form an arch-shaped structure. These rocks were laid down as layers of sand, mud, and clay under the sea. They were probably folded soon after, when a thick mass of sediment slid down a slope on the ocean floor.

Look carefully at the subduction zone on the right-hand side of Figure 3.6. The rocks near to the plate margin have been *folded* where the two crustal plates are being pushed together.

Types of folding

Figure 3.27 shows some of the ways in which rocks can be folded:

- An *anticline* is an arch formed where rocks have been folded upwards.
- A *syncline* is a trough formed where rocks have been folded downwards.
- *Overfolds* and *recumbent folds* are formed where rocks have been turned right over in part of the structure.
- In a *nappe*, the top half of a recumbent fold is pushed right forward, so that the rocks are fractured. A nappe is formed by a combination of folding and faulting.

The anticline in Figure 3.25 is a few metres across. Some folds are just small crumples in the rock, a few centimetres across. Elsewhere, there are large-scale folds which may be tens of kilometres across, and hundreds of kilometres long.

5 Make a sketch to show the pattern of folding in Figure 3.25. Label the different types of fold in this structure.

Fold mountains

Where rocks which have been folded are uplifted by earth movements and eroded, there is usually a very mountainous landscape. The world's highest mountains, the Himalayas, Andes, Rockies, and Alps, have been formed from rocks which have been strongly folded near to a plate margin, then uplifted and eroded.

In *fold mountains* like these, the landforms are related to the structure of the rocks in quite a complex way. The valleys are not usually in synclines, and the highest mountain peaks are not usually anticlines. The rocks have been eroded so much that there has to

3.25 Folded rocks near the east coast of Barbados.

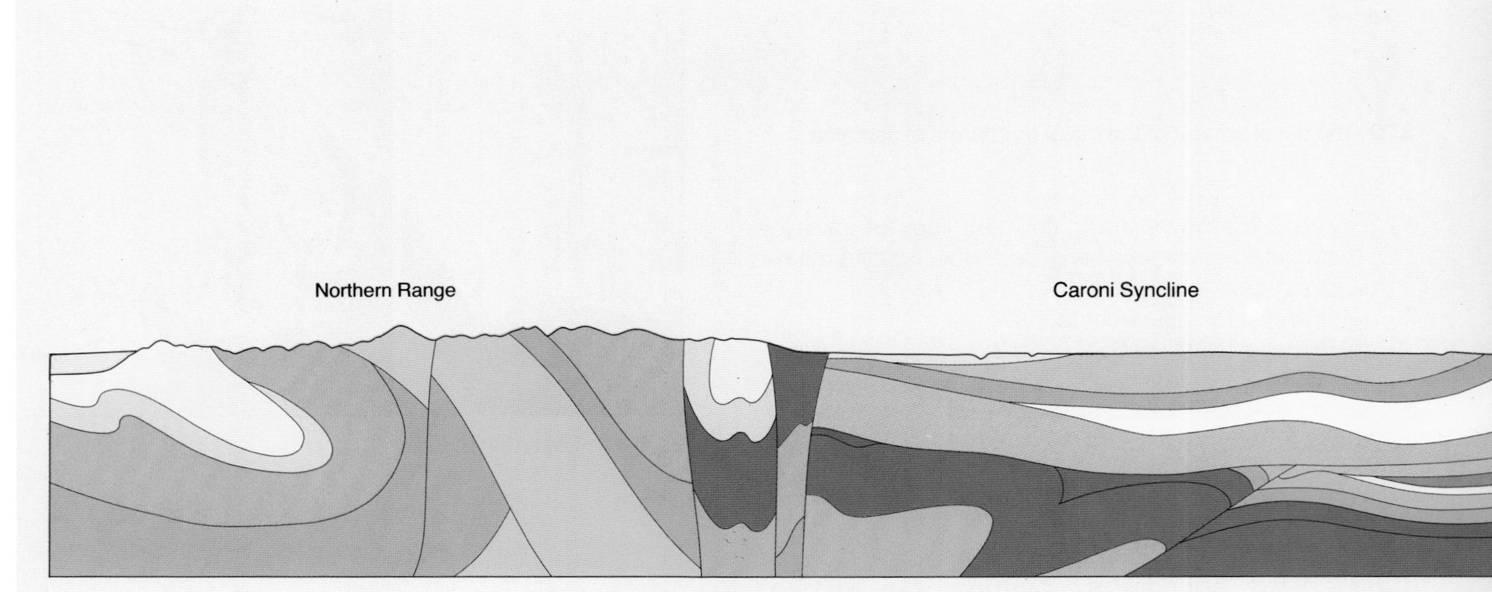

3.26 A cross-section of Trinidad.

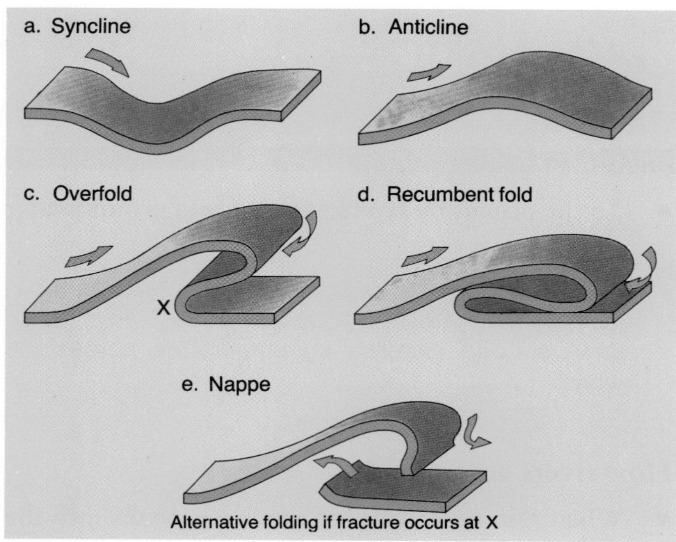

3.27 Types of folding.

be a very careful geological investigation before the way in which they were originally folded can be understood.

Folded rocks in Trinidad

Figure 3.26 shows how the landforms of Trinidad have been influenced by folding:

- The Northern Range are fold mountains, made up of metamorphic rocks. The diagram shows how the rocks have been overfolded, so that they reach the surface at an angle of approximately 30°. The highest point in the Northern Range is the Cerro del Aripo, which is 940 m high.
- In the Caroni syncline, the rocks have been folded downwards. The syncline has been filled in with mud, sand and other material, so it is a very flat, low-lying area.
- The rocks in the Central Range have been folded into a series of synclines and anticlines. The rocks are more easily eroded than those of the Northern Range, and the folding has not been so intense, so the hills are not nearly as high. The highest point in the Central Range is Mount Tamana, which is 308 m high.
- The Siparia syncline is another low-lying area, but the landscape here is not as flat as in the Caroni syncline.
- The Southern Range consists of a few small groups of low hills, formed of rocks which have been folded into synclines and anticlines.

Faulting and folding combined

Most mountain areas are formed by a combination of folding and faulting.

- Long Mountain in Jamaica is a horst, but the top of the mountain has also been folded upwards to form an anticline.
- The Blue Mountains in Jamaica have been pushed upwards by faulting; but they are made up of rocks which have been strongly folded in the past.
- If you study Figure 3.26 carefully, you will see that the Northern Range and the other areas of high ground in Trinidad have been pushed upwards by faulting. There is a very sharp boundary between the Northern Range and the Caroni plain, which is formed by a major fault line, the El Pilar fault. This fault is associated with the southern margin of the Caribbean plate.

4 • RIVERS

4.1 The hydrological cycle

There are 1,500 km^3 of water on or near the earth's surface.

This water circulates between the oceans, the atmosphere, and the land surface of the earth. This pattern of circulation is known as the *hydrological cycle*.

Water is stored in the oceans, in the ice caps, as groundwater, and in lakes. At any one time:

- 97.3% of the world's water is salt water in the oceans and seas.
- 2.1% is stored in the ice caps of Greenland and Antarctica.
- 0.6% is stored in the soil and in rocks.
- 0.01% is in rivers and lakes.
- Only 0.001% is held in the atmosphere as clouds and water vapour.

Water is *transferred:*

- To the atmosphere by evaporation and transpiration.
- From the atmosphere by precipitation, as rain or snow.
- To the oceans by rivers, streams and groundwater seepage.

1 How would the hydrological cycle be affected by:
(a) A long drought?
(b) A sudden increase in temperature across the world?

How rivers are formed

- When rain falls, some of the water soaks into the soil.
- When the soil is *saturated*, and can hold no more water, the excess rainwater starts to flow across the surface. It flows in small rills or as a continuous sheet of water. This is *overland flow*. It dries up soon after the rainstorm has finished.
- Surface flow runs into rivers and streams, which are usually permanent features of the landscape.
- Some of the water in the soil is evaporated, or taken up by plants.

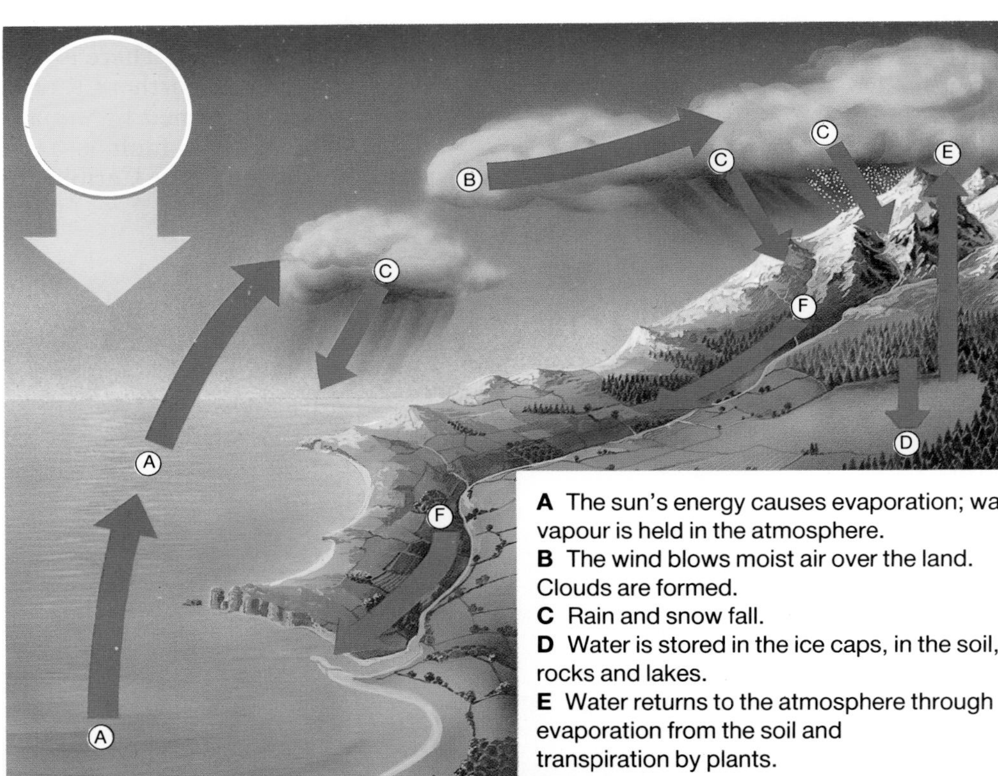

4.1 Hydrological cycle.

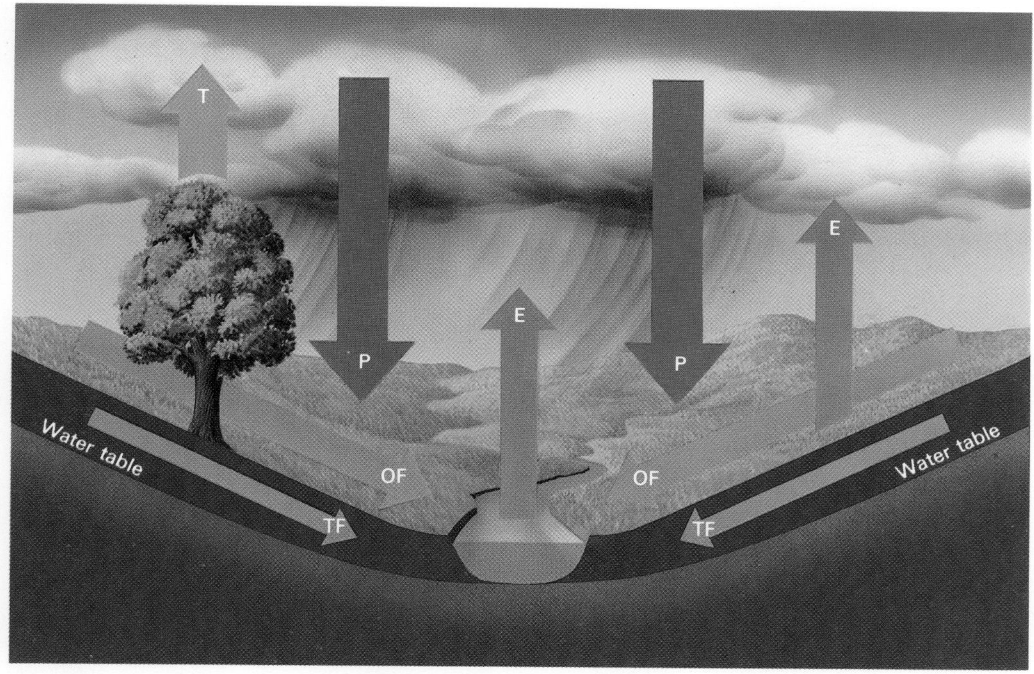

4.2 How water flows into rivers.

- Some soil water seeps slowly into rivers and streams over a long period. This is called *throughflow*.
- Soil water also sinks into rocks further below the surface. Rocks below the *water table* are saturated.
- Some of this *groundwater* eventually finds its way into rivers and streams.
- Rivers and streams carry excess water out of the *drainage basin*.

2 Explain in your own words what is meant by:
 (a) The hydrological cycle.
 (b) Overland flow.
 (c) Throughflow.
 (d) The water table.
 (e) Groundwater.

4.2 Drainage Patterns

There are many rivers in areas where:

- Rainfall is high, and
- The rocks cannot absorb large amounts of water very quickly.

There are very few rivers in areas where:

- Rainfall is very low, or
- Water flows through the rocks very easily, so that they can soak up rainfall quickly.

Radial drainage

Grenada has a radial drainage pattern. The rivers flow outwards from the main volcanic peaks in the centre of the island.

Trellised drainage

In parts of the Northern Range in Trinidad, there is a trellised drainage pattern. There are bands of metamorphic rock running east–west. The main rivers run north or south, cutting across these bands of rock. The *tributary* streams erode more easily along the east–west grain of the bands of rock; so they generally

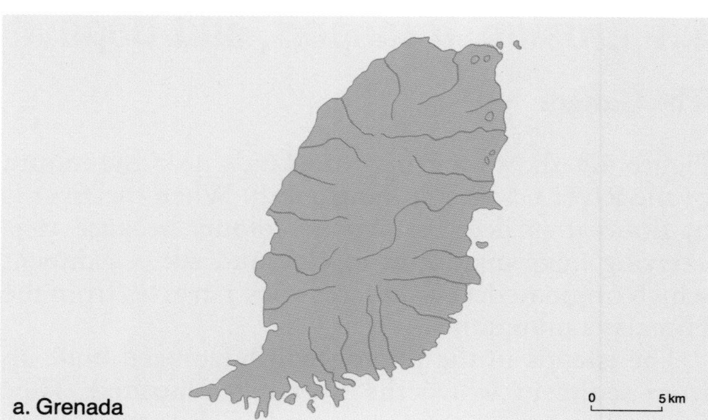

4.3 Drainage patterns.
(a) A radial drainage pattern – Grenada.

run east–west, roughly at right angles to the main river. Taken as a whole, the drainage pattern has the appearance of a rectangular grid.

Dendritic drainage

The Essequibo river basin has a dendritic or 'tree-shaped' drainage pattern. The main river is the 'trunk' of the tree; the larger tributaries like the Cuyuni and the Mazaruni are the main 'branches'; and the smaller tributaries form a pattern like little branches and twigs.

1 Look at Figure 3.16. What type of drainage pattern is there in northern St Vincent?

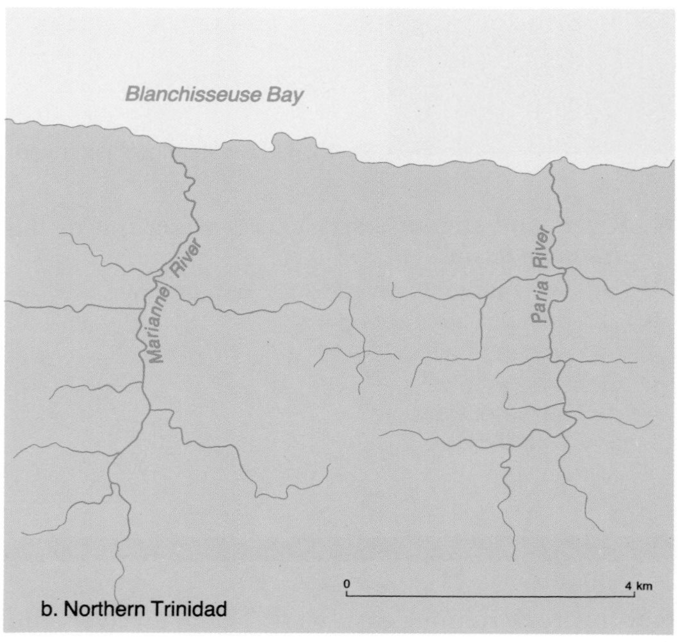

(b) A trellised drainage pattern in northern Trinidad.

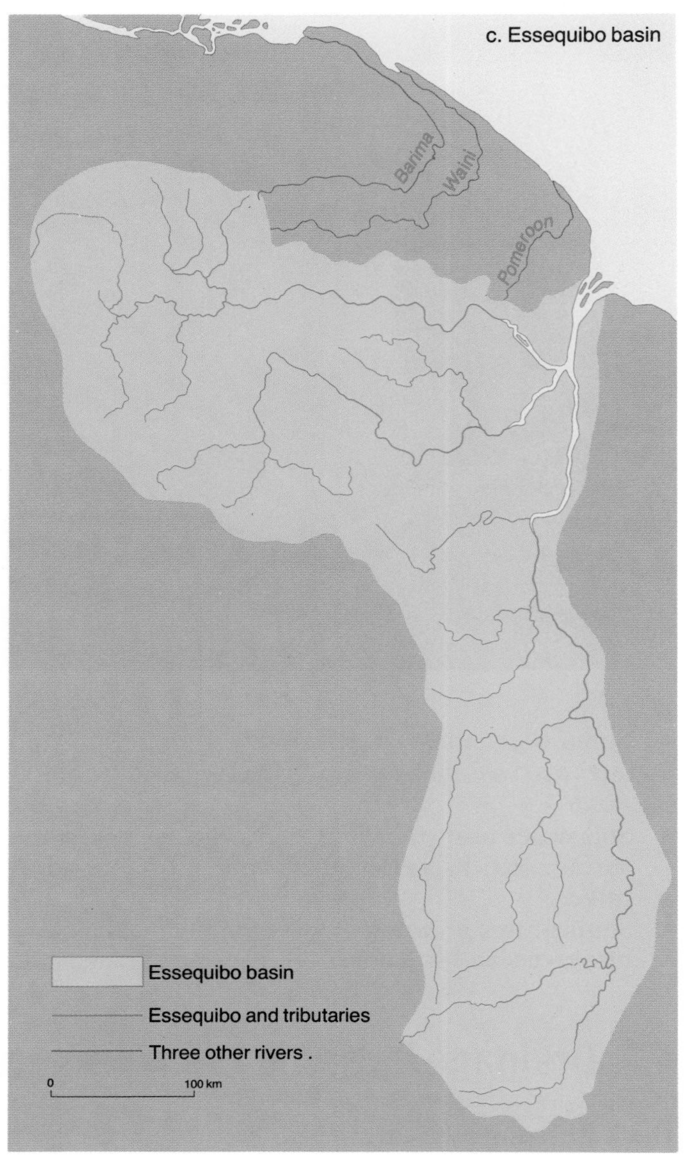

(c) A dendritic drainage pattern in Guyana.

4.3 Erosion, transport, and deposition

The Ganges

Figure 4.4 shows a group of islands near the mouth of the River Ganges in Bangladesh. When the river is in flood it is deep brown in colour, because it is carrying huge quantities of clay and silt – sediment which originated as weathered rock particles from the Himalaya mountains.

The islands in the photograph have been built up from sediment which the river has deposited. They are still growing, as more mud is deposited every year. The land is very low-lying, and is flooded every year during the *monsoon* or rainy season; but it has been settled by landless farmers, even though they risk losing their lives in a bad flood.

The Ganges transports 1,500 million tonnes of sediment to the sea every year, more than any other river in the world.

The rivers of the Caribbean islands, and even Guyana, are all much smaller than the Ganges. But they have all shaped the landforms of their valleys and drainage basins by:

- *Eroding* rock, weathered material and soil.
- *Transporting* it downstream.
- *Depositing* sediment along their valleys and in the sea.

4.4 Islands in the Ganges.

2 The Ganges drains an area of more than 2 million km^2. Use your atlas to make a sketch map of the drainage basin of the Ganges and its tributaries.

Rivers and energy

River water in a mountainous area has *potential energy*, which allows it to:

- *Flow* towards the sea, and overcome the friction between the water itself and the channel through which it runs.
- *Erode* the material on its banks and bed.
- *Transport* the material it has eroded.

The potential energy of the river can also be used to generate *hydroelectric power*, and for many other purposes.

A small river flowing slowly across flat terrain needs almost all the energy it has to overcome friction and flow towards the sea.

A large, fast-flowing river has much more energy available for erosion and to transport material downstream.

Erosion

There are several different processes by which rivers can erode.

Hydraulic action This is the force of the river water itself acting on the bed and banks. Hydraulic action is particularly powerful when river-flow is very fast.

When a river becomes *turbulent*, the sudden pressure changes produced by jets of water and imploding air bubbles can break up a well-jointed rock very quickly. This process is known as *cavitation*.

Solution River water can dissolve some of the minerals in rocks, soil, and weathered material. Solution is particularly important in limestone areas, but all rivers carry significant quantities of dissolved salts – even though we think of them as fresh water.

Abrasion or corrasion This is the process by which stones, sand grains, and other particles carried by the river are thrown against the bed and banks and help to erode them.

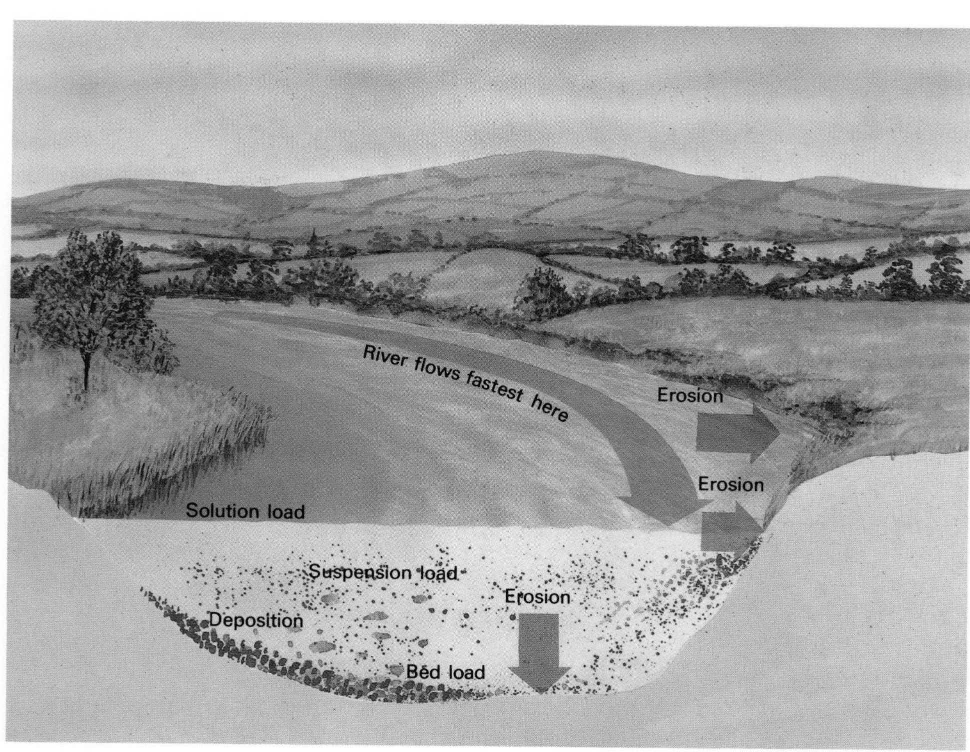

4.5 Erosion, transport and deposition.

Transport

Rivers transport material through:

- *Traction:* stones and boulders are rolled along the river bed. Material moved by traction is called the *bedload.*
- *Suspension:* fine clay particles float along in the river water.
- *Solution:* as we have seen, some minerals are actually dissolved in the water.
- *Saltation:* sand particles are often 'bounced' along the river bed.

Deposition

When a river does not have enough energy to transport all the material that has been eroded upstream, then some of its load will be deposited.

A river will have less energy available when:

- The *gradient* of the river is reduced; for example if it leaves a mountain range and flows into a flat lowland.
- The *volume* of the river is reduced. This may happen if it flows into a dry area where evaporation is high, and no new water is being added to it; or along the whole course of a river during a drought.
- The *velocity* of the river is reduced.
- The river flows into the *sea* or into a *lake*.

If a river does not have enough energy available, it will not deposit its entire load at once. The material it carries is often sorted out by size like this:

- Large boulders will be deposited first. They can only be moved when the gradient of the bed is very steep, and the river is full of storm water after a flood.
- Gravel and small stones are the next to be left behind. Many rivers deposit an *alluvial fan* of coarse material when they leave a mountain area.
- Silt can be carried along even when the river is flowing quite slowly; but most rivers deposit silt along their valleys. There will usually be a silt deposit left on the valley floor after a flood.
- Fine *clay* particles settle very slowly. There may be clay deposits on the bed of a lake, or clay mixed in with silt on the valley floor.
- The *salts* which are carried in solution are not usually deposited at all. They are carried into the sea, where they remain. Salt will only be deposited when a river dries up completely in a desert area; or flows into an enclosed 'salt lake' like the Dead Sea, where the salts are concentrated by evaporation until the water becomes completely saturated, and salt crystals form on the lake floor.

4.4 Meanders, flood plains, and deltas

Flood Plains

Where a river has deposited material along the valley floor, it usually builds up a *flood plain.* The flood plain of a small river may be only a few metres across; but some flood plains are tens of kilometres wide, and may contain thick layers of sediment.

Meanders

Most rivers flowing across a flood plain have a *meandering* course. Meanders are produced like this:

- There will usually be one part of a river channel where the current is flowing fastest.
- Where the course of a river is straight, the zone where the flow is fastest will follow a spiral pattern as it moves downstream.
- When the fastest flow is close to one bank of the river, then that section of bank will be eroded more quickly.
- Because of this, the course of the river curves.
- The curves become more pronounced until there is a well-developed pattern of meanders in the flood plain.

Meanders often take a regular shape. As a rule:

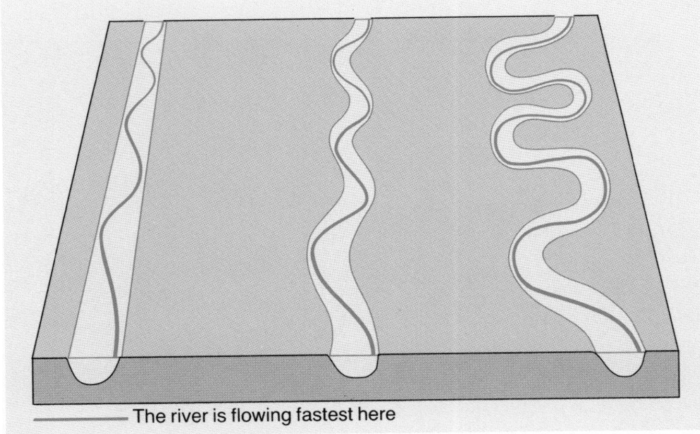

4.6 How meanders develop.

- The length of each meander will be about ten times the width of the channel.
- The width of each meander will be about 14–20 times the width of the channel.

Changes in the course of a river

A meandering river in a flood plain can change its course quite rapidly as Figure 4.7 shows.

Sometimes the 'neck' of a meander becomes very narrow. It may even be cut off in a flood, when the river finds a shorter and faster course for itself.

When this happens:

- The old meander becomes a crescent-shaped channel of almost stagnant water.
- Silt is deposited at each end of the channel, so that an *ox-bow lake* is formed.
- Eventually the ox-bow lake dries out. It becomes an *abandoned meander*.

Deltas

A delta is a wedge of flat land built up from silt and alluvium where a river flows into the sea or into a lake. *Distributaries* are channels which branch off from the main river on a delta. The distributaries usually make a fan-shaped pattern.

One of the largest deltas is that of the Mississippi, on the southern coast of the USA. Every year, 590 km^3 of river water flow down the Mississippi into the Gulf of Mexico, carrying 450 million tonnes of sediment. The sea here is relatively calm, not too deep, and has a small tidal range. This means that the river delta has built up rather quickly. The river here is constantly changing its pattern of flow, so the location of the delta has shifted several times over the past few thousand years.

1 Refer to your atlas, and make a sketch map in your exercise book to show the deltas of:
(a) The Mississippi. (c) The Niger.
(b) The Ganges. (d) The Yallahs River.
Use a scale to compare the size of these four deltas.

2 Explain why deltas do not form very easily:
(a) On coasts where there are large waves.
(b) Where the sea next to the river mouth is deep.

Levees

Along the lower course of a river, the river banks may sometimes be higher than the rest of the flood plain. High river banks, or *levees*, are formed like this:

- After a period of heavy rain, the river is swollen with flood water, which contains sediment from higher up the valley. The river floods the flat ground along the valley floor.
- The flood waters move more slowly than the main channel, and cannot carry as much sediment. Most of the sediment is deposited quite near to the main river channel.
- When the flood waters recede, a thick deposit of mud is left along the river banks. After this process has been repeated many times, a levee is formed.
- Where levees have been formed, a tributary stream may not be able to join the main river very easily. It runs almost parallel to the river for some distance before joining at a *deferred junction*.

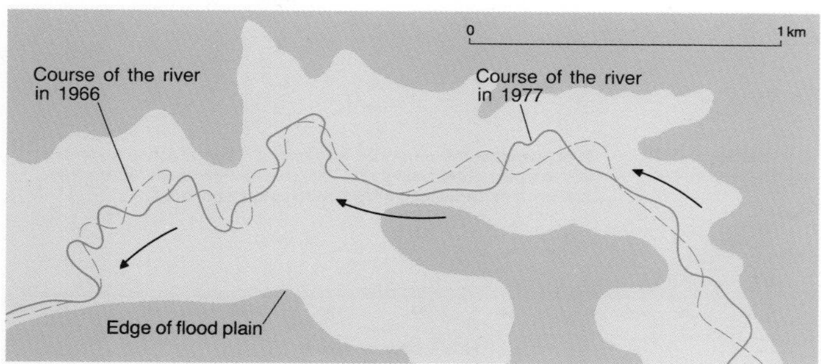

4.7 How the course of the Roseau River in St Lucia has changed.

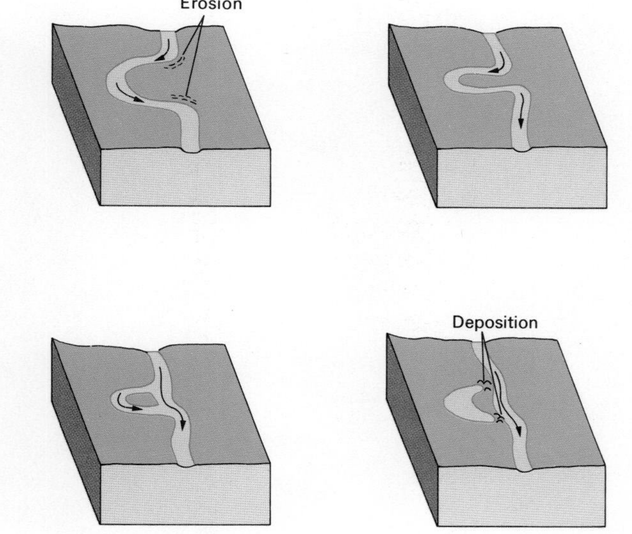

4.8 How an ox-bow lake is formed.

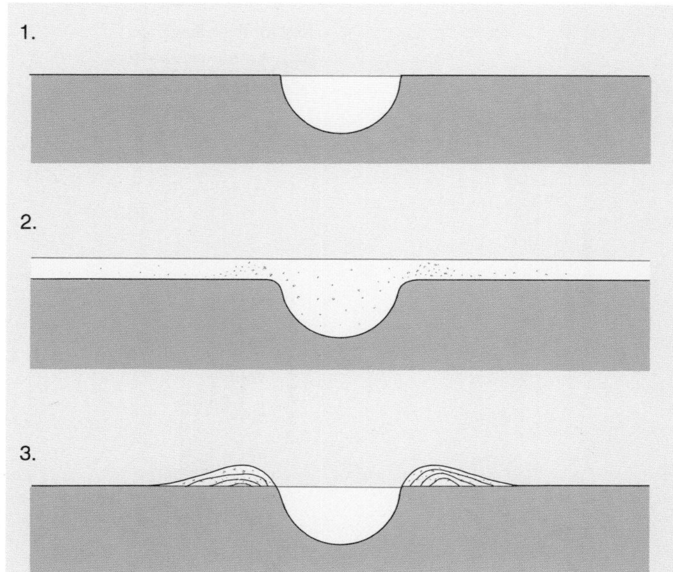

4.9 How levees are formed.

4.5 The Yallahs River

Figure 4.11 shows the Yallahs River basin in eastern Jamaica. Figure 4.10 gives some information about the flow of the river.

1 Why does the river carry more water at Llandewey than at Mahogany Vale, and more at Mahogany Vale than at St Peters?
2 Where does the river have most energy available for erosion?
3 Where is the flow of the river most *variable*?
4 Explain carefully in your own words why the river *erodes* more rapidly and *transports* more material after heavy rain.

The upper course of the river

This part of the river valley runs through a very mountainous area, where the rocks have been *uplifted* and *faulted* in recent geological times. Near St Peters, the river runs along a major fault line.

Some of the rocks are resistant to erosion, but in many places there are alternating layers of sandstone and shale which become very unstable when it is wet.

This is a high rainfall area. In the Blue Mountains, it is more than 4,000 mm per year; and much of the rain falls in torrential downpours.

The river is eroding its bed all the time, cutting *down* through the rocks. This is why it has a narrow, steep-sided valley. The cross-section of the valley is shaped like the letter V.

When there is a rainstorm, material moves rapidly down the valley sides:

- Rain action washes huge quantities of soil and loose material down to the river. It has been estimated that rain wash removes 100 tonnes of

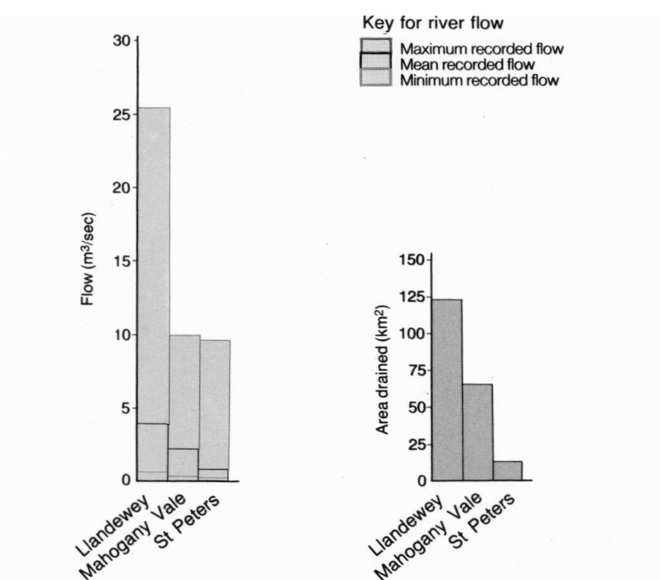

4.10 The Yallahs River: drainage and river flow.

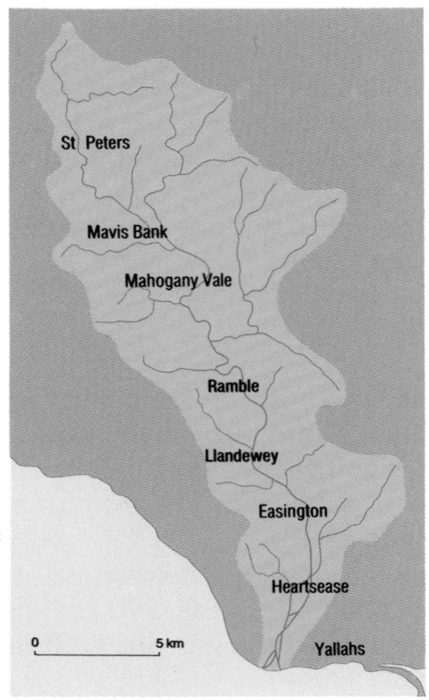

4.11 The Yallahs River Basin, Jamaica.

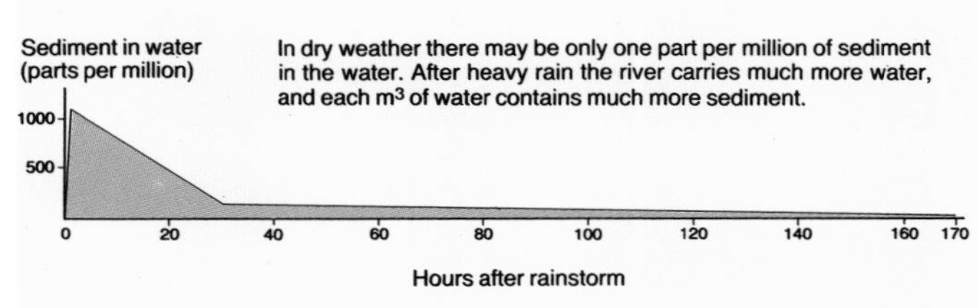

4.12 The amount of sediment carried after a rainstorm.

4.13 The Yallahs River near Mavis Bank.

soil per hectare per year where the land has been cleared for cultivation.

- There are many slumps and slides where layers of shale or masses of unconsolidated material are saturated by the rainwater and become unstable.

Figure 4.12 shows the effect of a heavy rainstorm on the amount of sediment carried by the river.

After a storm is over, it is quite easy for the river to carry away fine silt particles. But many of the large boulders remain on the river bed. They will not be moved again until the next major flood, or until they are broken up in the river.

There are some very large river boulders, many metres across, which could not be moved even in the largest floods that have been recorded. The present-day river valley may still be showing the effects of the rainfall pattern several thousand years ago, when the climate was much wetter than it is today.

4.14 Interlocking spurs in the Yallahs River basin.

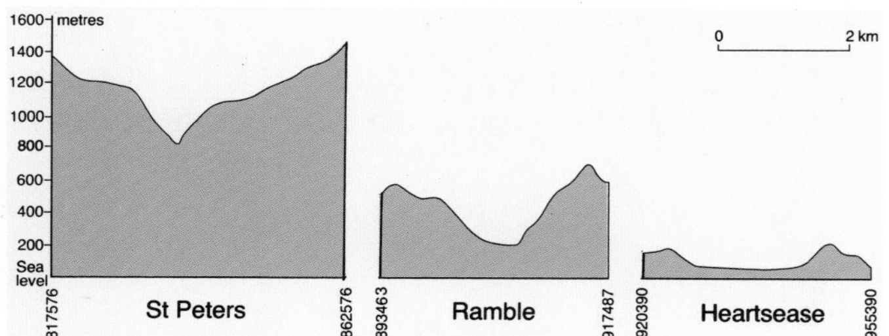

4.15 Three cross-sections of the Yallahs River valley.

In this part of the valley, the course of the river swings from side to side through the hills. Because the valley is narrow, and has a zigzag course, there are *interlocking spurs* of hillside in the bends which block the view along the river.

The middle course of the river

Further downstream, the valley is wider, and its sides are not so steep. There is a small flood plain in the valley floor.

There are several large meanders, which are widening the river valley, like this:

- In a meander curve, there is rapid erosion on the outer bank. The valley sides are cut away from below. There is a steep slope or *river cliff*.
- On the inner bank, the current is much slower. The river usually *deposits* material here. This is called a *slip-off slope*.
- The valley sides are not so steep where they meet the flood plain on the inner side of the meander, because they are not being cut away from below. Soil and loose rock are not washed down this slope as quickly as on the outer bank, and the slope has had time to stabilise, so slumping and sliding are much less likely.
- The end of a spur is often *truncated* when it is eroded by a meandering river.

The lower course of the river

In the lower course of the river, there is a wide flood plain, where material which has been eroded further up the valley has been deposited.

At the mouth of the river, a *delta* has been built up from material deposited in the sea. Even on the river delta, there is a high proportion of coarse material,

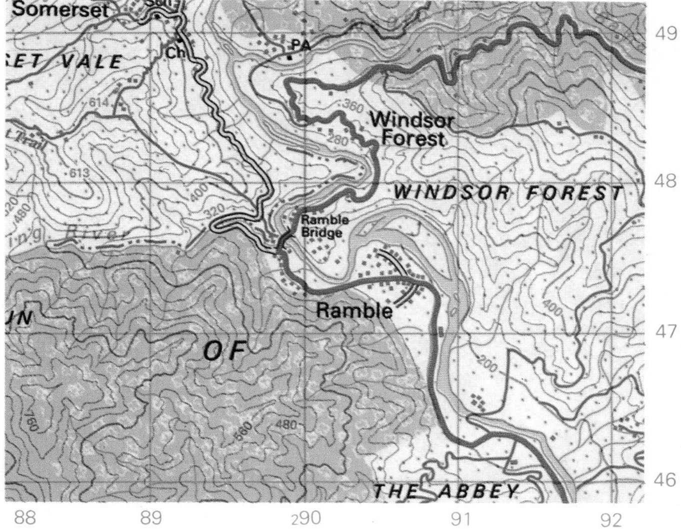

4.16 The middle course of the river at Ramble. 1:50 000

4.17 The lower course of the Yallahs River.

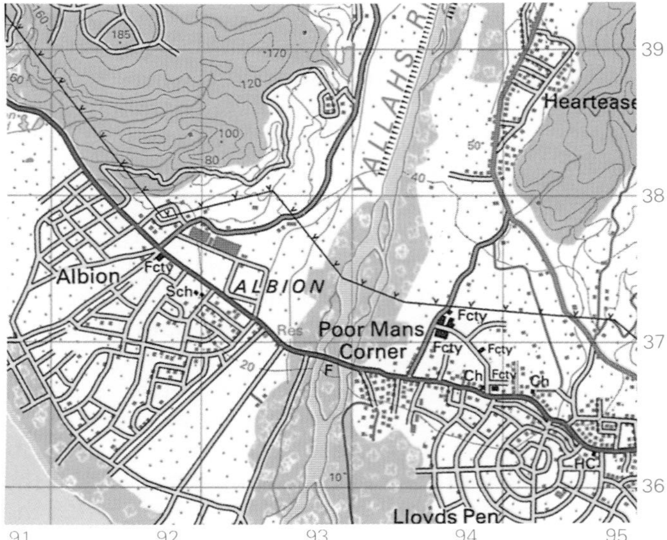

4.18 The lower course of the river and the delta. 1:50 000

boulders, pebbles, and coarse sand. Many other river deltas are made of silt, clay, and fine sediments.

The Yallahs River has a *braided* course. The river is wide and relatively shallow; and the channel is broken up by many small islands, which are made up of sand, gravel, and stones. Some of these islands have vegetation growing on them; others are just shifting sandbanks which move whenever the river is in flood.

Rivers usually have a braided channel when:

- They run down a steep slope from a high mountain area.
- They are carrying a large amount of sediment, particularly coarse sand, gravel, and boulders which are not easy to transport in periods of low water.

5 Make a labelled sketch map of the river valley at Ramble. You should show:
   (a) The river cliff, where the valley sides are being undercut by the river.
   (b) The inner bank of the meander.
   (c) The flood plain.

6 Use Figure 4.17 and 4.18 to make a sketch of the lower Yallahs valley. Show the braided river course, and comment on land use in the river valley.

7 Read through Section 3.4 again, and write down one way in which the landforms of the Yallahs valley are influenced by:
   (a) The *structure* of the area (faulting, rock types, etc.).
   (b) The *processes* by which the landscape is being altered (rainstorms, river flow, landslides, etc.).
   (c) The amount of *time* since the area was uplifted.
   (d) The *history* of the area and climatic change.

You should remember that in other river basins, where the influences on landform development will be different, the features which develop in the river valley will not necessarily be the same. The river channel may not be braided; the valley sides may not be so steep; the flood plain may be made up of fine sediment. There is no fixed set of features associated with the upper, middle, or lower course of every Caribbean river.

8 Compare the landforms of the Yallahs valley with those of a river basin in an area which you have visited.

4.6 The valley sides

Where a river has cut downwards, the material on the valley sides tends to move downhill. Loose soil and weathered material moves most easily – but even large masses of solid rock can become unstable if the conditions are right. These processes are known as mass movement or mass wasting.

Rain action

Rainwater can move individual particles of loose material downhill, like this:

- *Splash action:* a heavy raindrop throws up the soil when it hits the ground. On a slope, most of the particles that have been disturbed end up further downhill. Even on a 10° slope, three-quarters of the particles which are disturbed move in this direction.
- *Rill action:* when rainwater collects in a small channel, it flows downhill, carrying soil and other material along with it.
- *Sheet action:* very heavy rain flows over the surface of the ground as a continuous sheet of water, which can wash off loose soil over a wide area.

Rain action is very effective on sand or bare soil, where there is little or no vegetation to interrupt the downhill flow. If there is grass growing, it traps soil particles, and stops them from being moved too far; and in a forest, the force of the falling rain is broken by the leaves and branches before it drips to the ground. Where there is no vegetation, all the loose material is sometimes stripped off a steep slope, leaving the bare rock exposed.

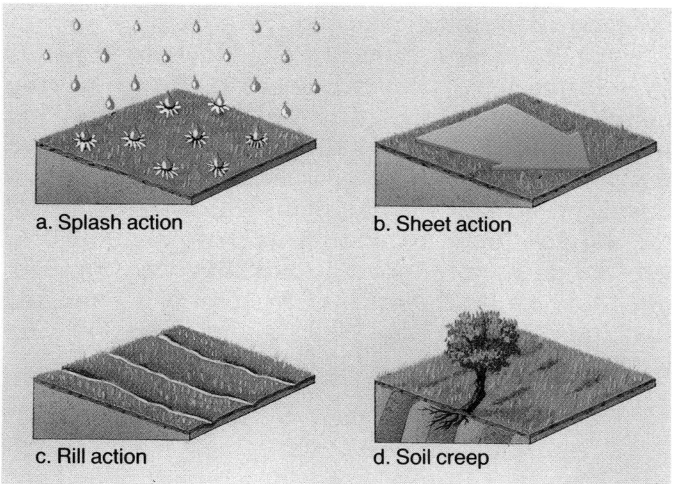

4.19 Rain action and soil movement.
(a) Splash action. (c) Rill action.
(b) Sheet action. (d) Soil creep.

Soil creep

On some slopes, a layer of soil moves gradually downwards at a rate of perhaps 1 mm per year. This sort of movement is very hard to observe, but it can sometimes be detected when a post or tree is slowly pushed over from a vertical position, and begins to lean downhill.

Slumps and slides

A whole section of hillside can sometimes slip downhill as a block – either rapidly or in a series of small earth movements.

Slumps and slides are most common:

- On steep slopes.
- Where there are rocks like shale and clay which become slippery when they are wet.

Figure 4.20 shows the main types of slumping and sliding movement.

Rockslides occur when there is a layer of slippery

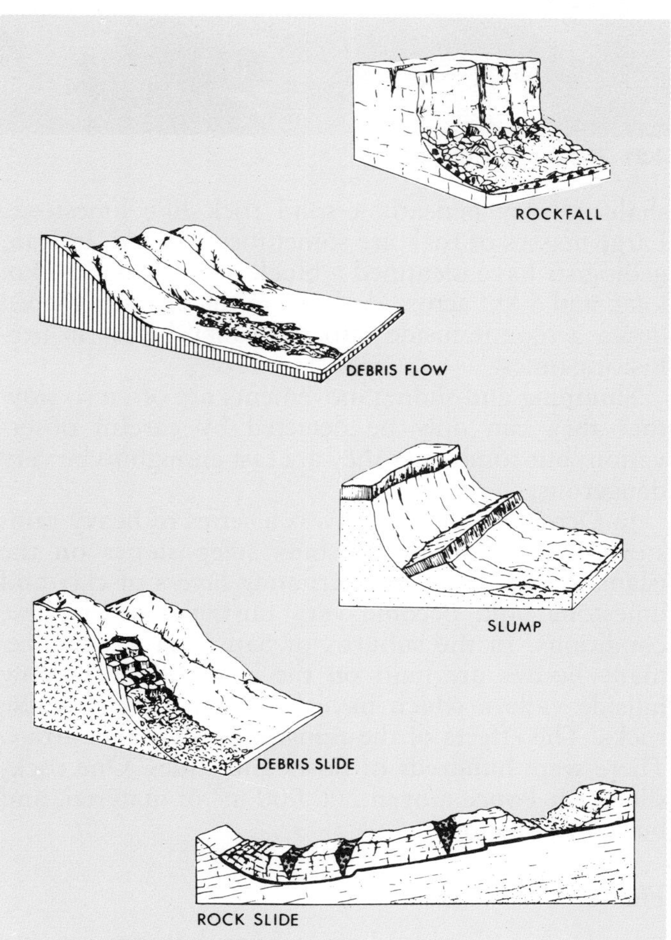

4.20 Slumps, slides and flows.

4.21 The Armero mud flow.

shale or clay beneath a solid rock like limestone. Large masses of rock are sometimes affected. In Iran, geologists have identified a block of limestone 14 km long, and 5 km across, and 300 m thick which slipped down a mountainside into the valley below in prehistoric times.

Slumping and sliding movements are often so slow that they can only be detected by careful observation; but sometimes they are fast enough to be very dangerous.

In October 1985, there was a series of heavy rainstorms in Puerto Rico. Many steep slopes on the island are made up of alternating layers of clay and limestone, and become very unstable under these conditions. In the suburbs of San Juan and Ponce, many houses are built on the sides of the narrow hillside valleys which have been cut through these rocks. The effects of the rainstorms were disastrous. There were hundreds of flows and slides. One rockslide near Ponce moved 200,000 m^3 of material, and buried 127 people.

Flows

A mass of sand, or mud, or loose rock fragments can, under some conditions, start to flow downhill like a liquid. Material in a flow does not move as a block; and flows are generally much faster than slumps and slides.

Mudflows often start after very heavy rain when a thick layer of mud is completely saturated with water. Mudflows can reach speeds of 50 km per hour, or more; a large mudflow which is moving rapidly will obliterate everything in its path.

Some of the most dangerous mudflows are triggered by volcanic activity. In November 1985, the Nevado del Ruiz volcano erupted in Colombia, producing a large quantity of ash. The heat of the eruption melted the volcano's ice cap, and sent a torrent of water down the sides of the mountain which picked up all the ash and loose material in its path. A number of very large, rapidly moving mudflows were formed, one of which hit the town of Armero. It is estimated that 20,000 people were killed, and over 60,000 were left homeless.

1 Explain carefully why there are so many slumps and slides in the Yallahs River valley.
2 Which part of the valley would have most slumps and slides? Give reasons for your answer.
3 Look carefully at Figures 6.1 and 6.2. What type of mass movement is shown?

4.7 Waterfalls

Erosion surfaces

The cover of the book shows the Kaieteur Falls in Guyana, where the Potaro river plunges down from a broad plateau over a steep escarpment. This waterfall is nearly five times as high as Niagara. There are other falls elsewhere in Guyana which are almost as spectacular.

The plateaux and escarpments of western Guyana were formed like this:

- Over a long period, a wide area of ancient rocks was eroded down almost to sea level. A relatively flat landscape – an *erosion surface* – was produced.
- The erosion surface was uplifted by earth movements to form a *plateau.*
- The edges of the plateau were eroded. A new erosion surface was formed just above sea level. A steep slope or *escarpment* separates the two surfaces. The surface of the plateau is relatively level and has not been eroded very much; but the escarpments are gradually worn back so that the size of the plateau is reduced.
- After another phase of uplift, a third erosion surface was formed. Only small remnants of the original surface now remain.

Scientists studying the rocks and landscapes of Guyana have identified at least six erosion surfaces.

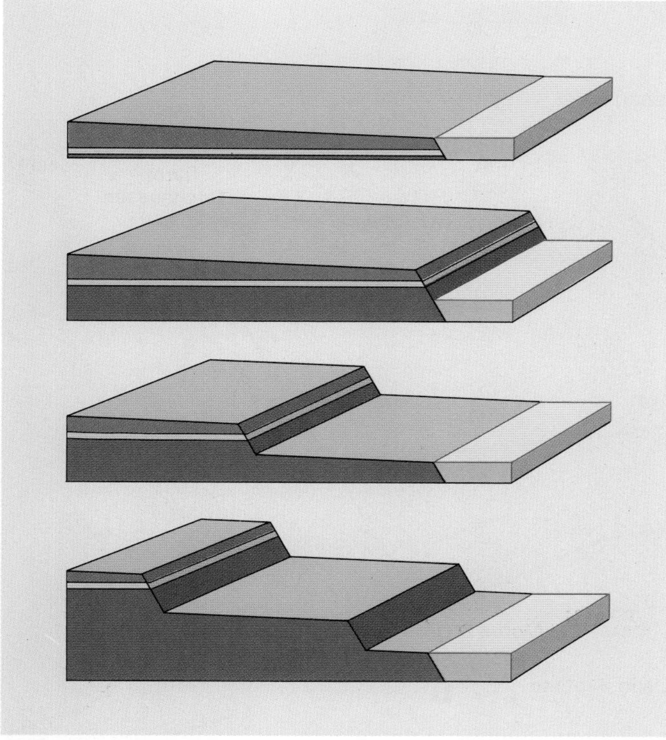

4.22 How erosion surfaces are formed. Surfaces like these are large scale features, up to several hundred kilometres across.

The oldest surfaces were formed tens of millions of years ago. The highest surface is the summit of Mount Roraima, 2,770 m above sea level. The youngest and most recent is 75–90 m above sea level.

Where rivers flow across old erosion surfaces, they have wide, open-sided valleys which merge gradually into the surrounding plateau.

When they flow across an escarpment, there will be a waterfall or a steep, fast-flowing section with rocks and rapids. The river has been *rejuvenated* by the uplift of the old erosion surface.

Erosion at waterfalls

At a waterfall, when a river plunges vertically downwards, a tremendous amount of potential energy is released.

The water at the bottom of the fall erodes through hydraulic action when it hits the ground. There is a lot of turbulence, and rocks are broken up by cavitation.

A deep *plunge pool* is cut into the rock at the base of the waterfall. The plunge pool is also cut back beneath the fall, so that an overhang is produced.

Eventually the lip of rock at the top of the waterfall collapses. The waterfall has retreated a few metres upstream.

After this process has been repeated many times, a long *gorge* is produced below the fall. The Victoria Falls on the border between Zambia and Zimbabwe have been retreating for the last two million years, and the gorge below the falls is now 110 km long.

In some places, a waterfall which has retreated a long way upstream may be reduced in height until it is replaced by a stretch of *rapids*, where water flows very fast down a steep slope and rocks are exposed at the surface, but the river does not plunge vertically downwards.

1 Make a labelled sketch of the Kaieteur Falls. Your sketch should show
   (a) The plateau.
   (b) The escarpment.
   (c) The waterfall.
   (d) The plunge pool.

The Trafalgar Falls

Waterfalls are also produced when a river crosses a band of rock which is *resistant* to erosion. In central Dominica, east of Roseau, a lava flow forms a gently sloping plateau. Above the plateau there are high volcanic peaks. The edge of this plateau is at 500 m above sea level; at this point there is a steep escarpment. Where rivers cross the escarpment, there is either a stretch of rapids or a waterfall. The largest and most spectacular of these waterfalls is the Trafalgar Falls.

4.8 Rising sea levels

20,000 years ago, there were ice sheets, several hundred metres thick, covering much of Europe and North America, and many other parts of the world. When this ice melted, worldwide sea levels began to rise.

It has been estimated that sea level rose by over 100 m in the period between 15,000 and 6,000 years ago. Sea levels may still be rising – but at a much slower rate than before.

Figure 4.24 shows the lower part of the Roseau valley in St Lucia. This river valley has been influenced by rising sea levels.

1 Draw a cross-section of the valley from 'A' to 'B'.
2 Calculate the average gradient of the valley sides along this line. Remember that the scale of the map is 1:25,000 and that heights are in feet.

The valley has an unusual cross-section. There is a sharp break between the steep valley sides and the flat valley floor. The floor of the valley consists of a thick deposit of alluvium, with the Roseau river meandering slowly across it.

The valley cross-section was formed like this:

1 When sea level was much lower than at present, the river cut a deep, steep-sided valley.
2 Sea level rose rapidly, and the original river valley was flooded by the sea, to form a long narrow inlet, or *ria*.
3 The river deposited mud and silt in the calm waters of the ria.
4 The ria has now been completely filled in, to form a flat valley floor. A slight fall in sea level probably helped to dry out the ria.

The lower course of many Caribbean rivers consists of a flat and often badly drained flood plain which was formed in this way. In these river valleys, there is often a sharp transition from the *upper course*, where the river has a narrow, steep-sided valley, to the *lower course*, where the river meanders slowly across a flat flood plain.

Where an area has been uplifted, so that sea level appears to have *fallen*, rivers will cut down rapidly, like the Yallahs, eroding a narrow, steep-sided valley.

3 Describe three ways in which the Roseau valley contrasts with the valley of the Yallahs River.

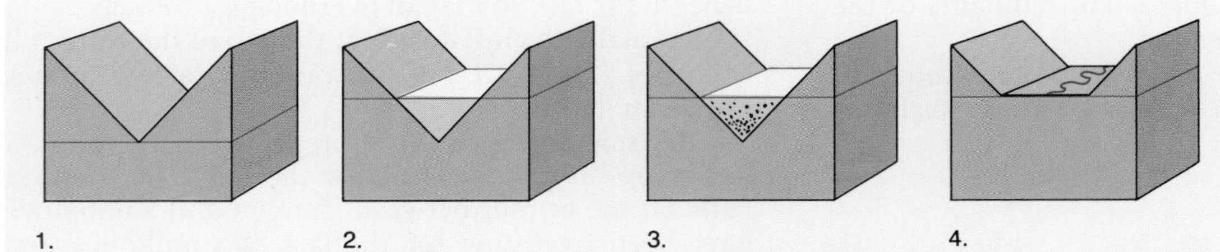

4.23 How sea level changes have affected the development of the Roseau River valley.

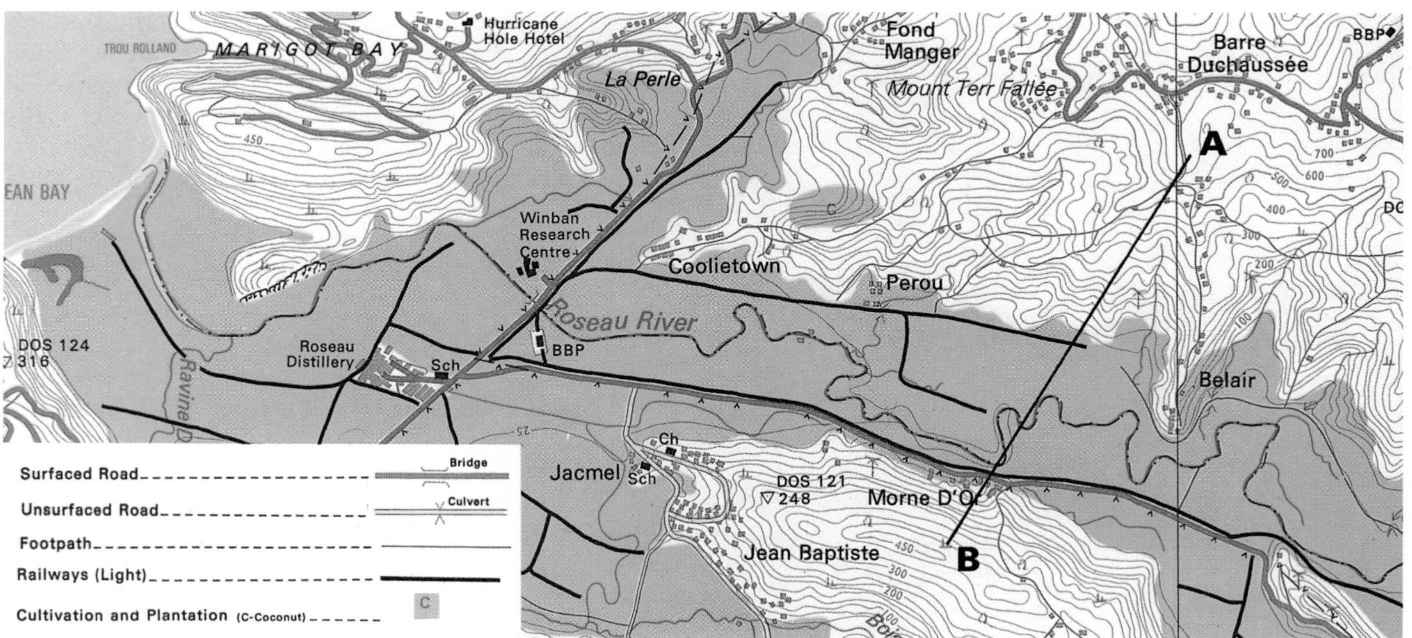

4.24 The Roseau River valley, St Lucia. 1:25 000

5 · LIMESTONE LANDSCAPES

5.1 Limestone

Limestones are rocks which are made up mainly of *carbonate* minerals. They are sedimentary rocks which were laid down under the sea, or sometimes in fresh water. There are large areas of limestone in all of the larger Caribbean islands and Belize; the Bahamas are made up almost entirely of limestone; and there is limestone in Barbados, and many of the other smaller islands.

There are many different types of limestone:

- Some limestones are composed mainly of coral.
- Other are composed mainly of shells and similar material.
- Some limestones are made up of small fragments of carbonate derived from microscopic sea creatures.
- Many limestones consist of almost pure carbonate. They are usually white when they have been freshly broken.
- Others contain a high proportion of mud and other material.

Limestone is an important resource:

- Many types of limestone can be cut into blocks for use as a building material.
- Limestone is the main raw material used to make cement. It is also used in the alumina and iron and steel industries.
- Limestone can be crushed to make an *aggregate* for use by the construction industry.

Limestone weathering

The landforms which develop in limestone areas are very different from those on other rocks. This is because limestone is weathered in a very distinctive way. Limestone landforms are known as *karst* landscapes.

Limestone consists mainly of calcium carbonate ($CaCO_3$).

Rainwater reacts with carbon dioxide in the atmosphere and in the air which is trapped in the soil to form a weak carbonic acid (H_2CO_3).

This carbonic acid reacts with the limestone to produce calcium bicarbonate:

$H_2CO_3 + CaCO_3 = Ca(HCO_3)_2$.

Calcium bicarbonate is soluble, and can easily be washed away by rainwater.

Drainage patterns on limestone

Most limestones contain pores, fissures and joints which water can pass through. These are enlarged when rainwater begins to dissolve the limestone. This means that limestone is a *permeable* rock – water can usually flow through limestone very easily.

When a large river enters a limestone area, it may flow through it; but sometimes it will disappear down a *sink hole*, and flow underground through a *cave* for a considerable distance.

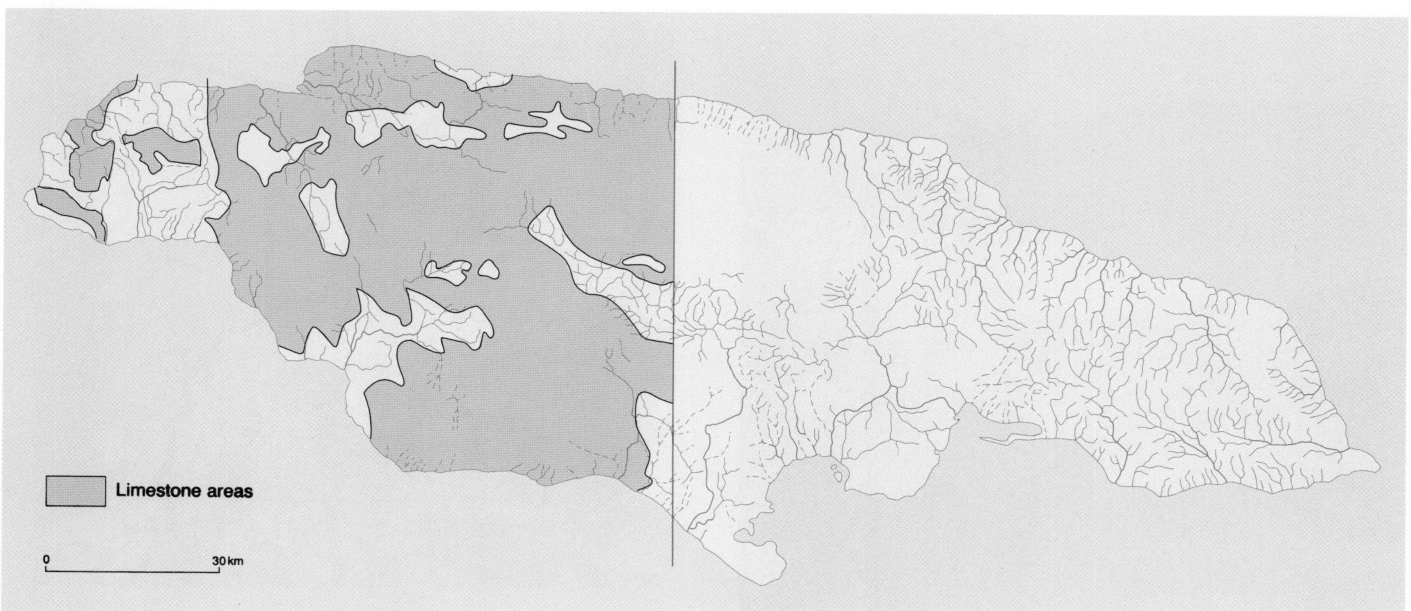

5.1 Drainage patterns in Jamaica.

Further downstream, there will be a *resurgence*; this is a very large spring, where a full-sized river flows out of the ground.

Figure 5.1 shows the main rivers of Jamaica. The location of the limestone areas in the western part of the island has been shown; but limestone areas in the eastern part of Jamaica have not been marked on the map.

1 What do you notice about the pattern of rivers in the limestone areas?
2 Make a copy of the map outline in your exercise book. Mark in:
   (a) Two areas in eastern Jamaica which seem to be made of limestone.
   (b) Four rivers.
   (c) Two sink holes.
   (d) Two resurgences.

Not all rivers in limestone areas flow underground. Sometimes there is too much rainwater for the underground passages and caves to carry; and if there are too many impurities in the limestone, the fissures can be blocked by mud.

The Great River in Jamaica runs through a limestone area. Like many limestone rivers, it has cut rapidly *down* through the rock by dissolving it, so it flows through a narrow, steep-sided gorge.

5.2 Jamaica

The way landforms develop in a limestone landscape will depend on:

- The type of limestone.
- The climate of the area.
- The amount of time that the area has been exposed to weathering and erosion.

There are many different types of karst landscape in the Caribbean, and only a few of them can be described in this chapter.

In Jamaica, there are many different types of limestone. The purest is the White Limestone, which covers many parts of the island.

In some places, the limestone areas of Jamaica have been exposed to weathering and erosion for more than 10 million years.

The limestone has been broken up by a large number of faults. Figure 3.23 shows the major fault lines.

5.2 A polje in Western Jamaica.

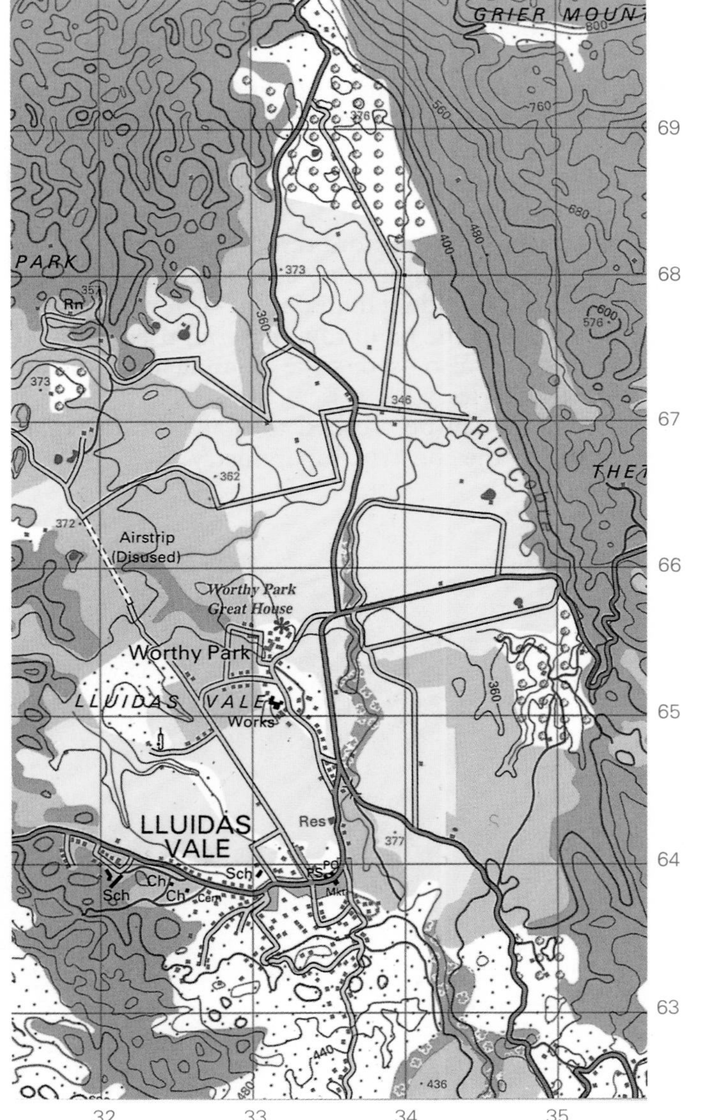

5.3 A polje at Lluidas Vale, Jamaica. 1:50 000

Poljes

Look at Figure 5.2. There is a very sharp contrast between the steep, wooded hillsides in the background, and the broad, flat valley floor. This photograph shows a *polje*. There are many poljes in the limestone areas of Jamaica. Many of them have formed in grabens, where a block of limestone has been faulted downwards by earth movements. A large depression is filled with alluvium, brought in by surface and underground rivers and streams from the surrounding area.

A *mogote* is a small hill, formed of a block of resistant limestone which has not been weathered away. Hills like these, and also the hills at the edge of the polje, are being undercut; water which collects on the alluvium eats away at the base of these hills, and gives them a very steep profile.

Sometimes a polje is completely flooded in wet weather, when there is too much rainwater to drain away through the limestone. A large polje around Newmarket in western Jamaica has been flooded many times this century. In 1979, after heavy rain, a temporary lake formed there which covered over 300 ha, was 30 m deep at one point, and lasted for more than five months.

Figure 5.3 shows a polje at Lluidas Vale in central Jamaica.

1. Make a sketch map of the polje to show:
   (a) The edge of the polje.
   (b) The drainage pattern.
   (c) A mogote.
   (d) A major fault line which runs through grid references 335 700 and 355 635.
2. Comment on:
   (a) The drainage pattern of the area.
   (b) The influence of the major fault line on the landforms.

Cockpit country

To the south of Falmouth, there is a large area of *cockpit karst*. The rock here is very pure White Limestone, with a criss-cross pattern of jointing. It has been weathered and eroded to form a maze of small hills and depressions. The hills have very little soil, and are covered with thick forest and woodland. Pockets of red soil have collected in some of the depressions or cockpits. Sometimes these are cultivated; but they have to be reached by a long, winding path from the nearest settlement. There is no permanent

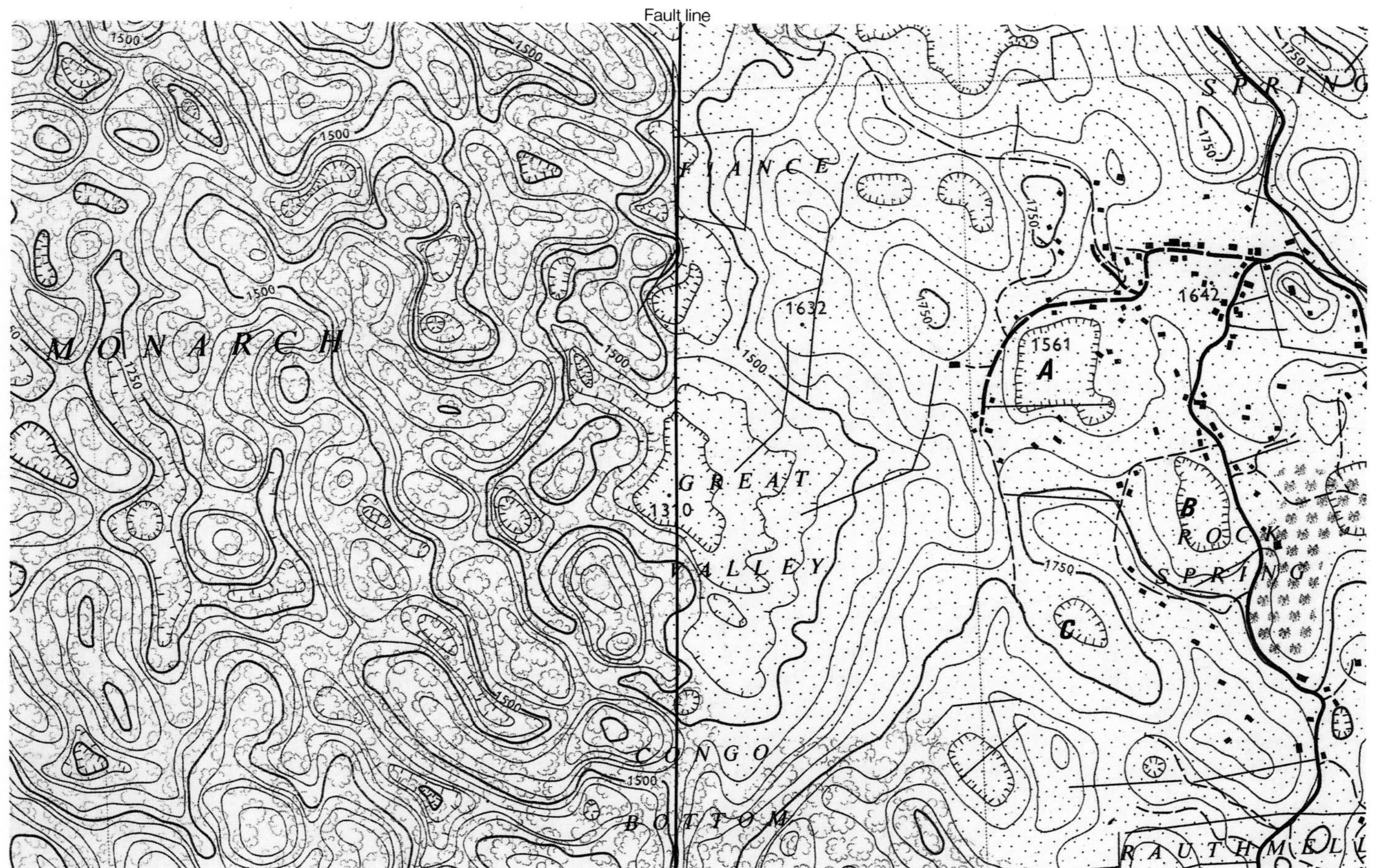

5.4 Cockpit country near Albert Town, Jamaica. Scale 1:10 000. Contour interval 50 feet.

5.5 Cockpit country, south of Albert Town.

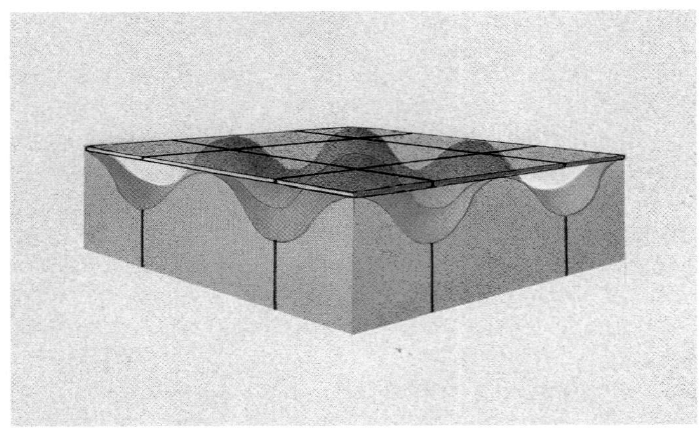
5.6 How cockpits are formed.

surface water in most of the cockpit country.

Cockpits are formed like this:

- The limestone has a criss-cross pattern of joints.
- The rock is dissolved fastest near to the joints, because this is where water collects.
- A deep, star-shaped depression is formed where two joints meet.
- Small hills are left away from the joints. Where the pattern of jointing is regular, the hills are arranged in rows.

Figure 5.4 shows an area on the edge of the cockpit country, near to Albert Town. To the west of the fault line, the surface rock is White Limestone; to the east, there is Yellow Limestone, which contains a much higher proportion of impurities.

3 The area west of the fault line covers 1.1 km^2. How many *hills* and *cockpits* does it contain?

4 Is there any evidence that the hills and cockpits are arranged in straight lines?

5 Describe the contrast between the areas of White Limestone and Yellow Limestone under these headings:
(a) Relief.
(b) Land use.
(c) Settlement.
(d) Communications.

5.3 Barbados

The Barbados landscape

The karst features of Barbados are very different from those of Jamaica, because:

- The limestone is very permeable. Water flows very easily through large fissures in the coral.
- The coral cap has not been exposed to weathering and erosion for more than 600,000 years anywhere in the island, and in most places for a much shorter time.
- The rainfall is 1,500–2,000 mm over most of the island. This is less than in many other parts of the Caribbean.
- As the island was uplifted, large-scale joints developed in the coral cap. Most of these radiate outwards from the centre of the main anticline.

Figure 5.8 shows a limestone landscape in Barbados.

- Over most of the island, there is no surface drainage. The rivers and streams all flow underground.
- Most of the land in the limestone areas is flat or gently sloping. Most of the original limestone surface has not been altered very much by erosion.
- There are many shallow depressions where the limestone has been dissolved more rapidly. Geologists refer to these as *dolines*. There are also dolines at the points marked 'A', 'B', and 'C' on Figure 5.4
- There are many narrow, steep-sided *dry valleys*. When the weather is very wet, there may be a stream in the valley bottom for a short time; but these temporary watercourses do not have time to erode the valley very much. These valleys were probably formed in the past, when rainfall was much higher than it is today.
- The dry valleys mostly follow a radial pattern, along the lines of the main joints in the coral cap. A dry valley is shown on Figure 6.18.
- At the edge of the coral cap, the Oceanic rocks may become completely saturated in wet weather. In the past, there have been rockslides, when a large mass of limestone has slipped downhill over the wet clay.
- A number of steep slopes or *terraces* were also formed when the island was uplifted. They are described in Section 6.5.

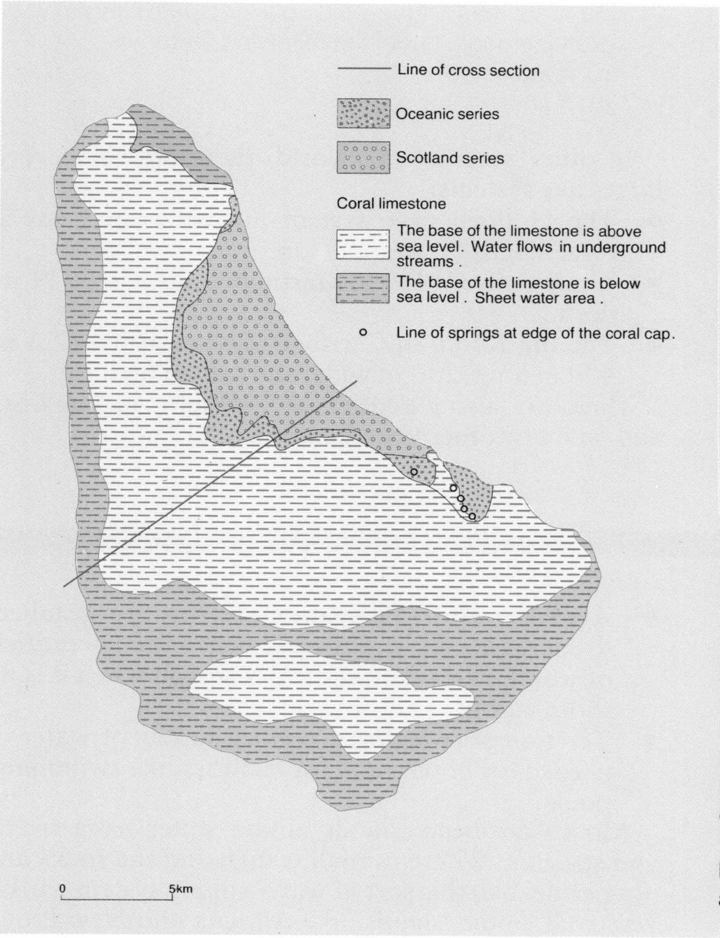

Line of cross section

Oceanic series

Scotland series

Coral limestone

The base of the limestone is above sea level. Water flows in underground streams.

The base of the limestone is below sea level. Sheet water area.

Line of springs at edge of the coral cap.

0 5km

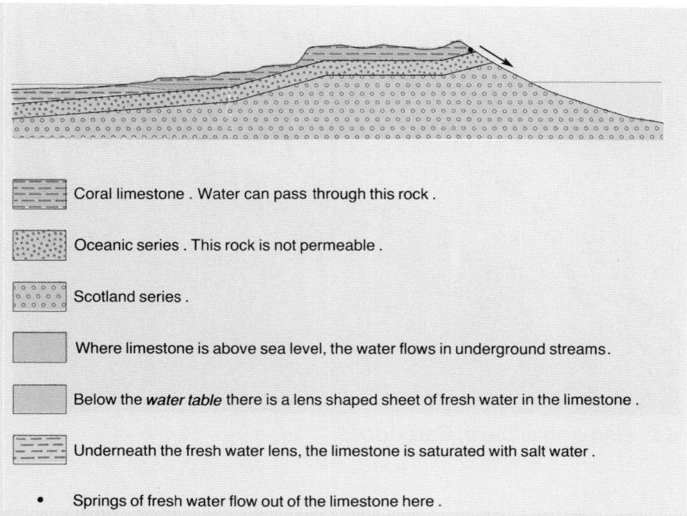

Coral limestone. Water can pass through this rock.

Oceanic series. This rock is not permeable.

Scotland series.

Where limestone is above sea level, the water flows in underground streams.

Below the *water table* there is a lens shaped sheet of fresh water in the limestone.

Underneath the fresh water lens, the limestone is saturated with salt water.

Springs of fresh water flow out of the limestone here.

The Scotland series sandstones and clays were laid down under the sea 60–70 million years ago.

The Oceanic series rocks are fine white clays, locally known as chalk, which were laid down in deep-sea conditions. They are not permeable, and become very slippery when they are wet.

The coral limestone cap was formed as the island was uplifted by earth movements over the past 600,000 years. It has been arched upwards to form two broad anticlines, one in the centre of the island and one in the south.

In the Scotland District in the east of the island, the coral cap has been eroded away. The Oceanic and Scotland series rocks are exposed at the surface.

5.7 The structure of Barbados.

5.8 A limestone landscape in Barbados.

1 Look carefully at Figure 5.8.
   (a) Make a sketch to show the dry valleys.
   (b) What do you notice about the pattern of land use?

Caves

In Barbados, almost all of the drainage system is underground.

One of the major cave systems has been developed as a tourist attraction. At Harrison's Cave, visitors can see a small part of a huge underground cave system. They travel to 50 m below the surface in an electric vehicle.

Sometimes the water in a cave carries more dissolved calcium carbonate than it can hold. When this water drips from the roof of the cave, it leaves some of the mineral behind. Over the years, the drips build up, forming:

- Stalagmites, which grow up from the cave floor.
- Stalactites, which grow down from the roof.
- Pillars, which join the roof to the floor.

5.9 Harrison's Cave, Barbados.

2 Make a sketch of the inside of Harrison's Cave in your exercise book. Label the following features:
(a) A stalactite.
(b) A stalagmite.

In other parts of the world, there are some very large cave systems:

- The Holloch cave system in Switzerland has a total length of over 100 km.
- The Gouffre St Pierre Martin in France is 1,311 m deep.
- The Big Room in Carlsbad Cavern in the USA is 400 m long, 230 m wide, and 100 m high.

There are also extensive cave systems in Jamaica, and on many other Caribbean islands.

5.4 Groundwater resources

Water as a resource

Too often, we take water for granted. In most parts of the Caribbean, there is clean, fresh water available whenever we turn on a tap. There is no need to go to a shop to buy water – and too frequently the water supply is wasted or misused as a result.

Many parts of the world do not have a reliable or safe water supply. In some parts of Africa, women have to walk for five or six hours to fetch water. Under these conditions, water is used very sparingly – on average people use less than 5 litres per person per day for washing, drinking, and cooking.

In the Caribbean, people use more water. In Barbados, for example:

- People taking water from standpipes use an average of 45 litres per day.
- People with a piped domestic supply use 140 litres per day.
- Total water use for all purposes averages 400 litres per person per day.

1 Make a bar graph to illustrate these figures.
2 List the ways in which your family uses the domestic water supply.
3 How would you cut back on water use if you had to walk several kilometres to fetch every bucket of water?

As an economy develops, more and more water is needed each year. Water is needed for:

- *Domestic use:* more people have a piped water supply, modern bathrooms, washing machines, and other appliances.
- *Industrial use:* more factories are built. All use water for cleaning and sanitation, and some use large amounts of *process water*. An alumina plant may use as much as 10 million litres per day.
- *Agricultural use:* irrigation systems are installed to increase yields. They use enormous quantities of water, and use it in the dry season when it is in short supply.
- *The tourist industry:* a regular supply of water is needed for hotels, and for facilities like swimming pools.

Most Caribbean islands obtain water from rivers and streams. Where rainfall is high and the rocks are not permeable, this sort of water supply system works very well. Some islands, like Antigua and New Providence, have a water supply problem.

Barbados has a fairly dry climate, very few rivers and streams, a high population density, and a high demand for water for all purposes. In spite of this, there is a reliable supply of pure, fresh water; the geology and structure of the island ensure a steady supply of groundwater for human use.

Groundwater in Barbados

Look at Figure 5.7. When rain falls on the coral cap, it sinks into the ground very rapidly. Bare coral rock can absorb over 60 mm of rainfall in one hour. Water flows downwards very rapidly, through pore spaces and fissures which have been enlarged by *solution*. When the water reaches the base of the coral cap, it reaches the impermeable Oceanic series rocks. At this point it begins to flow laterally.

Some of the underground water flows east until it reaches the steep slope at the edge of the Scotland District. Here there is a *spring line* at the junction of the coral cap and the Oceanic series rocks. Small streams of water emerge from the hillside.

Most of the water flows away from the Scotland District, in a series of underground rivers and streams, like the one which can be seen in Harrison's Cave.

In the centre of the island, the base of the coral cap is 275 m above sea level; but along the west and north-east coasts, and in much of the south of the island, part of the coral lies as much as 60 m below sea level. In this zone, there is a *water table* just above sea level, below which the rock is permanently saturated.

Not all of this water can be used. There is salt water which has seeped in from the sea, as well as fresh water from the underground rivers and streams.

Salt water is slightly denser than fresh water. This means that the fresh water can float on top of the sea water. Near the coast, the heavier sea water acts as a sort of dam, which ponds back the water from the underground streams. The fresh water forms a lens-shaped layer, locally known as *sheet water*. The freshwater lens is between 10 and 30 m thick.

Fresh water is extracted by tapping the flow at:

- Springs on the southern part of the Scotland District rim.
- Wells which tap underground rivers and streams.
- Wells in the sheet-water areas.

The freshwater lens acts as a *store* for rainwater. Water is added to the store by underground streams from the centre of the island, and by rainfall in the coastal areas which seeps down through the rock. The store can hold only a limited amount of water – when it is full, fresh water will seep out into the sea along the coast.

For a short time, it is possible to pump water out of the store faster than it is being added; but this cannot go on indefinitely. When too much water is pumped from a well, salt water is sucked up from below and in from the side to replace it. Pumping then has to stop until the freshwater lens has been re-established. In the long term, there is a limit to groundwater extraction. The water is a *renewable* but *finite* resource.

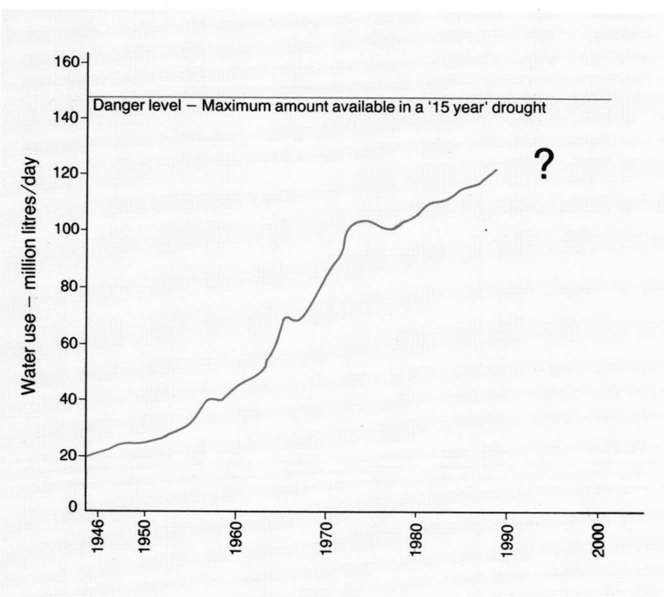

5.10 Water use in Barbados.

Is the water supply adequate?

In an average year, when rainfall is neither very high nor very low, it should be possible to extract about 229 million litres per day.

In a severe drought, this rate of extraction would not be possible. In the sort of drought that occurs about every fifteen years, only about 149 million litres can be extracted. And in a really bad drought, there would be even less water available.

Figure 5.10 shows the increase in water consumption between 1946 and 1986. The average growth rate was 5.9% per year.

4 What were the reasons for the increase in demand for water?
5 What is the trend likely to be in future years?
6 Copy the graph into your exercise book, and add a dotted line to show your estimate of future water needs, up to the year 2025.
7 Do you think that Barbados will face a water supply problem in the future?

Most people think that the rate of increase in the demand for water will slow down, and that the demand for water in the year 2000 will be between 136 and 183 million litres per day. But this might still be too much in a really dry year.

Alternatives

If a water shortage does develop, how can it be tackled? There have been many suggestions:

- *Creating extra stores for fresh water:* small dams could be built across the Scotland District rivers.
  POTENTIAL: 33 million litres per day.
  COST: 17 cents per 1,000 litres.
- *Increasing the flow of water into the freshwater lens:* small dams across dry valleys on the coral cap would hold back storm water. It would sink into the limestone instead of running into the sea.
  POTENTIAL: 2.4 million litres per day.
  COST: 21 cents per 1,000 litres.
- *Importing water by tanker:* islands like St Thomas and New Providence have had to obtain fresh water like this. Dominica is the nearest island which *might* be able to sell water to Barbados.
  POTENTIAL: 5.9 million litres per day.
  COST: $2.21 per 1,000 litres.
- *Desalination of salt water:* Aruba has used desalinated sea water since 1926. Antigua, St Thomas, and New Providence also have desalination plants. There have been some operating difficulties, but

desalination technology may improve in the future.
POTENTIAL: 45 million litres per day, just from brackish groundwater.
COST: At least 35 cents per 1,000 litres, and probably more.

- *Reducing the demand for fresh water:*
  - Publicity campaigns can make users more 'water-conscious'.
  - Water-saving showers and other appliances can be installed.
  - Water can be 'recycled'; this already happens in sugar factories.
  - Salt water can be used instead of fresh; the Barbados Light and Power Company already uses salt water for cooling.
- *Use of meters:* another way of reducing demand is to meter water, and charge customers for what they use. This system is now being introduced.
  POTENTIAL: it is estimated that 10% of all domestic water use is now wastage. This could be reduced to 5% with greater public awareness. The demand for water was actually reduced by 5% in 1973–6.

8 Which of these ideas seem most promising? Can any be rejected out of hand?
9 Do any of these suggestions have hidden *costs*? Or undesirable side-effects?
10 Are there any hidden *benefits*? Might some proposals improve other aspects of the human environment?

Groundwater pollution

Groundwater supplies can be damaged by over-use; they can also be damaged by *pollution*. Sewage, oil, and industrial and agricultural chemicals, are all a potential threat to the water supply. If a major source of drinking-water is contaminated, it may be many years before it is safe to use again.

In Barbados, the water supply at all the pumping stations is tested at regular intervals, to make sure that it is safe.

Land use around the pumping stations is also controlled. There is a zone around each major well where no new building is allowed, and a wider zone where building is very strictly controlled.

11 Look at Figure 5.11. How far from central Bridgetown has the built-up area spread:
(a) To the north?
(b) To the south-east?
(c) To the north-east?

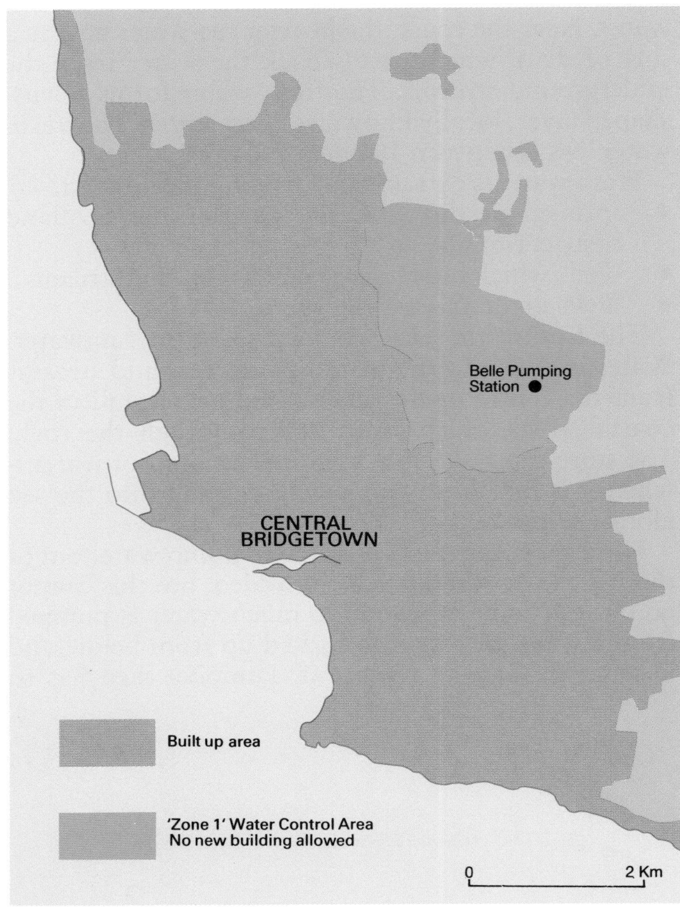

5.11 Pollution control and the growth of Bridgetown.

6 · COASTS

6.1 Marine erosion

6.1 A limestone cliff in Barbados.

Waves contain energy. When they break, the energy in the wave may:

- *Erode* material from one part of the coast.
- *Transport* it to a different place.
- *Deposit* it there to form a new feature.

In Figure 6.1, the rocks and reef in the background are being eroded by the waves, to produce sand; the sand has been deposited to form the beach; and the beach sand is being stirred up and transported from place to place in the turbulent 'white water' where the waves are breaking.

Waves erode through:

- *Hydraulic action:* this is the force of the water in the wave itself. Cavitation can be very important here, when bubbles implode in turbulent water.
- *Solution:* sea water can dissolve some minerals in the rocks.
- *Abrasion or corrasion:* waves throw sand and small stones against the shoreline, and wear it back.
- *Attrition:* sand grains and small stones are thrown against each other in the breaking waves. They are broken up and worn into a rounded shape.

A considerable amount of energy is released when big storm waves are breaking. At Wick in Scotland, a block weighing 2,600 tonnes was removed from the harbour breakwater during one storm; and at Cherbourg in France, another storm threw rocks weighing more than three tonnes over an eight-metre wall.

Marine erosion is fastest:

- On 'high-energy' coasts which are exposed to the full force of powerful waves.
- Where the rock is soft and unconsolidated.

6.2 The north-east coast of Barbados near Pico Tenerife.

Waves can erode the coastline very quickly. On the island of Krakatoa in Indonesia, volcanic ash was eroded from the shoreline at a rate of over 50 metres per year in the period after the 1883 eruption.

Cliffs

Figure 6.1 shows a cliff which has been formed by marine erosion on a limestone coast. Limestone is a resistant rock, unlike clay or volcanic ash. Notice these features:

- Marine erosion is concentrated at sea level. At this point, there is often a *notch* where the waves have eaten back into the rock.
- The rock above the notch has been undercut. When it projects too far, a section of cliff will break off.
- Rubble accumulates at the base of the cliff. It protects the rock against further erosion for a time; but eventually it will be broken down and removed by attrition.
- As the cliff is worn back, a *wave-cut platform* is developed. The platform is not being eroded, because it is too far below the surface of the sea.
- The cliff is steep, because it is made of a well-consolidated rock which will not collapse easily, and because the base of the cliff is being eroded.

The land along the coast in Figure 6.2 consists of soft Oceanic series clays. Material like this can slump and slide into the sea. A vertical cliff face cannot develop.

1 Make a labelled sketch to show the difference between these two stretches of coast.

Caves, arches, and stacks

It is quite common to find an isolated pillar of rock, or *sea stack*, forming a small island in the waves.

Figure 6.3 shows how many sea stacks are formed:

- Many rocks contain joints and fissures. These are often enlarged by hydraulic action to form a *cave*.
- Caves can be extended by wave action until they run right through an exposed headland. A *natural arch* joins the tip of the headland to the shore.
- The roof of the natural arch will eventually collapse, leaving an isolated sea stack, which will then be removed by erosion.

Headlands

Because hard rocks resist erosion, they often form islands or headlands on exposed coasts which are being worn away by wave action.

Read through Section 3.5 again. In southern St Lucia:

- Intrusive volcanic rocks in dykes and sills are very resistant to marine erosion.
- Lava flows and consolidated volcanic ash are also resistant to erosion.
- Ignimbrite flows, sand, and alluvium can be eroded very easily.

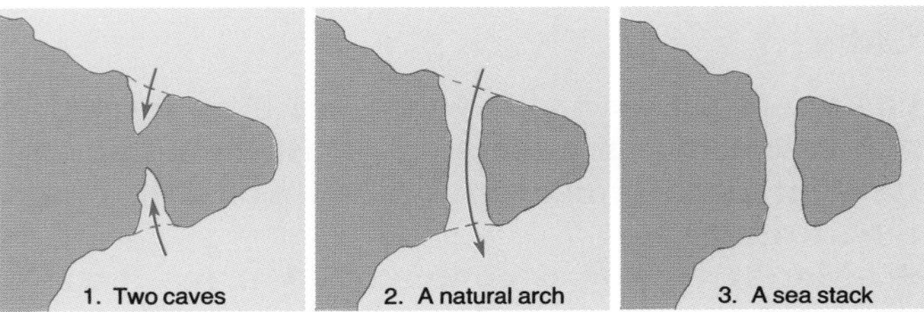

6.3 Caves, arches and stacks.

6.4 A natural arch in a limestone cliff on the coast of Barbados.

2 Comment on Figure 6.6. What do you notice about the main headlands on the east coast of Trinidad?

3 Look at Figure 6.5. Write a few sentences to explain the location of the main coastal features in southern St Lucia.

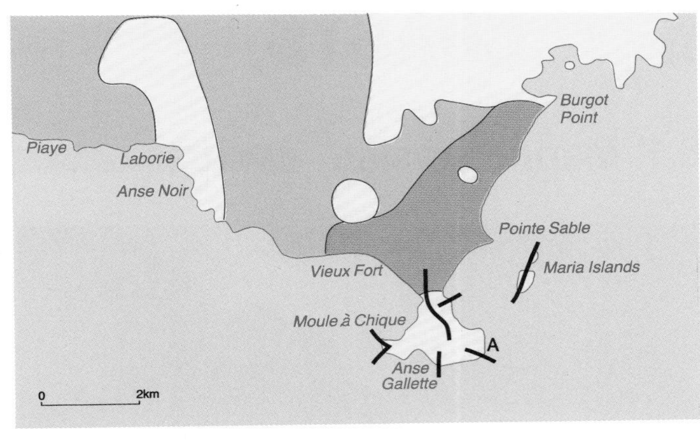

6.5 Coastal features in St Lucia.

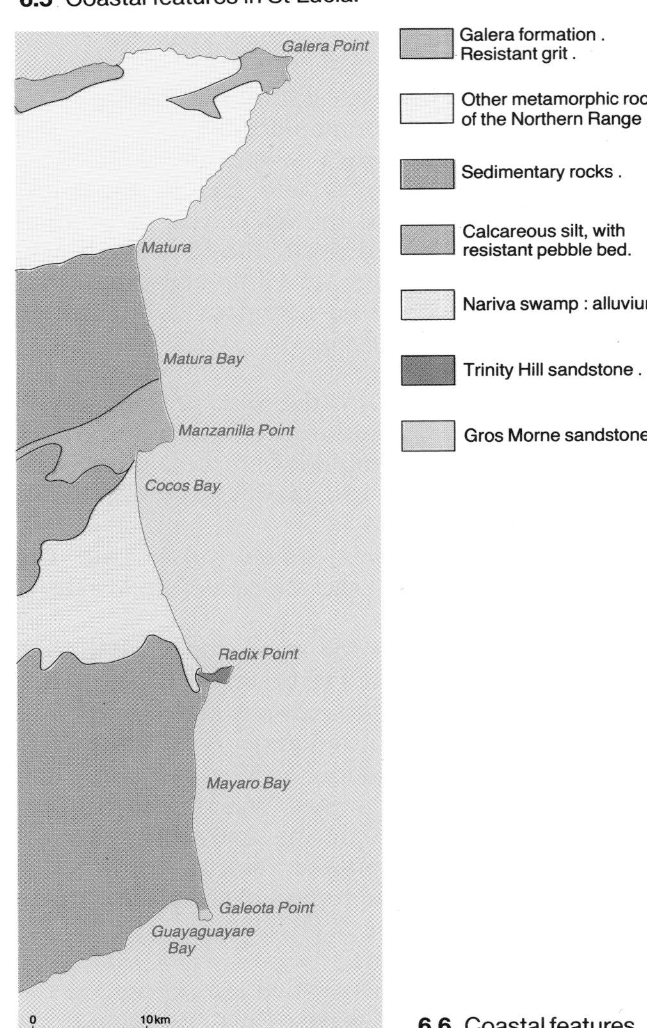

6.6 Coastal features in Trinidad.

6.2 Waves

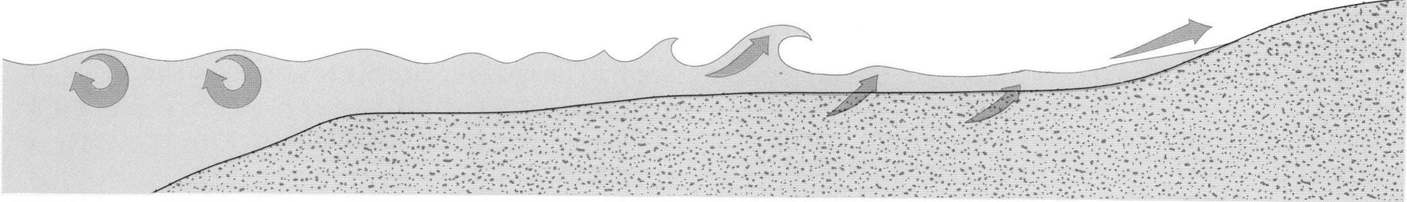

6.7 Waves.

Most waves are formed by wind blowing across the surface of the sea.

In deep water, waves seem to move forward; but the sea water is not moving with them. Each particle of water moves round in a circular pattern whenever a wave passes.

Because the water is not being carried forward, a surfer who is too far out to sea will not be carried along by the waves, but will just bob up and down in the same place.

There are many different types of wave.

Waves which have been formed by strong winds a long way off usually have a long wavelength and quite a flat profile. These waves will take a long time to pass any particular point. Waves which have travelled a long distance across open water are known as *swell*.

Waves which are caused by strong winds within the local area have a much steeper profile and a shorter wavelength. Waves like these bring very choppy conditions for small craft out at sea.

How waves break

Waves break when they move into very shallow water. When the depth of the sea is less than the height of the wave:

- Friction with the bottom increases, and the wave moves more slowly.
- The waves 'bunch up' because they are moving more slowly. The wavelength becomes shorter.
- The pattern of water circulation in the wave is now elliptical, not circular.
- The front of the wave becomes steeper.
- The water at the top of the wave starts to move forward faster than the wave itself.
- The top of the wave tumbles forward, and the wave breaks.

Breakers

Waves do not all break in the same way.

- *Spilling* breakers fall forwards. A great mass of foaming surf rushes up the beach, and then flows back again.
- *Plunging* breakers are much steeper. The crest of the wave curls forward over a large air pocket and then plunges vertically downwards.
- *Surging* breakers develop on very steep beaches. The wave slides up and down the beach, and there is not so much turbulence – the water has less white foam.

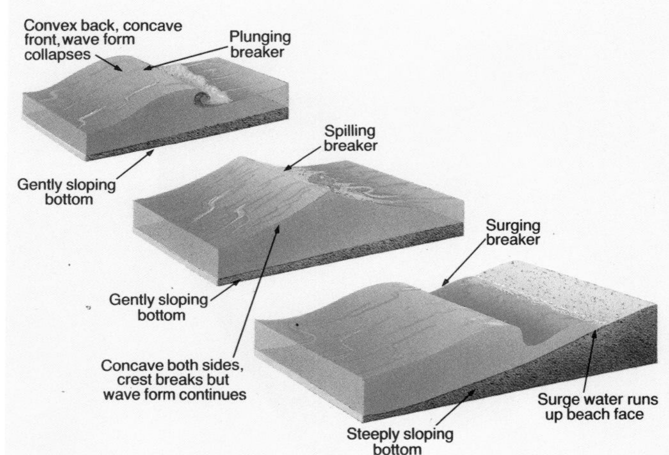

6.8 Plunging, spilling and surging breakers.

Constructive and destructive waves

If you stand in the surf where the waves are breaking you will feel the effect that the wave energy is having on the beach. A breaking wave churns up the loose sediments, so that they are suspended in the turbulent water. When surf runs up the beach, it takes a cloud of sand particles and even small stones with it. These are carried up the beach by the *swash*. Then the water starts to flow back down the beach. This is the *backwash* of the wave; it drags sediment from the beach back into the water.

Constructive waves build the beach up. The swash carries more material than the backwash. Waves are more likely to be constructive when the front of the wave is not too steep, and the wavelength is long in relation to its height. Spilling breakers are usually constructive.

Destructive waves erode the beach. The backwash drags more material down the beach than the swash has carried up. These waves generally have a steep profile. They have a shorter wavelength than constructive waves of the same height, and there are more waves per minute. Plunging breakers are usually destructive.

Constructive and destructive waves can change a beach very quickly. It has been estimated that as much as 15,000 m^3 of sand may be shifted in a few weeks on a fairly sheltered beach less than 1 km long on the west coast of Barbados.

Wave refraction

Waves begin to be affected by the seabed when the depth of the water is less than half the wavelength. If there is sand, the passing waves will begin to disturb it at this point.

Friction with the seabed slows the waves down. Figure 6.9a shows how waves approach the shore. The wave at 'C' has slowed down where it is passing through shallow water close to the beach. This part of the wave lags behind the rest. This means that the wave is bent or *refracted*. From the beach, the waves seem to be moving directly towards the shore.

1 Look at Figure 2.20. Make a sketch to show how the waves are being refracted as they approach the shore.

Bays and headlands

Figure 6.9b shows how waves are refracted on a bay-and-headland coast. The arrows show how the energy of a long section of the wave is concentrated on a short stretch of cliff on the headland, while the energy of a short section of the wave is spread out over a long stretch of coastline in the bay. Wave erosion is more powerful on the headland. The profile of the waves will also be altered. In the bay, they are much more likely to be *constructive* waves.

Because the waves in the bay are often constructive waves, a *bay-head beach* may be built up in locations like this.

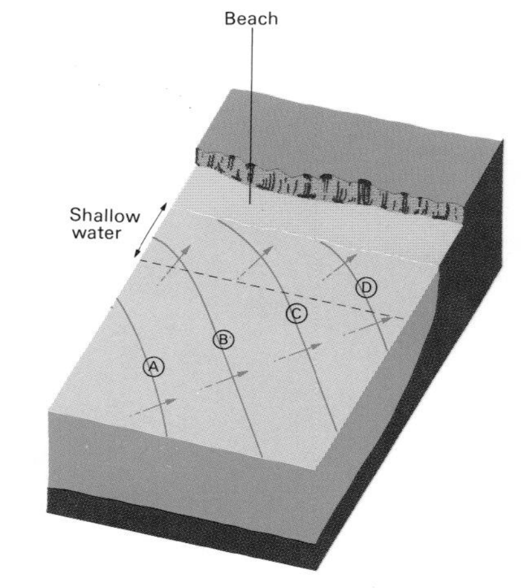

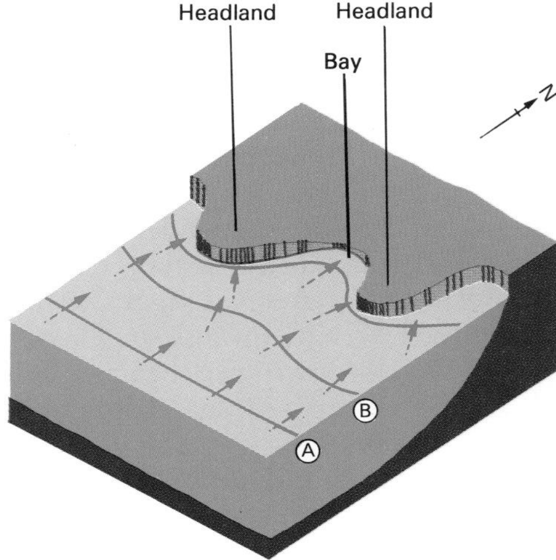

6.9 Wave refraction.
(a) on a straight coast
(b) on a bay and headland coast

Windward and leeward coasts

On most Caribbean islands, there is a contrast between:

- Rough conditions and exposed *high-energy* coasts on the windward side.
- Much calmer, *low-energy* coasts on the leeward side.

Figure 6.10 shows the contrast between the east coast and the west coast in Barbados. Except under storm conditions, the waves on the leeward side of the island have been refracted through almost 180° before reaching the shore and have almost no energy left for erosion.

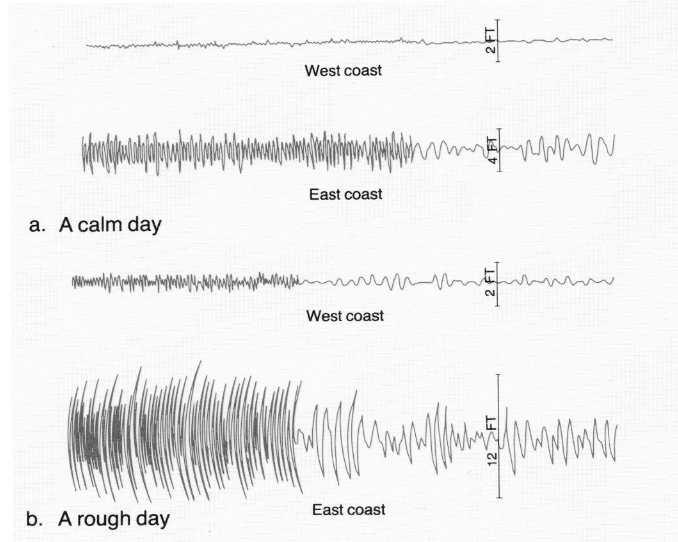

6.10 Wave height on the east and west coasts of Barbados.

6.3 Beaches, spits, and tombolos

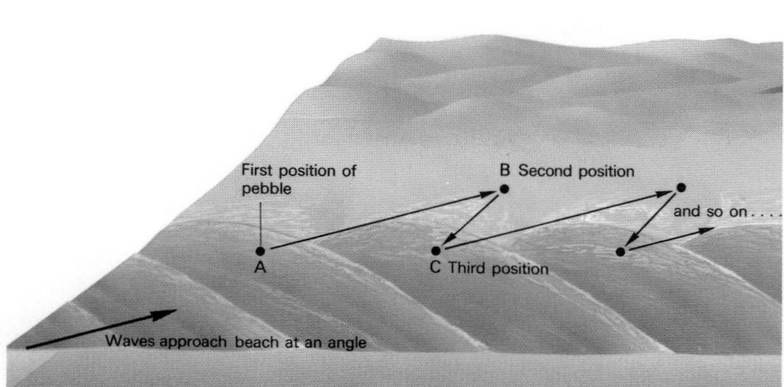

6.11 Longshore drift.

Longshore drift

When waves approach the shore at an angle, sand and other material is moved gradually sideways like this:

- Swash moves a particle of sand *diagonally* up the beach.
- Later on, backwash moves it *straight* down the beach.
- The particle has been moved slightly along from its original position.
- After this process has been repeated many times, the particle will have been moved to the point shown on the diagram.

Over a long period of time, a large quantity of material can be moved in this way. This process is called *longshore drift*.

Material which has been eroded by wave action is frequently transported by longshore drift before being deposited on a beach. The shape of the beach, and the type of material on it, will be influenced by the direction of longshore drift.

Tombolos

Figure 6.12 shows Scotts Head in Dominica. Find Scotts Head in your atlas. Waves from the east are refracted as they approach the south coast of the island, and are coming from the south-east by the time they reach the shore.

Material which has been eroded along the south coast is carried west by longshore drift. Scotts Head was probably once a separate island; but longshore drift has built up a *spit* of sand and pebbles which now joins it to the rest of Dominica.

When the sea is rough, destructive waves will remove material from the spit; but under normal conditions, new material will be carried along the shore to build it up. The hard rock of Scotts Head itself is resistant to erosion, and protects the end of the spit.

6.12 Scotts Head, Dominica.

A spit of sand or stones joining an island to the mainland is called a *tombolo*.

1 Draw a diagram to show how the Scotts Head tombolo was probably formed.

The Palisadoes

Figures 2.10 and 2.20 show a much larger tombolo – the Palisadoes in Jamaica.

Kingston Harbour was originally an open bay of shallow water, containing some small islands. One of these islands is now the site of Port Royal. Material from the Hope River and elsewhere on the south-east coast of Jamaica began to build up a spit near Harbour Head in the south-east corner of the bay. This spit now reaches almost the whole way across the mouth of the bay, and joins the small islands near Port Royal to the mainland.

2 How long is this tombolo?
3 What type of waves would you expect to find:
   (a) On the north side of the Palisadoes?
   (b) On the south side of the Palisadoes?
4 Why has mud and other material started to accumulate on the northern side of the spit?
5 How has this tombolo been altered by human activities?
6 From what direction do waves now enter Kingston Harbour?
7 Draw a diagram to explain how the smaller spit which leads to Fort Augusta may have been formed.

Beach	Wave action	Rock types	Type of material on beach (%)			Average size of material
			Shell, and limestone	Quartz	Other volcanic material	
Pointe Sable	Windward coast, but protected by reef and offshore islands.	Large offshore coral reef. Some volcanic material nearby.	80	8	12	0.2mm
Anse Gallette	Exposed to storm waves and refracted waves from south. All small particles washed away.	Lava, conglomerate, and other hard volcanic rocks.	0	Rounded pebbles and boulders of volcanic origin.		50 to 500mm
Piaye	Much less exposed; waves refracted from south-east.	Soft volcanic material from pyroclastic flow.	1.5	55	43.5	0.69mm

6.13 Three beaches in St Lucia.

Three beaches in St Lucia

The form of a beach is influenced by many factors, including:

- The direction of longshore drift.
- The nature of wave action on the beach itself.
- The types of rock in the surrounding area.

Figure 6.13 gives some information about three very different beaches in St Lucia which are also shown in Figure 6.5(a).

8 Why does Pointe Sable have more shell, coral, and limestone than the other two beaches?

9 Why is the material on Anse Gallette much larger in size than the material elsewhere?

10 Why are the pebbles and boulders at Anse Gallette rounded in shape?

11 Why is there no beach at all at the point marked 'A' on the map?

Cuspate forelands

The Maria Islands protect the coast at Pointe Sable from the full force of wave attack. The waves will be refracted round the islands; north of the point, they will approach from the north-east, and to the south they will approach from the south-east. This means that longshore drift has been gradually moving material towards Pointe Sable from the north and the south. The beach has been gradually built outwards to form a *cuspate foreland.*

There are cuspate forelands like these on many Caribbean islands.

Lagoons

Sometimes a spit stretches right across a bay. When this happens, the stretch of water behind it is cut off from the open sea, and becomes a *lagoon.* Within the lagoon:

- There will be no large waves.
- Mud and silt will accumulate on the lagoon floor.
- Mangroves and other plants will start to grow.
- Open water will gradually be replaced by swamp, and then by dry land.

12 Look at Figure 6.14. Make a sketch to show:
(a) Two bay-head beaches.
(b) A tombolo.
(c) A lagoon of open water.
(d) A partly filled lagoon.
(e) A completely filled lagoon.

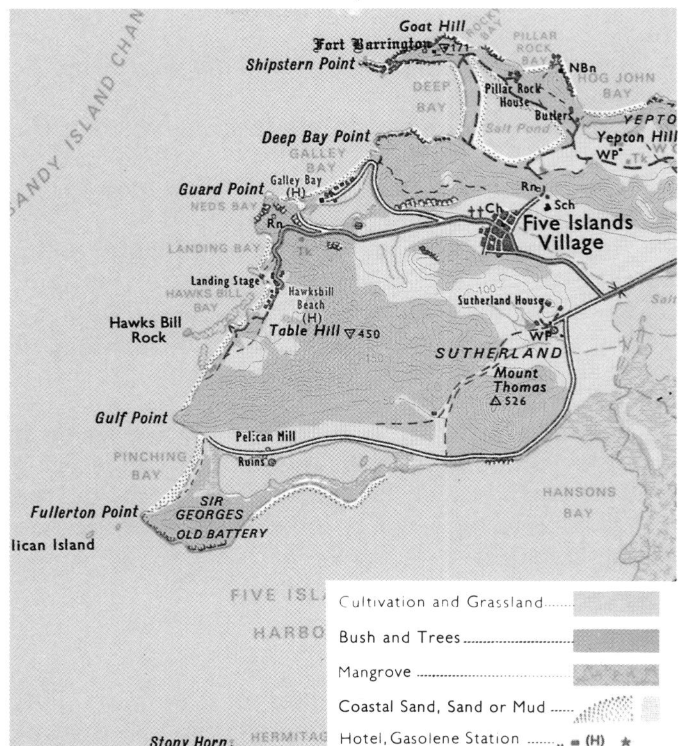

6.14 The west coast of Antigua. 1:50 000

Currents

The way material moves along the shore is also affected by marine currents. Along the coast of Guyana and Surinam, there are currents which transport material from the south-east to the north-west.

13 Look at Figure 4.3c. Describe how marine currents have affected the mouths of the Pomeroon, Waini, and Barima rivers.

6.4 Submerged coasts

Read through Section 4.8 again.

Coastal landscapes everywhere in the Caribbean have been affected by the worldwide rise in sea level over the past 20,000 years.

Estuaries

In Guyana, there is a flat coastal plain, part of which has been flooded by the sea. The lower part of the Essequibo valley is now under water – the river ends in a broad *estuary*. There is no delta, although silt and alluvium are now being deposited in the river mouth.

Large parts of the Guyanese coastlands lie below present-day sea levels. In the past, they were protected against marine erosion by a thick belt of mangrove swamp, which broke the force of the waves and held the deposits of sediment together. Along much of this coastline, the mangroves have now been removed. That is why it is necessary to protect the coastline artificially with a sea wall.

1 Look at a map of Brazil in your atlas. Name one large river that enters the sea through an estuary. Make a sketch map of this estuary.

2 Look at a map of north-west Europe. Name one river that enters the sea through an estuary, and a country where sea walls are needed to protect the land against erosion.

Rias

Figure 6.16 shows the effect of rising sea levels in a more mountainous area. It shows part of the south coast of Grenada.

Many small river valleys have been flooded by the sea, to form inlets known as *rias*. Several small hills were cut off from the mainland when the sea level rose, and now form separate small islands.

The rias have very calm water, almost completely sheltered from the waves. Even though the rivers flowing into the rias are small, the inlets are being filled in quite quickly by sediments; and the sediments are being stabilised by mangroves. Elsewhere, small bay-head beaches are being built up.

The headlands between the rias are exposed to attack by the waves. They are being actively eroded, and cliffs are being developed as the coastline is pushed back.

3 Draw a sketch map to show how the south coast of Grenada may look when the rias have been filled by sediment, and the headlands have been eroded back by the sea.

Section 4.8 describes how an old ria has been completely filled in by sediment to form the Roseau valley in St. Lucia.

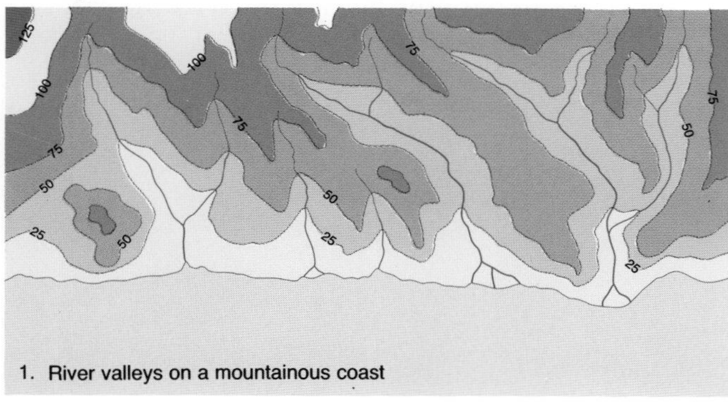

1. River valleys on a mountainous coast

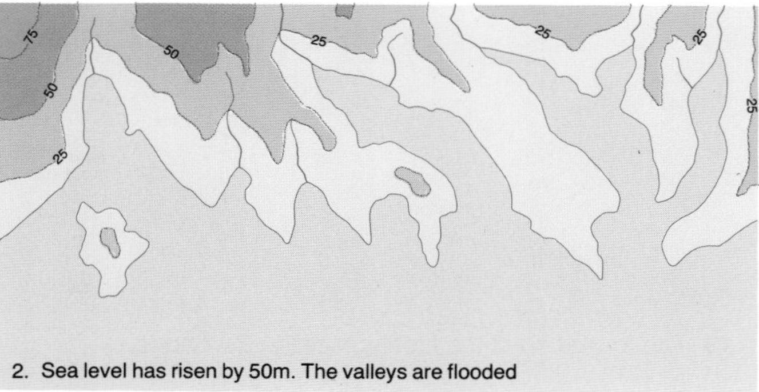

2. Sea level has risen by 50m. The valleys are flooded

6.15 How rias are formed.

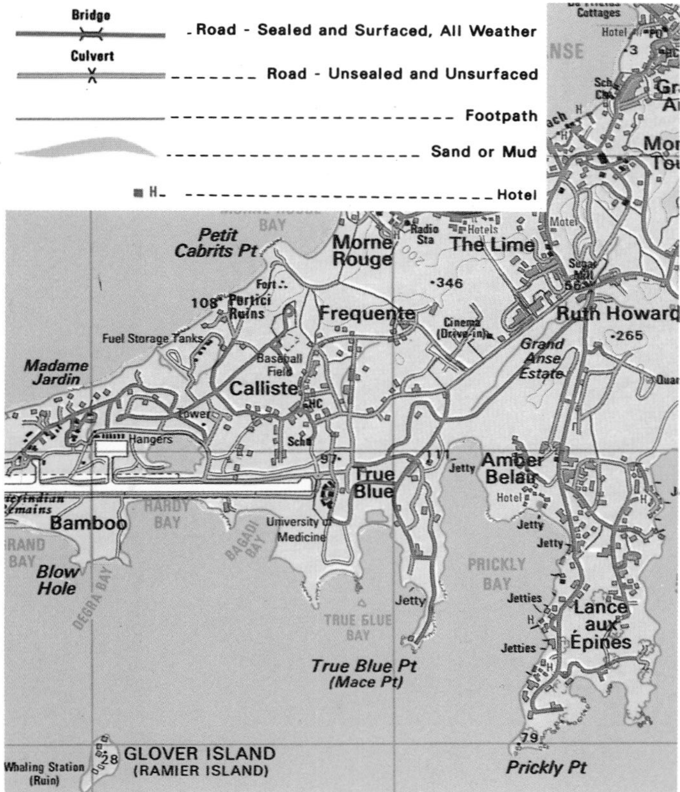

6.16 Rias on the south coast of Grenada. 1:50 000

6.5 Emergent coasts

Figure 6.17 was taken in Barbados. It shows a line of cliffs, a wave-cut platform, and a sea stack. In the background there is a cave.

6.17 An old shoreline near the north-east coast of Barbados.

The photograph was taken at about 30 m above sea level. These features represent an old shoreline, which was formed about 125,000 years ago.

There are several old shorelines like this in Barbados. They are also known as coral *terraces*.

Figure 6.18 shows part of the west coast of Barbados.

1 Draw a cross-section from 'A' to 'B'.
2 Make a sketch map to show:
 (a) A coral terrace.
 (b) A dry valley.

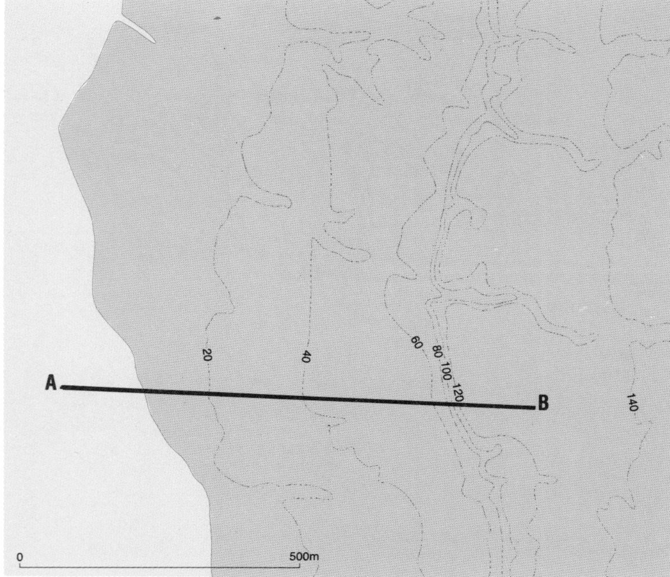

6.18 A Barbados coral terrace. The heights are in feet.

The Barbados *first high cliff*, which is shown in Figure 6.17, was formed like this:

- About 125,000 years ago, sea levels throughout the world were much the same as they are now.
- Then an ice age started. The climate of the Caribbean did not change very much, but sea level fell because of the water locked up in the ice sheets.
- For over a million years, the earth movements described in Chapter 3 have been pushing Barbados upwards at a rate of about 0.3 m per 1,000 years. This movement continued through the ice age.
- When world sea levels rose again about 20,000 years ago, the sea did not reach the first high cliff, because the island had been raised by over 30 m during the ice age. Instead, the old shoreline forms a coral terrace, and a new cliff is being eroded at the present-day sea level.

There are coral terraces of this type on emergent coasts in many other parts of the Caribbean: in Cuba, Hispaniola, Puerto Rico, and Jamaica.

The island of Jamaica is actually being slowly *tilted* by earth movements:

- In the north, there is an emergent coastline, with as many as seven coral terraces in some places.
- In the south, the coastline is being slowly submerged. There are wide swampy areas which are being filled in with alluvium; and offshore there is a broad shelf of shallow water which was once dry land and has now been flooded by the sea.

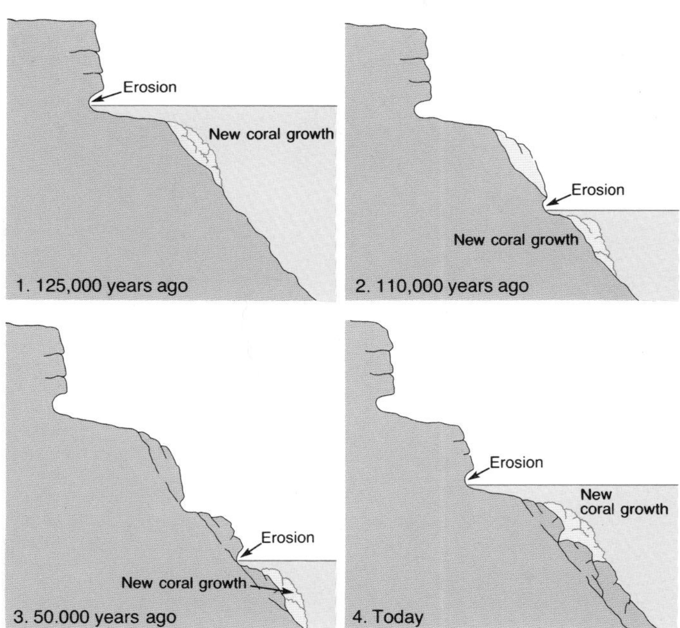

6.19 The formation of the first high cliff in Barbados.

6.6 Marine pollution

Kingston Harbour, north of the Palisadoes, is a valuable resource for many reasons:

- It provides a sheltered *harbour*, which is used by over 2,000 ships every year.
- It is a centre for the *fishing* industry, which employs about 2,000 people. The Harbour provides small fish for bait, and is a breeding ground for deep-sea fish.
- It is used for swimming, sailing, and water sports; the Harbour is an important *recreational* amenity.
- Much of the shallow water around the Harbour has been used for *land reclamation*; it has provided several large industrial sites and land for the airport runway.
- It is the main dumping-ground for all the industrial, domestic, and commercial waste produced in the Kingston area.

In the past, all these different uses were more or less compatible with one another:

- Kingston was a small city, and produced only a limited amount of waste.
- The water in the Harbour circulates. Every day, tidal currents move clean water into the Harbour from the open sea, and move some of the Harbour's water out again.
- If only a small amount of waste is put into the Harbour, it will soon be washed out again by tidal currents.
- Land reclamation was on a small scale, and did not alter the pattern of water circulation very much.
- Sailing ships had little effect on water quality.
- The Harbour was safe for swimming and as a source of food.

Kingston is now a large industrial city. *Pollution* of the Harbour has become a serious problem:

- The Harbour has been polluted with organic matter. A certain amount of organic matter provides useful nutrients for marine life; but too much can be disastrous. The bacteria which feed on decomposing organic waste may use up all the oxygen in the water, and cause other more developed organisms to asphyxiate. When there is too much decomposing organic matter and not enough oxygen, the water will begin to *smell* very bad.
- The Harbour has also been polluted with oil and other chemicals which may be poisonous to marine life.

Pollution comes from a number of different sources:

- Over 40 million litres of semi-treated sewage is pumped into the Harbour every day.

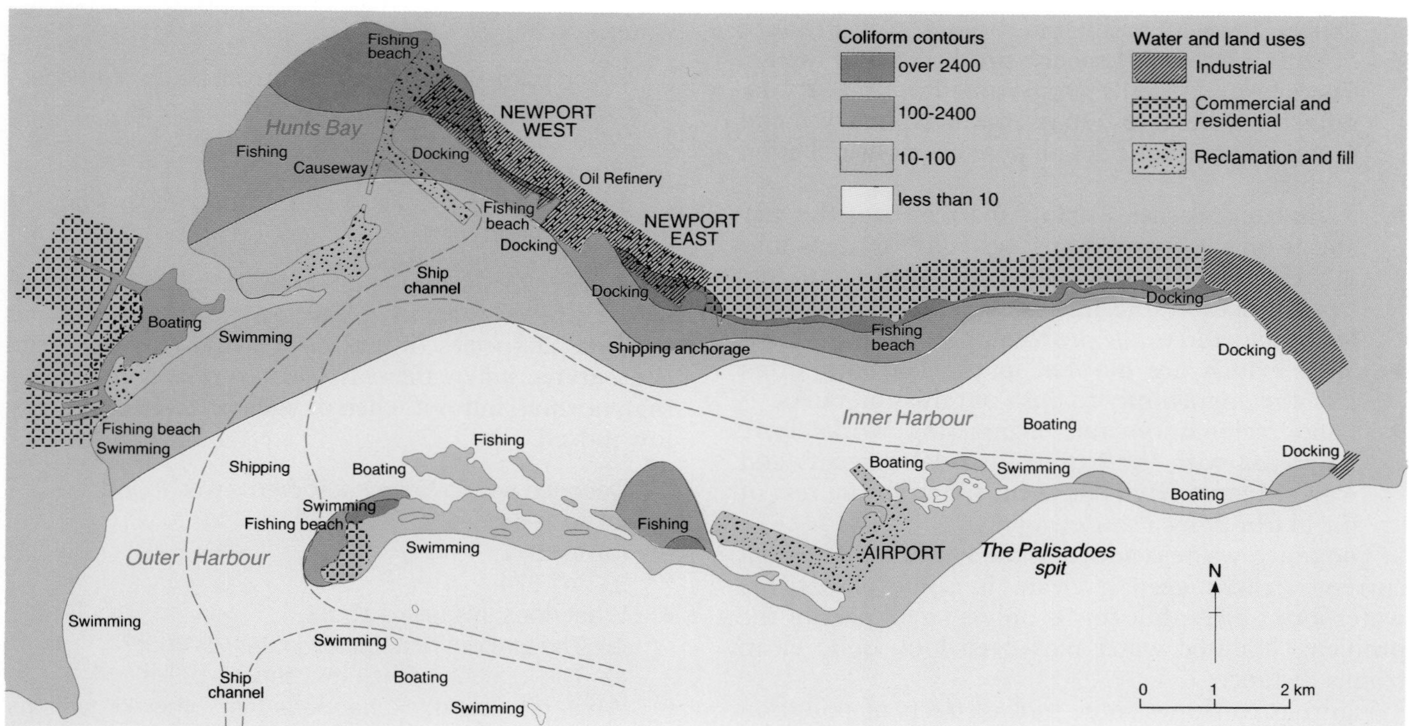

6.20 Pollution in Kingston Harbour.

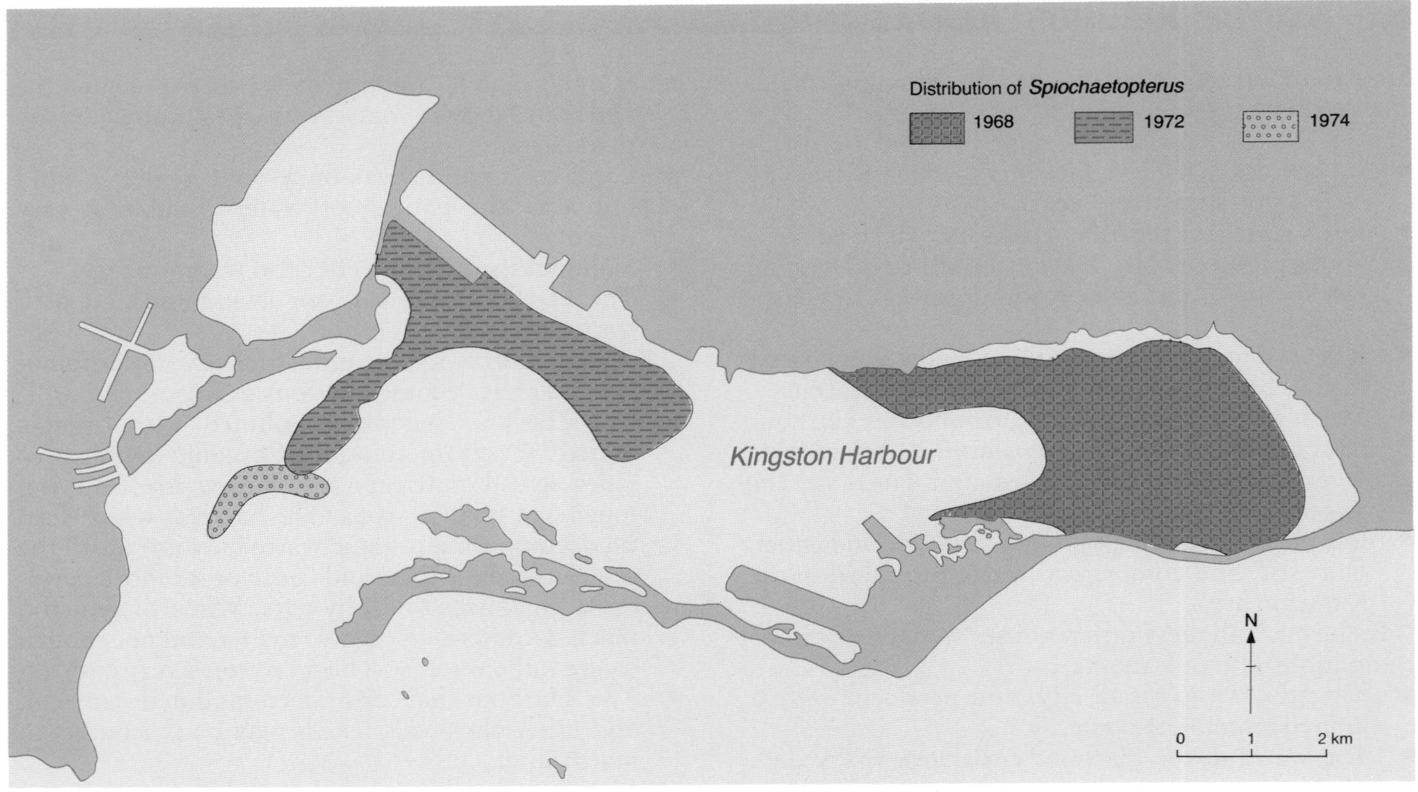

6.21 Distribution of *Spiochaetopterus* in Kingston Harbour.

- Many industrial plants add to the pollution problem. Food-processing factories – canning plants, dairies, breweries, slaughterhouses – all produce organic waste. A tannery produces acid waste. There are oil spills from time to time at the refinery. Detergents, soap products, heavy metal products, and pesticides all pose a serious pollution problem.
- Rainwater washes organic matter from the city and from the surrounding agricultural areas into the Harbour. During heavy rain, the nutrients from agricultural fertilisers are washed out of the fields, and add to the problem.
- Ships which are moored in the Harbour often take the opportunity to flush out their oil tanks.
- Land reclamation and engineering works have interfered with the pattern of tidal currents and waves. Hunts Bay is now cut off from the rest of the Harbour by a causeway.

Too much waste is added to the Harbour. The tidal currents cannot keep it clean. In some places, the water *looks* dirty; but this is only a small part of the problem. Polluted water may even look quite clean from a distance.

Figure 6.20 shows some of the effects of pollution by sewage. It shows the distribution of coliform bacteria, which originate in the human digestive system. These bacteria are quite harmless; but where these organisms are present in large numbers, it is likely that there will be other more dangerous ones in the water, too.

1 Which parts of the Harbour would it be most dangerous to swim in?
2 Which beaches:
   (a) Would be safest?
   (b) Would be most accessible for people living in Kingston?

Figure 6.21 shows the effect of increasing pollution levels on one small organism (*Spiochaetopterus oculatus*, a species of marine worm). This organism can survive when there is less oxygen in the water than normal, but not when oxygen levels become very low indeed.

3 Describe where *Spiochaetopterus* was found:
   (a) In 1968.
   (b) In 1972.
   (c) In 1974.
4 What does this tell us about:
   (a) The amount of pollution in the Harbour?
   (b) The location of the most serious pollution?
5 What do you think happened to other organisms which need more oxygen than *Spiochaetopterus*?
6 What effect would this type of pollution have on:
   (a) The fishing industry?

(b) Residents of Kingston who are not involved in fishing?

When organic pollution is very bad, there may be a *plankton bloom* or *red tide*. Large numbers of plankton appear, to feed on the bacteria which are decomposing the surplus organic matter. When plankton blooms occur, there is too little oxygen for most forms of marine life. The water body may be nearly 'dead'.

Plankton blooms have become quite common in Kingston Harbour during the period from June to November.

Can pollution be cut down?

Several ways of reducing the pollution problem in Kingston Harbour have been suggested – but none of them provides an easy answer:

- Building a new sewage plant which would treat the effluent more thoroughly and reduce its organic content before it is pumped into the Harbour.
  Problem: a project like this would be very expensive, and would take a long time to complete.
- Forcing all industries to treat their waste before dumping, or dispose of it elsewhere.
  Problem: this would increase the costs of manufacturing industries and make them less profitable; and there are few possible disposal sites that would not affect the Harbour in some way.
- Prosecuting ships that flush out their oil tanks.
  Problem: this might be difficult to enforce, and would only remove one source of pollution.
- Providing a direct connection between the eastern part of the Harbour and the open sea. This would allow clean water to enter the most polluted area. A new channel about 18 m deep and 500–800 m wide across the eastern end of the Palisadoes would be needed.
  Problem: This would be very expensive. A long bridge would be needed, so that the road to the airport and Port Royal could cross the channel. It is difficult to predict what effect a channel like this would have on the pattern of currents, and on beach erosion; or how far it would help to solve the pollution problem.

7 What effect might a channel through the Palisadoes have on longshore drift?

8 How might this affect the road, the airport, and Port Royal?

9 What do you think would be the best way of reducing pollution in Kingston Harbour?

6.7 Coral

Cliffs are formed by marine erosion; beaches and spits are formed by deposition; but many tropical coastlines are dominated by constructional landforms – the coral reefs.

Figure 6.22 shows the structure of a reef in the Caribbean.

The main frame of the reef is built up by coral *polyps*. These are small, soft-bodied creatures which use the calcium carbonate dissolved in sea water to build up a hard 'casing' of limestone to protect themselves. These tiny polyps live in colonies, or large groups. Layer after layer of limestone is added to the colony as new polyps build on top of the structure. Each species of polyp builds a colony with a distinctive shape. Elkhorn coral grows well in shallow water. Other corals grow where the water is deep.

Other organisms also live on the reef. These include algae, fish, sponges, sea eggs, and shellfish. There may be ten or a hundred times as much life in the reef as there is in the surrounding open sea. Many of the other creatures also produce hard skeletons, which help build up the structure of the reef around the framework of coral.

Only the surface layer of the reef is made up of live coral. Between the reef and the shore there is usually a shallow lagoon, the floor of which is made up of dead coral, sand, and rubble. On the seaward side, the reef slopes down more steeply; at the base of this slope there will also be an accumulation of sand and rubble.

Barrier reefs

Figure 6.22 shows a *fringing reef*, close to the shore,

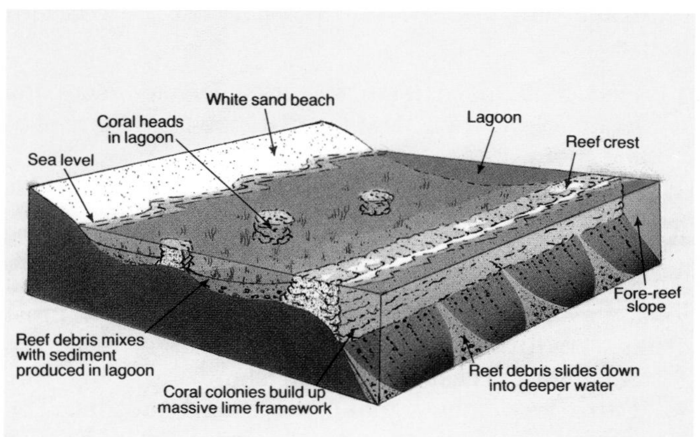

6.22 A fringing reef.

and separated from it by a shallow lagoon. There are fringing reefs off the coast of many Caribbean islands, including Barbados, Tobago, and Antigua.

A *barrier reef* may be many kilometres from the shore. Barrier reefs are formed like this:

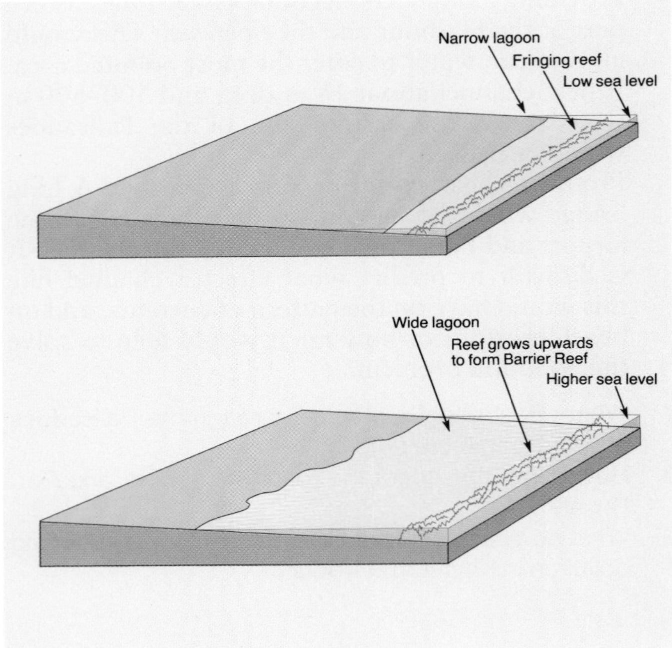

6.23 The development of a barrier reef.

- A fringing reef develops in the sea next to a low-lying coastal area.
- Sea level rises. The coastal plain is flooded, but the coral reef is able to grow upwards fast enough to keep pace with the increasing depth of the sea.
- A barrier reef is formed at a considerable distance from the new shoreline.

Wave action on a barrier reef may pile up dead coral to form a series of low-lying islands.

The world's largest barrier reef is off the coast of Australia, and the second largest is off the coast of Belize.

1 Find both these reefs in your atlas. Measure the length of the reefs, and the distance from the reef to the shore.

Atolls

An *atoll* is a ring-shaped coral reef, which may be a long way from the nearest land. This is how most atolls were formed:

- A fringing reef surrounds an island.
- Earth movements make the island subside. The fringing reef grows upwards to form a barrier reef.

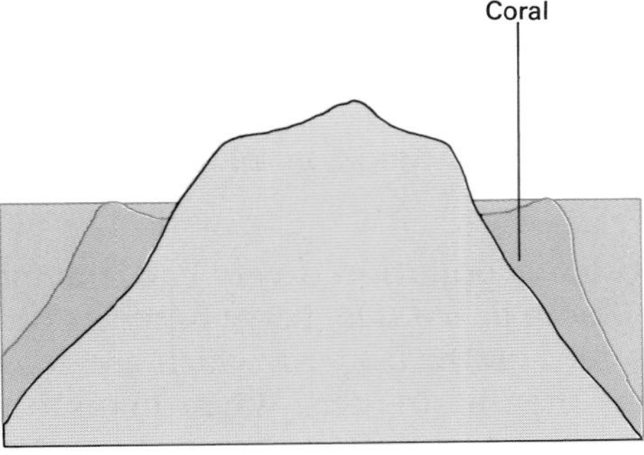

(a)
Island with fringing reef

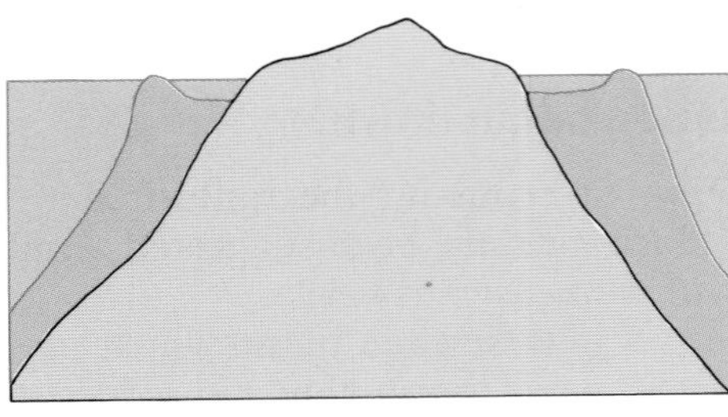

(b)
Island subsiding
Formation of barrier reefs

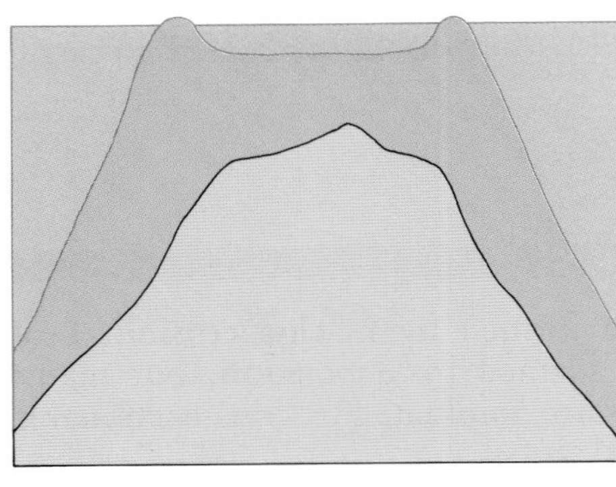

(c)
Subsidence continues
Formation of coral atoll

6.24 How coral atolls are formed.

- Subsidence continues until the island disappears; but the reef continues to grow upwards.

There are many coral atolls in the southern Pacific ocean.

Where coral grows

Coral polyps will only grow well in certain conditions:

- The temperature of the water must be between 23 °C and 30 °C. This is why there are very few coral reefs outside the tropics, or where there are cold sea currents.
- Sunlight must be able to penetrate down to where coral is growing. Coral will grow only in fairly shallow water.

- Coral must grow where the water has the right amount of salt. There are few reefs near to the mouths of large rivers.
- Coral needs to grow in clean water. Muddy water damages coral because it shuts out sunlight and because silt particles choke the coral polyps. Organic pollution damages coral, because it causes oxygen starvation. The growth of the coral is held back, it often becomes diseased, and may eventually die.

How reefs are damaged

A well-developed fringing reef is a self-constructed, self-repairing breakwater which protects the coast of an island from erosion.

A coral reef is a valuable resource – which depends on the maintenance of the right environmental conditions. Unfortunately, the fringing reefs which surround many islands have been very badly damaged by human activities.

When it was first settled, Barbados was almost completely surrounded by a fringing reef. Now, most of the reef is simply a ridge of dead coral, and even the parts which are still alive are in very bad condition.

The first real damage to the reef came quite soon after the English settlement. The original forest cover held the soil together, and during heavy rain the fresh water seeped gradually into the ground. In the seventeenth century, almost all the forest was cleared, so that the land could be used for growing sugar cane. This meant that after heavy rain, fresh water flooded into the sea, carrying a great deal of mud and soil with it.

2 Explain why these changes damaged the coral reef.

3 Explain how these more recent developments have caused further damage to the reef:

(a) More sewage and other organic material is washed into the sea along the south and west coasts.

(b) Urban development means that more rain falls on hard surfaces like roads, housing developments, or the airport, and runs straight into the sea.

(c) Agriculturalists are using far more chemical fertilisers than ever before.

(d) Explosives have been used illegally in some areas to kill fish.

(e) There are more oil spills from passing ships.

A healthy coral reef contains creatures which produce 250–1,250 tonnes of calcium carbonate per hectare in a year. Some coral will be removed from the reef by wave erosion, particularly when there is a hurricane or major storm; but over a long period of time there will be a balance between erosion and new growth. But when a fringing reef is in bad condition:

- The reef crest is eroded by the waves, and is further below the surface than before.
- Waves do not lose so much energy on the reef, and still retain most of their erosive power when they reach the shore.
- Sand is removed from the beaches by destructive waves. Along the south and west coasts of Barbados, the beach has virtually disappeared in some places, and houses along the shoreline are threatened by erosion.
- Marine pollution encourages the growth of algae, or sea moss, along the reef. At certain times of year, this is washed onto the shore in large quantities, and causes a further problem.

4 Explain why the tourist industry will suffer if the coral reef is badly damaged by pollution.

5 The government of Barbados has constructed a sewerage system, and plans to provide sewerage for the south and west coasts of the island, too. Sewage will be treated to make it safe.

(a) How will this help reduce the coastal pollution problem?

(b) Which types of marine pollution will not be dealt with by this project?

7 • WEATHER AND CLIMATE

7.1 The atmosphere

The atmosphere is a very thin layer of gas. It is difficult to say how high the earth's atmosphere extends. There is no sharp boundary at the top of the atmosphere – the air gradually gets less and less dense until it becomes very difficult to distinguish from empty space.

Most of the atmosphere is very close to the earth's surface:

- The earth has a radius of 6,320 km.
- Half the gas in the atmosphere lies within 5.5 km of the earth's surface.

In cities like La Paz, 3,600 m above sea level, the air is already becoming quite thin. Travellers who visit places like this may suffer from 'soroche' or mountain sickness. After a time, the body becomes accustomed to altitudes like these, but in places like the high peaks of the Andes and the Himalayas, the air becomes so rarefied that climbers need to take their own oxygen supply with them.

Although there is still some gas held by the earth's gravity at heights of 1,000 km or more:

- 90% of the atmosphere is within 16 km of sea level.
- 99.9% is within 50 km of sea level.

The gases in the atmosphere

Almost all the atmosphere is made up of two gases, oxygen and nitrogen; but there are three others which play a very important part in the world's weather system and are essential for the survival of life on earth. They are:

- Water vapour, which produces clouds, rainfall, and snow. If the water vapour in the atmosphere were condensed, it would form a layer 50 mm deep in the tropics; but only 1 mm deep at the poles, where the air can hold less moisture.
- Ozone, which screens out the sun's harmful ultra-violet rays, and is concentrated in a layer about 50 km above sea level.
- Carbon dioxide, which helps maintain the temperature of the earth, and which is needed by plants for photosynthesis.

1 Refer back to Figure 4.1. Describe the part which atmospheric water vapour plays in the hydrological cycle.

The troposphere

At the surface, weather conditions vary enormously. In the Arctic, there may be still, dry air, with a clear sky and temperatures of −20 °C. At the same time, somewhere in the tropics, there may be a hurricane, with heavy rain, wind-speeds of 200 km per hour, and a temperature of 30 °C.

The weather systems which affect us all develop within the troposphere – the lowest layer of the atmosphere, where the air is relatively dense. The troposphere is about 8 km thick at the poles, and about 16 km at the equator.

7.2 Energy in the atmosphere

The energy which drives a hurricane – like the energy in all the world's weather systems – is derived from the sun.

The sun has a surface area of 6,000,000,000,000 km^2. The temperature of the sun's surface is 6,000 °C; each square metre of this surface is giving off enough energy to power 600,000 light bulbs.

The earth is a tiny speck in space, 149 million km away from the sun. Only a tiny fraction of the sun's energy falls on the earth's surface. At this distance, the sun's rays are spread out over a wide area, and are not nearly so intense – but even so, each square metre of the earth's atmosphere receives on average enough energy from the sun to keep 3½ light bulbs alight, 24 hours a day, all the year round.

Not all of this energy reaches the surface of the earth. Quite a high proportion is absorbed by the atmosphere, or else reflected back into space.

The carbon dioxide heat trap

Like the sun, the earth's surface gives off radiation.

The sun is very hot. Because of this, it gives off *short-wave* radiation – mostly visible light, ultra-violet light, and infra-red radiation. Most short-wave radiation can penetrate easily through the atmosphere.

The earth is much cooler. Because of this, it gives off *long-wave* heat radiation.

The atmosphere is transparent. It lets *in* most of the visible light and infra-red radiation from the sun. But the atmosphere does not let *out* most of the long-wave heat radiation which the earth gives off.

The carbon dioxide and water vapour in the air are not 'transparent' to heat radiation. They form a small proportion of the gas in the atmosphere, but they play a very important part in the world's weather system. They act like a blanket which prevents heat from escaping into space.

The average air temperature near the earth's surface is 15 °C. If there were no carbon dioxide in the atmosphere, then the temperature of the earth would average −3 °C. The seas would be permanently frozen solid.

The energy that heats the atmosphere comes from the sun; but the air is really heated from *below*, by long-wave heat energy from the surface of the earth. This is one of the reasons why temperatures are lower in mountain areas. The blanket of air above the ground is thinner, and the earth's heat energy can escape more easily.

In the tropics, the temperature averages 26 °C at sea level; but it is −80 °C at the top of the troposphere. This is even colder than the South Pole in the middle of the winter.

1 If a car is parked outside in the sun, it will get much hotter than the air around it. Why is this?
2 Some scientists think we are burning so much coal, oil, and wood that the amount of carbon dioxide in the atmosphere is being increased. What effect might this have on the world's climates?
3 It is also thought that chlorofluorocarbon gases from aerosol spray cans may be destroying the ozone in the upper atmosphere. What effect would this have on human life?

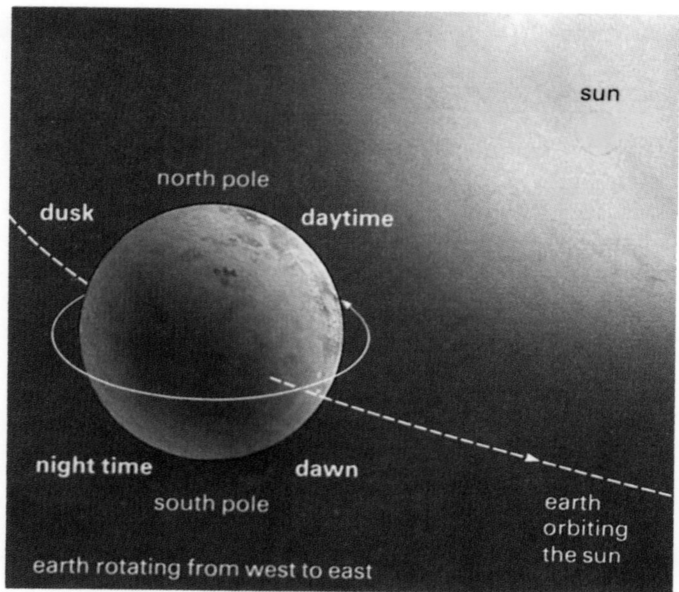

7.1 The earth and the sun.

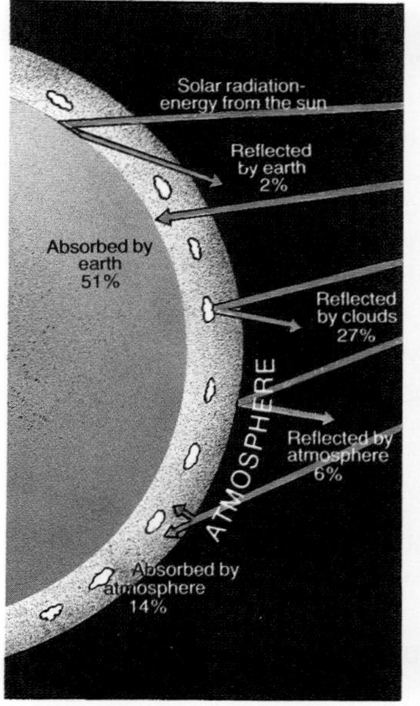

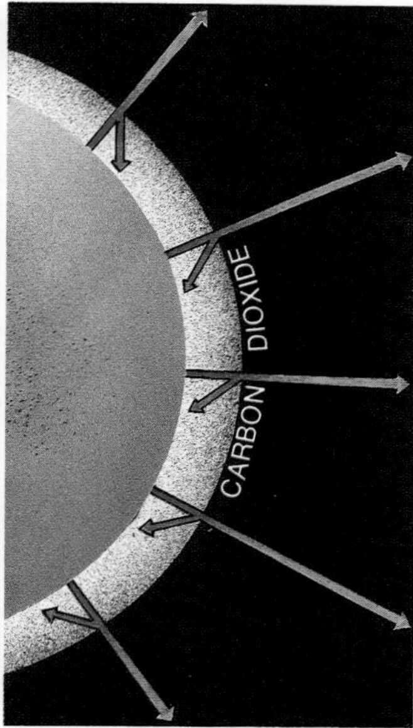

7.2 What happens to solar radiation. The right hand diagram shows that most of the heat energy which the earth gives off is trapped by carbon dioxide and water vapour in the atmosphere.

How solar energy is distributed

The sun's energy does not fall evenly on the earth. At any one time:

- There will be one place where the sun appears to be directly overhead. The sun's rays will seem very powerful here, because:
  - They are concentrated in one small area.
  - They travel vertically down through the atmosphere.
- Half the world will be lit by the sun. There will be some solar radiation, but it will not seem quite so powerful, because:
  - The sunlight is spread out over a wider area.
  - The sun's rays travel down through the atmosphere at an angle to the surface. They have a longer journey through the air, and a higher proportion of their energy will be filtered out by the atmosphere.
- Half the world will be dark, and will not be receiving any energy directly from the sun.

7.3 The seasons

The June solstice

The axis around which the earth rotates is tilted at an angle of 23½°.

In June, the northern hemisphere is tilted towards the sun. At the *solstice* on 21 June, it is midsummer in this hemisphere, and:

- Everywhere north of the Arctic Circle will have sunlight for 24 hours a day. This is the 'Land of the Midnight Sun'.
- Elsewhere in the northern hemisphere, the sun will be above the horizon for more than twelve hours a day. In Canada and Northern Europe, the nights will be very short.
- At the Tropic of Cancer, the sun will be directly overhead at midday.
- In the Caribbean, the day will be slightly more than 12 hours long, and temperatures may be a little above the annual average.
- At the equator, the sun will not be quite overhead at midday; it will be 66½° above the horizon. The sun will be above the horizon for exactly 12 hours.
- At the Tropic of Capricorn, the sun will rise only 43° above the horizon, and there will be much less solar energy than in the northern hemisphere.
- Further south, the days will be quite short, and the sun will be low in the sky.
- South of the Antarctic Circle, the sun will not rise above the horizon. It will be dark for 24 hours a day, and no solar energy will be received.

The equinoxes

At the *equinoxes* on 21 March and 23 September:

- Everywhere on earth will have exactly 12 hours' sunlight.
- At the equator, the sun will be exactly overhead at midday.
- At the tropics, the sun will be 66½° above the horizon at midday. There will be almost as much solar energy available as at the equator.
- Nearer the poles, the midday sun will be lower in the sky. At the Arctic and Antarctic Circles, the sun will rise to only 22½° above the horizon, and there will only be about 30% of the amount of solar energy at the equator.
- Very close to the poles, the sun will be above the horizon for 12 hours a day; but it will be only just above the horizon, and will provide almost no energy.

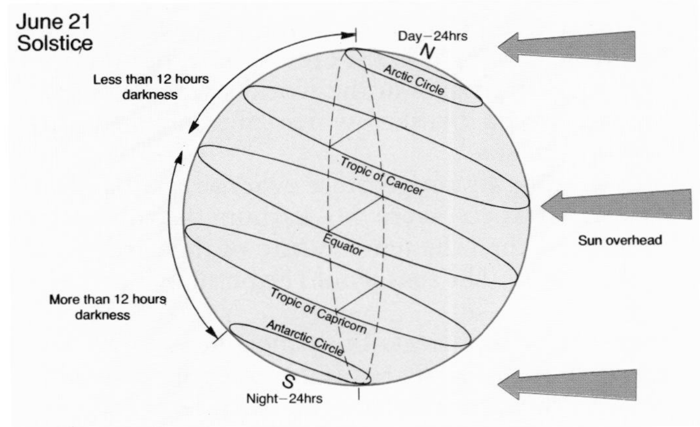

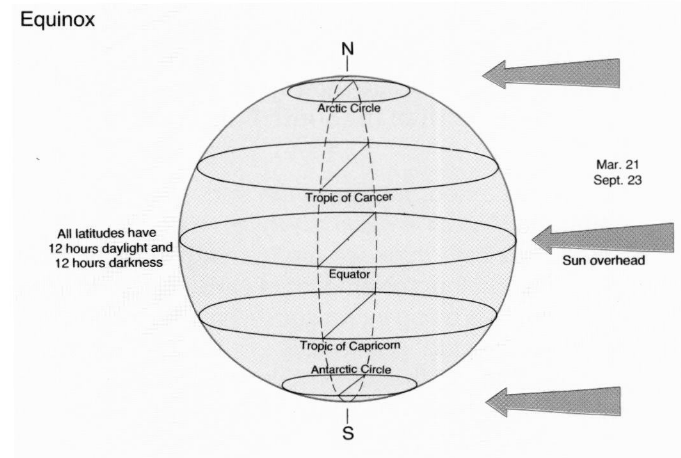

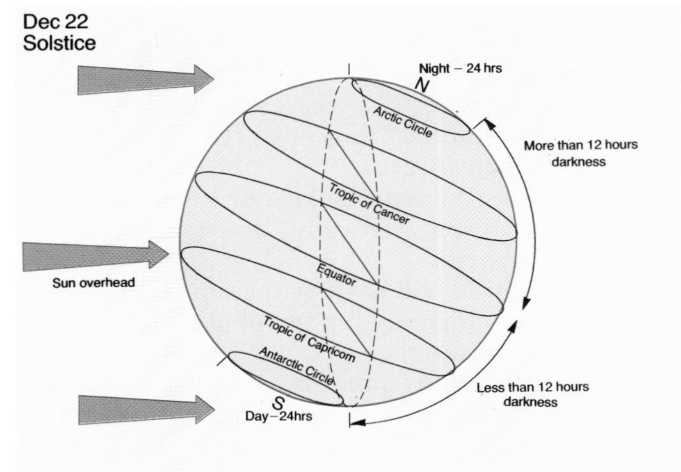

7.3 The seasons.

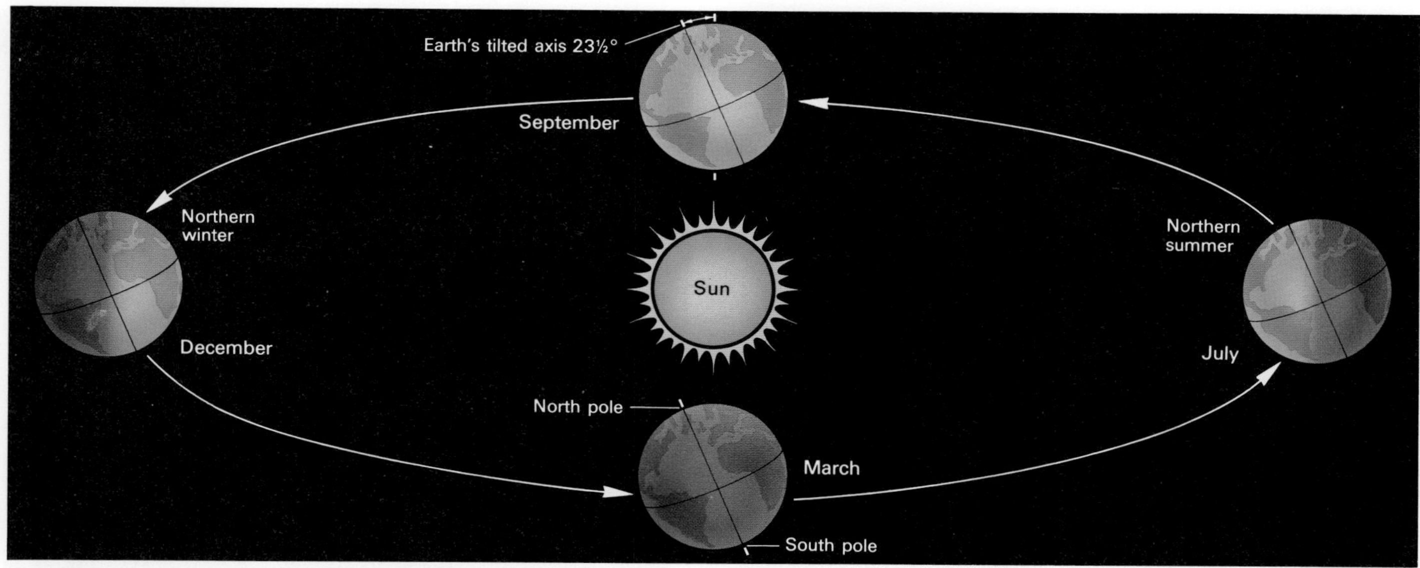

7.4 The seasonal movement of the earth around the sun.

1 Describe what conditions will be like at the solstice on 22 December, in the northern hemisphere winter:
(a) In the Arctic.
(b) At the Tropic of Cancer.
(c) At the equator.
(d) At the Tropic of Capricorn.
(e) In the Antarctic.

7.4 Time zones

As the earth rotates, the point where the sun is overhead moves from east to west.

There are 360 degrees of longitude, and 24 hours in the day. Every hour, the point where the sun is directly overhead moves 360⁄24 or 15° to the west. At this place, it will be midday, local time. Everywhere else on the same line of longitude, the sun will be highest in the sky at exactly the same time.

When we compare the time at different places, it is often convenient to use Greenwich Mean Time (GMT). Midday GMT is the time when the sun is highest in the sky at the old Royal Observatory at Greenwich, near London – exactly at 0° of longitude.

When it is 12.00 midday Greenwich Mean Time, it will be:

- 12.00 midday at Accra, Ghana, and everywhere at 0°.
- 11.00 a.m. at Las Palmas in the Canaries, and everywhere at 15° west.
- 8.00 a.m. in Barbados, and everywhere at 60° west.
- 6.00 a.m. at Merida in Mexico, and everywhere at 90° west.

1 Use your atlas to find out what the time will be at:
(a) Baranquilla, Colombia? (b) Manaus, Brazil?
(c) Oran, Algeria? (d) Denver, USA?
(e) New Orleans, USA? (f) Cook Islands, Pacific?

It will be:

- 1.00 p.m. at Catania, Italy, and everywhere at 15° east.
- 3.00 p.m. at Mogadishu, Somalia, and everywhere at 45° east.
- 6.00 p.m. at Dakha, Bangladesh, and everywhere at 90° east.

2 What time will it be at:
(a) Alexandria, Egypt? (b) Lahore, Pakistan?
(c) Kobe, Japan? (d) New Caledonia, Pacific?

Kingston, Jamaica is at 76° 47′ west. That means that the sun is highest in the sky at 5 hours, 7 minutes and 8 seconds after midday Greenwich Mean Time. Montego Bay is 1° 9′ further west. The sun reaches its highest point 4 minutes and 36 seconds later than at Kingston.

It would obviously not be convenient if every town and village calculated the exact time when the sun was overhead, and used that moment as midday, local time. For this reason, the world has been split into *time zones*. When travellers go from one zone to another, their watches must be adjusted by one hour. On long air journeys, a greater adjustment will be needed.

The air journey from London to Antigua takes eight hours and twenty-five minutes. Local time in

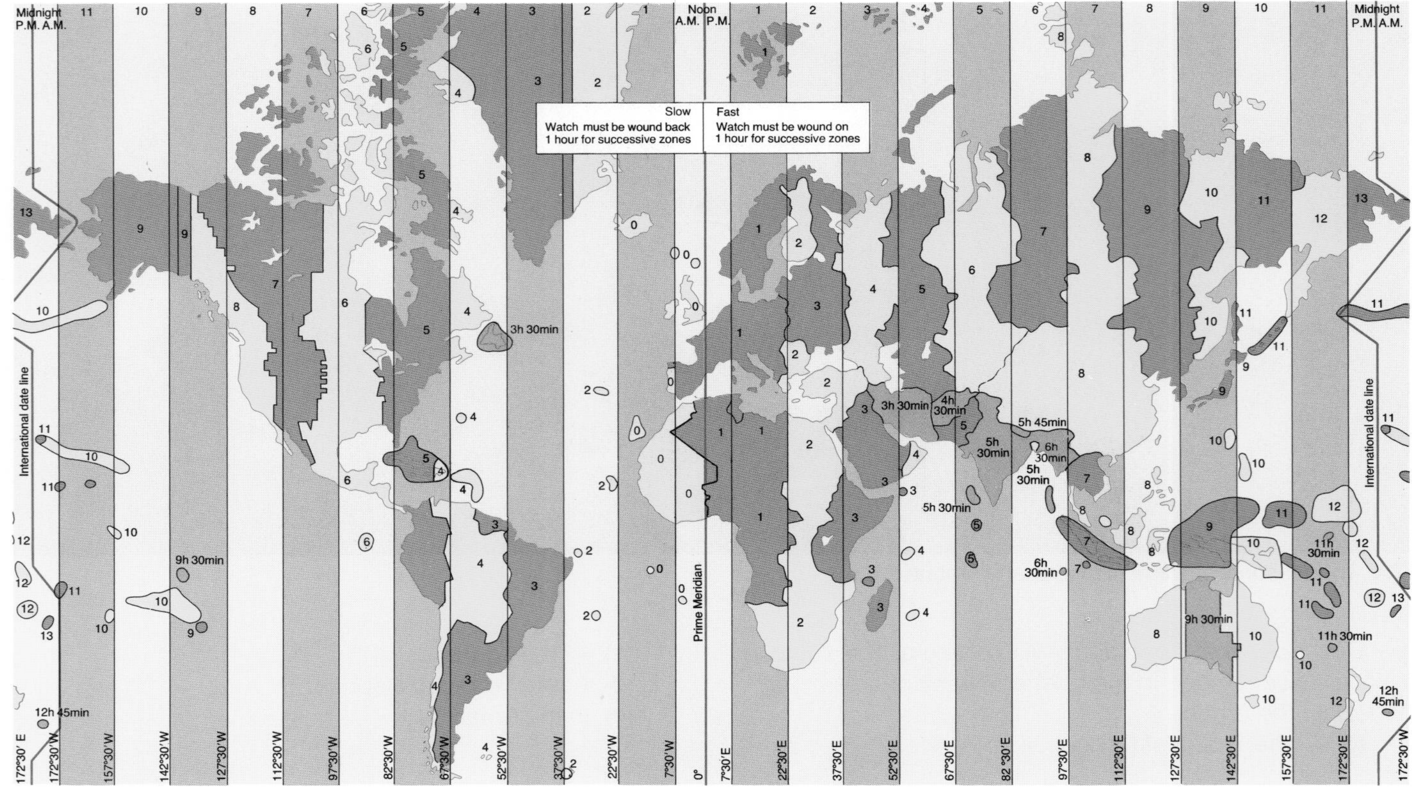

7.5 Time zones.

Antigua is four hours earlier than Greenwich Mean Time. If a traveller leaves London at 12.00 midday GMT, arrival in Antigua will be at 8.25 p.m. GMT; but his watch should be adjusted to read 4.25 p.m., local time.

Large countries are divided into several time zones. The Soviet Union has eleven time zones. When it is 6.00 a.m. GMT, it is 9.00 a.m. in Moscow – but it is already 8.00 p.m. in the eastern part of Siberia.

The only large country which is not divided into time zones is China. The whole country uses one time zone. At Hangzhou in eastern China (120° E) the sun is highest in the sky at 12.00 midday local time; but Kashi (Kashgar) in Xinjiang (Sinkiang) region is almost 4,000 km further west (75° E). At Kashi, the sun does not reach its highest point until 3.00 p.m., and does not set until after 9.00 p.m.

Calculating local time

You may be asked to calculate the difference in local time for two places. It can be done like this:

- For places in the same hemisphere (east or west)

Write down the longitude of the first place, e.g. Miami	80° W
Write down the longitude of the second place, e.g. Vancouver	123° W
Find the difference between the two	43°
Divide the result by 15°	2.866
Round off to the nearest whole number	3

Miami is further *east* than Vancouver. Local time must be three hours *ahead*. Vancouver is further *west* than Miami. Local time must be three hours *behind*.

- For places in different hemispheres

Write down the number of degrees west, e.g. Buenos Aires	58° W
Write down the number of degrees east, e.g. Auckland	173° E
Add the two	231°
Divide the result by 15°	15.4
Round off to the nearest whole number	15

Auckland is in the *eastern* hemisphere. Local time must be 15 hours *ahead*. Buenos Aires is in the *western* hemisphere. Local time must be 15 hours *behind*.

3 The BBC broadcasts the World News from London at 11.00 GMT. At what time will this broadcast be heard on the radio in:
(a) Barbados?
(b) Jamaica?
(c) Hong Kong?

4 A sports event takes place in Seoul, South Korea, at

12.00 midday, local time. If it is televised and transmitted by satellite, at what time will it be seen in:
   (a) Trinidad?
   (b) Moscow?
   (c) Los Angeles?
5 A relative is working for a short time in Sydney, Australia. She is in her office from 9.00 a.m. to 5.00 p.m. If you want to telephone her at work, what would be a good time to call, in your local time?

The International Date Line

When it is 12.00 midnight GMT, and Monday is just beginning:

- In New Caledonia, at 165° E, the clocks will be 11 hours ahead. The time will be 11 a.m. on Monday morning.
- In the Cook Islands at 165° W, the clocks will be 11 hours behind. It will be 1 p.m. on Sunday afternoon.
- At 180° longitude, it will be exactly 12.00 midday. But on one side of the line, it will be midday on Monday; on the other side it will be midday on Sunday.

This line of longitude – 180° – runs right through some countries. The town of Gisborne in New Zealand is right on the line. It would obviously be inconvenient if it were Sunday in some parts of the town, and Monday in others. The whole of Gisborne – and the whole of New Zealand – treats the day as *Monday*; but there are other islands on the same longitude which treat the day as Sunday. They are on the other side of the International Date Line, which zigzags through the middle of this time zone. One part of the zone is 12 hours *ahead* of Greenwich Mean Time; the other part is 12 hours *behind*.

7.5 The circulation of the atmosphere

Energy transfer

The tropics receive solar energy all the year round.

The middle latitudes receive as much solar energy as the tropics during the summer months, but much less in the winter.

The Arctic and Antarctic receive as much solar energy as the tropics for a short period in the summer, because the days are so long; but much less in the spring and autumn; and none at all during the winter months.

Taking the year as a whole, the atmosphere receives much more energy in the tropics than in the other regions.

When a liquid or a gas is heated in one place, it will begin to flow. Currents start to redistribute the heat energy so that it is spread more evenly. There may be other changes, too. It is because the atmosphere is heated *unevenly* that we experience winds, rain, clouds, and snow. These weather phenomena develop because the atmosphere is flowing and circulating. It is a fluid in which energy is being transferred from the tropics to the polar regions. If the atmosphere did not flow and circulate, the tropics would be even hotter, and the Arctic and Antarctic even colder.

1 When you are at home, heat a saucepan of water. Make a careful note of the changes you can observe in the water as it comes to the boil:
   (a) Is it possible to predict roughly where the air bubbles will begin to form?
   (b) Can you predict exactly what will happen to any small drop of water once the liquid is boiling really fast?

It is possible to describe in general terms how the atmosphere circulates to transfer heat energy – but it is not possible to say exactly what the weather will be like in a particular place at a particular time.

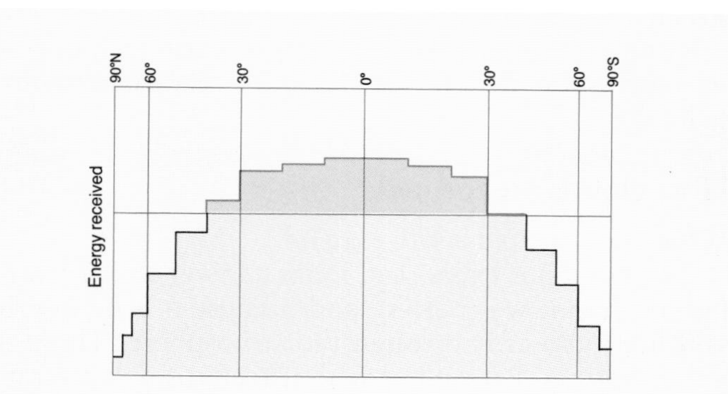

The earth receives most energy in the tropics

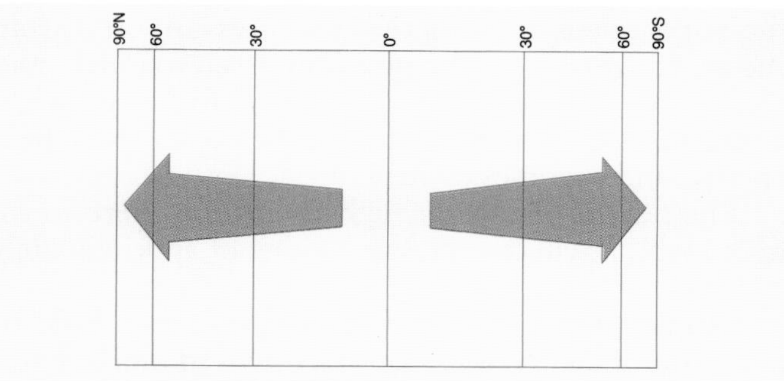

Energy is transferred towards the poles by the world's wind system and ocean currents

7.6 Energy transfer.

Energy is transferred from the tropics towards the poles by winds and ocean currents.

Even today – when we have the aid of satellite photography and know quite a lot about the upper atmosphere – we do not fully understand how this energy transfer takes place; and what we do understand cannot easily be summarised in a few pages. But it is important to know something about the heat transfer process so as to understand the main features of the worldwide pattern of weather and climate.

Water in the atmosphere

Air can hold more water when it is warm.

If an airtight container is placed in a refrigerator, drops of water will appear on the inside. The air has cooled down, and cannot hold so much water – so the water vapour inside has condensed.

If the container is warmed, the drops of water will disappear. The air can hold more water and the liquid will evaporate.

Tropical air with a temperature of 30 °C can hold about seven times as much water vapour as cold air with a temperature of 0 °C; and about 100 times as much as very cold arctic air with a temperature of −30 °C.

When air contains as much water vapour as it can hold, it has a *relative humidity* of 100%. Air which contains half as much water vapour as it can hold has a relative humidity of 50%.

If air is heated, the amount of water vapour it contains will remain the same; but its relative humidity will fall.

How clouds are formed

When air is heated it will expand.

Because it has expanded, it has a lower *density*. It is lighter than it was before; and because it is lighter, it will float upwards through the atmosphere. There is an *updraught*. Passengers who travel in small aircraft will be familiar with updraughts – which can give them quite a bumpy ride in some conditions.

When air starts to rise, and moves upwards through the atmosphere, then there is less pressure on it from the air above. It is not being compressed so much, and this makes it expand. It needs to use up energy when it expands outwards – so it uses up its own heat energy, and becomes cooler.

When air is rising through the atmosphere in an updraught, it will cool down at a rate of approximately 1 °C per 100 metres.

Because the air is cooling down, it cannot hold so much water. When it has cooled down so much that it cannot hold all its water vapour, clouds will start to form. Tiny drops of water condense around particles of dust and electrically charged air molecules.

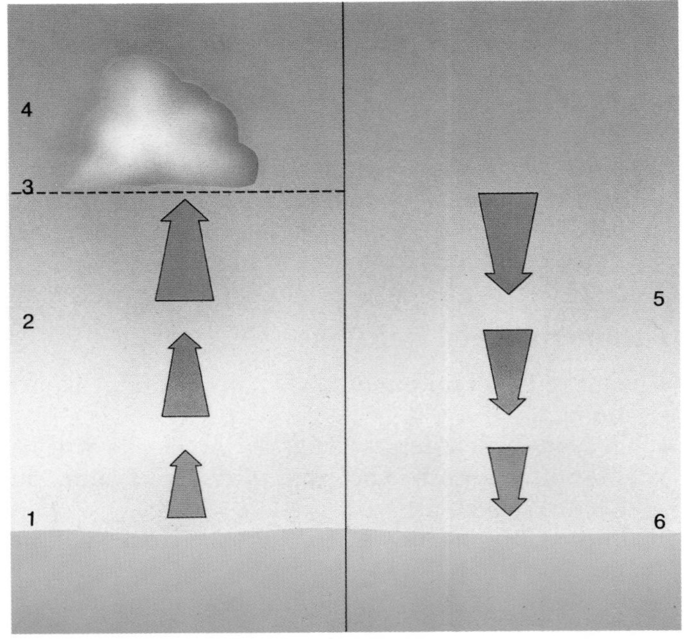

1 When air is heated, it begins to rise.
2 The air expands and becomes cooler.
3 When it reaches the condensation level, it cannot hold all its water vapour.
4 Clouds begin to form.
5 A descending air current is compressed and warmed.
6 When it reaches the surface, it will feel warm and dry.

7.7 How clouds are formed.

These droplets are so light that they can remain floating in the air; but under some conditions, clusters of ice crystals or much larger drops of water are formed. These fall down through the atmosphere as rain, or, in colder climates, as snow.

When air sinks, it will contract. Just as air is cooled when it expands, it warms up when it contracts. Because the air is getting warmer, it can easily hold all the water vapour it contains. Currents of air which are moving downwards through the atmosphere will generally feel warmer than the surrounding air, and they will be very dry.

Air pressure and winds

Air pressure is the total weight of the atmosphere at any particular place. Air pressure is measured in *millibars*. On average, the air pressure at sea level is 1,013 millibars; but the exact figure varies from place to place. Where an air current is *rising* upwards through the atmosphere, air pressure is *low*; where air is *sinking* downwards, air pressure will be *high*.

If the earth did not rotate, then air would flow very quickly from places where pressure is high to areas of low pressure. But because the earth rotates, this does not happen.

The earth rotates from west to east. Because of the rotation of the earth, winds which blow *towards* the equator are deflected, so that they come from the *east*; and winds which blow *away from* the equator are deflected so that they come from the *west*. This means that:

- Winds in the northern hemisphere are deflected to the *right*.
- Winds in the southern hemisphere are deflected to the *left*.

Look at Figure 7.8. When there is a local area with very low pressure, winds do not blow straight *into* it. They blow *around* it. They blow in:

- An anticlockwise pattern in the northern hemisphere.
- A clockwise pattern in the southern hemisphere.

Around an area of high pressure, wind directions are reversed.

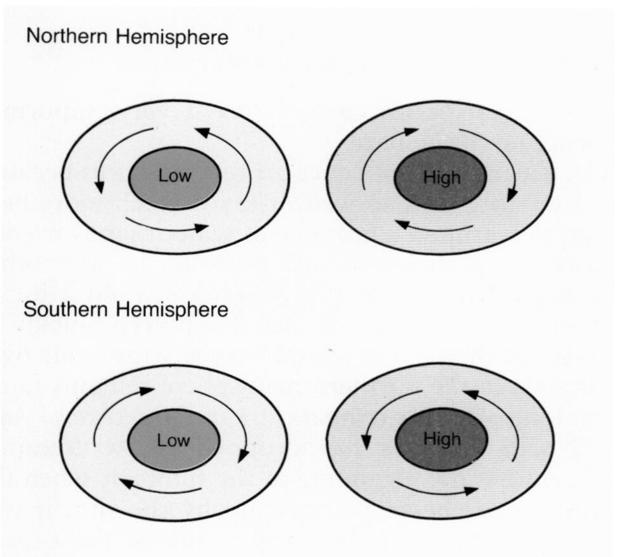

7.8 Air pressure and wind patterns.

The world wind system

Most of the energy that is transferred from the tropics towards the poles is taken by the world's wind system.

The ITCZ (Inter-Tropical Convergence Zone) The atmosphere receives most energy near the equator. Here there is a zone of warm air where air pressure is generally low. There are many updraughts, so atmospheric conditions can be unstable. Thick clouds form frequently, and rainfall is usually high.

The trade winds In the tropics, surface winds are sucked in steadily towards the ITCZ; but they do not blow directly towards the equator, because of the rotation of the earth. They are deflected, so that they blow from the *east*.

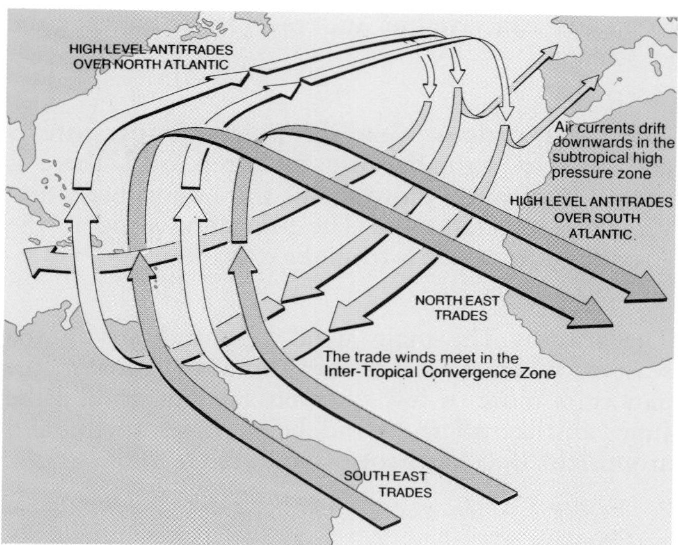

7.9 The trade winds and the anti-trades.

These are the trade winds. They were given this name because they were very important for world trade in the days of sailing ships. They are the *prevailing winds* in the Caribbean and many other tropical areas. The trade winds blow from the north-east in the northern hemisphere, and from the south-east on the other side of the equator.

In the Caribbean, fine high-level clouds can often be seen moving to the *west*. This is because upper-level winds blow steadily away from the ITCZ. These winds are the Antitrades. The Antitrades are important in the world's climate because they take heat energy away from the equator and towards the poles.

The subtropical high-pressure zone On the poleward side of the trade-wind belt, at about 30° north and south of the equator, there is a zone where air from the upper atmosphere drifts slowly downwards. When this air reaches the surface, it is very warm and dry. Most of the world's deserts are here. This region is sometimes known as the Horse Latitudes. Air pressure is usually quite high here, particularly over the oceans in the summer months and over the continents during the winter.

The westerlies Beyond this belt of high pressure, in the middle latitudes, the prevailing wind is from the *west*. This is a zone where a tremendous amount of heat energy is transferred away from the tropics and towards the poles. Unlike the trade winds, which blow steadily, the westerlies are very stormy, changeable winds. Air pressure is usually very low, and rainfall can be high.

To the north and south of this zone, there are two narrow bands of very fast upper-level westerly winds, known as the *jet streams*. An aircraft which is flying to the east can save fuel and travel faster by using the jet streams.

The polar regions Near the poles, air pressure is usually very high. Because the air is cold, there is usually not much moisture in the atmosphere, and very little precipitation. The prevailing wind in the Arctic and Antarctic is from the east.

The seasons The main wind belts move with the seasons. When the sun is overhead at the equator, the pattern is more or less symmetrical; but around the June solstice, all the wind belts move north; and around the December solstice they move to the south.

2 Figure 7.10 shows the wind belts over the Atlantic in January and July. What do you notice about the position of:
(a) The ITCZ?
(b) The subtropical high pressure zone?
(c) The jet streams?

Ocean currents

Heat energy is also transported towards the poles by the ocean currents. In the western part of every ocean, between latitudes 5° and 45°, there is a warm current, which takes tropical heat energy into the middle latitudes. The best-known of these currents is the Gulf Stream, which flows from the Gulf of Mexico through the North Atlantic to the edge of the Arctic Ocean.

When the Gulf Stream reaches the Arctic, the water is so cold that anyone falling into the sea would die of exposure in a few minutes; but it is still far warmer than any other area of sea at the same latitude. Because of the Gulf Stream, the sea around the island

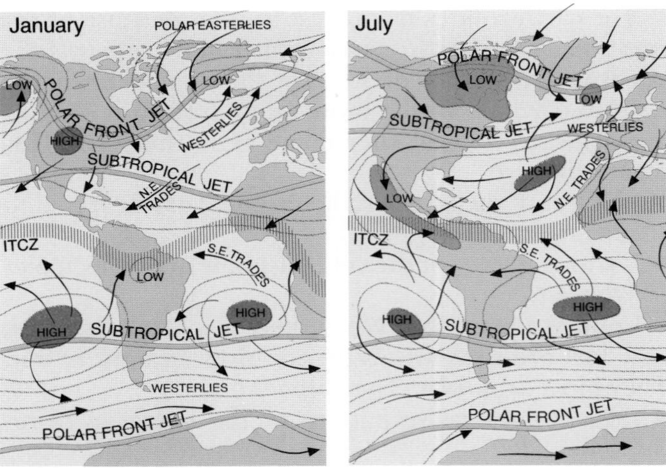

7.10 The wind systems over the Atlantic.

of Spitzbergen at almost 80°N does not completely freeze up even in the middle of winter.

How the oceans affect air temperatures

Near the sea, ocean currents are a very important influence on the climate.

The oceans also influence air temperatures because they can store heat so well. It takes much more heat energy to warm up a gramme of water than is needed to warm a gramme of air, or rock, or any other substance. This means that water can hold a lot of heat energy, and will not cool down very quickly at the start of the winter season. In the winter, air over the oceans in the northern hemisphere remains fairly warm long after the temperature in the centre of Asia and North America has dropped below freezing-point. And at the beginning of the summer, when the continents are being warmed up by the sun, it will take a long time for the temperature of the oceans around them to rise.

7.6 Climate

Figure 7.11 is a picture of the earth taken from a satellite 30,000 km above the equator on 3 August 1980.

In a photograph like this, it is possible to make out the main features of the world wind system. There is a broad belt with many clouds stretching across South America and the Pacific Ocean, to the north of the equator. There is clear, dry air in the subtropical high-pressure zone, in Northern Mexico, over the middle Atlantic, and in South America. The 'westerlies' in the mid-latitudes are really two belts of *circulating* wind systems; winds here blow from the west more often than from other directions, but not for the whole time.

We can learn something about the world's climate from a photograph like this; but it really only tells us what conditions were like on a particular day.

Climatic maps, on the other hand, are based on information which was collected at a large number of weather stations over a long period. They show the general worldwide pattern of temperature and rainfall; but they do not necessarily tell us what the weather will be like on a particular day.

There will be some days in July and August when Europe and southern Canada are much hotter than the Caribbean – but these places do not have a warmer *climate* than we do. They simply have warmer *weather* for a few days in the summer.

7.11 A satellite photograph of the western hemisphere at 23.00 GMT on 3 August 1980.

Verkhoyansk in Siberia is the coldest place in the inhabited world. The average January temperature is −50 °C, and even in July, the average is only 15 °C. But the highest temperature ever recorded there is 35 °C, which is 2 °C more than the record for Fort de France in Martinique.

The climate of a place is, in a sense, its 'average' weather. A description of the climate is partly a summary of the sort of weather conditions that can be expected in a normal year:

- How much rain can be expected over a year? What is the *average annual rainfall*?
- Which months are usually the wettest ones? What is the *seasonal distribution of rainfall*?
- How much does temperature vary over the year? What is the *annual temperature range*?
- What is the average temperature of the warmest and the coldest month?
- Do frosts occur; and if they do, when are they expected? What is the *frost-free period*?

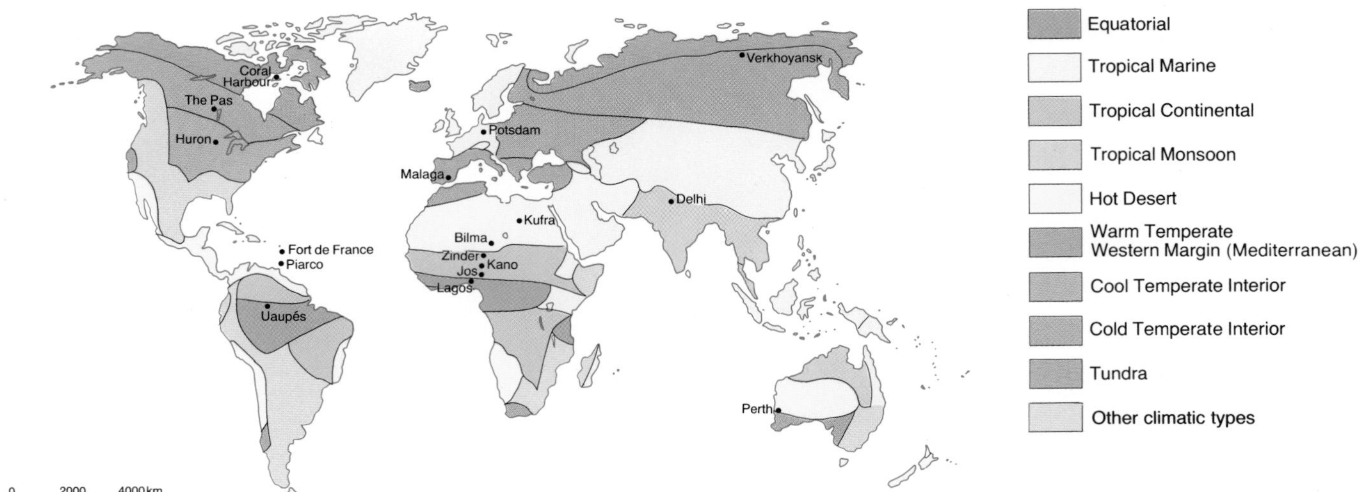

7.12 The climates of the world.

- Are there any months when it is too cold for plants to grow? What is the *growing season*?
- What is the *prevailing wind*?

But these 'averages' are not enough to give a real picture of what a climate is like. The 'extreme' events that do *not* occur every year are also part of the climate:

- Do hurricanes affect the area?
- What is the longest period of dry weather that can be expected?
- How much rain is likely to fall in a really heavy storm?

1 Which of these people would be mainly interested in knowing about the weather, and which would need to know about the climate? Which elements of the weather or climate would each of them be particularly concerned with?
   (a) An engineer designing a new fishing harbour.
   (b) A fisherman deciding whether to go to sea on a particular day.
   (c) A travel agency deciding whether to sell August holidays in the Caribbean?
   (d) A family planning a picnic on a holiday weekend.

The pattern of world climate

Figure 7.12 shows the world's main types of climate.

On a world scale, the climate of an area will be affected by:

- Latitude.

2 How would latitude affect the climate of a place located at:
   (a) 66° 30′ N?
   (b) 23° 30′ S?

- The world wind system.

3 In what ways would the climate of a place in the Horse Latitudes be different from that of a place which is affected by the ITCZ for much of the year?

- The pattern of ocean currents.

4 How would the climate of a coastal area be affected by:
   (a) A warm current like the Gulf Stream?
   (b) A cold current like the Humboldt current?

- The distribution of land and sea.

5 How will the *annual temperature range* in a small island be different from that of a weather station in the middle of a continent?

- Major mountain areas.

6 How will the climate of the Andes and the Himalayas be different from that of the Amazon basin or northern India?

World climate maps can be a little misleading, for these reasons:

- There are no sharp boundaries, as on a map, between climatic types. Around a desert area, for example, there will be a transition zone which may be several hundred kilometres wide. Within this zone, there will be a gradual change from *humid* to *arid* conditions.
- Conditions can vary within each climatic region. The Caribbean islands all have a tropical marine climate – but, as we shall see in Section 7.11, there are important variations in climate between different parts of the region.
- Knowing about the climate does not necessarily tell us what the weather will be like on a particular day.
- There is more than one way of classifying climates. Your atlas, or another textbook, may group the world's climates in a different way.

7.7 Types of climate

Equatorial climates

Near the equator, the sun is always high in the sky at midday, and there is very little seasonal variation in weather conditions.

Many equatorial areas are influenced all the year round by the zone of low pressure and unstable rainy weather conditions near the equator. But this zone changes position over the year; it moves north when it is summer in the northern hemisphere, and back south when the sun is overhead at the Tropic of Capricorn.

Rainfall is usually high – usually over 1,500 mm and sometimes over 3,000 mm. There is some rainfall all the year round, but in some regions with an equatorial climate, there are two *very* rainy seasons. There is one rainy season when the zone of unstable weather around the ITCZ is moving north; and another when it is moving back to the south.

Temperatures are generally around 27 °C, but the air is usually very humid, so it may *feel* very hot. The annual temperature range is very low, usually around 3 °C. There is usually a greater contrast between daytime and night-time temperatures than between the warmest and coolest month.

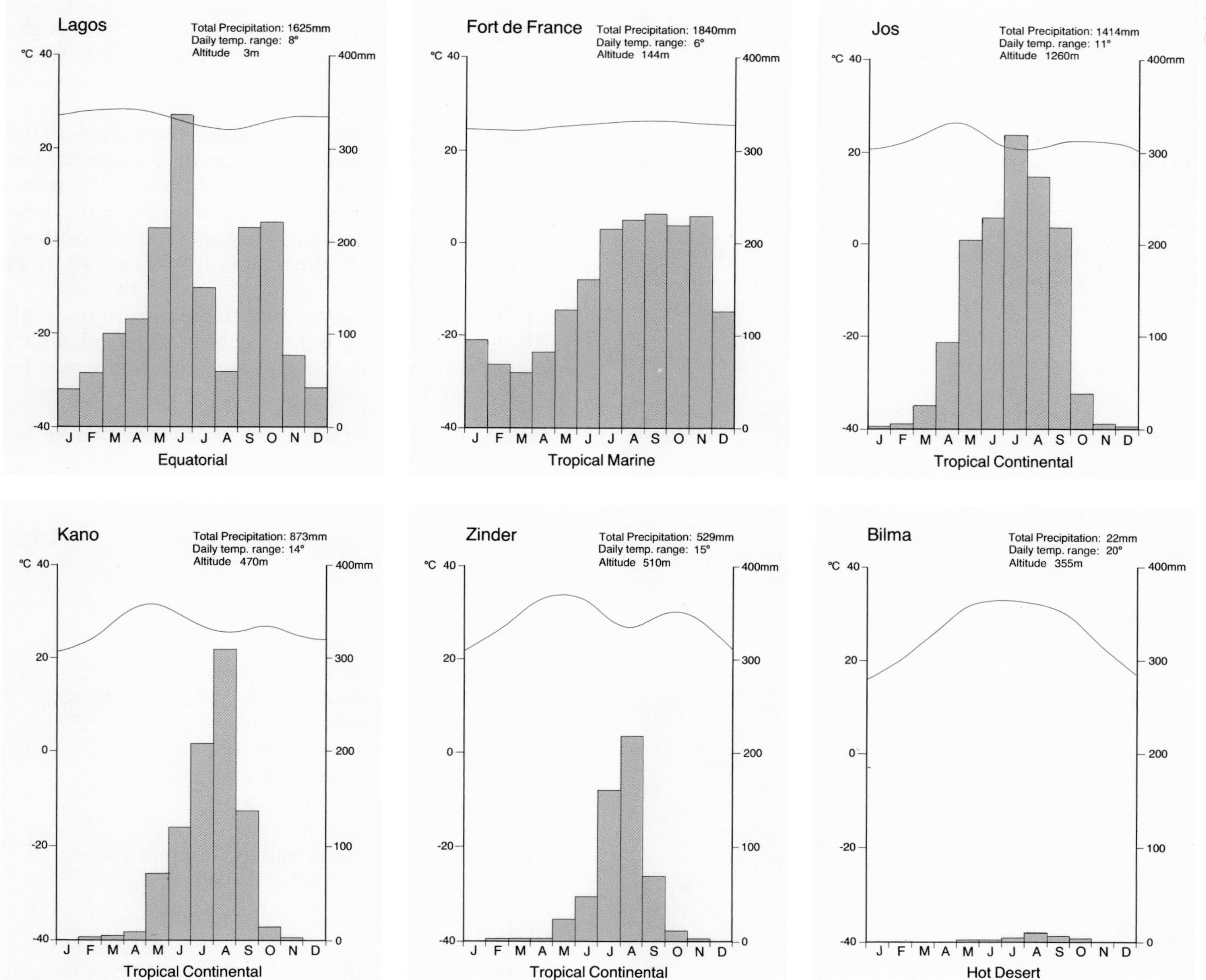

7.13 Climate graphs.

Tropical marine climates

Further away from the equator, areas like the Caribbean islands have a tropical marine climate.

The sun is never low in the sky at midday, and there is no cold season; but there is a definite pattern of seasonal variation.

There is a wet season, when atmospheric conditions are unstable, and part of the region may be influenced by the ITCZ; and a dry season with stable conditions and much less rainfall.

However, the contrast between the wet and dry seasons is not very sharp. There are no hurricanes or tropical storms in the dry season, but there are many minor disturbances which produce rain at any time of year. The trade winds blow all year round in this region, and they are moist winds which have passed over a warm ocean surface.

Temperatures are generally similar to those in an equatorial climate; but areas further away from the equator may have a short cool period, when they are affected by winter air from temperate latitudes.

Tropical continental climates

In continental climates, there is a much sharper contrast between the wet and dry seasons.

During the dry season, winds blow from the same direction as the trade winds; but they are hot, dry winds from the continental interior. An example is the *Harmattan* wind which blows over West Africa from the Sahara desert.

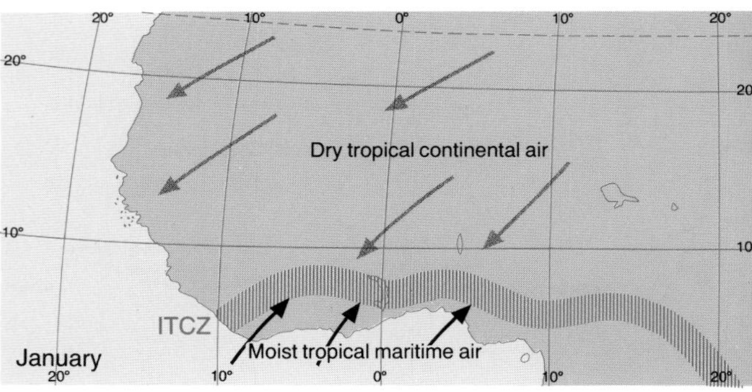

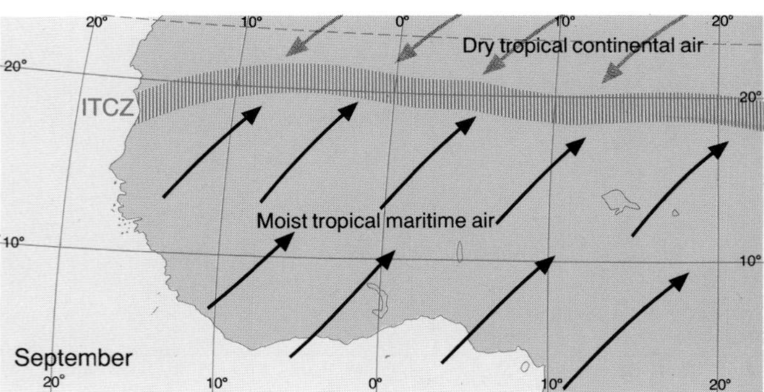

7.14 The wind systems which bring wet and dry weather to West Africa.

In the rainy season, these areas are affected by the equatorial zone of low pressure and unstable atmospheric conditions. In the northern hemisphere, the wettest months are usually July and August, just after the time when the sun is overhead at the Tropic of Cancer. In the southern hemisphere, the wettest months are usually January and February.

In West Africa, the wind often blows from the south-west during the rainy season, and moist air from the Atlantic Ocean penetrates several hundred kilometres inland. Near the coast, the wet season may last for as long as seven or eight months, and produce 1,500 mm of rain; but further north, the wet season is much shorter. In countries like Niger, Mali, and Chad, the rainy season is very short – and very unreliable. Quite often, the moist, unstable air does not penetrate this far north, and there is a drought year. Crops fail and livestock are slaughtered. When there are several drought years in succession, there is a tremendous amount of human suffering.

In tropical continental climates, there is a sharp contrast between daytime and night-time temperatures. This is because there is often very little water vapour in the air, and most of the earth's long-wave heat radiation can pass straight through the atmosphere into space. After dark, the temperature may fall by as much as 15 or 20 °C.

In the winter, the night-time temperature may fall to 10 °C, or even less; and in the hottest period, which is just before the rains, the daytime temperature may be well over 40 °C.

1 Refer to Fig. 7.13. Compare the climate graphs for Jos, Kano, and Zinder, under these headings:
   (a) Number of months with over 50 mm of rain.
   (b) Total annual rainfall.
2 Why are temperatures lower at Jos than the other two weather stations?
3 Name two areas of the world which have:
   (a) An equatorial climate.
   (b) A tropical marine climate.
   (c) A tropical continental climate.
4 Compare the climate graphs for Lagos, Kano, and Fort de France under these headings:
   (a) Temperature of warmest month.
   (b) Temperature of coolest month.
   (c) Annual temperature range.
   (d) Total annual rainfall.
   (e) Number of months with over 50 mm of rain.
   (f) Names of three wettest months.

Hot deserts

At about 15°–30° north and south of the equator, in the central and western parts of the major land masses, there is a region of high atmospheric pressure, the subtropical high-pressure zone. All the year round, warm dry air from the upper atmosphere drifts slowly downwards.

Offshore there are cold currents. When air from the sea blows inland, it is warmed by the land. This means that its relative humidity falls; it seems drier, because warm air can hold more moisture.

There is little chance of rain clouds forming here. There may be no rain for years at a stretch in the heart of the hot deserts; but there are signs that the climate was once much wetter. There are old river beds and lake shores, and ancient paintings on rock surfaces show that water-loving animals like the hippopotamus once lived in areas where they could not possibly survive today.

When the Harmattan wind blows, desert air spreads south from the Sahara into west Africa. This happens when the sun is overhead near the Tropic of Capricorn and the world wind belts have shifted to the south.

Monsoon climates

The monsoon is a seasonal pattern of winds and rainfall. Many areas in Asia and Australia have climates which are strongly influenced by the monsoon.

During the winter months, when temperatures in Siberia are very low, a large area of high pressure forms over eastern Asia. Winds at the surface blow *outwards* from this anticyclone – and because they are in the northern hemisphere, they are deflected to the *right*. Cold, dry continental air blows outwards across most of the coastal areas of Asia; most places on the mainland do not have much rain at this time of year.

In the summer, the temperature of the land mass rises rapidly. The air becomes unstable, and a large area of low pressure is formed. The low pressure is

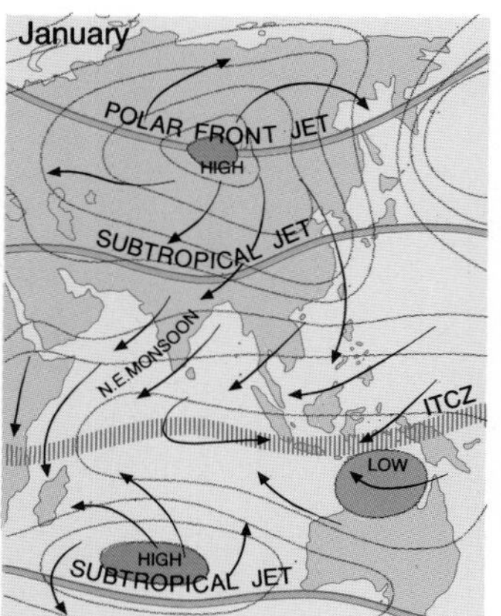

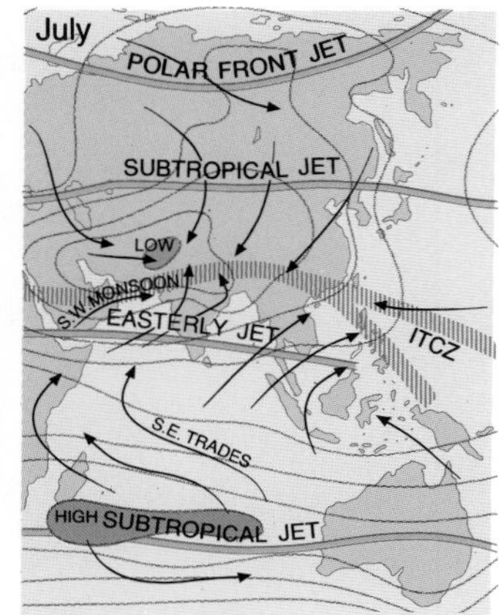

7.15 Monsoon wind patterns in Asia.
(a) Cool dry winds blow outwards from Siberia in the winter,
(b) Warm moist winds blow inwards towards northern India in the summer.

centred over northern India, where temperatures are highest. Winds blow into this low-pressure area, and are deflected to the *right* to make an anticlockwise pattern.

When moist maritime air moves over a hot land surface, it becomes very unstable. There are strong upward air currents, and heavy rainstorms.

Figure 7.15 shows the pattern of air circulation which causes the monsoon. The monsoon is not simply the result of seasonal temperature changes over Asia, however. It is also affected by:

- The pattern of high-level winds, particularly an easterly jet stream which blows over southern Asia in the summer months.
- The mountain barrier of the Himalayas.

A tropical monsoon climate

In northern India, the monsoon winds bring three distinct seasons:

- The *cold weather* lasts from November to early March. The wind blows from the north, and the air is very cool, clear and dry. The daytime temperature is 20–25 °C for most of this period; at night it is around 10 °C.
- The *hot weather* begins in April. There is very little wind, the humidity starts to increase, and the temperature rises. Daytime temperatures reach 35, 40, and even 45 °C. Even at night, it is only a little under 30 °C. Conditions are very unpleasant; it is almost impossible to do any work in the hottest part of the day.
- The *monsoon* starts quite suddenly in June or July. The rains spread across India from the south-east. It is not quite so hot during the rainy season, and conditions are much less oppressive. In most parts of India, the rains continue for three or four months; then they finish almost as abruptly as they began, and the cold weather starts.

The monsoon is not completely reliable. Sometimes the rains start late; and sometimes there is much less rain than in a normal year. Farmers in India depend on the monsoon, and when it fails, the results are disastrous.

Warm temperate western margins

On the poleward side of the hot deserts, there are regions which have a strongly seasonal pattern of rainfall – but where the rainy season is in the *winter*.

During the summer, the zone of high pressure and warm dry air from the hot deserts moves away from the tropics to influence this region. There is almost no rain, and the sky may be cloudless for days at a time.

In the winter months, when the world wind belts move towards the equator, this region is affected by the *westerlies*. These are very turbulent winds which transport a great deal of heat energy towards the poles. Where cold polar air meets warm air from the tropics, circulating wind systems known as *mid-latitude depressions* bring wet and sometimes stormy weather. These depressions are kept out of the warm temperate regions in the summer, when air pressure is high; but they cross it quite frequently in the winter months.

There is a much greater temperature range than in the tropics. In the summer, temperatures average almost 30 °C in the daytime, falling to just over 20 °C at night. In the winter, it is about 15 °C cooler; but because this is a *warm* temperate climate, there is no month with an *average* temperature of below 6 °C.

Some coastal areas are free from frosts, so that subtropical crops like oranges can be grown; but in the mountain areas, it can snow quite heavily.

This is often called the Mediterranean climate, because it is best-developed around the shores of the Mediterranean Sea, between Europe and Africa.

5 Compare the climate graphs for Bilma, Malaga, and Delhi under these headings:
   (a) Temperature of warmest month.
   (b) Temperature of coolest month.
   (c) Annual temperature range.
   (d) Total annual rainfall.
   (e) Number of months with over 50 mm of rain.
   (f) Names of three wettest months.

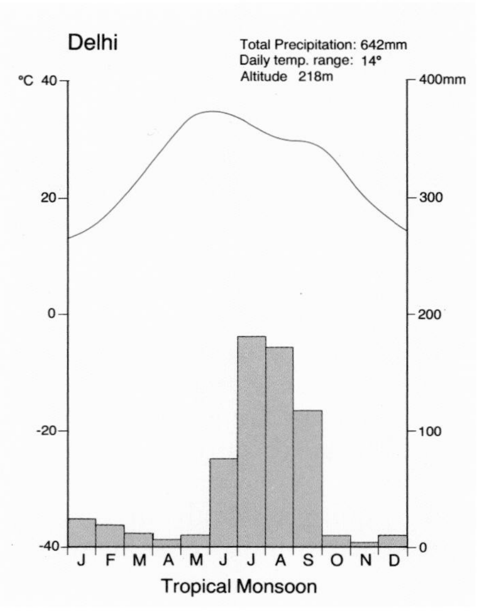

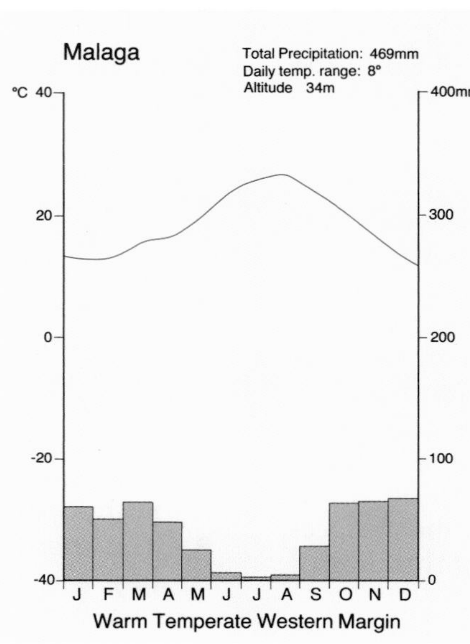

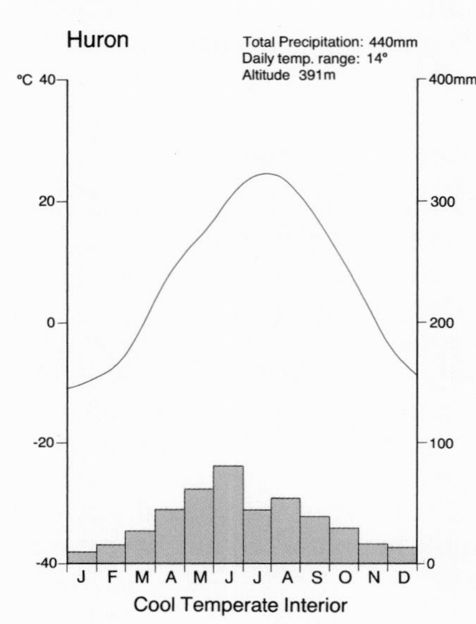

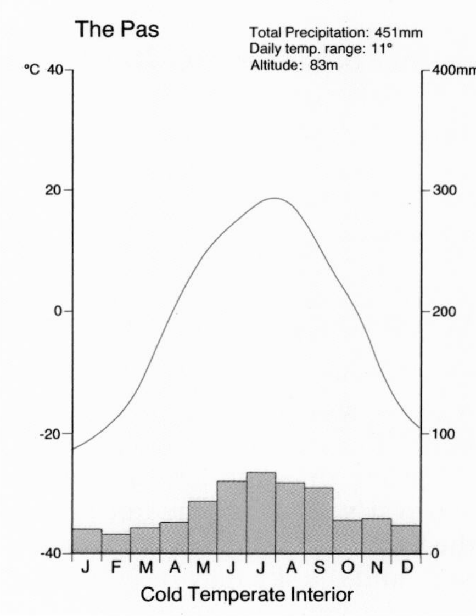

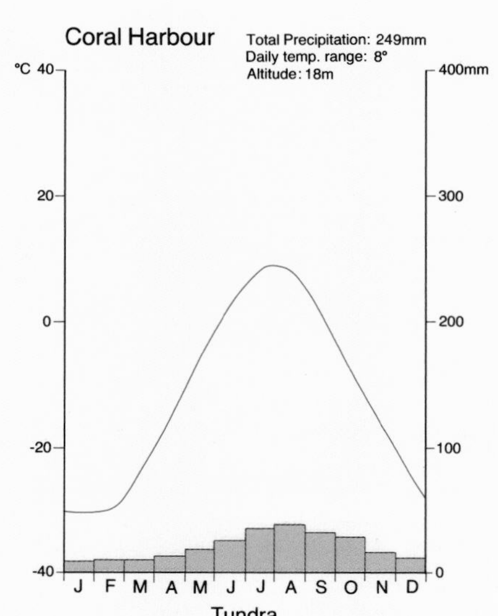

7.16 Climate graphs.

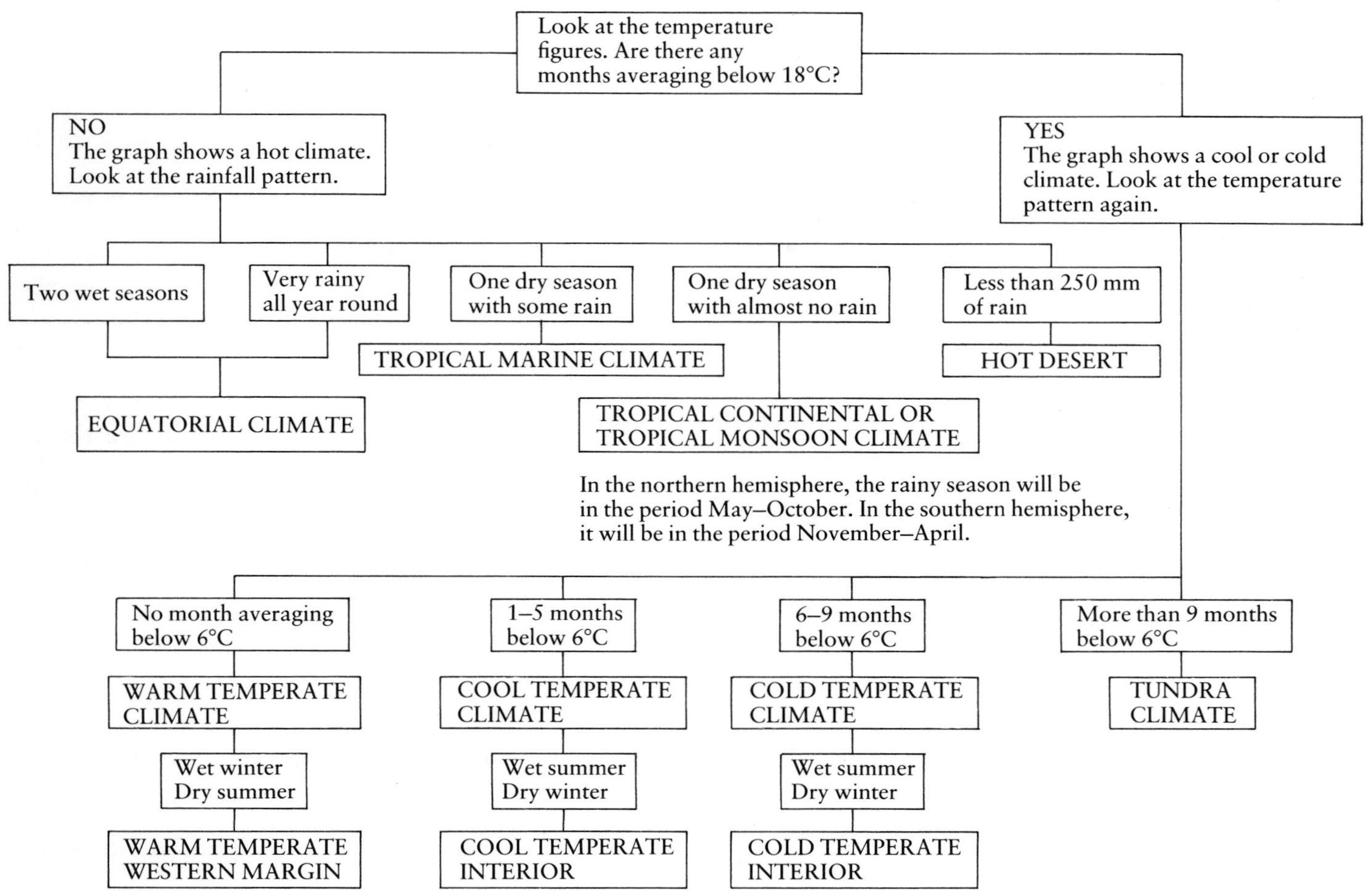

In the northern hemisphere, the coldest month will be January.
In the southern hemisphere, the coldest month will be July.

Note: There are many different types of monsoon climate. Some monsoon climates are quite cold.
It is often difficult to tell a tropical monsoon climate from a tropical continental climate, but as a rule the tropical monsoon climate has:
- A higher rainfall
- A short rainy season lasting from June to September.

7.17 Identifying climatic types. If you have monthly temperature and rainfall information you can usually identify the climate quite easily.

	1		2		3		4		5		6	
	Temp.	Precip.	Temp.	Precip.	Temp.	Precip.	Temp.	Precip.	Temp.	Precip.	Temp.	Precip.
J	–1	44	21	0	–50	4	23	7	26	284	25	77
F	0	39	23	0.5	–44	8	24	12	26	261	25	61
M	3	32	27	0	–30	21	22	22	26	284	25	27
A	8	42	33	0	–13	25	19	52	25	263	26	71
M	13	47	37	0.2	2	5	16	125	25	329	27	129
J	17	66	39	0	12	25	14	192	25	244	26	269
J	18	71	38	0	15	33	13	183	24	234	26	243
A	18	71	38	0.5	11	30	14	135	25	186	26	213
S	14	45	36	0.3	3	13	15	69	26	160	26	144
O	9	47	32	0.1	–14	11	16	54	26	164	26	151
N	4	46	27	0	–36	10	19	23	26	190	25	212
D	1	40	22	0.2	–46	7	22	15	26	270	25	153
Total precip. mm.		590		2		155		889		2869		1750
Daily temp. range °C	8		15		14		10		9		9	

7.18 Weather station statistics.

Temperate interior climates

The sea is a very good store of heat. The influence of the sea *moderates* temperature changes on islands and on the margins of the continents.

In the interior of the large continental land masses of the northern hemisphere – in North America, northern Asia, and eastern Europe – there are large areas where temperatures fall below 0 °C for several months in the winter.

- There is a *cool temperate interior* climate where temperatures average below 6 °C for one to five months every year. Most plants cannot grow when the temperature is below 6 °C.
- There is a *cold temperate interior* climate where temperatures average below 6 °C for six or more months. In cold temperate climates, the temperature may fall to −20 °C, or even lower, in the middle of the winter.

When the air is very cold, it will become denser. Air pressure at the surface will rise. A high-pressure area, or *anticyclone*, will form. In the winter, there are major anticyclones over North America and Asia. The air is cold, dry, and very stable. Precipitation is very low, but there is a thin layer of snow. It is only because the air is so still and dry that it is possible to survive at these very low temperatures.

In the summer, the land mass heats up quickly. The snow melts, and temperatures rise very fast. Even in the places which are coldest in winter, it may average over 20 °C in the daytime in the summer months.

When the land mass is warm, pockets of air are heated from below, and become unstable. There are updraughts, and rain clouds form. In these interior climates, most of the rain falls in heavy showers during the summer months.

Tundra climates

Along the shores of the Arctic Ocean, winter temperatures are not quite as low as in the interior of the continents; and the land mass does not warm up so quickly in the summer.

There is a very short growing season – there are less than three months with an average temperature of over 6 °C. Even in the warmest month, it may still be below 10 °C.

The air is cold, and can hold very little moisture. Annual rainfall and snowfall usually totals less than 250 mm – about the same as in the hot deserts. But the ground is usually moist, because the low temperatures mean that there is very little evaporation.

Polar climates

The least hospitable areas in the world are the ice caps of Greenland and Antarctica, where even the daytime temperatures in the warmest month are usually well below 0 °C.

6 Refer to Figure 7.16. Compare the climate graphs for Huron, The Pas, and Coral Harbour under these headings:
   (a) Temperature of warmest month.
   (b) Temperature of coldest month.
   (c) Annual temperature range.
   (d) Total annual rainfall.
   (e) Number of months with over 30 mm of rain.
   (f) Number of months with an average temperature below 6 °C.
   (g) Number of months with an average temperature below 0 °C.

7 Figure 7.18 gives temperature and rainfall statistics for six weather stations. They are Verkhoyansk, USSR; Uaupés, Brazil; Potsdam, German Democratic Republic; Kufra, Libya; Piarco, Trinidad; and Perth, Australia. (They are not in that order.)
   (a) Draw a climate graph for each of these stations.
   (b) Say which climatic type each graph shows. Give reasons for your answers.
   (c) Find each station on the map. Use Figure 7.17 to decide which climate type each of the places on the list should have, and label each climate graph with the right name.

7.8 Recording weather conditions

Figure 7.19 shows a weather station. There are many weather stations in the Caribbean. Every airport has one, and there are others at agricultural research stations and other institutions. Some have a large number of recording instruments; others measure only rainfall or temperature.

7.19 Reading a rain gauge in a weather station in Barbados. In the background there are three Stevenson screens.

Temperature

In the Caribbean, we experience quite a narrow range of temperatures. It is unusual for a day to be hotter than 33 °C or for night-time temperatures to fall below 18 °C. Although it sometimes feels too hot or too cool, it is never really difficult for the human body to cope with these conditions.

Human body temperature is approximately 37 °C. When it is hotter than this, it is very uncomfortable indeed.

Below 0 °C, water freezes. Snow can fall, and lie on the ground. Even when there is no snow, there may be a *frost*; a thin layer of ice crystals forms on the ground.

In some parts of Siberia, it is colder than −50 °C at night in the winter. Even in these conditions, it is possible to survive out of doors for short periods, provided that warm clothing covers the whole body, and everything is kept completely dry.

1 Look back to the climate graphs in Figures 7.13 and 7.16. Estimate the maximum daily temperature for the hottest month at each station like this –
   (a) Find the daily temperature range.
   (b) Divide this number by two.
   (c) Add the result to the average for the hottest month.
2 Now estimate the minimum daily temperature for the coldest month by subtracting half the temperature range from the average for the coldest month.
3 Which climates have a maximum temperature of above 37°? Which have a minimum of below 0°?

Recording temperature

Temperature is measured with a thermometer.

Mercury, like most materials, expands when the temperature rises. A thermometer is simply a thin glass tube containing mercury. When it is hot, the mercury expands, and rises up the tube to show the new temperature.

Temperatures usually vary over a 24-hour period. It is possible to record the highest daytime temperature,

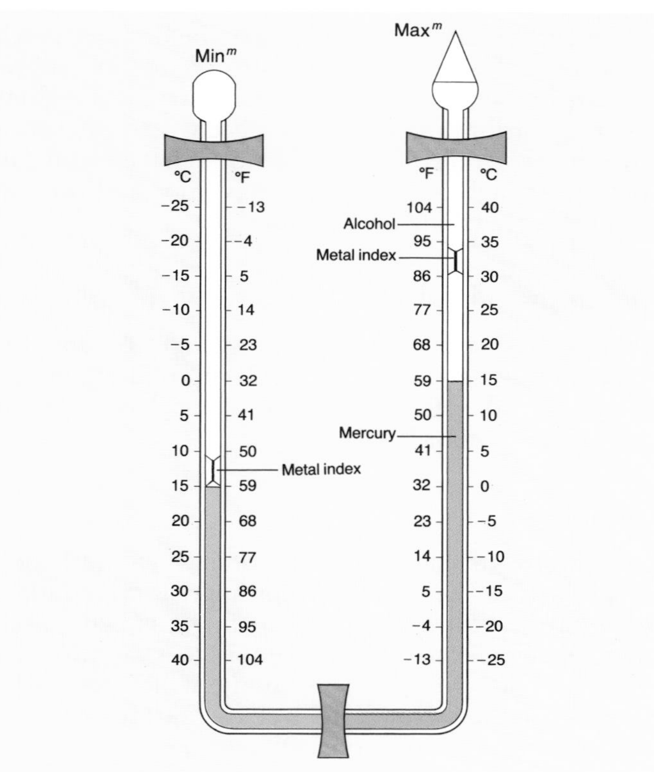

7.20 A maximum/minimum thermometer.

and the lowest temperature at night, with a maximum–minimum thermometer like the one in Figure 7.20.

If a thermometer is placed in direct sunlight, it will show a very high temperature indeed – which is not really the temperature of the *air* near the ground that day. Thermometers should be kept in a *Stevenson Screen* like the one in Figure 7.19. The instrument is in a place where it is protected from direct sunlight, and where the air can circulate freely.

4 Look carefully at the thermometer in the diagram:
 (a) What is the actual temperature?
 (b) What are the maximum and minimum temperatures recorded since the thermometer was last set?

Precipitation

There are no really dry areas in the Caribbean. In deserts, it may not rain for several years at a stretch; but even in the driest parts of this region, the average annual rainfall is almost 1,000 mm. In the wettest areas it is as much as 6,000 mm.

In the temperate regions, the air is cooler, and does not contain so much water vapour. Rainfall is generally less intense than it is in the Caribbean. In cool climates, precipitation generally forms in the clouds as snow – as clusters of ice crystals. It will either fall to the ground in this form, or melt as it passes through warmer air in the lower part of the atmosphere, and fall as rain.

Sometimes raindrops freeze again before they reach the ground. These frozen raindrops are not like snow; they are known as hailstones. Even in tropical regions like the Caribbean, there have been rare occasions when hail has fallen – large hailstones have formed in cold air at high altitudes, and have not had time to melt before reaching the ground.

Measuring rainfall

Rainfall is measured with a *rain gauge*. A funnel is placed inside a copper can 120 mm in diameter. Every day, the amount of rain that has fallen is measured in a glass bottle.

Humidity

If you wet your finger and blow on it, it will feel cool. This is because the water on your finger is evaporating. Some of the heat energy in your finger is being used up to change the water from a liquid to a vapour.

When you are hot, your body will sweat. The purpose of the sweat is to wet the surface of your skin, so that evaporation can take place and your body can cool down.

When relative humidity is high, it is hard for evaporation to take place. Your body does not cool down so much when it sweats, so you will feel more uncomfortable.

In hot weather, it is very uncomfortable when the relative humidity is much over 75%. Humid conditions are also very unpleasant when it is cold, because moist air is better at conducting heat away from the human body.

Measuring humidity

Humidity is measured with a *wet-and-dry-bulb thermometer*. This instrument consists of two separate thermometers. One of them – the dry bulb – is an ordinary thermometer which shows the air temperature. The other has the bulb of mercury at its base wrapped in a bag of damp muslin.

When the air is dry, the water in the muslin will evaporate very quickly, and the wet-bulb thermometer will be much cooler. When the air is damp, and

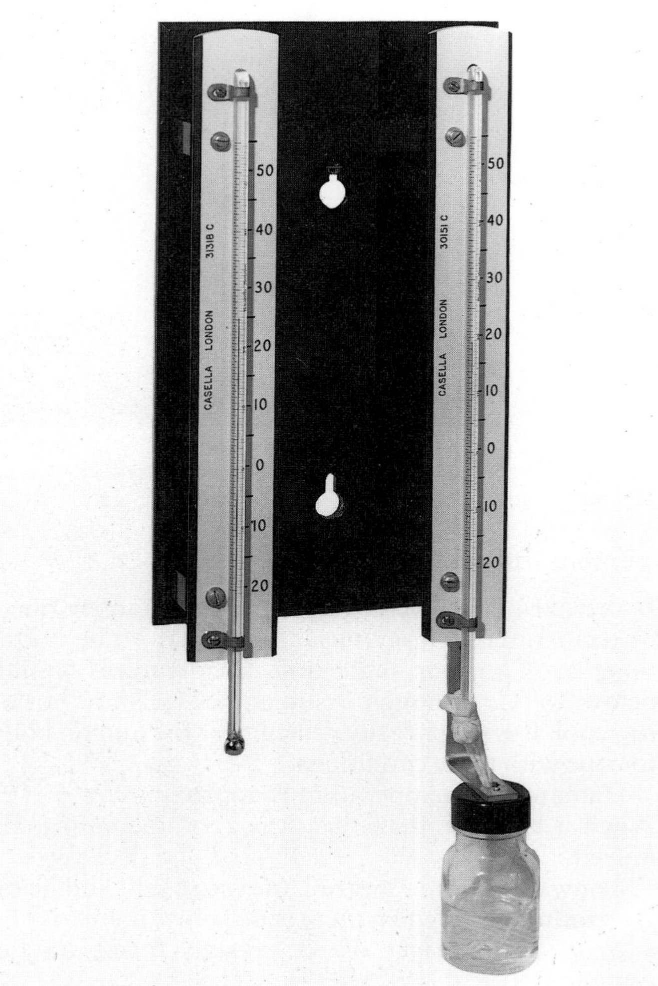

7.21 A wet and dry bulb thermometer. The wet bulb is on the right.

relative humidity is high, evaporation will be much slower. There will be much less difference in temperature between the two instruments. When the air is completely saturated, there can be no evaporation, and both thermometers will show exactly the same reading.

There are tables which show the relative humidity for wet- and dry-bulb readings at any particular air temperature.

Air pressure

We can feel changes in temperature and humidity, and we can see clouds and rain; but changes in air pressure are not immediately noticeable. We cannot feel the change when pressure drops from 1,020 to 990 millibars; but we have seen how important air pressure is in the development of weather and climate patterns.

Measuring air pressure

Atmospheric pressure is measured with a barometer.

There are many types of barometer. One common type is the *aneroid barometer*.

As much air as possible is pumped out of a small metal box. When air pressure is high, the top of the box will be pressed downwards very slightly; when pressure falls, the top of the box will rise upwards again.

These movements are barely noticeable, but a lever mechanism attached to the box exaggerates them, so that they can be recorded.

In a barograph, the recording is done automatically. A vertical drum is placed next to the barometer; this drum rotates slowly, and the changes are recorded on a strip of paper by a pen which is attached to the lever mechanism of the instrument.

7.22 A barograph.

Air pressure maps

Air pressure is shown on a weather map by *isobars*. These are lines like contours – except that they join up places with the same air pressure, rather than places at the same height above sea level.

Figure 7.23 shows atmospheric pressure over the Caribbean. Air pressure has been shown for certain points; and on part of the map, the isobars have been drawn in.

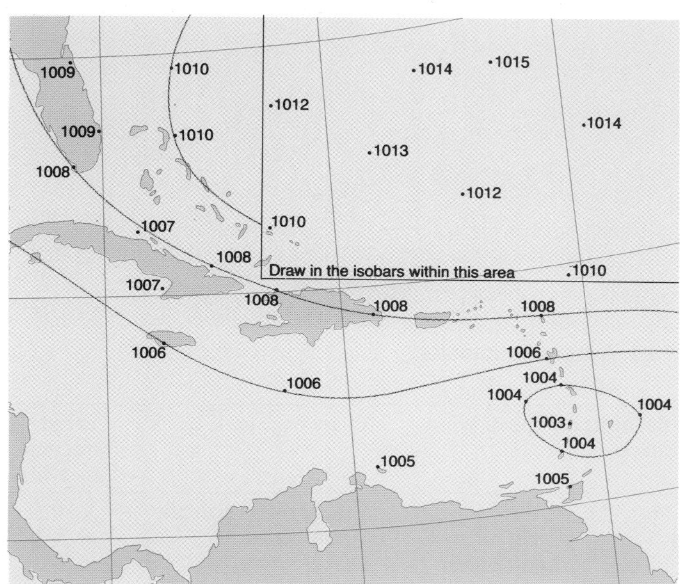

7.23 Air pressure over the Caribbean.

5 Copy the map into your book, and draw in the isobars for the rest of the map.

6 Shade in the area with *high* air pressure (over 1,014 millibars) and the area with *low* air pressure (below 1,004 millibars).

7 Study Figure 7.8 and draw in symbols to show the way the wind is likely to be blowing around the area of low pressure.

8 When there is a sharp drop in air pressure, there will usually be a strong wind. When there is a gradual fall in air pressure, there will be a gentle breeze. Show on your map the areas where the wind will be blowing most strongly.

Winds

Winds in the Caribbean nearly always blow from the east or north-east; but in some parts of the world, they are quite changeable.

A wind vane is used to determine which direction the wind is blowing from. This is probably the simplest weather instrument to make. The pattern of changing wind direction can be recorded on a *wind rose*.

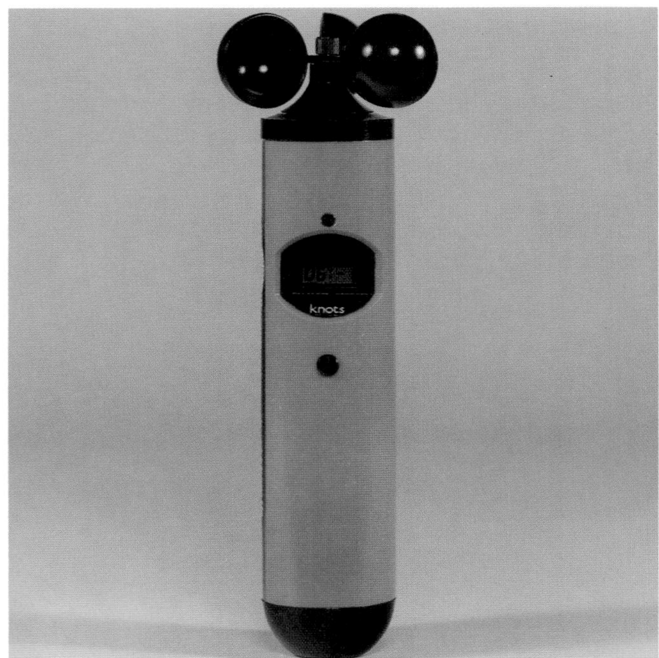

7.24 A cup anemometer.

Beaufort force	Type of wind	Effect over land	Speed (metres/ second)
0	Calm	Smoke rises vertically	>0.5
1	Light air	Smoke drifts	0.5–1
2	Light breeze	Leaves rustle, wind felt on face	2–3
3	Gentle breeze	Leaves and small twigs move; light flags exended	4–5
4	Moderate breeze	Raises dust and paper; small branches move	6–8
5	Fresh breeze	Small trees sway; small waves on water	9–11
6	Strong breeze	Umbrellas used with difficulty; telephone wires whistle	12–14
7	Moderate gale	Large trees sway; difficult to walk against the wind	16–17
8	Gale	Breaks twigs off trees; very hard to walk against wind	18–21
9	Strong gale	Slight damage to houses; large branches down	22–24
10	Storm	Trees uprooted; serious damage to buildings	25–28
11	Violent storm	Widespread damage	29–35
12	Hurricane	Disastrous results	<35

7.25 The Beaufort scale.

9 Study the wind rose in Figure 7.44:
(a) Which is the prevailing wind?
(b) Which four wind directions are next in frequency?
(c) Which wind directions are least frequent?

Although there are sometimes violent storms in the Caribbean, wind speeds are generally rather low. The trade winds usually blow at 10–22 km/hr (3–6 m/sec). In middle latitudes, hurricanes do not develop; but, particularly in the southern hemisphere, the normal everyday winds are much stronger. In the Falkland Islands, for example, the wind reaches *gale force* (over 57.5 km/hr or 16 m/sec) on one day in five.

Wind speed can be estimated using the *Beaufort Scale*. This is a systematic way of describing the effects of the wind.

More accurate measurements can be made with a *cup anemometer*. When the wind speed increases, the anemometer will rotate faster and faster. The velocity of the wind can be read off from a device at the base of the instrument.

Clouds and sunshine

Clouds are formed when water droplets are condensed in a rising current of air that has cooled until the relative humidity is 100%.

Cloud cover is usually estimated by eye. The proportion of sky which is covered by cloud is recorded.

Over the whole day, the amount of sunshine can be measured more accurately with a sunshine recorder. This is a glass sphere which concentrates sunlight onto a strip of paper. When the sun is shining, a burn mark appears on the paper; as the sun moves across the sky, the position of this burn mark moves. At the end of the day, the number of hours of sunshine can be worked out by looking at the length of burn mark on the paper strip.

7.26 A sunshine recorder.

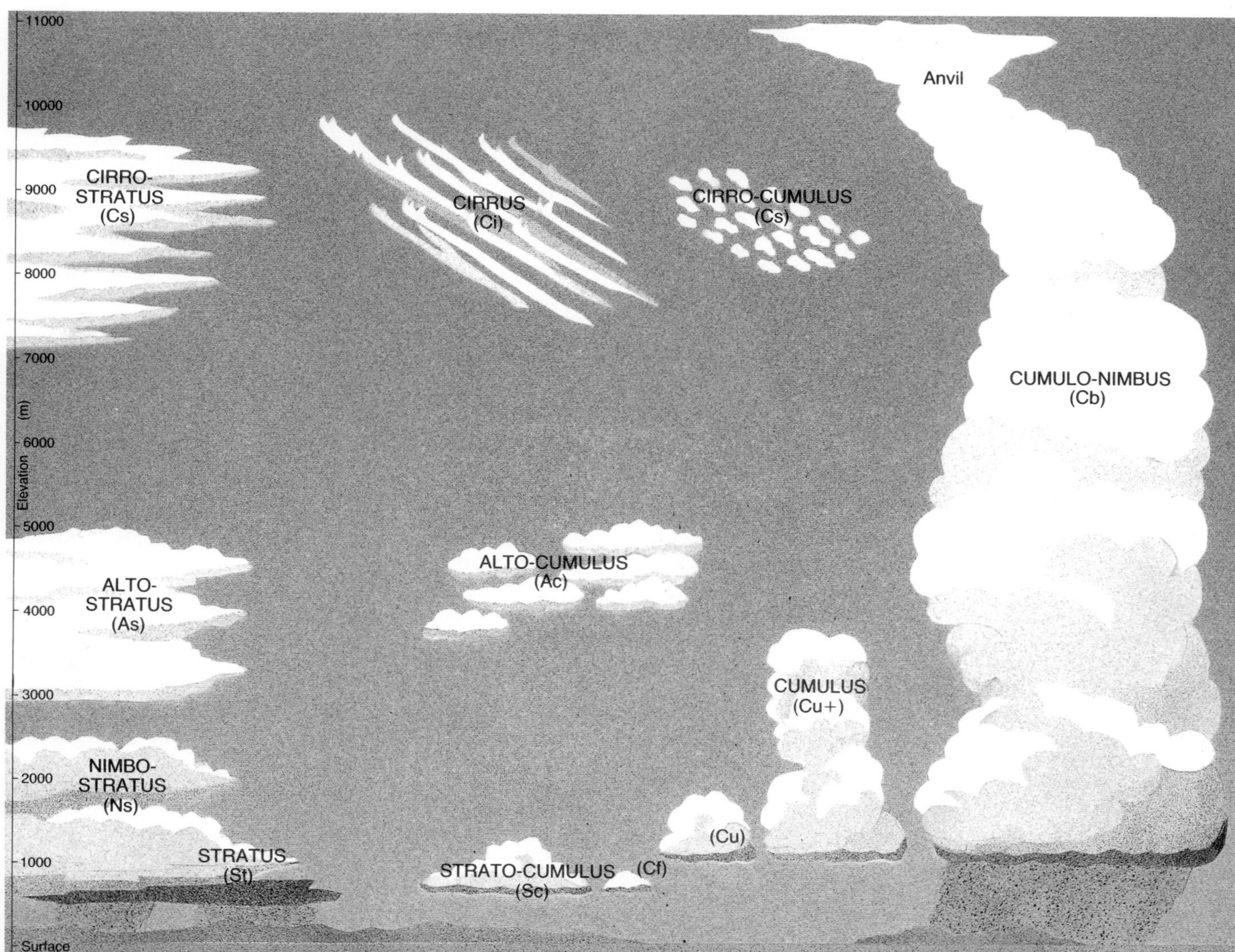

7.27 Types of cloud. There are many different types of cloud. The type of cloud which forms depends on how stable the atmospheric conditions are, an what types of air current are in play. The main cloud types can be classified as follows.

	Water clouds Low altitude clouds made up of water droplets.	**Ice clouds** High altitude clouds made up of ice crystals.	**Mixed clouds** Tall clouds which reach upwards from low altitudes to high altitudes.
Layer clouds These form in stable conditions at the boundary between two layers of air at different temperatures which are gliding past each other.	*Stratus* Low cloud forming dull, overcast skies.	*Altostratus* A high layer of grey cloud which may bring light rain. *Cirrostratus* A wispy white layer cloud through which the sun can be seen.	*Nimbostratus* These are dark grey layer clouds which give an overcast sky and bring steady and persistent rain.
Heaped clouds These form when the atmosphere is unstable. Small pockets of air form updraughts and drift upwards until they reach the point where water droplets can form.	*Cumulus* These are dense, low level clouds with a puffy appearance. The upper part of the cloud is white, but seen from below the cloud looks grey.	*Cirrus* These are white, streaky clouds formed out of ice crystals which are being pulled along by high level winds.	*Cumulonimbus* High dense clouds which form when there are strong updraughts and very unstable atmospheric conditions. These clouds bring heavy rain and sometimes thunder storms.
Intermediate clouds The lower atmosphere is unstable, but a warm layer prevents the cumulus clouds from developing upwards. The clouds look like heaped clouds, but are arranged in layers.	*Stratocumulus* Layers of low level cumulus clouds, often arranged in a fairly regular way.	*Cirrocumulus* Small puffs of cloud which form at high altitudes. They are often formed between two layers of air moving in different directions.	Because intermediate clouds cannot develop very far upwards, they are not tall enough to form mixed clouds.

7.9 Weather maps

Clouds and rain form well above ground level. Many of the weather systems which affect us develop in the upper part of the troposphere. To help detect them, and monitor their development, the largest weather stations use *Rawinsonde Balloons*. These are released twice a day, and can travel to a height of 25 km. They take measurements of humidity, temperature, and pressure, and transmit their readings back to the ground automatically.

The larger weather stations transmit their measurements to the US National Weather Service in Washington in the USA. This is one of three World Metereological Centres; the other two are in Moscow and Melbourne, Australia. In Washington, the data are collected, and

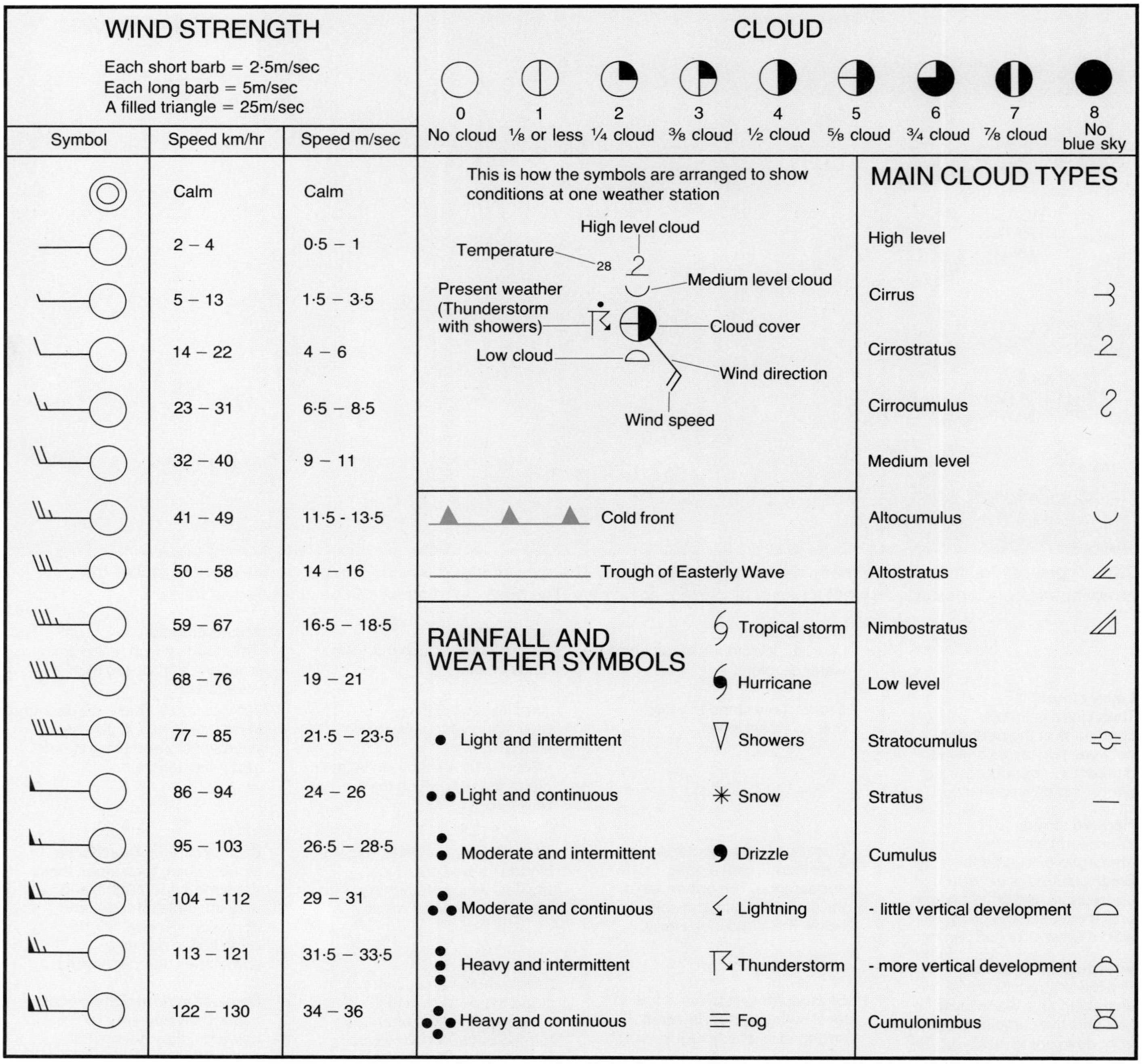

WIND STRENGTH

Each short barb = 2·5m/sec
Each long barb = 5m/sec
A filled triangle = 25m/sec

Symbol	Speed km/hr	Speed m/sec
	Calm	Calm
	2 – 4	0·5 – 1
	5 – 13	1·5 – 3·5
	14 – 22	4 – 6
	23 – 31	6·5 – 8·5
	32 – 40	9 – 11
	41 – 49	11·5 - 13·5
	50 – 58	14 – 16
	59 – 67	16·5 – 18·5
	68 – 76	19 – 21
	77 – 85	21·5 – 23·5
	86 – 94	24 – 26
	95 – 103	26·5 – 28·5
	104 – 112	29 – 31
	113 – 121	31·5 – 33·5
	122 – 130	34 – 36

CLOUD

0	1	2	3	4	5	6	7	8
No cloud	⅛ or less	¼ cloud	⅜ cloud	½ cloud	⅝ cloud	¾ cloud	⅞ cloud	No blue sky

This is how the symbols are arranged to show conditions at one weather station

High level cloud
Temperature 28
Medium level cloud
Present weather (Thunderstorm with showers)
Cloud cover
Low cloud
Wind direction
Wind speed

Cold front

Trough of Easterly Wave

RAINFALL AND WEATHER SYMBOLS

- Light and intermittent
- Light and continuous
- Moderate and intermittent
- Moderate and continuous
- Heavy and intermittent
- Heavy and continuous
- Tropical storm
- Hurricane
- Showers
- Snow
- Drizzle
- Lightning
- Thunderstorm
- Fog

MAIN CLOUD TYPES

High level
- Cirrus
- Cirrostratus
- Cirrocumulus

Medium level
- Altocumulus
- Altostratus
- Nimbostratus

Low level
- Stratocumulus
- Stratus
- Cumulus
- - little vertical development
- - more vertical development
- Cumulonimbus

7.28 The main weather symbols.

7.29 Releasing a Rawinsonde balloon.

sent out again; a weather station in the Caribbean will receive information from stations in most of North America, parts of South America, from ships in the Atlantic and the Caribbean, and from some stations further afield.

This information can be used to prepare a weather map. A weather map records weather conditions over a wide area, and is very useful in preparing a weather forecast.

The larger weather stations also receive information from weather satellites. There is an *orbiting* satellite, which passes over the Caribbean twice a day, and transmits pictures direct to the weather stations from a height of 300 km; and there is a *geostationary* satellite, which is always over the same place, 30,000 km above the equator, over Brazil, and transmits a small-scale photograph of a much larger area via Washington.

Satellite pictures have made it far easier to watch the development of weather systems. In the past, it was particularly difficult to tell what was happening over the oceans; there were only a few scattered reports from ships to rely on, and these did not provide nearly enough information.

A professional weather map contains a great deal of information about past weather conditions, changes in atmospheric pressure, wave patterns at sea, humidity, and visibility. There are also more than 200 different symbols in use. The weather maps in the next section have been simplified; they only give information about a few weather stations, and many symbols are left off.

7.10 Caribbean weather systems

Cold fronts

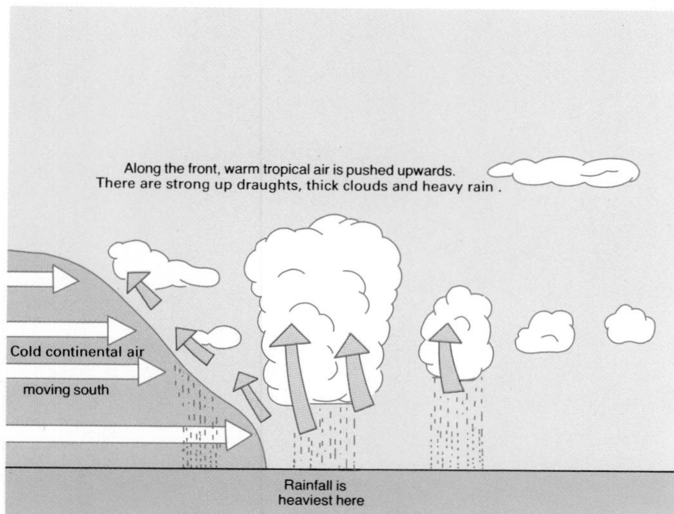

7.30 A cross-section through a cold front.

During the northern hemisphere winter, cold air from the North American continent sometimes blows south over the Caribbean.

When this happens, there is quite a sharp boundary between the cold, dry continental air moving in from the north and the warm, moist tropical air over the rest of the Caribbean. This boundary is known as a *cold front*.

To the north of the cold front, there will be a strong northerly wind. The continental air is warmed quite quickly by the sea beneath it. The air will still feel cold to a person who is used to tropical weather; but it will be much warmer than when it left the North American continent.

The cold continental air pushes underneath the warm tropical air as it moves south. This makes the air mass very unstable. There are strong updraughts, and the weather becomes very cloudy.

The air is most unstable at the cold front itself. Here, there is a sudden change in temperature, the sky

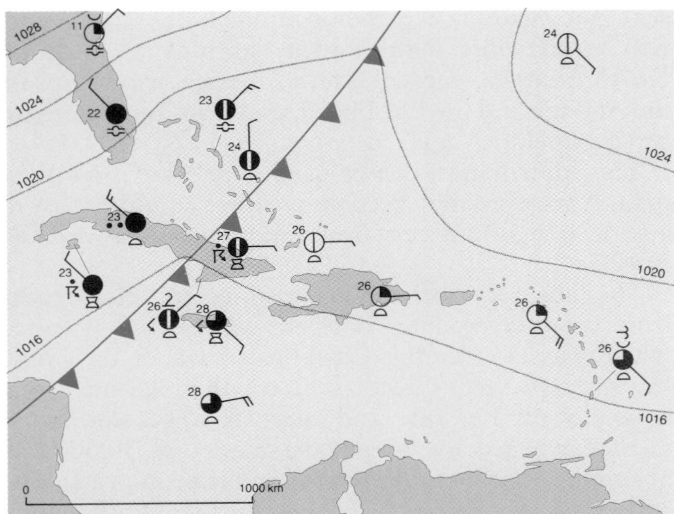

7.31 A cold front over the Caribbean, 6 December 1986.

is often completely overcast, and there may be very heavy rain.

A few hundred km south of the cold front, the conditions will be completely different. There may be a light wind from the east, and bright sunshine. It is difficult to tell that there is a cold front approaching.

In Jamaica, these outbreaks of cold continental air are known as *northers*. They bring cloudy weather, strong cold winds, and heavy rain to the north coast of the island.

1 Why are northers a problem for:
   (a) Farmers?
   (b) Fishermen?
   (c) The tourist industry?

Weather maps: a cold front and anticyclone

On 6 December 1986, there was cold, winter weather over the North American continent. Cold air was spreading south into the Caribbean and east over the Atlantic. At the same time, there was an anticyclone over the middle Atlantic, to the north-east of the Lesser Antilles.

2 Look carefully at Figure 7.32. Make a sketch showing the main areas of cloud.

3 Describe carefully what weather conditions were like:

7.32 A cold front: 6 December 1986.

(a) 1,000 km north-west of the front, in northern Florida.
(b) Up to 500 km north of the front, in the northern and central Bahamas, western Cuba, southern Florida, and the Cayman Islands.
(c) Up to 400 km south of the front, in eastern Cuba, the southern Bahamas, and Jamaica.
(d) 800–1200 km south-east of the front, in the Dominican Republic and the Lesser Antilles.

4 Was there rain in every section of the cold front?
5 Describe carefully what weather conditions were like 1000 km north of Antigua.
6 Explain how the direction of the wind in the eastern Caribbean was affected by the anticyclone over the Atlantic.
7 What can you learn about weather conditions from:
(a) The satellite picture?
(b) The weather map?
8 Make a sketch showing how the isobars bend suddenly where they cross the cold front.

Anticyclones

Look back to Figure 7.10. North of the Caribbean, there is generally an *anticyclone* or high-pressure area over the middle Atlantic. This anticyclone often extends over part of the Caribbean region as well. It is sometimes known as the Bermuda–Azores high.

Winds circulate in a *clockwise* direction round a northern hemisphere anticyclone. So when the Bermuda–Azores high is close to the Caribbean, the wind on its western side will blow from the south-east.

The air within the anticyclone is drifting slowly downwards. As it moves down, it is compressed by the air above, and is gradually warmed. Usually, there is a layer of warm air between 2,000 and 3,000 m above the surface. Updraughts cannot usually penetrate through this layer of warm air. Cumulus clouds may form below it, but they remain scattered, fluffy, white 'fair weather' clouds, which cannot grow to the size where they can produce rain.

Easterly waves

For most of the year, trade winds blow across the Caribbean. From time to time, weather systems develop in the trade wind belt which bring unsettled weather and rain to the region. These weather systems generally develop more frequently in the rainy season. Easterly waves are one of the types of weather system which affect the Caribbean in this way:

- To the west of the wave, the wind is blowing from the north-east, and is subsiding slowly downwards. As it moves through this part of the weather system, the air is being warmed, and its relative humidity is falling. There are very few clouds, or none at all. The weather will be dry and sunny.
- As the wave approaches, the wind direction will move round towards the east, and there will be more clouds.
- In the 'trough' of the wave, the air is very unstable. There are thick clouds, and heavy rain. Air pressure is a little lower than normal.
- To the east of the 'trough' the wind blows from the south-east. There are many strong updraughts in this part of the wave. There is a thick cover of cumulus clouds, and the sky may be completely overcast. There will be light rain in some places.

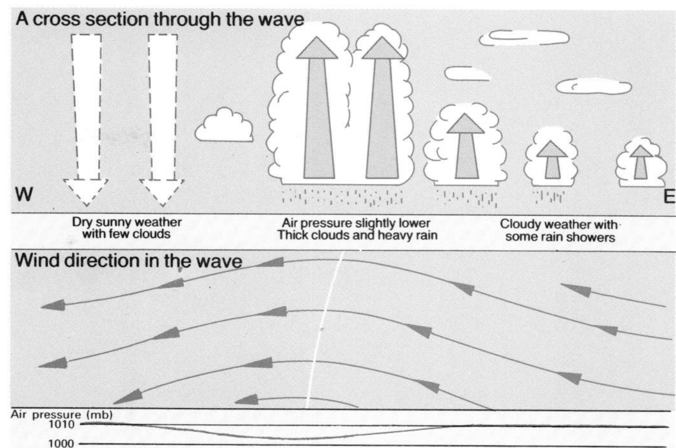

7.33 An easterly wave.

Easterly waves are large-scale weather systems, up to 2,000 km across. The wave trough moves from east to west across the region at 20–35 km/hr, so the whole system will take up to four days to pass any particular point.

The Inter-Tropical Convergence Zone

When the ITCZ is over the Caribbean, atmospheric conditions are unstable. There are strong updraughts, thick clouds, and heavy rainfall.

On world maps, the ITCZ is often shown as a continuous feature, running right round the earth. In reality, there will only be unstable conditions and heavy rain in some parts of this broad belt at any one time.

The ITCZ affects Trinidad and the southern part of the Caribbean during the northern hemisphere summer. It is usually furthest north in September, almost three months after the sun is overhead at the Tropic of Cancer. The zone where there is maximum convergence usually passes over Guyana twice; once in June, when it is moving north, and again in November, when it is moving back to the south. Each time it passes, there is heavy rainfall. During the northern hemisphere winter, the ITCZ is over the Amazon basin.

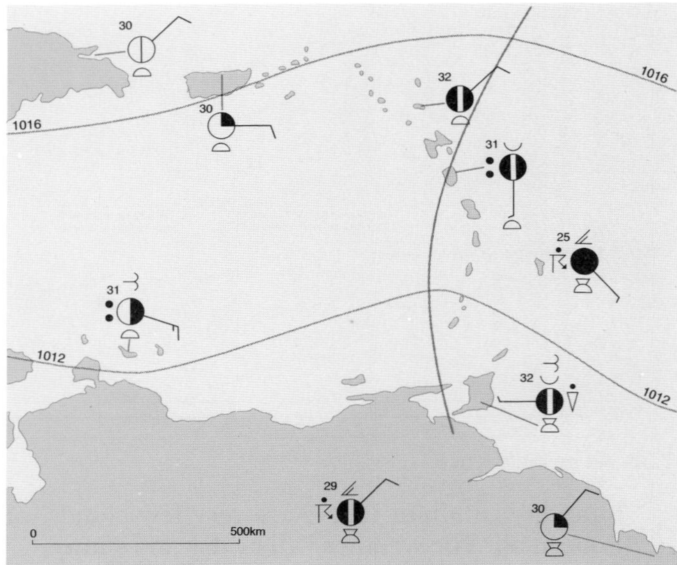

7.34 An easterly wave, 25th September 1986.

Weather maps: an easterly wave and the ITCZ

On 25 September 1986, an easterly wave was moving across the Lesser Antilles. At the same time, Trinidad and northern Venezuela were affected by cloud and rain associated with the inter-tropical convergence zone.

9 Describe carefully what weather conditions were like:
   (a) In the Dominican Republic and Puerto Rico, 600 to 1,000 km ahead of the wave trough.
   (b) In Dominica, very close to the trough of the wave.
   (c) In Venezuela and Trinidad, in the area affected by the ITCZ.
   (d) In northern Guyana, to the south of the ITCZ.

Hurricanes

Figure 7.35 shows the structure of a hurricane:

- In the centre of the hurricane, air pressure is very low. It is usually below 985 mb, and sometimes as low as 860–890 mb. There are strong *updraughts* over most of the weather system.
- Around the centre of low pressure, there is a strong revolving wind system. Look back to Figure 7.8 to check on the way winds rotate round a low-pressure area. In the northern hemisphere, they rotate in an anticlockwise direction.
- Wind speeds are very high. Near the centre of the storm, they may reach 360 km/hr (100 m/sec).
- There is a spiral pattern of enormous cumulonimbus clouds. Some of the clouds tower up to a height of 16 km. Where the clouds are thickest, there is very little light even at midday.
- At a high level, there is a canopy of cirrus clouds. Above 9 km, the winds spiral *outwards* from the centre of the hurricane.
- In some hurricanes, there is very heavy rain. During one hurricane in 1909, more than 2,400 mm of rain was recorded over a four-day period at Silver Hill in Jamaica.
- Right at the centre of the storm, there is an *eye*, 20–50 km across. In the eye, conditions are very different. There are light winds, blowing at perhaps 10–20 km/hr (2.75–5.5 m/sec) and there may be no rain falling.
- Around the eye, there is a wall of dark clouds.
- Within the eye, there is a strong *downwards* current of air. Because of this, the air there is very warm, and there are no low-level clouds.

Hurricanes are very powerful weather systems. They help to transfer energy from the tropics towards the poles. In a hurricane, an enormous amount of energy is transferred; but taking the year as a whole, much more energy is transferred by less spectacular systems which operate for more of the time.

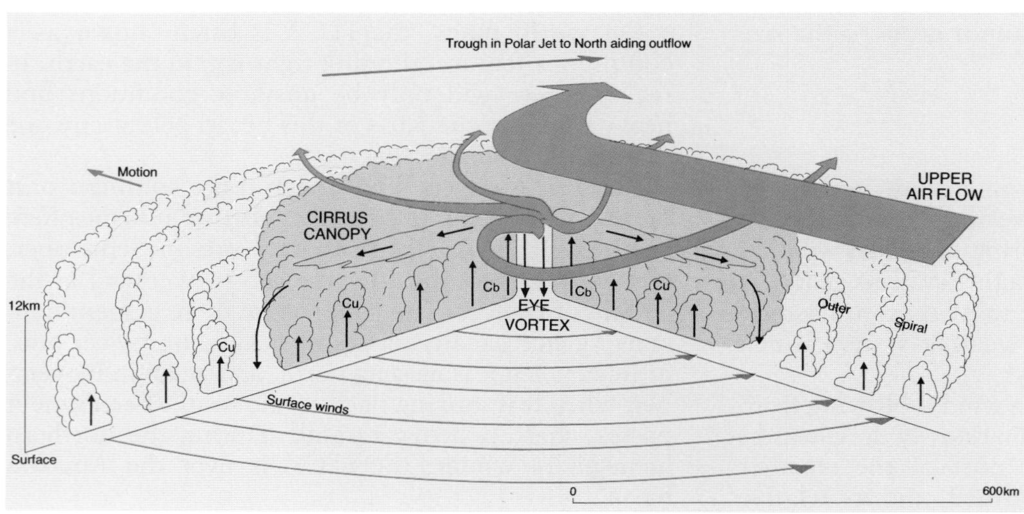

7.35 The structure of a hurricane.

How hurricanes develop

Hurricanes start as minor disturbances in the atmosphere over the tropical oceans. There are many disturbances in this zone over the year; but a few of them become much stronger than the others:

- A tropical depression has wind speeds of 51–61 km/hr (14–16 m/sec). There is a definite centre of low pressure at the surface, and the beginnings of a revolving wind system.
- A tropical storm has winds of 62–116 km/hr (17–32 m/sec). It may cause quite serious damage.
- In a hurricane there are winds of 117 km/hr (32.5 m/sec) or more, and the effect can be devastating.

Nobody is quite sure why some tropical disturbances develop into tropical storms, and why some tropical storms develop into hurricanes while others do not. But we know that:

- All hurricanes develop over the sea.
- The surface temperature of the sea must be at least 26 °C. Evaporation from a warm sea surface is the main energy source for a hurricane.
- Hurricanes do not usually develop in the belt between 9° N and 9° S. This is because wind systems do not spiral round low-pressure areas in the same way when they are very close to the equator.

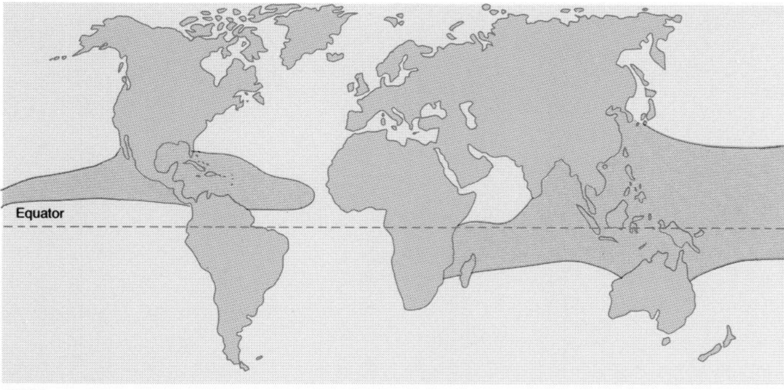

(a) areas of sea with a temperature over 27° in summer

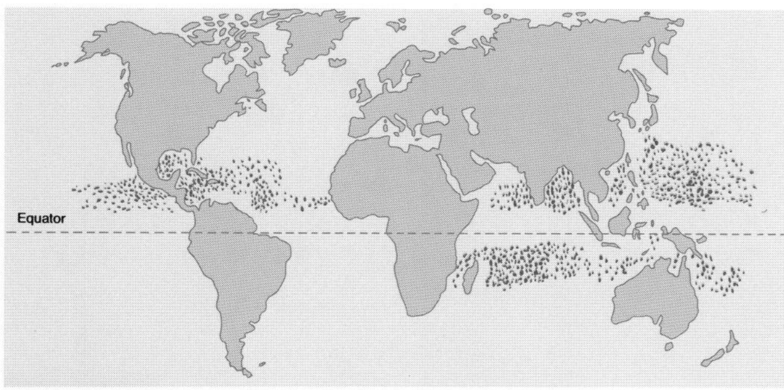

(b) places where hurricanes have started

7.36 Where hurricanes start.

- Where a hurricane is developing, there is a *divergent* pattern of upper-level winds. This allows air to be drawn in at the base of the weather system, to feed the updraughts.

When a tropical storm has developed into a hurricane, it continues to grow in size and pick up strength. A fully developed hurricane may be an enormous weather system, 1,500 km across.

How hurricanes move

Hurricanes do not stay in the same place. The centre of the storm may move several hundred km over a 24-hour period.

- Ahead of a hurricane, there is calm weather. Humidity is high, so the air feels hot and sticky. At sea, there may be a strong swell, as waves arrive before the storm itself.
- As the hurricane approaches, the cloud cover builds up, and winds become stronger. There may be rain showers.
- Near the centre of the storm, winds are very strong.
- When the eye passes, the wind drops suddenly. Many accidents are caused when people go outside during this period, thinking that the hurricane has passed.

Hurricanes do not usually move towards the equator; but the movement of a hurricane is very hard to predict. Figure 7.37 shows some hurricane tracks over the North Atlantic. On rare occasions, hurricanes may even back-track, to hit an area they have already devastated a few days before.

Hurricanes can only form in the tropics; but once they have formed, they can move into temperate regions. Hurricanes often hit the south and south-east coasts of the United States. When a hurricane moves over a land area, there is not so much evaporation; so the weather system cannot sustain itself. Over the North American continent, hurricanes die away after one or two days. But sometimes, a hurricane moves across the North Atlantic. It changes its character, and becomes a mid-latitude storm; but the 'tail end' of a hurricane like this can devastate areas like the north-east coast of the USA and the Atlantic coastlands of Europe.

10 Look at Figure 7.37 and at atlas map of the same area. For each of the hurricanes shown:
   (a) At approximately what latitude and longitude did a tropical depression form?
   (b) How many days did it take to build up to hurricane strength?
   (c) How many days did it remain at hurricane strength?
   (d) Which countries did the centre of the hurricane cross or pass very close to?

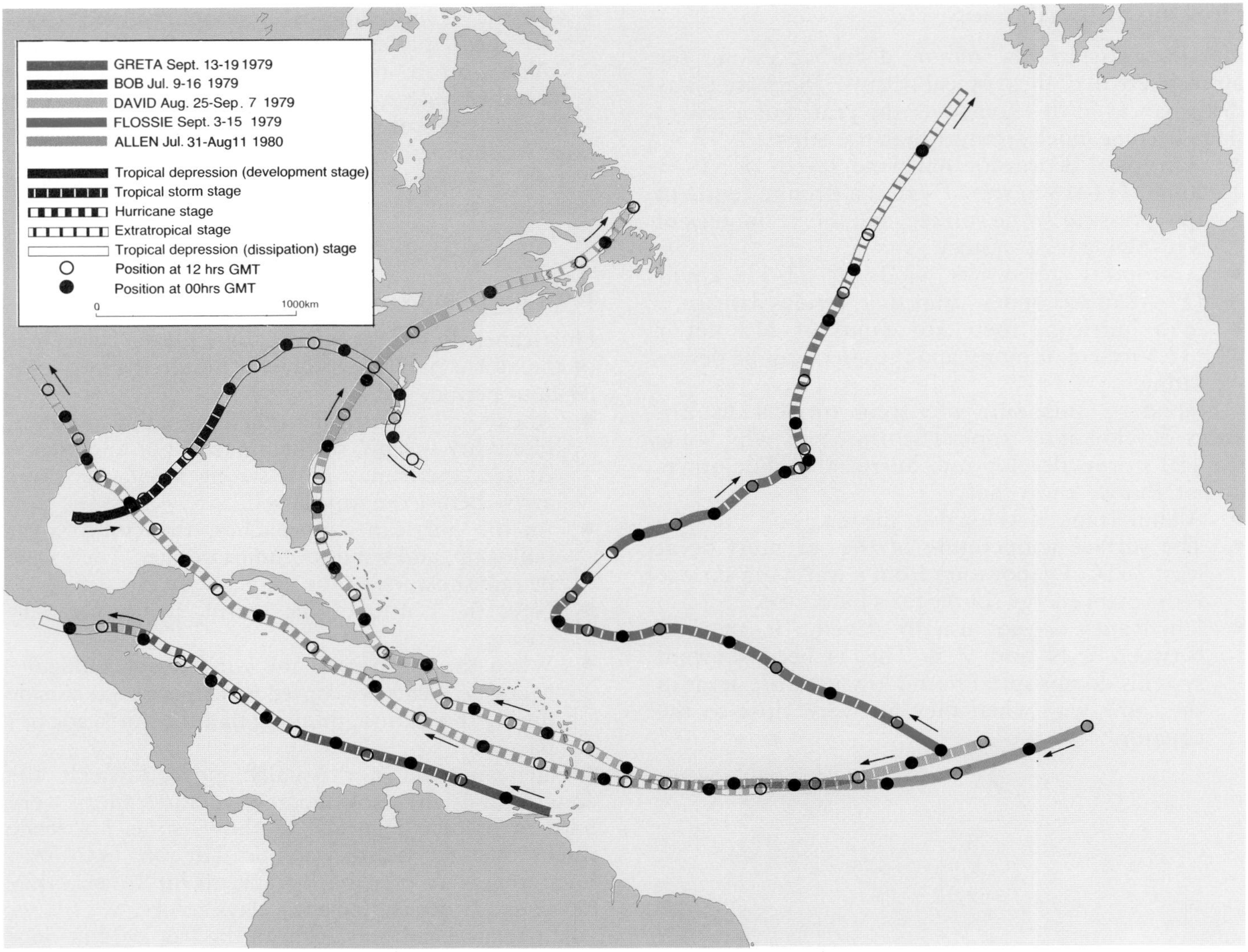

7.37 Some hurricane tracks over the Caribbean and North Atlantic.

7.38 Hurricane Allen, 00hrs GMT, 5 August 1980.

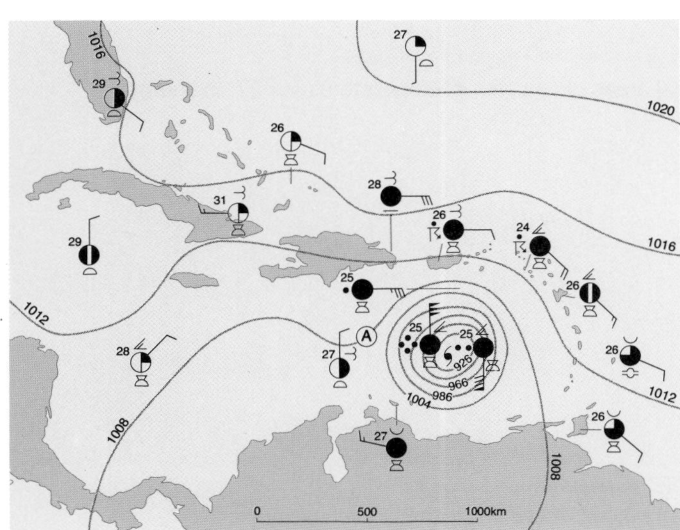

7.39 Hurricane Allen at 00.30 GMT on 5 August 1980.

Hurricane Allen

Look back to Figure 7.11. There is a spiralling mass of cloud just east of the Caribbean. This is Hurricane Allen.

Figures 7.38 and 7.39 show the position of the hurricane approximately 24 hours later, at 00 hrs GMT on 5 August 1980. One hour later, the US National Weather Service in San Juan, Puerto Rico, gave out this advisory statement:

'Hurricane Allen most intense hurricane in Eastern Caribbean this century . . . A hurricane watch is in effect for the south-west section of the Dominican Republic and the south-west peninsula of Haiti . . . Reports from Air Force reconnaissance indicate that Hurricane Allen has continued to strengthen during the evening. The central pressure is now down to 915 mb . . . The centre of Hurricane Allen is located near latitude 14° 48′ N longitude 67° W . . . It is moving slightly north of due west at about 32 km/hr . . . No change in speed or direction is expected during the next 24 hours . . . Highest winds are now 257 km/hr. Hurricane force winds extend outward 64 km in all directions from the centre . . . Residents of the Dominican Republic and Haiti in the hurricane watch area should listen for later advisories.'

Weather maps: a hurricane

11 Look carefully at Figure 7.38. Make a sketch to show the spiral pattern of cloud in the hurricane. Make sure that the eye is shown clearly. Label the diagram.

12 Describe carefully what weather conditions were like:
- (a) In the middle Atlantic, north-east of the Bahamas.
- (b) In the central Caribbean, 500 km west of the eye of the hurricane.
- (c) 50 km west of the eye.
- (d) 200 km east of the eye.
- (e) In Barbados, which was close to the centre of the storm approximately 24 hours before.

13 If the hurricane continues to move at the same speed in the same direction, when will it pass point 'A', which is 384 km west of the eye on the weather map?

14 Give a weather forecast for point 'A' for the next 48 hours.

15 Look at Figure 7.39. What countries did the centre of the hurricane pass over? Did the hurricane move as predicted in the Weather Service statement?

Storm surges

Hurricanes can be very damaging. Some of the worst damage is caused by *storm surges*.

Over the ocean, low air pressure near the centre of a hurricane causes the surface of the sea to dome upwards by about 0.5 m. When the storm moves into shallow coastal waters, this may be transformed into a surge of water up to 6 m high. At the same time, there are giant breakers, moving at about half the speed of the wind.

In low-lying coastal areas, the effects can be devastating. In 1970, a cyclone, or Indian Ocean hurricane, killed more than 200,000 people in the Ganges delta.

16 Look back to Section 4.2, and explain why storms in this region are so damaging.

17 Which areas in the Caribbean would be at risk from storm surges during a hurricane?

Storm surges can also cause serious damage on the low-lying south and south-east coasts of the United States. On 9 August 1980, Hurricane Allen was threatening coastal areas in the Gulf of Mexico, and the US National Weather Service issued this advisory statement:

'Outer fringes of severe hurricane Allen spreading across South Texas and north-east Mexico . . . Tides of 5 to 7 metres near and just north of landfall area . . . Hurricane warnings are in effect for the Texas coast from Brownsville northward to High Island . . . Rising tides have cut off escape routes from offshore islands . . . Highest sustained winds are 275 km/hr and the central pressure is 917 mb . . . The hurricane has been moving westward for the past few hours . . . Heavy rains of 150 mm or more will spread inland along the hurricane track later this morning and afternoon . . . details on possible inland flooding will be issued.'

18 Look at Figure 7.37 and make a sketch map to show:
- (a) The position of the centre of hurricane Allen at 00 hrs on 9 August 1980.
- (b) The track of the hurricane.
- (c) The area of the Texas coast covered by the hurricane warning.

19 Were wind speeds faster or slower when the hurricane was in the eastern Caribbean?

Taking precautions

20 Look at Figure 7.40. In what months is there a risk of hurricanes in the Caribbean?

In the past, hurricanes could hit anywhere in the Caribbean almost without warning. Today, with the benefit of satellite photographs and modern weather forecasting, it is possible to *monitor* the development of a tropical disturbance which looks like developing into a hurricane, and *inform* the public when there is danger of a hurricane or tropical storm striking a particular area.

It is possible to limit the extent of hurricane damage

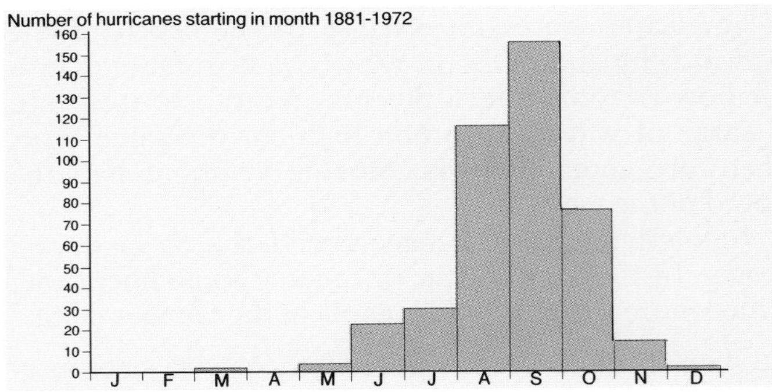

7.40 When hurricanes start.

7.40a Damage caused by Hurricane Gilbert in Jamaica.

by taking precautions. These are:

- Long-term precautions, like making sure that buildings are designed to stand up to hurricanes, and taking out hurricane insurance.
- Medium-term precautions, like making sure that every household has emergency supplies during the hurricane season; keeping buildings in a good state of repair; and removing dangerous limbs from trees.
- Short-term precautions, to make sure that everyone is safe when there is a hurricane warning from the meteorological service.

21 What emergency supplies should a household have in store?

22 What should be done to protect buildings when there is a hurricane warning?

23 What disaster relief agencies operate in your country, and what preparations have they made for dealing with an emergency?

Hurricane Gilbert

The most damaging hurricane this century, struck the Caribbean on 10–17 September 1988. Gilbert affected the Eastern Caribbean as a weather system bringing strong winds and heavy rain, but the real damage was done in Haiti, Jamaica, the Cayman Islands and Mexico. Wind speeds rose to over 250 km/hr. Almost 300 people were killed – 160 of them outside the Mexican city of Monterrey, where the Santa Catarina river swept away four buses in flood waters five metres deep. The hurricane passed directly over Jamaica, from east to west. The effect was devastating – many crops were totally destroyed, many buildings were ruined, power and telephone lines were brought down, and large trees were torn up by their roots.

7.11 Caribbean climates

Most parts of the Caribbean have a tropical marine climate. But there are important variations in weather patterns within the region, based on:

- Large-scale factors, such as latitude, the world wind system, and the position of the main land masses.
- Small-scale factors, like the relief of the surrounding area.

The main weather systems all affect different parts of the Caribbean:

- The ITCZ mainly affects Guyana and Trinidad, although it may influence weather systems as far north as Barbados and the Windward Islands.
- The Bermuda–Azores high mainly affects the north-east part of the region.
- Cold fronts are more frequent and more clearly marked in countries like the Bahamas, Cuba, and Jamaica. They do not affect Guyana at all.
- Hurricanes do not develop south of 9°N. They do not affect Guyana, and are also almost unknown in Trinidad.

Rainfall patterns

The northern part of Guyana has an equatorial climate, with two rainy seasons. There is one rainfall maximum in June, when the ITCZ is moving north, and another in December, when it is moving back towards the south.

In southern Guyana, the Rupununi savanna has a tropical continental climate. There is one rainy season. During the rest of the year, the weather is very dry. In the dry season, pressure is low over the Amazon basin; air from southern Guyana is drawn into this low-pressure region, and dry air from the upper atmosphere drifts down to replace it.

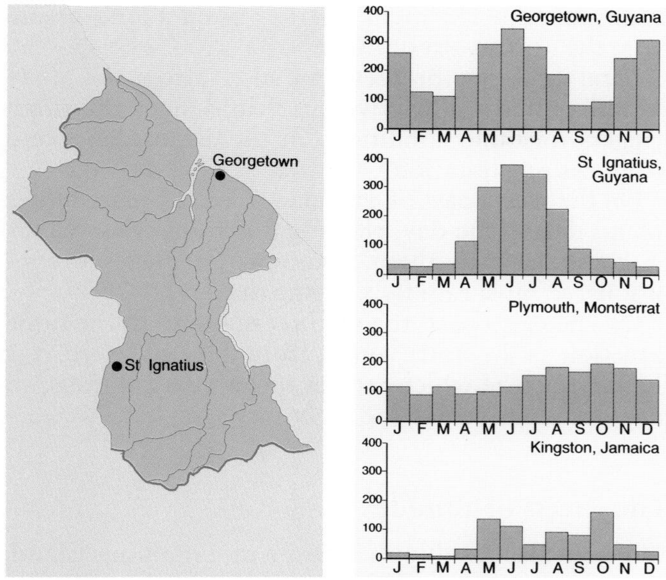

7.41 Rainfall patterns at four Caribbean weather stations.

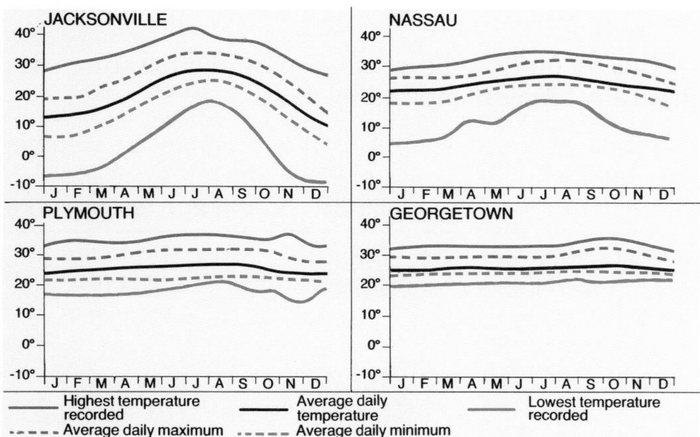

7.42 Temperature variations at four Caribbean weather stations.

Over the rest of the Caribbean, there is one rainy season and one dry season; but there is no clear boundary between the two, and rain can fall at any time of year.

1 What are the five wettest months in:
(a) Georgetown? (c) Plymouth?
(b) St Ignatius? (d) Kingston?

In Jamaica, Cuba, and Hispaniola, there are two rainfall maxima, one at the beginning of the wet season, and one at the end. This is not an effect of the movements of the ITCZ, which never reaches this far north. This pattern is probably related to an upper-atmosphere low-pressure system from North America, which brings unstable conditions to the Greater Antilles in May and October, but moves further west in July and August.

The cool season

We have seen how cold air from the North American land mass can affect the northern part of the region during the winter months.

For most of the time, the Bahamas and Cuba are just as warm as the rest of the Caribbean; but sometimes a cold front brings a sudden drop in temperature. This means that *minimum* temperatures are much lower than elsewhere in the region, and *average* temperatures in the winter months are a little lower.

Cold air is warmed by the sea as it moves south. Jacksonville in Florida has a very mild climate for the USA, but quite severe frosts can occur. In the Bahamas, there are no frosts. Further south, the effects of a cold front are less noticeable, and Guyana is never affected by cold air from North America.

2 Make a table in your exercise book to compare Jacksonville, Nassau, Plymouth, and Georgetown under these headings:
(a) Average temperature of the warmest month.
(b) Average temperature of the coolest month.
(c) Annual temperature range.
(d) Highest temperature ever recorded.
(e) Lowest temperature ever recorded.

Land and sea breezes

On a sunny day, the air over an island heats up much more quickly than the air over the surrounding sea. When this happens:

- There are strong updraughts over the island.
- A *sea breeze* develops as cooler air from around the island is drawn inwards.

Figure 7.43 shows some of the effects of a sea breeze around a Caribbean island.

- There are large cumulus clouds formed by updraughts over the centre of the island.
- Around the island, there is a ring of clear, dry air moving downwards. There are very few clouds within 50 km of the coast.

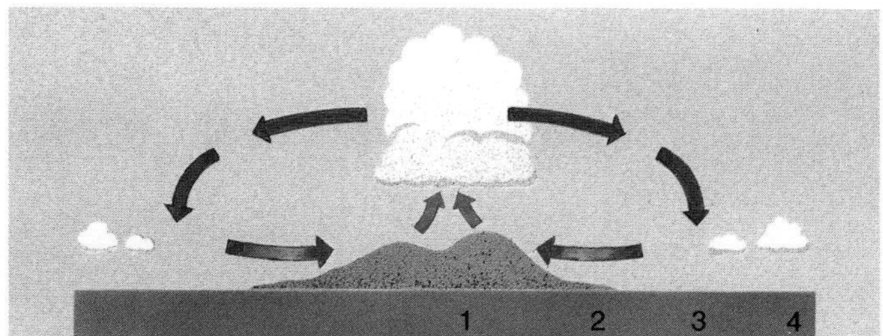

1 The air over the centre of the island warms up quickly. There are updraughts. Large cumulus clouds may form.
2 Air is drawn in around the coast. This is the sea breeze.
3 Here there is a current of dry, descending air. There are no clouds.
4 Further out to sea, there may be small cumulus clouds.

7.43 How a sea breeze develops.

- Further out to sea, there may be many small cumulus clouds.

At night, the land will be cooler than the surrounding sea. There may be a *land breeze* if updraughts over the sea draw cool air outwards.

There may be quite complex wind patterns where land and sea breezes interact with the trade winds.

Figure 7.44 shows a wind rose for the Palisadoes, on the south coast of Jamaica. The sea breeze combines with trade winds to blow from the south-east during the day. At night, there is often a land breeze from the north-west or north.

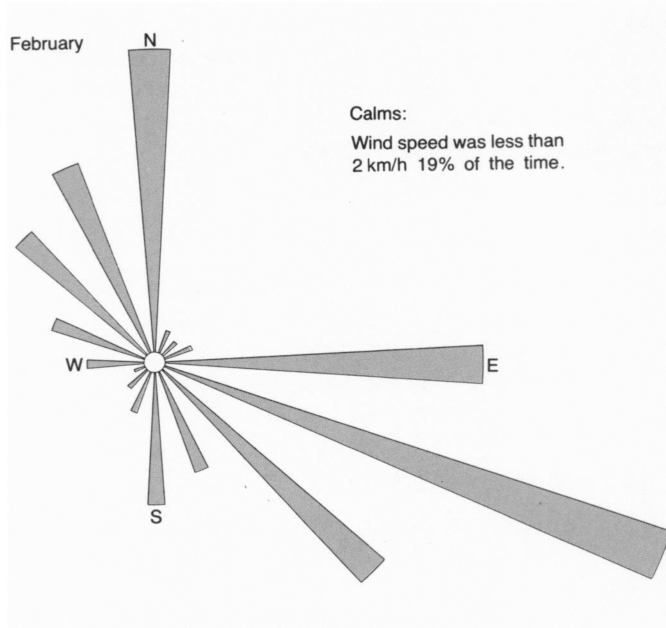

7.44 A wind rose for the Palisadoes, Jamaica.

Land and sea breezes can also affect the daily rainfall pattern. When two airstreams meet, this often triggers unstable conditions in the atmosphere, and produces precipitation.

On the west coast of Trinidad, the sea breeze blows inland during the day, slowing down the trade winds or colliding with them. This creates unstable conditions, so most rain falls during the *day*.

On the east coast, the sea breeze blows in the same direction as the trade winds, from the east. Here, it is the land breeze which creates unstable conditions, so most rain falls during the *night*.

The effects of altitude

When an air mass blows across a mountainous island, it is forced upwards. This means that:

- The air expands, because there is less pressure on it from above.
- The air uses heat energy to expand, and becomes cooler.

This is one of the reasons why temperatures are generally lower in mountain areas.

3 Look at these figures for three Jamaican weather stations:

	Altitude	Average temperature
Cinchona Gardens	1493 m	17.4°C
Empire Nursery	649 m	21.9°C
Palisadoes	3 m	27.1°C

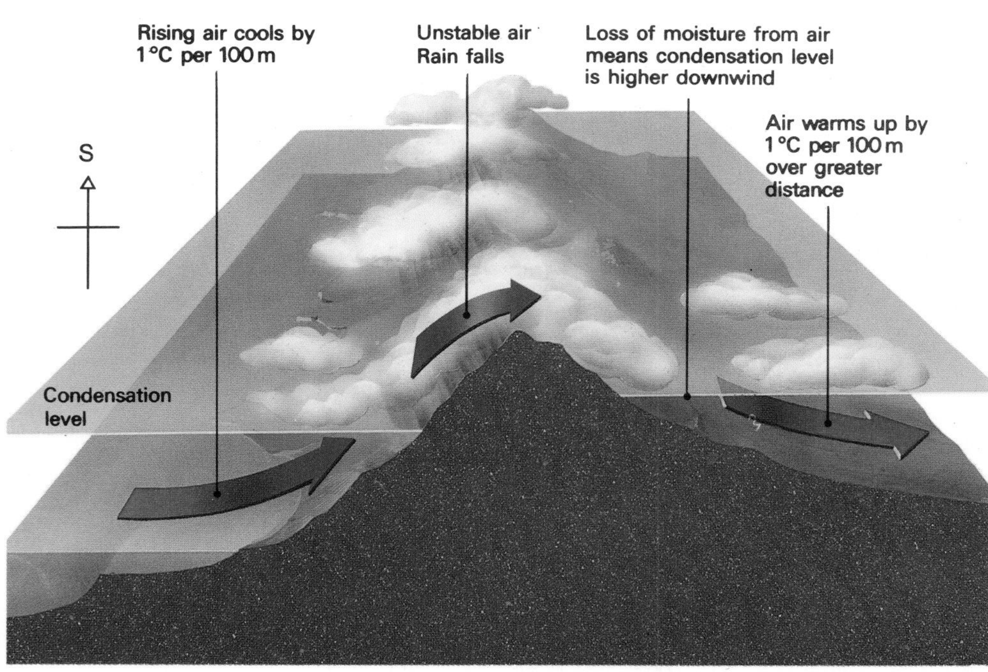

7.45 How relief affects rainfall and temperature.

(a) What is the difference in average temperature between:
  (i) Cinchona Gardens and Empire Nursery?
  (ii) Empire Nursery and Palisadoes?
(b) What is the difference in altitude?
(c) Work out the average fall in temperature for every 100 m of altitude.

If atmospheric conditions are stable, then the air that is forced over a mountain range will simply sink down again on the other side; but if the atmosphere is unstable, then powerful updraughts will be triggered within the air mass.

- Clouds form over the mountains, and there may be heavy rainfall.
- On the leeward side of the mountains, the air will move downwards again. It will contract and become warmer.
- Because the air has lost much of its moisture in the mountain area, it will be dry and warm after it has crossed the mountains.

The dry area on the leeward side of a mountain range is called a *rain shadow*. Look back to Figure 7.41. Kingston has a low rainfall because it is in the rain shadow of the Blue Mountains.

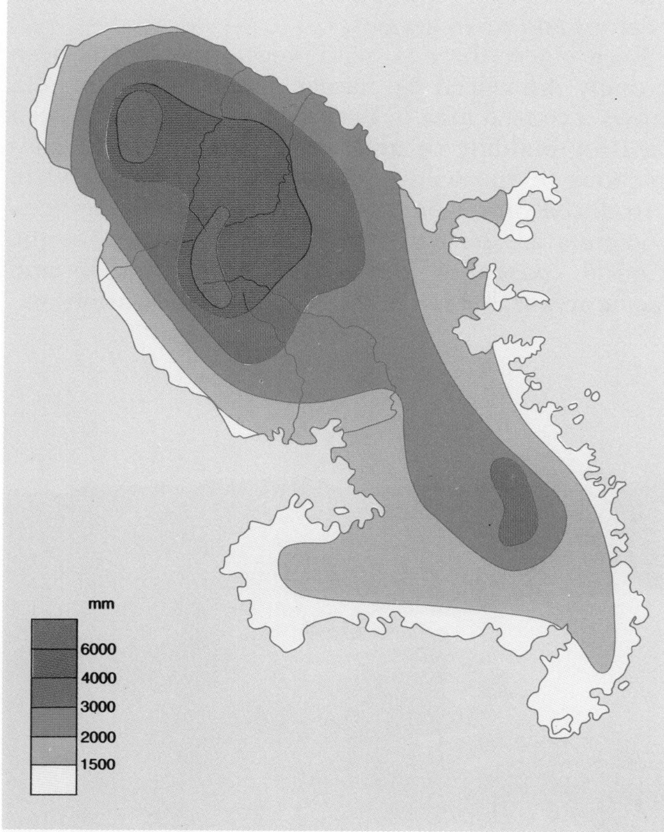

7.46 Rainfall patterns in Martinique.

4 Figure 7.46 shows the effect of altitude on rainfall in Martinique. Compare this map with a relief map in your atlas. What is the average rainfall:
  (a) Near the summit of Mont Pelée?
  (b) On the low hills in the south of the island?
  (c) On the west coast?

In a large island, like Jamaica, the pattern of relief and rainfall will be complex. The relief will also affect the *seasonal* pattern of rainfall, because the weather systems at certain times of year may bring rain to particular parts of the island.

- In February, during the dry season, there is very little rain except in the Blue Mountains. These are high enough to trigger rainstorms even when the atmosphere is relatively stable.
- In May, all parts of Jamaica are much wetter, and the rainfall is much more evenly spread. There is much more rain in the western part of the island.
- In December, the northers bring high rainfall to the north coast, east of Discovery Bay.

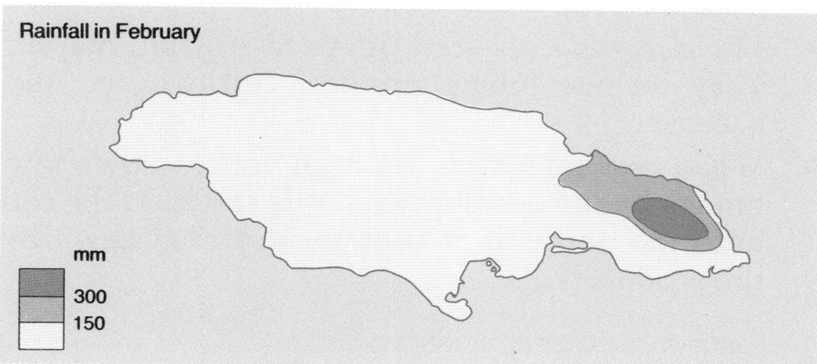

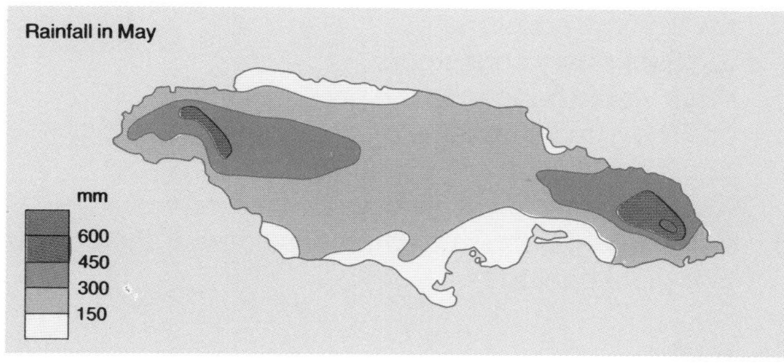

7.47 Rainfall patterns in Jamaica.

8 · VEGETATION

8.1 Ecosystems

The different plants and animals of a forest area relate to each other in an *ecosystem*:

- The main *inputs* to the system are rainwater, sunshine, and minerals.
- Two of these inputs – rainwater and nutrients – can be stored in the soil.
- The *producers* are the green plants. They grow by making direct use of rainwater, sunshine, and minerals.
- The *primary consumers* are animals which feed directly off the plants, like parrots, tapirs, bees, and monkeys.
- The *secondary consumers* feed off the primary consumers and off each other. They include lizards, jaguars, spiders, and birds of prey.
- The *decomposers* feed off dead organic matter. They include fungi, termites, earthworms, and bacteria.
- When organic matter has been broken down into humus by the decomposers, it is stored in the soil until the nutrients it contains are used again by the producers.

1 List some other species which are:
   (a) Producers.
   (b) Primary consumers.
   (c) Secondary consumers.
2 What would happen to the producers if:
   (a) The climate became much cooler?
   (b) There were a long drought?
   (c) There were fewer minerals and nutrients available?
3 What would happen to the consumers if there were less plant growth?

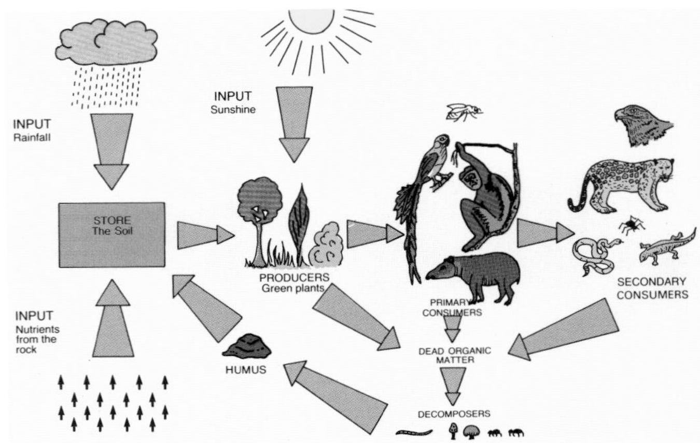

8.1 A forest ecosystem.

Soil, climate, and human activity

Plant life is affected by *climate* and *soil* conditions.

Breadfruit, like many tropical species, will only grow where there is never cold weather. It will be killed if there are even a few days with temperatures below 5 °C.

Aloes, cacti, and succulent plants will only grow where rainfall is low. These plants will rot in a wet climate.

Wallaba will thrive in acid soil conditions, where most other trees will not grow.

It is often possible to learn a great deal about the climate and geology of an area by studying its plant life. Some plants can almost be used as a climatic indicator or as a soil-testing kit.

Plant life is also affected by *human activity*. Today, there are no completely untouched 'natural' environments anywhere in the world. In many areas, wild plants have been replaced by buildings and roads, or by crops and sown grasses.

Even where there is 'wild' vegetation, it has been strongly influenced by human activities. Figure 8.2 shows a coastal area in Barbados which has not been used for building or agriculture. But the most conspicuous of the wild plants – the coconuts – were introduced into the region by European settlers. Coconuts are part of the natural vegetation of the tropical coastlands and islands of the Indian and Pacific oceans, but not of the Atlantic or the Caribbean.

8.2 Coastal vegetation.

World vegetation patterns

When we look at a world map, the relationship between climate and vegetation shows up very clearly. Figure 8.3 shows the worldwide distribution of some of the most important types of vegetation. Compare this map with Figure 7.12 in Section 7.6.

4 What types of vegetation are associated with these climatic types:
(a) Equatorial?
(b) Tropical continental?
(c) Cool temperature interior?
(d) Cold temperate interior?

But you should read the comments on the world climate map in Section 7.6 carefully again. Remember that world-scale maps like this can be very misleading. Some of the problems connected with using a map like this will be explained in this chapter.

Biomass

Figure 8.4 shows how fast plants grow in different types of environment. It shows the total amount of *biomass* or plant and animal matter which grows on a square metre of land in a year – the amount of extra growth which plants like trees put on, and the total amount of growth for smaller annual plants which develop during the year.

Plant growth is fastest where there is plenty of warmth, sunlight, and moisture.

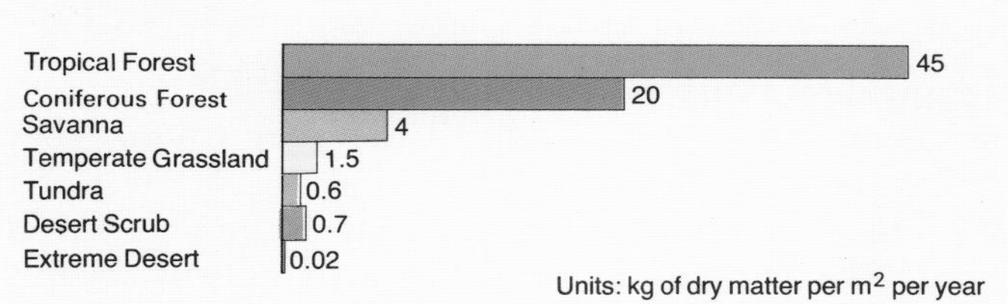

8.4 The average amount of plant growth in different areas.

- When plant roots cannot extract moisture from the soil, new growth cannot take place.
- Photosynthesis is possible only when the temperature is above 6 °C.

There are some areas where it is moist enough and warm enough for rapid plant growth all the year round. This is true of the tropical rain forests.

There are other regions where it is always too dry or too cold for plant growth. These include the ice caps and sandy deserts.

In most parts of the world, conditions are sometimes suitable for plant growth; but there is a season when it is too dry or too cold, and little plant growth can take place.

5 In which climatic types is plant growth restricted by:
(a) A *cold* season?
(b) A *dry* season?

6 Look back to the climate graphs in Figure 7.16. How long is the cold season in:
(a) Huron?
(b) The Pas?
(c) Coral Harbour?

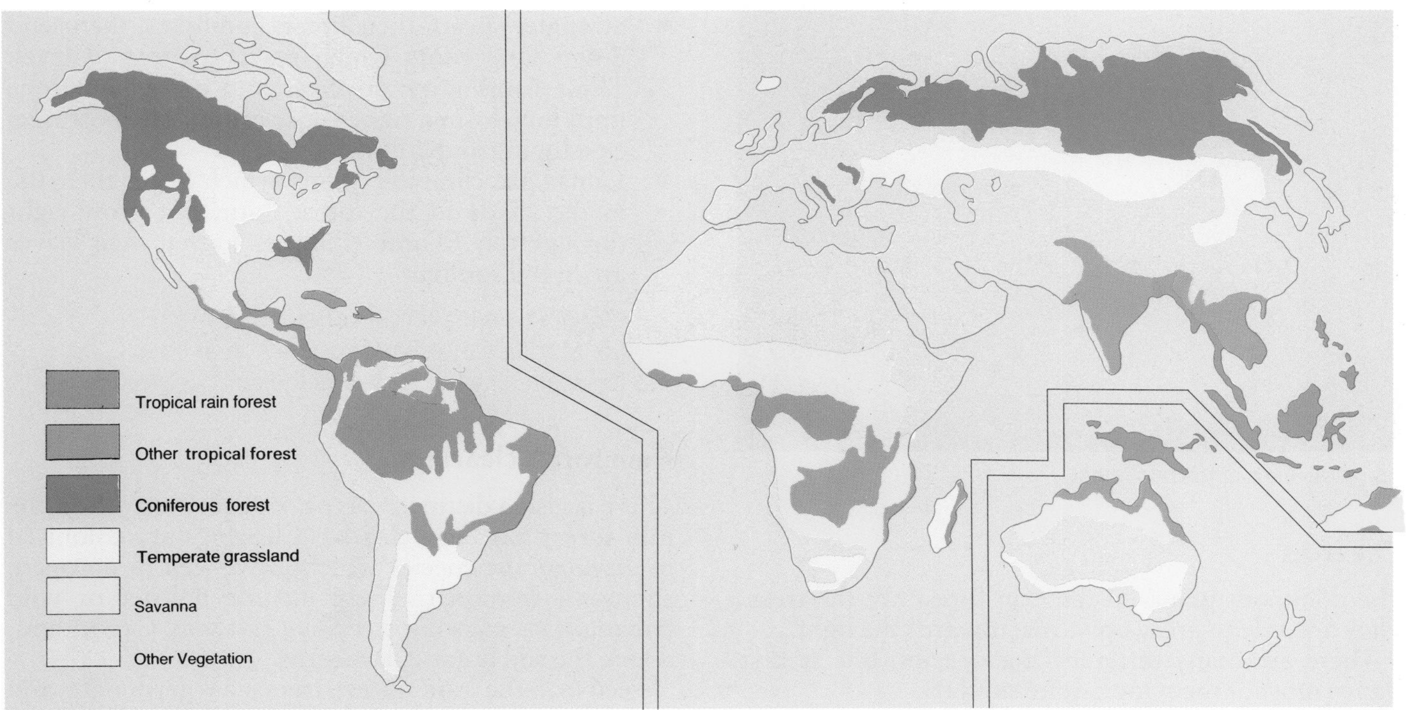

8.3 World vegetation patterns.

8.2 Tropical rain forests

Tropical rain forests are found where:

- Temperatures are high all the year round; they are generally about 25 °C.
- There is no real dry season. Rainfall is over 2,000 mm, and is distributed fairly evenly throughout the year.

There is more plant growth in the rain forest than in any other type of plant community. There is also a greater variety of different species.

It has been estimated that there are between one and two million different plant and animal species in the world. About 40% of these species can be found in the tropical rain forest – which covers only about 6% of the earth's land surface. Most of the smaller species have not yet been given a name – and most of those which have been named have not yet been studied. A handful of surface soil or plant litter from a rain forest is quite likely to contain at least one small organism which is not yet known to science. The larger plants and animals are also very varied. One hectare of rain forest will generally contain about forty different types of tree.

The rain forest is a very complex environment; but when an area of forest is studied carefully, it is possible to see how the plant community is structured.

1 Look at Figure 8.3. List three countries where there are tropical rain forests.

8.5 An air view of the rain forest.

The trees

The dominant plants in the rain forest are the trees. They are able to grow upwards, towards the light.

There are many different tree species, but at first glance most of them look quite similar:

- They have a tall, straight trunk, with no leaves or branches for most of its length. Any leaves near the ground would be useless for photosynthesis, because it is so shady there.
- They have a well-defined crown, where all the leafy growth is concentrated.
- Leaves are dark green and leathery. This protects them from the intense sunshine.
- Leaves generally have a *drip tip*, which helps them dry off quickly after heavy rain. A dry leaf is much more efficient for transpiration and photosynthesis.
- The bark is generally smooth and very thin. Some trees, like cocoa, have fruit which grows straight out of the trunk.
- Many trees have 'plank buttresses' growing out from the lowest part of the trunk. These may help provide extra support for the tallest trees.

The other plants

Most of the other plants in the rain forest depend on the trees for support or nutrition:

- Parasites get their nutrition by drawing on the resources of the host plant. They will damage its growth.
- Epiphytes live on another plant, but have their own sources of nutrients and moisture. The Bromeliads, for example, have thick leaves which are arranged to form a container for water and nutrients. Insects help to bring nutrients into the container.
- Stranglers begin their life as epiphytes, then send down long roots which reach to ground level. These roots grow stronger and more numerous until they form a tight noose around the host tree, enveloping and killing it.
- Lianas are climbing plants which begin their life in the shade of the forest floor, but grow right through the 'B' and 'C' layers so that their leaves are in full sunlight.

2 Explain how the forest vegetation:
(a) Modifies the climate on the forest floor.
(b) Maintains the fertility of the soil.

Rain forest clearings

There is also a distinctive type of vegetation where the rain forest has been cleared. Clearings are colonised by *opportunist* species which grow well in an open, sunny environment. These include Balisier or wild banana, fast-growing trees like the Bois Canot, and, where the soil is good, tree ferns.

Seeds of the rain forest trees can germinate and start to grow underneath these plants. They will eventually overtop the opportunist species, and start to shade them out. Eventually, the true rain forest community will re-establish itself, and the opportunist species will not be able to survive because the environment is too shady for them.

3 In pure rain forest vegetation, these opportunist species are quite rare. Why are they so common in the Caribbean islands?

'A'-layer or emergent trees are 30–45 m high, and have wide spreading crowns.

The tops of these trees are exposed to the full force of the sun's rays; this is an open, windy environment. There is quite a wide daily temperature range. Some epiphytes and parasites, and many birds and insects, live in the crowns of the emergent trees, but in this part of the forest they must be able to cope with strong sunshine and a limited water supply.

8.6 Rain forest vegetation.

'B'-layer or canopy trees are 18–27 m high. Their crowns are rounded or elongated, and packed more closely together to form an almost continuous cover. There are large numbers of birds and insects, and also many mammals, such as sloths and monkeys, which do not often come down to ground level. Epiphytes and parasites are very common. The canopy is an open and sunny environment, but it is more sheltered than the emergent layer, and more moisture is available.

'C'-layer or lower-storey trees are 8–14 m high. Their crowns are quite closely packed together. There is much less light at this level – most has been filtered out above. There is much less wind, and the air is humid. Epiphytes and parasites are adapted to a shady and moist environment. Birds, insects, and mammals are very common.

In the shrub layer there is very little light. Photosynthesis is difficult, and the young trees and other plants do not grow quickly.

When a tall tree dies and collapses, a clearing will be created. Suddenly, light will be available. The young trees will have an opportunity to grow quickly. One or two of them will succeed in growing fastest, and these will shade out the others again, closing up the temporary opening in the canopy.

Only about 1% of the sunlight actually reaches ground level. The air is very still and humid. Temperatures are very steady. Moisture is plentiful, but there is not enough light for photosynthesis. This is why there is very little undergrowth in a rain forest.

Among the tree trunks, plank buttresses, and the stems of the lianas, a few plants manage to grow. Saprophytes are plants which get their nourishment with the help of root fungi which help them to use the organic matter in the soil.

Some mammals, such as tapirs and deer, live at this level. Their diet includes fruit and seeds which fall to the ground, young plants, and roots.

There is little organic matter on the floor of the rain forest. Plant litter is broken down very quickly by the decomposers, and then taken up very quickly by the plant roots. It is *recycled* very quickly in this plant community. But there is a continuous supply of new plant litter.

Although the trees are very tall, they usually have a shallow rooting system. Most of the organic matter is snatched up before it has a chance to penetrate to any great depth in the soil.

8.3 Grasslands

Tropical savannas

In regions with a tropical continental climate, there is a well-marked dry season. Plants must be able to survive a period when lack of moisture restricts their growth.

Most rain forest plants cannot survive in this environment. They would not be able to cope with the dry season.

The plants which do grow well in this climate:

- Have features which help them make good use of what water there is available in the dry season.
- Or have a seasonal pattern of growth, and become dormant during the annual drought.

One very common type of vegetation in these regions is tropical grassland or savanna – a wide expanse of open grassland with trees growing singly or in groups.

Savanna vegetation grows very fast during the wet season, because temperatures are high and there is plenty of moisture; but during the dry season, growth is restricted. This means that the total amount of biomass produced over the year is less than in the rain forest – although it is much higher than in some other types of environment.

1 Look at the climate graphs for Jos, Kano, and Zinder (Figure 7.13).
   (a) How many dry months are there at each station?
   (b) Why will evaporation be very fast in the dry season?
   (c) Are there any months when low temperatures will restrict plant growth?
2 Look at Figure 8.3. List four countries where there are savannas.

Savanna plants and animals

The tallest trees are around 20 m high. They often have wide, spreading crowns. Most of them have features which help them conserve water in the dry season, such as small, leathery leaves, which reduce transpiration, or a thick bark. The baobab has a large, swollen trunk which can store water. Many trees have deep roots, which can extract water from far below the surface.

The air is dry, so very few epiphytes can grow; and because there is no continuous tree canopy, very few animals live in the branches.

There are large numbers of grazing animals – zebras, giraffes, antelopes, and elephants; and there are large carnivores like lions. There are also small rodents which can burrow and feed on bulbs and roots when water is scarce.

Most savanna grasses grow in *tussocks* or large clumps. During the wet season, the grass may grow to 3 metres, about the height of full-grown sugar cane.

8.7 Dry season savanna vegetation in northern Nigeria.

In the dry season, there are many fires; the ground is covered with burnt grass and many patches of bare earth are exposed.

There is a strong seasonal pattern to plant growth. Read this description of the savanna:

'Between February and April, after the fires have passed, the trees come into new leaf and flower. It is remarkable the way many species produce their new flowers and foliage at the very driest part of the year. At about this time too, the burnt tussocks send up fresh green shoots.

'During the rainy season, the tree canopy becomes denser and the grass grows apace. The most beautiful time is undoubtedly the early rains, when the grass is green and short, the monocotelydons (orchids and lilies) are in flower, and the trees in young foliage and flower. Many trees have brightly coloured young leaves.

'Towards the end of the rainy season (September and October) the grasses flower. During the dry season, the grass becomes dry, and sooner or later it is burnt. The ground is then incredibly bare and blackened, and the trees charred and usually leafless. The savanna may remain in this dreary and apparently dead state for weeks.'

(R. Keay, *An Outline of Nigerian Vegetation*)

3 Why do the trees produce flowers and new leaves just *before* the rainy season starts?
4 Does the vegetation in the area where you live have a seasonal pattern of this sort?
5 Which Caribbean trees produce flowers or fruit:
   (a) At the beginning of the rainy season?
   (b) In the middle of the rainy season?
   (c) During the dry season?

8.8 The savanna in the wet season.

6 List the differences between savanna trees and rain forest trees.

Fires and savanna vegetation

Savanna vegetation is often associated with a tropical continental climate; but there are many ways in which the distribution of savanna vegetation is rather puzzling:

- In West Africa, there is a *gradual* transition from an equatorial to a tropical continental climate; but a very *sharp* boundary between the closed forest and the savanna.
- When a stretch of savanna is fenced off and protected, the number of trees often increases quite fast. Open grassland may be replaced by closed forest in only twenty or thirty years.
- Rocky slopes in savanna regions are often drier than the flat plains – but they are often covered with thick thorny woodland rather than grass.

Many researchers think that fires play an important part in the development of savanna vegetation.

- During the dry season, most savanna areas are swept by fierce fires which burn up the dead grass.
- Savanna trees are fire-resistant. Features like thick bark mean that they can stand up to scorching flames.

Where there is no dry season, it is always too wet for a forest fire to spread. In a desert area, there is not enough vegetation to feed a fire. But in the savannas, there is enough plant material to keep a fire going; and there is a dry season when fires start easily and spread fast.

Fires can be started by natural causes, such as lightning; but most savanna fires seem to be the result of human activity:

- Hunters start fires to drive game into a trap.
- Herders start fires to encourage fresh new grass.
- Farmers start fires to clear the vegetation and prepare the ground for cultivation.

7 Why would *annual* plants like grass grow well in areas which are regularly burnt?

Temperate grasslands

In many areas with a cool temperate interior climate, plant growth is restricted both by the *cold* in the winter, and by the lack of *moisture* in the summer when evaporation is high.

In these regions, there are wide stretches of grassland vegetation – the Prairies of North America, the Steppes of Europe and Asia, and the Pampas of temperate South America.

In some ways, these temperate grasslands are quite similar to the tropical savannas:

- Grasses are the dominant plants.
- The climate is drier than in the neighbouring forest areas.
- There are some wooded areas on steep slopes and in the river valleys.
- There are many grazing animals – buffalo, deer, and antelope for example. There are also small burrowing rodents like the prairie marmot.

Many researchers think that fires have played an important part in the development of this type of vegetation, too.

But there are important differences between the temperate grasslands and the tropical savannas:

- Over most of the prairies, there are no trees at all; grassland stretches as far as the eye can see.
- The grass is generally shorter. In the wettest parts of the prairie, there is tall grass up to 1 m high; but generally the grass is around 50 cm high, and in the drier areas it does not grow much over 20 cm.
- The grass does not usually grow in tussocks.
- Temperate grasses are usually more nutritious for domestic animals than the grasses of the savannas.
- Temperate grassland soils are usually very rich in organic matter.

The original wild forms of many crops, such as wheat, and of many farm animals, such as cattle, were found in an environment very similar to that of the prairies and steppes. Today, these areas are so well suited to the European type of farming, that there is very little of the original vegetation left. Even where the grasslands have not been ploughed up for cereal cultivation, they have been altered out of all recognition by commercial grazing and other activities.

8 List three countries where there are temperate grasslands.

9 Make a labelled sketch to show some of the differences between temperate grasslands and savannas.

8.4 Coniferous forests

Some of the largest areas of forest in the world are found in North America and Asia, in regions with a cold temperate interior climate. This environment is very unlike that of the rain forest, so a very different type of vegetation grows here.

The pattern of plant growth in this climate is *seasonal.*

In the *winter*:

- Temperatures are far too low for plant growth.
- There are only a few hours of sunlight each day, so photosynthesis would be limited even if temperatures were higher.
- All the water in the ground is frozen. It is locked up in ice crystals, and is not available for the plant roots to take up.

But in the *summer months*:

- The air is quite warm. Midday temperatures are often above 20 °C.
- There are long hours of sunlight. At midsummer, photosynthesis can take place almost 24 hours a day.
- The snow melts when moisture is most needed, during the spring, when temperatures are beginning to rise and there is plenty of daylight.
- Most rain falls in the summer, just when it is most useful for plant growth.

It does not matter how far the temperature falls below freezing in the winter months. No plant growth can take place then, anyway. What is important for the trees is that there should be a few months every year when the temperature rises significantly above 6 °C, there is plenty of sunlight, and there is enough water for plant growth.

Coniferous forest trees

Most of the trees in the coniferous forest are evergreen. They can start using sunlight for photosynthesis right at the start of the growing season. They do not waste valuable time growing new leaves in the spring. The trees are cone-shaped; this helps them shed snow easily. Too much snow on the branches in winter would cause them to break. They have a thick bark, which helps protect them from the cold, and waxy, needle-shaped leaves, which do not lose much moisture in the winter when there is no liquid for the roots to take up.

Compared with the rain forest, there are very few different species. Often a *stand* consisting mainly of one species covers several square kilometres.

There are no lianas or epiphytes in a coniferous forest.

Evergreen trees cast a heavy shade all year round. There are very few other plants growing, because there is little light at ground level.

Because temperatures are low, plant litter rots slowly. The ground is covered with a layer of dead needles.

Animal life

Most of the animal life is at ground level; there are herbivorous animals like deer and porcupine, and predators like the wolf, lynx, and mink. A few animals, such as the squirrels, spend part of their life in the trees.

During the summer, insects breed rapidly. There

8.9 A coniferous forest in winter.

8.10 Coniferous trees have needle-shaped leaves.

may be swarms of flies or mosquitoes. There are also large numbers of insect-eating birds. In the winter, there are few insects; there are only eggs ready to hatch out in the spring. Almost all the birds migrate south when the weather is cold, and many animals *hibernate* at this time of year.

1 List three countries where there are coniferous forests.
2 List the differences between the tropical rain forest and the cold temperate coniferous forest.
3 Explain how plant and animal life in the coniferous forest is adapted to *cold* conditions.

Resources

Wild plants and animals can provide useful resources for human society.

1 What resources can be obtained from:
   (a) Tropical rain forests?
   (b) Savannas?
   (c) Temperate grasslands?
   (d) Coniferous forests?
2 Which of these are renewable resources?
3 Is the natural environment damaged when these resources are used?

8.5 Caribbean vegetation

There are many areas of rain forest or savanna in the Caribbean, but there is also a wide variety of other vegetation types.

There are distinctive vegetation patterns in:

- Dry environments.
- Coastal environments.
- Mountain environments.
- Environments with special soil conditions.

In all of these areas, there is some reason why true rain forest vegetation cannot develop.

Mountain environments

Figure 8.11 shows a photograph taken in low cloud, near the top of Mont Pelée in Martinique. Many Caribbean mountain peaks are hidden in cloud for most of the time. This means that there is a very distinctive environment there:

- The atmosphere is saturated with millions of tiny water droplets.
- There is very little sunshine.
- The ground is almost always moist.
- Temperatures are quite low by tropical standards: generally around 15 °C.
- Rainfall is very high: up to 6,000 mm.
- There are often strong winds; and the impact of storms and hurricanes is completely devastating.

1 In what ways is this a favourable environment for plant growth?
2 In what ways is it an unfavourable environment?
3 Why could rain forest not develop in a mountain area?

Elfin woodland

On the high peaks, where it is very cloudy, cool, and windy, the vegetation is *elfin woodland*.

The ground is covered with dwarf trees only 1–2 m high. The trees find it almost impossible to grow upwards, so they stretch along the ground, and their branches take on strange contorted shapes. The trees are often completely covered with epiphytes, mosses, and lichens. There are also small flowering plants. Many of the epiphytes and flowering plants are Bromeliads.

8.11 Elfin woodland on Mont Pelée, Martinique.

Montane forest

On the middle slopes of Caribbean mountains, there is generally a *montane forest*:

- The trees are not as tall as in the rain forest; they generally reach a height of 10–12 m.
- There is one one tree storey.
- The trees become very leafy; they need as many leaves as possible to get sunlight for photosynthesis in cloudy conditions.
- The trunks and branches of the trees are covered with mosses and lichens which thrive in the damp atmosphere.
- There are many epiphytes growing on the trees.

8.12 Montane forest in St Lucia. The trees are covered with mosses and epiphytes.

Special soil conditions

There are some forest areas in the Caribbean with specialised soil conditions, where most types of tree would not grow well. In these areas, there are often large *stands* where one species predominates over several square kilometres:

- In the *white sand* belt of Guyana, the soil is very acid and does not hold nutrients at all well. Wallaba and Damara are very common trees here because they can cope with these conditions.
- In the *marsh forests* of north-west Guyana, there are *pegasse* soils which consist of a heavy clay covered with a layer of spongy peat between 0.3 and 4.0 m thick. These soils are flooded and waterlogged most of the year. Even in the dry season they are still very damp. Most trees would die in these conditions, because their roots could not breathe properly, but Dalli trees grow well. There are large stands of Dalli in Guyana and Surinam.
- There are also large stretches of *Mora* forest in Guyana and Trinidad, in areas where drainage is a little better, but it is still too moist for most other species to thrive.

Dry environments

In most Caribbean climates, there is a dry season. For part of the year, there is not enough water in the soil for plant growth to take place. Rain forest is replaced by other forms of tropical woodland, or by savanna.

Where there is:

- High annual rainfall.
- A short dry season with some rain.
- A soil which retains water well.

Then the woodland will be almost the same as true rain forest.

Where there is:

- Low annual rainfall.
- A long dry season with very little rain.
- A soil which drains rapidly, or a permeable rock like limestone.

Then there will be a very different type of vegetation.

Semi-evergreen forest

In areas with a moderate rainfall, the vegetation looks rather like true rain forest, particularly during the wet season; but there is less plant growth, and the structure of the plant community is simpler:

- There are only two tree storeys, not three.
- Many trees shed their leaves in the dry season, or have very small leaves. This helps them to save moisture.
- There are fewer epiphytes than in the rain forest, because the tree canopy is often very dry.
- During the dry season, the ground is covered with fallen leaves. These do not decay until the earth becomes moist again.
- There is a definite seasonal rhythm to plant growth. Many trees flower during the dry season, so that their seeds will be ready just when the rainy season begins.

Dry woodland

Where there is a long dry season, the vegetation is very different from the rain forest, because:

- Rain forest plants have plenty of moisture, but have to fight their way up towards the sunlight.
- Plants in the dry woodland have plenty of sunlight, but need features which will help them to make good use of the available water.

These are the main differences:

- The biomass of the dry woodland is much lower; lack of moisture limits plant growth.
- There are fewer different species.

- Trees are smaller than in the rain forest; the tallest trees are generally 15–25 m in height.
- There are few lianas and epiphytes.
- Most trees shed their leaves in the dry season, or have small leaves.
- The bark of the trees is thick and often cracked. Thick bark helps the tree to retain moisture.
- The trunks of the trees are often crooked, and start to branch out quite near to the ground.
- Although plenty of light penetrates through the trees during the dry season, there are very few herbaceous plants at this level. The ground is usually covered with old leaves, dead wood, and other plant litter, which would have decayed very quickly in the humid rain forest environment.

8.13 Scrub vegetation in Grenada in the dry season. Most of the trees have lost their leaves.

Thorn scrub

There are few patches of undisturbed dry woodland left in the Caribbean. Most areas of dry woodland are near to the coast, and at some point they have been cleared:

- Some areas were once thought suitable for cultivation.
- Most have been used as a source of wood and charcoal.
- Almost all have been used as grazing for goats, sheep, and cattle.

The dry woodland is a very fragile environment. When the tree cover has been removed, there are few other plants to protect the soil. Rainstorms wash the soil away very quickly. With a thinner layer of soil, less water is retained after a rainstorm – more of the rainfall runs straight down the hillside, or sinks into permeable rocks below.

This is why so many areas of the Caribbean are now covered with dry scrub vegetation. The high forest does not grow back; instead there are small trees, shrubs, and cacti. The tallest plants are generally about 3 m tall.

All the plants are adapted to dry conditions:

- Their leaves are small, and often have a waxy or hairy surface to cut water loss.
- Some plants, like cacti, have no leaves at all.
- Some plants are *succulents* which can store water.
- Some plants have very deep roots, which can reach water far below the surface.

In areas which are used for grazing, the plants which can survive best are those which have spines or thorns to protect themselves.

4 Are there any ways in which dry woodland is similar to savanna vegetation?

5 What are the main differences between dry woodland and savanna?

6 Why are there so few herbaceous plants at ground level?

Coastal vegetation

Look back to Figure 8.2. Sandy coastal areas like this have a distinctive type of vegetation. Most plants will not grow on beach sand, because:

- Water drains quickly through the loose sand.
- The sand has a high salt content which would kill most plants.
- Beach sand is unstable; seedlings find it difficult to establish themselves.
- There is no humus in beach sand, and few nutrients.

Next to the sea there is a strip of bare sand where nothing grows.

A little way inland, there are a few plants which can grow by creeping across the loose surface and sending down shoots. These plants help to stabilise the sand. Organic matter and nutrients can start to accumulate.

A little further from the sea, there are a few woody plants like Fat Pork and Sea Grape. The soil can hold water for longer and has a lower salt content.

The next zone has quite a wide variety of plant life. There are large Sea Grapes, Machineels, and many smaller bushes and flowering plants. There is a gradual transition from this zone to dry woodland or scrub, where Fat Pork, coconut, and Sea Grape are replaced by other species, and the salt content of the soil is no longer particularly high.

7 How does coastal vegetation help to protect beaches from erosion?

Mangroves

Mangroves grow in coastal areas where mud is being deposited – in shallow bays, in lagoons, in estuaries, and in deltas. These are difficult environments for most plants, because:

- The soil is permanently waterlogged, so that plant roots cannot breathe.
- The mud is disturbed every day by tidal currents, so that most seeds find it difficult to germinate and establish themselves.
- The water is too salty for most plants to grow in.

Mangroves are trees and shrubs which can grow in these conditions:

- Some mangroves have stilt roots. The trunk begins above the surface of the water, and the tree can breathe through the exposed portion of the root.
- Other mangroves have separate breathing roots – shoots which grow up from the main root system through the mud into the air where they can breathe.
- Some mangroves have seeds which germinate while they are still on the tree. When they drop to the ground, they have already developed into small plants with independent rooting systems.

Mangrove swamps do not appear at first glance to be very useful areas; but they are an important part of the coastal environment:

- Mangrove roots stabilise the mud which is brought down to the coast by rivers and streams. Instead of being washed out to sea, the mud gathers round the roots of the mangroves. Gradually, the swamp will be converted to solid ground, and new areas out to sea will be colonised by young mangroves.
- Mangroves provide a breeding-ground for young fish. There is plenty of food for them here, and they are comparatively safe from predators. Crabs, molluscs, and many different types of bird also thrive in the mangrove swamps.
- Mangrove wood is not good for construction, but it can be used to make charcoal. When a mangrove is cut back for charcoal, it will grow again in a few years. This means that charcoal extraction does not damage the environment. In one small mangrove swamp in St Lucia, research by secondary school students showed that at least 2,700 bags of charcoal were being produced every year, enough to provide an income for several local families.
- Mangrove swamps can be used as nature reserves. In Trinidad, the Caroni swamp is a home for many species of bird. At dusk, the Scarlet Ibis can be seen there in large numbers. For this reason, the swamp has been developed as a tourist attraction, and there are boat trips every day for bird-watching, fishing, and photography.

8 What resources can be obtained from:
   (a) Dry woodland?
   (b) Coastal vegetation?
   (c) Mangrove swamps?

9 Look back to Figure 2.10:
   (a) Make a sketch map to show the location of the mangrove swamps.
   (b) Why has a mangrove swamp developed here?

10 How could the natural environment of a mangrove swamp be damaged?

8.14 Mangroves in Trinidad. Mangroves are an important breeding ground for young fish.

8.15 Making charcoal in St Lucia.

9 · SOILS

9.1 Weathering

9.1 Part of a weathered limestone building.

9.2 A new building being constructed from freshly cut limestone blocks.

Most rocks are formed deep below the earth's surface. They are formed at very high temperatures, and under tremendous pressure from the rocks above; they are formed away from air and water.

When these rocks are exposed at the surface, conditions are very different. Temperatures are much cooler, and the great weight of the rocks above has been taken away. Rocks at the surface are exposed to wind and rainwater. Under these conditions, the rocks begin to break down; they are *weathered.*

Figure 9.1 shows part of an old limestone building. The effect of weathering on the rock can be seen clearly.

Physical, chemical, and biotic weathering

Rock is weathered in many different ways:

- Even before the rock is exposed at the surface, it begins to expand and crack as the rocks above are eroded, and their weight is taken away. *Joints* are formed in the rock. This process is called *pressure release.*
- At the surface, small cracks in the rock fill up with water when the ground is damp. In cold climates, this water often freezes. When water freezes, it expands by about 9%; this means that there is not enough room in the joints for the ice. The ice crystals press out against the sides of the crack. When this process is repeated many times over, the pressure of the ice can split the rock. This is known as *frost shattering* or *freeze–thaw weathering.*

Frost shattering and pressure release are both forms of *physical weathering.* They break up the rock; but they do not soften it or change its colour. *Chemical weathering,* on the other hand, affects the actual minerals which make up the rock. The rock rots away as a result of the action of air and natural acids:

- Some minerals, like rock salt, can be dissolved by water. This is known as *solution.*
- *Hydrolysis* occurs when minerals react with water, but do not actually dissolve. Feldspar is a hard, rock-forming mineral; but it reacts with water to produce *clay* minerals.
- *Oxidation* is a form of chemical weathering which occurs when a mineral reacts with the oxygen in the air. When an object made of iron is left exposed to the atmosphere, it will oxidise; rust will form on the surface. Many other rock-forming minerals can also be altered by oxidation.
- *Carbonation* is a distinctive type of chemical weathering which is particularly important in limestone areas. It has been described in Section 5.1.

Plants and animals may sometimes help to break down the rocks beneath them, particularly if the rocks are already soft or unconsolidated. This is sometimes called *biotic weathering.* Biotic weathering includes both physical and chemical processes.

- Tree roots growing in joints in the rock may help to split it up.
- Burrowing animals and earthworms may help to break up the rock.

9.3 A coarse-grained igneous rock.

- When dead plants and animals decay, acids are produced which can play an important part in chemical weathering.

1 How can you tell the building in Figure 9.1 is not new?
2 Figure 9.2 shows some recently cut limestone blocks. In what ways do they look different from the weathered limestone in Figure 9.1?
3 Figure 9.3 shows a coarse-grained igneous rock. The light-coloured grains are feldspar. The glass-like *quartz* grains are more resistant to chemical weathering. What will happen to the rock if the feldspar is affected by hydrolysis?

The effect of climate

Weathering is affected by the climate.

In a cold climate, frost shattering will be an important form of weathering, and there will be many slopes made up of coarse, angular rocks and boulders.

In a warm climate, most chemical reactions take place at a much faster rate when temperatures are high.

Many types of chemical weathering can only take place when there is some moisture on the ground.

4 In what type of climate will chemical weathering act more quickly?
5 Name two types of climate where chemical weathering will act very slowly.

The effect of rock type

Weathering is also affected by the type and structure of the rock.

Some minerals, like quartz, are usually very resistant to chemical weathering. Rocks which contain a high proportion of these minerals will generally weather more slowly than rocks which are composed of less resistant minerals.

We have already seen how limestone is affected by carbonation.

6 Explain why a closely jointed rock will be affected more quickly by:
(a) Frost shattering.
(b) Chemical weathering.
(c) Biotic weathering.
7 Describe the type of material which is produced by frost shattering.

9.2 The soil

In most situations, rocks are weathered not by one process acting alone, but by a combination of physical, chemical, and biotic weathering – and a mixture of fragments and particles of different sizes is the result:

- *Clays* are particles less than 0.002 mm across, which are formed by the chemical weathering of minerals like feldspar.
- *Silt* particles are larger. They are between 0.002 and 0.02 mm across.
- *Sand* generally consists of minerals which are quite resistant to chemical weathering, like quartz. Sand particles are between 0.02 and 2 mm across.
- *Gravel and small stones* are fragments of rock larger than 2 mm across.

In most places, solid rock is not exposed at the surface. Instead, there is a cover of gravel, sand, silt, and clay which conceals the rock below.

This cover of weathered material is the starting-point for soil formation; but soil is not simply broken-up rock. It contains much else besides rock particles and fragments. Figure 9.4 shows what a small section of soil may contain.

What the soil contains

In addition to the basic framework of rock fragments, soil will contain:

- *Water:* the soil will absorb moisture after rain, and release it gradually in dry weather. Even a soil which appears completely dry and dusty will contain some moisture clinging to the solid particles; but unfortunately, this water clings to them so tightly that it is not available for plant growth.
- *Air:* except in a completely sodden and water-

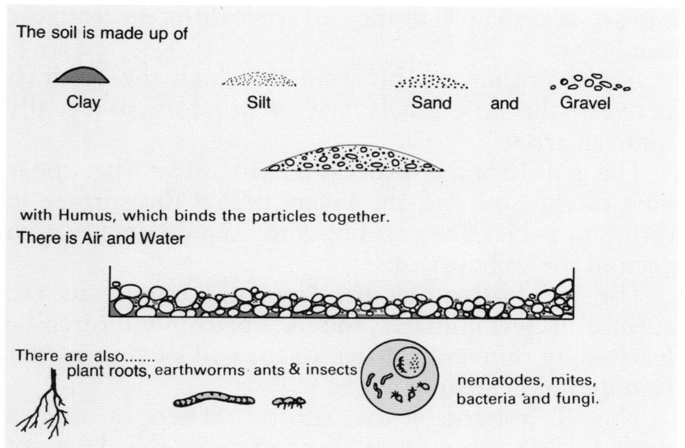

9.4 What the soil contains.

logged soil, there will be air trapped in the spaces between the soil particles. About half of the volume of the soil will usually consist of air.

- *Living matter:* soil looks 'dead' to the casual observer; but most soils house enormous numbers of living organisms. In some environments, there are several million earthworms living in each hectare of soil; and in most places, a handful of garden soil will contain several million bacteria and micro-organisms. Living matter in the soil will include plant roots, insects, burrowing animals, nematodes, and fungi. It has been estimated that there is about 1,800 kg of living matter in a hectare of soil.
- *Humus:* many soils are covered with a litter of dead leaves; but even more important is the dark-coloured material – humus – which is produced when bacteria and fungi break down organic matter. Some soils contain hardly any humus at all; others as much as 15–20%. Humus plays a very important part in the soil, because:
  - Humus helps the soil to retain water.
  - Humus holds on to the mineral nutrients like calcium and potassium which are needed for plant growth.
  - Humus gives the soil a *crumb* texture by sticking sand, clay, and silt particles together into larger units. This improves the soil, because the air spaces between the crumbs make it easier for plant roots and other living organisms to breathe and grow.

Soil-forming processes

It takes a long time for a well-developed soil to form. Fragments of weathered rock gradually develop into mature soil as a result of the *soil-forming processes.*

These processes include:

- *Weathering:* weathering does not stop when the rock has been broken up. Sand, silt, and clay continue to be altered by chemical weathering – in fact, they are altered much faster than minerals in solid rock, because they are exposed on all sides to the action of the soil water and the natural acids which it contains. Weathering of the soil particles releases more mineral nutrients into the soil.
- *Leaching:* rainwater dissolves minerals near the surface of the soil, and washes them away when it drains through the ground. The minerals are deposited again deeper below the surface – or else they are carried along with the rainwater into rivers and streams, and are taken out of the area altogether.
  - Sandy soils are leached very quickly, because water drains through them very fast.
  - Clay soils are less easily leached, because they drain more slowly, and also because the surface of the clay minerals holds on to the nutrients in the soil very firmly.
  - Humus holds minerals and nutrients very well, so that soils with a high proportion of organic matter are usually resistant to leaching.

  Strongly leached soils have very few nutrients in their surface layers, and are said to be *acid.* Leaching is also known as *eluviation.*
- *Capillary action:* if a glass tube full of fine sand is placed in a jar of water, the water will move slowly up the sand. It is being sucked upwards because the very small capillary spaces between the sand particles attract water. When water evaporates from the surface of the soil, more water is attracted up from below by capillary action to replace it.
- *Illuviation:* when soil water contains a very high proportion of salts and other minerals in solution, these are deposited back onto the solid particles in the soil. This process is known as illuviation.

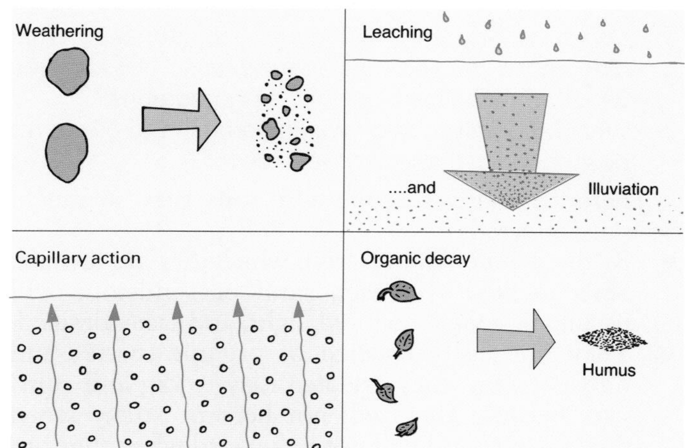

9.5 The soil forming processes.

In a wet climate, water generally moves down through the soil, and illuviation takes place below the surface. In some warm and fairly dry climates, water moves *up* through the soil at certain times because of capillary action, and there is illuviation near to the surface of the soil.

- *Organic growth and decay:* humus is added to the soil when there is a plentiful supply of dead organic matter, which decays steadily, and is not removed too quickly. Under these conditions, a dark-coloured soil with a good crumb structure can be formed. Where there is little plant and animal life, and where organic matter breaks down very quickly, then the soil will contain very little organic matter.

Soil horizons

When a cross-section of the soil is exposed – in a new road-cutting, or where a pit has been excavated – you can see that the soil at the surface is different from the soil below.

A soil *profile* can be seen, in which the contrast between the different layers, or *horizons*, is usually quite clear.

The soil-forming processes will affect the upper part of the soil and the layers below the surface in different ways. They will operate in a distinct way in each of the soil horizons.

The 'A' horizon is the 'topsoil', closest to the surface. In wet climates, the 'A' horizon will often be leached by rainwater. Most of the soil's living matter is in the 'A' horizon.

The 'B' horizon is the 'subsoil'. There is often a considerable amount of illuviation in this layer of soil.

The 'C' horizon consists of weathered parent material with little organic matter. This layer has not been altered very much by any of the soil-forming processes.

9.3 Why soils vary

There are many different types of soil. Soils can vary:

- In *colour*: they may be red, black, brown, yellow, or almost white.
- In *depth*: there may be anything from a few millimetres to tens of metres of soil before unaltered bedrock is reached.
- In *texture*: soils may be stony, sandy, or may consist of almost pure clay.
- In *structure*: some soils have a well-developed *crumb* structure, others may have a structure of horizontal *plates*, or vertical *columns*, or larger *blocks*.
- In *chemical composition*: soils may be acid, or neutral, or alkaline; they may contain large or small quantities of the main plant nutrients; they may contain too much salt, or other substances which are dangerous to certain plants.

1 Compare the soils in Figures 9.8 and 9.9. What differences between the two types of soil can you detect from the evidence of the photographs?

2 What other information would you need to give a full description of these two types of soil?

There are many reasons why soils vary so much. Soils are affected:

- By the *parent material* from which they are formed. Soils formed on beach sand or sandstone will usually be coarse-textured, light, and easily drained. They are easily leached of organic matter and nutrients, but they are also easy to dig and cultivate because they will not become sticky when they are wet and will not bake hard when they are dry.

3 Figure 9.8 shows a soil which has been formed on clay. In what ways will a soil which has been formed on clay differ from a soil formed on sand?

- **By the *climate*. In cold environments, chemical reactions generally work more slowly. Soils tend to be shallow, and partially decomposed organic matter can stay in the soil for a long time. In tropical environments, soils are usually much deeper, and organic matter is more likely to break down very quickly.**

4 Explain how leaching and illuviation would be affected by:
(a) A very wet climate.
(b) A very dry climate.
(c) A climate with a strong contrast between the wet season and the dry season.

- **By the *relief* of the land surface.**

5 Refer back to Figure 2.10, and the cross section in Figure 2.18. Explain:
(a) Why the soil at grid reference 770 470 may be very thin.
(b) Why the soil at grid reference 776 495 may be much deeper.

6 Draw a sketch cross section to show the sort of area which will have a *waterlogged* soil where few crops can grow well.

- **By the *vegetation* and *animal life* of the area.**

7 Study Figures 9.4 and 9.5, and make a list of the ways in which the soil may be influenced by:
(a) Vegetation.
(b) Animal life.

There are other ways in which vegetation can affect the soil, which cannot be shown so easily in a diagram. Nitrogen is an important plant food; but plants cannot use nitrogen from the air. First of all it is *fixed* in the soil, in compounds which can be taken up by the plant. Bacteria which are associated with the roots of certain plants can *fix* nitrogen in the soil in this way. Under certain conditions, they may fix as much as 600 kg of nitrogen in a hectare of soil each year.

- By the *drainage* of the area. When a soil is completely waterlogged, many of the bacteria which decompose organic matter cannot survive. Partly rotted plant and animal remains will gradually accumulate – they form a thick layer of black spongy material known as *peat*. There are many areas of peat in swamps and lagoons in the Caribbean; and the *pegasse* soils of Guyana contain a high proportion of peaty material.

8 Can leaching and illuviation take place in a waterlogged soil? Explain your answer.

- By the amount of *time* the soil-forming processes have been operating. Soils on beach sand or recent volcanic ash will not have a mature soil profile, because the soil-forming processes have not been operating on them for very long.

9 Besides beaches and areas of recent volcanic activity, where else will there be young soils which have not had time to develop a mature profile?

Soil fertility

Soils are often described as 'fertile' or 'infertile'; but these terms are not always very precise. Think about these two statements:

- The soils of the tropical forests are very fertile, because they can support an enormous variety of plants and animals, and the rate of plant growth is very high.
- Tropical forest soils are very infertile, because they produce low crop-yields when they have been cleared for agriculture, and deteriorate quickly until they can only grow a few weeds.

A soil is agriculturally productive if it has good physical and chemical properties. A good soil would:

- Be deep enough for plant roots to grow downwards without hitting solid rock.
- Be a *loam* soil with a good mix of sand, silt, and clay particles.
- Have a good crumb structure, with plenty of humus to hold the soil particles together.
- Retain water well in dry periods.
- Drain freely after heavy rain.

It would also:

- Have a good supply of the main plant nutrients.
- Contain enough clay minerals and humus to hold the nutrients for the plant roots to take up.
- Be free of concentrations of salt and other toxic substances.
- Be neither too acid nor too alkaline.

However, soil fertility is not fixed. Human activity is one of the most important influences on the quality of the soil.

10 How will soil be affected if:
(a) It is ploughed regularly for several years?
(b) Manure and organic matter are added to it?
(c) Leguminous plants are grown there?

9.4 Some soil types

Classifying soils

Because soil can vary so much over a short distance, it is very difficult to classify soils on a worldwide basis, or to draw a world soil map.

But because so many of the soil-forming processes are controlled by the climate and the vegetation, it will usually be possible to make some generalisations about the soils of a large natural region.

Zonal soils

Podzols and *chernozems* are referred to as *zonal* soils, because they are associated with a particular type of climate and vegetation. Zonal soils were first identified by Russian soil scientists in the nineteenth century.

Podzols are strongly leached, acid soils associated with the coniferous forests of Europe, Asia, and North America. The name is derived from a Russian word meaning ash-grey.

Chernozems are associated with temperate grasslands – with the prairies and the steppes. There is very little leaching of the soil profile in this environment, and a considerable amount of organic matter can accumulate in the soil. The word 'chernozem' comes from the Russian for 'black earth'.

There is a strong link between climate, soil, and vegetation. But, as we have seen, there are also other influences which cause soil to vary from place to place. Not all podzols are in coniferous forests. There are podzols associated with other types of temperate vegetation – and even some soils which closely resemble podzols on very sandy parent materials in areas of high rainfall in the tropics. In the coniferous forests, not every soil is a true podzol; and there are soils in the prairies and steppes which are not chernozems.

A podzol

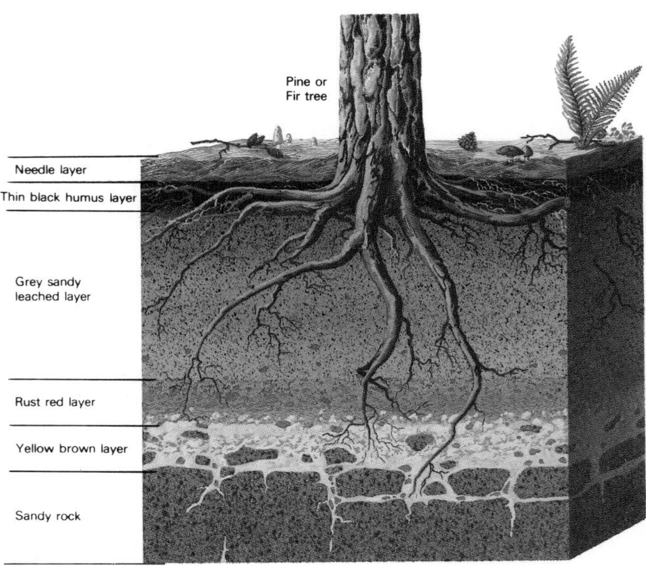

9.6 A podzol.

At the surface, there is a layer of pine needles and plant litter. The pine needles turn black as they decompose. Decomposition is quite slow, because of the cold climate, and because of the waxy surface of the needles. Below the needles, there is a layer of humus – which is quite acid, because of the chemical composition of the needles and the way they decompose.

Few earthworms can survive in an acid podzol. This means that the soil is not mixed up very much, and there is a sharp boundary between the different horizons.

The organic acids in the humus are dissolved by rainwater, and help to leach the layer below. Most of the 'A' horizon has been strongly leached, and contains very few nutrients. Almost all the clay minerals are broken down into iron and aluminium oxides, and are washed away. The sandy material which is left behind is very pale in colour, and very acid in its chemical reaction.

There is another sharp transition at the top of the 'B' horizon.

There is a considerable amount of illuviation, and some humus is deposited here, in combination with iron and aluminium oxides. This gives the soil a darker colour. In the B horizon there may also be a thin, hard layer of illuviated mineral compounds called an iron-pan.

The lower part of the 'B' horizon is stained reddish or yellow-brown by iron and aluminium oxides.

A chernozem

9.7 A chernozem.

The surface of the soil is covered with plant litter and dead grass, and the upper part of the soil is stained almost black by plant humus. Without the humus, the surface material of a chernozem would be pale grey in colour. There are also many plant roots in the upper part of the soil and the soil has a well-developed crumb structure.

There is just enough rainfall to leach out the harmful sodium and potassium salts, but other minerals, like calcium, can accumulate. The soil has a slightly alkaline reaction. Clay minerals do not break down in this environment, so the soil has quite a high clay content.

There are many earthworms and other burrowing animals. They mix up the soil, and there are no sharp changes in colour between the different horizons, but the lower part of the soil profile is paler in colour. Some calcium carbonate is washed down from the surface layers, and accumulates here in hard, pale lumps called *nodules*.

1 List four important differences between podzols and chernozems.
2 Are there any similarities between the two types of soil?
3 List the ways in which each of the soil-forming processes described in Section 9.2 has influenced the formation of these two types of soil.

Latosols

9.8 A latosol.

Well-drained soils in humid tropical climates are generally known as *latosols*.

In tropical environments, silicates and clay minerals break down far more quickly than in temperate climates. Silicates are generally leached out of the soil profile, but iron and aluminium compounds generally stay behind. The upper part of a podzol is white or grey because it consists mostly of silicates; but the upper part of a latosol is red or yellow because it contains a high proportion of iron and aluminium compounds.

In a latosol, there is usually a cover of plant litter but organic material decomposes very quickly. Partly rotted material and humus does not build up at the surface.

The upper part of the 'A' horizon may contain quite a lot of humus. It has a darker colour than the soil below but nutrients in the soil are quickly taken up by plant roots. Because there is a continuous supply of humus, the soil near the surface usually has a neutral reaction.

Salts are leached out of the soil very quickly because of the heavy rainfall; and most clay minerals break down very quickly. Those which do not break down are usually not so good at holding on to soil nutrients.

The lower part of the soil profile is quite acid and leaching extends quite a long way down the soil profile; there is no zone of illuviation where humus and other materials are deposited.

There is chemical weathering far below the surface in a humid tropical environment. Weathering may extend ten, twenty, or even a hundred metres below the surface.

There are many different types of latosol. The *ferrisols* which form on many recent volcanic rocks are generally very productive. But other latosols which form on old, highly weathered rocks, are much less fertile. Some latosols contain *laterite* or *ferricrete*, a hard brick-like substance which forms when all the silicate has been leached out. Laterite makes soil drainage and plant growth very difficult.

4 List four important differences between latosols and podzols.

5 Are there any similarities between the two types of soil?

Rendzinas

9.9 A rendzina.

Rendzinas are *intrazonal* soils. They are associated with a particular type of parent material – limestone. The influence of climate and vegetation on intrazonal soils is not so great.

Rendzinas are shallow, dark-coloured soils with a high proportion of organic matter. They generally have a good crumb structure, and are slightly alkaline in their reaction.

The soil is rich in humus and very dark in colour. Earthworms and other soil animals thrive in this environment. Because of this, the soil is well mixed.

In a rendzina there are often lumps of weathered limestone quite close to the surface and the pale colour of the parent rock contrasts sharply with the dark soil.

6 List four important differences between rendzinas and chernozems.

7 Are there any similarities between the two types of soil?

10 · MANAGING THE ENVIRONMENT

10.1 A traditional society

Styles of resource management

Look back to Section 1.1. We have seen how the natural environment can provide human society with a wide variety of resources; and how both renewable and non-renewable resources must be used carefully to avoid damaging the environment.

There are several different styles of resource use:

- Most traditional societies use a wide variety of resources from the natural environment; and use them in a way which does not usually upset the long-term balance of the ecosystem.
- Some modern institutions are organised in a way which allows them to go into an area and exploit one resource and earn a high profit for a few years, but does lasting damage to the environment. When the resource has been used up, they can move on.
- Modern scientific resource management looks at the natural environment as a whole. Many resources are used, including some which would not have been available to a society without the benefit of new technology. Renewable resources are used in a way which makes sure that they will be available in the future; and non-renewable resources are exploited carefully.

Amerindian subsistence farmers

Some Amerindian groups in Guyana still operate a system of *subsistence agriculture*. They use the resources of the area they live in to produce their own food and all the necessities of daily life. Almost everything used in this farming system is locally produced. The community is virtually self-sufficient.

The main farming method used is *shifting cultivation*. First of all a small area of forest is cleared. The vegetation is cut back in a period when the weather is dry, and then burnt. Burning kills off the weeds, and the ash which is left gives a boost to the fertility of the soil. Then the crops are planted. Cassava is the most important, but maize, bananas, yams, and sweet potatoes are also cultivated. The first harvest is generally a good one, but soil fertility declines rapidly as the nutrients and organic matter are leached out of the soil. Weeds also begin to establish themselves, and compete with the crops for the available nutrients. The second harvest is not so good. In most areas, the land cannot be cultivated successfully for more than two years in succession. After this, the land is abandoned, and a new area is cleared.

Abandoned clearings quickly revert to forest. This is because they are generally less than one hectare in size; and also because some of the original vegetation is left when the land is cleared. After twenty or thirty years, the fertility of the soil has been fully restored.

In many ways this is an efficient farming system:

- Very little *capital* is needed. No fertiliser or farm machinery has to be purchased.
- Very little *labour* is used. There is no ploughing, and little need for hand weeding.
- There is no permanent damage to the forest *environment*.

But shifting cultivation can only operate successfully where there is a large area of *land* available for clearing.

For the Amerindians, subsistence farming is not a 'job', but part of a way of life in which they cater for all their basic needs.

High protein foods Most of the crops grown are starchy foods, but the diet is varied and nutritious. Hunting and fishing are still important. Fish can be shot from the river bank with a bow and arrow, or trapped.

Housing Permanent village houses are solid, well-constructed waterproof dwellings which make use of the most suitable materials in the local environment. In the forests, they are built with a timber frame, bark walls, and a shingle roof.

Transportation The rivers are by far the best transport routes. There are many types of river craft. On land, loads of up to twenty kilos can be carried on the back in a basketwork container called a *warishi*.

Food processing The most important crop is bitter cassava, which must be carefully prepared before it is safe to eat. It is grated on an oblong board with sharp stone chips, then squeezed to extract the juice. The juice is poisonous when raw, but can be boiled to make cassareep, which is the preservative used to make pepperpot. The dry cassava meal is sifted, pounded and soaked. This produces cassava flour, which can be used to make cassava bread or baked dry to use as *farine*.

Crafts Pottery is made from local clay. There are large and small containers, beautifully shaped and decorated with animal figures or geometric patterns. These are used for cooking and storing food. There are also special earthenware water coolers. Basketwork is important, too. Some containers have several layers, and remain waterproof even when they are submerged in a river. Hammocks are also woven from homespun wild cotton, from palm fibre, and from silk grass.

1 List some of the goods which a small community like this *cannot* produce for itself.
2 Which of these goods are *necessities*?

Amerindian society today

Amerindian peoples have a distinctive language and culture. They have an unwritten literature, only some of which has been recorded; and traditions of music and dance are also an important part of their way of life. But of course not everything is perfect in the traditional way of life.

3 What are the advantages and disadvantages of the traditional Amerindian way of life?

Before the colonial period, the Amerindians were the only inhabitants of the Caribbean. Today they are only a small proportion of the population; but there are still substantial Amerindian communities in Guyana and Belize, and smaller groups in Dominica and Trinidad. Elsewhere, there are no 'pure' Amerindians; but many people who do not realise it have some Arawak or Carib ancestors.

Where there are Amerindian communities, their way of life is changing rapidly today. Some Amerindians live in towns or cities, or farm in relatively accessible areas growing crops for sale and earning a cash income. Others work in gold and diamond mining, or take jobs on cattle ranches in the Rupununi savannas. It is also possible to earn money by selling basketwork, hammocks, and other craft items.

10.1 An Amerindian house in a forest clearing.

With a cash income, manufactured goods can be bought. A hundred years ago, trees were felled with a stone axe; today axes are made of steel. Cutlasses are in common use. People with money can buy modern clothing, guns, medicines, and rum; and canoes can be driven by a powerful outboard motor.

10.2 Forest clearance

Destroying the rain forest

In Brazil, and elsewhere in the tropics, modern farmers have been clearing huge areas of rain forest with government help.

Large-scale cattle ranching has been introduced into Amazonia, because beef fetches a good price on the world market. But cattle are not originally rain forest animals. They eat grass; and grass does not grow well in the forest. So huge areas have been cleared of trees, and sown with grass. Some cattle ranches cover several hundred square kilometres; they are as large as one of the Windward Islands.

When the land is cleared like this, there is no way of maintaining soil fertility.

1 Read Section 8.2 again. Explain what effect removing the trees will have on:
(a) The temperature of the air near the ground.
(b) The humidity of the air near the ground.
(c) The supply of plant litter and organic matter.
(d) Leaching of minerals and nutrients.

When the trees are removed, the soil is *degraded* very quickly. All that is left in some areas is sandy and gravelly material that cannot hold water or nutrients for very long. Ploughing and cultivating the land simply make matters worse, and fertilisers do no good, either, as they are simply washed away from the surface horizons in the first heavy shower of rain. When a hard layer of laterite is formed, soil conditions are even worse.

A few years after it has been cleared for grass, an area that once supported a rich growth of forest plants will produce nothing but a few weeds. Many areas that were cleared in the 1950s and 1960s have already been abandoned. In these areas, it may take hundreds of years for the soil structure to recover.

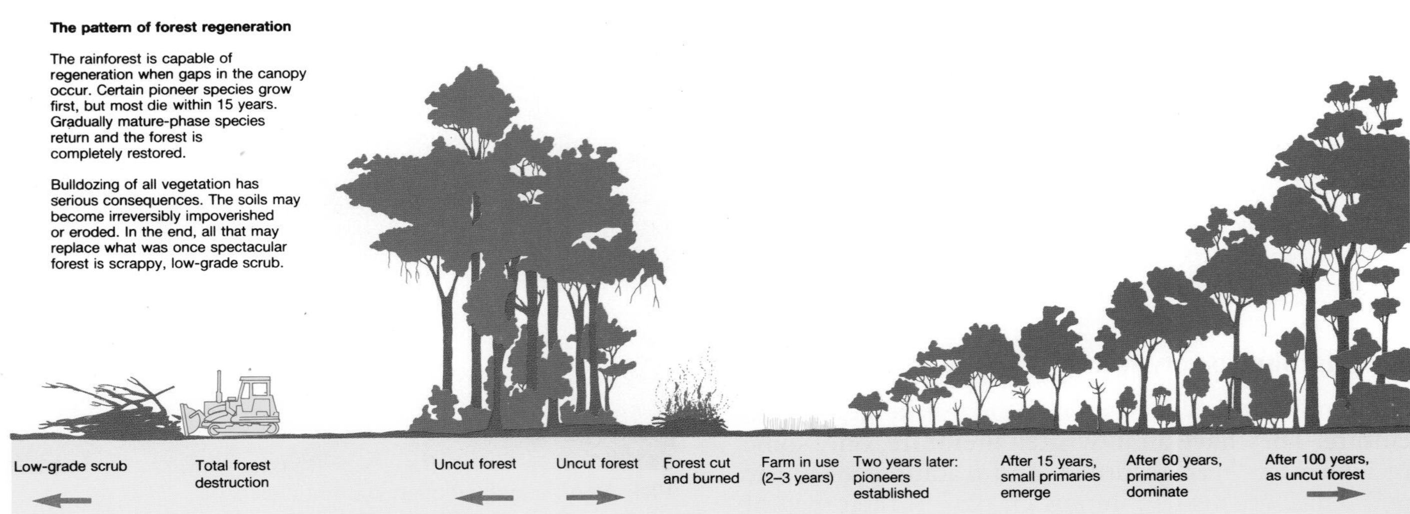

10.2 What happens when rain forest is destroyed.

It has been estimated that:

- About 15% of the earth's land surface was tropical forest in 1950.
- By 1975, the figure had fallen to 12%. About half of this was true rain forest.
- If clearing continues at the present rate, only 7% of the earth will be tropical forest in the year 2000.
- Most of the remaining forest may have gone by the year 2100.

In an average year, the area of forest which is destroyed throughout the world is about the same as a country the size of Guyana.

2 What can be done to protect the world's rain forests?

The human impact

When a rain forest area is taken over by modern settlers, there is often conflict between the newcomers and the tribal groups who live there. Conflicts like these are now going on in modern Brazil, in the areas which are being cleared for 'civilised' settlement. Even where there is no open confrontation, some of the worst damage may be done by well-intentioned missionaries, who undermine a group's sense of identity and self-respect.

In the past many tribal peoples were completely shattered by their first contact with modern society:

- In the nineteenth century, whole groups were hunted to extinction in Tasmania and Tierra del Fuego.
- In many Caribbean islands, the Amerindians were virtually wiped out by the effects of forced labour and imported diseases.
- The Amerindians of North America were systematically driven from their lands in the nineteenth century as successive treaties with them were broken by white settlers.

3 Imagine that you are a member of a small Amerindian group in northern Brazil. You have heard rumours about outsiders coming into your area, but so far your group has had no contact with them. Then one day some strangers appear; they are cutting down trees as the first stage in a road-building operation. You do not fully understand what they are doing, but they appear to be friendly and leave objects which seem to be gifts. How should your group react? Should you make contact, or move away as fast as you can, or attack with bows and arrows, or just wait quietly and see how the situation develops?

Forest plants: potential resources?

Many cultivated plants, including rubber, bananas, yams, and cocoa, originated as rain forest species. Many other plants produce drugs; a quarter of the medicines which doctors now prescribe originated in rain forest species. A few years ago, for example, it was found that a plant called the Rosy Periwinkle, which grows in Madagascar, can be used to treat children suffering from leukaemia. It has been suggested that the Amazon rain forest may contain the materials for many new anti-cancer drugs.

A wild form of maize has been found growing in a forest in Mexico. It is disease-resistant, and grows as a perennial. When it is crossed with cultivated maize, a new seed may be developed which will benefit farmers and consumers.

10.3 Amerindians exploited the rain forest for their own needs, such as canoes like this.

Research into new ways of using the rain forest without destroying it is now going on. It is hoped that this research can be applied before it is too late.

The Caribbean forests

Four hundred years ago, almost all the Caribbean islands were covered with rain forest, semi-evergreen forest, dry woodland, or mangrove. Today, most of the original forest cover has been removed, and the remaining woodland has almost all been altered by human activity:

- In Barbados, about half of the natural woodland was removed within twenty years of the first European settlement, and most of the rest had gone by the middle of the eighteenth century. The settlers cut down trees because they needed *land* for cultivation, *timber* for construction, and *firewood* for fuel. On the whole island, there is only one small area of about twenty hectares which has never been clear-felled.
- In Tobago, almost all the land was cleared for sugar plantations in the seventeenth and eighteenth centuries. Much of the land which was cleared can no longer be cultivated. But the original dry woodland has not grown back. Instead it has been replaced by thorn scrub.
- Guyana has much more forest left than any other Caribbean country. But even here, most of the coastal forest has been removed so that the land can be cultivated; many areas away from the coast have been used intensively for timber; and large areas have been completely cleared for bauxite mining.

4 Make a sketch map of an area about 5km across which you know personally. Using map evidence and your own knowledge, shade in the areas where the natural vegetation has been:
(a) Completely removed.
(b) Greatly altered by forestry, grazing, mining, or other activities.
(c) Left largely unchanged.

5 What are the *reasons* why natural vegetation has been removed or altered in your area?

10.3 Soil erosion

How soil erosion starts

The removal of the forest cover causes some very serious problems. Most of these problems are related to *soil erosion*.

It is quite normal for some soil to be removed from a hillside every year by the processes of mass wasting described in Section 4.6. Every year, a small amount of rock at the base of the soil profile will be broken up by weathering. This will replace the soil which is eroded, and the depth of the soil will remain the same.

1 Read section 4.6 again. Explain why rain action and mass wasting are very slow in a forest environment.

When land is cleared for cultivation, the soil is eroded much more quickly. The top 5 cm of soil may take anything from 200 to 5,000 years to form, depending on the climate, rock type, and the type of weathering; but this much soil can often be removed in ten years if too much bare earth is left exposed on sloping ground. When this happens, the soil is being used up like a non-renewable resource. It may produce good crops for a few years, but after that the land will be useless.

Soil is eroded in a number of different ways:

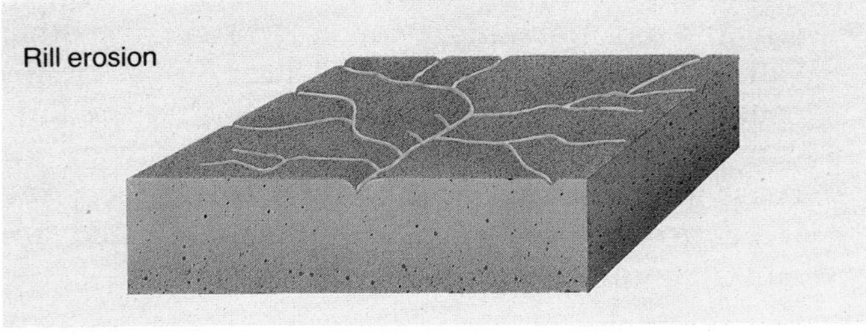

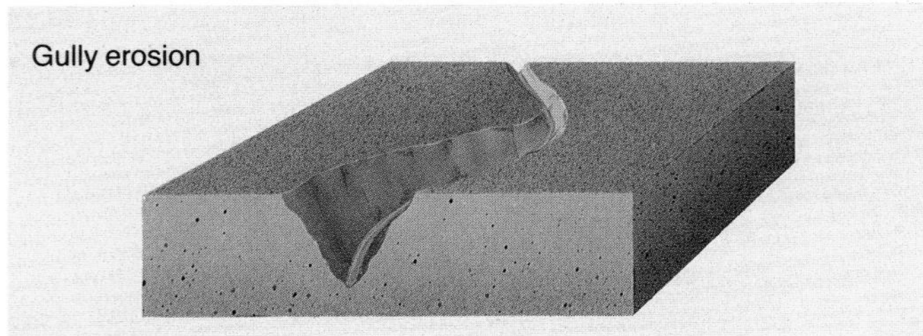

10.4 Sheet erosion, rill erosion and gully erosion.

- *Sheet erosion*: each storm takes away a thin layer of soil over a wide area. The farmer may notice that the soil seems to be getting lighter in colour, as the surface layer which contains most of the humus and organic matter is washed away; or it may seem as if 'rocks are growing' in the field, if sheet erosion exposes stones which were previously hidden from sight.
- *Rill erosion*: caused by rainwater flowing downhill in a small channel, carrying soil particles with it. At first, these small channels will disappear when the land is ploughed; but rill erosion may be the first stage in the development of gully erosion.
- *Gully erosion*: this starts when water flowing down a hillside cuts a deep channel through soft rock. Once a gully has formed, it branches out and spreads uphill very quickly. Soon a big area of land is completely useless.
- *Wind erosion*: this is a serious danger in dry areas, especially if the land is flat and there are no trees or natural windbreaks. The wind simply blows away fine soil particles in a 'dust storm'. Figure 10.8 shows the effects of serious wind erosion.

Soil erosion is not always noticed in its early stages; but by the time it is really obvious, it may be too late.

2 Read the paragraph on humus in Section 9.2. Explain why humus is important for maintaining the soil structure, and in helping the soil store water and plant nutrients.

The amount of humus in the soil will begin to decrease if land is badly farmed. When the humus content is too low, the soil will start to lose its structure. Instead of being stuck together in crumbs, the fine soil particles will separate. They will form a fine dust which can easily be washed away in a rainstorm or blown away by the wind.

Small farmers in Haiti

Like most Caribbean countries, Haiti is mountainous. Only about 20% of the land is flat. When Columbus discovered the island of Hispaniola, he described the mountains like this: 'All are most beautiful, of a thousand shapes, and all accessible, and filled with a thousand kinds of tall tree, and they even seem to touch the sky.'

3 Compare the landscape described by Columbus with the scenery shown in Figure 1.3.

As late as 1920, about 60% of Haiti was still covered with forest, and there was a thriving timber

10.5 Soil erosion in Haiti. Even though there has been some replanting in this area, and the land is cultivated in ridges, soil is still eroded rapidly on the steepest slopes.

industry which exported mahogany for making furniture. Today, almost all the forest has been removed. At most, 9% of the country is covered with low-grade woodland or thorn scrub. In many areas, it would be hard to find a full-grown mahogany tree still standing.

Haiti has a population of six million, which is still increasing by more than 100,000 every year.

Three-quarters of the people still live in the countryside; and the only work available for the rural population is small-scale farming. Most farmers grow vegetables, a cereal crop, beans, and coffee; they may also keep a few goats and chickens. The farms are very small. In Haiti, there are on average more than four people for every hectare of agricultural land. This means that there is barely enough food grown to feed the family, and very little surplus to sell.

The average income in rural Haiti has been estimated at around $50 US per person per year.

Under these conditions, small farmers are interested in making whatever short-term return they can from every patch of land:

- When there is any possibility of growing crops, the trees are cut down and uprooted so that the ground can be cultivated.
- Any small area of woodland which remains is used for firewood and making charcoal. About 10,000 people earn their living by making charcoal, which is the only fuel available for most rural families.
- Woodland and scrub are used for grazing goats. Goats will eat leaves, and will even chew at small branches. When there are too many goats, the land is *over-grazed* and the effect on the vegetation is devastating.

It has been estimated that a third of the land area of Haiti now shows the effects of extreme soil erosion or is completely sterile, and that a further 60 km^2 is lost every year.

The effects of soil erosion

When the soil has been badly eroded, the land will start to produce less. However hard a farmer works, the results will be worse and worse. Eventually, the land will not be worth cultivating. But loss of agricultural output is not the only problem related to soil erosion.

A river basin in Haiti

The Artibonite is the largest river in Haiti. Its river basin drains much of the centre of the country, and part of the Dominican Republic as well.

This river is an important resource. In 1956, the Peligre dam was built so that better use could be made of the river water for irrigation. In 1972, generators were installed at the dam, so that the energy of the river water could be used to generate electricity for the capital, Port au Prince.

The hill slopes in the upper part of the river valley

have been cleared for cultivation. This has caused a serious soil erosion problem. Because of soil erosion, the river carries more sediment than before, and the lake behind the dam has almost completely silted up. In dry weather, no electricity can be generated. During a drought in 1977, power was cut for five hours every day in Port au Prince for this reason. In a few years the dam will be useless.

Flooding is another result of the removal of the forest cover. A forested hillside soaks up the rain in wet weather, then releases it over a long period of time. It acts rather like a sponge. Rivers running through a well-wooded area do not dry up easily, and very rarely flood. They flow steadily, because water is always trickling into them from the soil along their banks. When the forest has been removed, there is a sudden rush of water straight after heavy rain; and then the river may dry up quite soon afterwards.

The maximum peak flow of a river after heavy rain is twice as high when a forest is replaced by cultivation, and four times as high when it is replaced by bare earth.

Flooding and soil erosion have damaged the irrigation system in the lower Artibonite valley. Floods damage the canals; then they are silted up by sediment. And when there is a drought, many of the irrigation canals simply dry up.

Many of the rural roads in Haiti become impassable in the wet season because of flooding. In Port au Prince, flood water from other rivers which drain the surrounding hills can drown people who live in slum areas near to watercourses, and leaves a thick layer of mud on main roads; but this does at least mean that officials in the capital have some idea of just how bad the soil erosion problem is.

Other Caribbean countries

There has been serious soil erosion in many other parts of the Caribbean. Some of the worst affected areas have been:

- The Yallahs River valley in Jamaica, where steep slopes were cleared for cultivation in a high rainfall area. The problem was particularly bad here because much of the land was used to grow coffee. This crop leaves most of the soil bare and exposed to the effects of rain action.
- The Scotland District of Barbados. In the past, sugar was grown here on steep slopes with unstable clays and soft rocks. These slopes are often affected by large-scale slumps and slides, as well as rainwash. They should not have been cultivated at all.
- The Northern Range in Trinidad is another area where there has been rapid soil erosion, caused by heavy rainfall on steep slopes which should never have been cleared for cultivation.

Soil erosion is not limited to areas with steep slopes. Even an area with quite a gentle slope can be affected if the soil is left exposed. In Barbados, there is only 50 cm of soil in many coral limestone areas where slopes are quite gentle. In some places, over 15 cm of this thin layer of soil has been washed away. Some agriculturalists are worried about the effects of replacing sugar cane, which protects the soil quite well, with crops like cotton and some vegetables, which do not.

4 On an outline map of the Caribbean, show the location of the three areas listed, and of any other areas where you know that there is a soil erosion problem.

Controlling soil erosion

There are many possible ways of reducing soil erosion in an area which is at risk:

- Land around a gully can be fenced in, and planted with grass and small trees.
- Check dams can be built across gullies to slow down the flow of water. Even a barrier of brushwood is of some use in a small gully.
- Steep hillsides can be terraced. Terraces convert a sloping hillside into a series of steps, so that rainwater does not rush straight downhill.
- Some crops can be grown in ridges, which run along the slope, and also prevent water from running straight downhill. Ridges are rather like small-scale terraces. They are much easier to construct, but do not work very well on a really steep slope.
- When the land is ploughed, furrows which run straight up and down the slope are disastrous, because they actually encourage the formation of rills and gullies. Contour ploughing, which follows the slope of the land, is much less damaging.
- A suitable cropping pattern is probably the most important conservation measure of all. It is much better to plant a mixture of different crops, rather than one single crop, which will leave the soil completely unprotected after the harvest.
- Planting different crops in strips which run along the contours is also useful. When one crop has been harvested, only a narrow band of soil will be left exposed; the runoff water will not be able to gather speed or do any real damage.
- Tree crops are very useful, because their roots help to stabilise the soil all the year round. It is also a good idea to plant a cover crop to protect the soil on land which has just been harvested. Before the next crop is planted, the cover crop can be fed to animals or ploughed back into the soil.
- The farmer should also try to maintain the amount of humus in the soil. Soil which has a good crumb

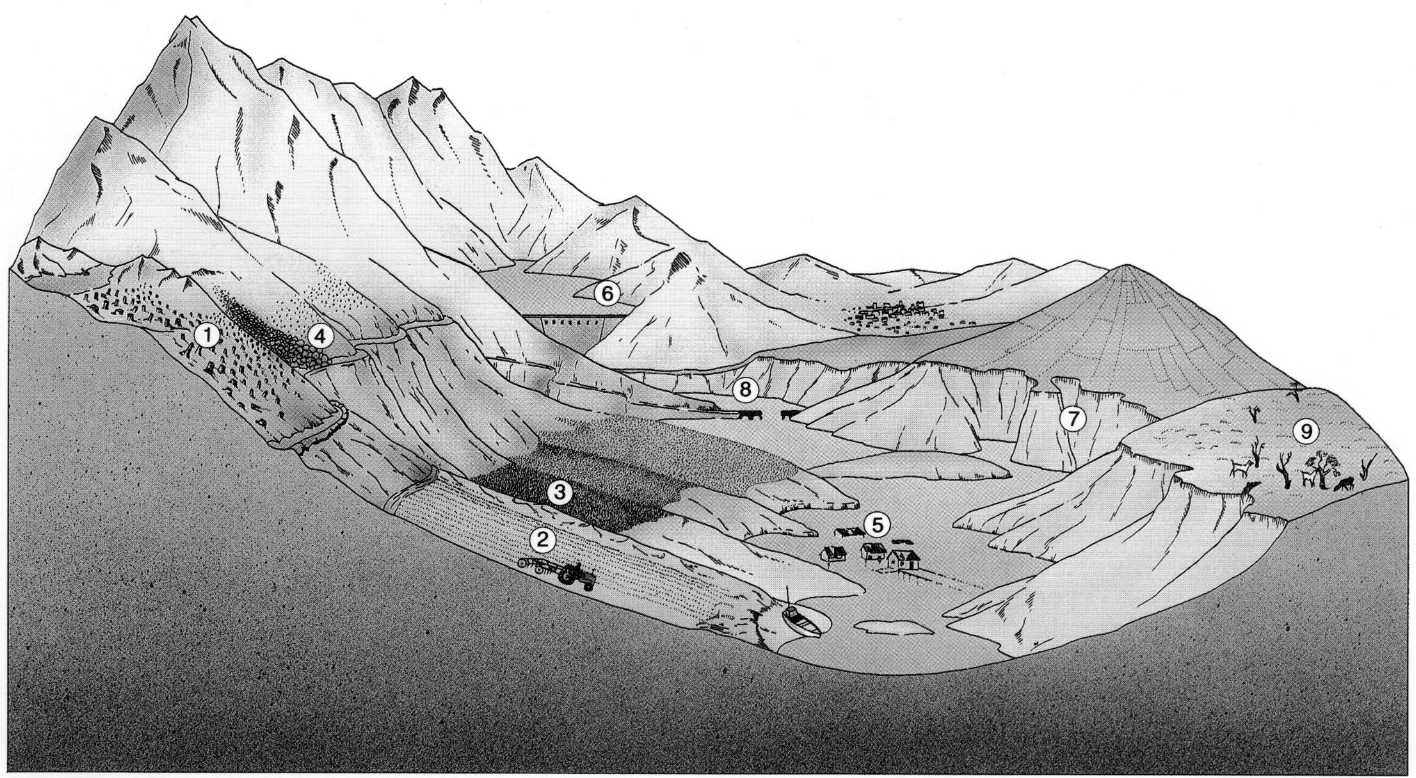

10.6 Soil erosion and its results.

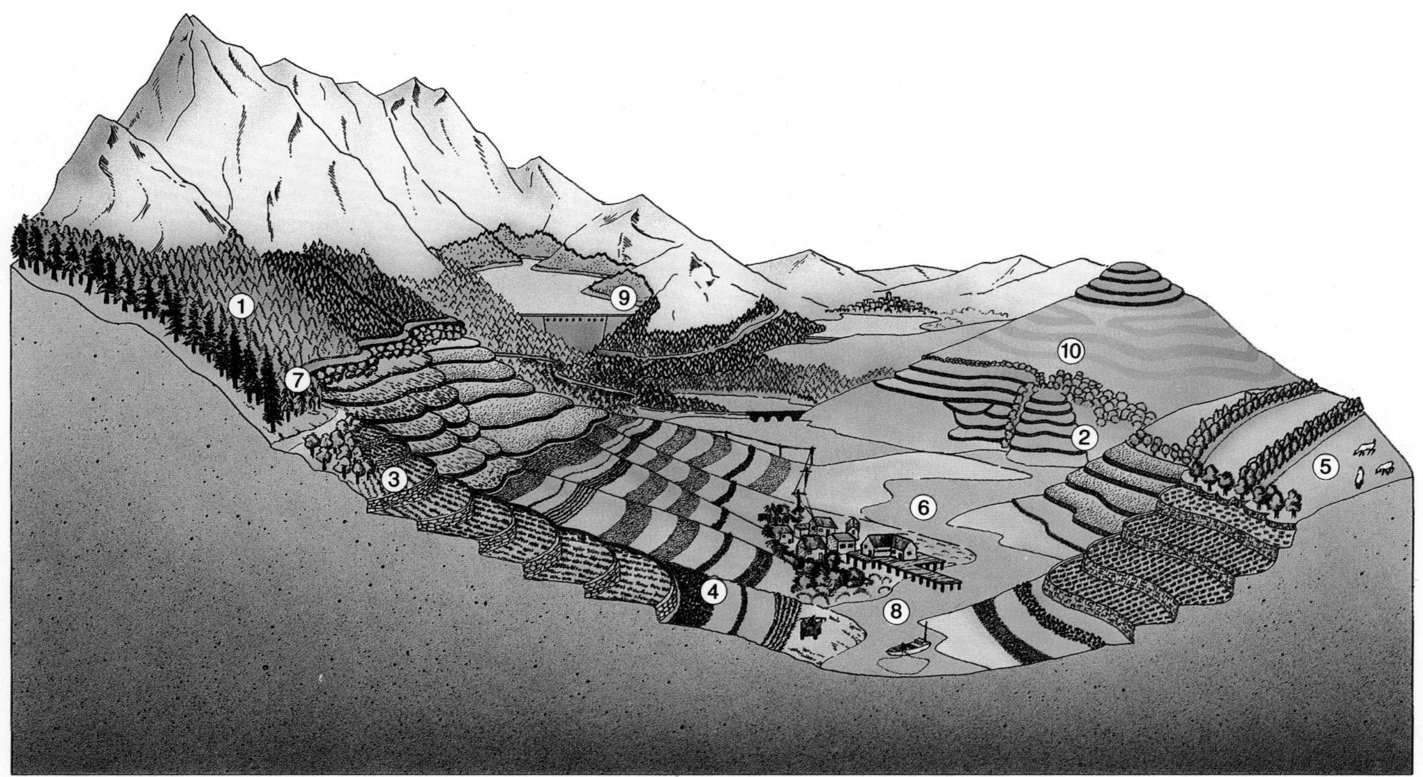

10.7 Controlling soil erosion.

structure is much less likely to be eroded by the wind or the rain.
- Some areas are simply not suitable for cultivation at all. On very steep slopes, the land should be used for pasture, or, in some cases, forest.

Some of these erosion control methods can achieve spectacular results. An experiment at Smithfield in the parish of Hanover in Jamaica showed that when yams were grown on a steep slope, the soil loss was:
- 135 tonnes of soil per hectare when they were planted in lines running up and down the slope.
- 17 tonnes per hectare when the yams were grown in terraces.

Unfortunately, the most effective soil conservation methods are often expensive to adopt:
- Making ditches and waterways on land with a 7–15° slope can reduce soil erosion by ⅔.
- Building full-scale bench terraces reduces erosion by ⅚; but it costs three times as much.

It is easy to implement an ideal soil conservation programme on a small experimental plot. It is much less easy to persuade many thousands of small farmers to adopt the same conservation methods on their holdings.

5 Which methods of soil erosion would be most expensive?
6 Which would be easier for a small farmer to adopt?
7 Look at Figure 10.6:
(a) Describe the poor farming and land-use practices at each of these numbers: 1, 2, 3, 9.
(b) Describe the effect that soil erosion is having on agricultural land, communications, water resources, and settlement at each of these numbers: 4, 5, 6, 7, 8.
8 Look at Figure 10.7
(a) List the soil conservation methods which are shown at each of these numbers: 1, 2, 3, 4, 5, 10.
(b) Describe the beneficial effects of soil conservation at each of these numbers: 6, 7, 8, 9.
9 Make a sketch in your exercise book to illustrate:
(a) Terracing.
(b) Contour ploughing.
(c) A check dam.
(d) A good cropping pattern.

Controlling soil erosion in Haiti

In the past, it has proved very difficult to control soil erosion in Haiti:
- Check dams and terraces are expensive to build. Farmers do not have the money for this sort of construction activity.
- Governments have often been corrupt and inefficient, and have made very poor use of the limited resources available.
- There are very few people in Haiti with an advanced training in agriculture, who can give practical advice in the field to small farmers.
- There are laws to limit tree-cutting and the making of charcoal; but as there is no other source of fuel in rural areas, these laws are impossible to enforce.
- Peasant farmers are mainly concerned with making sure that their families have enough food to get through the next week. Conserving trees and soil to maintain production in ten years' time may sound like rather an abstract objective.

A few check dams were built by farmers and overseas aid agencies; but there were not nearly enough, and those that were constructed were mostly damaged by flooding. And when trees were planted on unused land, they were very quickly eaten back by goats.

More recently, the Pan-American Development Foundation has started a programme which aims to persuade peasant farmers to plant and care for trees which can be used as a *cash crop*. Peasant farmers who take part in the scheme must agree to plant at least 250 trees on their own land. The aim is for the trees to be planted in cultivated areas, where they will be protected from goats. The trees chosen are species which will be useful to the farmer, such as:
- *Leucaena*: this is a Mexican species which can grow up to 10 m in three years. The leaves and small branches can be fed to small animals, and the roots of the tree fix nitrogen in the soil. The seedlings establish themselves very easily, and the tree can also be *coppiced*; if it is cut back, new shoots will grow from the stump. Leucaena is a good source of fuelwood and charcoal.
- *Casuarina*: this tree originated in Australia, but is now quite common in the Caribbean. It will grow on poor soil. The wood makes good charcoal, and can be used for rafters.

Under good conditions, a tree can produce $1.50 US worth of charcoal in four years. The farmer will earn money from a tree crop like this if it is properly looked after.

10 Work out the cash value of 250 fully grown trees after four years.

The young trees are provided free, because they are quite cheap to grow, and because the project brings long-term benefits to the whole community.

In the first five years of the project, almost 20 million young trees were planted; and, unusually for tree-planting schemes in Haiti, most of the seedlings survived and began to grow. The project aims to spread the idea that trees can be a useful cash crop. However, it still has a long way to go. It is estimated that the equivalent of 40 million trees are cut down for use as wood and charcoal every year.

11 What are the advantages and disadvantages of this method of controlling soil erosion?

10.4 Soil erosion in the USA

It is not only developing countries which suffer from soil erosion. In the USA, it is estimated that:

- One-third of the total volume of soil in the country has been lost in the four centuries since commercial farming began. Most of this soil has been lost in the last hundred years.
- One-third of the agricultural land now has a serious soil erosion problem. About three billion tonnes of soil are lost through wind and water erosion every year.

Some of the worst soil erosion occurred in the dry grasslands of Oklahoma in the 1930s.

When these areas were first opened for settlement, in the late nineteenth century, they had rich chernozem soils with a high humus content. Rainfall was low, but *dry farming* produced very good crops; after each harvest, the soil was left fallow for one year before a new crop was planted. During this period, the ground was tilled to keep it free of weeds, and to retain moisture. This worked well for about forty years; but the humus content of the soil was falling all the time.

10.8 Wind erosion in Oklahoma in the 1930s.

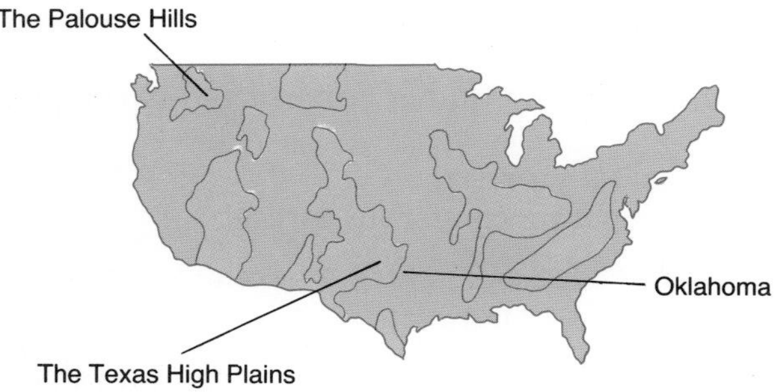

10.9 The areas where soil erosion is worst in the USA.

The soil began to lose its crumb structure, and became more like a fine powdery dust. Then there was a series of dry years, and the effects were disastrous. The loose soil was simply blown away every year by the wind. One four-day storm in 1934 removed 300 million tonnes of soil, and darkened the sky as far away as New York. Even in the Atlantic Ocean, thick deposits of dust had to be cleaned off the decks of ships.

Where soil erosion is worst

Figure 10.9 shows the areas where soil erosion is worst today. These include:

- The High Plains of Texas. About 17% of US soil erosion is in this state.
- The Palouse Hills of Washington State. About 80,000 ha of the Palouse has lost most of its topsoil.

Soil erosion is fastest where:

- There are large quantities of unconsolidated sediment.
- Crops like tobacco or cotton leave most of the soil bare, even while they are growing.
- The rainfall pattern is uncertain.
- There are wide treeless plains with no *windbreaks*.
- There are steep slopes which encourage rain erosion.

It is most dangerous where any of these factors are present:

- The soil is very thin, and hard bedrock will be exposed very quickly.
- The 'B' and 'C' horizons are much less fertile than the 'A' horizon.
- There is a hard layer such as an iron-pan, or an accumulation of calcium carbonate below the surface, which will be exposed by soil erosion.

10.10 Soil conservation measures in the mid-west of the USA.

The situation today

Many farmers in high-risk areas now take care to reduce the amount of soil erosion:

- Land which was not suitable for cereal crops has now been returned to pasture.
- Contour ploughing, strip cropping, and terracing are now encouraged.
- Some dry areas are now irrigated. Many parts of Oklahoma now grow grain again, because farmers can pump up groundwater which accumulated in rainy periods during the ice ages.
- Many farmers now use 'conservation tillage': the land is not ploughed; weeds are killed with herbicides; and the new crop is sown under the stubble from the previous harvest.

Not everyone is agreed on how serious the soil erosion problem is in the USA today.

There is an optimistic view:

'We know enough today to make sure that a disaster like the dustbowl of the 1930s can never happen again. Responsible farmers now all use good soil conservation practices; and modern fertilisers mean that many soils are actually more productive than ever before.

'Most parts of the country do not really have a soil erosion problem; and even where there is erosion, material is simply being moved around from one place to another, which does not matter very much. The best soils are several metres thick, so the loss of a few centimetres from the top does not matter very much. Anyway, erosion is a natural process; there is no way it can be stopped completely.'

And there is a pessimistic view:

'In some places, soil erosion is now much too fast to cope with; many areas will soon be completely useless for farming, if they have not been wrecked already.

'Using fertilisers just masks the problem. If there is no humus to hold the nutrients, they will be leached out of the soil very quickly. "Conservation tillage" is dangerous, because it encourages farmers to use large quantities of herbicides when we do not know enough about their long-term effects. And irrigation water from the ice ages is a non-renewable resource which we should be using very carefully indeed.

'Large-scale modern machinery makes contour ploughing very difficult; many farmers now plough up and down the slope again.

'Whenever cereal prices are high, people still plough up dry land which should really be left under grass.'

1 Why might a prosperous commercial farmer use methods which encourage soil erosion?

2 Compare the soil erosion problem in the USA and Haiti under these headings:
(a) Causes of soil erosion.
(b) Types of soil erosion.
(c) Ways of preventing soil erosion.
(d) The present situation.

10.5 Wood

The uses of wood

The Amerindians relied on forest products for all their needs: for food, clothing, and shelter.

We still rely on the forests for one major raw material – wood.

Wood is used:

- For construction.
- For making paper
- For making cardboard and other packaging materials.
- For fuel, and for making charcoal.
- As a source of cellulose for making artificial fibres.
- And for many other purposes.

1 List five objects in the room where you are sitting which are made out of wood.

2 Could any of these objects have been made out of another raw material instead?

Worldwide, over three billion cubic metres of wood is cut every year. This would be enough to bury the island of Barbados with a pile of timber seven metres high.

It has been estimated that the demand for timber for paper-making, industry, and construction will *double* over the next fifty years.

Where wood is produced

Most of the world's timber comes from two types of forest:

- Tropical rain forests.
- Cold temperate coniferous forests.

3 Read Sections 8.2 and 8.4 again. What are the main differences between these two types of forest?

Figure 10.11 gives some statistical information about some of the world's main timber-producing countries, and about some Caribbean timber-producers.

	Total wood production (000m^3)	Percentage of world production	Percentage used for fuel and charcoal	Plywood production (000m^3)	Paper production (000 tonnes)	Balance of trade in timber and wood products ($1,000,000 US)
Some major world producers						
USA	438,000	14	23	18,000	62,000	4,900 net imp.
India	239,000	8	92	180	2,000	200 net imp.
Brazil	222,000	7	74	900	3,800	850 net exp.
Canada	161,000	5	4	1,800	14,200	10,500 net exp.
Sweden	53,000	2	8	66	6,900	4,650 net exp.
Japan	33,000	1	2	7,300	19,300	5,415 net imp.
Nigeria	92,000	3	92	65	15	200 net imp.
Some Caribbean producers						
Belize	164	..	77	–	–	1 net imp.
Cuba	3,130	..	88	2	110	190 net imp.
Dominican Republic	970	..	99	–	9	59 net imp.
Guyana	200	..	6	–	–	In balance
Haiti	5,800	..	96	–	–	5 net imp.
Jamaica	117	..	32	–	18	48 net imp.
Trinidad and Tobago	57	..	28	–	–	132 net imp.
World total	3,050,000	100	52	44,000	188,000	

Source: FAO Yearbook of Forest Products, 1984.

10.11 World wood production.

4 Which of the countries listed produce more than 100 million m^3 of timber?
5 Which produce timber mainly from coniferous forests?
6 Which produce timber mainly from tropical forests?
7 Which use most of their production for fuel and charcoal?
8 Which produce more than 1 million tonnes of paper?
9 Which three Caribbean countries produce most timber?
10 What proportion of world production do these three countries account for?
11 What do these three countries use most of their timber production for?
12 Which of the countries in the table are industrial countries? Which are low-income countries?

The last column shows the balance of trade in timber, sawn wood, wood pulp, paper, and similar products. Some of the countries are net exporters; others import more than they export.

13 Which countries are net exporters of timber and wood products?

14 Guyana exports every year wood to the value of more than $6m. US. What wood products does Guyana import?

15 Figure 10.12 shows total wood output for seven of the world's leading timber-producing countries. Use the information in Figure 10.11 to construct a bar graph showing the paper production for these six countries. Do not forget to *label* your graph properly, include a *scale*, and show the *source* of your information.

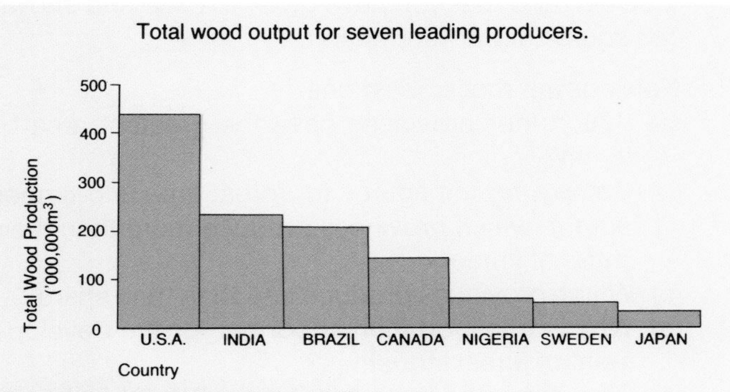

10.12 Total wood output for seven leading producers.

A renewable resource

In principle, forests are a renewable resource. In a properly managed forest, new trees are planted every year to replace the ones which are cut. Timber production can be maintained at a constant level.

Some countries have even increased their production because they have planted with young trees land that was previously unproductive. Trees can be grown like a crop, so that they are protected while they are growing and harvested when they are mature.

Elsewhere, forests are exploited in a destructive way. Huge areas are felled. All the trees are cut down, and no attempt is made to provide for the future.

10.6 Forestry in Canada

Canada is one of the world's leading exporters of timber and forest products.

These industries play an important role in the Canadian economy:

- Over 45,000 people are employed in lumbering. This is only 0.4% of the Canadian labour force; but there are also more than 200,000 jobs in industries like pulp and paper-making which are directly connected to forestry.
- More than 3,000 communities across Canada are one-product towns, which are more or less totally dependent on lumbering and forest industries.
- Canada is the world's largest exporter of wood pulp and newsprint. Timber and wood products make up 12% of Canada's exports.

Forest industries are well developed in Canada, because:

- Canada has a vast area of forest; more than 4.4 million km^2, or 45% of the country.
- There are large stands of useful species which are relatively easy to exploit.
- Most coniferous forest trees have tall, straight trunks, so they are easy to transport, and easy to cut into useful lengths as required.
- Most of the coniferous species are ideal for pulp and paper-making.
- Canada is a developed country, with a good transport network. The capital and the technical knowledge needed to set up successful timber-processing industries were available.

There are three types of forest in Canada. These are:

- The northern coniferous forests of the Canadian Shield.
- The temperate deciduous forests.
- The western coastal forests.

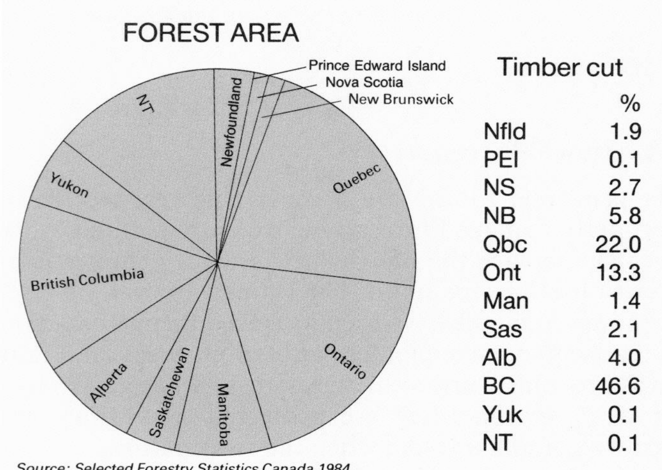

Timber cut	%
Nfld	1.9
PEI	0.1
NS	2.7
NB	5.8
Qbc	22.0
Ont	13.3
Man	1.4
Sas	2.1
Alb	4.0
BC	46.6
Yuk	0.1
NT	0.1

10.13 Proportion of forest area in Canadian provinces and territories. (Inset table shows % of timber cut.)

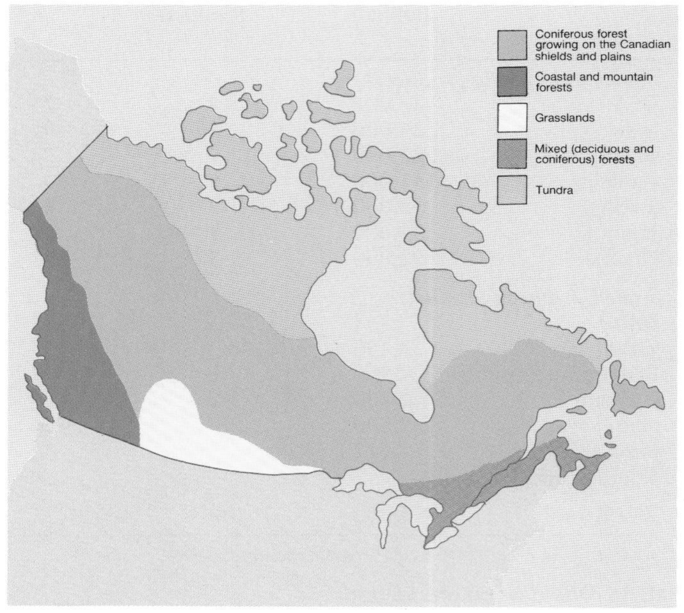

10.14 Forest areas in Canada.

The coastal forests of British Columbia consist mainly of coniferous trees. But the climate here is much rainier than that of the Canadian Shield, and the growing season is longer. This means that biomass productivity is much higher. A tree may grow to a height of 40 m in 75 years in the coastlands of British Columbia; in Saskatchewan or Manitoba, trees would grow only 18 m over the same period. Douglas firs, which grow near to the Pacific coast, can reach 80 m in height. They have tall, straight trunks and are very easy to saw.

1 In Figure 10.13, there is a divided-circle diagram, which shows the proportion of the forest area of Canada which is in each of the twelve provinces and territories. Use the information in the table to construct a second divided-circle diagram, showing the proportion of total timber output in each of these areas. Make sure that your diagram is properly labelled, and that you have given it a *title* and shown the *source* of the information.

2 Now answer these questions:
   (a) Which four provinces have the greatest area of forest?
   (b) Comparing the figures for forest *area* and timber *output*, which provinces produce more than their share of timber?
   (c) Which provinces produce less than their share?
   (d) Why is transportation important for the development of forest industries?
   (e) Give *two* reasons why British Columbia has a much higher output than the Northwest Territories.

Forest management

More than 90% of the productive forest area of Canada is owned by provincial and federal governments. This means that it should be possible to manage these forests in the public interest, so that they are used as a renewable resource. Government agencies use air photographs and ground surveys to assess the quality of the timber in the areas they manage, and then sell private companies the right to extract wood from a specified stretch of forest within a given period. Planned harvesting of trees should allow the forests to be managed on the basis of a *sustained yield*:

- If it takes 80 years for a tree to reach its full size.
- And 1/80 of the forest area is felled every year,
- By the time the last stretch of forest has been cut, the first will have grown back to maturity.
- So the yield of timber can be maintained indefinitely.

Even so, there are worries about the management of the Canadian forests – and there have been for some time.

'The sight of immense masses of timber passing my window every morning constantly suggests to my mind the absolute necessity for looking into the future of this great trade. We are recklessly destroying the timber of Canada, and there is scarcely a possibility of replacing it.'

(Sir John A. Macdonald in 1871)

'One-eighth of Canada's productive forest has deteriorated to the point where huge tracts lie devastated, unable to regenerate a merchantable crop within the next 60 to 80 years. Every year some 200,000 to 400,000 ha of valuable forest are being added to this shameful waste.'

(The Science Council of Canada in 1983)

Even a hundred years ago, it was clear that the 'unlimited' forest reserves of North America were actually finite and needed to be used carefully. But for a logging company concerned about next year's profits or a politician who is concerned to create jobs and cut taxes before the next election, increasing production now may seem more important than safeguarding future supplies which will be used in eighty years' time.

Replanting

If an area of cleared forest is left, the first trees to establish themselves are often birch and aspen. These deciduous trees produce light seeds, which can be blown a long way by the wind. They also grow well in an open, sunny environment. Unfortunately, they are not nearly as valuable for timber as the coniferous species.

There are two ways of solving this problem:

10.15 Using a chain saw.

- A cutting pattern which avoids clearing a large area at any one time helps the process of natural regeneration.
- Some areas of cleared forest are replanted with seedlings of productive tree species.

Unfortunately, replanting is expensive. The replanted areas have to be fertilised, weeded, kept free of pests, and later thinned; and there is no financial return for many years. It is planned to increase the amount of replanting in the near future, but at present:

- 800,000 ha of forest are cut every year.
- Only 200,000 ha are properly seeded or replanted.

Clear-felling and selection cutting

The easiest way to extract timber is to cut all the trees in a section of forest at once, leaving only a few areas on steep slopes or on river banks.

In some types of mixed forest, trees are taken out by selection cutting. Fully grown trees of one or two species are used; the rest are left to continue growing.

3 Explain why clear-felling:
  (a) Makes better use of forest roads.
  (b) Reduces transport costs.
  (c) Disrupts wildlife more than selection cutting.
  (d) Increases the risk of soil erosion.

About 80% of the timber obtained in Canada is extracted by clear-felling.

Mechanisation

One reason why the industry employs only a small proportion of Canada's workforce is that the advanced

10.16 Moving lumber.

machinery and equipment which is now in use allows one person to do what would in the past have been the work of several men:

- Mechanical feller-bunchers can grip a tree, cut it, and stack it; then bunch several trees together and transport them to a collecting point.
- Skidders (specially designed vehicles with huge rubber wheels) can pull tree trunks to a forest road.
- In the sawmills, there is electronic equipment to control the sawing, trimming, and drying of the wood; lumber sorting is also automated.

The average output per worker is 46% higher in British Columbia than in the adjacent regions of the USA.

Cutting waste

One way of increasing production without damaging the environment is to cut down on waste:

- Small fragments of wood are used to make products like particle board and wood pulp. Half the wood used for paper-making is now wood chips, reject lumber, or sawmill residue.
- Waste wood, sawdust, and bark can also be used to generate electricity.
- The stump of the tree is cut much lower than before. Only 30 cm is usually left behind.
- Pests and diseases destroy timber equivalent to 11% of the annual cut. Pests are controlled by chemical spraying; or in a safer and more efficient way by introducing bacteria, parasites, or predators which cut down the pests through *biological control.*
- Forest fires destroy timber equivalent to 8% of the annual cut. Landsat data are now used to predict where fires are likely to start; to find them once they have started there are infra-red scanners which can detect a burning cigarette from a helicopter flying at 300 m. 'Water bomber' aircraft can then be used to put out the fire.

4 Explain why:
(a) Using the forest as a non-renewable resource can bring high profits for a few years.
(b) Forest conservation is expensive.
(c) Forest conservation is essential for the future of the industry.

5 What is the best way of ensuring that good conservation practices are adopted?

Acid rain: a threat to the forests?

Forests are not just useful sources of an important raw material. They are places where people can go to relax, and enjoy a peaceful outdoor environment. Unfortunately, many stretches of forest are now threatened by distant industrial pollution.

Electricity generating stations, metal smelters, and diesel engines produce emissions of waste products like sulphur dioxide and nitrogen oxides. Near to the source, there will be a plume of dirty-looking 'smoke' and perhaps an unpleasant smell in the air. At a distance, the air usually *looks* clean; but chemicals may be producing weak acids which change the nature of the rainfall over a wide area. About two million km^2 of North America now receives rainfall which is about ten times as acid as unpolluted rain.

It is easy to miss the signs of acid rain damage when the problem is in its early stages. But by the time the signs are obvious, it may be too late.

In some parts of Europe, about a third of the forest area consists of dead and dying trees because of acid rain pollution.

It should be possible to cut the emissions which cause acid rain at source, by using cleaner fuels, or by burning them in a different way.

Nobody knows how much this would cost, but it would not be cheap. It has been estimated that for the USA, cutting sulphur dioxide emissions by 10 million tonnes would cost between $2.5 billion and $4.7 billion per year.

6 Should expensive measures to control acid rain pollution be adopted? Explain your answer carefully.

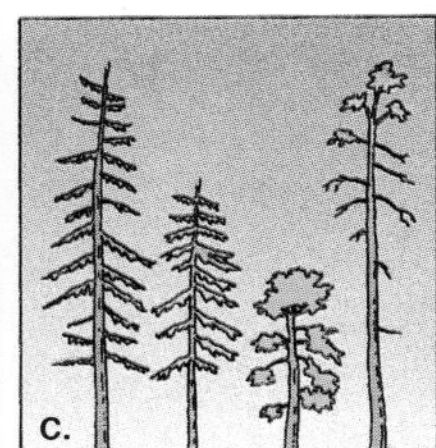

10.17 The effects of acid rain.

10.7 Forestry in Guyana

Most of Guyana is covered with forest, but the *natural* and *human* environment has not been ideal for the extraction of lumber and the development of forest industries:

- Most Guyanese forests are mixed tropical rain forests. There are few large stands where a single species is the *dominant* tree over several square kilometres.
- Loggers who are interested in only a few of these species have to travel a long way before they can extract a worthwhile amount of timber.
- This means that a much greater length of forest road and trail is needed to get each cubic metre of timber out of the forest than in countries like Canada.
- The Guyanese rivers provide the main transport routes to the interior; but they are interrupted by rapids and waterfalls, so long-distance river transport is not easy.
- There is no pulp and paper industry, and other wood-processing industries are not nearly so well-developed as they are in Canada.

Trees and their uses

Every type of tree grows in a distinctive way, and produces wood of a particular type.

For some purposes, like making charcoal, it does not matter very much what type of tree is used. Charcoal is generally made from low-grade timber from the more accessible areas.

But for many purposes, there are only certain types of wood which can be used. These types of timber fetch much higher prices; they are the ones which are sought out by the loggers, and which are easiest to sell on the export market:

- In the very early days of the logging industry, the most important products were logwood, which was used for making dye, and letterwood, which was used for printing.
- Wallaba has a straight grain and can be split easily. It also resists rot. This means that it is useful for making transmission poles, posts, and shingles.
- Crabwood and purple heart are decorative woods which are easy to work. They are suitable for making good-quality furniture.
- Greenheart is a very dense wood, which sinks in water. It does not rot easily, and is resistant to termites. This means that it is suitable for flooring and construction. It is used throughout the world for marine construction. More than half of the wood exported from Guyana is greenheart.

To broaden the base of the industry, an attempt is now being made to interest buyers in other types of timber. This will mean that more timber can be extracted and sold from each hectare of forest. It will make logging operations easier to run.

The importance of transportation

Transport difficulties have held back the development of the logging industry in Guyana:

- In the early days of the industry, logs were pulled to the river bank by a group of 12–16 men working together. Smaller logs were placed on the ground as rollers, to make the job less difficult; but this was back-breaking work, and wood could not be extracted more than 1 km from the river.
- When oxen were used, a little later, logs could be dragged further. It was worth while to fell trees up to 3 km from the river bank.
- From the 1920s, the largest concerns started using winches, pulling the logs along on a wire rope with a truck engine or an agricultural tractor. Logs could be transported for 5–10 km, using a series of different winching points.
- A few years later, the first real forest roads were made. Trucks and trailers could take the logs direct to the sawmill. The first trucks and trailers were economically viable up to a distance of about 20 km.
- Logging was also extended further up the rivers. With careful organisation and timing, it was possible to transport timber through the rapids on some of the major rivers.
- Large logging concerns now use many different types of heavy machinery, such as bulldozers, road construction equipment, and heavy trucks. It can be profitable to transport timber overland for up to 100 km.

10.18 Some logs can be floated to the sawmill.

Today, about 25% of the forest area of Guyana is accessible for logging. But in any one year, only about 70 km^2 is actually used. This is a tiny fraction of the accessible area.

Extracting timber

These are the main operations in the logging industry today:

- *Felling*: a fully grown tree is cut with a chain saw. Only large trees of the most useful species are felled. When an area is logged, about 10–15% of the timber is removed.
- *Bucking*: the smaller branches are cut off, so that the main trunk can be moved more easily.
- *Stumping and skidding*: the log is dragged to a loading-point on a forest road. It is either pulled by a skidder, or else winched by tractor. Only the largest logging companies use skidders.
- *Loading*: the logs are loaded onto a four-wheel-drive truck.
- *Road transportation*: forest roads are narrow mud tracks where driving conditions are very difficult. Trucks wear out very quickly. In some parts of Guyana, logs are taken all the way to the sawmill by road.
- *River transportation*: river transport is not easy in Guyana, because rapids, rocks, and sandbanks make it difficult to use large boats; and many hardwood logs will not float on their own. On the most difficult stretches of river, 4 to 6 logs are taken along by a small wooden boat called a *ballahoo*. Elsewhere, larger vessels called *punts* can transport about ten times as much timber. On the lower part of the river, larger operators use big steel *pontoons*.

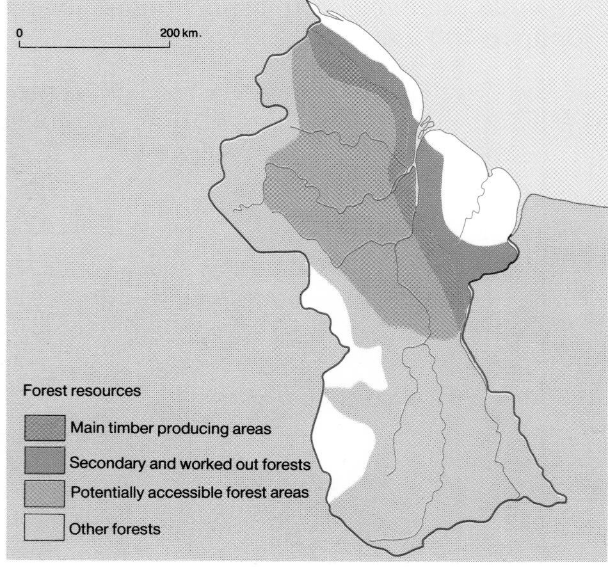

10.19 Main forest areas in Guyana.

1 How many of these operations are concerned with transportation?
2 Every time a log is loaded onto a truck or a boat, the cost is increased. Why is this?

Where timber is extracted

Figure 10.19 shows the main forest areas of Guyana.

3 What do you notice about the distribution of:
   (a) Secondary and worked-out forests?
   (b) The main timber-producing areas?
   (c) The potentially accessible areas, which will be the next areas to be used?
   (d) The other forests, which are unlikely to be cut on a large scale in the near future?

Working conditions

Loggers have to work in remote areas, sometimes several hundred kilometres from the nearest town. They have to use chain saws, bulldozers, and heavy trucks in difficult conditions for long periods. This makes the industry a very difficult one to work in.

4 Explain why:
   (a) Accidents and injuries are common, unless careful precautions are taken.
   (b) It is difficult to keep equipment in good condition.
   (c) It can be difficult to attract skilled and experienced workers to the industry.

Forest management

When all the trees from the most valuable species are extracted over a large area the forest may become *degraded*. The pattern of regrowth is badly disrupted. The valuable trees which have been extracted are replaced by less valuable species.

The most accessible areas of forest in Guyana are now classified as *secondary* and *worked-out* forests. These areas can still be used for extracting low-grade timber and for making charcoal; but there are very few of the more valuable trees left.

In recent years, there have been moves towards much more careful control of the industry by the Guyana Forestry Commission, which encourages loggers to work in a way that will produce a sustained yield of high-quality timber. However, it is not easy to persuade the logging companies to change their methods.

5 Compare timber production in Canada and Guyana under these headings:
   (a) Natural environment.
   (b) Transportation.
   (c) Equipment used.
   (d) Cutting patterns.
   (e) Uses of timber.

10.8 Land management in St Lucia

If the forest cover is removed in the upper part of a river valley, this can cause problems throughout the whole drainage basin. If a drainage basin is studied and managed as a whole, then these problems can be dealt with at the same time. Look back to Figure 4.24.

The lower part of the Roseau valley contains some of the best agricultural land in St Lucia; but in the late 1970s, production in this area fell sharply.

For many years, steep hillsides in the middle part of the river valley have been cleared for cultivation. No soil conservation measures were used on much of this land. In the period 1966–77 alone, there was a 14% increase in the amount of cleared land.

As a result:

- Peak river flow in flood periods increased dramatically.
- There was an even greater increase in the amount of sediment carried by the river and by rainwater draining down the valley sides.
- The course of the river began to change very quickly. This caused the loss of 7 ha of farmland every year.
- In the dry season, river flow was much less. Water supply began to run low just when water was needed for irrigation and other purposes.
- The lower valley floor is very flat, and has a heavy clay soil. Field drains are needed to make this area productive. Because of soil erosion, many field drains were choked with sediment.

Bananas, the main crop, are very easily affected by poor drainage conditions. The top layer of soil should be well aerated so that a healthy root system can develop. The water table should be at least 60 cm below the surface or the growth of the plants will be held back, and they will be easily damaged by strong winds. If the fields are flooded for several days, then the plants may be killed outright.

1 Why has forest land been cleared?
2 How can clearing be controlled?
3 Look back to Section 4.8. Explain why the valley floor is so flat.

Further up the river valley, the results of deforestation have been just as bad:

- In the 1930s, St Lucia used to export timber. Today, the island imports over 12,000 m^3 every year, mainly from the southern part of the USA.
- Some valuable tree species are becoming very rare. The Laurier Canelle used to be one of the most valuable sources of timber; its wood is durable and easily worked. In the past, the tree was cut indiscriminately and not replanted. This species is now almost extinct on the island.

10.20 Cultivation and grazing on a steep slope in St Lucia.

- When trees are removed, other wildlife is also threatened. The flat red seeds of the Bois Pain Marron are one of the most important foods of the St Lucia parrot; but the tree is often cut for timber. Partly because of this, the parrot is now a threatened species. Numbers have fallen from over 1,000 in the early 1950s to between 100 and 150 today. The parrot species which once lived in Martinique and Guadeloupe are now extinct. It is important to make sure that St Lucia's national bird escapes this fate.

Forest conservation and production

In the upper part of the Roseau valley, the Forest Management Plan is a careful attempt to increase timber production, control soil erosion, and conserve the natural environment at the same time.

There are to be three different categories of forest:

- *Protection forests*: 45 km^2.
  Protection of the natural environment should be the first priority in areas where there are:
  - Slopes over 30°.
  - Unstable soils.
  - Important water catchment areas.
  - River banks which need protection.
  - Habitats for rare and endangered species.

  In these areas, timber should not be cut at all. Large clearings which already exist should be planted with native St Lucian trees if regeneration is too slow.

- *Protection/production forests*: 16 km^2.
  Here there should be some controlled harvesting of mature trees. So as to keep damage to neighbouring trees to a mininum, heavy equipment should not be used except for large and valuable trees like the Gommier. Cutting should be organised so that no big open clearings are created, because experience has shown that open clearings are colonised by less valuable 'opportunist' species which need a lot of light.
- *Exploitation forests*: 6.7 km^2.
  These are areas which are to be organised mainly for timber production, with a controlled programme of planting and felling. A fixed area of land is to be planted each year with species like Blue Mahoe or Honduras Mahogany which provide valuable timber and grow quite quickly. These areas will be harvested mechanically on a twenty-year cutting cycle, so that there will be a *sustained yield* of timber for construction, furniture-making, fuelwood, and charcoal. Large and small landowners will be encouraged to invest in forestry. Many areas of dry coastal woodland will be managed and planted with species like leucaena on a planned basis for charcoal production.

A small island like St Lucia cannot become self-sufficient in timber; but a management scheme like this could increase local production from 700 m^3 to almost 3,700 m^3, which is enough to bring a substantial saving in foreign exchange.

4 What other benefits will result from planned forest management?

The *Taungya* system

There are laws against clearing land in the forest reserve in St Lucia. Farmers who begin to grow crops there without permission can be fined up to $740 US for the first offence.

These laws are very difficult to enforce. Most people who clear land do not see that they are causing problems. They simply feel that they need to earn a living, and may not know about the harmful effects of soil-erosion. Prosecuting large numbers of small farmers would just make the Forestry Officers very unpopular.

It is much more sensible to provide a constructive alternative for people who need land. For this reason, the *taungya* system has been introduced. Originally developed in Africa, this system combines agriculture and forest management. It operates like this:

- The Forestry Division clears a small area of land, and plants it with young trees.
- The plot is allocated to a small farmer.
- The farmer grows a suitable crop between the seedlings.
- The farmer keeps the ground free from weeds, which might damage the growth of the young trees.
- When the trees have grown to a size where they will compete with the food crop for nutrients, the farmer is allocated another plot and moves on.

5 What are the advantages of this system for:
(a) The farmer?
(b) The Forestry Division?

6 Compare the methods used to control soil erosion in Haiti and St Lucia.

10.21 Tree seedlings are cultivated for use in replanting schemes.

Managing the lower Roseau valley

In the lower part of the river valley:

- The course of the river has been stabilised by careful land management. An area of 70 ha within the meander belt is set aside for protection. Within this zone, plants which stabilise the soil, like elephant grass, are encouraged. No crops which leave the soil unprotected are allowed.
- Artificial levees along each side of the meander belt protect the rest of the valley floor from flooding.
- Field drains are repaired where necessary, and properly maintained. The layout of the drains has been rationalised.
- Special measures will be needed for a very swampy area near the river mouth. Possibly an earth dam should be built to keep out flood water; the area within the dam could then be kept dry by pumping.

10.9 Conservation in the USA

To the early settlers, the North American continent seemed to have unlimited resources. Forests, grasslands, and mountains stretched for thousands of kilometres. Even in the middle of the nineteenth century, it took several months to travel from coast to coast, and huge areas had never been used for large-scale agriculture, mining, or forestry. Good land management was seen as a matter of bringing unused resources into production.

Today, over much of the continent, there is very little 'natural' vegetation left. Some areas of grassland and forest are now productive agricultural land; others have been used for construction or mining; and others have been badly damaged by soil erosion or pollution. It has been clear for some years that good land management is not just a matter of maximising production.

National Parks

As early as 1872, the Yellowstone area of what is now Wyoming was declared a *national park*. Today, there are 47 national parks, managed for the benefit of the public by the federal government. Within these areas, the first priorities are conservation and recreation. The land is protected from forms of land use which wiii destroy the natural environment.

The Yosemite National Park

The Yosemite National Park in California covers a huge area, more than 3,000 km^2. It is almost two-thirds as large as Trinidad. The highest point, Mount Lyell, is almost 4,000 m above sea level.

There are many different types of vegetation here. The Mariposa Grove is a forest of giant sequoia trees, many of which are more than 10 m across, and one of which is 64 m high. Near the mountain peaks, there is arctic alpine vegetation, which is quite similar to tundra. Altogether, there are 1,200 species of flowering plant, 75 types of mammal, and 220 different birds.

By setting aside one small part of the state of California, many different types of wildlife have been protected.

The Yosemite National Park is a major tourist attraction. There are 2.6 million visitors every year. Catering for their needs is an industry in itself. The National Park Service and a private organisation, the Curry Company, have 3,400 employees between them.

Visitors come to the park because they want to relax in peaceful surroundings or take part in outdoor activities after a year in one of the large cities of California or an urban or suburban environment elsewhere in the USA.

Many different activities are available for the visitors. There is skiing, swimming, rock-climbing, fishing, and boating. There are six-day mule trips through the mountains. There are almost 2,000 km of trail for backpacking; and for those who do not wish to do anything energetic, there are free shuttle buses and 'tourmobiles'. There are several large hotels, and a number of well-appointed camp-sites.

Unfortunately, this amount of recreational use can become a source of environmental problems. Some visitors may damage trees, start fires, or leave litter. Thefts of purses, wallets, cameras, and radios are increasingly common. Some activities are forbidden; no motorboats are allowed, for example. But there are visitors who break the rules. Every year, there are deaths from parachuting, which is illegal in the Park. There are more deaths associated with activities like

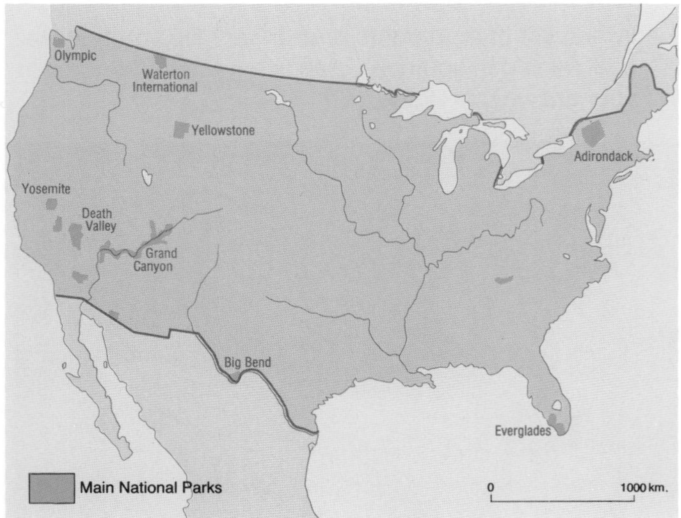

10.22 Some of the National Parks in the USA.

10.23 Yosemite National Park

rock climbing and hang gliding, caused by visitors who ignore basic safety rules.

So as to prevent the 'wilderness' from becoming overcrowded, there is a strict limit on the number of backpackers. Only 4,000 are allowed into the 'back country' at any one time. The others have to wait their turn.

1 Explain why national parks on the scale of Yosemite would be impossible to set up in most Caribbean countries.
2 Are there any national parks, wildlife parks, or nature reserves in your country? If so, write a brief description of one of them under these headings:
   (a) Location.
   (b) Types of natural vegetation.
   (c) Animals and birds.
   (d) Ownership and management.
   (e) Facilities for visitors.
3 Explain carefully why national parks and wildlife reserves can benefit the tourist industry.
4 Explain why careful management of these areas is necessary.

Resource use and conservation

In southern Utah and the adjacent parts of Arizona and Colorado, there is an area of mountain and desert 400 km across which contains six national parks, five national forests, three national monuments, and the Glen Canyon National Recreation Area. There are many rare plant and animal species, and some of the finest natural scenery in the world. The region is famous for its clear, unpolluted air.

Under the surface, there are important mineral resources. There are reserves of uranium and coal; tar sands, which contain petroleum, and permeable rocks containing large quantities of groundwater. At present, there are uranium mines in the area, and groundwater is used by cattle farmers; but the coal reserves are largely unused.

A few years ago, a proposal was made to develop a large coal mine, covering 40 km^2. This would be an *open-cast* coal mine; vegetation, soil, and rock would be stripped from the surface so that the coal could be removed. Coal, which is a black shiny rock, would be crushed, and mixed with groundwater to form a *slurry* which can flow down a pipeline to two proposed electricity-generating stations. The electricity would be transmitted to Los Angeles and other cities in California, more than 600 km away.

At its nearest point, the coal mine would be only 8 km from the Bryce Canyon National Park.

A large-scale proposal like this is naturally very controversial.

Some local residents are in favour of large-scale coal-mining:

'We need jobs in this area. If the development goes ahead, the population will increase from 10,000 to almost 100,000, and there will be many prosperous small businesses, not to mention the jobs in the mine and the electricity station. The development is not actually inside the national park boundary, and anyway the land will be reclaimed after mining. The soil will be replaced, and planted with vegetation.

'The US is becoming too dependent on imported oil. Around 1.4% of the nation's coal reserves are in southern Utah, and we can't afford to tie them up for ever just because there are some national parks in the area. There are plenty of wilderness areas in other parts of the United States.'

Other people are very concerned about the implications:

'This is a small community, and unemployment is not high. There is no need for thousands of people to move here from other parts of the USA.

'If the coal mine goes ahead, a huge area will be scarred by open-cast mining, and all around there will be disturbance from dust and blasting. The electricity plants will pollute the atmosphere over a wide area – and they may cause further damage through acid rain. You cannot treat a national park as an isolated museum piece. If an area next to the park is devastated, the park will be damaged, too.

'Even if the land is reclaimed after mining, it will be impossible to restore the natural ecosystem exactly as it was. We will have created an artificial environment.

'This is a desert area, and groundwater resources are very precious. If we pump millions of litres down a slurry pipeline, there may not be enough left for the cattle.

'We should put more effort into developing renewable energy resources, like solar power. And even if we do need to use more coal, there are plenty of reserves elsewhere in the country.'

5 Which set of arguments is stronger? Do you feel that coal mining in southern Utah is a good idea? Explain your answer carefully.

10.24 Bryce Canyon National Park, Utah.

11 · Fishing

11.1 Fishing in the Caribbean

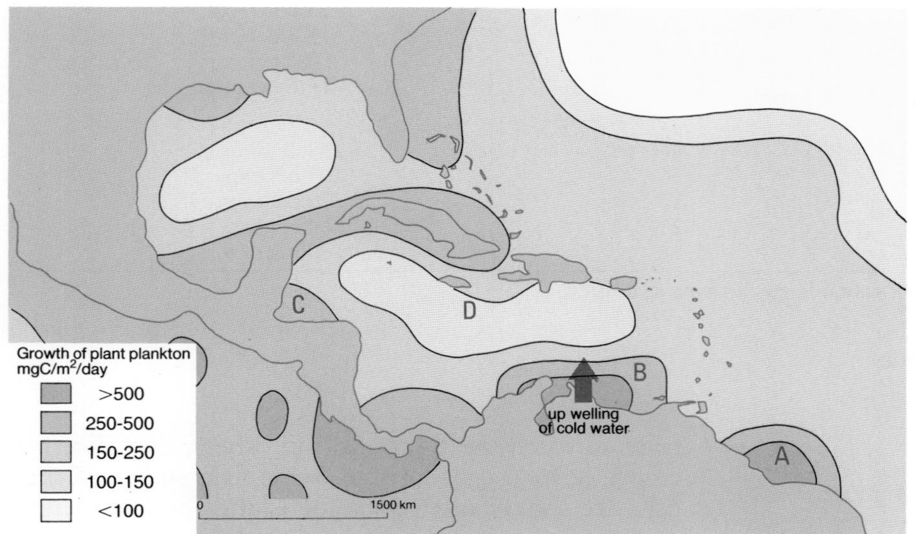

11.1 Fishing grounds in the Caribbean. Fish are most plentiful where plankton grow most rapidly.

TEMPERATURE IN °C

12 14 16 18 20 22 24 26 28 30

DEPTH IN METRES

50 100 150 200 250 300 350 400

11.2 The thermocline. There is.a sharp drop in temperatures 120–175 metres below the surface.

Where fish are found

When we compare different land environments, it is very obvious that some are more productive than others. The desert looks different from a rainforest, and a savanna looks different from an ice cap. When we compare marine environments, the differences are not so obvious, but they can be just as important.

Marine life depends on plant plankton; this is a collective term for a multitude of tiny organisms which fix the sun's energy through photosynthesis. Plant plankton thrives where there is plenty of sunlight, and a good supply of nutrients.

Most sunlight is absorbed near the surface of the oceans. Below 100 metres, the sea is almost dark; plankton cannot grow here, and nutrients can accumulate unused.

In temperate oceans, currents mix the water, so the nutrients in the surface layers are constantly being renewed by water from the ocean depths. But in tropical oceans, there is a zone called the thermocline 120–175 metres below the surface, which separates the warm surface waters from the cold bottom waters. There is usually very little mixing of the waters on each side of this boundary zone. Above the thermocline, there is plenty of light, but all the nutrients are quickly used up. Below the thermocline, there are plenty of nutrients, but there is not enough light for plankton to grow.

We do not eat plankton. But they are important because they are the *producers* of the marine ecosystem. They provide food for *primary consumers* such as flying fish, and for *secondary consumers* such as sharks, dolphins, and humans.

Tropical seas are generally poor in marine life; but there are some productive areas where there are:

- Winds and ocean currents, which cause an up-welling of nutrient-rich bottom water.
- Rivers which bring nturients from the land into the marine ecosystem.
- Coral reefs where living coral, reef fish, and crustaceans recycle the nutrients, so that they are not lost to the open sea.
- Other shallow areas, like seagrass meadows and mangrove swamps, where nutrients can easily be brought up from the bottom.

1 Figure 11.1 shows the distribution of nutrient-rich and nutrient-poor areas in the Caribbean and adjacent seas. Using information from the map and from your atlas, explain the location of:
(a) The nutrient-rich areas 'A', 'B', and 'C'.
(b) The nutrient-poor area at 'D'.

2 Read through Section 8.1 again. Explain the meaning of the terms 'producers', 'primary consumers', and 'secondary consumers'.

	Total fish catch (000 tonnes)	Average fish consumption (kg/person/year)	Balance of trade in fish ($000,000 US)
Some Caribbean countries			
Antigua and Barbuda	2.2	18	0.9 net imp.
Barbados	6.5	27	2.2 net imp.
Belize	1.6*	7	5.5 net exp.
Cuba	199.6	19	125.7 net exp.
Dominican Republic	13.2	8	4.6 net imp.
Guyana	32.4	25	22.6 net exp.
Jamaica	9.6	17	18.8 net imp.
St Vincent and the Grenadines	0.5	10	0.3 net imp.
Trinidad and Tobago	3.6	14	14.6 net imp.
Some major fishing countries outside the Caribbean			
Japan	12,021.2	86	3,261 net imp.
USSR	10,593.0	25	165 net exp.
USA	4,814.0	17	2,779 net imp.
Canada	1,220.6	21	864 net exp.
Nigeria	373.8	16	133 net imp.

* The Belize fish catch includes a high proportion of valuable species such as lobster.
Source: FAO Yearbook of Fishery Statistics, 1984.

11.3 Fisheries statistics, Caribbean and worldwide.

The fishing industry

3 Study Figure 11.3, and answer these questions:
   (a) Which two Caribbean countries have the largest fish catch?
   (b) In which two countries does the average person eat most fish?
   (c) Which major Caribbean fishing nations are close to the good fishing grounds shown on Figure 11.1?
   (d) Japan has the world's largest fish catch. Why is it a net *importer* of fish?

Fish imports

Most Caribbean islands are net importers of fish.

As long ago as the eighteenth century, slave-owners were bringing in salt cod from Canada to provide a cheap source of protein for the plantation workers. Salt cod is still imported – and so are canned tuna, sardines, and mackerel, as well as frozen fish products. On some islands, about half the fish consumed is imported.

4 Which imported fish products are on sale in your local stores?
5 What are the countries of origin?
6 How do they compare in price with local fish?
7 If fresh fish were more readily available, would people still prefer the processed foreign product?
8 Which Caribbean countries are net exporters of fish?

Fishing and economic development

Traditional fishing methods vary a great deal from island to island. In some areas, fishermen use small traps to catch small reef fish; in others, they dive for conch, sea eggs, or lobster. Some fish, such as flying fish, are sought after on some islands and not eaten on others. Some fishermen use lines, some use nets. Some use small canoes based on the Amerindian dugout; others have boats 15 m or more in length and equipped with ice and inboard motors.

But there are some problems which affect small-scale fishing on most Caribbean islands. Boats are generally small and cannot travel far. Marketing is not well developed, so it is not easy to sell fish to people who do not live near the sea. Fish are plentiful at some times of year, but scarce at others. Incomes suffer when catches are small; but also when a sudden glut drives prices down. If there is no way of storing fish, then any remaining at the end of the day must go to waste.

Most governments are now trying to develop and modernise their fishing industries so as to:

- Cut down on the level of imports.
- Provide a better supply of high-protein food.
- Increase the standard of living of the fishing population.
- Provide additional employment.
- Produce enough fish to process and export.

But expanding the fishing industry does not just mean providing better equipment and larger boats so that more fish can be caught. There are other problems to consider. Think about the following questions.

9 What will happen to fish prices if the size of the catch is suddenly doubled?
10 What equipment and organisation would be needed to run a successful fish-canning or fish-freezing industry?

11 What happens when fishermen land too much fish for local consumption, but too little for a full-scale freezing or canning operation?
12 What problems are caused when there are big seasonal variations in the fish catch?
13 Will new equipment lead to better catches, or just to *overfishing*, where too many fish are caught, and the fish population falls, sometimes almost to the point of extinction?

Traditional fishing methods have many strong points. People who have spent all their lives in fishing communities will know a lot about the sea and marine resources; about the pattern of waves and currents; and about where fish can be found at a particular time of year. Their methods are not usually environmentally damaging, and do not use expensive imported equipment.

Traditional fishermen are well aware of the dangers of overfishing, and usually avoid areas where there is a drop in yield so that fish stocks can recover.

The Serrana Bank

Now think carefully about this description of fishing in the 1950s.

'Serrana Bank (off the coast of Nicaragua) is a small cluster of coral rock and sand islands, uninhabited, and best known as a sea-bird rookery. Boats from Belize, the Caymans, and Jamaica, were collecting hundreds of thousands of tern eggs a year. The largest island in the banks scarcely exceeds a few hectares . . .

'In 1957, the US research vessel Oregon *anchored off the south side of Serrana Bank. We observed a small driftwood shelter on one of the outer islets. When we went ashore, we found in the shelter eight Hawksbill Turtles lying on their backs, with their front flippers tied to prevent escape. Realising that we were inspecting private possessions, we returned to the ship. Shortly, two small dugout canoes appeared. There were two men in each canoe. The man in the stern was paddling, while the man forward was furiously bailing out with coconut shells, barely able to keep a freeboard of 5 or 10 cm. When the canoes reached the shelter of the home islet, the men returned our waves of welcome.*

'We joined them ashore, and learned that they were a team of fishermen from Old Providence Island (in Belize). They explained that during the spring and summer months, an Old Providence company put parties ashore on various banks from carrier vessels. Their tour of Serrana Bank was for 30 days . . . They lived on dumplings, fish, lobster, and birds' eggs. Salt brine for curing the catch was prepared by boiling down sea water. Their hooks were hand-made from iron nails and their line was hand-made hemp line with a . . . strength of not more than 9 kilos.

'As their provisions were . . . limited, we returned that evening with fresh food, circle hooks . . . and a 1,000 m roll of nylon twine. We learned that their dried catch was marketed on Old Providence Island. They were paid a fee or salary, with no incentive for producing over a minimum catch. The profit incentive for undertaking such a tedious and precarious life came from the opportunity to catch Hawksbill Turtles, for the shell brought a good price. They captured beached females before egg-laying, because fresh Hawksbill eggs were a prized delicacy, and they could be sold or bartered.

'The next day we took the fishermen to their grounds in outboard-powered dories. Using the new hooks and lines over 140 kilos of snapper and grouper were quickly caught by the fishermen. They were not particularly pleased because they had reached their minimum quota and still had 20 days to wait for the relief vessel. Our offer to return them to Old Providence was declined, since it was still the mating season, and perhaps more Hawksbill Turtles would appear.'

H. R. Bullis, *Proceedings of Gulf and Caribbean Fisheries Institute*, 1978

11.4 Boats ready for fishing from a small beach.

14 What were the main *technical* problems with this system of fishing?
15 Why were the fishermen not particularly pleased when these technical problems were put right?
16 What problems were connected with the system of payment, preserving, and marketing?
17 Why was the procedure for catching turtles very bad from a conservationist's point of view?
18 Were there any strong points in this fishing system?

Fishing co-operatives in Belize

Belize has excellent fishing-grounds in the lagoon between the mainland and the barrier reef, and in the three outer coral atolls. There are breeding-grounds for fish in mangrove swamps and in seagrass meadows along the coast.

Belize now has a very successful fishing industry. Export earnings from shellfish alone are now more than $6 m. US per year. The industry is successful because the fishing-grounds are a valuable resource; and because the industry is organised and managed in a way which allows it to make good use of the opportunities which are available.

Between 1960 and 1968, five fishermen's co-operatives were formed. Today, the co-operatives have over 1,400 members, and there are many shore-based jobs in processing and administration. Organising a well-run co-operative has several advantages.

Produce can be marketed on a larger scale. A big co-operative is in a far stronger position than individual fishermen when it comes to negotiating an export price for conch or lobster with a buyer in the USA. The co-operative buys the fishermen's catch, processes it, and organises sales. At the end of the year, the profits are distributed to the members as a 'second payment'.

The co-operative can also make loans for the purchase of items like outboard motors, and even for fishermen who want to buy large long-distance trawlers. Some of them now also have funds for educational purposes, for pensions, and to provide sick pay.

The most valuable catch is shellfish, mainly conch and lobster. They are caught by trapping and diving. But it will be difficult to increase catches, because there is a real danger of overfishing. Lobster landings are now stable at around 900 tonnes per year, but conch catches have been dropping since the early 1970s.

To conserve stocks:

- There is a closed season for conch and lobster, at the time of year when most breeding takes place.
- Young lobster and conch below a minimum size are not used. This gives them a chance to mature.
- Each co-operative has an annual quota, which cannot be exceeded.

11.5 Weighing lobster tails in a processing plant in Belize.

If there is overfishing, recovery is slow, because conch take between 4 and 6 years to reach maturity. If the fishing industry is to expand, the best prospect is to increase the catch of scale-fish, not shellfish. These are already exported to the USA, Jamaica, Honduras, and Guatemala. But if scale-fish production levels are to be increased without overfishing, there will have to be a move to deep-sea fishing in large vessels beyond the barrier reef. This would not be easy for the co-operatives to organise.

There have been problems with the fishing industry in Belize:

- Sometimes, fishermen sell their catch illegally across the border in Honduras or Mexico, where they may get a slightly higher price.
- There are no successful co-operatives in the south of the country. Fishing-grounds are just as good here, but most fish are caught by small farmers for their own use; part-time fishermen do not feel the need to increase their cash income by taking a larger catch and selling it.

But in spite of these problems, the fishing industry has made a real contribution to the development of Belize.

Small-scale fishing in the Grenadines

Mayreau is a tiny island in the Grenadines. It is only 2.5 km^2 in area, and has a population of 130. It is a difficult place to make a living. The dry season lasts for five or six months, and at this time of year fresh water is in short supply. People grow pigeon peas and maize, and keep livestock; but in a very dry year the crops will fail, and many animals will have to be slaughtered.

Fishing is the main source of employment on Mayreau. Fishermen use small wooden boats to catch fish, using pots and nets. Many young men also go skin-diving to catch extra fish and lobsters.

Mayreau fishermen have had low incomes, because:

- Sailing-boats cannot travel far in a day, so fishing-grounds are limited.
- There is no cold-storage facility on the island.
- There is no ready market for fish close at hand.

Recently things have begun to change on Mayreau. The Caribbean Council of Churches, through CADEC, has initiated a *small-scale* development scheme. Full-scale freezing facilities or deep-sea trawlers would not be appropriate for a small island like Mayreau, but a few more modest improvements can make a real difference to people's lives.

CADEC has given small loans to help fishermen repair boats, buy new tackle, or invest in an outboard motor. With a motor, a boat can travel further in a day. Fishermen can use more distant grounds, or set and check traps in one place and then set a net in another. And high-income catches like lobster can be taken to other islands for sale without the need for a middle man.

Modernising the fishing industry in Barbados

Barbados has quite a large and well-developed fishing industry. There are over 600 boats in operation, mostly diesel-powered and 7–11 m long. During the main fishing season, from December to June, the main activity is deep-sea fishing for flying fish, king-fish, shark, billfish, and dolphin. The larger fish are caught with lines, usually when boats are on their way to the flying fish grounds; flying fish are caught with lines and gill nets.

At other times of year, some fish species migrate elsewhere, and there is also a danger from storms and hurricanes. Smaller fish can be trapped on the island's fringing reef, but total catches are much smaller, and fresh fish is less widely available.

Boats generally go to sea around dawn, and return in mid-afternoon. Fish are landed at 25 different points around the island; but over half the catch is sold at the three largest fishing centres: Bridgetown, Speightstown, and Oistins. Generally the proceeds are split fifty-fifty between the boat-owner and the fishermen.

There is still a need to improve the industry, so as to cater for the local and tourist population, cut down on imports, and make fish more easily available all year round.

The Oistins Fisheries Project is an attempt to solve some of these problems. Its most important feature is an ice-making plant and cold store. Ice is sold below cost to fishermen, and they have been encouraged to invest in larger boats which can carry ice on board. In the early 1950s, the Barbados fishing fleet was made up of small sailing vessels with little equipment. Today, there are over 60 large ice boats which have facilities such as ship-to-shore radio, direction-finders, sleeping-quarters and a galley, so that they can remain at sea for several days at a time.

The project also includes a jetty, where boats can take on fuel or unload their catch; boat repair facilities; and an improved fish market where fish can be inspected for quality and sold on ice in clean conditions.

19 A distinctive approach to fisheries development, suited to local conditions, has been developed in Belize, in Barbados, and in the Grenadines. Summarise the characteristics of these three fishing systems under these headings:
(a) Equipment and methods.
(b) Organisation and marketing.

11.6 The Oistins Project in Barbados: the fish market.

11.2 Fishing in British Columbia

Fishing in Canada

Look back to Figure 11.3. Canada is one of the world's major fishing nations. The Canadian fish catch is more than four times as large as that of all the Caribbean nations put together. Canada is also the world's leading exporter of fish products; it accounts for 8% of world fish exports.

Fishing is an important part of the Canadian economy; although not nearly as important as forestry and wood products. There are 78,000 fishermen, or 0.6% of the labour force; and 27,000 more jobs in fish-processing. Fish products make up 1.5% of Canadian exports.

Fishing is an important export industry in Canada, because:

- The waters off the Atlantic and Pacific coasts are temperate seas, with no thermocline. There is also a pattern of ocean currents which ensures a good supply of nutrients.
- There is a regular supply of fresh fish. Canning and freezing factories can be kept well supplied; and because there are processing plants in the main fishing areas, there is less danger that fish will go to waste when there is a glut. About 90% of the fish caught in Canada is frozen, chilled, canned, cured, or salted before it is sold.
- Because fish-processing is well-developed, canned, salted, and cured fish are available for sale to export markets.
- Canada has a much smaller population than other major fishing nations like the USA, the USSR, and Japan. This means that there is a substantial amount available for export even after the local market has been satisfied.

11.7 Fishing grounds off North America.

1 Look at Figure 11.7. Explain why the seas off the coast of British Columbia and eastern Canada are such productive fishing-grounds.

Fishing on the Pacific Coast

British Columbia, on the Pacific coast, is one of the most important fishing regions of Canada. It accounts for 14% of the total fish catch.

In some ways, the industry is a specialised one. In most years, various types of salmon make up more than 75% of the catch, by value.

Salmon-fishing

Salmon are *anadromous* fish. They spend most of their lives in the open ocean, but return to rivers in order to spawn. When the eggs hatch, the young fish make their way to the sea.

Before the European settlement, the Amerindian peoples of the Pacific coast had large villages by the river banks. Salmon and other fish were the main source of protein in their diet; but more than that, fishing was the mainstay of their culture, economy, and way of life.

Today, canned salmon from commercial fisheries is an item on supermarket shelves in many different countries. Salmon-fishing is still economically important; but attitudes to fishing have completely changed.

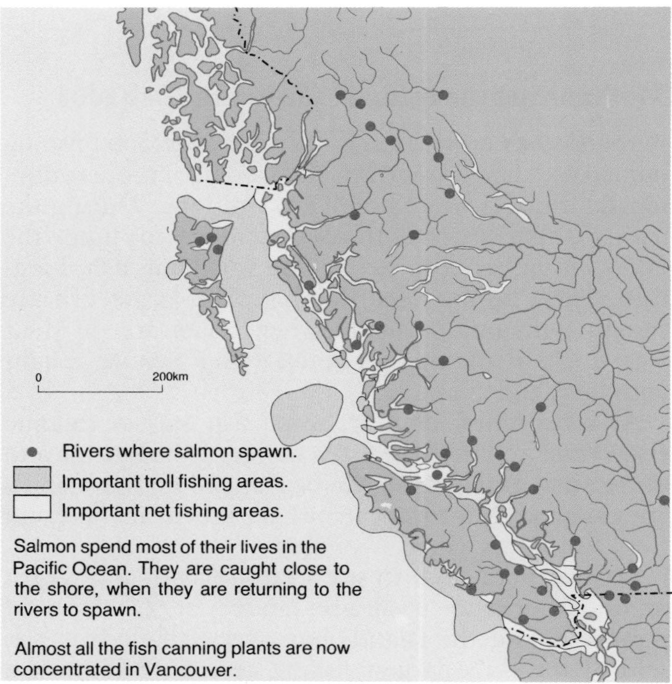

11.8 Salmon fishing in British Columbia.

11.9 Salmon fishing at Alert Bay, British Columbia.

Salmon-fishing today

Salmon are generally caught in small boats rather than huge ocean-going factory ships:

- Troll fishing takes place up to 200 km from the shore. A sturdy vessel with a two-man crew catches fish with a large number of lines and lures.
- Nearer the shore, fish are caught with purse-seine nets. A larger boat with a crew of about five, which is equipped with electronic fish-detection gear, encircles a shoal of fish with a circular net, and draws it in.
- In the river mouths, there are small one- or two-man vessels using smaller gill nets, which are pulled in with a power drum.
- In the rivers, fish are caught by individual recreational fishermen using lines. Sports fishing accounts for only 4% of the catch; but it is important because it provides the basis for much of the tourist industry, and because much more is involved than just the commercial value of the fish.
- Amerindians now account for only a small proportion of the recorded fish catch. Fish are caught in rivers and along the coast by a variety of methods – hooks, harpoons, nets, weirs, and fish traps. Fishing is still an essential part of the culture of Amerindian fishing communities.

Overfishing

With any fishing industry, overfishing is always a potential problem. Salmon are particularly vulnerable, because their movements are so predictable. For the individual fisherman, the temptation is always to improve his equipment and fish a little further out to sea so as to get to the salmon first as they approach the shore. It would be easy to fish the salmon almost out of existence.

A recent government report asserted: 'We have spent far too much on catching fish, and too little on managing and producing them.'

However:

- Nets are now made with a large mesh, so that small fish are not caught.
- There are hatcheries on some of the rivers, where young fish are protected until they are large enough to be released.
- A system of licensing has been introduced, limiting the amount of fish a boat-owner can catch.
- Government has bought some of the existing vessels and scrapped them so as to reduce the number of boats.

The aim is not to expand the fish catch, but to develop a small but efficient commercial fishing industry which uses the Pacific salmon as a renewable resource; and to leave enough fish for the Amerindian communities and also for sports fishermen.

Theoretically, the Amerindians are given priority in fishing policy; but in practice they are always the first to suffer when there is overfishing, because they depend more on fisheries than anyone else, and because they catch fish near the shore, after the commercial boats have taken what they can.

Pollution

Over the past century, there have been many changes in land use in the river basins of British Columbia. Some of these changes have been very damaging for anadromous fish like the salmon. In the Fraser River, which is the largest on the Pacific coast of Canada, fish stocks have been reduced by 50% since 1900.

2 How would freshwater and anadromous fish be affected by:
   (a) Intensive logging along the river valley?
   (b) Increased soil erosion?
   (c) The construction of dams for irrigation and water supply?
   (d) Acid rain?
   (e) An increased amount of organic waste in the river?

3 Compare the fishing industry in British Columbia with that of one Caribbean country. Make a note of the similarities and the differences under these headings:
   (a) Types of fish caught.
   (b) Equipment and methods.
   (c) Fish-processing.
   (d) Exports and imports of fish.

12 · Agriculture

12.1 Agricultural systems

12.1 Planting rice seedlings in China.

12.2 Growing grapes in France.

12.3 Sheep farming in New Zealand.

The pictures on this page show agricultural landscapes. Human societies are using the land as a resource to produce crops or livestock.

1 Which crops or livestock can you identify in these pictures?
2 Which would be used for food, and which for other purposes such as clothing?

Agricultural landscapes are extremely varied. The way agricultural land is used will depend on factors like:

- the *climate*: is it hot or cool? Rainy or dry? Is the climate dependable, or does the weather vary greatly from year to year? What is the risk of strong winds, droughts, or floods?
- The *soil*: does it retain plant nutrients well? Does it drain easily, or is it liable to become waterlogged? Is it sandy, or is it a clay soil?
- *Relief*: is the land flat or mountainous? Does it slope smoothly, or is it broken by gullies and sudden steep slopes?

These are some of the aspects of the *physical environment* which influence agriculture. Equally important is the *social and economic* environment in which farmers work. This includes factors like:

- *Land ownership*: is the land owner-occupied, or rented? Is it divided into small farms, or run as large estates?
- *Technology*: what techniques are available for cultivating the land, maintaining soil fertility, limiting the growth of weeds, and controlling pests and diseases?
- *Demand*: is there a ready market for agricultural products? Which ones are in demand? Are prices rising or falling?

There are many other physical and socio-economic factors which influence agriculture. The availability of *water* may determine whether irrigation is possible in a dry area. The level of *wages* may make it worth while to purchase a piece of labour-saving machinery. The role of government is very important. In many countries, governments have changed the pattern of land ownership, made technology available to small farmers, and set the prices for which agricultural products are sold.

Agriculture is often said to be influenced by *historical* factors. What this means is that the social and economic environment was very different at some stage in the past, and that the influence of this historical environment can still be seen in the way farmers operate today.

3 Look again at the photographs on this page. Can you identify ways in which the agricultural landscapes have been influenced by:
(a) Physical factors such as climate, soil, relief, and irrigation water?
(b) Social and economic factors, such as land ownership, technology, demand and government policies?
(c) Historical factors – the way in which social and economic factors operated in the past?
4 Which set of influences is hardest to detect, just by looking at the pictures?

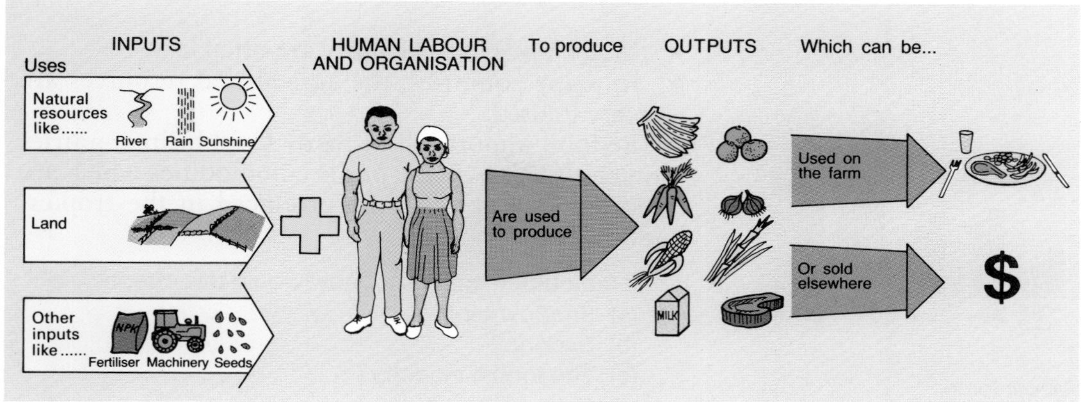

12.4 A farming system.

Farming systems

Every farming system:

- Uses natural resources and land . . .
- Along with other inputs like tools, machinery, seeds, and fertilisers . . .
- As the basis for human labour and organisation . . .
- So that outputs are produced, which can be . . .
- Taken elsewhere for sale or consumed on the farm.

There are many ways of classifying farming systems:

By the type of product:

Pastoral farming	*Mixed farming*	*Arable farming*
Mainly animal products, including: • Dairying • Beef production • Sheep-farming • And other activities	Animal products and crops	Mainly crops, including: • Cereal-growing • Fruit-farming • Sugar cane • And other activities

By the size of the farm units:

Small-scale farming	*Medium-scale farming*	*Large-scale farming*
A small family farm		Estates, plantations, and ranches

By the main purpose of the farm unit:

Subsistence farming	*Semi-subsistence farming*	*Commercial production*
Almost all the output is consumed on the farm; farming is a household activity and a way of life for the family	Some of the output is consumed on the farm, and some is sold	Almost all the output is sold; the farm is run purely as a business

12.5 Classifying farming systems.

5 Using these categories, how would you classify:
(a) The farming systems shown in Figures 12.1 to 12.3?
(b) The different types of farm unit in the area where you live?

Subsistence and commercial agriculture

At the time of the Arawaks and the Caribs, the economy of the Caribbean was based on subsistence agriculture, as well as hunting and fishing. A traditional Amerindian farming system is described in Section 10.1.

For much of the colonial period, agriculture in most of the Caribbean was *commercially* orientated. Large plantations grew tropical crops for sale at high prices in Europe and North America. Sugar was the main commercial crop, but there were others, too. Very little land was used to grow food. It was more profitable to import food, and use the limited amount of good agricultural land to produce crops for sale.

After the abolition of slavery, other types of agriculture began to develop in the region. Much of the top-quality land was still owned by plantations producing export crops; but these were less profitable than before. Large areas were now used by *peasant farms*. These are small family farms producing many different field and tree crops and a few livestock products. Much of the output is consumed by the farm family; but some is sold, either locally or for export.

Agriculture and development

Figure 12.6 shows how the percentage of the labour force employed in agriculture has changed over the past twenty years in seven different countries.

6 What do you notice about:
(a) The percentage of people who work in agriculture in industrial countries like Canada and Japan?
(b) The pattern of change in all seven countries?

There is a worldwide trend for fewer people to work in agriculture:

- When farming techniques improve, fewer workers can often produce an increased output.
- As economies develop, more jobs are available in manufacturing, commerce, and tourism.
- Many people leave agriculture because they *believe* conditions will be better elsewhere.

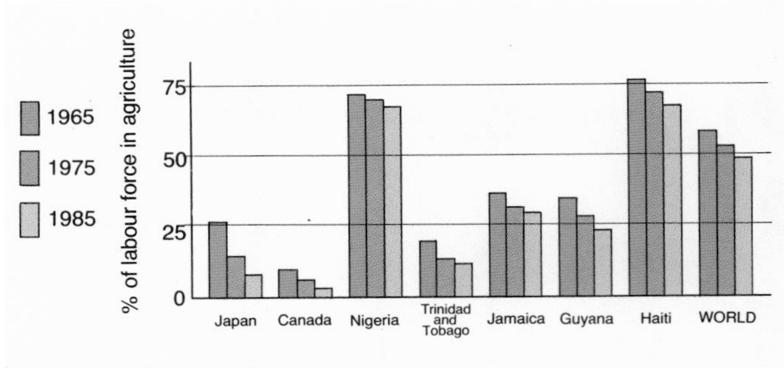

12.6 Changes in the agricultural labour force.

However, it is very dangerous for a developing country to neglect agriculture.

Agriculture has an extremely important role to play in the economic development of the Caribbean. Agriculture can:

- Earn foreign exchange when export crops are sold abroad.
- Reduce the need for food imports.
- Provide employment for large numbers of people.
- Produce raw materials for food-processing industries.
- Encourage the development of industries producing fertiliser, packaging materials, and other inputs.
- Promote the development of an efficient transport system.

Unfortunately, there are many problems facing agriculture in the Caribbean today:

- The Caribbean has a falling share of many export markets.
- The price of many agricultural commodities is unstable, and much too low for profitable production.
- Wage levels in agriculture are often low.
- In many countries, the agricultural resources are very limited.

The food import bill of many Caribbean countries is much too high. Some of the commodities which are imported cannot easily be produced in the tropics; but others can.

7 If agriculture collapsed, how would this affect:
 (a) Employment?
 (b) Exports?
 (c) The tourist industry?
 (d) Manufacturing?
8 List six imported food products which are on sale in your country. Which ones could have been produced in the Caribbean?
9 Very few young people choose a career in agriculture. Why do you think this is?

In this chapter we will look at three farming systems:

- Peasant farming.
- Commercial arable farming.
- Commercial pastoral farming.

We will look at:

- How each system is operated.
- How each system is influenced by physical, social, economic, and historical factors.
- What problems are associated with the operation of each system today.
- How these problems are being dealt with.

For each farming system, we will contrast the way it is operated in the Caribbean with other areas outside. We will look at:

- Peasant farming in Nigeria.
- Commercial arable farming in the Canadian prairies.
- Commercial pastoral farming in the Great Plains and the Mid-West in the USA.

12.2 Peasant farming in the Caribbean

Pure subsistence farming is very unusual in the Caribbean; but peasant farms which mix production for family use and production for sale are very common.

This type of farming grew up after emancipation, when freed slaves settled areas which had previously been uncultivated, or when unprofitable plantations were broken up into smaller units.

From the beginning, there was a mix between commercial and subsistence production. Some items, like cloth and metal tools, have always been imported goods, which peasant farmers have had to buy. This meant that they always needed a cash income.

The proportion of land which is worked by small farmers varies a great deal; but peasant agriculture is important in every Caribbean country:

- In St Christopher and Barbados, most of the land is still owned by large sugar estates; but small farmers make good use of the land they have available, and grow a high proportion of the locally produced fruit and vegetables.
- In Haiti, some of the big French-owned plantations were broken up into small units after independence. Since then, many new areas have been cleared by peasant farmers. But unfortunately most holdings are too small to bring in a reasonable income, and there are other reasons why it is difficult to farm successfully.

	Large scale commercial farming	Traditional peasant farming
Size of farm	Usually over 100 Ha	Under 10 Ha
Land ownership	Owned outright	Often owned; but sometimes rented
Equipment and technology	Modern technology – large scale machinery, chemical fertilisers and pesticides	Traditional technology – cutlass and hoe – organic fertiliser
Labour	Wage labour	Family labour, with some help from neighbours
Specialisation	One or two crops – usually no livestock, except in specialised pastoral farms	Many different crops – usually some livestock
Markets	Produce exported – sold on world market	Produce used by family or sold locally

12.7 Commercial farming and peasant farming. These are some of the contrasts between large-scale commercial farming and traditional Caribbean peasant farming.

12.8 A peasant farm in Dominica. The building is for storage.

Peasant farming and land quality

Where there is a mixture of large estates and peasant farms, the plantations often occupy the best land, because:

- When plantations were being established, the best land was cleared for cultivation, and the least promising areas were ignored.
- If any plantations were established on marginal land, they generally failed financially and were broken up into smaller units.

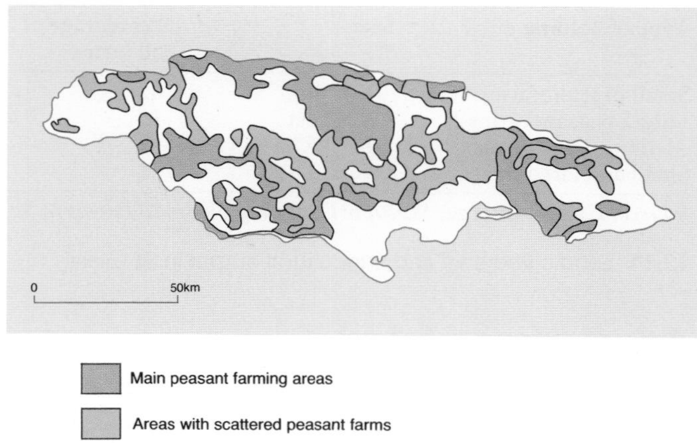

12.9 The main peasant farming areas in Jamaica.

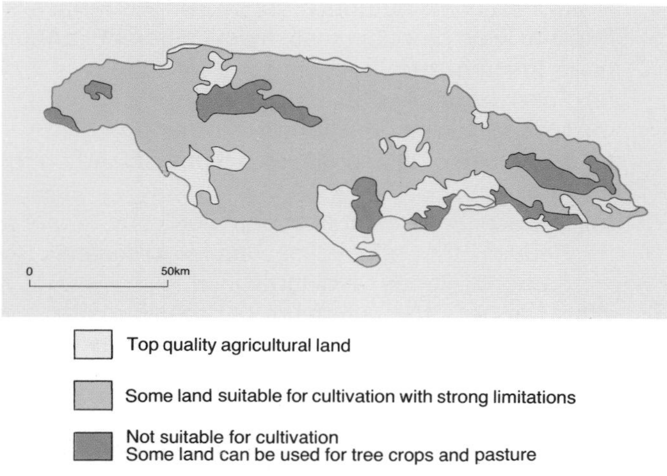

12.10 The quality of agricultural land in Jamaica.

1 Figure 12.9 shows the main peasant farming areas of Jamaica. Compare this map with Figure 12.10, which shows the quality of agricultural land on the island. What pattern do you notice?

Production on peasant farms

Peasant farmers often make very good use of the land they occupy. In St Lucia, 97% of all farm units are peasant farms. They occupy only 33% of the agricultural area of the country; but small farmers produce 68% of the banana crop.

1 Look carefully at Figure 12.11:
   (a) Draw proportional circles to show the percentage of the agricultural *area* in peasant farms, and the proportion of total *output* they produce.
   (b) What type of farming appears to make best use of the available land area?

Type of holding	Size	Percentage of all farms	Percentage of agricultural area	Percentage of agricultural output
Small peasant farms	0–1.9 ha	82	14	60
Larger peasant farms	2–9.9 ha	15	19	
Medium-sized farms	10–19.9 ha	2	9	40
Small and large estates	Over 20 ha	1	58	

Source: Calixte George, *Multiple Cropping on Small Farms in St Lucia: Preliminary Observations*, 1981.

12.11 Land ownership and agricultural output in St Lucia.

A peasant farm in St Lucia

Figure 12.12 shows a peasant farm in St Lucia.

2 Give two reasons why the house is located where it is.
3 Why are most of the tree crops grown near the house?
4 Make a list of the outputs produced on this farm.
5 Explain why producing so many different outputs helps the farmer to:
  (a) Feed the family.
  (b) Maintain an income all the year round.
  (c) Make use of all the different types of land on the farm.
  (d) Reduce the amount of soil erosion.
  (e) Reduce the effects of natural disasters like droughts, floods, and hurricanes.
6 What happens to the amount of organic matter and humus in the soil:
  (a) When the land is in cultivation?
  (b) When the land is left fallow?
7 How does the farmer use:
  (a) Thin, dry, sandy soil which is exposed to the wind?
  (b) Thick, heavy soil which is sheltered from the wind?
8 List the *differences* between this farming system and Amerindian subsistence farming.
9 What *similarities* are there between the two farming systems?
10 Explain why peasant farmers and their families:
  (a) Have to work very hard.
  (b) Have to organise different types of work very carefully.
11 Why would it be difficult for a large commercial farm to operate this type of farming system?

Farming strategies

Peasant farmers have very limited resources:

- They have only a small area of land.
- They do not usually have land with the best soil and climate conditions.

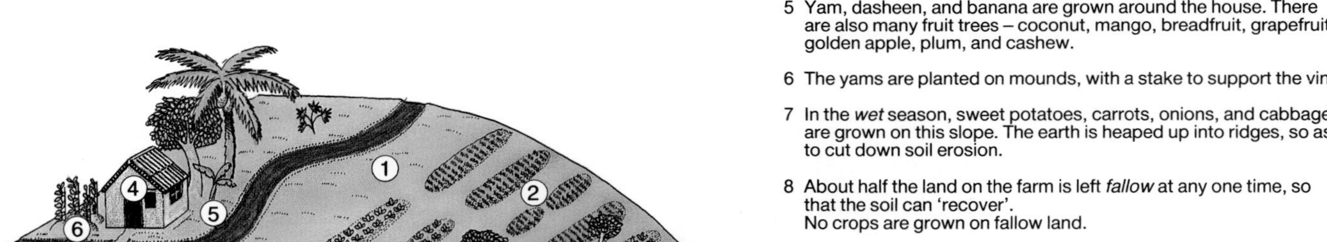

12.12 A peasant farm in St Lucia.

- The weather is always uncertain. There may be a drought, or heavy rain, or a hurricane.
- It is not easy to obtain extra finance for investment, or to see the farm through a bad period.

The farmer has to produce enough food for most of the family needs. He must have enough over for sale to provide a cash income to buy farm equipment, clothing, and a whole range of other items.

This is not an easy task. Most small farmers work hard, and at the end of the year the total cash income may not add up to very much. But in most parts of the Caribbean their accumulated experience has developed a method of farming which is suited to the natural environment and to the economic and social conditions they have to deal with.

No two peasant farms are exactly the same. Every small farmer faces the same *problem*, trying to make a living from a small area of land. But the exact pattern of land use, and the *solution* arrived at will depend on the *physical*, *social*, and *economic* environment of the farm.

For example:

- In a *dry* environment, cassava or pigeon peas may replace dasheen as the main food crop.
- If the land is flat and *badly drained*, the farmer will have to dig ditches, and cultivate the land in ridges to prevent waterlogging.
- If the farmer does not *own* the land outright, fruit trees may not be planted, because the benefit may go to someone else.
- If there is a *large family* to help with the farm work, more food crops will be grown. An elderly person living alone might leave much of the land in pasture, which does not need so much labour.
- On a very *small farm*, there is usually a need for another source of income, like fishing or handicrafts.
- With a *large farm*, it may be possible to invest in another business, like a minibus or a small shop. Somebody else can then be employed to do some of the heavy work on the farm.

Peasant farming and economic development

Many people believe that small farms always have low yields, and that this is a very inefficient form of agriculture. This is not usually true. But there are problems with peasant farming as an agricultural system in the Caribbean.

A recent survey in St Lucia showed that:

- Most peasant farmers are middle-aged or elderly. Only a very small number are under 30 years old.
- More than half the farmers interviewed could not read and write well. Very few had had secondary education, and none had been to agricultural college.
- Almost half said they would prefer *not* to work in farming.

Similar results could probably have been obtained from a survey of this sort in most other Caribbean countries. There are other problems, too:

- Land ownership is often uncertain.
- It is often difficult to obtain capital for investment.
- Marketing is often badly organised, so that farmers do not receive a good price for what they produce, and cannot always be sure of making a sale.
- In many areas, farmers do not receive technical help, so that they do not hear of innovations which might help improve output.
- Praedial larceny can be a very serious problem: fruit and vegetable crops may be stolen in the field just as they get ripe.

Many of these problems can be overcome if social and economic conditions are right, and appropriate government help is available.

In Sections 12.5 and 12.6 we will look at two areas where small farmers have started to operate on a more commercial basis, and have begun to earn a higher income by producing consistent outputs of high-quality produce.

13 Explain carefully why peasant farming is important for the economy of the Caribbean, under these headings:
   (a) Employment.
   (b) Food production.
   (c) Making use of the available land resources.
   (d) Other reasons.

12.3 Peasant farming in Nigeria

Nigeria is a very large country, covering more than 924,000 km^2. It is more than four times the size of Guyana, and more than eighty times the size of Jamaica. It is a very varied country, too.

Figures 12.13a–d give some information about the climate and vegetation of Nigeria, and about the main food crops.

1 Look back to Sections 7.7, 8.2, 8.3, and 9.4. Write a few sentences about the climates, vegetation types, and soils of Nigeria. Describe the contrasts between the north and south of the country.

2 What are the main food crops in:
   (a) Northern Nigeria?
   (b) Southern Nigeria?
   (c) The mountainous east of the country?

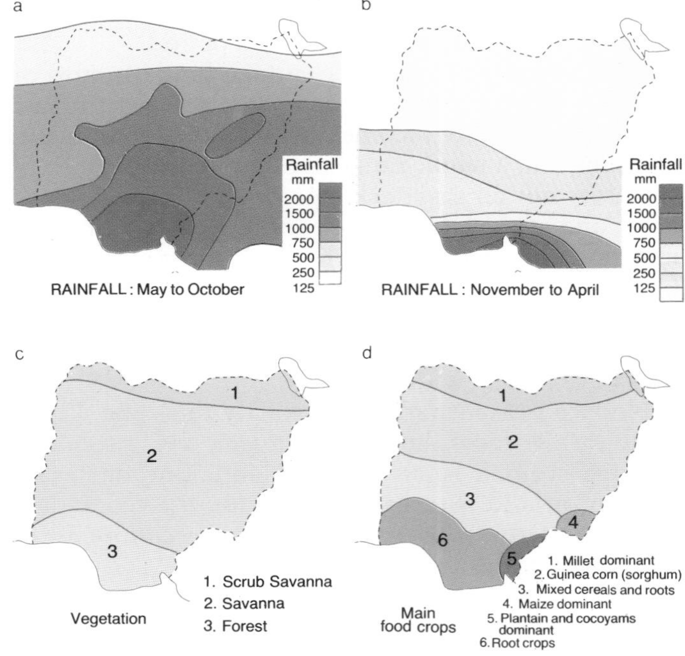

12.13 Nigeria: rainfall, vegetation and soils.

The social and economic environment of Nigeria is just as varied as the physical environment. Lagos is a sprawling modern city of over two million inhabitants. Elsewhere, there are remote country districts where, at first glance, an outsider might think that conditions had barely changed in the last hundred years. There are many different ethnic groupings each of which has its own culture and traditions, and there are many different languages and religions.

For all these reasons, there are many different types of peasant farming, and no one farming system is really 'typical' of Nigeria as a whole.

A village in southern Nigeria

Poka is a large village in southern Nigeria, about 75 km east of Lagos. It is situated on a flat coastal plain. Figure 12.14 shows how the land around the village is used:

- Immediately around the village ('A'), the land is divided into tiny garden plots. These are well manured, and produce several crops a year. Yams, peppers, and other vegetables are grown here. There are also many fruit trees.
- A little further away from the village ('B'), there are small fields, each measuring around 0.2 ha. These fields are also manured, but not so heavily as the garden plots. Some of the fields are in fallow; next year they will be cultivated again. This land is used to grow maize, melons, and cassava.
- In the next zone ('C'), the land is not manured. The land is divided into family sections up to 4 ha in size, which are used for tree crops like rubber, cocoa, and kola nuts. The kola nuts are used as a stimulant. They are taken apart and chewed. Gifts of kola nuts are important on many social occasions. Some of the land under the trees is used to grow cassava, maize, and eddoes.

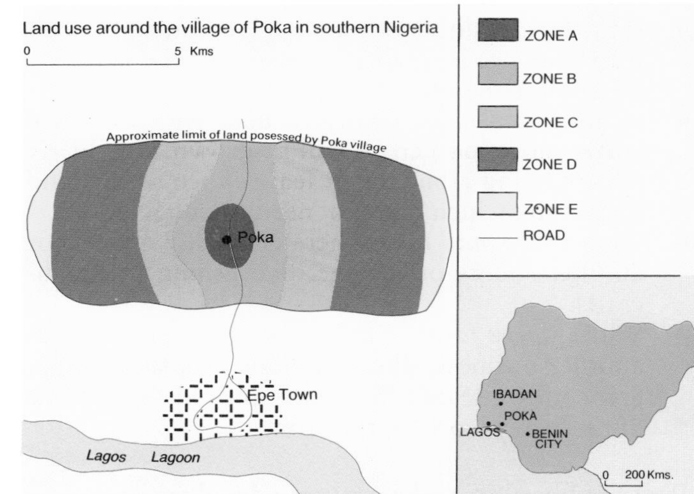

12.14 Land use around the village of Poka in Southern Nigeria.

- At 3 km or more from the village ('D'), farmers clear fields which are cultivated for up to three years, and then left fallow when most of the humus in the soil has been used up. After a fallow period of perhaps five years, fertility has been restored and the land can be cleared again. Cassava, groundnuts, maize, and melons are grown here; there are no tree crops except for oil palms. Some of the farmers build temporary shelters next to their fields, so that they do not have to go straight back to the village when they

12.15 Peasant farmers in Plateau State, Central Nigeria.

have finished working. There is still some forest left, which has not been cleared for cultivation.

- The land which is furthest from the village ('E') is still forest. Firewood, wild fruits, and other forest products are collected here. Cooking oil and palm wine are prepared for the fruit and sap of the oil palm. A few tiny plots have been cleared for food crops. These will be abandoned after one or two years. People who are working in this area usually build camps, so that they do not have to keep going back to the village.

3 Including the forest area, how much land is used by the people who live in the village?

4 The settlement is a prosperous one. Why is it an advantage to be located:
(a) On a main road?
(b) Relatively near to Lagos?

5 Explain carefully why tree crops help maintain the fertility of the soil.

6 How is soil fertility maintained:
(a) Near to the village?
(b) In the zones which are furthest from the village?

7 Yams only grow well where the soil has a good structure and contains a good supply of nutrients. Cassava will grow well even with poor soil conditions. Write a few sentences commenting on the location of the areas where *yam* and *cassava* are grown.

8 Compare farming in Poka with the peasant farm described in section 12.2, or with another peasant farm which you know. List the *similarities* and *differences* under these headings:
(a) Physical environment.
(b) Crops grown.
(c) Land in fallow.
(d) Maintaining soil fertility.

9 Are there any ways in which farming in Poka is similar to the system of shifting cultivation described in Section 10.1?

The village community

There are temporary camps and shelters on the land which is furthest from the village; but all the permanent dwellings are in one central settlement. This village is a close-knit community in which many families are related.

Houses in this part of Nigeria are built of bricks and dried clay, which is plastered with cement after completion. Houses are much larger than in the Caribbean, because they are occupied by an extended family, which may consist of a household head, one or two wives, children, and several other relatives. The house of a wealthy person may contain 15 or 20 rooms, and may be one or two storeys high.

In most parts of Africa, it is not usual to own farm land outright. A family member may have the right to use a particular piece of land for a particular purpose and for a certain period; but this does not mean that the land is personal property which can be bought or sold. Most families will cultivate several plots, so that they can have some land of each type.

10 Compare Poka village with a rural community in the Caribbean. List the *similarities* and *differences* under these headings:
(a) Houses.
(b) Family structure.
(c) Land ownership.

The development of African farming

Pure subsistence farming in Africa belongs to the distant past. A thousand years ago, there were already farming villages all over the region. Within the villages there were specialist crafts like weaving, metalwork, and pottery. There were several prosperous towns and cities, and the tribal groups in many areas had been brought together in extensive kingdoms and empires.

In a farming village today:

- Farmers produce crops or livestock for sale.
- Many villagers travel to towns and cities to work, and return with their savings.
- The cash income is used to buy manufactured goods. These may include items like colour televisions and videos.
- Social customs are often changing, too. In the past, a guest staying in a village would offer kola nuts as a gift. Today, a bottle of whisky or gin might be more acceptable.

To an outsider, the farming system in an African village may look as if it has remained unchanged for centuries; but present-day farming systems are the result of a series of innovations by peasant farmers over a long period of time:

- *Cassava* was introduced to Africa from South America or the Caribbean in the sixteenth century. Cassava-growing spread rapidly from village to village when farmers discovered that it was a valuable source of food which could grow well in difficult conditions.
- *Cocoa* is an important cash crop. It was introduced to the African mainland by a Ghanaian at the end of the last century. Peasant farmers began to grow it on a large scale because it provided a useful cash income.
- *Permanent cultivation* is another innovation. In the past, the farming system in most parts of West Africa was quite similar to shifting cultivation. The land was cultivated for a few years, and then left fallow for an extended period. Population has now increased in many areas, and it is no longer possible to leave the land uncultivated for such a long time. Villagers in places like Poka have been able to cut down on the fallow period, because they make good use of manure and tree crops.

Unfortunately, there are many parts of Africa where the farming system is not evolving so smoothly. Population has increased, and the fallow period has been cut down from 20–30 years to 5 or 10. If the soil is poor, or there is not enough manure, and if tree crops do not grow well in the area, then the land begins to deteriorate. Every time the land is cleared, it produces less; and if there is a disaster such as a drought, the community faces starvation.

12.4 A commercial crop: sugar cane

The early sugar industry

In the Caribbean, sugar is grown on a large scale as a commercial crop for the world market.

The Caribbean was almost the first area in the tropics to be systematically colonised by Europeans. The colonies here were used to grow tropical crops for consumption in Europe.

12.16 St Nicholas Abbey in Barbados. This old plantation house is one of the three oldest domestic buildings in the western hemisphere.

Sugar was much the most important of these crops. A new and convenient way of sweetening and preserving foods, it almost revolutionised European cooking and eating habits. Demand grew rapidly. At one point about two hundred years ago, the price of a tonne of sugar in England was £60. This was equivalent to two years' wages for a skilled manual worker at the time. In this period, growing tropical agricultural products was very profitable. Plantations – and sugar plantations in particular – dominated all aspects of life in the Caribbean.

Even in islands where there is no commercial sugar-growing today, the influence of the plantation period can still be seen in the landscape, and in the economy and social structure.

- Ruined sugar mills are thick on the ground almost everywhere; in St Vincent alone, the sites of 160 small sugar mills have been identified.
- Many plantation great houses are still standing. Some of them, like Worthy Park and Rose Hall in Jamaica, are imposing eighteenth-century mansions.
- Many place-names are the names of sugar plantations. The name may be derived from the owner's surname, or his original home, or a landscape feature, or a public figure or great event. It may be English, French, Spanish, or Dutch.

12.17 Morgan Lewis windmill in Barbados. Early sugar mills were also powered by water on islands where there were fast flowing rivers, or by oxen.

- Property boundaries and roads often follow the pattern laid out by colonial adminstrators and estate proprietors several centuries ago.
- Commercial cane-farming affected the physical geography of many islands when woodland was cleared for agriculture. The settlers had little experience of tropical agriculture. In islands like Antigua and Tobago there was disastrous soil erosion on unsuitable land which was cleared for sugar-growing.
- The most significant effect of the plantation economy was on the society and population of the Caribbean. Most people living in the region today are wholly or partly descended from African slaves who were brought in to work on the sugar estates, or from indentured labourers, mostly Indian, who were brought here at a later date.

The sugar industry today

Almost every country in the world now produces some sugar. Tropical countries grow *sugar cane* and temperate countries grow *sugar beet*.

1 Look at Figure 12.18:
   (a) Which countries are the world's three leading sugar *producers*?
   (b) Which countries are the three leading sugar *exporters*?

2 What proportion of the world sugar crop is grown in:
   (a) Cuba?
   (b) The Dominican Republic?
   (c) The USA?
   (d) The Commonwealth Caribbean?

	Production (000 tonnes)	Exports	Imports
The main Caribbean producers			
Barbados	101	78	–
Belize	110	96	–
Cuba	7,889	7,209	–
Dominican Republic	921	722	–
Guyana	258	230	–
Haiti	50	–	18
Jamaica	210	152	24
St Christopher and Nevis	27	25	–
Trinidad and Tobago	80	62	28
Some leading producers outside the Caribbean			
European Community	13,860	4,291	1,339
USSR	8,600	175	4,477
USA	5,415	364	2,275
Brazil	8,451	2,609	–
China	5,200	200	–
India	7,016	41	–
Australia	3,439	2,651	–
World production			
Beet sugar	32,247		
Cane sugar	61,753		
Total	99,000	27,537	26,394

Source: International Sugar Association Sugar Yearbook, 1985.

12.18 Caribbean and worldwide sugar statistics.

3 Name four countries which grow sugar cane, four countries which grow sugar beet, and two countries which grow both.

The world sugar market

When many countries have a poor sugar crop, there is a worldwide sugar shortage, and the price of sugar rises rapidly. The last time this happened was in 1974, when the sugar price rose at one point to $1,320 US per tonne.

High prices benefit sugar producers, while they last. But generally, they do not last very long. The next year, the main consuming countries may have a good crop; and the main exporters may have been tempted to produce more sugar for sale. If this happens, the world sugar price will fall rapidly.

Luckily, most Caribbean countries are protected by special marketing arrangements. The European Community, Canada, and the United States all buy sugar from many Caribbean countries at a guaranteed price. The Soviet Union also buys sugar from Cuba at above the world market price.

4 Look at Figure 12.20:
   (a) What manufactured goods would a sugar grower have to buy to use as inputs?
   (b) Explain why producers who sold sugar on the world market would have faced serious difficulties in 1982–5.

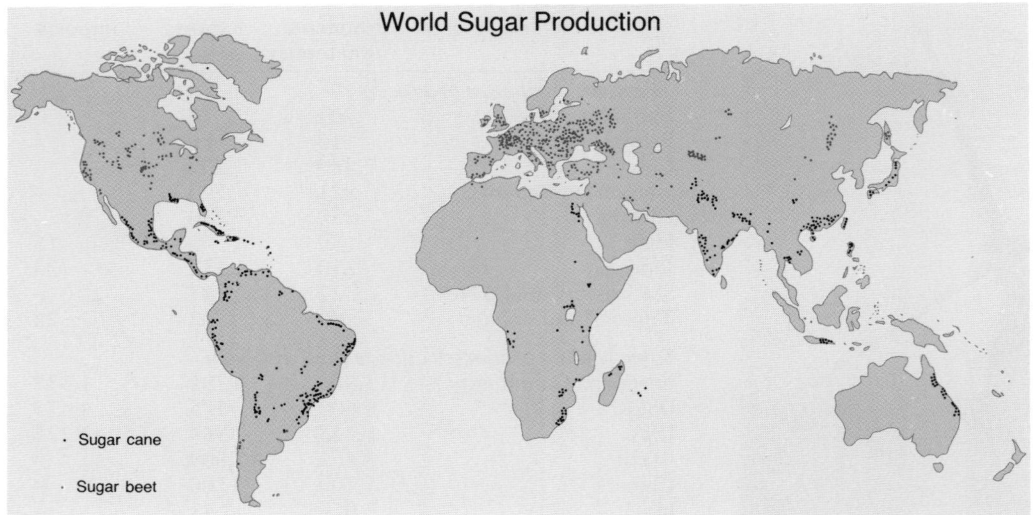

12.19 Where sugar is grown today.

5 What would be the effect on world sugar prices of:
(a) A very good harvest in Brazil?
(b) A cut in production by the United States?
(c) A cut in production by Jamaica?

The decline of the sugar industry

As world sugar prices are low and unstable, only producers who are efficient and who farm land which is suitable for sugar-growing can survive. This is why most of the old plantations and estates no longer grow sugar, and some islands have no commercial sugar-growing at all.

Even where sugar is still the main crop, it is much less important to the economy than it was forty years ago.

Driving around Barbados, a visitor would think that the island still depended on sugar. Most of the agricultural land is still planted with cane, and there sometimes seems to be an endless expanse of canefields stretching as far as the horizon.

In spite of this:

- Employment on the estates has fallen from 22,500 jobs in 1946 to less than 8,000 today.
- The sugar industry earned 55% of the island's foreign exchange in 1946, but brings in less than 10% today.

6 What economic activities have replaced sugar as the major source of employment in the Caribbean?

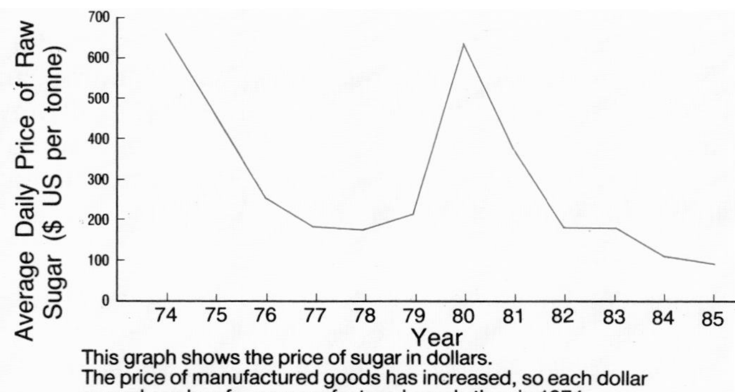

12.20 World sugar prices, 1970–1985.

How sugar cane is grown

Fields are prepared for planting by deep cultivation. On large estates, heavy crawler tractors are used to pull disc harrows and sub-soilers, which break up the lumps of earth. After cultivation, furrows are made in the field, and stones are picked off where necessary. On most soils, over 200 kg of fertiliser is needed for every hectare for a good crop of cane.

Pieces of cane stalk are placed in the furrow, and covered with soil. They will send up new shoots. Seed is used only for breeding new varieties. Rows of cane are planted, between 1.2 m and 1.6 m apart. Other crops are often grown between the rows of young cane.

Weeds must be controlled. This can be done by hoeing, with a cultivator, or by using herbicides.

In some countries, fields are burnt before harvesting. Elsewhere, burning can have a disastrous effect on soil quality and on the next year's yield. The harvest starts soon after the beginning of the dry season.

Traditionally, cane has been cut by hand, but estates in many countries now use mechanical harvesters. After the harvest, cane is transported to the factory.

New shoots spring up from the roots of the old crop. They produce the next year's growth of cane, the first *ratoon* crop. There is no need for replanting, but fertiliser must be applied again, and some cultivation between the rows may be necessary. There will generally be about four ratoon crops before the field is ploughed and replanted.

12.21 A sugar estate in Barbados. The farm buildings are grouped around the plantation house.

Small farmers and large estates

In most Caribbean countries, sugar cane is grown by:

- A few large estates, which are specialised commercial operations.
- A large number of small farmers, many of whom produce several crops, some mainly for home use and some for sale.

In Jamaica, for example, there are:

- Nine large estates which cultivate 19,700 hectares and produce 46% of the cane. Five of these estates are government-owned.
- 20,000 small farmers who cultivate 23,000 hectares of cane and produce 54% of the crop.

Mechanisation

Changes in agricultural technology and economic conditions have influenced farming practices. Forty years ago, large commercial estates used oxen to pull the ploughs, and manual labour to reap the cane. There was no suitable machinery then, and wages were so low that there was little incentive to develop new techniques.

Before mechanisation, it would have taken a dozen workers two days to cut and load the cane from a one hectare field. With mechanisation, the same job can be done by two people in half a day.

7 Why have the larger estates in some Caribbean countries now introduced mechanisation?

8 Why would small farmers find it difficult to mechanise production?

9 How would farming practices be affected if:
(a) Wages were increased by 50%?
(b) Smaller, cheaper harvesters were introduced?

10 Would mechanisation be suitable for;
(a) A country with many manufacturing industries and high wages?
(b) A country with high unemployment in rural areas?
Explain your answer carefully.

12.22 Mechanical harvesting of green cane in Barbados. Machinery for cutting unburnt cane was developed here, and it is now in use in many other parts of the world.

Where sugar cane grows well

11 Compare Figure 12.19 with Figure 7.12 in Section 7.6, which shows the main world climatic types. Which climates appear to be suitable for growing:
(a) Sugar cane?
(b) Sugar beet?
(c) Neither of these two crops?

Sugar cane can be grown in most tropical environments, but it cannot be grown *cheaply* and *easily* everywhere in the tropics. If the climate, relief, soil conditions, or land drainage are not good, then either costs will be higher or yields will be much less.

Sugar cane grows best where rainfall is between 1,250 and 2,500 mm per year:

- Where there is too much rain, the sugar content of the plant will be too low. More cane will be needed to produce a tonne of sugar in the factory.
- Where there is not enough moisture, the growth of the cane will be held back. In very dry climates, irrigation will be needed; and someone will have to pay for it.

Cane is quite sensitive to the seasonal distribution of rainfall:

- Dry weather just after cane has been planted makes it difficult for the plants to establish themselves.
- Dry weather just before and during the harvest makes it easier to reap the crop and increases the sugar content of the cane.
- In Guyana, there are two rainy seasons, and two relatively dry seasons. Some fields can be reaped in the first dry season, and others in the second dry season. Much better use can be made of the sugar factories, and workers are less likely to be laid off for long periods.

Sugar cane is not affected very much by variations in temperature conditions within the tropics:

- Sugar cane needs a long growing season, with temperatures above 20 °C for most of the year; but it can be grown in the subtropics, where there is a short cold season, and can even withstand occasional frosts.

Relief is becoming increasingly important:

- It is cheaper to grow cane on wide expanses of flat land. Broken relief makes it much harder to use modern machinery; and there is a danger of soil erosion on sloping ground.

Cane can be grown on many different types of soil, but deep soils with a fairly heavy texture are best:

- On light, sandy soil, cane needs more moisture, and more fertiliser has to be used. This makes farming costs higher, and there is more of a risk of crop failure in dry weather.

Good drainage is also important:

- Where the soil does not drain well, an expensive system of field drains has to be built and maintained.

Where sugar cane is grown in Trinidad

Figure 12.23a shows the main sugar-growing areas of Trinidad. Figures 12.23b–d show relief, rainfall, and soil conditions on the island. Unfortunately, it is not possible to show detailed variations in soil conditions on a small-scale map; many areas of central and southern Trinidad have acid, poorly drained, or infertile soils.

12 (a) Explain why sugar is grown in area 'A'.
   (b) Explain why sugar is not grown in areas 'B', 'C', 'D', and 'E'.

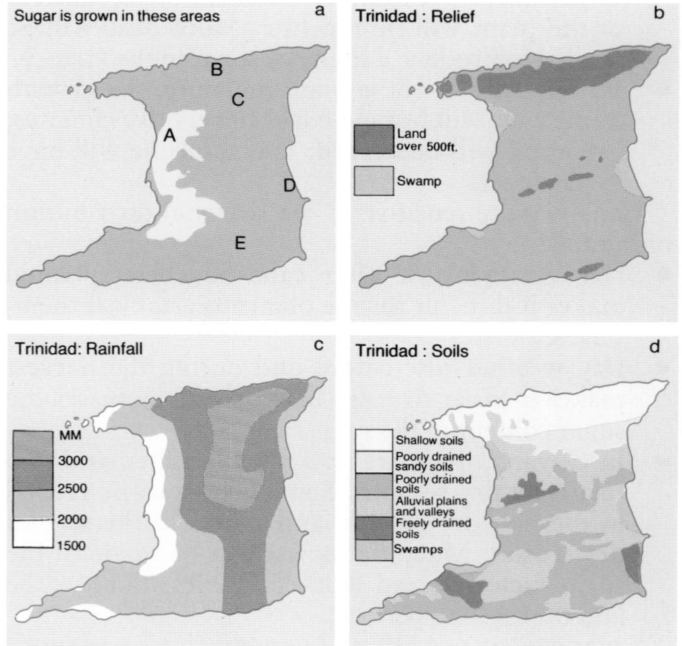

12.23 Where sugar is grown in Trinidad.

Worthy Park estate

Look back to Figure 5.3, which shows the Lluidas Vale polje in central Jamaica.

Most of the land in the polje belongs to Worthy Park estate, a large, privately-owned sugar plantation.

13 Give the grid reference of:
   (a) The Great House.
   (b) The sugar factory.

14 Why is the land in the polje suitable for sugar-growing?

15 Describe the *relief* and *land use* of:
   (a) The polje.
   (b) The land to the north-east and north-west of the polje.
   (c) The land to the south of the polje.

16 What type of farming system would you find in the area south of the polje?

17 Besides sugar, what other crops are grown in the polje?

Land drainage in Guyana

The first European settlers in Guyana found a wide expanse of coastal swamp, about 1–2 metres below sea level at high tide. This was not a promising environment for agriculture, and coastal areas like this in French Guiana and northern Brazil have remained virtually empty. Coastal areas in Guyana and Surinam are closely settled and cultivated because they were colonised by English and Dutch settlers in the days of high sugar prices and slave labour.

12.24 A sluice gate or *koker*. When the gate is opened at low tide, water from the drainage canal can flow into the sea.

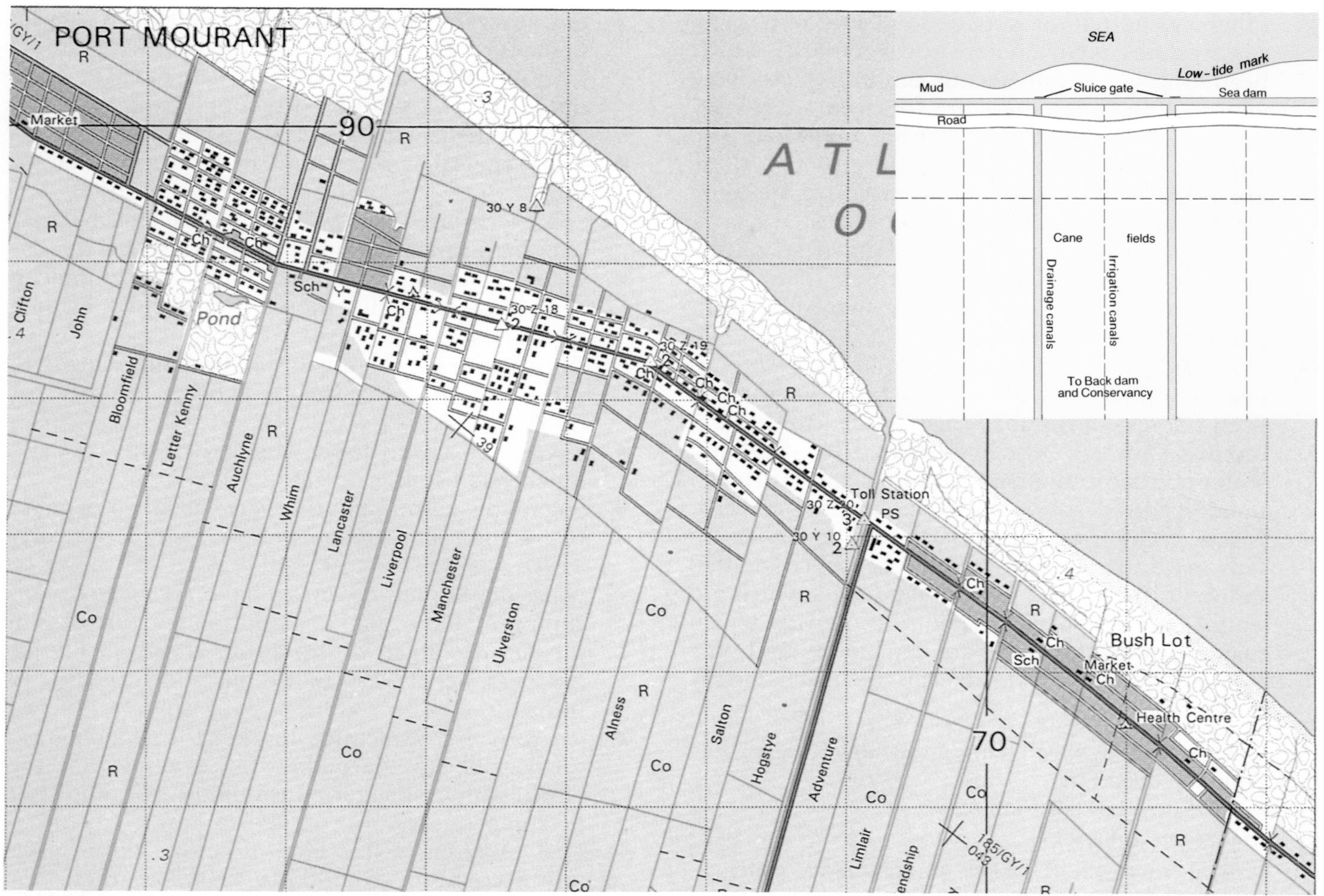

12.25 Cultivation and settlement on the coast of Guyana. The old sugar plantations are named and their boundaries can be clearly seen on present day maps.

12.26 The land drainage system in Guyana.

The early sugar estates were away from the coast, along the river banks; but the soil here soon lost its fertility, and it was found that the coastal swamps had much more potential. The settlers had the technology for land drainage, because low-lying areas in England and the Netherlands were being drained for agriculture at this time.

New plantations were laid out, in a regular, geometric manner. They each measured 377 m along the coast, and stretched inland for 2,825 m. The initial land grant was the 'first depth'; later on, second and third depths might be added, so that the estate became a narrow strip of land which extended several kilometres inland.

Water was kept out by a sea dam, and by a 'conservancy dam' at the southern end of the estate. On the eastern and western boundaries, there were 'sideline dams'. The marshy area to the south of the estate was known as a conservancy. Water from the conservancy was brought onto the estate for use in dry periods along an irrigation canal.

Water was fed into a main drainage canal from a network of smaller channels which divided the estate into rectangular fields 4–5 ha in area. At the mouth of the main drainage canal was a sluice-gate which could be opened to allow water to flow into the sea at low tide.

Each square kilometre of cane needed about fifty kilometres of drainage canals and ditches.

Figure 12.25 shows an area of old sugar-growing land on the Guyanese coast. It is a regular, planned landscape. The way in which this physical environment is used today is strongly influenced by historical factors from the days of high sugar prices, slave labour, and Dutch and English settlement.

Sugar cane growing in Guyana

The need for a land-drainage system has given the Guyanese sugar industry a very distinctive pattern of organisation.

- A drainage system is expensive to maintain. Almost all the smaller plantations eventually went bankrupt. Some were amalgamated, and others went out of production. The remaining sugar estates in Guyana are now very large. At the beginning of the nineteenth century, there were almost 400; today there are fourteen, all owned by one government corporation, Guysuco. The largest estate covers 70 km^2, and although there are some small farmers, they account for only 12½% of total production.

- The system of canals gives Guyanese sugar-growers access to irrigation water. They have more protection against drought than their competitors in some other countries.
- Some Guyanese estates use *flood fallowing* to restore soil fertility. After the last ratoon crop has been harvested, the fields are flooded for several months. The silt which is carried by the flood water contains important minerals and nutrients; flooding also destroys weeds, old roots, and trash.
- Mechanisation is much harder to introduce in Guyana. Cane has not traditionally been planted in long furrows, but in *cambered beds* which aid drainage. These beds are laid out in a way which makes it difficult to operate machinery, and only a small number of fields can be mechanically harvested.

18 List the ways in which sugar-growing in Guyana has been influenced by:
 (a) The physical environment.
 (b) Historical factors.

19 Look at Figure 12.25. Make a sketch map to show:
 (a) The area which is now cultivated.
 (b) The area of swamp which has not been drained.
 (c) The main road.
 (d) The canals.
 (e) The area which is used for settlement.

20 The map is at a scale of 1:50 000
 (a) Calculate the total area of the map extract.
 (b) Measure the distance along the main road.

The future of the sugar industry

The sugar industry often seems to have a poor image. It is associated in people's minds with badly paid and unpleasant work, with the past, and with dependence on others.

Sugar is certainly not nearly as profitable as it once was, and the Caribbean countries generally have very little influence on the world market.

It is impossible to say what the future for sugar production in the Caribbean will be; but the following facts are worth considering:

- The world price of sugar is less than the cost of production, even for the most efficient growers.
- For several years in the early 1970s, prices were high and the industry was profitable.
- Caribbean producers do not sell most of their output at the world price, but through special arrangements with their trading partners.
- These special arrangements may not continue for ever.
- Some territories, like Martinique, have deliberately chosen to run down their sugar industries.
- Other countries, like Cuba and the Dominican Republic, are still among the world's leading producers.
- People who eat too much sugar are more likely to suffer from tooth decay, diabetes, obesity, or heart disease.
- Sugar is a cheap food which the body can use quickly as a source of energy.
- Sugar consumption in the USA has fallen from 45 to 34 kilos per person per year since the early 1970s.
- Most developing countries have a very low consumption, but sugar consumption may increase in the future. Sugar consumption is only 4.1 kilos per person per year in China, and 8.0 kilos in India.
- There is a considerable market for sugar within the Caribbean. Barbados, for example has the world's highest sugar consumption: 64 kilos per person per year.
- New sweeteners like High-Fructose Corn Syrup now account for over 40% of the US market.
- Compared with fruits, vegetables, and specialist crops, sugar produces fewer dollars' worth of output from each hectare of land.
- Sugar cane provides good protection against soil erosion, compared with cotton and many vegetable crops.
- Sugar is the raw material for many profitable industries, such as food-processing and rum-refining.
- New uses are being developed for sugar. In Brazil, for example, alcohol made from sugar is used as a motor fuel.
- At today's prices, alcohol is a far more expensive fuel than petroleum.
- Sugar exports earn foreign exchange to pay for imported goods.
- Many of the inputs used by the sugar industry have to be imported; and the need for these inputs rises when the industry is mechanised.

21 Taking all these facts into consideration, do you feel that the sugar industry in the Caribbean has a healthy future? Give reasons for your answer.

12.5 Bananas

Banana exports

Bananas first appeared in the temperate countries in the last century as a luxury item, exotic and highly priced. Sailing-ships, and then steamships, would rush a few bunches to Europe or the USA before they spoilt. Now, the banana is an everyday item there, just as English apples are in the Caribbean; most people in temperate countries consume 5–10 kilos a year.

This is possible because there is:

- An efficient production system in the exporting countries.
- An efficient marketing system in the importing countries.
- An efficient transport and distribution system connecting the two.

Growing bananas for export is a major industry for the Windward Islands, and quite an important activity for Jamaica.

In St Lucia:

- Bananas are the second most important earner of foreign exchange, after tourism.
- There are over 6,000 registered banana-growers. This is around ⅙ of total employment.
- Cardboard boxes for packing bananas make up over 25% of manufacturing output.

Caribbean bananas and world trade

The banana trade is very important to the small countries of the eastern Caribbean, but they play only a very small role in the world market. The whole of Caricom accounts for under 1% of the world banana production, and for about 2½% of total exports and world trade.

Three large US-owned companies, United Brands, Castle and Cooke, and Del Monte, organise about 70% of world banana trade. They supply about 90% of the US market, and own some very large banana plantations, principally in Latin American countries, where the US has traditionally had a great deal of political influence and widespread economic interests.

In the Commonwealth Caribbean, the industry is organised in a very different way. In the Windward Islands, for example, there are:

- More than 15,000 growers who actually produce the fruit.
- Four Banana Growers' Associations which purchase the fruit from the farmers and supply them with fertilisers and other inputs.

The Windward Islands specialise in supplying one small part of the world market – the UK. Also involved in the industry are:

- Geest, a British company which buys fruit from the Banana Growers' Associations, ships it to the UK, and distributes it there.
- The Ministries of Agriculture on each island, which give general support to all agricultural activities.

12.27 Bananas from the Caribbean on sale in the UK.

	Production (000 tonnes)	Exports (000 tonnes)
Some Caribbean producers		
Antigua and Barbuda	1	–
Barbados	1	–
Cuba	220	–
Dominican Republic	320	6
Dominica	37	33
Grenada	14	9
Guadeloupe	153	131
Haiti	235	–
Jamaica	160	11
Martinique	205	156
St Vincent and the Grenadines	33	30
St Lucia	80	65
Some leading producers outside the Caribbean		
Colombia	1,200	945
Costa Rica	1,100	1,003
Ecuador	1,705	906
Honduras	1,300	830
Panama	1,100	660
World total	42,460	6,828
Some leading importers		
	Imports (000 tonnes)	
Canada	278	
France	443	
Japan	682	
UK	309	
USA	2,665	

Source: FAO Year Books, 1984 and 1985.

12.28 Bananas: world production and trade.

- The UK Advisory Committee on Bananas, where representatives of WINBAN (The Windward Islands Banana Growers Association), the Jamaican producers, the importers, and the UK Ministry of Agriculture meet so as to plan ahead and ensure that the right amount of fruit is imported.

1 Look at Figure 12.28:
   (a) Which are the four leading banana-producers in the Caribbean?
   (b) Which are the four leading banana-exporters?
   (c) Which two Caribbean islands do you think export large quantities of bananas to France?

Production difficulties

Collecting fruit from thousands of growers on four islands, and delivering it in peak condition to thousands of retail shops on another continent in a short space of time is a complex business:

- If there is too much fruit, it cannot be sold, and the price plummets.
- If there is too little fruit, other producers take more of the market.
- If there is poor-quality fruit, the customers buy elsewhere.
- If costs are too high, the producers' profit margin disappears.

The 1970s was a difficult period for the Windward Islands banana industry. Figure 12.29 shows how production fell during this period. Prices were low – too low to meet marketing and shipping expenses and still leave even an efficient medium-scale grower with a reasonable profit. At the same time, the UK market was gradually lost to other producers and weather conditions were not favourable.

2 Use the information in Figure 12.29 to explain the fall in production in the 1970s.

Since 1980, the banana industry in the Windward Islands has recovered. An industry based on a large number of small growers can produce good-quality fruit at a competitive price.

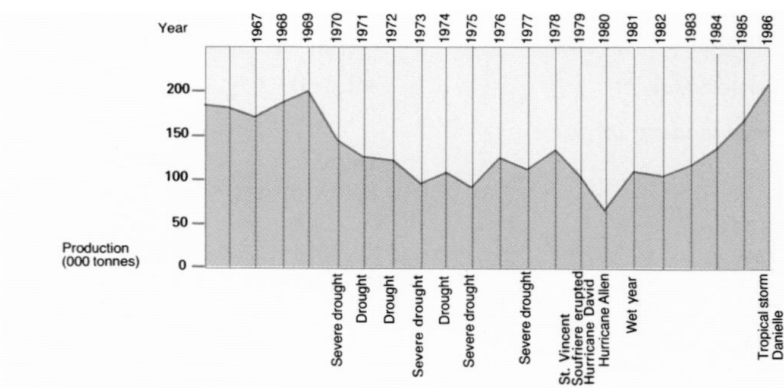

12.29 Windward Islands banana production, 1965–1983.

Banana yields

Banana yields in the Caribbean are generally much lower than in some other exporting countries. Internationally, the most efficient producers achieve yields as high as 25 to 30 tonnes per ha, and WINBAN has actually managed to get better results than this using the best available techniques in St Lucia. But many small growers get as little as 10 tonnes of marketable fruit per ha, and in some cases results are actually much worse than this.

There are several reasons for this:

- Some Caribbean farmers grow bananas on unsuitable land, which is really too dry or has poor soil.
- Countries like Cameroon and Ecuador do not suffer from hurricane damage.
- Production in Central America is generally on very large estates, organised into 'divisions' of up to 120 km^2, which are worked by several thousand employees under one management team. Very large plantations like these can afford facilities like aerial spraying and private rail lines.

3 Caribbean growers need to increase yields, cut costs, and increase their market share. Would large estates on the Central American pattern be a good idea?

4 Do very large estates have any disadvantages from the social point of view?

Where bananas grow well

- *Temperatures* should be high all year round. Even a short period with low temperatures damages bananas. They cannot be grown commercially in 'subtropical' areas like Florida.
- *Rainfall* should be high, too, A prolonged dry season damages the crop, unless there is water for irrigation. Total annual rainfall should be at least 1,500 mm.
- *Soils* should be deep and well-drained. Artificial fertilisers are needed to maintain nutrient levels.

Bananas are grown in small quantities for domestic consumption throughout the Caribbean, but the main export industries are concentrated in certain countries.

5 Why are the Windward Islands major banana-exporters?

6 Why are few bananas grown in Antigua or Barbados?

7 Which types of environment are suitable for growing sugar cane but not suitable for bananas?

How bananas are grown

The WINBAN Research Centre at Roseau, St Lucia, carries out research into all aspects of the banana industry. It is the largest agricultural research centre in the eastern Caribbean and has a worldwide reputation.

It is important to ensure that growers are aware of the results of the research. WINBAN prepares leaflets, posters, films and radio programmes, as well as training growers and agricultural extension workers.

Extension officers visit farmers to assess the strong and weak points of their existing farming practices, and persuade them to adopt new methods where appropriate. In the Windward Islands, there are over 100 banana extension staff.

Every year, more than 3,000 soil samples are analysed, to determine the exact fertiliser requirements of a particular piece of land. Fertiliser should be applied regularly in the correct amounts, depending on soil and rainfall conditions and the stage of growth of the plants.

Correct pruning and weed control are essential, to ensure that the available nutrients are used to produce fruit and not waste growth. Plants should be sprayed to protect them from nematodes, banana borers, slugs, and other pests. Props help to prevent wind damage.

Sleeving with blue diothene bags protects the fruit from field marks, and hastens ripening.

Where possible, bananas should be boxed in the field. Careful transport from the field is important. Rough roads and poor packing damage the fruit, so that it cannot be sold. Cableways can be used to take the bunches to boxing plants without bruising.

Bananas are loaded onto the ship on *pallets*. This cuts down the need for labour at this point. The journey to the UK takes one week. On the ship, the fruit is kept at a temperature of 13.5 °C, and ventilation is carefully controlled.

In the UK, bananas are loaded into containers, and taken to a depot to finish ripening. The next stage is distribution to the point of sale.

8 List the inputs which are used by the banana industry.

Most small farmers have adopted some improved practices in banana cultivation. A recent survey showed that:

- 98% were pruning their bananas, and using some form of weed control.
- Over 90% were propping their plants to prevent wind damage, and using some fertiliser (though not necessarily using the correct quantities of the right type of fertiliser).

However, very few kept proper farm records and accounts, or sent soil samples away for analysis.

Small farmers, commercial crop

Bananas fit in very well with the small farmer's cropping system:

- They provide quick returns. The time from planting to harvest is less than a year.
- They bring in a steady income. They can be harvested all the year round.
- There is a guaranteed market for good-quality fruit.
- They are not just an export crop. Bananas can be used as a food crop for the family or sold locally.
- They fit in well with food crop production, and can easily be grown in mixed cropping systems.

9 How do bananas compare in these respects with:
(a) Sugar cane?
(b) Citrus?
(c) Carrots?

Peasant farmers may grow as many as fifteen or twenty different crops on one or two small parcels of land. Bananas may be grown under tree crops like coconuts, breadfruit, or mangoes; then other plants like maize or sweet potatoes may be planted between the bananas. Almost all the 'banana land' on some islands is under some form of mixed cropping system.

Leguminous crops like cowpeas are very useful for intercropping, because they fix nitrogen in the soil and cut down on the amount of fertiliser needed. Research by WINBAN has shown that careful inter-

12.30 Large growers sometimes use cableways to transport bananas without bruising.

12.31 Most growers in the Windward Islands now pack bananas in the field.

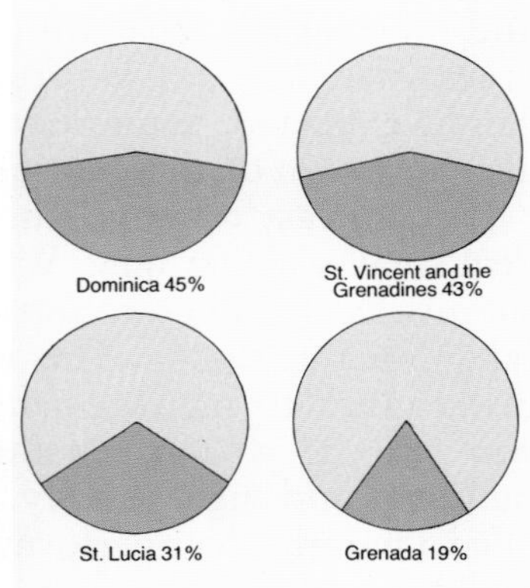

12.32 Bananas as a percentage of total exports.

cropping does not damage banana yields, and increases overall production from the land significantly.

10 Look carefully at the cropping system in Figures 12.8 and 12.12. What are the advantages of a mixed cropping pattern for:
   (a) Soil conservation?
   (b) Feeding the farm family?
   (c) Providing a year-round cash income?
11 Are there any disadvantages to this type of cropping system?

St Lucia Model Farms

12 Refer back to Section 4.8:
   Write a description of the landforms of the lower Roseau valley.

Like most of the top-quality agricultural land in St Lucia, the lower Roseau valley was originally a large sugar estate. It was bought by Geest in the early 1960s. By that time, bananas were a much more profitable proposition than sugar, and this was seen as an opportunity for a large commercial firm to grow bananas with maximum efficiency in the eastern Caribbean.

The results were disappointing. Yields were low, about 15 tonnes of fruit per ha of land, and some of the high-quality land was not even in cultivation.

13 Why was this an unsatisfactory situation for:
   (a) Those working on the estate?
   (b) The owners of the land?
   (c) The government of St Lucia?

In 1982, an organisation called St Lucia Model Farms was given the task of breaking up the estate into smaller farms. For the first time, people living in the villages round the edge of the estate were to have the opportunity to run farms on good land, first as tenants, then as owners. The first smallholders took possession in 1983. When the project is complete, there will be 115 small farms of 2 hectares each on the valley floor, which will specialise in producing bananas for sale, and 60 hillside farms of between 4 and 6 hectares which will grow other crops, such as limes, mangoes, passion fruit, and pineapples, which can be exported. Some root crops and vegetables can also be grown on these farms.

It is not easy to move from estate work to independent small-scale farming. Where plantations have been subdivided in other countries, production has often fallen for this reason. This is why careful attention is being given to management and supervision. There will still be a 'nucleus farm' near the old estate buildings and sugar factory. Smallholdings are visited once a month; their performance is assessed, and they will be told if their weed control or pruning, for example, is not sufficiently thorough. Advice is always available for farmers who need it, and the smallholders build up accounts with a central fund which can be used to buy inputs such as fertilisers, boxes, or pesticides.

So far, the project has been a real success. Yields have increased to 25 tonnes per hectare on the smallholdings which are now in operation. With yields like these, the farmers can pay the substantial rent which is needed to cover land purchase and central administrative costs, and still have enough over for saving and family expenditure.

14 List the ways in which the production system operated by small farmers in the lower Roseau valley is different from traditional Caribbean peasant farming.

One-crop economies?

Twenty years ago, the Windward Islands were highly specialised economies, dependent on:

- One export crop, bananas.
- One major buyer, Geest Industries.
- One overseas market, the UK.

These provided a large percentage of the foreign exchange the Islands needed to buy goods from abroad.

In some years, St Lucia depended on bananas for over 90% of its export earnings.

An overspecialised economy is very vulnerable to:

- Natural disasters, like hurricanes, which can wreck the banana crop.
- Diseases, like Panama disease, which almost wiped out the Jamaican banana industry in the 1920s and 1930s.
- Changes in the exchange rate. Bananas for the UK are priced in pounds, so whenever the value of the pound against the EC dollar is reduced, growers get less for their fruit.
- Changes in the marketing arrangements for bananas in the UK.

For a small island, there are also advantages in specialised export agriculture:

- Top-quality research into growing and marketing the crop is possible if researchers concentrate their efforts on one or two crops.
- It is easier to spread information about new agricultural techniques.
- It is possible to make sure that the right inputs are available, and to start manufacturing some of these inputs within the island.
- It is possible to set up specialised transport and marketing systems for a perishable crop like bananas.

15 Figure 12.32 shows bananas as a percentage of total exports for the four Windward Islands in 1983. Were any of these countries too dependent on one export crop? Explain your answer carefully.
16 How can the transport and marketing system which has been developed for bananas help to increase the export of other fruit and vegetable crops?

12.6 Small-scale farming in Trinidad

Look back to Figure 12.6. The number of people working in agriculture in Trinidad and Tobago fell very rapidly in the period 1965–85, because there were many other types of work available in manufacturing and services. However, many small farmers have become very prosperous by operating a *market gardening* system. They earn a steady income by producing high-quality fruit and vegetables for sale on a small area of land.

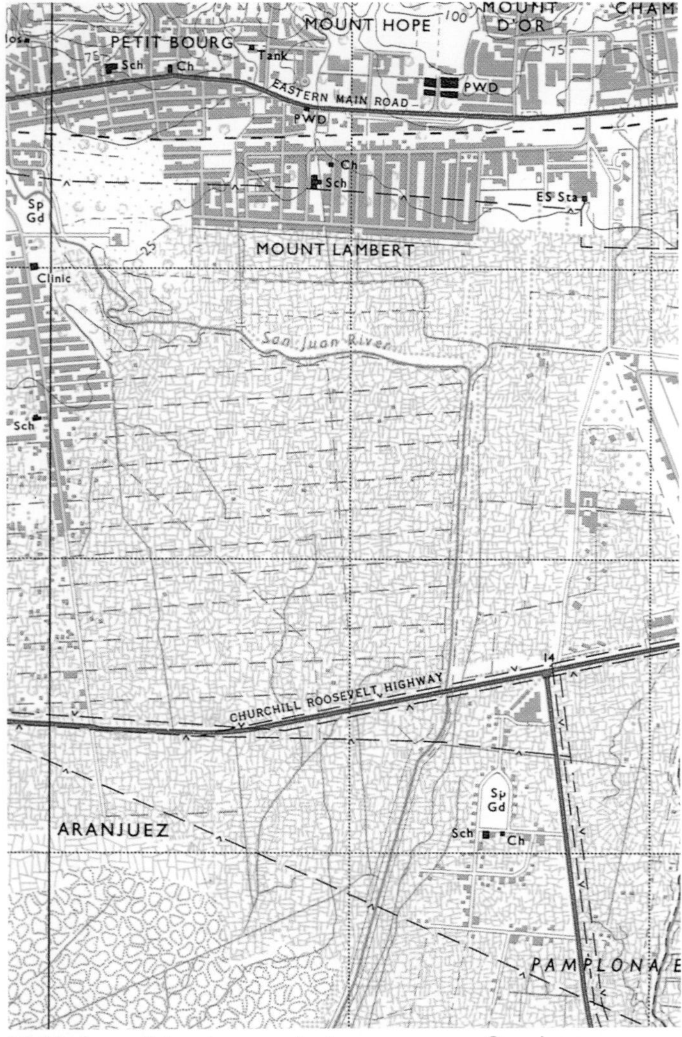

12.33 A small farming area in Aranguez, near San Juan, Trinidad. Scale 1:25 000. Contour interval 25 feet

Vegetable Garden

Vegetable-growing in Aranguez

The Aranguez valley, east of Port of Spain, is an old sugar estate, which has been split up into a large number of small tenant farms. No sugar cane has been grown there for more than forty years, and the small farmers produce vegetables for sale.

12.34 Irrigated vegetable growing in Aranguez, Trinidad.

These farmers have been successful because:

- Most of the area has good loam soil, which holds moisture well in dry weather and remains workable when it is wet.
- There is a good supply of irrigation water. A dam was built across the San Juan river in the 1930s; water from the dam supplies irrigation channels which run across the land approximately 90 m apart.
- There is a huge demand for fresh vegetables in Port of Spain and the surrounding area.

Figure 12.34 shows part of a vegetable farm. The land is divided into large beds, which measure approximately 6.5 by 90 m. Between the beds, there are ditches, which can be used to take water from the main irrigation channels.

The farm is in immaculate order. There are no weeds to be seen between the neat rows of vegetables. This farm grows sweet peppers, cauliflower, tomatoes, eggplant, beans, spinach, and other crops. The land is kept well fertilised, with chicken manure and bagasse as well as chemical fertiliser. Each piece of ground produces several crops every year, so although the farm measures only 0.8 ha, it brings in a satisfactory income for the farmer and his family.

Running a farm like this is hard work. Because of the small size of the farm, it is not worth buying any heavy machinery. But the farmer hires a tractor when the ground needs to be cultivated; a drainer when the ditches need to be shaped; and a bush-cutter when land needs to be cleared. He also owns a spray pack for applying pesticide, and a water pump for irrigation.

When there is a busy period, temporary farm workers are taken on; but there is no permanent hired help.

Some problems

There are some problems with farming in the Aranguez valley, however:

- Insects and other pests often attack the growing crops. Chemical sprays are expensive, and do not always seem to be effective.
- Praedial larceny is a serious problem. Many farmers sleep in a shelter in the fields when a crop is ready to be harvested.
- Some holdings are very small. Some holdings are as small as 0.2 ha, which is not enough to provide a reasonable income.
- Vegetable prices are very unpredictable. If there is a *glut* of one crop, the price will be very low. If there is a *shortage*, the farmer will make a good profit.
- Some farms are flooded when there is heavy rain; when this happens, growing crops may be a total loss.
- In dry weather, there is not always enough irrigation water for all the farmers.

In spite of these problems, this farming system is a very successful one. Forty years ago, the houses in the village were built of mud, with roofs thatched with carat palm leaves. Today, there are substantial concrete-block houses, with a full range of modern services.

1 Make a sketch map of the Aranguez area. You should show:
   (a) The main roads.
   (b) The farm access roads.
   (c) The San Juan river.
   (d) The built-up areas.
   (e) Sloping land.
2 Compare market gardening with traditional peasant farming. List the *similarities* and *differences* under these headings:
   (a) Size of farm.
   (b) Crops grown.
   (c) Equipment and technology.
   (d) Markets
3 What can be done about the problems which affect small farmers in Aranguez?
4 Look at Figure 12.33. Can the area which is used for this type of farming in Aranguez be expanded?

Growing citrus in Siparia

Near Siparia in southern Trinidad, there are many hilly areas where the soil is a red-brown sand with a low humus content. Most land of this type is not used for agriculture. It would not be suitable for intensive vegetable-growing. However, it can be used for pasture and tree crops.

A typical farm in this area would be about 16 ha in size. It would grow coffee, cocoa, and many different types of fruit. The main crop is citrus. Most citrus farms in Trinidad grow oranges and grapefruit to sell in bulk for juicing; but this farm has taken a different approach. Most of the land is planted with trees which produce high-grade fruit like ortaniques and tangerines for eating. There is a high demand for good-quality fruit, and the whole crop can be sold from the roadside stall, in Figure 12.35. By selling direct, the farm gets more money for the fruit; and the consumers pay less than they would in a supermarket.

12.35 Selling citrus by the road provides a convenient marketing outlet.

There is also pasture land on the farm. The sheep which are grazed there provide manure for the fruit trees. Most of the fruit trees are young; but when they are larger, the sheep will be able to graze beneath them to control the weeds.

There is no need for heavy machinery. There is a bush-cutter, and two four-wheel-drive vehicles for transportation. Artificial fertiliser has to be used to maintain soil fertility, and there are chemical sprays to control pests.

A medium-sized farm like this can be worked with family labour, although in this case there is one full-time employee. Because the farm is a successful one, all the family members are able to earn a cash income which makes farm work more attractive than any other avenue of employment.

5 Why would this area not be suitable for vegetable-growing?
6 Why is it possible to work a farm of this size with only family labour?
7 List the differences between this farm and the Aranguez farms under these headings:
   (a) Size of farm.
   (b) Crops grown.
   (c) Relief and soil.
   (d) Marketing.

12.7 Farming in the Canadian Prairies

12.36 A prairie landscape.

Figure 12.36 shows a rural landscape in the Canadian prairies:

- The land is almost completely flat.
- There are very few trees.
- Most of the land is being used for one crop, wheat.
- The land is divided into large, rectangular fields.
- The town in the foreground has a regular, planned layout. The streets run at right angles to each other in a grid plan.
- A railway line runs through the settlement.
- Next to the railway line, there are large elevators which are used to store grain.
- There are several large pieces of agricultural equipment outside a dealer's office near the railway.
- Outside the village, there is very little rural settlement.

1 In what ways does this scene contrast with a rural landscape in the Caribbean islands?
2 Are there any similarities?
3 Which Caribbean landscapes would have most similarities with the one shown in the photograph?

The prairie provinces are the most important agricultural region in Canada. They cover a vast area, 1.75 million km^2, or 20% of the national territory; and this includes almost 80% of the country's farm land.

Within the prairie provinces, there is an area of temperate grassland vegetation known as the *prairies*. This is the most productive agricultural area. To the north of the prairies, these three provinces contain large areas of coniferous forest and tundra vegetation.

The natural environment

4 In the Canadian prairies, there is a cold temperate interior climate:
   (a) Refer back to Section 7.7 and describe the main features of this type of climate.
   (b) Give two reasons why conditions in the summer are favourable for plant growth.
   (c) Why is plant growth impossible in the winter?
5 The southern part of the prairie provinces has temperate grassland or *prairie* vegetation. Refer back to Section 8.3, and describe the main features of this type of vegetation.

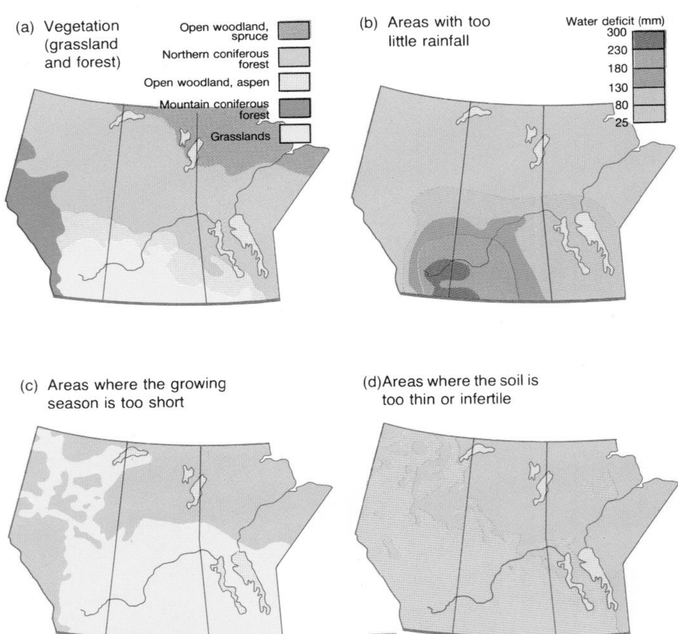

12.37 The Prairie provinces: physical environment.
(a) Vegetation.
(b) Areas with little rainfall.
(c) Areas where the growing season is too short.
(d) Areas where the soil is too thin or infertile.

12.38 Posters like this one attracted settlers to the prairies.

6 Many areas with temperate grassland vegetation have *chernozem* soils:
   (a) Refer back to Section 9.4 and make a labelled sketch to illustrate this type of soil.
   (b) Explain why this type of soil is agriculturally productive.

7 Figures 12.37a–d show some of the aspects of the physical environment which influence agriculture in the prairie provinces:
   (a) Make one sketch map to show the area which is most suitable for agriculture.
   (b) Explain why agriculture can be difficult in the south-west part of the prairie provinces.
   (c) Give two reasons why agriculture is not possible in the north-east part of the prairie provinces.

The settlement of the prairies

The prairies have a regular, planned landscape because they were settled very recently. Some of the children who came out with their parents to cultivate new land in the early years of this century are still alive today.

The prairie provinces are a very productive agricultural region, but they were settled very late, because;

- They are an interior region, and Canada was settled from the coast.
- There is a long, cold winter. This made conditions very difficult for the early settlers.
- There are very few trees. It was difficult to build warm houses or obtain enough fuel. Some early settlers built 'sod houses' out of turf, and had to burn animal dung to keep warm.
- Over large areas, there are no surface streams, and fresh water is difficult to obtain.

The first European settlers came to Manitoba in 1812–13. Travelling from eastern Canada was so difficult that they came into the region from the north, via Hudsons Bay. Life was hard at first. Agriculture was almost on a subsistence basis, and there was very little money to buy supplies from outside. The first shipment of wheat was not made until fifty years after the settlers arrived.

By the end of the nineteenth century, it was a great deal easier to settle the prairies, because of the development of:

- The steel plough, which made it much easier to cut through the thick mat of grass and cultivate the soil.
- Steel windmills, which could pump up groundwater where there were no surface streams.
- Reaper-binder machines, which meant that a farmer and his family could cut a big field of wheat without hired help.
- New varieties of wheat, which could ripen where there was a short growing season.
- Dry-farming techniques, which made it possible to grow wheat where rainfall was very low.

- The railway, which linked the prairies with the big cities and ports of eastern Canada. The Canadian Pacific Railway was completed in 1883–5. Over the next thirty years, a whole network of branch lines was added. All the agricultural land was within easy reach of a railway station by horse and cart.

8 Explain why the railways were so important for the development of a commercial farming system in the prairies.

The newly settled lands were laid out as a regular grid. We can still see traces of this pattern in Figure 12.36. Land was granted to the railway companies, to encourage them to open up new lands for settlement. The Canadian Pacific Railway alone received 100,000 km^2 of farmland. New settlers were allocated quarter-sections of government land for a nominal sum. After they had farmed the land successfully for three years, they became the owners.

The Canadian government printed pamphlets in 20 languages to publicise the scheme, and distributed them in eastern Canada, the USA, and Europe. In many parts of Europe, peasant farmers and landless labourers were desperately poor. The offer of virtually free land must have sounded like a dream, and there was a rush of new settlers. In 1900, there were just over 10,000 farms on the prairies; by 1914, there were 250,000; and most of the good land had been occupied.

Environmental problems

When the prairies were first settled, the soil produced between 1.15 and 1.70 tonnes of wheat per hectare. But after a few years, yields fell by about 30%. When there was a run of dry years, a serious soil-erosion problem developed, and many farmers went bankrupt. Some unsuitable areas had been settled, and these were converted back from agricultural land to pasture, or else, in some cases, irrigated.

9 Section 10.4 describes how soil-erosion problems developed in a temperate grassland area of the USA during the 1930s. Read through this section again:
  (a) Explain why yields fell after the land had been cultivated for a few years.
  (b) Explain what is meant by *strip cropping* and *conservation tillage*.

Prairie farming today

Wheat farms are now very large. Almost half are over 300 ha, and 13% are over 640 ha. But in spite of their size, nearly all the work is done by family members; at most, one or two hired helpers may be taken on for a few weeks during sowing or harvest.

12.39 Combine harvesters.

Machinery is a major item of expenditure; so are fuel, fertilisers, pesticides, and other chemicals.

This is an *extensive* form of agriculture. The output from each hectare of land is not so great, but farmers have a very high income because they use such a large area of land.

In Canadian agriculture, the trend is towards large farms which use less human labour and more machinery, chemicals, and other equipment.

In the last century, 80% of the Canadian labour force worked in agriculture; today the figure is less than 5%.

Over the period 1961–81:

- The number of farms fell by 34%
- The percentage of farms larger than 450 ha increased from 4.7% to 11.3%.
- The number of tractors increased by 108,000.

The farming year

The seasonal pattern of wheat farming is like this:

- After the snow melts in the spring, the ground is very wet; but as soon as it is dry enough, which is usually in May, fields are ploughed and wheat is sown. The seeds are spaced mechanically 25 mm apart for the best results. Within a week, the fresh green shoots of young wheat begin to appear.
- While the wheat is growing, the fields must be fertilised two or three times. The growth of weeds must also be controlled, and the crop must be sprayed to protect it from pests and diseases. Growing wheat is green in colour.
- Towards the end of the summer, in August or early September, the wheat ripens. It turns to a golden-yellow colour. The crop must be harvested very quickly, before the first frost. A combine harvester allows one person to cut 20 ha of wheat in one day; but even at this rate, the farmer must work very quickly on a large farm to get the crop

in at the right time. The combine cuts the wheat, and separates the grain from the straw and the waste material.

- The wheat is then transported to the nearest grain elevator. There is virtually no physical work to be done on the farm during the winter months, unless there are livestock to be cared for. There may be a considerable amount of paperwork, because a large farm is a major business operation; but many farming families spend the winter in a city, or in the southern part of the USA, or even in the Caribbean.

10 Draw a diagram to compare the farming year in:
(a) A Canadian wheat farm.
(b) A sugar plantation in the Caribbean.
(c) A peasant farm in the Caribbean.

The world market

Wheat is in many ways an ideal export crop:

- It can be stored for long periods without deteriorating.
- It is cheap and easy to transport.
- There is a strong demand for wheat in many countries which cannot grow enough to meet their own requirements.

11 Look at Figure 12.41:
(a) Which three countries are the world's leading wheat producers?
(b) Which country is the leading exporter of wheat?
(c) Why do some of the biggest producers still need to import wheat?

12 What would happen to the world price of wheat if:
(a) There is a very bad harvest in the USSR?
(b) Canadian farmers grow much more wheat?

	Percentage of world production	Wheat yield (kg per hectare	Population (000,000)	Percentage of world exports
China	16.7	2,951	1,052	Net importer
USSR	16.3	1,647	275	Net importer
USA	12.9	2,519	237	37
India	8.7	1,873	747	Net importer
France	5.7	6,008	55	13.2
Canada	4.7	1,746	25	18

Source: FAO and *UN Yearbooks*, 1985.

12.41 Wheat production statistics.

13 Make a bar graph to show the average yield of wheat per hectare of land in each of the six countries.

14 Figure 12.40 shows the main routes used to export wheat. Which route would be used to send wheat to:
(a) China?
(b) The Caribbean?
(c) Western Europe?

As with almost all agricultural commodities, the price of wheat on the world market is very unpredictable. If Canadian farmers produce a very large amount of wheat, their income may even *fall* if the price is much lower than it was the previous year.

The aims of the Canadian government are:

- To have an efficient production system, and keep costs low.
- To help maintain prices at a reasonable level.

The federal government attempts to influence the wheat market through the Canadian Wheat Board:

- The Board limits the amount of grain each farmer can produce, to avoid the danger of over-production.
- When a farmer delivers wheat to the Board, a down payment is made straight away.

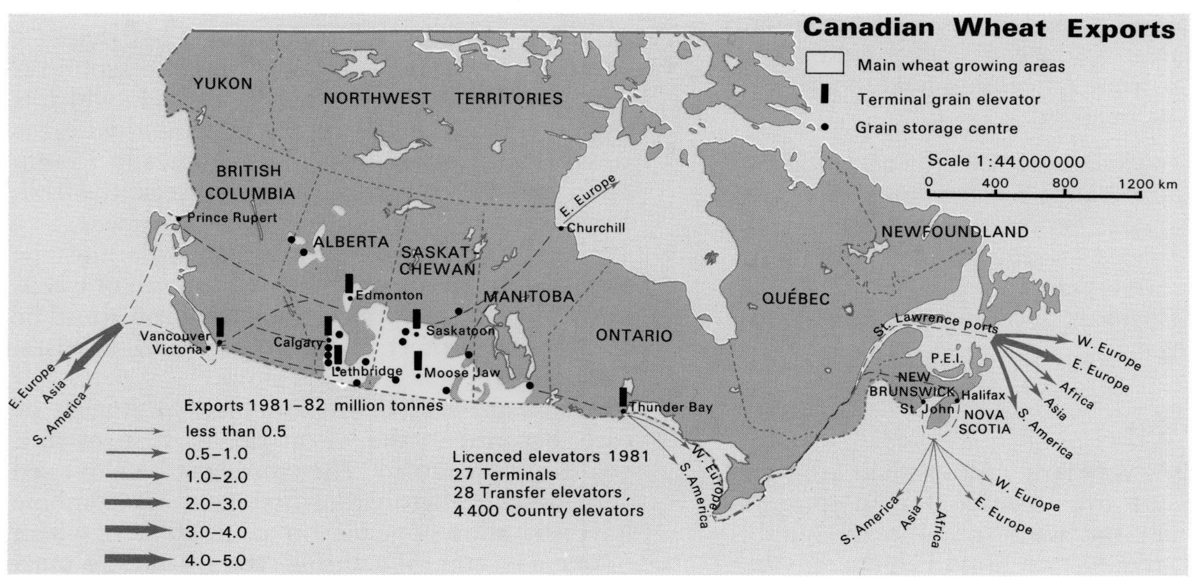

12.40 How wheat is exported from Canada.

- The Board negotiates the sale of wheat on the world market. If prices are too low, grain is stored until there are more buyers. Because the Board is a large organisation, it is in a position to get a good price.
- When the wheat has been sold, farmers receive an extra payment.

Droughts, pests, and plant diseases are all natural hazards which can cause major problems for the farmer. But today, the economic environment is at least as important for the commercial farmer. If a farmer has borrowed money to buy land and machinery, and then sees interest rates go up at the same time as wheat prices fall, then the farm will be in financial trouble even if the harvest is a good one.

The economy of the prairies

The prairie provinces are often classed as a wheat-farming area. But this does not give a full picture of their economy today.

In many parts of the prairies, other arable crops or livestock farming are now more important than wheat-growing. This is because:

- It is important to limit wheat production so as to maintain prices.
- Dry areas in the south-west of the Canadian prairies are more suited to livestock farming.
- The land in the *park belt* to the north of the prairies is more suitable for dairy farming and for other crops like rapeseed and barley, which ripen more quickly than wheat.

Wheat-growing is more important in Saskatchewan than in the other prairie provinces, but even here more than one-third of the farms specialise in other grains or in livestock production, and most of the wheat farms have some other activity as well.

When they were first settled, the prairies were agricultural communities. Since then, farms have become larger and use more machinery; and other economic activities have become more important:

- More than half the population of the prairie provinces lives in five large cities.
- Mining and oil extraction in Alberta bring in much more money than agriculture.
- Manufacturing in Manitoba brings in more money than agriculture.
- Even in Saskatchewan, only 25% of the labour force is still in agriculture.

12.8 Cattle in the Caribbean

Animals are raised in many different farming systems. In the Caribbean:

- Many small peasant farmers keep a few cattle, goats, sheep, or chickens.
- There are also large specialised pastoral farms where large numbers of animals are kept on a commercial basis.

Many commercial pastoral farmers raise poultry, pigs, sheep, or other animals. But cattle are probably the most important animals for commercial farmers in the Caribbean.

Some cattle are kept mainly for slaughtering for *beef*; others are kept mainly for milk and *dairy* products.

	Cattle slaughtered (000)	Average carcass weight (kg)	Total beef production (000 tonnes)
Some Caribbean producers			
Belize	7	162	1
Cuba	880	165	145
Dominican Republic	329	177	58
Guadeloupe	28	146	4
Guyana	15	133	2
Haiti	185	180	33
Jamaica	78	205	16
Martinique	21	171	4
Puerto Rico	152	161	24
Trinidad and Tobago	8	175	1
Some leading producers outside the Caribbean			
Canada	4,180	234	980
China	3,219	88	283
India	1,115	80	89
Japan	1,576	352	555
Nigeria	1,750	126	221
USA	40,045	275	10,994
World total/average	229,938	200	46,072

Source: FAO Yearbook, 1985.

12.42 World beef production statistics.

Beef cattle in the Caribbean

1 Look at Figure 12.42:
  (a) Are any Caribbean countries major beef producers?
  (b) Which Caribbean countries produce most beef?
  (c) What do you notice about the average weight of beef cattle in:
    – The USA, Japan, and Canada?
    – Nigeria, India, and China?
    – The Caribbean?
  (d) Make a bar graph to show average carcass weight of beef cattle in the USA, Jamaica, and Nigeria.
  (e) India has a very large population. Why are so few cattle slaughtered there?

Cattle farming in the tropics

Wild cattle originated in a temperate environment, and most of the more productive modern breeds were developed in countries like Britain and the USA. Beef cattle like Herefords and Angus, and dairy breeds like Friesians, Holsteins, and Jerseys do not always thrive easily in tropical conditions:

- Tropical grasses are generally less nutritious than those of temperate countries. Cattle do not gain weight so quickly if there are less nutrients in each mouthful of feed.
- Cattle suffer from heat stress in full sunlight. They need shade in the middle of the day. They will not normally make use of open unshaded pasture at this time.
- Diseases like tick fever, foot rot, and mastitis are a serious problem. They lower milk production for dairy cattle, and reduce the productivity of animals which are being kept for beef.

The Creole cattle which were traditionally kept in the Caribbean could cope well with heat, stress and poor pasture, and were disease-resistant. But they did not produce nearly as much milk or meat as the temperate breeds.

Cattle-farmers in the Caribbean have now developed ways of dealing with some of these problems:

- New breeds have been developed for the tropics. In Jamaica, cross-breeding of Indian and European breeds with local Creole cattle has led to new beef and dairy breeds such as the Jamaica Red Poll and the Jamaica Hope.
- There have been some major disease-control programmes. In Puerto Rico, there was a successful drive to eradicate the cattle tick. In Cuba, the number of veterinary surgeons has increased from 220 in 1959 to 3,516 in 1983; and the number of outbreaks of bovine tuberculosis has fallen from 1,074 in 1967 to 6 in 1983.
- There has been research into improved pasture management. Grasses and legumes which can provide relatively nutritious pasture on water-logged soil or in dry conditions have been identified. In Martinique, the amount of useful feed growing on dry land was almost tripled after the pasture was irrigated and fertilised.

The buffalypso

Water buffalo were first brought to Trinidad from India in 1903. They were used for many years as draught animals by small farmers and on the sugar plantations, to pull carts and for ploughing. When they were old, they were slaughtered; the carcass would produce a small quantity of rather tough meat.

Buffalo cannot be interbred with cattle. But from 1949, buffalo have been bred selectively in Trinidad to produce meat. A new breed, the buffalypso, has been developed. Buffalypso are much more solidly built than traditional buffalo. A mature animal weighs 380–450 kg, and produces high-grade meat which is marketed as beef.

12.43 Many small farmers keep cattle; but breeding and grazing is often haphazard.

12.44 The buffalypso have been bred for meat. Contrast the shape of these animals with the creole cattle in photograph 12.43.

Buffalypso are an ideal beef animal for the tropics. They have a thick skin, which makes them resistant to ticks and other parasites. They can thrive on low-grade pasture, with only small amounts of extra feed.

Today there are approximately 6,000 buffalypso in Trinidad and Tobago. Most of the beef in the country is still imported, but there have been profitable exports of live animals to other countries for breeding. Calves are sold for breeding at $1,000 to $1,500 US per head, and shipments of around 100 animals have been sent to Guyana, Cuba, the USA, and ten other countries in the Caribbean and Latin America.

A pastoral farm in Trinidad

The Circle A Ranch near Waller Field in Trinidad is a successful commercial pastoral farm. There is a herd of 150 buffalypso, as well as cattle, Black Belly sheep, pigs, and horses.

The ranch is on low-quality soil, which has developed on white silica sand. The soil is acid, and holds few nutrients. Until the 1950s, the land was not used for agriculture at all. Today, there are 16 ha of woodland, and 90 ha of pasture.

The buffalypso are kept on the pasture for most of the time. During the dry season, they are given low-grade supplementary feed.

Less labour is needed here than in most types of arable farming. There are only three full-time employees.

If there is water available, buffalo like to wallow in it during the hottest part of the day. This keeps them cool, and helps them to gain weight faster. The land at Circle A Ranch is very dry, however, so there is not enough surface water for this to happen.

2 Compare the buffalypso in Figure 12.44 with the creole cow in Figure 12.43. Explain why the shape of the buffalypso makes it a better animal for meat production.

3 Explain why the land at Circle A Ranch would not be suitable for arable farming.

4 List the ways in which the buffalypso is more suited to tropical conditions than temperate breeds of cattle.

Cattle in Guyana

Guyana is a large country. Although only a small proportion of the land is used for pasture, this is enough to make Guyana self-sufficient in beef, and to make the aim of self-sufficiency in dairy products by 1992 a realistic one.

Most of the cattle are concentrated in two parts of the country, the coastal plain and the Rupununi savannas.

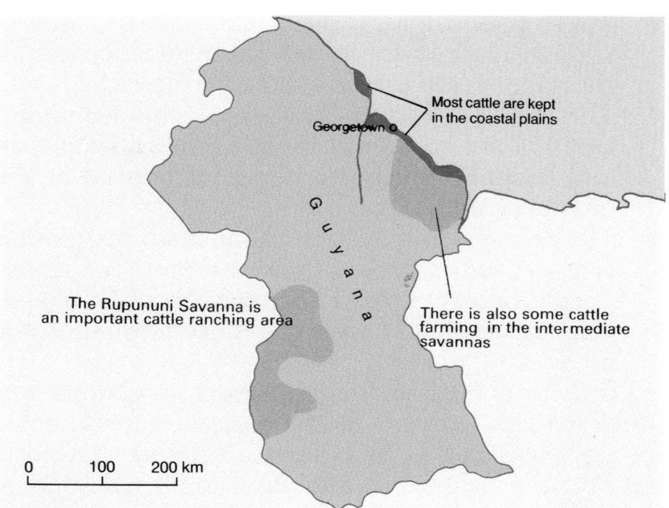

12.45 The main cattle farming areas of Guyana.

The coastal plain

Cattle are kept by small farmers and by specialised commercial operations in many areas of the coastal plain which were formerly used to grow rice or other crops.

This is the most *accessible* part of Guyana. There is good road transport to Georgetown and the other large towns. Cattle are kept for milk as well as for beef.

Most of the cattle are Creoles, but the local breed has been improved over the years by imported bulls.

The commercial farmers are trying to increase production by:

- Improving the quality of the pasture. New grasses and legumes are being introduced.
- Preserving grass as *silage*. This means that feed can be made available when it is needed, all the year round. There should be no shortage of feed in the dry season or in very wet weather.
- Increasing the numbers of pure-bred dairy cattle. Recently, large numbers of Holstein cattle have been imported from the United States.

Climate, soil, and accessibility mean that these areas have a great deal of potential for cattle farming. At present, 0.8 ha of pasture are needed for each head of cattle; but with improved management, the most efficient commercial operations will soon be able to reduce the area of pasture needed to 0.2 ha.

The Rupununi savannas

There is a large area of tropical grassland in southern Guyana which is also used for cattle-raising. The physical and human environment here is very different from that of the coastlands:

- There is a tropical continental climate, with a strongly marked dry season. During the dry season, shortage of feed can be a serious problem.
- The natural pasture grasses of the Rupununi savanna are not as nutritious as the sown grasses and legumes which are being introduced in the coastal areas.
- The area is a long way from the main population centres, and transport routes are not well developed. There is no road link to the rest of Guyana. This means that commercial dairy farming is not possible.

Cattle from the Rupununi savannas are slaughtered in the town of Lethem, and the carcasses are flown to Georgetown. This is an expensive form of transport, but beef is a valuable commodity, so air transport is worthwhile.

Because the quality of the pasture is poor, at least 10 ha of land are generally needed for each animal.

Farms have to be large. Some of them may measure as much as 200 km^2.

5 List the contrasts between cattle farming in the Rupununi savannas and cattle farming in the coastal plain.

	Number of dairy cows (000)	Average annual milk yield (kg per cow)	Total milk production (000 tonnes)
Some Caribbean producers			
Antigua	6	1,000	6
Barbados	7	1,296	9*
Cuba	680	1,471	1,000
Dominican Republic	249	2,000	498
Haiti	93	238	280
Jamaica	50	1,000	50
Puerto Rico	202	1,797	363
Trinidad and Tobago	6	1,705	10
Some leading producers outside the Caribbean			
Canada	1,722	4,762	8,200
India	28,130	658	18,500
Japan	1,462	5,046	7,377
New Zealand	2,220	3,559	7,900
Nigeria	1,200	295	354
USA	11,115	5,844	64,954
World total/average	222,423	2,059	458,023

*These figures include traditional dairy farmers as well as commercial producers selling milk to Pine Hall dairy. Milk yields are much higher than average on the commercial farms.
Source: FAO Yearbook, 1985.

12.46 Dairy farming: world patterns.

Dairy farming in the Caribbean

6 Study the statistical information in Figure 12.46:
(a) Which five Caribbean countries produce most milk?
(b) What do you notice about the average milk yield in:
- The USA, Japan, and Canada?
- Nigeria, India, and Haiti?
- Other Caribbean countries?

(c) Make a bar graph to show average milk yields in the USA, Cuba, and Haiti.

Traditional dairy farming

Until recently, most Caribbean countries had a very small-scale dairy industry. Milk production was mainly a sideline for farmers:

- Plantations often kept a few cattle to supply fresh milk for their own use.
- Peasant farmers might keep a *house cow* or two, to provide milk for the farm family and a few neighbours.

Cattle were grazed on land that was not needed for other purposes; for extra feed, they were given cane tops, cut grass, and any extra feed that was available. Breeding was haphazard, and milk yields were low. There was a health risk from unpasteurised milk, and there was no organised marketing and distribution system to make fresh milk available to the general population.

Very little capital was needed for this sort of dairying. Not much milk was produced, but there was no need for imported feed and equipment, or for any purchases from off the farm. This was a *low-input – low-output* system.

12.47 Dixie Farm in Barbados. Cattle are fed on the 'zero grazing' system.

Some problems with dairy farming

The development of dairy farming in the Caribbean has been held back by problems connected with the physical environment, such as poor-quality pasture, heat stress, pests, and diseases; and storing fresh milk is always a problem in a tropical climate.

There are also problems connected with the social and economic environment:

- In a small country it is hard to pay for top-quality imported bulls. Inbreeding damages the long-term health of the dairy herd.
- There are not enough dairy calves. Older cows are often kept in production, even though they may barely be producing enough milk to pay for the feed they consume.
- Most people do not use very much fresh milk. In many cases, people are used to evaporated or condensed milk, which is imported or made from imported milk powder.
- Some countries do not have a dairy which can *pasteurise* fresh milk to make it safe for human consumption.

A modern dairy farm

Dixie Farm in the south-east of Barbados is a commercial livestock farm. There are several thousand chickens, Black Belly sheep, and a herd of dairy cattle.

The farm covers 16 ha. The land is no different in climate, soil, or relief from the surrounding canefields; both types of production can be carried on profitably in the same environment.

There are approximately 100 cattle, including young calves. This gives an average of seven per hectare, quite a high figure for the Caribbean. The cattle are Holsteins, a black and white breed that was developed in northern Germany and North America for milk production. There is no bull on the farm, so cattle are bred by *artificial insemination*.

The farm uses a 'zero grazing' system. The cows remain in the milking shed all day; the pasture land is sown with grass which is cut and fed to them in the form of chopped fresh grass, hay, or silage. They are also given *concentrates*, supplementary high-nutrient feed which is purchased to maintain a high level of milk output. 400 grammes of concentrate must be fed to the cows for each litre of milk produced.

Zero grazing uses more labour and more machinery than traditional methods, but the pasture land can be used very efficiently.

There are only four workers on the farm, including the manager, because there is a lot of specialised machinery. There are machines to cut the grass, bale it for hay, chop it for silage or green feed, and to scrape manure from the floor of the cattle shed. Milking by machine saves labour; and is also much more hygienic than milking by hand.

No one farm is 'typical' of modern dairying in the Caribbean. Some farms have several hundred cows; others have under ten. Instead of zero grazing, some farms use continuous cropping of large areas of pasture; others stake cattle out in the field, or subdivide the pasture into small paddocks. Some producers have very little pasture of their own, and bring in most of their feed from outside. What is typical is a trend towards larger units, which are specialised dairy farms, and which have very careful technical and financial organisation.

Marketing milk

Fresh milk must be processed very soon after it is produced to make pasteurised milk, butter, cheese, milk powder, or other dairy products.

Farmers can only plan their production if they are confident that their milk can be sold. Organising the processing and sales is usually too complex for the individual medium-scale farmer.

The 33 commercial dairy farms in Barbados all sell their milk at a guaranteed price to the Pine Hill Dairy, which collects fresh milk every day in refrigerated trucks, and takes it to a central plant outside Bridgetown to be pasteurised, packaged, and distributed for sale.

Since the dairy was opened in 1966, commercial milk production has expanded from 1,800 tonnes in the late 1960s to 4,546 tonnes in 1986.

7 Draw a diagram to show the operation of:
   (a) Traditional Caribbean dairying.
   (b) A modern dairy farm.

8 Why does a modern dairy farm need a large amount of capital?

9 Are there any other reasons why small farmers would find it difficult to operate a modern dairy enterprise?

10 How does Dixie Farm deal with each of the problems which have affected Caribbean dairying?

11 Which problems would be difficult for an individual farm enterprise to deal with?

12 What are the *advantages* and *disadvantages* of:
   (a) The modern approach to dairy farming?
   (b) The traditional approach?

13 List the differences between the farming systems at Dixie Farm in Barbados and Circle A Ranch in Trinidad.

12.9 Cattle in the USA

Refer back to Figure 12.42. The USA produces 24% of the total world output of beef. The average person in the USA eats 110 kg of beef every year; this compares with an average annual beef consumption of:

- 32 kg in Brazil.
- 10 kg in Trinidad and Tobago.
- 6 kg in Nigeria.

Beef production is by far the most important sector of US agriculture. Beef and other livestock products make up almost half of total farm output in the country.

Beef cattle in the Great Plains

Look at Figure 12.48 and 12.49. Most of the western half of the USA has:

- An average annual rainfall below 500 mm.
- A population density below 50 persons per km^2.

Running from north to south across the western half of the USA is a broad belt of temperate grassland known as the Great Plains. The climate here is very variable:

- Winter temperatures are very low.
- Summer temperatures are very high.
- Rainfall varies a great deal from one year to another.
- The length of the frost-free period can also vary.
- There are very strong winds, which can cause rapid soil erosion.
- Hailstorms can devastate a field of growing crops.

This is a difficult area for agriculture. Figure 12.51 shows land-use patterns in the Great Plains. Some areas are used for growing wheat. The 'wheat belt' extends north into the Canadian prairies. But the western part of the Great Plains is too dry for arable farming. Most of the land is low-grade pasture, which is used for cattle ranching.

1 Look at Figure 12.50:
   (a) Comment on the difference in land-use patterns between Illinois, Iowa, Nebraska, and Wyoming.
   (b) Make a bar graph to show the average value of farmland per hectare in these four states.

Cattle ranches

A large cattle ranch may cover several hundred square kilometres. Cattle ranches need to be large because the *carrying capacity* of the land is very low. In some

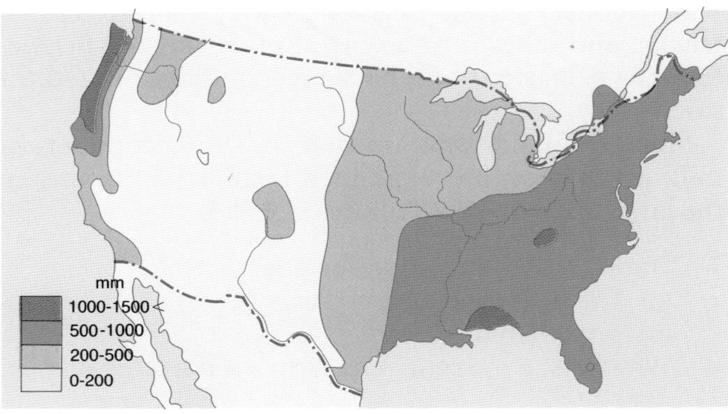

12.48 The United States: rainfall.

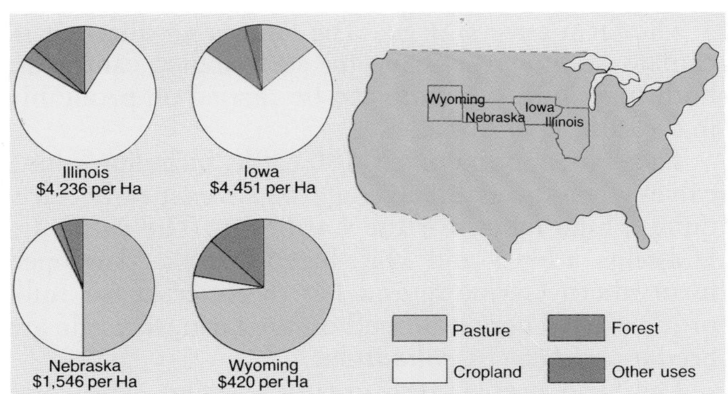

12.50 Land use in the United States showing value of farmland.

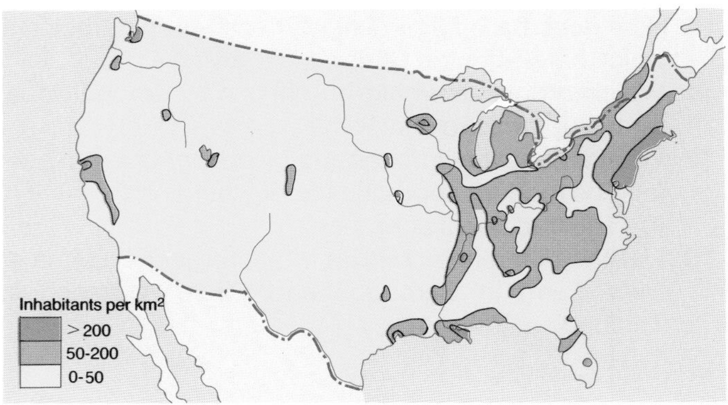

12.49 The United States: population density.

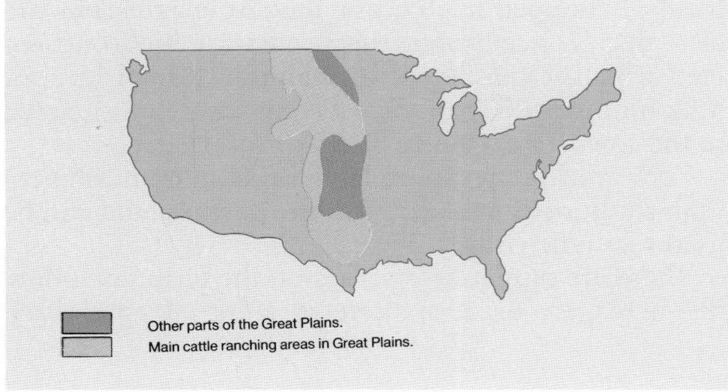

12.51 The Great Plains.

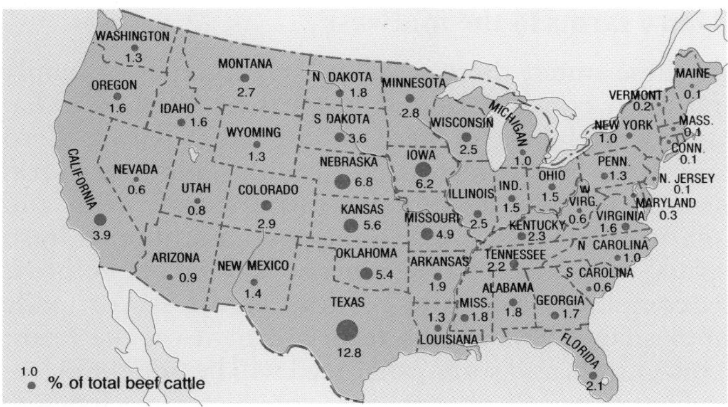

12.52 Beef cattle in the United States.

parts of the Great Plains, an animal needs 20 ha of grazing land; so an area of 100 km^2 is needed to support a herd of 500 cattle. King Ranch in Texas covers 3,340 km^2.

The cattle are mostly Hereford and Angus. These are breeds which were developed in the UK in the nineteenth century for beef production. The animals put on weight in the rump, and in other parts of the body which produce high-grade meat.

In Texas, in the southern part of the Great Plains, many of the cattle are Texas Brahmans. This is a breed of humped cattle which was developed by crossing Indian Zebu cattle with European breeds. Texas Brahmans cope well with hot conditions and poor pasture.

Calves are born in the spring. They spend the first six months of their lives with their mothers on large areas of pasture. After 8–10 months, the calves are weaned. They are rounded up, dehorned, castrated, vaccinated, and branded. Some calves are sold at this stage, but most ranches keep them for another year. During the winter, they are pastured for much of the time in most areas; but they are also given feed, such as silage or alfalfa.

During the summer, the young cattle are pastured again; but before the cold weather starts, the animals which are not required for breeding are sold to *feedlots*.

Feedlots

Ranches are *extensive* farming systems, making use of large areas of low-grade land; feedlots are *intensive* operations where large numbers of cattle are kept on a small area of land. Cattle do not graze on a feedlot; they are fed according to a carefully planned programme which is designed for maximum weight gain in as short a time as possible. The aim is for each animal:

- To eat 2–3% of his body weight per day.
- Include 0.6–1.35 kg of protein in his intake.
- Achieve a weight gain of 1–1.35 kg per day.

A large feedlot may contain as many as 20,000 cattle in small pens. They are given concentrates, grain, and vitamin supplements. On average, 10 kg of grain are fed to cattle to produce 1 kg of meat. For roughage, the animals are given silage made from maize (corn), and other material such as plastic pellets.

Feedlots are located:

- On irrigated land in the western states, where fodder crops like hay and alfalfa can be grown in the summer for winter use.
- In the midwest, where large quantities of maize and soybeans are grown for fodder.

2 Look at Figure 12.52:
   (a) Which states have most beef cattle?
   (b) Which of these states are:
      – Western states with extensive cattle ranches and some feedlots?
      – Midwestern states with feedlots for fattening cattle?
      – States in other parts of the USA?
   (c) Why does Wyoming have a large area of pasture, but a comparatively small number of beef cattle?

3 Compare cattle farming for beef in the USA with cattle farming in Guyana. What are the *similarities* and *differences* between the farming systems in the two countries?

Dairying in the USA

The average US household spends 7% of its food budget on dairy products. Most people in the USA drink large quantities of fresh milk, and more milk is used to make butter, cheese, and other items.

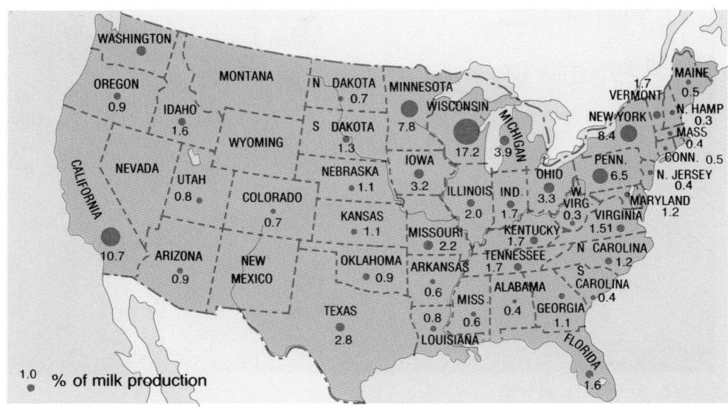

12.53 Dairy farming in the United States.

Traditionally, there has been some dairy farming in all states of the USA, producing milk for the local market, and a specialised dairy region in the midwest, producing fresh milk, butter, and cheese for the whole country.

4 Look at Figure 12.53:
   (a) Which states have most dairy farming?
   (b) Compare Figures 12.53 and 12.48. What pattern do you notice?
   (c) Compare Figure 12.53 with Figure 12.52. What *differences* do you notice between the distribution of beef and dairy cattle?

A dairying region

The northern-part of the US midwest is a specialised dairying region because:

- The climate is moist, and fodder crops grow quickly.
- The growing season is quite long, but sometimes not long enough for most varieties of maize (corn) to ripen.
- The landscape is too hilly for large-scale arable farming. It is not suitable for modern ploughs and combine harvesters in some places.
- The soil is reasonably fertile, but not ideal for arable farming.

Much of the milk which is produced in the midwest is consumed within the region. But most is transported to other parts of the USA by road, dried or frozen for use in the food-processing industries, or made into butter and cheese.

The state of Wisconsin accounts for:

- 17% of US production of fresh milk.
- 25% of the butter.
- 40% of the cheese.

12.54 A feeding lot.

Dairy farms in the midwest

In these states, there is still a large number of family farms. A typical farm would measure 100 to 150 ha, and would have a herd of 50 to 75 cows. Zero grazing is very common. Most of the land in the farm is used to grow feed for the cattle, mostly grass and maize. The grass is fed to the cows as chopped fresh grass, or as hay, or silage; maize is often cut before it is completely ripe, and is either used fresh or made into silage. Not all the feed is grown on the farm; concentrate and some other feed will be bought in.

Some small dairy farms are quite highly mechanised. Cattle may be fed mechanically; cultivation of fodder crops is highly mechanised; milking is always by machine. Because of mechanisation, farms are larger then they were; the number of farms fell by 55% over the thirty years 1952–82. But dairy farming still employs quite a large number of people. Even a small family farm will have one or two helpers.

5 Compare dairy farming in the midwest with:
   (a) Cattle ranching in the Great Plains, and
   (b) Commercial dairy farming in the Caribbean.

6 Canadian arable farmers can leave their farms for a long period each year. Explain carefully why this would not be possible for a dairy farmer.

12.55 A milking shed.

13 · Manufacturing

13.1 Types of industry

Primary, secondary, and tertiary industry

Primary industries make direct use of the earth's *natural resources*. The main primary industries are agriculture, mining, forestry, and fishing. They produce things which can either be used directly as they are, like fresh fruit and fresh fish, or which can be used as *raw materials* for other industries.

1 What natural resources are used by:
   (a) A farmer growing sugar cane?
   (b) A Caribbean fisherman?
   (c) A lumber company in Canada?

Secondary industries are also known as *manufacturing industries*. They produce processed and assembled goods. Many secondary industries use raw materials which have been produced by primary industries: canning fruit, freezing fish, or making cement. But some manufacturing industries do not make direct use of primary products; they simply assemble or reprocess what other secondary industries have produced. The inputs for a factory which makes computers or clothes have already been through several stages of manufacturing and processing.

2 What secondary industries would make *direct* or *indirect* use of these primary products:
   (a) Sugar cane?
   (b) Wood?
   (c) Iron ore?

Tertiary industries do not produce anything which you can pick up and take away. They provide a service for members of the public or for another industry. Transportation and retailing are service industries. They ensure that manufactured goods are available in the right place and when they are needed. Hospitals and schools are tertiary industries which provide an essential service to the community. Other tertiary industries include tourism, banking, and insurance.

3 Look at this list of activities. Classify them into three groups – primary, secondary, and tertiary industries:

hairdressing	computer programming
shipbuilding	mining bauxite
selling clothes	air traffic control
dairy farming	making clothes
fashion design	making butter

Classifying manufacturing industries

There are several different ways of classifying manufacturing industry.

By the type of technology

- *Craft industry*: small-scale family-owned industries which generally use local materials and traditional technology to produce goods for the local market, for export, or for the tourist trade.
- *Factory industry*: larger-scale industries using modern machinery and employing a sizeable workforce to produce goods for the national or international market.

By the nature of the manufacturing process

- *Heavy industry*: industries like iron and steel, oil-refining and aluminium smelting, which operate in very large factories with a great deal of expensive machinery and equipment, and where a big volume of raw materials is used.
- *Light industry*: industries where less raw material and heavy machinery is used per employee. In *labour-intensive* industries, wages account for much of the cost of the finished product, and employers try to keep wage costs to a minimum.

By the pattern of ownership

- *Small businesses*: a small company or an individual owns and manages a single factory or workshop. Small businesses may operate successfully in craft industries, or in some high-technology fields like electronics.
- *Multinationals*: these are at the other extreme. One large holding company owns and controls operations in many countries. Very large companies produce and sell a wide range of different goods and services, and may own hundreds of well-known brand names.

By the type of product

This is probably the most obvious way of classifying industries into different groups and subgroups, such as:

- Food, drink, and tobacco-processing.
- Clothing and textiles.
- Wood and wood products.
- Paper, printing, and publishing.
- Chemicals and oil-refining.
- Metal products.

13.1 A manufacturing system.

A manufacturing system

Figure 13.1 shows how manufacturing industries operate.

They take in raw materials and other *inputs*.

These are processed or assembled in the factory by human labour and machinery to make a *product*, which is distributed to shops, warehouses, or other customers, either in the same country or overseas. These provide the *market* for the product.

4 Compare Figure 13.1 with the farming system shown in Figure 12.4. In what ways are the two systems alike? In what ways are they different?

Industrial location

Manufacturing industry is very unevenly distributed.

This is true on a *world scale*, if we contrast advanced industrial countries like the USA, West Germany, or Japan with less developed countries in Africa, South Asia, or Latin America.

This is true on a *regional scale*, if we contrast major industrial cities like Tokyo or Detroit with agricultural and mountain regions in the USA and Japan.

It is also true on a *local scale*, when we contrast industrial and residential areas in a large city, or look at the distribution of factories in a small island.

To operate successfully, an industry will need:

- A good supply of *raw materials*.
- A reliable and reasonably priced *energy supply*.
- Good *transportation* facilities – by land, by sea, and by air.
- Good *infrastructures*, such as: water supply, telephone service, waste disposal.
- A reliable *workforce*; sometimes with specialised skills if they are needed for a particular industry.
- A good *market* for the finished product.
- *Government policies* which provide direct or indirect help for industry, and ensure that transportation and infrastructures are adequate.

No location would have *all* these advantages. Industrialists deciding where to locate a factory will always have to weigh up the advantages and disadvantages of different possible sites. One location might be close to an agricultural area which provides raw materials for processing; another might be close to a town where there are many potential workers and a good market for the finished product.

5 Look at Figure 13.2. Which of the numbered locations would be suitable for:
 (a) A factory making jams and fruit juices?
 (b) A printery producing advertising literature for shops and offices?
 (c) A big clothing factory with several hundred employees?
 (d) A heavy chemical industry causing serious air pollution?
 (e) None of these factories?
 Explain the reasons for your answers carefully.

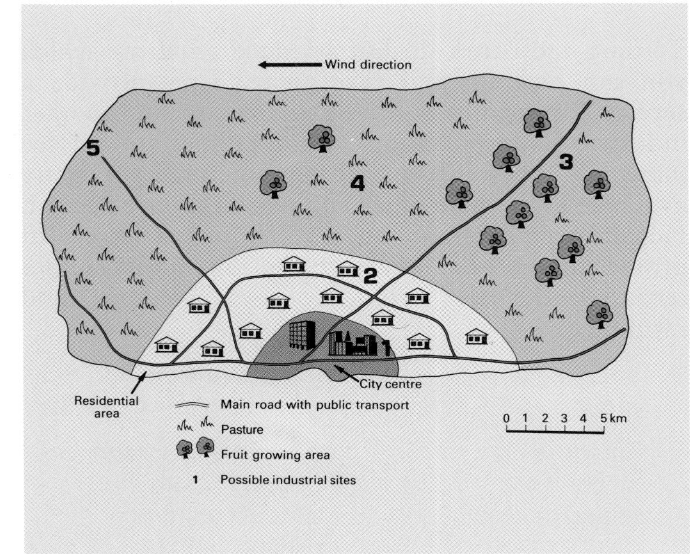

13.2 Industrial sites on a Caribbean island.

13.2 Manufacturing in the Caribbean

In the past, the Caribbean was not a major manufacturing region. The Caribbean countries were colonies which produced raw materials for Europe and North America:

- Sugar and cocoa were grown in the Caribbean; but chocolate was made in Europe.
- Cotton was grown in the Caribbean; but textiles were made elsewhere.
- Bauxite is mined in the Caribbean; but there is still no aluminium smelter in the region, and no prospect at all of an aircraft industry.

During the colonial period, almost all the manufactured goods used in the region were imported. There were only small-scale craft industries, where earnings were very low, and a few larger factories processing local primary products.

Some of the first industries to be set up were baking bread, printing newspapers, and bottling drinks. All of these industries made *bulky* or *perishable* products, which had to be made near to the market.

Government policy

Many new manufacturing industries have been established since the 1950s. Governments encourage new industries because:

- *Manufacturing provides jobs*: there will be well-paid management jobs as well as unskilled work on the factory floor. Reducing unemployment is a priority for all Caribbean governments.
- *Manufacturing reduces imports*: foreign exchange can be saved when local products can be substituted for goods from abroad.
- *Manufacturing increases exports*: manufactured goods can be sold abroad. More money is earned by exporting local products if they are processed first. But many factories also need to import their inputs from overseas.
- *Manufacturing provides government revenue*: most industries pay taxes, and also fees which help to cover the cost of ports, airports, and other infrastructures. Government revenue from industry can help to improve essential services for the local population.

Caribbean governments have tried to develop three types of manufacturing. These are:

- Heavy industries like oil-refining and bauxite-processing which are based on Caribbean *raw materials*.
- Industries which produce goods for the local *market*, sometimes with imported materials, like flour-milling and automobile assembly. These are *import substitution* industries.
- Industries which import materials and components, then use Caribbean *labour* to produce goods for export. These are *enclave* industries.

In this chapter, we will look at:

- Industry in St Vincent, a small country with few manufacturing industries.
- Light industry in the Caribbean: clothing, food-processing, and electronics.
- Heavy industry in Trinidad and Tobago, where there are many large industrial plants based directly or indirectly on two local resources, oil and natural gas.
- Bauxite: an industrial raw material which is very important for two Caribbean countries, Jamaica and Guyana.
- Manufacturing outside the Caribbean, in two industrial countries, Japan and the USA, and one less developed country, Nigeria.
- Manufacturing in Haiti: two approaches to industrial development in the poorest country in the western hemisphere.

13.3 Industry in a small island: St Vincent

Small islands are not always easy places for manufacturing industries to operate in. In the case of St Vincent:

- The local market is very small. Only a few types of manufacturing industry can operate on a small enough scale to make a profit by producing for a market of around 100,000 people.
- There is no manufacturing tradition on the island. There are very few skilled mechanics and technicians, and most potential employees have never worked in a factory before.
- Arnos Vale airport has a 'short' runway and cannot take long-haul jets, so freight has to be flown in or out in a two-stage operation through an island like Barbados. This can cause delays.
- Kingstown Port has no large-scale mechanical container-handling equipment.
- Electricity supplies have at times been subject to quite frequent interruption.
- There is a shortage of local capital for investment; and many people with investment capital prefer to use it in importing, retailing, tourism, property, or even outside of St Vincent altogether.
- There are few industrial raw materials produced

13.3 Campden Park industrial estate, St Vincent. The flour mill is on the left.

locally, although local agricultural products are used by one or two manufacturing concerns.

Government policies attempt to deal with some of these problems:

- Industries can produce for the export market. St Vincent and the Grenadines is a member of the East Caribbean Common Market and Caricom; and the Lomé Convention and the Caribbean Basin Initiative give some types of manufacturer access to markets in Europe and the USA.
- Infrastructures and transport facilities have been improved. In recent years, cargo-handling and container-storage facilities at the port have been improved and there have also been improvements at the airport.
- An industrial estate has been built at Campden Park, and another is planned for Rutland Vale. New factory units have been constructed by the government's Development Corporation (Devco), fully serviced and with good road access. This means that new businesses can rent factory space and start production with the minimum of delay.
- Small businesses which need capital can borrow from the Small Industry Credit Scheme, which is funded by the Caribbean Development Bank.
- There has been a major drive to attract foreign investment to the island. For new businesses, there are 'tax holidays' of between ten and fifteen years, when major tax concessions are granted.

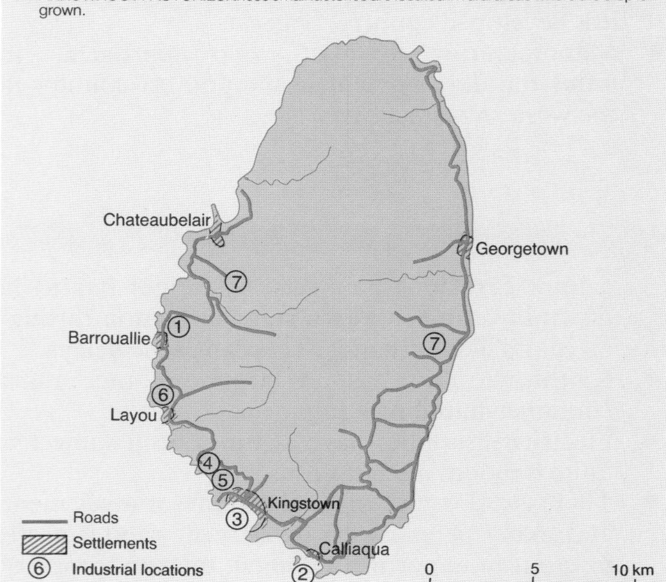

13.4 The location of industry in St Vincent.

1 Compare your own country with St Vincent as a location for manufacturing industry under these headings:
(a) Size of local market.
(b) Skilled labour.
(c) Transport facilities.
(d) Raw materials.
(e) Government help for manufacturing industry.

Industrial development

In 1984, there were just over 2,100 manufacturing jobs on the island. This is about 5% of the island's total workforce. Secondary industry still employed far fewer people than agriculture or the public services.

Some industry has developed; but there is still a long way to go.

Of the new industries:

- Some are based on local *raw materials*.
- Some are import substitution industries, based on the local *market*.
- Some are *enclave* industries, importing their raw materials and exporting their finished products.

2 This is a list of some of the manufacturing industries in St Vincent. Classify them into the three groups listed above:

making tennis equipment — baking bread
arrowroot-processing — flour-milling
making cable TV parts — bottling soft drinks
printing — distilling rum
making cardboard boxes for bananas

Industrial location in St Vincent

3 Explain why:
   (a) Almost all the manufacturing industries are located in or near Kingstown.
   (b) Some small factories are located away from Kingstown.

4 Comment on the location of the industrial estate at Campden Park.

An enclave industry

St Vincent Children's Wear is a US-based company with a factory employing over 200 workers on the Campden Park estate. They produce children's dresses to be sold under the 'Polly Flinders' label. All the raw materials are purchased centrally in the USA, and the entire output of the factory is air-freighted back there for pressing, bagging, and final packaging; and almost all the dresses are sold there.

The garments are manufactured in the Caribbean because wage rates are far lower than in the USA. Even after paying for air freight, manufacturing costs are around ⅓ of what they would be in the US.

The parent company started to manufacture in the Caribbean in the 1960s, with factories in Barbados and Guyana. The Barbados factory is still in operation, employing 500 workers; but wage rates in Barbados have risen, and it is now cheaper to make the simpler designs elsewhere.

13.5 St Vincent Children's Wear.

Besides those who work in the factory itself, there are over 1,200 women who work at home, hand-stitching the smocking which is used on the bodice of most designs. Most of these women manage to complete around a dozen pieces every week.

St Vincent is a suitable location because:

- It is an English-speaking country relatively close to the US.
- Many people are prepared to work for what is, by US standards, a very low rate of pay.
- As one of the first big industrial employers on the island, the company found it easy to recruit staff.

But there have been problems with operating in St Vincent:

- Electricity supply has at times been unreliable. At one point in 1983, there was no power for two days each week. Now the factory has bought an emergency generator of its own; this is an extra cost, but one which would pay for itself very quickly if it were needed again.
- Air-freighting through another island can be unreliable. A large consignment of finished goods may have to be shipped out in several batches. This can make it hard to meet delivery dates.
- Transportation for workers can be difficult. The minibus service past the estate is not always reliable.
- Almost all employees are new to factory work. Establishing a regular routine is not easy. Although productivity is as high as in the Barbados factory, it is not always easy to recruit good supervisory staff for quality control.

All these are short-term problems, which can be dealt with by good management.

In the long term, a more serious problem is competition from Asian producers like China. Chinese-made dresses of a similar type can be landed in the US at a price 20–30% below that of clothing made in the Caribbean. Even firms with an established reputation are finding their profits squeezed. If wage rates in St Vincent rise – and everyone clearly hopes that living standards on the island will be increased over the next few years – then it will become very hard to attract *labour-intensive* enclave industries to the island.

5 What benefits does an enclave industry like this bring to St Vincent?

6 Several government policies are aimed at attracting enclave industries like this. Which of these policies cost money?

7 What are the disadvantages of this sort of industrial development?

8 Should wages be held down so as to keep manufacturing costs low?

13.4 Light industry

A craft industry

13.6 Finished earthenware pots displayed for sale.

Figure 13.6 shows pottery made near Chaguanas, on the southern main road in Trinidad. This is a *craft industry*:

- Clay is dug at Carlsen Field, a few kilometres away.
- The clay is *wedged* to remove air pockets, and *thrown* on a potter's wheel. It is shaped to make large plant-pots, small lamps for the Diwali festival, and other items.
- The pots are fired in a simple *kiln*. The kiln is heated with firewood, which is also obtained locally.
- When they have been fired, the pots are displayed for sale. Business is usually very brisk.
- All the work is done by family members. Some of the jobs are highly skilled. These skills are passed on within the family.

Very little capital is needed to set up a business like this. Craft industries using local raw materials and skills to produce items which are in demand are often very profitable.

1 Explain why it is useful for this industry to be located:
   (a) Near to good sources of firewood and clay.
   (b) On a busy main road.
2 Why can craft industries be set up with very little capital?
3 What other items can be made by craft industries?
4 How can craft production benefit from the tourist industry?

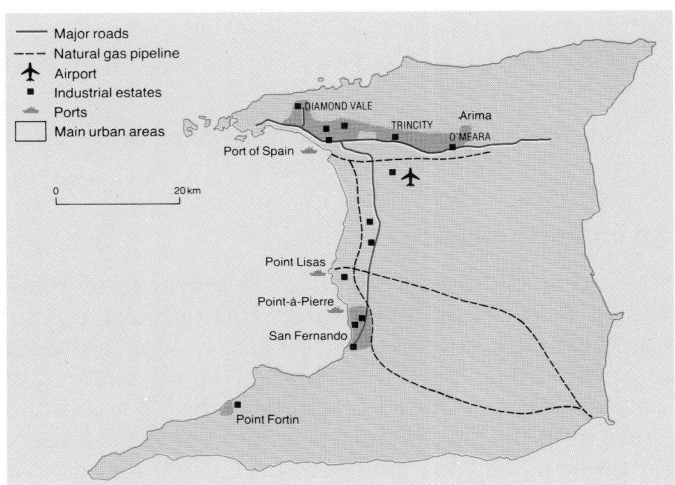

13.7 The location of the main industrial estates in Trinidad.

Industrial estates

Today, most light industries in the Caribbean are factory industries. Many of these industries are located on industrial estates, like the Campden Park industrial estate in St Vincent. Some industrial estates have been set up by government agencies, like Devco in St Vincent or the Industrial Development Corporations (IDCs) in Barbados, Jamaica, and Trinidad and Tobago. Others are privately owned.

5 Explain carefully why many industries choose to locate their factories on industrial estates.
6 Figure 13.7 shows the location of the main industrial estates in Trinidad. Comment on the location of these estates.

Industry in Jamaica

A large island like Jamaica provides a much better environment for manufacturing industry than St Vincent;

- The local market is much larger. The population is over 2,300,000. Many industries can make a profit by producing for a market this size.
- There are two international airports, with frequent direct flights to Europe, North America, the Caribbean, and Latin America.
- There are two deep-water ports with container-handling facilities, and several other ports, some equipped for bulk handling of specialised cargoes.
- Agriculture and mining provide several useful industrial raw materials.

And as in the rest of the Caribbean, government policies have also encouraged industrial development. The Jamaica Industrial Development Corporation

13.8 An industrial estate in Kingston, Jamaica. See grid reference 683 483 on Figure 2.10.

has constructed several industrial estates. There are tax incentives for new businesses and overseas companies. There are training programmes to increase the number of skilled workers, and consultancy programmes for management.

Free zones

Many enclave industries are located in *free zones*. Materials and other inputs can be brought into the free zones duty-free, if the finished products are shipped straight out of the country again for export.

Most of the factories in the free zones are owned by companies from the USA and Canada. But some are owned by firms from Hong Kong; if they assemble goods in Jamaica, it is easier to sell in the USA. Some overseas firms set up joint ventures or partnerships with Jamaican companies.

Many clothing factories in the free zones, and some outside, operate under a US customs regulation which allows clothing into the USA duty-free if it is made from US cloth which has simply been stitched and finished overseas. Factories which operate on this basis employed 11,000 people in Jamaica in 1985.

The location of industry in Jamaica

Figure 13.10 shows the main manufacturing areas of Jamaica.

7 Which two areas have most manufacturing industry?

8 Why is such a high percentage of manufacturing industry located in these two areas?

Percentage of total manufacturing employment in parish (1984)			
1 Kingston and St Andrew	64.7	8 Hanover	0.5
2 St Thomas	3.3	9 Westmoreland	2.4
3 Portland	0.5	10 St Elizabeth	1.1
4 St Mary	1.8	11 Manchester	1.5
5 St Ann	1.5	12 Clarendon	4.0
6 Trelawny	3.2	13 St Catherine	12.1
7 St James	3.4		

Source: Ministry of Labour, Jamaica

13.9 The percentage of Jamaican manufacturing employment in each parish (1984).

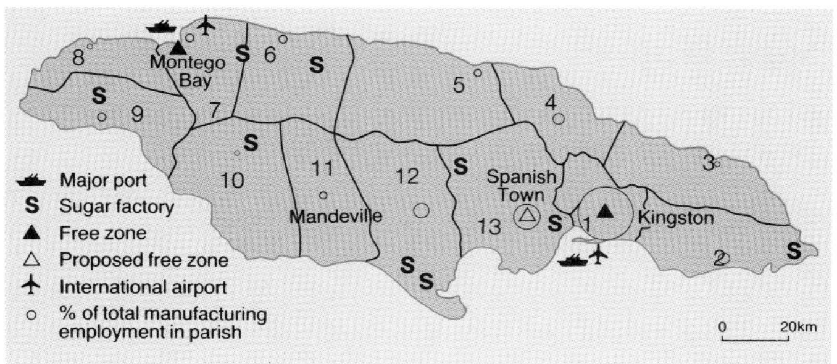

13.10 The location of industry in Jamaica.

9 Comment on the location of:
(a) The free zones.
(b) Sugar factories.

Figure 13.11 shows the percentage of the manufacturing workforce which is employed in different industries.

10 What percentage of the manufacturing workforce was employed in:
(a) Food-processing industries?
(b) Textiles and clothing industries?

11 Draw a divided-circle diagram to show the percentage of the workforce in these two industrial groups.

12 Which of the industries in Figure 13.11 would make some use of Jamaican raw materials?

	% of employment		% of employment
Meat and dairy products	4.0	Clothing	16.4
Preserving fruits and veg	4.4	Wood and furniture	6.2
Flour etc.	1.9	Paper and printing	6.8
Bakery products	6.2	Leather and rubber	1.9
Sugar	8.5	Chemicals	6.6
Confectionery, etc.	1.2	Oil refining, etc.	0.7
Miscellaneous foods	2.6	Non-metallic products	3.2
Beverages	6.6	Metal, machinery etc.	6.3
Tobacco	3.3	Electrical machinery	2.2
Textiles	0.8	Transport equipment	5.6
Footwear (incl. repairs)	1.6	Miscellaneous	3.0

Source: Ministry of Labour, Jamaica

13.11 The proportion of Jamaican manufacturing employment in each industrial group (1985).

Food-processing industries

Most foods which we buy today have been *processed*. They have been frozen, canned, baked, or dried before they are sold. There are many different types of food-processing industry in the Caribbean:

- Some of them process local agricultural products for export.
- Some of them process imported products for the local market.
- Some of them process local products for sale within the region.

13.12 A sugar factory in Barbados.

Sugar factories

Making sugar is a traditional manufacturing industry, based on an important local raw material.

In the early days of the sugar industry, every estate had its own sugar mill, powered by wind, running water, or oxen. These mills were inefficient, because:

- They could not extract all the juice from the cane.
- They produced low-grade, impure sugar in open pans.
- Many workers were needed to produce a small amount of sugar.

Figure 13.13 shows how a modern sugar mill operates. In a modern sugar factory, the machinery and equipment are designed to squeeze all the juice out of the cane and to produce high-grade sugar crystals. The machinery is much more energy-efficient; burning the *bagasse* produces enough electricity to power the factory, and often a surplus which can be sold to the local power company. Modern machinery is expensive; it is only profitable in a really large factory. That is why production is now concentrated in a few locations, and the older factories have now been closed down. In Barbados the number of sugar factories has, over the years, fallen like this:

1700	500 windmills
1944	60 factories
1969	17 factories
1989	4 factories

The number of jobs has also fallen. In 1946, there were more than 2,500 people working in the sugar factories during the crop season. Today, there are fewer than 900.

There has been a similar pattern of change in many old-established industries throughout the world:

- More efficient machinery and equipment.
- A few large factories instead of many small ones.
- Fewer jobs, because modern machinery needs less labour.

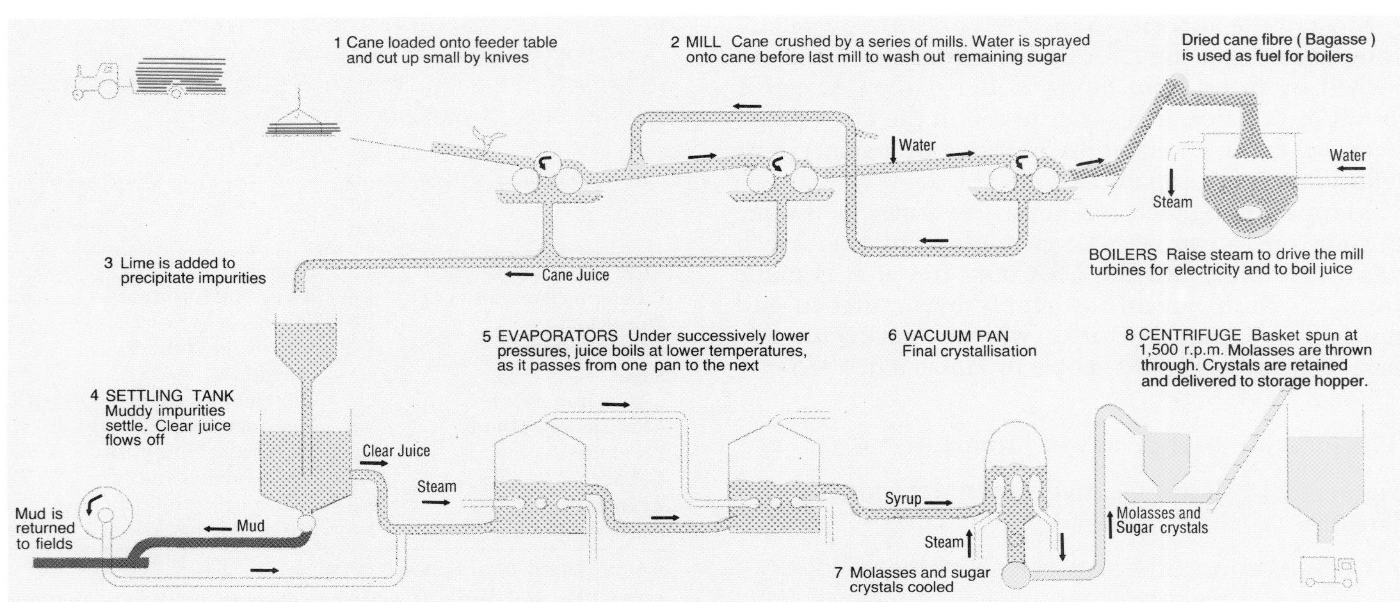

13.13 How sugar is produced from cane.

Nine tonnes of cane are needed to produce one tonne of sugar. A large number of trucks is needed to transport cane from the fields to the sugar factories. Transporting cane is an expensive operation.

13 List the main processes which are used to make sugar from cane.
14 Look at Figure 13.14. Comment on the location of the sugar factories.
15 If the sugar factories were located near to the port, how would this affect:
(a) Total transport costs?
(b) Traffic congestion in Bridgetown?

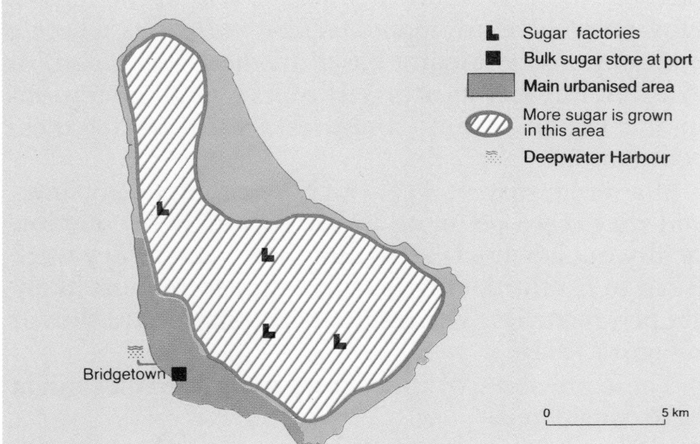

13.14 The location of sugar factories in Barbados.

Flour-milling

No Caribbean country can grow wheat; but several have flour mills which can process imported grain for the local market. They are import substitution industries, because they substitute a locally *processed* product for imported flour. One example is East Caribbean Flour Mills in St Vincent.

Wheat from Canada is brought in by bulk carrier to a wharf in Campden Park. The *by-products* from flour milling are used to produce animal feeds. They are mixed with maize from Canada, and a small amount of limestone from Barbados is added to provide calcium. There are 125 people working in the mill, which supplies all the flour consumed in St Vincent, and most of the flour for St Lucia, St Kitts, Antigua, Nevis, Dominica and Montserrat.

Like many industries which process bulky imported raw materials, flour-milling has a coastal location. It is a port industry. There are flour mills in similar locations on many other islands, including Barbados, Jamaica, and Trinidad.

16 All the raw materials used in the flour mill are imported. What *benefits* does an industry like this bring to St Vincent? How does the flour mill help the development of local agriculture?

Packaged foods

Catelli is a well-known brand name for packaged foods in Trinidad and the eastern Caribbean. Two companies, in Trinidad and Barbados, which are both linked to a large firm in Canada, produce spaghetti, macaroni, canned foods, and ketchup for the local market.

All the food items used at present are imported; but even so, many of the other inputs are locally produced. All the packaging materials used by Catelli Trinidad are locally made; and they represent a substantial proportion of the cost of the final product. In the future, it is planned to develop products which use local agricultural materials.

There are 120 employees in the Trinidad factory, which is on the western side of Port of Spain. It is not on an industrial estate, but is well located on a main road, near the main port, and in an area where it is easy to recruit staff.

13.15 Canning vegetables in the Catelli factory, Trinidad.

The clothing industry

Clothing industries have been established in the Caribbean for longer than almost any other type of manufacturing. There are clothing factories in almost every Caribbean island.

Clothing can be made on a very small scale, as a craft industry or family business. In 1946, there were 8,300 dressmakers and tailors in Barbados alone; they accounted for 45% of what was then classified as manufacturing employment. Today, many people still have some of their clothes made by a neighbour with a sewing machine and some other simple equipment; but most items of clothing are mass-produced in a factory.

17 List the ways in which a large clothing factory, like St Vincent Children's Wear, will be different from a small family dressmaking business.

There are many clothing factories in the Caribbean, because:

- The industry can operate successfully on a fairly small scale.
- Many people already have skills which are useful in the clothing industry.
- Textiles, and the other inputs used, are not usually locally produced. But they can easily be imported into the region.
- There is a sizeable local market for finished clothing. Some countries specialise in production for the local market.
- Clothing is a lightweight product, which can easily be exported. Some companies are enclave industries, which produce entirely for export.

Clothing imports

In most Caribbean countries, clothing stores sell:

- Locally produced goods.
- Imports from other Caribbean countries.
- Imports from outside the region.

Many Caribbean governments would like to encourage more people to buy locally produced items. There are many ways of doing this. In some countries, there is a high level of import duty on clothing from outside the region. This makes imported goods more expensive, and encourages people to buy the local product instead. Import controls restrict the number of items that can be bought from overseas, or ban certain items altogether.

18 If everyone bought locally produced clothing, how would that affect:
   (a) Clothing factories?
   (b) Unemployment?
   (c) The need for foreign exchange?
19 Why do many people prefer to buy imported goods?
20 Should imports from other Caribbean countries be treated in a different way to imports from outside the region?

Electronics

The electronics industry makes computers, calculators, and also important *components* for many other products like aeroplanes, video and audio equipment, military hardware, and automated industrial machinery.

Clothing and food-processing are traditional Caribbean industries where local firms can often operate independently on a small scale.

Electronics is another light industry. But it is a new industry; and it is also dominated by multinational companies producing high-technology products which will be sold in many countries. There are no fully independent Caribbean producers who design, manufacture, and market their products within the region. However, there are many *enclave industries* where a multinational company based in the USA, Japan, or Western Europe, locates part of its overall operations in the region. Many countries try to attract these companies.

	% of responses		% of responses
UK and Ireland	21	Mexico	6
Rest of Europe	34	Rest of Latin America	3
Japan	6	Canada	3
South-East Asia	12	Rest of World	7
Caribbean	8		

Source: Electronics File.

13.16 Countries where US electronics companies would consider opening a new factory.

In a recent survey, 39% of US electronics companies said they were planning to set up a new production facility outside the USA within three years. They were asked to list the countries where they were most likely to open factories. The results of the survey are shown in Figure 13.16.

These are some of the factors the companies might have considered:

- 'We want a country where people don't go on strike, and where they work hard all day.'
- 'We need a skilled workforce, so people can be trained quickly.'
- 'There should be good transport and communications. We want to get goods in and out of the country quickly and cheaply.'
- 'Wage levels have got to be low. We need to save money.'
- 'Some countries give financial help to foreign countries. That can be very useful.'
- 'Is there a suitable factory we can move into right away?'
- 'What's the political situation like? Is our investment going to be safe?'
- 'Is there a good local market for our products?'
- 'Are there research facilities there? Can we learn from local companies in our field?'
- 'Is it a clean working environment?'
- 'Our executives will have to travel down there from time to time, or even live there. Is it a pleasant place to live?'
- 'How many people can speak English? Will it be hard to communicate with people there?'

21 Do you think your own country would be a good location for a US electronics company to open a factory?
22 Read through the comments carefully, and compare your country with *two* other possible locations.

Working conditions

Electronics is a high-technology industry; but many of the people who work in the industry do low-technology jobs.

When a company opens a branch plant in the Caribbean, it is usually looking for a site for its routine *assembly* operations, not for research or for developing new products. Most of the jobs will be for low-paid, semi-skilled workers, not for computer engineers and professional staff. Working conditions can be very good; but sometimes the work is unpleasant. Read this description of a job in the electronics industry in one Caribbean island:

'Anselma, using her bare hands, dips one wire and then another into an open pot of molten lead-tin solder, a task she must perform 500 times a day to make her quota. Sometimes, in haste, she scalds herself. Waves of fume and heat rising from the solder burn her eyes and make her head pound . . . 'We must work two weeks to buy a pair of shoes, and it's only because of my children that I do the dip soldering, because I can't stay at home."'

When an international company is in economic difficulties, the overseas operations are often the first to be closed down.

Intel is an American electronics company which has assembly plants in many countries, including Puerto Rico, Israel, and Malaysia. Until 1986, it had a factory in Barbados which employed over 1,000 people; this was approximately 10% of the island's manufacturing workforce. In that year, which was also the end of the company's 10-year 'tax holiday', the plant was closed.

23 List the *advantages* and *disadvantages* of each of these types of industry for economic development in the Caribbean:
(a) Food processing
(b) Clothing
(c) Electronics

13.5 Heavy industry in Trinidad and Tobago

Energy resources

Some form of energy has to be used for every form of human activity.

In the past, *renewable* energy sources like wind power, running water, firewood, charcoal, or human and animal power were used.

Today, most energy is derived from *fossil fuels*, like oil, natural gas, and coal. They are non-renewable mineral resources. They provide human society with access to plentiful sources of energy in a convenient form; but, like other non-renewable resources, they will not last for ever. Fossil fuels can either be used directly, or used to generate electricity.

1 Two hundred years ago, what forms of energy would have been used in the Caribbean for:
(a) Land transport?
(b) Sea transport?
(c) Cooking food?
(d) Running a sugar mill?
(e) Lighting?

2 What forms of energy would be used for these purposes today?

3 Look at Figure 13.17:
(a) Which of the major energy sources are non-renewable?
(b) What energy source is used for atomic energy?
(c) What energy sources will be available when fossil fuels run out?

4 Look at Figure 13.18. Why do More Developed Countries use more energy than Less Developed Countries?

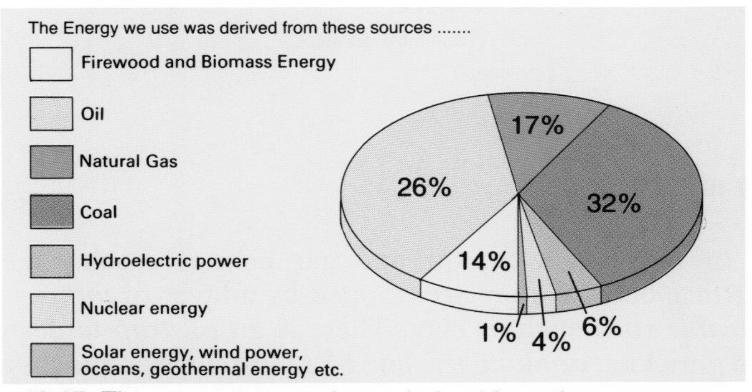

13.17 The energy we used was derived from these sources.

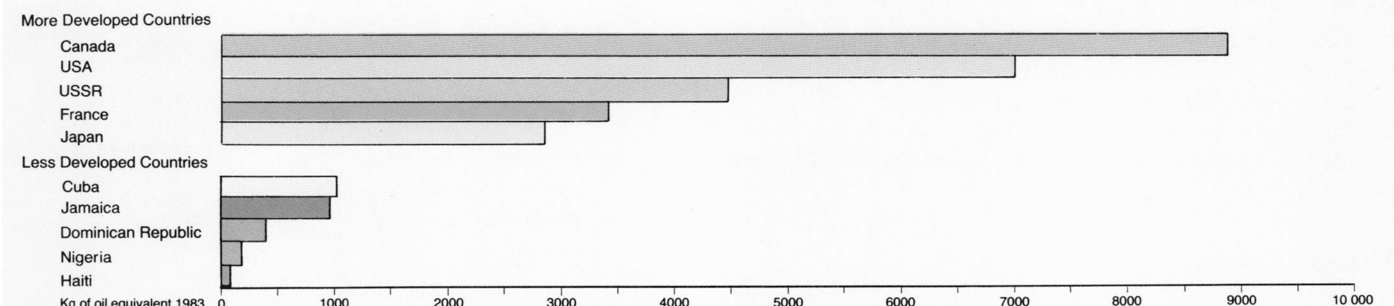

13.18 Energy consumption in ten countries. Average energy consumption per person 1983 (Kg of oil equivalent).

How oil and gas are formed

Oil and natural gas are called fossil fuels because they are formed from organic matter which was deposited in sediments beneath the sea many millions of years ago. As the layers of sediment built up, heat and pressure transformed the organic matter in the rocks into crude oil and natural gas. Most of the oil in Trinidad is found in rocks which were laid down about 10 million years ago.

Where oil and gas are found

Oil and gas are held in the pore spaces and joints of some layers of permeable rock.

Oil and gas are much less dense than rock. They often seep right to the surface, if there are no obstructions. The Pitch Lake in southern Trinidad is a large mass of oil and other substances which has found its way to the surface. *Manjak* is a dense, tarry substance formed of oil which has seeped to the surface. In the past, it was collected and used as fuel in Trinidad and Barbados.

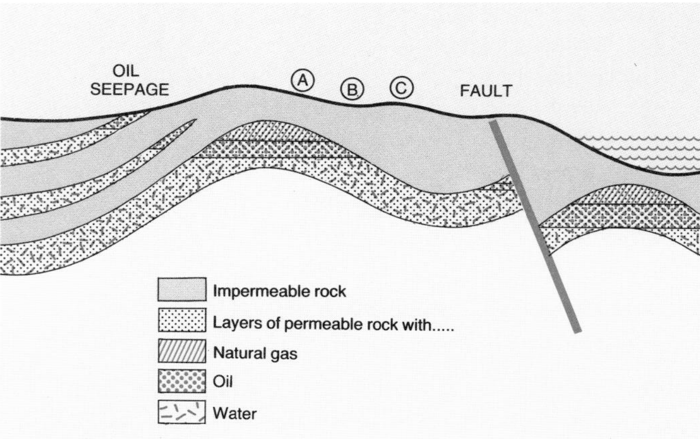

13.19 Oil traps.

In most oilfields, oil and gas cannot reach the surface because they are trapped by a layer of *impermeable* rock such as clay. There is an *oil trap* under an anticline, or along the line of a fault, or in a 'pinch-out' where a layer of permeable rock such as sandstone is sandwiched between two impermeable layers.

5 Look at Figure 13.19:
(a) How many oil traps are there?
(b) How many of the traps are anticlines?
(c) How many are under the sea?
(d) What would be extracted by a well at 'A', 'B', and 'C'?

A seismic survey

Careful work by geologists at the surface can identify anticlines and other structures where there may possibly be an oil trap. One method used to investigate rock structures below the surface is a seismic survey.

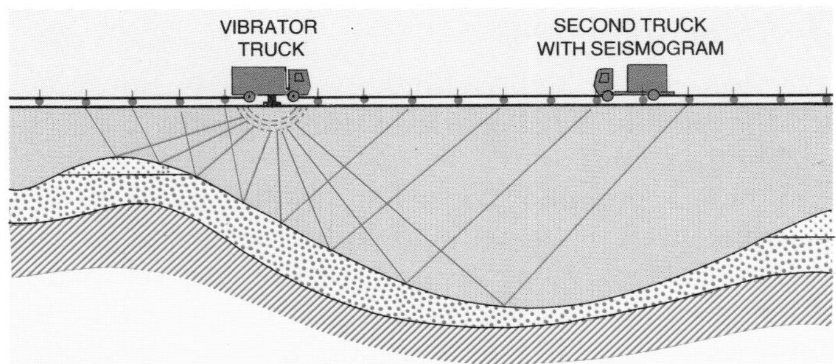

Shock waves from the vibrator truck are reflected by a layer of hard rock below the surface. The equipment in the second truck is used to predict the structure of the underlying rocks.
This drawing is not to scale.

13.20 A seismic survey.

However, the only way of being certain whether oil or gas can be found is to drill a well.

Drilling for oil

- A drilling *bit* is used to cut through the rock.
- The bit is turned by a square, hollow pipe called a *kelly*.
- The kelly is turned by a *rotary table*, which is powered by an engine.
- As the bit cuts downwards, lengths of round *drill pipe* are inserted between the bit and the kelly.
- The drilling equipment is held in place by a steel tower called a *derrick*.
- The complete structure used for drilling an oil or gas well is a *drilling rig*.

Drilling a well is an expensive business. An average oil well in Trinidad is over 1,100 m deep; the deepest well ever drilled on the island went down to more than 4,900 m. Drilling a well on land would cost around $2 m US. At sea, it would cost around four times as much.

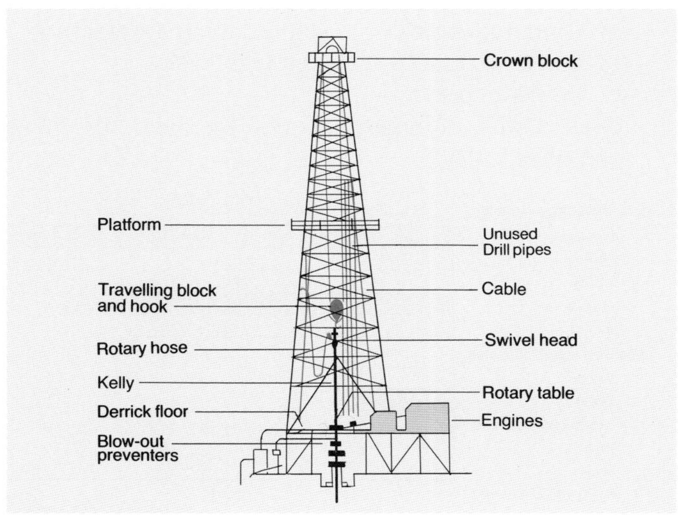

13.21 A drilling rig.

Oil production in Trinidad and Tobago

Most Caribbean countries rely on imported oil for almost all their energy needs. This can be very expensive. In Jamaica, for example, oil and petroleum products make up more than 32% of the total import bill. Trinidad and Tobago is the only Caribbean country which is a net exporter of oil.

	Percentage of total world oil production	Percentage of total world proven oil reserves
Trinidad and Tobago	0.3	0.09
Nigeria	2.6	2.3
Saudi Arabia	6.3	23.8
Rest of Middle East	19.2	56.3

Source: BP Statistical Review of World Energy, 1986.

13.22 Oil resources.

Trinidad was one of the world's first oil producers:

- Bitumen from the Pitch Lake was used to tar ships as early as the sixteenth century.
- The first oil well was sunk in 1857.
- Commercial oil production started in 1908.
- The first refinery was opened in 1912.

However, the industry has remained a small one by international standards, because oil resources are limited.

6 Look at Figure 13.22:
Write a few sentences comparing the oil resources of Trinidad and Tobago, Nigeria, and Saudi Arabia.

Much of the oil in Trinidad's reserves is difficult to extract. Costs are high, because:

- There are many small oil traps in the folded and faulted rocks of southern Trinidad. Because these oil traps are so small, wells have to be closely spaced.
- In many oilfields, there is no longer enough oil to flow naturally to the surface. It has to be forced out by injecting water, steam, natural gas, or carbon dioxide into the oil-bearing strata.
- 77% of the oil is now extracted from marine oilfields off the coast of the island. Drilling and extraction costs are much higher for a marine well.

Oil-refining

Crude oil is a black, tarry substance, made of a mixture of different chemicals. It is of no use until it has been *refined*. In a refinery, the different *fractions* of crude oil are separated out. Figure 13.24 is a simplified picture of how a refinery works:

- Crude oil is heated to 300 °C in a furnace. The furnace is usually fuelled by natural gas.
- In the furnace, all the fractions in the crude oil evaporate, and become gases.
- The gases are fed into a metal tower, 40 m high, called a *fractionating* column.
- The fractionating column contains horizontal trays. The trays have holes with *bubble caps* which allow vapours to pass through.

13.23 A drilling rig off the coast of Trinidad.

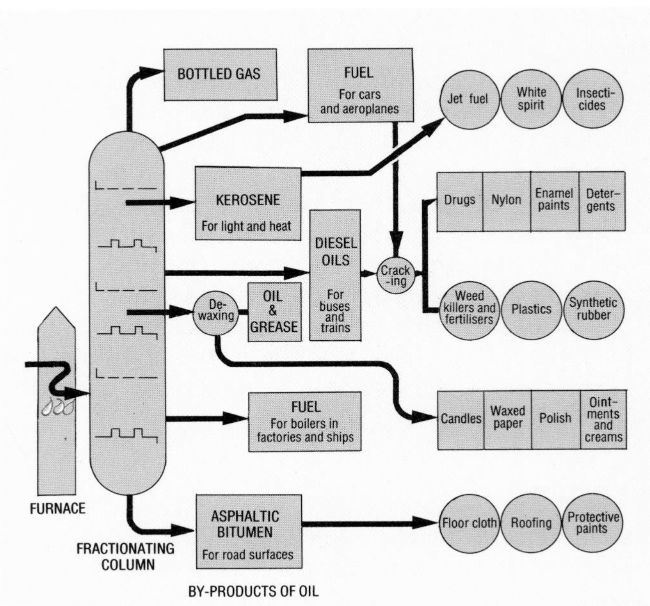

13.24 How oil is refined.

- As the gases pass from the furnace to the fractionating column, and then up the column, they cool down.
- Some fractions become liquid again at quite a high temperature. They separate out from the other gases at the bottom of the column.
- Other fractions do not become liquid again until the temperature is quite low. They travel to the top of the column, and condense there.

7 Look at Figure 13.24:
  (a) What fractions condense at the bottom of the column, and what are they used for?
  (b) What fractions condense at the top of the column, and what are they used for?

Most types of crude oil produce too much of the heavy fractions, like fuel oil, and not enough of the more valuable lighter fractions, like gasoline (petrol).

The large molecules that make up the heavy fractions can be split to produce lighter fractions by a process known as *catalytic cracking*.

Market	% of output		% of output
Trinidad and Tobago	27	Europe	17
Other Caricom countries	19	Others (mainly Japan)	15
Other Caribbean countries	12	USA	10

Source: Ministry of Energy and Natural Resources, *Annual Report*, 1985.

13.25 The main markets for Trinidad and Tobago refinery products.

Oil-refining in Trinidad and Tobago

There are two large refineries in southern Trinidad, at Pointe-à-Pierre and Point Fortin. Both are now run by a large government-owned company, Trintoc (Trinidad and Tobago Oil Company).

8 Look at Figure 13.26:
  (a) Why are both refineries in southern Trinidad?
  (b) Why are both on the coast?
  (c) Why is it an advantage for the Pointe-à-Pierre refinery to be located near San Fernando?

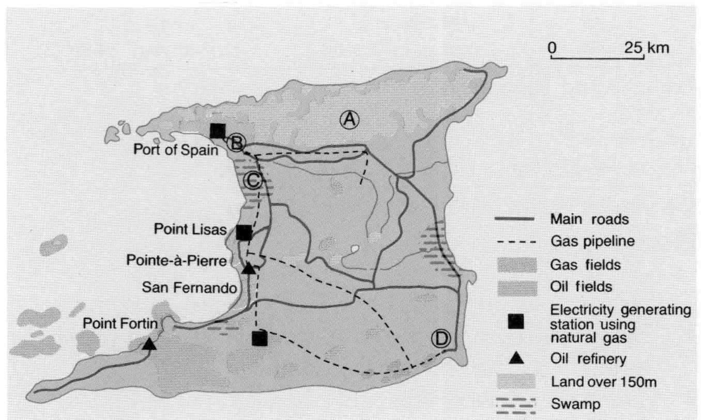

13.26 Trinidad and Tobago: natural gas, oil and heavy industry.

These two refineries were originally built by large international oil companies to:

- Refine oil from Trinidad for the local market and for export.
- Refine oil from other countries for the US market.

Offshore refining for the US was important in the Caribbean until the 1980s, because:

- Shallow water off the Gulf and Atlantic coasts of the US meant that the largest tankers could not unload there.
- In the 1970s, there was a tax advantage for offshore refineries in the Caribbean.

There were other offshore refineries in Aruba, Curaçao, the Bahamas, and elsewhere. The other countries with big offshore refineries were not oil producers.

Today, there is very little offshore refining for the US market. This is because:

- A specialised oil port has been built off the coast of Louisiana, where oil can be fed directly into the US pipeline system for distribution to refineries.
- The US tax system now favours refining within the USA.

The refineries in Trinidad and Tobago are in a much better position than the ones in countries where there is no local oil production; but even so they are working well below capacity. In 1985, refinery *throughput* was only 25% of what it had been in 1975. Only a small amount of overseas crude oil is now imported for refining; but 46% of the crude extracted in the country is now locally refined.

Figure 13.25 shows where refined products from Trinidad and Tobago are sold.

9 Make a bar graph to show the relative importance of the main markets.
10 Why is an industry in a stronger position if it sells to many different export markets?
11 Explain why the refineries are important to the economy of Trinidad and Tobago.

Natural gas

Natural gas is a much less convenient fuel than oil. It takes more than 950 m^3 of gas to provide as much energy as only 1 m^3 of oil; so gas is much more expensive to transport over a long distance.

In the past, most of the natural gas extracted in Trinidad and Tobago was just flared off. This was a very wasteful practice; but there was no easy way of using the gas. From the 1950s, some use was made of the gas to generate electricity and make chemicals; and today, more than 78% of the gas extracted is used. The rest comes out of the ground at such low pressure that it would cost too much to compress it and send it down a pipeline.

Of the gas which is used:

- 44% is used by the oil companies, in the oilfields and refineries.
- 17% is used to generate electricity. There are three large generating stations, at Penal, Point Lisas, and Port of Spain.
- 2% is used in cement manufacture and for various other purposes.
- 37% is used by heavy industries at Point Lisas on the west coast of Trinidad.

12 Make a divided-circle diagram to illustrate these figures.

Point Lisas

Figure 13.27 shows the Point Lisas industrial estate and port on the west coast of Trinidad. The estate covers more than 8 km^2, including 2 km^2 of reclaimed land.

Development work on this site started in 1976. The government of Trinidad and Tobago has at least a majority shareholding in the development company, PLIPDECO (Point Lisas Industrial Port Development Corporation), and in all the heavy industrial plants.

The Point Lisas development consists of:

- A port, with specialised bulk-handling facilities and container facilities for general cargo. A deep-water channel 3 km long and a turning basin have been dredged, so that large bulk carriers can be accommodated.

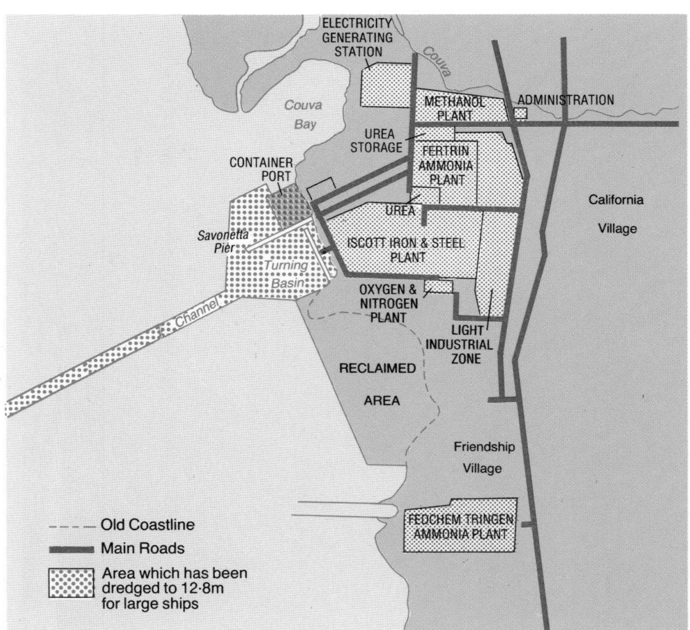

13.27 Point Lisas industrial estate and port.

- The largest electricity generating station in the Commonwealth Caribbean.
- The ISCOTT (Iron and Steel Company of Trinidad and Tobago) iron and steel mill, which is the only steelworks in the Commonwealth Caribbean.
- Three large chemical plants, making ammonia, urea, and methanol.
- An industrial estate for light industry.

Just south of the Point Lisas development is another large ammonia plant: this is Fedchem (Federation Chemicals), owned by a large private company, which has been operating since 1959.

14 In 1975, the land at Point Lisas was partly mangrove swamp and partly used for sugar cane. Figure 13.27 shows the old shoreline. List the ways in which the landforms and marine environment have been modified so that industrial development can take place.

Petrochemicals

Look back to Figure 13.24. Oil-refining does not only produce fuels. It also produces *hydrocarbons* – liquids and gases which can be used by the chemical industry to make a wide range of products, such as fertilisers, plastics, dyes, solvents, resins, paints, adhesives, drugs and textiles.

Natural gas can also be used to make important industrial chemicals.

Figure 13.29 shows the raw materials used to make the industrial chemicals which are produced in Point Lisas, and some of their uses.

Methanol and ammonia are sold to large industrial

13.28 Bulk loading facilities for urea, methanol and ammonia.

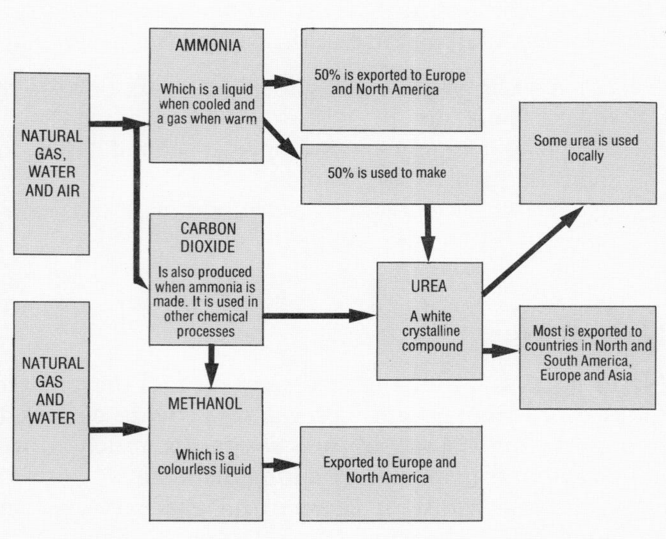

13.29 Natural gas and the chemicals industry at Point Lisas.

buyers in Europe and North America. With two major ammonia plants, Trinidad and Tobago is the world's second largest exporter, after the Soviet Union.

With the construction of these plants, Trinidad and Tobago has moved some way from being an exporter of raw materials towards being an exporter of more valuable manufactured goods. But even so the country is unlikely to be able to establish the full range of chemical industries which use chemicals like ammonia and methanol. There are too many specialised processes involved which need to operate on a large scale if they are to pay.

For example:

- Some of the 'first stage' raw materials needed to manufacture detergents are produced by the oil refineries at Point Fortin and Pointe-à-Pierre.
- There are two factories near Port of Spain which produce detergents.
- But there is an important 'intermediate-stage' chemical, alkyl benzene, which is not produced in Trinidad. It is imported by a company which uses it to make the main active ingredient for detergents.
- Many of the other products which are used in the 'final stage' of detergent manufacture, like water softeners and brightening agents, are also imported.

Heavy industry: location patterns

Heavy industries do not always have to be close to all their raw materials, but they need good transport facilities for any materials that have to be brought in. Water transport is much cheaper than land transport for moving heavy goods in large quantities.

Heavy industries take up a lot of space. They need to operate where there is a large vacant area of flat land with plenty of room for expansion.

For most heavy industries, a cheap energy source is essential.

In some countries, heavy industries have been established in remote areas, and towns have been built there to house the workers. But it is helpful if a large-scale industry is built reasonably close to existing settlements where there is a labour force available.

15 Look at Figures 13.26 and 13.27 again:
   (a) List the reasons why Point Lisas was a good site for heavy industry.
   (b) Give reasons why the sites marked 'A', 'B', 'C', and 'D' on the map of Trinidad would not have been suitable for this sort of industrial development.

16 Why is the urea plant next to the ammonia plant?

The iron and steel industry

The ISCOTT iron and steel plant at Point Lisas is a *mini-mill*. Although it is a large industry by Caribbean standards, it has a capacity of 700,000 tonnes, only a fraction of the output of a big integrated steel plant in Japan or the USA.

Many companies have opened up mini-mills in recent years. They are often outside traditional steel-making regions.

13.30 The ISCOTT iron and steel plant at Point Lisas.

The ISCOTT plant was planned to:

- Import iron ore from Brazil by bulk carrier.
- Use natural gas from Trinidad and Tobago's offshore fields as a cheap energy source to make steel billets and wire rod.
- Export the finished product. Most was to be sold on the US market.

Figure 13.30 shows how the plant is laid out:

- Iron ore from Brazil is unloaded at the wharf. Pure limestone is also imported from Curaçao.
- The ore has a 65% iron content. The direct reduction process produces pellets with an iron content of 92–95% for steel-making. Natural gas is used as a *reducing agent*.
- The pellets are stored in silos, and then in the open. They can either be exported, or used for steel-making at Point Lisas.
- In the *meltshop* there are two *electric arc* furnaces. Iron pellets are heated, along with lime, and alloy metals which are used to produce the right type of steel.
- Liquid steel is cast into *billets* 12 or 16 m long.
- The billets can either be exported, or reheated in a gas-fired furnace to 1,200 °C to make wire rods.
- Because this is a small steelworks, there is no attempt to produce the full range of products. ISCOTT specialises in producing billets and wire rods.

Using imported materials in the iron and steel industry is not a problem, because long-distance transport by bulk carrier is now very cheap.

The plant was built partly with capital borrowed overseas, and all the plant and machinery is imported. That is to be expected with a large-scale heavy industry. A successful steelworks can earn more than enough to service a loan covering its capital costs.

The most serious problem for the industry is finding a steady market for its products. The USA and the EC have imposed restrictions on imported steel so as to protect their own industries, so only a small percentage of total production can be sold there. A few companies in Trinidad process steel, but they do not use nearly enough to keep the plant in operation. There are small markets for steel products in Jamaica and Barbados. In 1986, the plant was working at approximately 70% of full capacity, and steel was being sold in Asia and South America.

Heavy industry in the economy

Heavy industries like those at Point Lisas:

- Are expensive to set up.
- Produce a high output.
- Produce goods which can be exported.
- Use a large area of land.
- But they do not provide many jobs.

In Point Lisas, the three chemical plants employ rather more than 500 people. The ISCOTT Plant employs 1,100.

17 Look at Figure 13.31. Which sectors of the Trinidad economy are most important for:
(a) Providing employment?
(b) Producing exports?
(c) Reducing the need for imports?

	Percentage of total employment	Percentage of total output	Percentage of total exports
Oil, oil refining, and natural gas	4.5	21.0	80.0
Heavy chemical industries	0.15	1.4	14.5
Light industries	8.9	9.0	2.7
Export agriculture and sugar	4.0	2.4	2.7
Other agriculture	8.5	3.0	–
Electricity, water, construction, and service industries	74.1	63.2	–

Source: Ministry of Finance and Planning, *Review of the Economy*, 1986.

13.31 Oil and heavy industry in the economy of Trinidad.

13.6 Bauxite

Large areas of Jamaica are covered with an infertile red clay which does not hold water well in the dry season. This clay does not *appear* to be a very useful resource. In 1867, a landowner sent away a sample for analysis; he wanted to find out why his land was so infertile. He was told that the red clay was *bauxite*, the ore from which aluminium is obtained.

There are also large deposits of bauxite in Guyana, buried under a thick layer of white sand in a belt of low-grade woodland to the south of the coastal plain.

Bauxite does not look like a valuable resource at first glance; but it plays a very important part in the economies of both Guyana and Jamaica.

Aluminium

Aluminium is the commonest metallic element in the earth's crust; but it is hard to extract the metal from the minerals which contain it. There was no practical industrial process for making aluminium until 1886. Until then, the metal was a scientific curiosity. Today, it is in common use for many purposes. Aluminium and its alloys are used in the manufacture of aircraft, trains, buses, overhead electric cables, cooking foil, and many other items.

1 Name two other items which are often made out of aluminium.

2 Aluminium is a lightweight metal which does not rust. Explain why this makes it suitable for *two* of the purposes it is used for.

3 Demand for aluminium has grown rapidly. Look at Figure 13.32. Draw a graph to show the increase in world aluminium production.

1886	production begins	1960	3,500,000 tonnes
1894	480 tonnes	1970	11,000,000 tonnes
1939	703,000 tonnes	1985	12,200,000 tonnes

13.32 World aluminium production.

How bauxite was formed

The *Guyanese bauxites* were formed by the weathering of rocks on an old erosion surface about 40 million years ago. Minerals containing aluminium silicate were broken down; the lime, magnesia, and silica they contained were leached out, leaving the iron and aluminium oxides behind.

After the bauxite was formed, the land was submerged beneath the sea, and the old erosion surface was covered, first by a layer of hard clay, then by white sand. The clay and sand form an *overburden* which protects the bauxite but which has to be removed before the bauxite can be mined.

There are three theories about the formation of the *Jamaican bauxites*, which are generally found in *limestone* areas:

- They may be formed from impurities which are left behind when a great thickness of limestone has been removed by solution.
- They may be derived from older igneous and metamorphic rocks, which are exposed at the surface in some places. Material from these areas may have been transported through the limestone by underground streams, and deposited in depressions where the streams emerge again.
- But it now seems more likely that bauxite is derived from volcanic dust. About 7 million years ago there were volcanic eruptions in what is now central Hispaniola. Igneous rocks in Haiti which were formed then have a similar composition to Jamaican bauxite. Several metres of volcanic dust were probably deposited in Jamaica in that period. The dust has now weathered to form bauxite.

Jamaican bauxite is not a continuous deposit. It is found in patches, where weathering conditions have been right. These patches usually cover between 0.5 and 30 ha, and are between 8 and 14 m deep. Most are in well-drained areas and at more than 400 m above sea level.

4 Look at Figures 13.33a and 13.33b:
   (a) List the main bauxite mining centres in Jamaica and Guyana.
   (b) What forms of transport are used to move bauxite in each of these countries?

How bauxite is mined

In *Guyana*, bauxite mining is a difficult operation, because it is necessary to remove a thick layer of overburden. In the first areas to be mined, the overburden was less than a metre thick, and could easily be removed with shovels. Today, bauxite is being extracted from areas with over 60 m of overburden. The overburden is removed like this:

- The land is debushed and cleared by bulldozer.
- The first layer of overburden is sand or sandy clay. This is removed with a *bucket wheel excavator* and taken to a disposal point by a system of conveyor belts. It can also be removed by *hydraulicking*: the overburden is gouged out with a jet of water. Almost 23,000 litres of water per minute is directed at the base of the overburden; the sand is artificially 'eroded' by the jet of water, and washed into a pool. The sand and water from the pool are pumped into settling ponds.
- The next layer of overburden is clay. This is removed with a *walking dragline*. This machine

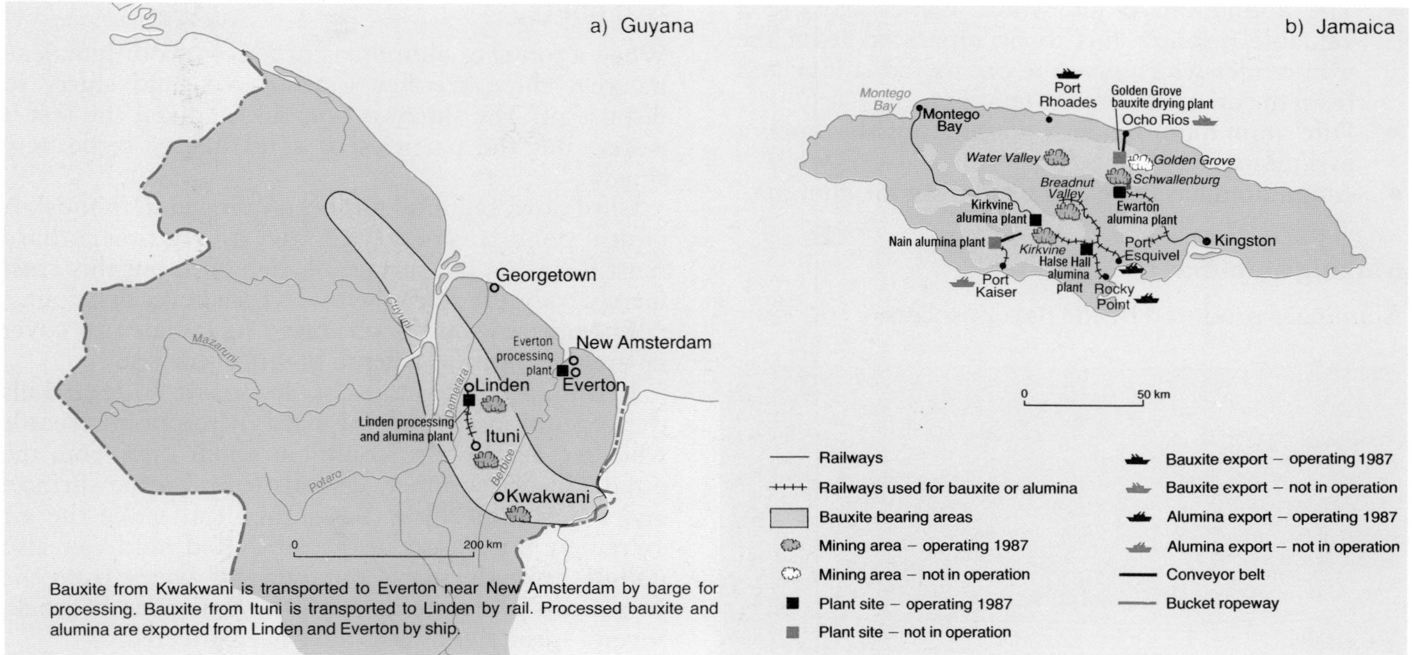

13.33 The bauxite industry in Guyana and Jamaica.

has a bucket which can scoop up 15 tonnes of clay on the end of a boom which is 60 m long. The boom can swing round and deposit the clay on land which has already been mined.

After the overburden has been removed, the bauxite is drilled and blasted with explosives, to break it up. Then it can be loaded into trucks or rail-cars, and transported to the bauxite plant.

In *Jamaica* there is no overburden to remove, and the bauxite is soft enough to be extracted without blasting. This means that there are fewer separate stages in the mining operation. When the land has been cleared and the topsoil removed, the bauxite can be dug out with a dragline or a rubber-tyred *tractor shovel*.

But mining is not a simple operation in either country. It must be very carefully planned and organised. Before a bauxite deposit is mined, there must be a careful geological investigation. The size of the deposit must be measured, and samples must be taken for testing so that the quality of the deposit can be determined. Mining also has to be organised so that *transport* costs are kept to a minimum.

In Jamaica, it has been estimated that building mining roads and hauling bauxite to a processing plant accounts for ⅔ of total mining costs.

Land reclamation

Bauxite mining uses a large area of land.

In Jamaica, there are regulations which ensure that:

- Land remains in agricultural use until mining begins.
- Land which has been mined is restored, so that it can be used for farming again.

When land has been cleared for mining, the top 15 cm of soil is removed from on top of the bauxite with a bulldozer. This layer of soil contains most of the nutrients and organic matter.

After mining, the land is smoothed and reshaped. Any limestone outcrops are removed by blasting. Then the soil is replaced, and the land is fenced and planted with grass. Weeds are controlled, and fertilisers are used if they are needed to restore fertility.

Most of the reclaimed land is used as pasture, but some is planted with trees to prevent soil erosion, and some is cultivated.

5 Jamaica is a relatively small country. If there were no land reclamation, how would this affect:
(a) Agricultural production?
(b) Soil erosion?
(c) The tourist industry?

6 Explain why land reclamation would be more difficult in Guyanese conditions.

Processing bauxite

Bauxite is an *ore*, in which natural processes have produced a high concentration of aluminium over a long period of time. Jamaican bauxite contains about 45% aluminium oxide; but to obtain the metal from the ore:

- The aluminium oxide which makes bauxite a valuable resource has to be separated from the iron oxides which give the ore its red colour and from the other minerals it contains.
- Pure aluminium oxide is a white powder known as *alumina*.
- Aluminium has to be extracted from the alumina.

Making alumina

Alumina is produced by the Bayer process:

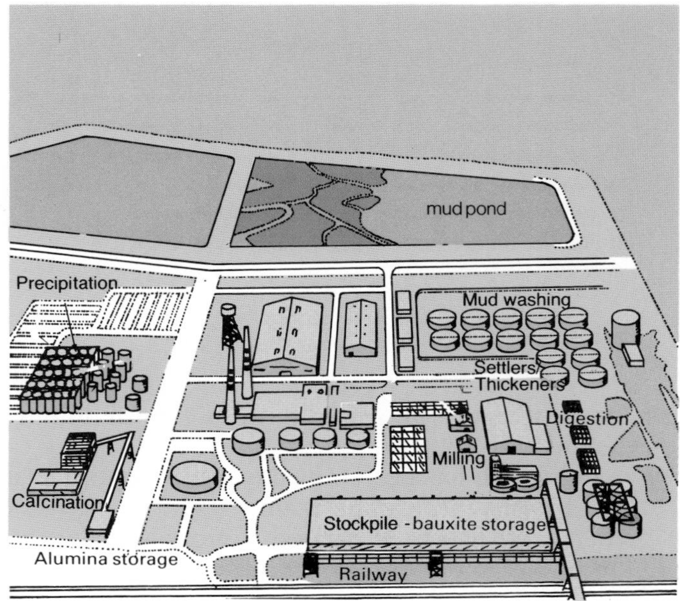

13.34 An alumina plant.

- The ore is ground with caustic soda to form a *slurry*.
- Bauxite slurry is fed into large pressure vessels called *digesters*, where a second stream of hot caustic soda is added. The caustic soda reacts with the alumina and dissolves it. The other minerals in the bauxite do not react with the caustic soda, and are not dissolved.
- After cooling, slurry from the digesters is fed into *settling tanks*. The liquid in the slurry, which has a high alumina content, is separated from the solids by a simple filtration process. The residue which remains is known as *red mud*. Disposing of the red mud is a major problem for the industry.
- The liquid which contains the alumina is filtered to remove any traces of red mud and cooled in *precipitation tanks* where the alumina is crystallised. Small alumina *seed crystals* are added to the solution. These increase the rate at which crystals grow. The crystals are separated out, sorted by size, washed, and dried. Then they are stored in silos.

Red mud

When a tonne of alumina is produced from Jamaican bauxite, there are five tons of red mud slurry to dispose of. The slurry is only 20% solids; the rest is water. But the particles of solid matter settle very slowly.

Until now, red mud has been dumped in 'ponds'. A typical pond covers 80 ha. After a long time, a hard crust forms on the surface of the pond; but this crust merely traps the slurry below, which never dries out.

Enough red mud is produced in Jamaica to cover an area of 3 km^2 to a depth of 4 m every year.

Red mud still contains some caustic soda. It kills the vegetation around the edge of the pond. People who live nearby also complain about dust from the ponds. In dry weather, crystals form on the surface; and when these blow away they can make the air extremely unpleasant to breathe. Red mud can also pollute groundwater. Contaminated water from the ponds can percolate through the limestone bedrock. Several springs and wells have been affected.

Scientists from McGill University in Canada and from the University of the West Indies have been investigating ways of dealing with the red mud problem:

- By improving the design of the settling tanks and adding certain chemicals to the red mud, it should be possible to produce a more concentrated slurry. There would then be less red mud to dispose of.
- If red mud is pumped onto a slope, instead of into a pond, it will spread out and form a thin layer which can dry off in the sun. The dried mud can then be cut up and stacked.
- It may be possible to process red mud to extract rare elements like scandium, which sells for $50 per gramme and is used in military research.
- It is possible to use red mud to make bricks. Unfortunately, these bricks contain very small amounts of radioactive gas. Careful investigation will be needed before it is decided whether red mud bricks are completely safe to use.

Making aluminium

Aluminum is produced in a *smelter*:

- The alumina crystals are dissolved in molten *cryolite*, in a container which is lined with *graphite*.
- A strong electric current is passed through the molten ore.
- The graphite lining on the container has a negative electric charge. It is a *cathode*.
- The alumina is broken down into aluminium and oxygen. The aluminium is attracted towards the negative charge in the container lining.

- Molten aluminium collects in the bottom of the container and is tapped off.

An aluminium smelter uses enormous quantities of electricity. Unless the electricity is very cheap, the cost of the aluminium will be very high. That is why smelters are usually located close to a cheap power source. Some smelters are in areas with large, fast-flowing rivers, where hydroelectricity can be generated. Others are located close to sources of cheap natural gas.

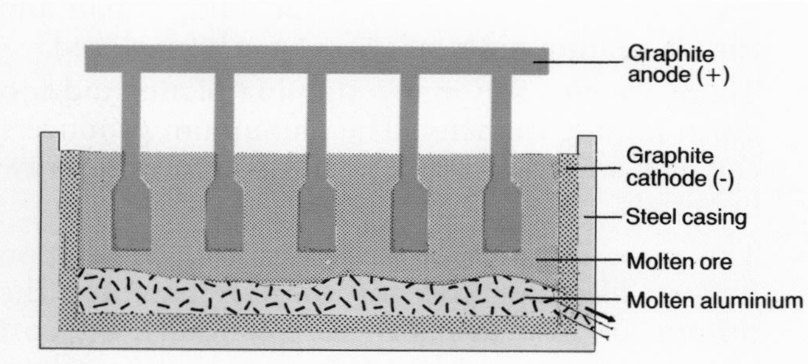

13.35 How aluminium is smelted.

7 List the different steps involved in mining baxuite, making alumina, and smelting aluminium.

Other uses of bauxite

Some Guyanese bauxite has a very high proportion of alumina. It is known as refractory-grade bauxite, and has many other uses. It can be used as a raw material for making:

- Firebricks for lining kilns and furnaces.
- Special cement for making concrete which can stand up to high temperatures.
- High-strength electrical porcelain for making electrical insulators.
- Anti-skid surfacing material for roads, bridges, factory floors, and airport runways.
- Aluminium sulphate and other chemicals.

For most of these purposes, refractory-grade bauxite is *calcined* by heating it to over 1,500 °C in rotating kilns 100 m long. This removes all the water from the bauxite. The calcined bauxite is shipped abroad for further processing.

In Guyana, the emphasis is now on the production of refractory-grade bauxite and calcined bauxite, rather than on metal-grade bauxite for making aluminium. This is because:

- Calcined bauxite fetches a much higher price.
- Many countries produce bauxite which can be used to make aluminium; but only a few produce refractory-grade bauxite for these other uses.

Managing the industry

Bauxite is a valuable resource. Everyone would agree that it should be used; but not everyone would have quite the same view of the resource.

8 Here are four contrasting points of view about the bauxite industry. For each of these statements, describe the type of person who would be likely to hold that point of view. Explain your answer carefully.

'Bauxite from the Caribbean is an important raw material for our smelters. We want to keep the cost down, and make sure that we have a reliable source of supply.'

'Bauxite mining will help develop our economy. We need to improve our transport system, and we need capital to improve agriculture, build hospitals and start new industries.'

'Working in the mine is not easy. But I earn much more than I could in farming, and I can rely on a steady income all year round.'

'I don't like the dust, or the noise from the blasting. But I get compensation from the company, and the men from the mine have plenty of money to spend in my shop.'

Bauxite mining started in Guyana in 1917, and in Jamaica in 1952. In both countries the industry was started by large companies from the United States and Canada which wanted to develop overseas sources of bauxite for their aluminium smelters.

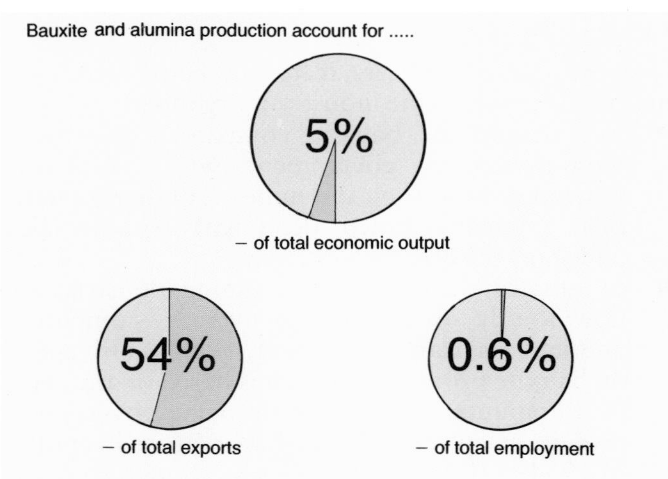

13.36 Bauxite in the Jamaican economy.

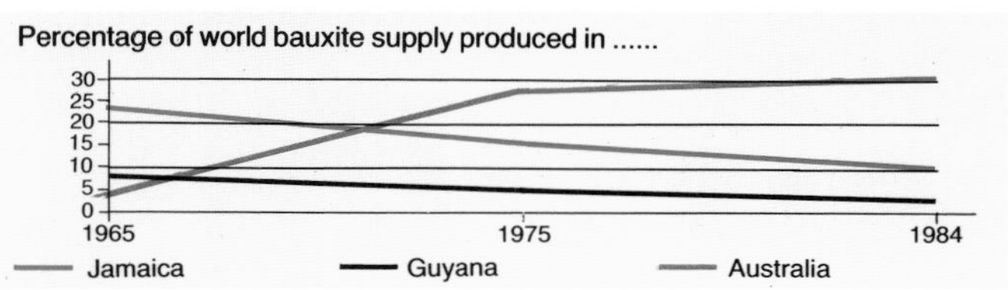

13.37 Bauxite production in three countries.

Most people would now agree that the Caribbean economies did not derive enough benefits from the industry in the past:

- After almost seventy years of bauxite mining, there is still no aluminium smelter in the region. Caribbean industries which use aluminium must import it from abroad.
- Almost all the machinery and equipment used by the industry is imported.
- There were several thousand new jobs; but mining and processing bauxite employs only a tiny percentage of the workforce.
- Almost all the top management positions were for overseas staff; and control of the industry was in the hands of overseas companies.
- New transport routes were opened up; but some of them were really only useful to the bauxite companies.
- Even where land is reclaimed after mining, there is always disturbance to the local community, and a serious pollution problem when mining is actually taking place.
- It was difficult to estimate a fair rate of tax, based on the value of bauxite, because the ore was 'transferred' to the parent company, not sold on the open market.
- Very few Caribbean nationals acquired detailed technical knowledge about the running of the industry. Even the geological information about the reserves was not made public by the companies.

Local control

Over the past twenty years, there have been big changes in the way in which the industry is organised:

- In Guyana, the bauxite companies have been *nationalised*. A government-owned company, Guymine, now runs the mines; another government company, Bidco, deals with bauxite sales and ships the ore overseas.
- In Jamaica, the mining and alumina industries are now jointly owned by the overseas companies and the Jamaican government. There is also a levy on bauxite production which is based on the price of aluminium. Because of the levy, government revenue from the industry has increased rapidly. In 1984–5, the bauxite levy was enough to cover 12% of government spending. The Jamaica Bauxite Institute carries out research into the industry and keeps a close watch on its overall development.

The world market

Caribbean bauxite and alumina producers are a small part of a worldwide industry. Local control over mining and processing does not mean that there is local control over the *world market* for bauxite and alumina. There is no 'instant solution' for some of the industry's problems.

- The demand for aluminium is not increasing as fast as it was before 1970. If every smelter in the world were working full-time, there would be too much aluminium, and the price would fall very quickly. In many countries, including Japan and the USA, aluminium smelters have been closed.
- There are also too many alumina plants and too much mining capacity. The aluminium producers can pick and choose where they will buy their raw materials.
- The price of the raw materials will depend on factors like the cost of *mining* bauxite; the proportion of *alumina* the ore contains; the cost of *transporting* bauxite or alumina to the smelter; and the level of *taxation*.
- The large aluminium companies buy a much smaller proportion of their raw materials from the Caribbean than before. Figure 13.39 shows how the 'market share' of one of the new producers has increased at the expense of Jamaica and Guyana.
- It would be diffucult for any Caribbean country to start a completely independent operation by building its own smelter. Jamaica has no cheap power source for generating electricity. Guyana has fast-flowing rivers, which could be used to generate hydroelectric power; but this is a resource which would cost a great deal of money to develop; and a new aluminium smelter would be a very risky investment.

The bauxite industry uses a non-renewable resource from the Caribbean. It has brought benefits to the region, but there have also been problems. The questions for the future are:

- How to maintain and increase sales.
- How to avoid polluting the environment.
- How to use bauxite mining and processing as a starting-point for developing other industries.
- How to ensure that people in the region benefit from the development of the industry.

13.7 Industry in Nigeria

Nigeria has a long tradition of craft industry; but there was very little large-scale manufacturing in the country until the 1950s.

Since then, the government has been encouraging the development of secondary industry. Nigeria has several advantages for industrial development:

- There is a large internal market. Nigeria has a population of over 90 million, so many consumer items can be produced on a really large scale.
- Nigeria is one of the world's leading oil-producers. Oil exports earn foreign exchange which can be used to buy machinery and raw materials for new industries.
- Oil money can also be used to improve the country's *infrastructure*; it can pay for roads, water supply systems, electricity generating stations, and so on.
- Many other industrial raw materials are produced in Nigeria. These include natural gas, iron ore, tin, and coal, as well as agricultural products like cotton and rubber.

Some development problems

However, there have also been some major problems with industrial development:

- Since 1980, the price of crude oil has fallen. There is less foreign exchange available from oil exports; but imports still have to be paid for, and money which was borrowed to help finance development during the oil boom still has to be repaid.

13.38 Craft industry in Nigeria: weaving cloth.

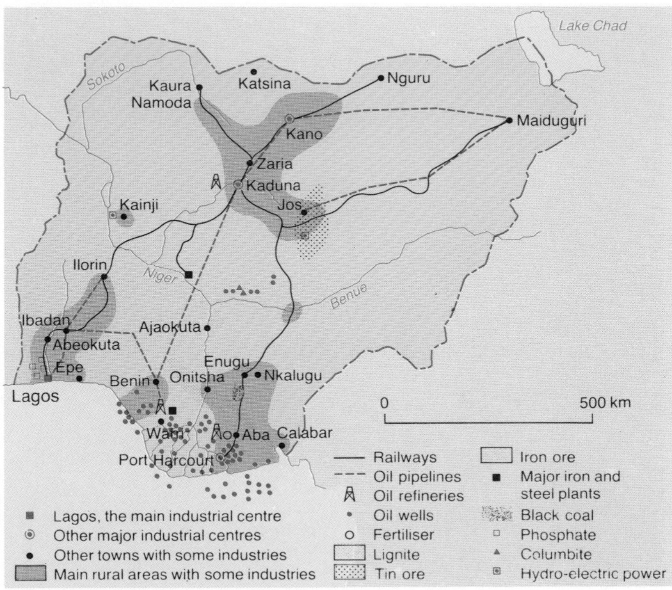

13.39 Industry and mineral resources in Nigeria.

- The population of Nigeria is growing rapidly. The urban population is increasing particularly fast. This makes it hard to provide schools, housing, hospitals, and other services.
- Nigeria is a very large country, with many very different ethnic groups. There have sometimes been very serious conflicts; the south-east of the country was devastated by a terrible civil war in 1966–70. Politicians have to be very careful to strike a balance between the needs of different regions of Nigeria.
- Agriculture has not developed nearly as fast as industry. Food production has not kept pace with the rising population, and many agricultural products which could be grown in Nigeria are imported: for example, Nigeria now imports 60% of its cotton.
- Many Nigerians prefer imported products to locally produced goods. It is difficult for local industries to compete with low-cost imports.
- There is a growing gap between the rich and the poor; and between urban and rural areas. In a country where some people are acquiring wealth very rapidly, there is a big temptation for officials and politicians to accept bribes.

Nigerian industry today

There is now quite a wide range of manufacturing industries in Nigeria. There are:

- Industries which process Nigerian raw materials. These include large-scale heavy industries using oil, natural gas, and iron ore; and smaller-scale industries which use agricultural raw materials

13.40 Lagos is a busy industrial city.

and forest products.
- Import substitution industries which process materials and components from abroad to produce goods for the local market. Some of these industries operate on a very large scale.

Lagos

Lagos is a huge, sprawling city with a population of more than two million. It has been estimated that Lagos contains:
- 25% of the bakeries in Nigeria.
- 25% of textiles production.
- 50% of furniture production.
- 50% of printing and publishing.
- 60% of plastics production.
- 100% of the production of electronic goods.

Lagos is the first choice for many manufacturing industries, because:
- It is Nigeria's largest single market for industrial goods.
- Lagos Port handles 70% of the industrial raw materials landed in Nigeria.
- Lagos has better air connections than any other airport in the country.
- Although there are plans for a new capital, most government agencies still have their headquarters in Lagos.

But there are problems with Lagos as an industrial location. Traffic congestion is so bad that it can take two hours to cross the city; and services like electricity, water supply, and telephones are very unreliable. It is also difficult to find suitable sites to build new factories.

If all the industrial growth is concentrated in Lagos, then migration to the city will increase, and it will become even harder to provide urban services. If the other parts of Nigeria are neglected, the gap between the rich and poor regions will become wider and there will be a danger of serious political conflict. Both the national government and the different states are encouraging manufacturing companies to move away from Lagos. Every big city in Nigeria now has some modern industry.

Breweries

There are 22 breweries in Nigeria, spread over 12 of the 19 states. Beer production is dispersed because:
- Beer is consumed in almost every part of the country.
- It costs more to transport beer than the raw materials which are used to brew it. Breweries save on distribution costs if they are located near their customers.
- Beer production can be profitable on a fairly small scale.
- State governments encourage breweries, because they can collect duty, which increases their revenue.

Breweries originally used an imported raw material, barley. But increasingly, they now substitute local products like sorghum and maize syrup, and use locally grown barley from the north of Nigeria. And about two-thirds of the packaging and other materials used in the breweries are locally produced.

Motor vehicles

As incomes have increased in Nigeria, there has been an increasing demand for cars and trucks. Two European firms, Volkswagen and Peugeot, import components from overseas, and assemble them in

13.41 Assembling cars in Lagos.

Nigeria. Volkswagen, like many firms which use imported materials, is located in Lagos; but Peugeot operates successfully in the northern city of Kaduna. Components are brought to Lagos Port in containers; and these containers are taken unopened by rail to Kaduna. This does not increase costs very much.

Many of the components and other inputs used in car assembly are now made in Nigeria, too. These include tyres, batteries, paint, radiators, exhausts, generators, clutches, and radios. About 30% of the components of the Peugeot are locally produced.

1 How does automobile assembly help in the development of other industries?
2 Why is it easier to manufacture components locally if only one or two types of car are being assembled?

Heavy industries

Oil is Nigeria's most important mineral resource. Most of the crude oil produced in the country is still refined abroad, and some refinery products are still imported. But there are several major refineries and petrochemicals plants.

Natural gas is another important raw material. However, not enough use is made of Nigerian natural gas. Even in 1984, 80% of the gas produced in the oil fields was still being flared off. Some gas is used to generate electricity, and there is a plant at Port Harcourt which uses gas to make fertiliser. There are plans to liquefy the gas, so that it can be exported or used in other parts of the country, but the cost of this project would be very high, and it has not yet been finalised.

13.42 Drilling for oil in the Niger Delta.

3 Make a sketch map to show the location of:
   (a) The main oil-producing area.
   (b) The oil refineries.
4 Why has one of the refineries been built in the northern part of Nigeria?
5 Why is natural gas more difficult to use than oil?
6 Why is it important to make good use of this resource?
7 Look at Figure 13.39. Besides oil and natural gas, what other mineral resources are there in Nigeria?

Iron and steel

Nigeria has huge oil and gas reserves, and also some iron ore and coal. As in many developing countries, the government has encouraged the development of an iron and steel industry. Steel is an important industrial material, but it is difficult for a developing country to produce it at low cost. Nigeria has steelworks which produce billets, and rolling mills which produce *steel sheet* which can be made into various products.

8 Compare the location of the two steelworks shown in figure 13.39 with Point Lisas in Trinidad. What are the advantages and disadvantages of each location?
9 Explain why Nigeria has a much larger market for steel products than Trinidad and Tobago.
10 Explain why many developing countries have made it a priority to build a steel mill.

There have been technical problems with the development of the steel industry. The rolling mill at Ajaokuta, for example, was designed to take 10-cm billets; but the steelworks at Warri originally produced 12-cm billets. The machinery at Warri had to be retooled to produce billets of the right size. This was an expensive process.

11 There has been a proposal to build a small steel mill in Lagos state. This mill would use scrap metal from local industries. It could supply the local market. Give one argument *for* and one argument *against* this proposal.
12 Compare the development of industry in Nigeria with industrial development in either Trinidad and Tobago or Jamaica, under these headings:
   (a) Resources.
   (b) Heavy industry.
   (c) Other industry.
   (d) Location patterns.
   (e) Industrial development problems.

13.8 Industry in Japan

Japan is probably the most successful industrial economy in the world; yet the country seems to have few advantages for industrial development:

- Japan is not very close to countries which import industrial goods.
- Japan does not have a privileged trading relationship with other countries.
- Very little outside capital has been invested in Japanese industry.
- Japan does not have a wide range of natural resources: 99.7% of the oil used in Japan, 99% of the iron ore, 92% of the coking coal, and 100% of the nickel, bauxite, cotton, and wool used by Japanese industry have to be imported.

The Japanese economy has been successful largely because the Japanese have made good use of the limited natural resources they do have. For example, only 15% of the country is suitable for agriculture; but Japan has rice available for export and produces 98% of the fruit it needs, as well as most of its meat and dairy produce.

The development of Japanese industry

Until 1856, Japan was cut off from the outside world. Foreign trade was forbidden. The country developed a self-sufficient economy. Peasant farmers, fishermen, craftsmen, businessmen, and traders provided all the goods and services that were needed.

Then Japan was forced to start trading with the West. The country began to modernise very rapidly. Outsiders still thought of Japan as a quaint little country where people lived in paper houses and made beautiful craft items; but the foundations of a modern industrial state were being laid.

At first, Japan exported silks and luxury craft items.

13.43 Dyeing a silk kimono by hand.

The first large-scale export industry was cotton textiles. This was a 'low-technology' industry where low wages gave Japan an advantage. In the 1930s, textiles made up half of Japan's exports. By then, Japan was also producing coal, steel, textile machinery, military equipment, and other goods.

Japan started a colonial empire. By 1940, Korea, Taiwan, and much of China were under Japanese rule. Then Japan entered the Second World War as an ally of Germany. By the end of the war, the economy was in ruins and most of the cities had been devastated by bombing.

Japanese industry recovered quite quickly from the effects of the Second World War:

- Steel production was 7.6 million tonnes in 1943. It was only 0.6 million in 1946; but by 1951, it was back to 6.5 million tonnes.
- By 1956, the Japanese shipbuilding industry was the largest in the world.

Industrial growth was far faster than anyone would have thought possible.

- By 1980, Japan was producing over 110 million tonnes of steel, more than any other country except the USSR.
- In the 1950s, one Japanese firm was still assembling British cars under licence. In 1960, 165,000 cars were produced. By 1983, the figure was over 7 million, and Japan was the world's leading car producer.
- Today, Japan is the world's leading producer of a whole range of goods, including aluminium, cameras, watches, washing machines, and motor cycles.
- Because of improved production methods, the output of the average Japanese worker increased by 42% between 1975 and 1980. In the USA, the figure was 15%.
- Because Japanese industry has been so successful, wage levels are now about the same as in Western Europe. Japan is no longer a 'low-wage' economy.
- There has been a shift away from low-technology industries. Textiles are now less than 5% of Japanese exports.

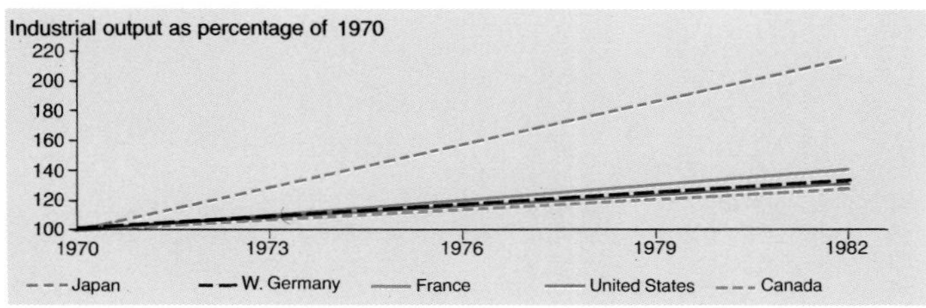

13.44 Manufacturing production has grown much faster in Japan than in other industrial countries.

Why Japanese industry has been successful

Japan is a very complex society, and one which is very different from our own. There is no 'easy' explanation for Japanese economic success; but several reasons have been suggested which may provide part of the answer:

- Japan has never been ruled by another country.
- Japanese consumers buy home-produced goods rather than imports.
- Investors put their money into Japanese industry, and do not send it overseas.
- Japanese workers are very loyal to their company. Long strikes are very unusual.
- Large firms give their workers regular wage increases and other benefits such as housing and health care.
- The company dominates every aspect of the worker's life. It even arranges leisure-time activities, and sometimes marriages.
- There is a good education system. Almost all students stay on after the school-leaving age, and more than one-third go to university.
- In the past, wage rates were quite low.
- Japanese people generally do not question those who are in authority.
- Japanese people are keen savers; and the banks invest their savings in industry.
- Government works carefully to develop Japanese industries. It is not easy for foreigners to sell industrial goods to Japan.
- Japan spends far less on defence than any other industrial country.
- When Japan began to trade with the West, it was already an advanced country, even if there was no modern factory industry.
- Japan has a big enough population to make large-scale production for the internal market profitable.

1 Which of these explanations seem reasonable?
2 List some of the *differences* between Japan and the Caribbean as an environment for industry, under these headings:
  (a) Natural resources.
  (b) History.
  (c) Attitudes and way of life.
  (d) Other factors.
3 Are there any *similarities*?

The location of industry

Most of Japan consists of remote mountain areas with a very low population and almost no manufacturing industry.

Japanese industry is concentrated in a narrow coastal strip running from the island of Kyushu in the south along the shore of the Inland Sea and the Pacific as far as the Kanto plain, just north of Tokyo.

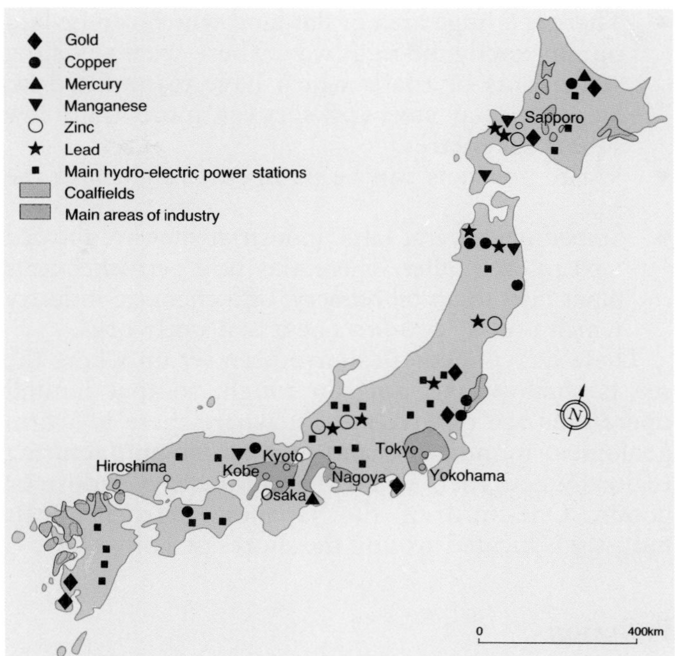

13.45 The main manufacturing regions in Japan.

Within this coastal strip, there are three major concentrations:

- Around Tokyo and Yokohama.
- Around Nagoya.
- Around Kyoto, Osaka, and Kobe.

These three districts account for more than half of the country's manufacturing output.

4 Look carefully at Figure 13.45. Do these three industrial concentrations have more natural resources than the rest of Japan?

These districts developed as industrial centres because they already had large cities and a dense rural population:

- There was a large labour force.
- There was a market for industrial goods.
- Communications with the rest of Japan and with the outside world were good.
- There was already a strong tradition of craft industry in the cities.

Heavy industries

Large-scale heavy industries like oil-refining, petrochemicals, electricity generation, and iron and steel are located along the coast, usually on land which has been reclaimed from the sea.

- A coastal site means that imported raw materials like iron ore or crude oil can be unloaded directly from a bulk carrier or tanker. Transport costs are very low.

- There is a huge area of flat land which can be laid out in exactly the right way. There are no existing settlements or roads which have to be fitted in. Some coastal steelworks cover more than five square kilometres.
- Waste products can be pumped straight into the sea.
- Sometimes several large industrial sites are located next to each other. There may be a petrochemicals plant next to an oil refinery, or a chemical industry which uses *by-products* next to a steelworks.

These heavy industries have been set up where the sea is shallow and not too rough, so that landfill operations are relatively easy; where there is a firm geological foundation; and in major manufacturing regions where there is a demand for heavy industrial goods. One-third of the Japanese petrochemicals industry is located around the shores of Tokyo Bay.

Pollution

'An extraordinarily beautiful body of water, dotted with innumerable islands, providing views of far mountain ranges and great expanses of seascape.'

(Description of the Inland Sea, 1951)

'The view from the ferry is a nightmare. On some islands, the vegetation has died off completely from the effects of pollutants. Over all hangs a pale sun, sometimes a faint yellow, sometimes a pinkish orange, in whose diffused light objects cast no shadow.'

(The same writer, describing the Inland Sea in 1976)

Until quite recently, the Japanese attitude to industrial pollution was that industrial growth was the overriding priority, and that too many controls would hold up the pace of development.

As a result, environmental damage has sometimes been disastrous:

- Over 70,000 people have been officially certified as having a disease caused by pollution.
- Many more people suffer from minor ailments related to air pollution.
- Smaller numbers have been crippled or killed by Minamata disease, which is caused by eating fish from water which has been polluted by mercury; or by Itai-itai disease, caused by eating rice which has been irrigated with water containing small amounts of cadmium.

Traditionally, Japanese culture has valued natural beauty and the natural environment very highly; and many people have found the effects of pollution very distressing. In recent years, the government has started to control pollution. The regulations on car exhausts are among the strictest in the world; and no firm could now be allowed to dump large quantities of a dangerous substance like mercury or cadmium in the water. But it will take many years to clear up the damage that has already been done.

5 Some developing countries look at pollution control as a luxury which they cannot afford to spend money on. Is this a sensible attitude?

6 Why is the Inland Sea particularly vulnerable to marine pollution?

13.46 A large steel mill. Heavy industries can be a major source of pollution.

13.47 This oil refinery near Yokohama is built on reclaimed land.

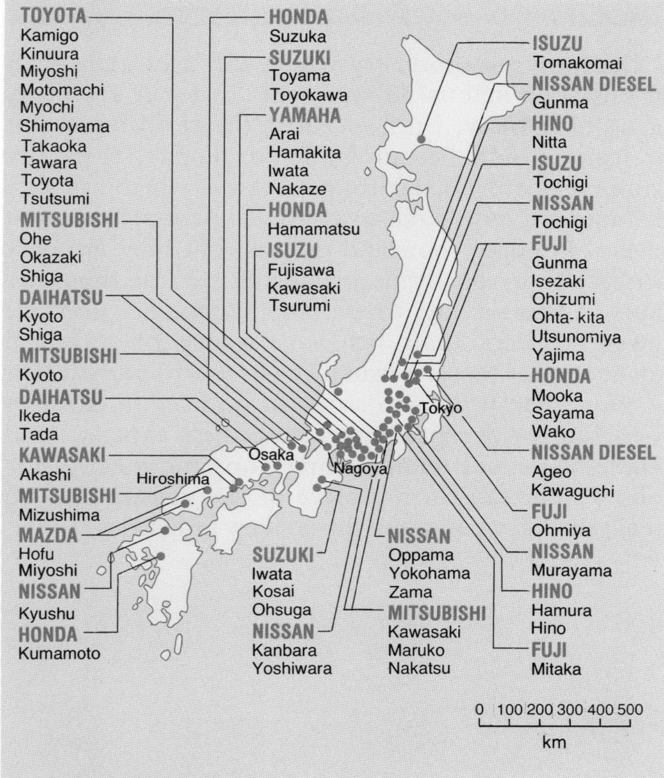

13.48 Motor vehicle plants in Japan.

7 The Japanese get almost half their animal protein from fish. How would their economy and diet be affected by widespread marine pollution?

Assembly industries

Factories producing cars and electrical goods are usually located in the big industrial concentrations, because they depend on a large number of smaller factories which supply them with *components*.

In Japan, there are twelve big companies producing cars and other motor vehicles; but there are over 8,000 which make parts and components for the motor industry. Many of these are small firms with fewer than 300 employees, but taken together, they employ more than twice as many people as the car industry itself.

These factories usually have a suburban location, because land in the city centre is too expensive. But the suppliers of components and the assembly industries are dependent on each other, and both need to be located in or near a major industrial concentration. Toyota even has a special industrial estate for components suppliers near to its main factory.

8 List five of the components which are used in the assembly of a motor car.

9 What difficulties would be faced by:
   (a) A components supplier located too far from a vehicle manufacturer?
   (b) A vehicle manufacturer with no components suppliers nearby?

Industrial dispersal

Since the 1960s, costs have been increasing for factories which are located in the three main industrial concentrations:

- Traffic congestion has worsened. It can now take several hours to transport goods across a big city.
- Land prices have increased enormously. Flat land with good communications costs far more than in other parts of Japan.
- There is a shortage of coastal areas which are suitable for land reclamation.
- Wages are much higher than in rural Japan.
- Heavy industry uses an enormous amount of water. In the industrial areas, there are sometimes water shortages, and some sources have been polluted. Where too much groundwater has been extracted, there has been a problem with land subsidence.
- There is a serious pollution problem. In heavy industrial centres like Kawasaki, air pollution causes respiratory diseases for many people.

Many industries have now started to move away from the most congested areas. This trend has been encouraged by the government; and road and rail communications have improved, so that it is now much easier for a company to transport components and finished products to where they are needed.

Usually, industries have moved to districts which are still within easy reach of the main centres, on the coast of the Inland Sea or within 200 kilometres of Tokyo; but there has also been an attempt to develop industrial centres at Mutsu in northern Honshu and Tomakomai in Hokkaido.

10 Look at Figure 13.48. How many motor vehicle plants are located:
   (a) In the three main industrial concentrations?
   (b) Near to the Inland Sea?
   (c) Within 200 km of Tokyo?
   (d) Elsewhere in Japan?

13.9 Industry in the USA

The Caribbean countries are small nations, trying to develop an industrial base for the first time. The USA produces more industrial goods than any other country in the world, and has had large-scale manufacturing industries for more than a century and a half.

In spite of this, most people in the USA do not work in manufacturing. Employment can be broken down like this:

- Primary industries: 4.1%.
- Secondary industries: 22.4%.
- Tertiary industries: 73.5% (including construction, electricity, water, etc.).

The percentage of people who work in manufacturing is actually falling. This is because of technical advances which mean that a small number of workers are able to produce a large quantity of high-grade goods.

Clothing is an industry which still uses quite a lot of unskilled manual labour; but costs can be cut by using machinery. Until recently, the cloth for a pair of jeans would be cut by hand. Today, there are computer-controlled cutting machines which can slice through a whole stack of cloth. These machines cost several hundred thousand dollars; but they are only profitable for big firms producing several thousand pairs of jeans a day. These large companies need far fewer workers than before. Because of technical advances like these, it usually costs less to *make* a pair of jeans than it does to *advertise* and *sell* it. Most of the selling price represents management expenses and wholesaler's and retailer's mark-up; and most of the jobs which transform a piece of raw cotton into an item you can wear are in the tertiary industries.

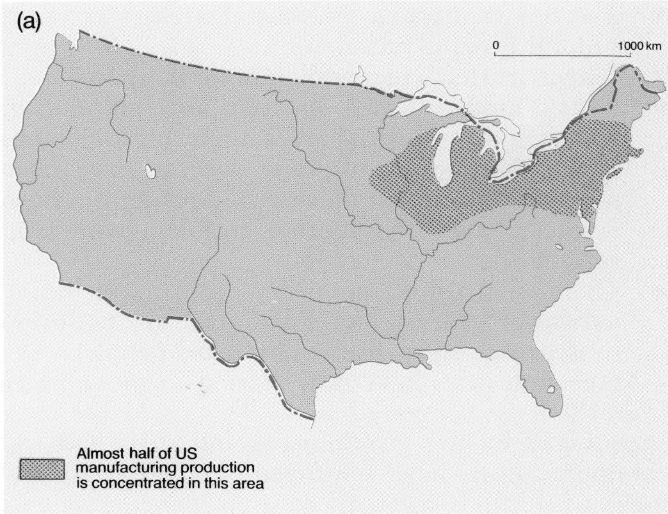

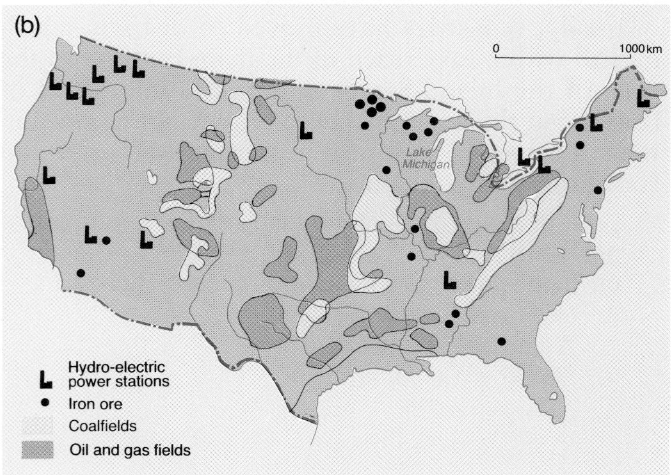

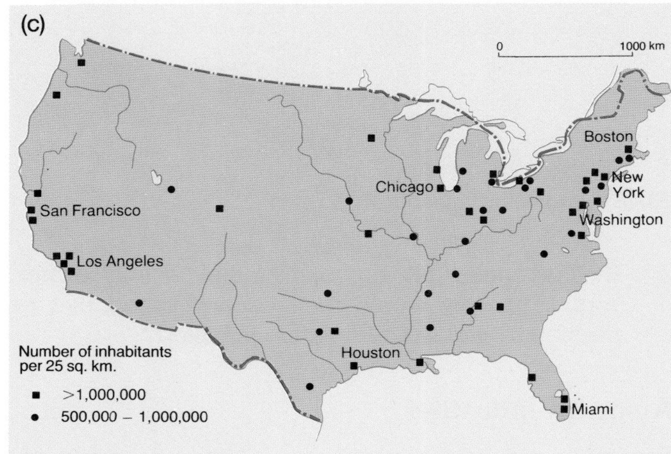

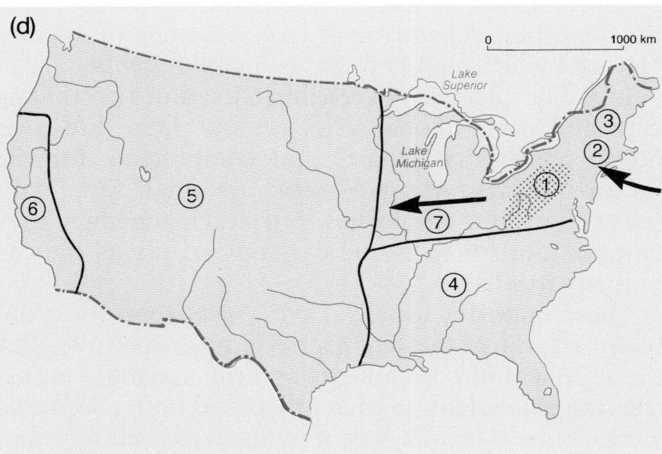

1. The first coalfields to be exploited
2. Immigrants from Europe arrived in the ports of the North East
3. Water power in New England helped early industrial development
4. The south was an agricultural area, which was devastated by the civil war
5. The west was not settled until the late nineteenth century
6. California was isolated from the main population centres
7. The mid-west was becoming a prosperous agricultural region

13.49 The manufacturing belt.
(a) Main manufacturing area. (c) Population centres.
(b) Mineral and power resources. (d) The US in the 19th century.

The manufacturing belt

Almost half of all industrial employment in the USA is concentrated in the *manufacturing belt* in the north-east of the country.

1 Study Figures 13.49a, b and c. Comment on the location of the manufacturing belt in relation to:
   (a) Coal.
   (b) Oil.
   (c) Hydroelectric power.
   (d) The market for industrial goods.

It is not easy to explain the location of the manufacturing belt in relation to present-day resource patterns. This region is important partly for historical reasons.

2 Look at Figure 13.49d. Explain why the manufacturing belt was the main industrial region of the USA in the second half of the nineteenth century, when it was becoming an industrial nation for the first time.

Over the past century, the percentage of manufacturing employment which is in the north-east has fallen, like this:

- 77% in 1870.
- 67% in 1910.
- 55% in 1970.
- 48% in 1980.

This is because industry has spread to areas like:

- The south, where wage rates are usually lower.
- California and Florida, where the population is rising, and there is a growing market for industrial goods.

Industry has also been able to spread into new areas because *transporting* manufactured goods and raw materials is now far quicker and cheaper than it used to be, and because there is *energy* for industrial development all over the United States.

The manufacturing belt covers a huge area. Many parts of the north-east are rural areas, with hardly any secondary industry. Manufacturing is centred in the areas shown in Figure 13.49a.

3 How far is it from Chicago to Boston?

4 Write down the names of five big cities in the manufacturing belt.

New England

In the nineteenth century, there were a large number of textile factories in New England. They used simple machinery, and employed a large number of workers. Raw cotton and wool were brought to New England to make the cloth, and energy came from water power or from coal. More than 21% of the industrial jobs in the United States were in this region in 1870, but the region has become less important and it now accounts for only 7.5% of all manufacturing jobs.

Today, the textiles industry is very different. Machinery is much more efficient, and fewer workers are employed. Electric power is used for energy. The old textile mills are obsolete, and almost all of the new ones which have replaced them are in the southern part of the USA or outside the country altogether. Over the past forty years, three-quarters of the jobs in the New England textile industry have gone.

However, New England is still an important manufacturing area:

- 70% of the handguns and rifles made in the USA are from New England.
- Aircraft engines and helicopters are manufactured in Connecticut.
- Boston is a major centre for the computer and electronics industries.

All these are light industries which employ a high proportion of skilled workers. The small-arms and aircraft industries employ specialised engineering workers. Electronics is a newer industry. Many of the assembly workers are unskilled; but there are many highly paid professionals developing and designing new products. Highly skilled scientific staff can be recruited in a big metropolitan area with well-established universities like Harvard and Massachusetts Institute of Technology

5 Explain why a well-established industrial region like this can remain prosperous, even if its main manufacturing industry moves elsewhere.

Iron and steel

A heavy industry can only make a profit if the cost of transporting the raw materials and the finished product is kept low.

There has been a large-scale iron and steel industry in the USA for over 150 years. During this period,

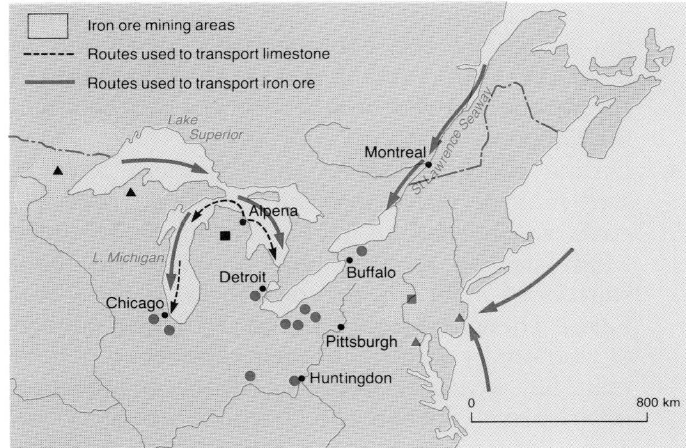

13.50 The US iron and steel industry: location patterns.

the *location* pattern of the industry has altered several times because of changes in:

- The raw materials used.
- The transport system.
- The technology of steel manufacturing.
- The markets for the finished product.

Figure 13.50 shows how the location pattern of the US iron and steel industry has developed:

- The first iron and steel plants were in eastern Pennsylvania. All the main raw materials were found in this area; there was iron ore, limestone, and coal which was of the right type for early steel-making technology. This area was also well placed for reaching the main markets for iron and steel products. At this time, during the first half of the nineteenth century, there were very few railways, and road transport was by horse and cart. So it was very important for everything the industry needed to be available within one small area. However, there was not much iron ore here, and it soon began to run out.
- In the second half of the nineteenth century, large-scale sources of iron ore were developed to the west of Lake Superior. However, nineteenth-century steel-making methods used much more coal than iron ore to make a tonne of steel. It was cheaper to take the iron ore to a coalfield than to take coal to the main mining area. Many new steelworks were built near Pittsburgh in western Pennsylvania, because there were good supplies of coal there, which could be mined more cheaply than the coal in the older coalfields to the east; and because iron ore could be taken most of the way from Lake Superior to Pittsburgh by water, with only a short *rail* journey to the city from the Lake Erie ports. Pittsburgh was also well placed for river transport; it is built at the point where the Allegheny and Monongahela rivers join to form the Ohio; and it was a good location to supply the growing market for steel products in the midwest.
- During the first half of the twentieth century, steel-making technology improved, so that less coal was needed to make one tonne of steel. Many steelworks were built closer to the main sources of iron ore, on the shores of the Great Lakes. These new steelworks received their supplies of iron ore by water; and their supplies of coal by rail. They were close to the big steel-using industries in cities like Chicago and Detroit which provided a *market*, and a source of *scrap* which could be used in the steel-making process. Some new steelworks were also developed at this time in the south and west of the USA. For a time, the Pittsburgh steel companies were able to slow down the growth of the new steel-making centres, by manipulating the pricing system; but this was ruled illegal. At the beginning of this century, almost half the steel output of the United States was concentrated in Pittsburgh; today, the figure is less than 10%.
- From the 1950s, the supply of high-grade iron ore from Lake Superior was insufficient for the needs of the US steel industry. New sources of iron ore were developed in Labrador and Quebec in eastern Canada. So that the steelworks on the Great Lakes could use this ore, the St Lawrence seaway was constructed. The seaway allows ocean-going vessels to travel from the Great Lakes to the St Lawrence and the Atlantic. At the same time, large steelworks were developed or expanded on *coastal* sites. Two of the largest coastal steelworks are quite close to the original US steel-making centres in eastern Pennsylvania.
- In recent years, *imports* from Japan and other countries have captured an increasing share of the US steel market. The big steel-making companies are one of the least profitable sectors of the US economy. They have reduced the size of their workforce, and some of the least efficient plants have been closed down. The most profitable producers are probably the newer *mini-mills*, some of them outside the traditional steel-making areas, which use cheap sources of energy to supply a specialised range of steel products.

6 List the ways in which the development of the location pattern of the US iron and steel industry has been influenced by changes in:
   (a) Raw materials used.
   (b) The transport system.
   (c) Steel-making technology.
   (d) Markets for steel.

The automobile industry

Only a small proportion of the industrial workers in the manufacturing belt are employed in the iron and steel industry; but many more are employed in industries which use iron and steel products.

One of the biggest employers is the automobile industry. The largest US motor vehicle companies all have their headquarters in Detroit, Michigan; and they have large assembly plants in Detroit itself and in other industrial cities nearby. There are some assembly plants elsewhere in the USA; but the majority are still in the western part of the manufacturing belt. In recent years, some of the large Japanese and European vehicle manufacturers have opened plants in the USA; and most of them have been located in this region, too. Mazda's plant is in Detroit, and most of the others are also in the manufacturing belt.

13.10 Industry in Haiti: two approaches

In the past, Haiti depended for its foreign exchange on the sale of agricultural products like coffee, sugar, and sisal. Sisal is a crop which thrives in badly eroded semi-arid areas where little else can grow; it produces a fibre which can be used to make string, rope, bags, and carpets.

Over the past 30 years, output of agricultural exports has stagnated. There has been a shift towards exporting manufactured goods.

Enclave industries

Most of the new factories are enclave industries, set up by US firms which produce a labour-intensive product. Wages in Haiti are very low. There are about 150 plants where Haitians stitch baseballs, assemble electronic components, or sew clothes for the US market.

These industries provide employment; but there are problems:

- All the materials, machinery, and components are imported. For every $1.00 of foreign exchange that these industries bring in, 50 cents goes straight out of Haiti again to pay for imported components.
- Haiti has to provide infrastructures like water, electricity, and roads. Water is a scarce resource; and electricity is sold to these factories below cost.
- When there is a downturn in the US market, these factories can be closed down.
- No use is made of the country's agricultural resources.
- The employees do repetitive work, and do not develop skills which would allow them to start a business of their own.
- Enclave industries can disappear as quickly as they arrive. After the overthrow of the Duvalier regime in 1986, an estimated total of 12,000 jobs was lost when overseas firms moved their operations out of the country.

A sisal co-operative

A few new enterprises have developed out of Haiti's traditional agricultural activities. One example is a sisal co-operative making floor-coverings for export to the Netherlands.

- The co-operative buys sisal directly from small farmers, at a price which is *above* what the farmers would normally get, but *below* the normal selling price of sisal in the city.
- 100 women in rural areas are paid to make twine from sisal fibre. They produce higher quality twine than the usual machine-made product; and the extra earnings from craft work have the effect of doubling their average family income.
- 250 women in Port au Prince are employed part-time to braid the twine into ribbons. These women are able to increase their earnings by 25–50% because of this extra work.
- A house in the city centre was rented for the next stage in the operation. The rent is about one-tenth of what would be charged for a similar-sized building on an industrial estate, and the location is more convenient for the workers.
- The ribbons are made into 30-cm squares which can be sewn together to make the floor-covering. This is a skilled job. Fifteen skilled male workers were engaged to do this work; and fifteen trainees were employed to learn the trade.
- There are also some other manual workers, an accountant, managers, and office staff. Altogether, about 450 people are employed on the project. In addition to their wages, they receive free medical care, school fees for their children, and emergency welfare payments. The co-operative makes a 10% profit, which can be invested in other new ventures.
- The original investment to set up the project was $12,000 US, which came from a small Netherlands development agency. This compares with an estimated $5,200,000 US to create 700 jobs in a recent proposal by a US agency for a rural development scheme.

1. What advantages does this sort of scheme have over enclave industry development?
2. Why is this sort of project difficult to start up?
3. How would the project be affected by:
   (a) Competition from other countries producing similar goods?
   (b) Changes in fashion for furniture and floor-coverings?

13.51 Small-scale manufacturing in Port au Prince; an open air welding shop.

13.11 Industry in India

13.52 A power station on the banks of the River Hooghly, Calcutta.

By any standards, India is a giant country. In area, it is the seventh largest in the world, and in population it is about three times the size of the USA and the USSR. Only China has more people.

But unlike the world's two superpowers, India is still a poor country with a largely rural economy. As much as 70% of the labour force is still in agriculture; and only a quarter of the population live in urban areas. The rest are scattered in tens of thousands of villages, many of which still do not have electricity or telephones.

A large proportion of the Indian population has a very low standard of living. The average income is about the same as that of Haiti, though prices in India are lower and standards of health and nutrition are rather higher.

Although most of the poor live in the countryside, the worst poverty is probably in the cities. Calcutta now has more than 10 million inhabitants, and every year there are more arrivals as people come to the city looking for work. In the poor districts on the outskirts of the city, there are shanty towns with no electricity, clean water, or sanitation, where most families are barely able to feed themselves from one day to the next.

However, the Indian economy also has a substantial modern sector. Agriculture in states like Haryana and the Punjab has been transformed by the 'Green Revolution'. There are many modern manufacturing industries; the engineering industries now earn three times as much overseas revenue as tea, the main agricultural export. There have been significant Indian initiatives in fields like nuclear energy, space research, and deep sea oil exploration. More than 60% of the population is still illiterate; but there are two million people with an advanced qualification in science, engineering, or agriculture. India has a higher manufacturing output than any country in the developing world, except Mexico and Brazil. And although it is estimated that a third of the world's poor people live in India, there are also perhaps 40 million in the business and professional class who have a very comfortable standard of living.

The Pattern of Industrial Development

India has a tradition of craft industry which stretches back for over four thousand years. In the past, every village produced its own cloth, pottery, leather and metal goods, and more specialised high quality products were traded over long distances. From the eighteenth century until 1947, most of India was under British rule. Although some large scale industries were developed by Indian businessmen at this time, large scale industrialisation did not really start until after independence in 1947.

The government of India has developed a strategy for economic development based on –

- A series of five-year economic plans
- A strong public sector
- Priority for large-scale heavy industry
- Self-reliance, with as wide a range of ocal industry as possible.

As a result of this approach, India now has many large state-owned companies producing steel, chemicals, paper, ships, engineering products and other goods. The public sector owns 60% of the

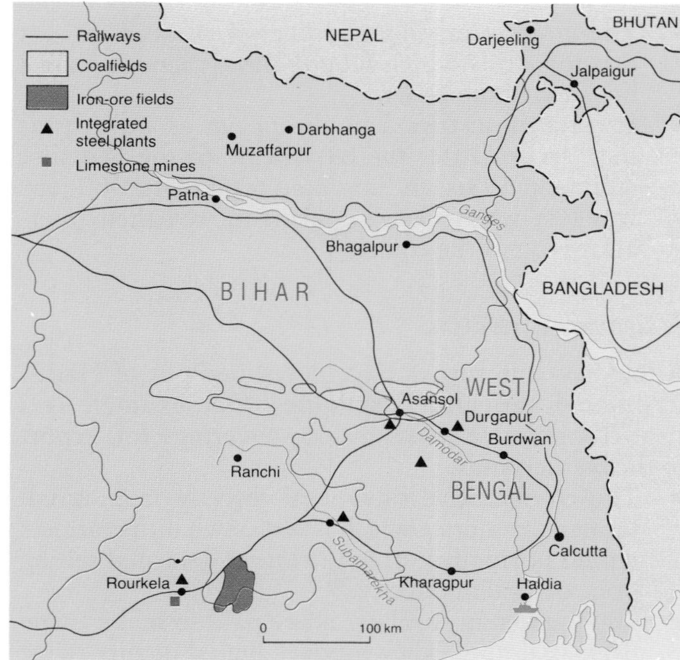

13.53 Bihar and West Bengal: the Lower Ganges Valley.

country's industrial capacity. Other industries – particularly the light industries which produce consumer goods – are privately owned.

Many people would say that this strategy now needs to be modified. Many locally produced goods could never compete internationally, either on quality or on price. The most common car, for example, is the Ambassador, which is simply a version of the Morris Oxford of the 1950s. Indian companies will now need to develop high quality, high technology goods.

The Lower Ganges Valley

Many manufacturing industries have been developed in the two states of West Bengal and Bihar, in the Ganges valley. This is because –

- Calcutta, the capital of West Bengal, used to be a major port and is still an important centre for transport, banking, and commerce.
- The Ganges Delta produces one of India's main export crops, jute. Processing jute fibre to make ropes, packing materials, and floor coverings is an important local industry.
- There are major deposits of iron ore, coal, and other important industrial minerals in these two states.

At independence, West Bengal was the richest and most industrialised state in India. Since then, however, it has lagged behind the rest of the country.

- The jute industry has stagnated. New materials have replaced traditional fibres for many uses.
- Government policy has favoured industrial projects in other parts of India. It is harder to get a permit for industrial development in an old-established region like Bengal.
- Industries in other regions benefit from transport and energy subsidies, tax concessions, and extra government orders.
- Of the 463 factories official classed as 'sick units', 108 are in West Bengal.

But West Bengal is still a major manufacturing region. It has only 3% of India's land area, but 8% of the population and 12% of the factories in the country.

1 Look at Figure 13.54. Compare the pattern of development in Bihar, West Bengal, and Punjab.

Small Scale Industries

There are more than 23 million jobs in small scale manufacturing industries in India. These industries employ 10% of the labour force – four times as many people as large scale factory industry. Small scale industries account for two thirds of the cotton textiles account for two thirds of the cotton textiles produced in India; and handicrafts, leather goods, clothing, and textiles produced by these industries make up about a quarter of manufacturing exports. A million rupees invested in small industries creates more than five times as many jobs as the same amount invested in large factories.

	Average income as % of national average	Rate of economic growth 1970–85
Punjab	163 (richest state)	4.8%
West Bengal	106 (sixth position)	1.0%
Bihar	59 (poorest state)	3.6%

13.54 Production trends in three Indian states.

Some small scale industries are traditional village crafts; but others are part of the modern sector.

There are now a number of industrial estates designed specifically for research-based small scale industries. One of these is near the town of Ranchi, in Bihar, close to the well-known Birla Institute of Technology. It contains small firms which use *appropriate technology* to make products such as electrical transformers, electronic control panels for irrigation schemes and hospital equipment, transmission clamps, and pharmaceuticals. Young people with the right training and commitment who develop a proposal for a product which is in demand can obtain the backing needed to begin production.

2 Explain why Bihar is a good location for research-based small industries.

3 Compare the pattern of industrial development in India with that of Trinidad and Tobago or Jamaica.

13.55 A busy street in Calcutta.

14 · Tourism

14.1 The travel industry

International travel is one of the world's growth industries. Internationally, there are now more than six million hotel employees and 17 million hotel beds; total tourist expenditure is equivalent to almost 5% of world trade: and there were 340 million foreign tourist arrivals in 1985.

There has been a big increase in foreign travel, because:

- Many people in the developed countries have more leisure time and more money to spend than ever before.
- International travel is now far quicker and cheaper than it used to be. To travel by ship from New York to Barbados in 1950 took four days. Today, the flight takes 4½ hours.

1 Will tourism continue to be a growth industry in the future? Give reasons for your answer.

2 Look at Figure 14.1a. Of the twelve countries where most tourists come from:
 (a) Which are important for Caribbean tourism?
 (b) Which have direct air connections to the Caribbean?

3 Which are the world's three most populous countries? Why do few tourists come from these countries?

Country	Money spent US $M		Money spent US $M
USA	16,036	Netherlands	3,010
West Germany	13,927	Switzerland	2,205*
UK	6,135	Mexico	2,174
Canada	5,049	Australia	2,162
Japan	4,609	Austria	2,154
France	4,267	Italy	2,094

*1983 figure.
Source: World Travel Overview, 1986–7.

14.1a People from these twelve countries accounted for two-thirds of overseas tourist spending in 1984.

Country	Money spent US $M		Money spent US $M
USA	11,385	Austria	4,485
Italy	8,578	Canada	3,401
Spain	7,761	Mexico	3,278
France	7,594	Switzerland	3,038*
UK	5,528	Singapore	1,993
West Germany	5,472	Belgium	1,664

* 1983 figure
Source: World Travel Overview, 1986–87.

14.1b Two-thirds of the money was spent in these twelve countries in 1984.

Country	Tourists (000)	Cruise ship passengers (000)	Money spent ($m. US)	Hotel rooms
Puerto Rico	1,532	419	689	7,710
Bahamas	1,368	1,136	870	12,090
Dominican Republic	660	91*	368	6,600
Jamaica	572	262	407	11,280
US Virgin Islands	412	679	532	4,150
St Maarten	398	146	150	1,910
Barbados	359	112	309	6,650
Aruba	207	72	121	2,060
Trinidad and Tobago	191	10	197	1,710
Martinique	190**	153	93	2,750
Guadeloupe	151**	69	95	3,490
Cayman Islands	145	259	86	2,060
Other Caribbean	990	641	498	15,580
Total for Caribbean	7,175	4,049	4,415	78,040
Percentage in twelve main destinations	86%	84%	89%	80%
Percentage in other Caribbean countries	14%	16%	11%	20%

* 1984 figure
** Hotel visitors only
Source: Caribbean Tourism Research Centre, *Statistical Report*, 1986.

14.1c Caribbean tourism: taken as a whole, the Caribbean ranked eighth as a tourist destination in 1984, coming after Austria.

Although international travel has grown in importance, many people still spend their holidays at home or in a tourist area in their own country. In the USA, for example:

- Only 10% of the population travel abroad in any year.
- More than half of the people who do go abroad travel to Canada or Mexico.
- Only 8% of those who go abroad, or 0.8% of the population, visit the Caribbean.

4 Look at Figure 14.1b. Of the twelve most important tourist destinations, how many are in:
 (a) Europe?
 (b) North America?

5 Name a major tourist attraction in each of these twelve countries.

Choosing a holiday destination

January is the coldest month of the year in Europe and North America. There is often snow on the ground, and in many countries it gets dark at around four in the afternoon. At this time of year, many people spend time looking through holiday advertisements in magazines and newspapers, and visit their travel agent to pick up travel brochures. At home, there are many points to discuss:

- Can the family afford a foreign holiday this year?
- Should they return to a place they know, or choose somewhere new?
- What is the best way to spend a few weeks abroad? Is there one holiday centre where there will always be something really enjoyable to do?

International tourism has a seasonal pattern. Many families find it easy to take a holiday together when the schools are closed in the summer months. Other people like to travel at Christmas. In most tourist destinations, the busy periods are generally those when the weather is best for tourist activities.

All Caribbean countries have some environmental resources that can be developed as tourist attractions. Some have good beaches; others have mountains, waterfalls, or good shopping facilities.

Not every tourist wants the same type of holiday:

- Some people like to try local food and drink; others prefer to stick to what they are familiar with.
- Some tourists want to understand something of the culture of the area they are visiting; others are not interested.
- Some people just want to lie on a beach all day; others want a more active holiday – sailing, hiking, or windsurfing.
- Some tourists are working people on a tight budget; for others, money is no object.

Each country needs a strategy for the tourist industry that:

- Starts from its potential resources for tourism.
- Identifies a group of tourists which can be attracted.
- Makes its tourist attractions accessible and develops tourist facilities.
- Fits in with its general pattern of economic development.

Not all tourists are from outside the Caribbean. On many islands, such as Tobago, Caribbean tourists play an important part in the tourist strategy.

14.2 Caribbean tourism

Resources for tourism

Tourism is a tertiary industry. Unlike agriculture and manufacturing, it does not produce anything that you can pick up and carry away; but the tourist industry is influenced by the natural and man-made environment just as much as primary and secondary industries.

1 List the resources which are used by the tourist industry in your country under these headings:
   (a) Natural environment;
   - *Climate*: sunshine, snow, winds, etc.
   - *Landforms*: beaches, mountains, rivers, waterfalls.
   - *Wildlife:* animals, birds, forests, flowering plants.

   (b) Human environment:
   - *Cities*: shopping, historic buildings, art treasures.
   - *Night-life*: theatres, music, food and drink, festivals.
   - *Sports events*, and facilities for outdoor activities.

2 Are there any potential resources in your country which have not yet been developed for tourism?

Besides the environment, there are other points about a holiday centre which should be considered:

- How accessible is it? What are the fares? Are there special rates available?
- What facilities have been developed for tourists? What types of accommodation are available? At what price? What entertainment is provided?
- Are tourists made to feel welcome? Is there a high crime rate?

3 Look at Figure 14.1c:
   (a) Which of the twelve main tourist destinations in the Caribbean are Caricom countries?
   (b) Name one country where a high proportion of tourists are cruise ship passengers.

4 Which were the three main tourist destinations in terms of:
   (a) Number of tourists?
   (b) Money spent by tourists?
   (c) Number of hotel rooms?

5 In 1984, more than 19 million foreign tourists went to the USA; this is more than twice the number who went to the Caribbean, and 130 times the number of tourists in the Cayman Islands. But tourism has much more influence on the Cayman Islands than on the USA. Explain carefully why tourists on a small island have more impact on:
   (a) The economy.
   (b) The environment.
   (c) The social structure.

6 Compare the impact on a Caribbean island of:
   (a) Tourists from the same country.
   (b) Tourists from elsewhere in the Caribbean.
   (c) Tourists from outside the region.

   List the advantages and disadvantages of each type of tourism.

Antigua

Figure 14.2 is an extract from a brochure advertising a package holiday in Antigua, costing $1,500–2,000 US for one week including air fare. In 1985, 140 thousand tourists visited Antigua and Barbuda, making the country the fourteenth most important destination in the Caribbean.

14.2 A package holiday in Antigua.

10 Make a sketch map of the photograph above showing the position of the tourist facilities.
11 What advantages does this stretch of coastline have for tourist development?
12 List the resources that are used by the tourist industry in Antigua.
13 What type of tourist would be attracted to Antigua?

Accessibility

Accessibility is very important to the development of the tourist industry.

Figure 14.3 shows some of the countries from which there are direct flights to Barbados.

14 Which is the most important measure of accessibility:
(a) The number of kilometres travelled?
(b) The cost of the journey?
(c) The time taken in travelling?

15 Which countries outside the Caribbean is it easiest to reach Barbados from?
16 Which countries do most of the tourists who visit Barbados come from?
17 Give *two* reasons why such a high proportion of tourists who visit Barbados are from the USA.
18 Refer to Figure 14.1. Name two countries which are important in the worldwide tourist industry, but which do not send many tourists to Barbados.

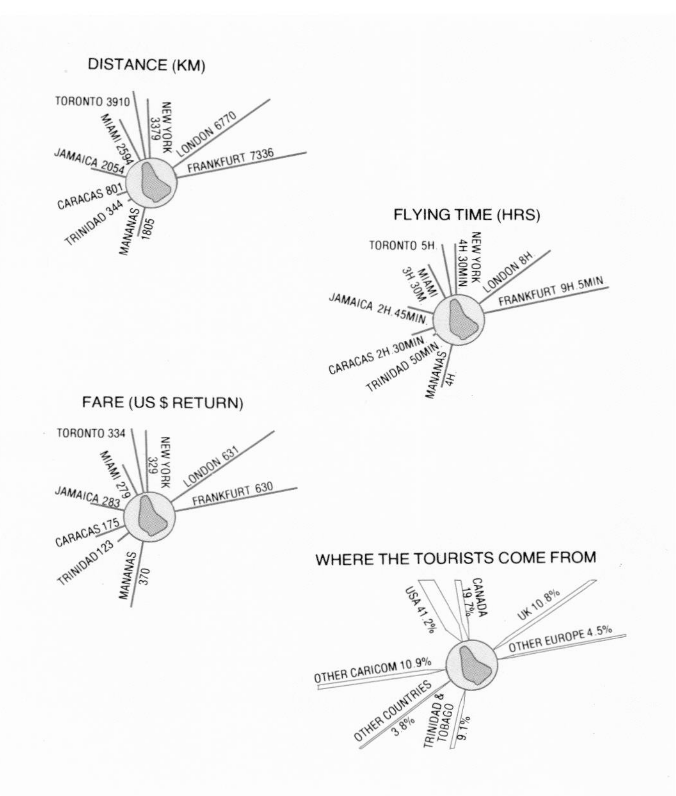

14.3 Travel to Barbados

Dominica

Fewer tourists visit Dominica than most other Caribbean islands. In 1985, 22,000 tourists visited Dominica. There are fewer tourists than on many other islands because:

- There are fewer white-sand beaches than on many islands.
- Many of the beaches on the windward side are too rough for safe bathing.
- There is very little flat land on the island, so it has not been possible to build an airport with a runway long enough to take intercontinental jets. There are no direct flights to Europe or North America.
- The climate is much wetter than in most of the other islands.

It is unlikely that Dominica will ever have mass tourism on the scale of Jamaica or Barbados and most Dominicans probably would not want that sort of development for their island, anyway. But the island has developed a smaller and more specialised tourist industry, based on its natural attractions:

'Dominica is an island of rainbows. Mists rise gently from lush green valleys and fall softly over blue green peaks. Rivers framed by banks of giant ferns rush and tumble to the sea. Trees sprout orchids. Along the mountain slopes, fields of bananas contrast with cocoa and lime trees, and cattle graze in the feathery shade of coconut palms. A young girl walks by, gracefully bearing a stalk of bananas on her head . . .' (Dominica Tourist Board leaflet)

Many tourists do not want to stay in a big international hotel, go to discos, and spend the day taking part in water sports. Most hotels in Dominica are quite small; they are often locally owned and family-run.

19 List the ways in which the tourist industry in Dominica contrasts with tourism in Antigua.
20 What are the *advantages* and *disadvantages* of a small-scale tourist industry?

14.4 The rivers, forests and waterfalls are the main tourist attractions of Dominica.

21 Many of the features described in the publicity material would be very familiar to someone from the Caribbean. Why would they attract an overseas tourist?

Jamaica

Figure 14.5 shows the distribution of hotels within Jamaica.

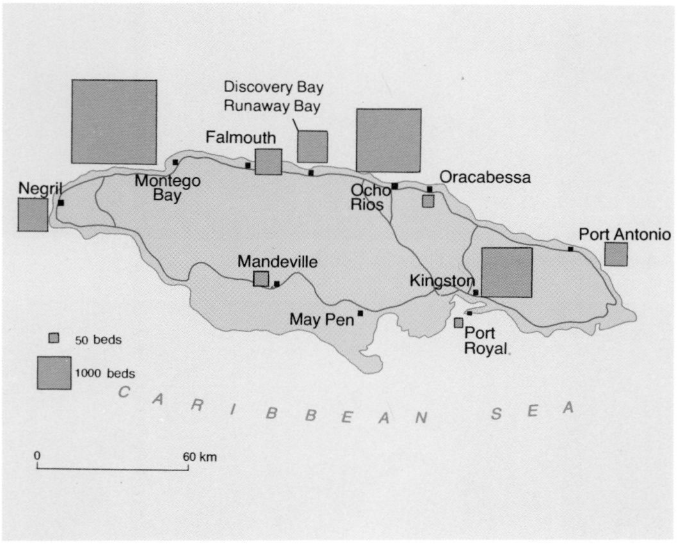

14.5 The main tourist areas of Jamaica.

22 Which are the main tourist areas?
23 What are the main reasons why hotels are located in:
(a) Montego Bay?
(b) Negril?
(c) Kingston?
(d) Port Royal?
24 Why are there so few hotels in:
(a) The central part of the island?
(b The south-west coast?

Figures 14.6 and 14.7 show Ocho Rios. The first was taken in 1959, before the town was developed as a tourist centre; the second was taken in 1987.

25 What natural features encouraged the development of tourism in Ocho Rios?
26 What changes were made to the landscape over this 16-year period? List the changes under these headings:
(a) Coastline.
(b) Roads.
(c) Buildings.
(d) Vegetation.

Figure 14.8 shows the seasonal pattern of tourism in Jamaica.

27 Which 3-month period is most popular with tourists?
28 Give three reasons why tourists come at this time of year.

14.6 Air view – Ocho Rios in 1959.

14.7 Air view – Ocho Rios in 1987

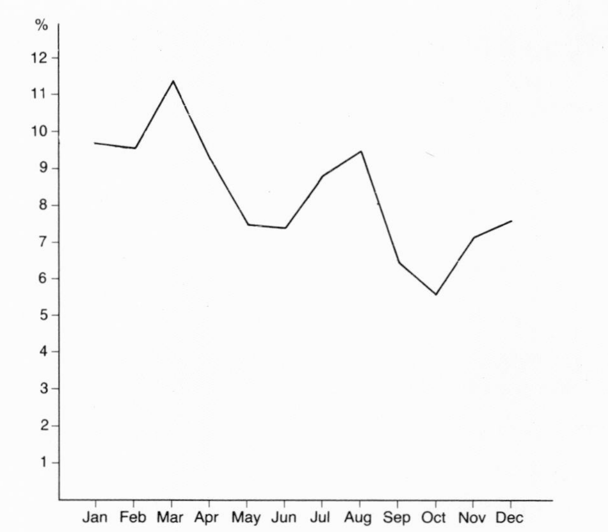

14.8 Tourist arrivals in Jamaica.

29 Why do more tourists come to Jamaica in August than in the other wet-season months?

30 There are very few tourists at some times of year. What problems does this cause for:
(a) Hotel management?
(b) Hotel staff?
(c) Airline companies?

The image of the Caribbean

Figure 14.9 is taken from a travel brochure advertising holidays in Haiti.

31 Does this picture give an accurate impression of conditions in Haiti?

32 What aspects of life in the Caribbean are usually shown in travel-industry publicity material?

33 What aspects of life in the Caribbean are not usually shown in travel brochures?

34 The Jamaica Tourist Board has used the slogan 'We're more than a beach, we're a country'. What do you think was the purpose of this slogan?

14.9 A luxury hotel in Haiti.

Providenciales

The Turks and Caicos Islands are a British Crown Colony, with a population of 8,000 and an area of 430 km^2.

There is virtually no commercial agriculture, and no large-scale manufacturing. The main traditional industries are fishing and salt-making; but tourism may provide the best long-term prospect for economic development. The islands have a dry climate, a beautiful coastline, and are surrounded by clear, unpolluted water.

There are 1,200 hotel beds on the islands, and about 500 people out of a total workforce of 4,000 are employed in hotels.

14.10 The Club Méditerranée development on Providenciales.

In the 1970s the British government began to negotiate with a big French tourist company, Club Méditerranée, about opening up a really large-scale tourist development in the islands. The company insisted that:

- The development should be on Providenciales Island.
- There should be a full-scale international airport there, even though there was already an international airport on Grand Turk.

After a long period of talks, a long-runway airport and several roads were built for the new development at a cost of $6 million US. A 300-room hotel complex has now been opened.

The hotel operates as an 'enclave industry'. Most of the food and other inputs used are imported. Most of the tourists spend very little money outside the hotel. The hotel operates on US Eastern Standard Time, one hour behind the rest of the Turks and Caicos. There are 175 staff. About half are local employees; but the senior management positions are filled by expatriates, and many of the manual workers are from Haiti.

As a result of this development, the number of tourists visiting the Turks and Caicos has increased dramatically. There are now 30,000 tourist arrivals every year, of whom almost half stay in the 'Club Méd' development.

35 Look at Figure 14.10. Has the hotel development affected the surrounding area?
36 How does a large-scale scheme of this sort benefit:
   (a) Unemployed people in the Turks and Caicos Islands?
   (b) International hotel operators?
   (c) Airline companies?
   (d) Building contractors?

Cruise ships

The Caribbean is one of the world's leading destinations for cruise ship passengers. In 1985, approximately 2 million tourists visited the Caribbean on cruise ships. Most of these passengers were from the USA, and most of the cruise ships are based in Miami. Figure 14.11 is a page taken from a cruise brochure.

37 Make a sketch map to show the route of the cruise.
38 List the main attractions on each island visited.
39 List three ways in which cruise ship passengers might use their time when a cruise ship is in port.
40 For the tourist, what are the *advantages* and *disadvantages* of this type of holiday?
41 How do cruise ships contribute to the economy of the islands they visit?
42 For the Caribbean islands, are there any *disadvantages* with this sort of tourism?
43 Look at Figure 14.1c:
   (a) Make a bar graph to show the number of cruise ship passengers visiting the main tourist islands.
   (b) Which islands have more cruise ship passengers than long-stay tourists?
   (c) Which islands are easiest to reach for a ship making a short cruise from Miami?

Tourism and development

Tourism plays a useful role in economic development; but many people also feel that the industry is something of a mixed blessing.

There are many different views:

- 'Tourism brings in foreign exchange: US dollars, pounds, and deutschmarks which help pay for the region's imports.'
- 'Much of this foreign exchange goes straight back to Europe and North America. Many tourists fly in on a foreign airline, and stay in a hotel which is owned by an overseas company; it has been estimated that 58 cents in every dollar spent by the average tourist is used immediately to pay for goods and services which the tourist industry buys from abroad.'
- 'The tourist industry provides a market for other local industries, such as agriculture and crafts.'
- 'Tourists often prefer to eat food which cannot be grown in the Caribbean. Souvenirs are often made in countries like Hong Kong and Taiwan.'
- 'Tourism helps to pay for infrastructural development which can be used by other sectors of the economy.'
- 'The infrastructure which is built is often expensive, and may not be suited to local needs.'
- 'Tourism may help to open up attractions which local people can enjoy. Harrison's Cave in Barbados, for example, was inaccessible until it was developed as a tourist attraction.'
- Tourism can make natural features less accessible for local people. Some of the best beaches in

The Grenadines & Orinoco River Cruise

OCEAN CRUISE LINES

from BARBADOS

For those in search of something a little out of the ordinary, KUONI is delighted to offer this unusual cruising holiday.
Because the yacht-like Ocean Princess is able to enter harbours often inaccessible to large ships, your journey will take you to the small untouched islands of the South Caribbean as well as the wilds of Venezuela's Orinoco River. At only 12,000 tons and refurbished in 1984, the fully stabilised Ocean Princess is the flag ship of Ocean Cruise Lines. She can carry up to 460 passengers and facilities on board include a swimming pool, health club, beauty salon, deck sports, piano bar, disco, boutique, two lounges with evening entertainment, cinema and small casino with a wide variety of watersports available from the ship. Superb cuisine, entertainment nightly and personalised service in the finest European tradition ensure that your stay aboard will be the experience of a lifetime. Combine it with a stay on Barbados and you have a Caribbean holiday that's irresistible.

Palm Island

The Ocean Princess off Palm Island

Ocean Princess

Cruise: 7 nights
Barbados: Optional extensions.

Day 1 Sun London/Barbados
Afternoon departure by British Airways scheduled service to Barbados arriving in the late afternoon. Transfer to the Ocean Princess in time for your sailing at 10 p.m.

Day 2 Mon Palm Island/Grenada
Wake up in Paradise as you anchor off idyllic Palm Island this morning. Enjoy a beach party at Palm Island with steel band, barbecue and rum punch. Time for a swim before sailing to Grenada, arriving in its delightful capital St. George's mid afternoon. Optional shore excursions show you this beautiful 'Spice Island'.

Day 3 Tue At Sea/Orinoco River
A relaxing day at sea to enjoy the ship's fine facilities. Around noon pass through the narrow channel that leads to the Orinoco and spend the rest of the afternoon admiring the passing scenery. Tonight is the Captain's Gala Cocktail Party and Dinner, where you will sample the sumptuous fare on board. Then it's showtime!

Day 4 Wed Cuidad Guayana/Orinoco
Early morning arrival at Cuidad Guayana, a modern boomtown located 180 miles up river. Weather permitting, take an excursion by air over Angel Falls to Canaima, a jungle camp located on a wine-red lagoon. We recommend you pre-book this excursion in the UK as space is limited. Another option is a tour of Cuidad Guayana including the city's exotic zoo. In the afternoon relax and enjoy the river and jungle scenes as you sail back to the Caribbean.

Day 5 Thu Tobago
Arrive in the afternoon and anchor off beautiful Pigeon Point. Tenders carry you in to its palm-fringed golden sand beaches for an afternoon of swimming and watersports, calypso music and rum punch. Join the optional glass bottom boat ride to Buccoo Reef or take an island tour.

Day 6 Fri The Grenadines/Mustique/ Bequia/St. Lucia
An enchanting morning as the Princess weaves through the picturesque Grenadines, past Mustique and Bequia. Later, the soaring Pitons of St. Lucia form a dramatic backdrop as you call at this beautiful island – a chance to visit La Soufrière volcano, as well as sample the local nightlife, as you don't sail until early morning.

Day 7 Sat Martinique
A full day on Martinique – a taste of France in the Caribbean with plenty of time to shop for perfumes, crystal and French fashions! Or take the optional excursion to see this unusual island past splendid beaches, tropical forests and on to St. Pierre, once buried by a volcano. Tonight there's the Captain's Farewell Banquet.

Day 8 Sun Barbados/London
Disembark after breakfast and transfer to the Discovery Bay Hotel where changing facilities will be available for you to enjoy your last day in the Caribbean. Please note that meals and the private use of a room are not included. Transfer from the hotel in time for your evening departure by British Airways scheduled service arriving in London Heathrow early Monday morning.

Opinion: In just one week, this island and jungle adventure gives you two unique travel experiences for the price of one.

HOLIDAY PRICES PER PERSON IN £ ex London INCLUDING FLIGHTS AND CRUISE

			02 Nov-09 Dec 7 nights	10 Dec-31 Dec 7 nights	04 Jan 7 nights	11 Jan, 18 Jan 7 nights	25 Jan-05 Apr 7 nights	12 Apr, 19 Apr 7 nights
Grade	**Description of cabin**	**Deck**	£	£	£	£	£	£
H	Inside, lower and upper berth	Various	—	—	—	1045	1114	—
G	Inside, two beds	Capri	925	1260	1026	1168	1237	1026
F	Inside, two beds	Belvedere or Pacific	1034	1383	1149	1213	1298	1149
E	Inside, two beds	Promenade or Pacific	1084	1467	1210	1254	1357	1210
D	Outside, two beds	Belvedere or Pacific	—	—	—	1339	1455	—
C	Outside superior, two beds	Pacific or Promenade	1181	1601	1320	1387	1510	1320
B	Outside superior, two beds	Lido or Riviera	1249	1682	1398	1442	1561	1398
A	Outside deluxe, two beds, sofa	Promenade or Riviera	1403	1874	1573	1592	1728	1573

14.11 A Caribbean cruise.

Mustique are now private; others may become overcrowded or polluted.'

- 'Local people come into contact with other ways of life; they may make friends with visitors from other countries, and meet people with a different outlook.'
- 'Contact of this sort is not always a good thing. It may lead to the spread of prostitution, petty crime, or drug trafficking. Most people do not meet tourists on equal terms; only when they are being paid to provide a service.'
- 'An area where there has been little economic development can often make money quite quickly from tourism.'
- 'The tourist industry can disappear as quickly as it arrives. Fashions change fast; and a few unfavourable news reports can lead to large-scale cancellations in a few days.'

44 Which of these statements sounds reasonable? Can you find any *evidence* to support them, from your own experience or from books and newspapers?

14.3 Tourism in Switzerland

The Swiss economy

Switzerland is a small country by European standards. It has a population of 6.4 million, and an area about 3½ times the size of Jamaica.

There are few mineral resources, and no oil or natural gas. Most parts of the country are too mountainous for arable farming. But in spite of this, Switzerland is one of the richest countries in the world, with a standard of living slightly higher than that of the USA. This is because:

- The limited resources for primary industry are well used. Agriculture, particularly dairying, is well developed; although there are some food imports, other products, like cheese, are exported. For energy, there is considerable use of hydro-electric power.
- Secondary industry concentrates on high-value products like surveying cameras, textile machinery, grain-milling equipment, pharmaceuticals, generators and diesel engines. Swiss engineering and management skills have made companies like Geigy, Bayer, Nestlé, and Brown–Boveri successful around the world.
- Switzerland is a world centre for tertiary industries like banking and insurance. Zurich is an international financial centre; certain types of people from many parts of the world find it useful to have a numbered Swiss bank account. Individuals and financial institutions in Switzerland have investments abroad equivalent to 2½ times the Gross National Product; the income from these investments is enough to pay for 12½% of the import bill.

Tourism in the economy

Switzerland does not in any sense depend on tourism.

Foreign exchange from tourism is enough to pay for only 3% of total imports. Investments abroad bring in four times as much money as tourism; and exports of machinery and equipment bring in more than eleven times as much.

Tourism is not an *alternative* to developing other sectors of the economy for a country like Switzerland. In fact the tourist industry brings more benefits to the country if agriculture, manufacturing, and other service industries are developed, too; the tourist is more likely to eat local food, buy locally made products, and change travellers' cheques in a locally owned bank.

One reason why tourism is important for the Swiss economy is that it helps to bring employment to remote mountain areas which do not have resources for large-scale agriculture and are not well located for manufacturing or other services.

Why tourists go to Switzerland

1 What can you learn from figures 14.12a–c about:
   (a) The natural resources used by the Swiss tourist industry?
   (b) The difference between tourism in the Caribbean and tourism in Switzerland?

14.12 Tourist attractions in Switzerland. (a) mountaineering (b) Ski-ing. (c) an historic city – Zurich.

14.13 Nineteenth century tourists in Switzerland.

The early tourist industry

Switzerland has a well established tourist industry. Tourists from other European countries have been visiting Switzerland for over two hundred years. Resorts like St Moritz were already well known a century ago. Skiing was introduced to Switzerland at this time by English visitors who had learnt the sport in Norway.

2 Figure 14.13 is a drawing from a travel book written in the nineteenth century. Are any of the attitudes shown in the picture relevant to tourism in the Caribbean today?

Where the tourists come from

3 List the seven single countries from which most tourists travelled to Switzerland.
4 Make a sketch map from an atlas to show the position of Switzerland in relation to other European countries.
5 Why do such a high proportion of the visitors come from West Germany?
6 Compare the countries of origin for tourists visiting Switzerland and Barbados:
(a) What are the main differences?
(b) What are the reasons for these differences?
7 The Rockies, the Andes, and the New Zealand Alps all have dramatic mountain scenery, lakes, forests, and winter snow. Why were the Swiss Alps developed for tourism earlier and more intensively than these other areas?

The main tourist centres

Scenically, Switzerland is a very varied country:

- The Alps are fold mountains which have been eroded by glaciers during the ice age. They are not densely populated, and only small areas on the valley floors can be cultivated.

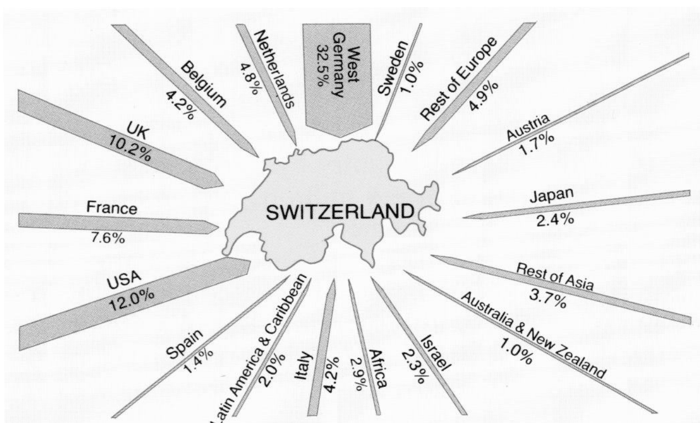

14.14 Where most of the tourists who visit Switzerland come from.

- The Swiss plateau contains all the large cities, and most of the rural population. It was also affected by glacial erosion and deposition. There are many large lakes.
- The Jura in the north-west are also fold mountains; but they are not nearly as high as the Alps. They consist mainly of limestone.

8 Figure 14.15 shows the main tourist centres of Switzerland:
(a) Name the five centres which each have more than 1 million visitor-nights per year.
(b) Which region contains most of the very large tourist centres?
(c) Which region contains a large number of smaller tourist centres?
(d) Which region would be most likely to attract:
– Business visitors?
– Winter sports enthusiasts?
– People who like mountain scenery?

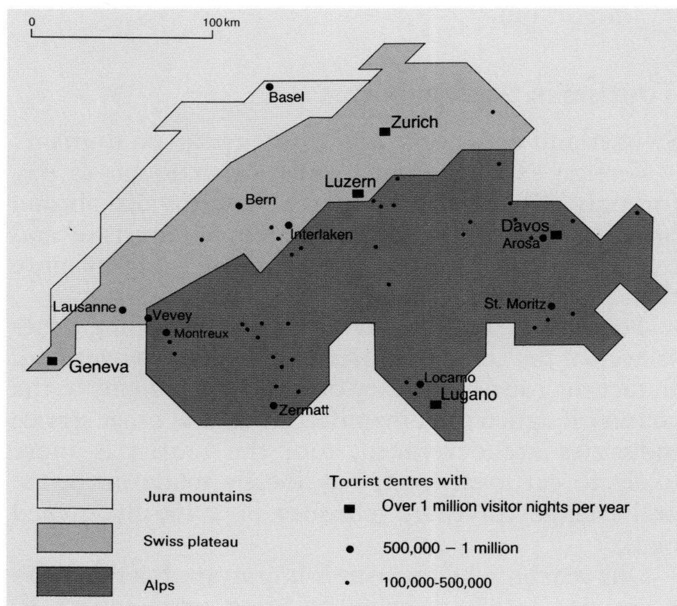

14.15 Switzerland: the main tourist centres.

15 · Population and settlement

15.1 Population distribution

Population density

Look at Figure 15.1. Area 'A' has a smaller population than area 'B'; but it is more crowded. It has a higher *population density*; there are more people for every square kilometre of land.

1 Work out the population density of area 'C'.

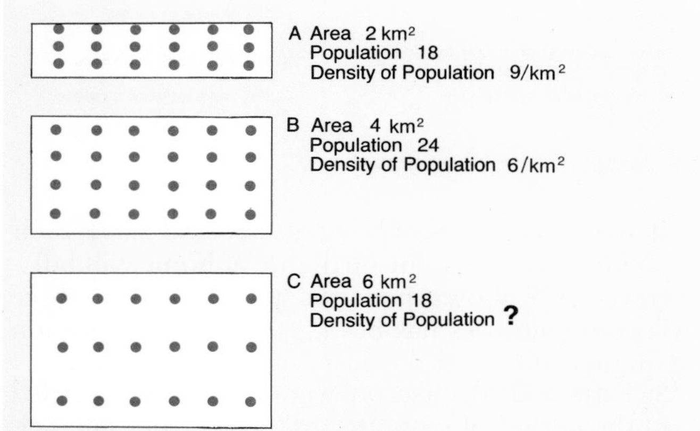

15.1 Population density.

World population patterns

The population of the world is very unevenly distributed. There are some small areas which are very crowded, and some large areas with a very low population density.

2 Look at Figure 15.2 and compare it with Figure 7.12 in Section 7.6:
   (a) Make a sketch map to show three areas with a very high population density, and four areas with a very low population density.
   (b) What do you notice about the population density of areas with:
   – Tundra climate?
   – Cold temperate interior climate?
   – Desert climate?
   (c) What are the reasons for this pattern?

International comparisons

Refer back to figure 1.4, which shows the average population density of some Caribbean countries. Figure 15.3a gives the population density of some countries outside the Caribbean.

3 Sort the countries into four groups:
   (a) Very low population density (under 10 per km^2).
   (b) Low population density (10–99 per km^2).
   (c) High population density (100–249 per km^2).
   (d) Very high population density (over 250 per km^2).

4 Make a bar graph to show the population density of Guyana, Cuba, the Dominican Republic, Jamaica, Trinidad and Tobago, and Barbados.

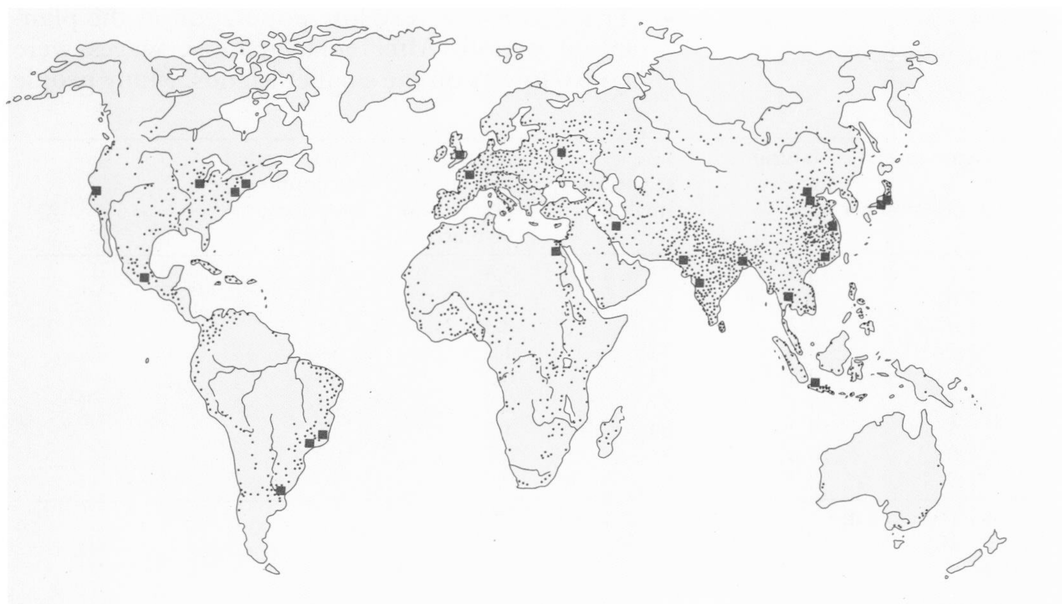

15.2 The world: population distribution.

5 Which of these statements is true:
   (a) All Caribbean countries have a high population density.
   (b) Some Caribbean countries have a very high population density.
   (c) Islands have a higher population density than Caribbean mainland countries.
   (d) Large islands have a lower population density than small islands.

6 Can you think of any reasons why:
   (a) Guyana has a lower population density than Trinidad and Tobago?
   (b) Dominica has a lower population density than Barbados?

Population growth

Study Figure 15.4. Population growth is affected by:

- Births and deaths.
- Immigration and emigration.

In small countries, migration is very important because:

- Unemployment is very high if a major industry runs into trouble.
- A large proportion of the population may emigrate if there are good opportunities elsewhere.

	Population 1984 (000)	Area (km^2)	Density of population (persons per km^2)
China	1,052,000	9,597,000	110
USSR	275,000	22,402,000	12
USA	237,000	9,373,000	25
Brazil	133,000	8,512,000	16
Japan	120,000	378,000	318
Switzerland	6,440	41,300	156

Source: UN Demographic Yearbook, 1984.

15.3a Population statistics for selected non-Caribbean countries.

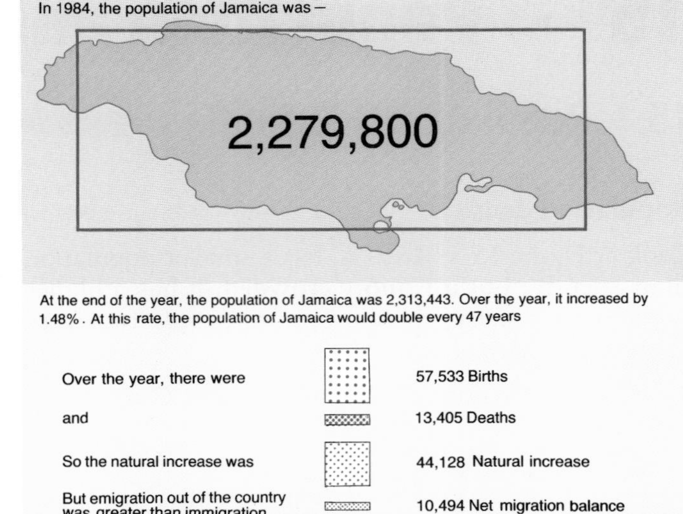

15.4 Jamaica: population growth.

- If many young people emigrate, and have their children overseas, the birth rate at home will fall.

Figure 15.5 shows how the population of three Caribbean countries has been affected by emigration and immigration over the past two hundred years:

- St Kitts and Montserrat were very closely settled in the period of plantation slavery. After emancipation, there was very little spare land, and wages were very low. Many people emigrated, first to Trinidad and Guyana, then to Panama and Bermuda, then to Britain and the USA. Many emigrants eventually returned, but others had families overseas and settled there permanently. Both islands now have about the same population as at the end of the eighteenth century.
- Trinidad had a very low population in the plantation period. After emancipation, wages were not so low as on the smaller islands. Many people

	Birth rate	Death rate*	Natural increase	Life expectancy (males)	Average annual population increase (%)	Time needed to double population (years)
	(per 1,000 population per year)					
Nigeria	50.4	17.1	33.3	**	3.4	21
Venezuela	35.2	5.6	29.6	65	2.9	24
Brazil	30.6	8.4	22.2	58	2.3	31
USA	15.7	8.7	7.0	71	1.3	54
Switzerland	11.5	9.1	2.5	73	0.2	347
Dominican Republic	33.1	8.0	25.1	57	2.9	24
Trinidad and Tobago	25.7	6.5	19.2	64	1.2	58
Cuba	16.6	6.0	10.6	71	0.7	100
Barbados	16.7	7.8	8.9	67	0.3	250

* Countries with many young people may have a low death rate even if health standards are poor.
** No recent figures available.
Source: UN Demographic Yearbook, 1984.

15.3b Population growth: some key statistics.

migrated there from elsewhere in the Caribbean, and indentured labourers were brought in from India and China to work on the plantations. In the 1950s and 1960s, when many people from other islands were migrating to the UK, emigration from Trinidad was much lower, although some people did go overseas. The population of Trinidad is now more than 350 times as high as it was in the late eighteenth century.

7 Look at Figure 15.3b. Explain why the rate of *natural increase* is not the same as the average annual population increase.
8 Which of the countries in the table has:
(a) The highest birth rate?
(b) The highest death rate?
(c) The longest life expectancy?
(d) The lowest rate of population increase?
9 What happens to the rate of population growth when:
(a) The birth rate rises?
(b) The death rate falls?
(c) Emigration increases?

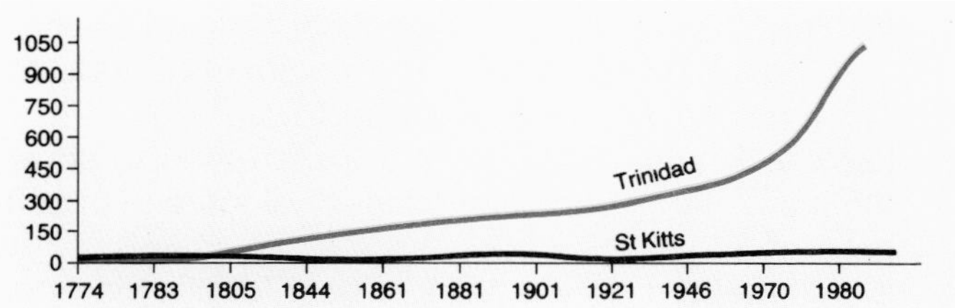

15.5 Population growth in Trinidad and St Kitts.

15.2 The population map

Guyana

The average population density of Guyana is four persons per km^2. But this figure does not give a very good picture of what conditions in the country are really like. As in any country, there are big variations in population density:

- There are many large areas in the interior which are completely uninhabited.
- On the coastal plain, there are many areas where the density of population is very high indeed.

Figures 15.6a–c show the distribution of population of the area between the Berbice and Corentyne rivers in eastern Guyana. Three different methods have been used to show population density:

- Figure 15.6a is a *choropleth* map. The population density of each administrative area has been calculated. Each administrative area has been shaded in, to show its average population density.
- Figure 15.6b is a *dot* map. Each dot represents 250 people. The dots have been placed carefully, to show where people actually live.
- Figure 15.6c is an *isopleth* map. Lines have been drawn to join the places where population density is the same, in the same way that contour lines join places which are the same height above sea level. The areas between these lines have been shaded in to show the population density. An isopleth map looks rather like a relief map with layer colouring.

1 Look at Figure 15.6a:
(a) What is the population density of New Amsterdam?
(b) How many communities had a population density greater than 100 per km^2?
(c) How many community areas were uninhabited?
2 Look at Figure 15.6b
(a) How many people live along the Berbice river, to the south of New Amsterdam?

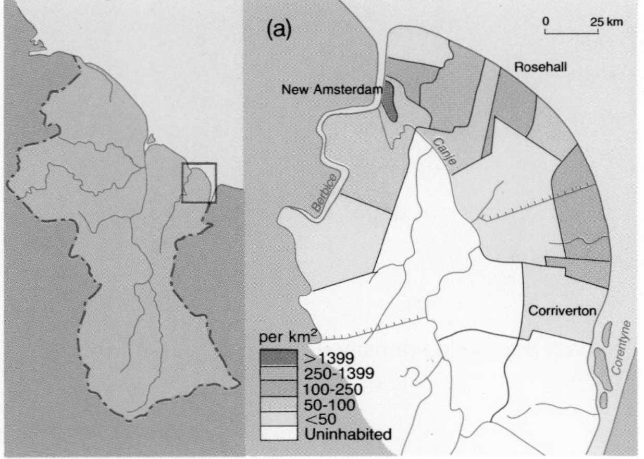

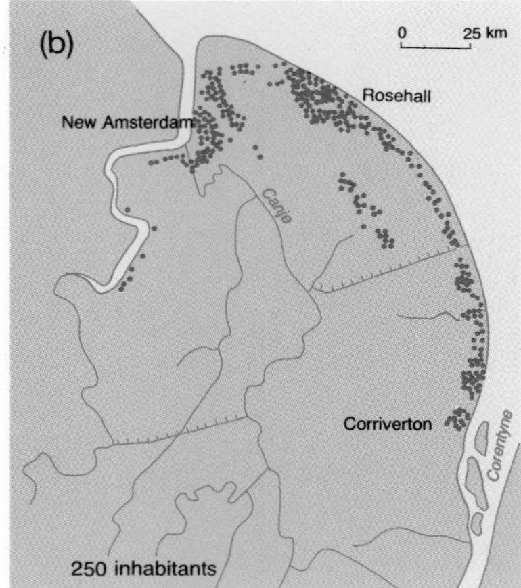

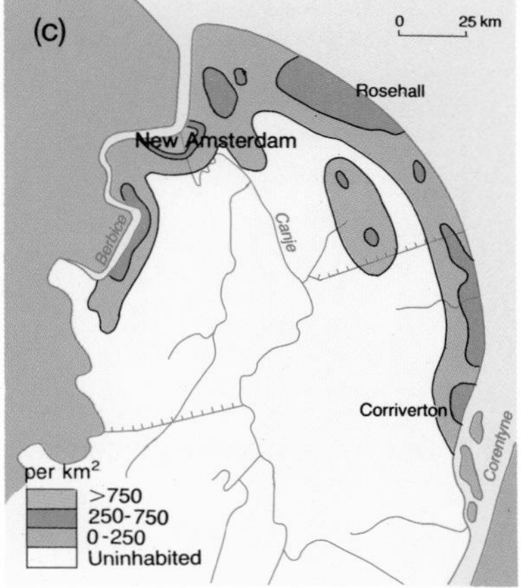

15.6 Eastern Guyana: population density.

(b) Find the administrative area containing Rosehall (15.6a). Which part of the community area do most people live in? Use map 15.6b.

3 Look at Figure 15.6c. Make a sketch map to show the areas with a population density of more than 500 per km^2.

4 Which method do you think is best for showing the distribution of the population within this part of Guyana?

5 Write a few sentences to describe the distribution of population in this part of Guyana.

6 Why do so few people live in the interior of Guyana?

Dominica

Figure 15.7 shows relief and population distribution in Dominica:

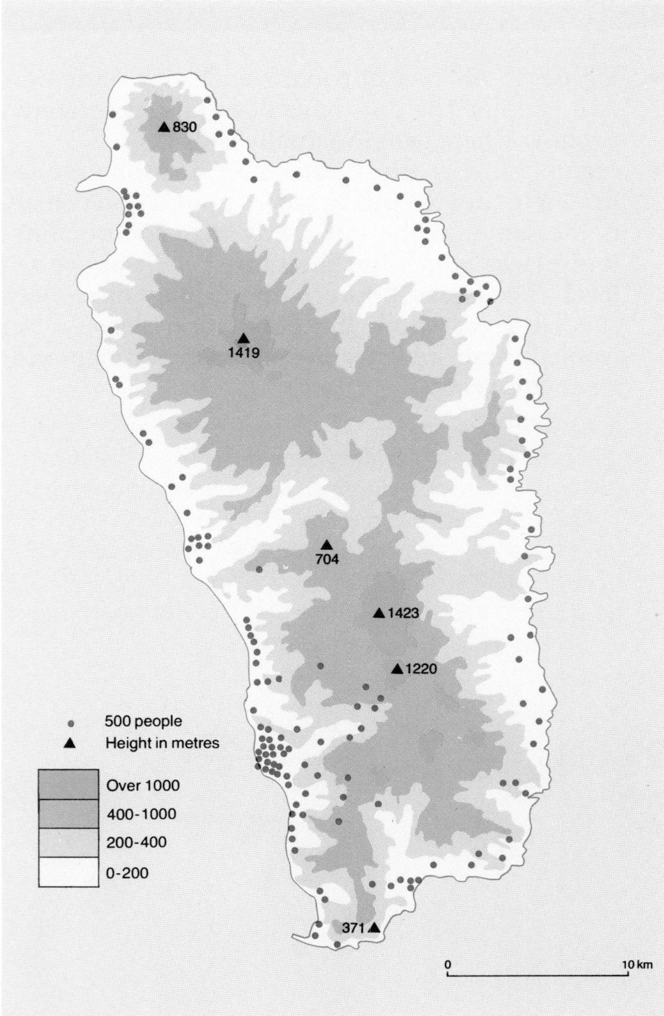

15.7 Dominica: population density.

- There are large uninhabited areas in the central part of the island.
- Most of the population lives near the coast.
- The density of population is quite high near to the capital, Roseau.
- There are some agricultural areas away from the coast with a moderate density of population.

7 What type of map is this?

8 Why is much of the interior of the island uninhabited?

9 Why is the density of population higher:

(a) Near the coast?

(b) Near Roseau?

10 Do any other islands have a similar pattern of population distribution?

Trinidad

Trinidad is a much larger island than Dominica, and the pattern of population distribution is less easy to understand at first glance. But it can be related to the resources, history, and agricultural and industrial development of the country.

Figure 15.8 shows the distribution of the population of Trinidad. Refer back to Figures 12.23 and 13.26 and to an atlas map of Trinidad.

11 What type of map is Figure 15.8?

12 Name two areas where population density is low.

13 Explain why population density is low in these areas.

14 Name two areas where population density is very high.

15 Explain why population density is high in these areas.

16 Name one part of Trinidad where population density is moderately high.

17 Explain why population density is high in this area.

18 What are the *disadvantages* of this type of map?

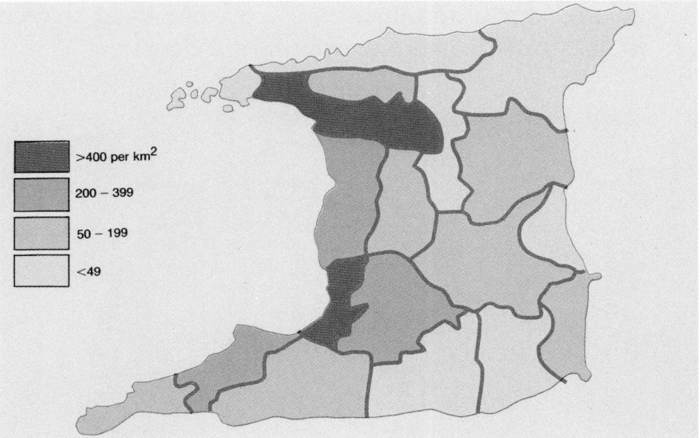

15.8 Trinidad: population density.

About half of the world's population lives in *rural* settlements. These are small settlements which provide few services for the people who live in them. People in rural settlements usually have to travel to a town or city if they need to use a supermarket or a hospital or a bank. In most rural settlements, many people work in agriculture.

There are many different types of rural settlement. There are:

- Nucleated settlements, where many houses are clustered together.
- Dispersed settlements, where the houses are scattered over a wide area.
- Linear settlements, where the houses are strung out along a road or a river.

Rural settlement in Dominica

On the west coast of Dominica, most of the land was once owned by plantations; but there was a strip along the shoreline three chains (60 m) wide, which was retained by the Crown.

After emancipation, anyone who was able to do so left the estates, and built a house on the Crown land. These free villagers earned their living by farming small patches of unoccupied land in the hills, which were not used by the estates, or from fishing. Today, many of these villages extend much more than 60 m inland. But they are still tightly *nucleated* settlements. All the houses are packed closely together.

Along the east coast, there were fewer plantations. In some places, there were stretches of good agricultural land which could be occupied by peasant farmers. There was no need for the houses to cluster together on the Crown land. There was room for a good-sized piece of cultivated land around each house. In many places the houses are not clustered together at all, and there is a completely *dispersed* settlement pattern.

There are some places which have been settled more recently. In some of these, the houses are strung out along a road, giving a *linear* settlement pattern.

1 Which settlement pattern is best for:
   (a) Reducing the amount of time farmers spend travelling to their fields?
   (b) Providing all households with road access?
   (c) Providing schools, shops, and other services for the rural population?

Coastal settlement in Guyana

Figure 12.25 is a large-scale map of part of the area covered by Figure 15.6. There is a nucleated settlement near to the sugar factory at Port Mourant, but along the coast to the east of the factory there is a long linear settlement along the main road. There are many settlements like this on the coastal plain and along the rivers in Guyana.

The linear settlement pattern evolved in the following way. After emancipation, many of the plantations in Guyana were bought by the former slaves. Plantation workers were desperately poor, by today's standards; but they grouped together and contributed small amounts from their earnings until enough money had been accumulated to buy the land.

When the estates were subdivided, everyone had a share of the best-drained and most accessible land, nearest the coast. The new holdings were long, narrow

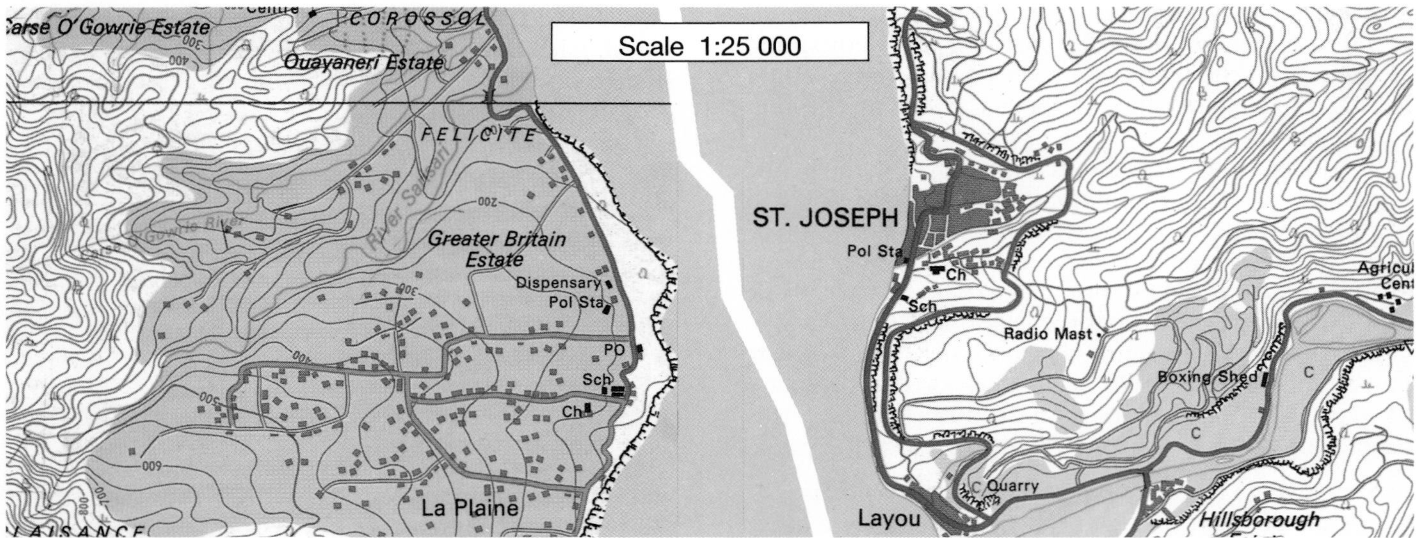

15.9 Dispersed settlement on the east coast of Dominica.

15.10 Nucleated settlement on the west coast of Dominica.

strips, running inland from the main road. When the original purchaser died, the land was often subdivided again, so that each of the heirs could have a portion. Eventually, some holdings were as little as 12 m wide, and ran inland for almost 3 km.

The land nearest the road was usually well used. There would be a house here, and ground provisions, fruit, bananas, and coconuts would be grown, mainly for family use. There would usually be some poultry, and a few sheep and goats. Further back, some families would grow rice or coconuts, or another crop for sale. But some of the households would not use the land for farming; many people earned a cash income from a non-agricultural job, or by spending periods of a few months in the gold fields of the interior.

2 Why would this pattern of settlement and land use make it difficult to:
   (a) Maintain drainage canals?
   (b) Make good use of land away from the coast?
3 Are there any advantages to this pattern of settlement?
4 Why is there a nucleated settlement near to the sugar factory on the land which is still used as a large sugar plantation?
5 Write a few sentences to describe the settlement pattern in Figure 3.16. Why are all the settlements located on or close to the coast?
6 Describe the settlement pattern in Figure 6.14.

15.4 A small capital: Kingstown, St Vincent

Urban settlements

A rapidly increasing proportion of the world's population lives in towns and cities. These are large settlements which provide services for the surrounding area. Very few people in towns and cities work in agriculture. In almost all Caribbean countries, the capital city is by far the most important urban settlement.

The origins of Kingstown

The first towns and cities in the Caribbean were built for European colonists and settlers. The major urban centres of today are almost all built on sites that were chosen in the sixteenth, seventeenth, and eighteenth centuries; to understand how these locations were picked out, we should try to imagine how the islands of the Caribbean looked to soldiers, merchants, and planters from the temperate countries who were establishing their ownership of their Caribbean colonies for the first time.

St Vincent was settled much later than some of the Caribbean islands. A mountainous and thickly forested island, it was declared 'neutral' by Britain and France in 1748; they agreed to leave it to the Caribs. However, there was some French settlement; then the English took possession of the island in 1763.

By the early nineteenth century, there was a white population of over 1,000; a 'free coloured' population of over 1,500; and more than 20,000 slaves. By this time, Kingstown was firmly established as the capital.

1 Look at the map of St Vincent in the early nineteenth century (Figure 15.11), and read the comments taken from two early descriptions of the island. Use your own words to explain why Kingstown was chosen as the capital rather than:
   (a) Georgetown, which was in the most productive sugar-growing area.
   (b) Owia, which has a natural harbour.
   (c) Calliaqua, which is well placed for reaching the east and west coasts.
   (d) Barrouallie, which was an important centre for the first French settlers in the eighteenth century.

The early settlement

Read this description of Kingstown in the early nineteenth century:

'The town consists of three streets, nearly a mile long, parallel to the sea, intersected by six others. There are about three hundred houses, the lower storeys are in general built with brick or stone, and the upper of wood, with shingle roofs; but there are a number of small wooden houses, which, however convenient they may be for the lower classes, give an air of poverty and inferiority to the whole. Three streams flow across the town, and add considerably to its cleanliness. The public buildings are substantial, but not elegant.'

2 Look at Figures 15.12, 15.13 and 15.14. What has changed about Kingstown in the past century and a half? What has remained the same?

The functions of Kingstown

Cities develop as centres of economic activity. People will often migrate to a city when they think that there are jobs available there; and will often move away when economic activity takes a downturn.

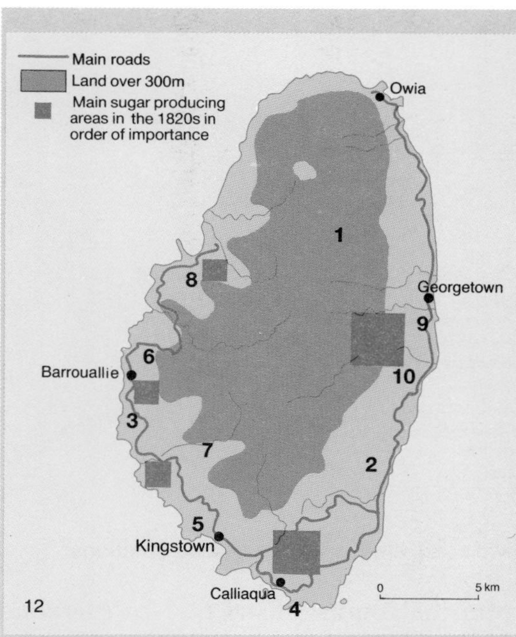

1 The internal parts are the most wild, broken, and inaccessible of any of the islands, some parts of Dominica excepted, consisting of an aggregate of deep ravines and chasms, perpendicular precipises, and conical-topped mountains, jumbled together in all the forms and appearances man can conceive.

2 The roads (here) are always dry and good, from the nature of the soil and the surface of the country.

3 On the Leeward coast, the (roads) are much inferior, the hills being higher. They are little frequented, the passage of the sea in canoes being more commodious.

4 Calliaqua
A very fine bay formed by a tongue of land and two islands which renders it a safer anchorage than Kingstown; (but) the entrance is narrow and dangerous.

5 Fort Charlotte
From the natural strength of this hill and the small extent of its summit, it was fixed on as a post to maintain the sovereignty of the island.

6 St Patrick
Here the land becomes much more . . . difficult of cultivation, and the fertitility decreases.

7 Buccament
The valley is the most beautiful and extensive on the island, well cultivated and containing eight sugar estates . . . At the bottom is a fine bay where ships . . . may anchor.

8 St David
The facilities for shipping produce, compared with the bold eastern coast, are great.

9 It is by far the most fertile and beautiful part of the island, and very healthy from having the regular sea breeze. The cane arrives to a greater perfection here than in most other parts of the island.

10 The properties encounter a serious embarrassment from want of bays and shipping places. From that defect they experience much risk and great danger in shipping their product.

15.11 St Vincent in the early nineteenth century.

15.12 Kingstown, St Vincent, in the early nineteenth century.

15.13 Kingstown today.

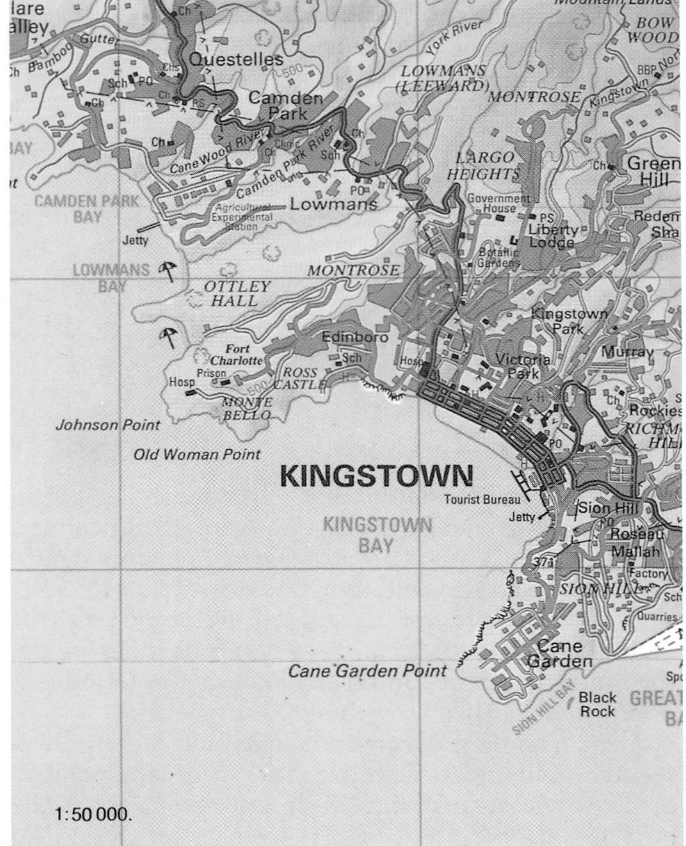

15.14 Kingstown.

The *functions* of a city are its main economic activities; they provide the main reason for its growth and development.

These are the main functions of Kingstown:

- Kingstown is a capital city. It provides government services for St Vincent and the Grenadines, and contains the headquarters of all the ministries as well as other public buildings.
- Kingstown is a centre for wholesaling and retailing. People travel from all over St Vincent to Kingstown to use the supermarkets, clothing stores, and other specialist shops; and small farmers travel to Kingstown to sell their produce.
- Kingstown is a centre for public services. The main hospital, more than half of the secondary schools, the Teachers Training College, and many other services are located in the capital.
- Kingstown is a port. It has the island's only deep-water harbour. Bananas and other agricultural produce are exported from Kingstown. The island's airport is at Arnos Vale, on the outskirts of the city.
- More recently, Kingstown has begun to develop as a manufacturing centre. There are a number of small factories in central Kingstown, and the island's main industrial estate is a few kilometres to the north.

3 Which functions do you think are important in explaining the growth and development of the city?

4 What do you think would appear to be the most important function of Kingstown to:
(a) A person from a rural area in St Vincent?
(b) A tourist visiting the island?

5 What major economic activities are *not* mainly located in Kingstown?

The growth of Kingstown

St Vincent and the Grenadines, like most Caribbean countries, is gradually developing from an agricultural economy into a more broadly based one with significant manufacturing and tourist sectors. In 1946, 53% of the workforce was in agriculture; by 1980, the figure had fallen to 29%. As a result of this process, the functions of the capital city have grown in importance, particularly over the past twenty years.

There is more government activity and more public-sector employment; there are more shops and private-sector services; there have been improvements to the port and airport; the Teachers College and Technical College have been established; there is a new hospital; and there have been new factories opened in Kingstown itself and in the surrounding area.

This means that there are more jobs available in the city than in most rural ares. For this reason, many people, particularly younger people, have moved to

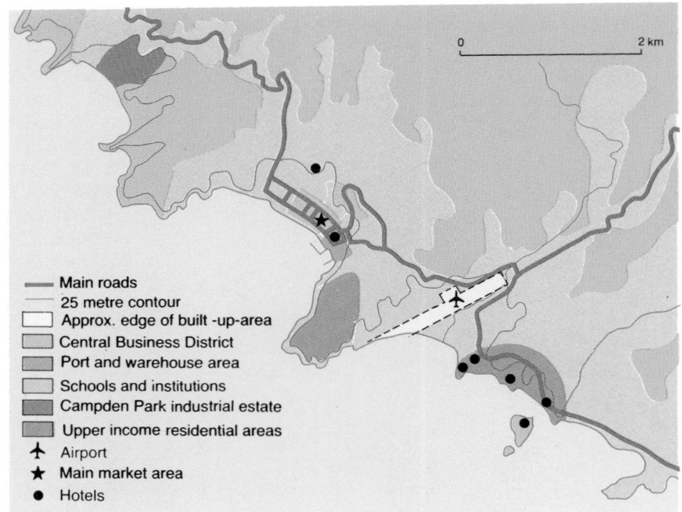

15.15 Kingstown: some areas with specialised functions.

Kingstown from the country districts. Not everyone will find a job, but the city is seen as offering a better chance of well-paid employment.

There are other reasons for moving to Kingstown, too. There is more entertainment, and more people to meet. Those who have young children may move to the city because health services are more accessible there, and educational provision may be of a higher standard.

Kingstown, like most Caribbean cities, has grown in population; but the population growth has not taken place in the older 'core' area of the city. Around the CBD, there is virtually no spare land for building. New housing is being built in suburban areas away from the city centre, and along the south coast of St Vincent in districts which most people would not consider to be part of Kingstown at all. It is quite easy to travel into Kingstown to work from a housing development 5 km or more from the city.

In the period 1970–80, the population of St Vincent and the Grenadines increased by 1.3% per year. But population growth varied from district to district. The total population:

- *Fell* by 0.3% per year in central Kingstown.
- *Increased* by 3.3% per year in the Kingstown suburbs, and by 2.2% in the district of Calliaqua on the south coast.

6 Look at Figure 15.14. Make a sketch map to show:
(a) The densely built-up area close to the CBD.
(b) The suburban areas, where there is more open space.

7 Is there a clearly defined boundary between the suburban areas and the open countryside?

8 How do the street plan and layout of the suburban areas contrast with the plan of the original historic core of Kingstown? What are the reasons for this contrast?

Contrasts within the city

In any city, the style of housing, the main land uses, the amount of traffic in the street, and the 'feel' of the urban landscape can alter completely over a very short distance. Sometimes the two sides of a street can be completely different in character.

Figure 15.15 shows how some of the functions of Kingstown are concentrated in particular areas.

One distinctive part of Kingstown, and of almost all cities, is the Central Business District (CBD). This is the oldest part of the town, where the original settlement was located; however, many of the original buildings have been pulled down and rebuilt so as to keep up with changing needs.

The CBD is the main focus of commercial activity. It contains the main banks and insurance companies, the large department stores and supermarkets, and a market area where fresh fruit and vegetables and other items are bought and sold.

Land values are very high in the CBD, so there is very little open space. The buildings are crowded very close together, and are usually several storeys high.

Many people come to this part of Kingstown to shop or do business, so the traffic in the streets is very heavy. This is the part of the city where traffic congestion is sometimes a problem, and where it is most difficult to find a parking place. The minibus routes all converge in the CBD; it is the focus for the island's road system. There are also many pedestrians, particularly in the main shopping periods.

The main public buildings are in the CBD. The Court House, where Parliament meets, faces the main square. The area where the public buildings are concentrated has a slightly different atmosphere, it is a little quieter, and the style of architecture is not the same. Public buildings are usually designed in rather a formal way; they are built to give a feeling of permanence and solidity.

Away from the CBD, there are other distinctive areas:

- There is a port area, with an area for warehousing next to it.
- There is an industrial estate to the north of the city.
- There is an area near the CBD which contains several schools and other institutions which have their own open space around them.
- There are residential areas; and here there is a contrast between high-income areas with luxury housing, mixed and middle-income areas, and some areas with low-quality housing which needs to be replaced.

9 Why are most large stores and other businesses concentrated in the CBD?

10 What type of shop would you be most likely to find in residential areas outside the CBD?

11 Explain the location of:
(a) The main tourist area.
(b) The airport.

Land reclamation

Kingstown is built on a restricted site. The small area of flat land in the city centre is surrounded by steep hillsides which are not really suitable for building large structures.

In 1968, the harbour was modernised. At the same time an area along the foreshore was reclaimed from the sea. Over the past twenty years, many schemes for making use of this area have been put forward.

In 1987, a scheme to use this area for a fish market, a jetty and quay, small shops, a bus terminal, and a car park was approved.

12 Explain why these uses are suitable for a waterfront site near the Central Business District.

13 Figure 15.16 shows the reclaimed area in 1985. What was the land being used for at that time?

Cities with specialised functions

Like most cities in the Caribbean, Kingstown has a wide variety of different functions. One or two urban settlements in some countries are more *specialised*. One function accounts for a high proportion of the town's economic activity, and is important in explaining patterns of growth. Oil has played an important part in the growth of San Fernando, Trinidad; Ocho Rios in Jamaica is to a certain extent a specialist centre for the tourist industry. There are also some smaller settlements, like Canaries and Anse La Raye in St Lucia, which specialise in fishing.

14 What are the main functions of these settlements:
(a) Belmopan, Belize?
(b) Bartica, Guyana?
(c) Linden, Guyana?

15.16 An area of reclaimed land. The Central Business District is on the right.

15.5 A large capital city: Kingston, Jamaica

The growth of Kingston

Kingston was founded in 1692, soon after the Port Royal earthquake. It rapidly became the main trading port for Jamaica, a busy city where sailing ships could dock. Kingston merchants grew rich by selling sugar, coffee, and other agricultural produce to the traders, and buying manufactured goods which they could sell on the island. The city was also a major centre for the slave trade.

A colonial trading centre needed:

- A sheltered harbour.
- Good roads to the rest of the island.
- A site with room for expansion and new development.
- Reasonably good building land, with a firm foundation for new construction.

1 Look at Figure 15.17. Explain why Kingston was a better trading centre than:
   (a) Spanish Town, the colonial capital.
   (b) Port Royal, the headquarters of the early buccaneers.
   (c) Delacree Pen, where the survivors of the Port Royal earthquake first set up camp after the disaster.

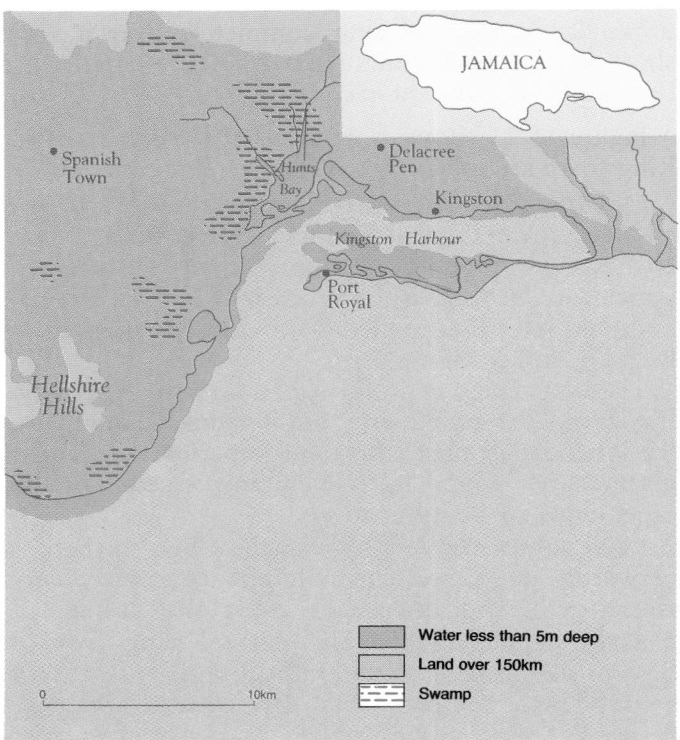

15.17 The site of Kingston in the late seventeenth century.

Kingston had a population of 5,000 in the year 1700. By 1774, there were over 11,000 inhabitants, and the city was four times the size of Spanish Town. In 1807, the population was probably 30,000.

The population of Kingston did not grow very fast during the nineteenth century. It remained a specialised trading city, at a time when the sugar industry and export agriculture were much less profitable than before.

After emancipation, many people became small peasant farmers. There was rapid population growth in many rural areas. In the city, living conditions were very poor for most people.

Read these descriptions of nineteenth-century Kingston:

'The houses are partially dilapidated and of course old. Though I have been through nearly every street, I have not seen a single house newly erected . . . On every block may be seen vacant lots, on which are crumbling the foundation walls of houses long in ruins.'

'One looks and listens in vain for the noise of carts and the bustle of city men; no one seems to be in a hurry; but few are doing anything, while the mass of the population are . . . in rags.'

Then the city began to grow more quickly again. In 1880, an observer wrote:

'There is a tendency among portions of the rural population to gravitate towards the towns, and Kingston especially. The class to which we refer are moved by a desire to obtain their livelihood by a means other than agricultural labour, and by the hope of that casual employment at high rates which is often to be obtained in the towns.'

Year	Population (000)		
	Kingston (parish)*	Kingston and St Andrew	Whole of Jamaica
1881	38.6	73.5	580.8
1921	63.7	118.3	858.1
1943	110.1	238.2	1,237.1
1960	123.4	419.4	1,609.8
1970	109.8	531.5	1,848.5
1982	104.0	586.9	2,190.4

* The parish of Kingston is now only a small part of the built-up area. Most of the built-up area is in the parish of St Andrew.

15.18 Kingston and St Andrew: population growth.

2 Look at Figure 15.18. Work out the population increase for Kingston and St Andrew in the period 1881–1943. What evidence is there for migration to Kingston at this time?

3 Why do you think that many people did not want to work in agriculture?

4 Were the migrants sure of finding regular work in Kingston?
5 Work out the proportion of the population of Jamaica living in Kingston and St Andrew in:
   (a) 1881.
   (b) 1921.
   (c) 1943.
   (d) 1960.
   (e) 1970.
   (f) 1982.
6 Draw a line graph to illustrate these figures.
7 Is the proportion of the Jamaican population living in Kingston and St Andrew still increasing?

The functions of Kingston

8 Look at Figure 15.19:
   (a) Which employment types are:
      – Concentrated mainly in Kingston and St Andrew?
      – Located mainly in other parishes?
      – Shared about equally between Kingston and St Andrew and other parts of Jamaica?
   (b) What are the main functions of Kingston and St Andrew today?
   (c) Kingston was a specialised city in the eighteenth century? Is this still true today? What new functions have developed since that period?
   (d) Write a few sentences explaining why the population of Kingston grew faster than the population of Jamaica in the period 1881–1970.

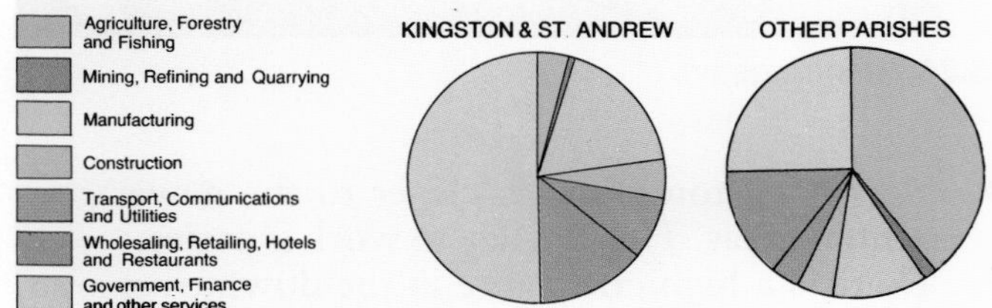

15.19 Employment in Kingston and St Andrew.

The Metropolitan Area

9 Look at Figure 15.20. Each of the small squares on the map represents an area of 2.25km^2. Calculate the approximate area of Kingston in:
   (a) 1750.
   (b) 1889.
   (c) 1920.
   (d) 1952.
   (e) 1980.
10 Why did the city not grow outwards very much in the period 1750–1889?

As the population of Kingston has increased, more and more land has been needed for construction, and the *built-up area* of the city has expanded outwards.

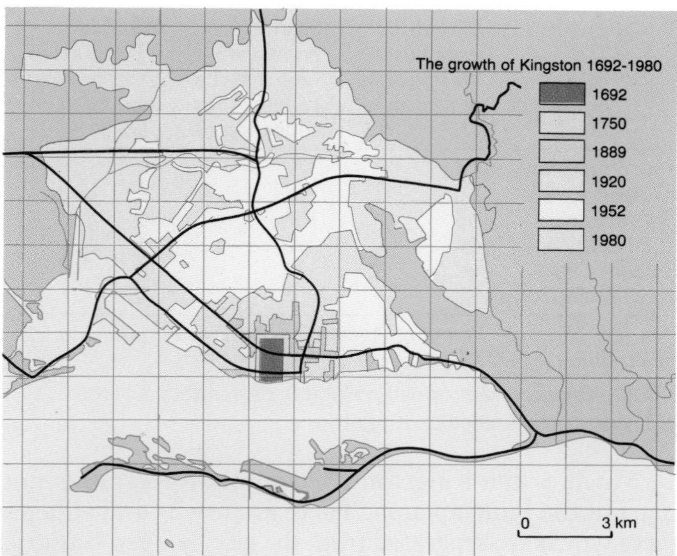

15.20 Kingston: The growth of the built-up area.

Figure 15.21 shows the boundary of:

- The parish of Kingston.
- The parish of St Andrew.
- The Kingston Metropolitan Area.
- The Kingston Metropolitan Region.

The parish of Kingston is now a very small part of the built-up area, and its population is now *falling* because land is needed for uses like industry and offices and there is less room for people to live in the area.

11 Look at Figure 15.18 again. Make a graph to show how the population of the parishes of Kingston and St Andrew changed between 1881 and 1985.
12 In which year was the highest population recorded for the parish of Kingston?

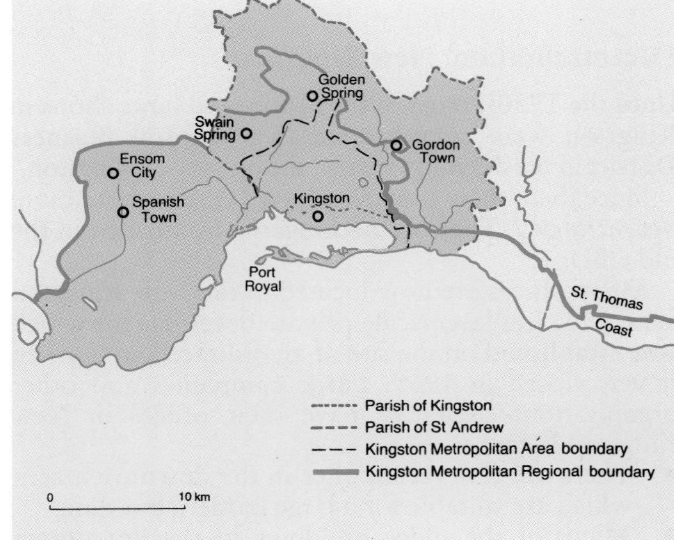

15.21 Kingston Metropolitan Region.

	Working population with jobs in Kingston (%)	School population who travel to Kingston for education (%)	Population who travel to Kingston for recreation (%)
Gordon Town	74	74	40
Golden Spring	60	62	26
Swain Spring	66	100	66
Spanish Town	14	12	4
Ensom City	64	36	35
St Thomas Coast	28	5	2

Source: National Planning Agency Urban Growth and Management Study: Final Report.

15.22 Kingston Metropolitan Region: dependence of the outlying communities on Kingston.

Much of the Kingston Metropolitan Region is not part of the built-up area. There are towns and villages here which are separated from the city by open country. But these settlements are included in the Metropolitan Region because people who live in them often work or shop or go to school in Kingston Metropolitan Area.

13 Look at Figures 15.21 and 15.22:
 (a) Which settlement is furthest from the centre of Kingston?
 (b) Which is the old established centre with its own history?
 (c) Which is most dependent on Kingston?
 (d) Which is least dependent on Kingston, and provides most services for its own inhabitants?

14 Which do you think is the most realistic definition of Kingston:
 (a) The parish?
 (b) The Metropolitan Area?
 (c) The Metropolitan Region?
 (d) The built-up area?
 Give reasons for your answer.

Decentralisation: New Kingston

Until the 1950s, most of the offices and large shops in Kingston were concentrated in a Central Business District in the downtown area, the old city of Kingston.

Since then, these functions have become more more *decentralised*. They are no longer concentrated in the old CBD.

Many offices are now located in the New Kingston area. This is a large-scale private development which was established on the site of an old racecourse when it was closed in 1959. Large companies and other organisations prefer to have their offices in New Kingston because:

- There are few vacant sites in the downtown area which are suitable for a large modern building.
- Many of the older buildings in the downtown area are cramped, and in a poor state of repair.

15.23 Downtown Kingston.

15.24 New Kingston.

- New Kingston is much closer to the newer residential areas. The journey to work is easier.
- There is a high crime rate in the downtown area. New Kingston is much safer for employees who work in the evenings.
- There is much less traffic congestion in New Kingston, because the streets are wider. It is also easier to park.

The New Kingston development has been a success. The largest hotels are located there. So are most of the banks and finance companies, and many embassies. Around the edge of New Kingston, many other sites are now being redeveloped for office use. The original owners of the land have made a large profit on their investment; land prices are now higher than those in downtown areas, and about five times as high as in other outlying office areas such as Halfway Tree or Constant Spring.

15 The grid reference of New Kingston on Figure 2.10 is 72 50. Make a sketch map to illustrate this sentence:

15.25 A shopping centre in suburban Kingston.

'New Kingston has a more central position in the built-up area than the downtown area, and is easily accessible by road.'

16 Compare Figures 15.23 and 15.24. List the ways in which the landscape of New Kingston contrasts with that of the old downtown area.

Decentralisation: shopping

There are still many shops in the downtown area of Kingston. The main market area is there, and there are also many well-established larger stores. But most of the newer stores and supermarkets are located in large shopping plazas away from the old CBD.

17 Compare Figures 15.23 and 15.27 with Figure 15.25. List the differences beween the suburban shopping centre, which is at grid reference 714 515, and the downtown area. What sort of people would find it convenient to use a suburban centre?

The port

Many other land uses have also been decentralised. The main port area used to be just south of the CBD. There were wooden 'finger piers', where ships could dock, and general cargo was loaded and unloaded. Along the waterfront, there were warehouses where goods could be stored.

The old finger piers are no longer suitable for modern shipping. There is now a modern port with container-handling facilities at Newport West, which has been built on reclaimed land. There are also specialised bulk-handling facilities at the oil refinery, the cement plant, and the flour mill.

20 Look at Figure 2.11. Make a sketch map to show the old port area.

21 Look at Figure 2.10. Make a sketch map of Newport West and Newport East. Show how the shoreline of the western part of Kingston Harbour has been modified by land reclamation. (The old shoreline is shown on Figure 15.19.)

Manufacturing industry

Look at Figure 15.26. There are manufacturing industries in many different parts of Kingston:

- In the downtown area, there are many small factories on restricted sites. Some of them have been established for a considerable time.
- Many modern factories are located in the Free Zone and in other industrial estates close to the port area.
- There are many factories in other parts of the city.

22 Look at Figure 15.26, and make a sketch map to show the parts of Kingston where most factories are located.

23 Look at Figure 2.10, and comment on the location of:
(a) The oil refinery (692 468).
(b) The cement plant (784 457).
(c) The flour mill (767 463).

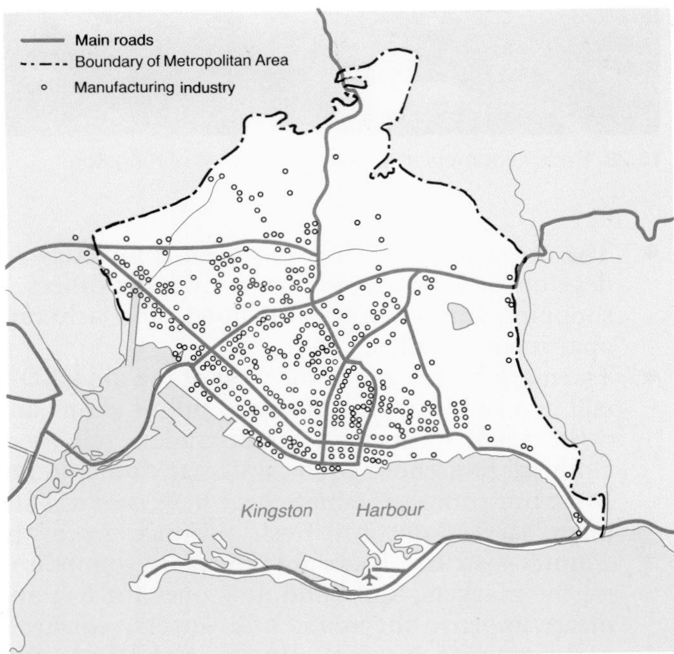

15.26 Kingston: the location of manufacturing industry.

The downtown area

Most people would not want the centre of Kingston to become too run-down.

In recent years there has been an attempt to revive the downtown area:

15.27 The market area in downtown Kingston.

15.28 Redevelopment in the waterfront area of Kingston.

- The old waterfront area has been completely redeveloped. It now contains many large offices, a shopping centre, a modern hotel, and a luxury apartment complex.
- The market area just to the west of the old CBD is still a very lively part of town, full of shops and other small businesses. Street traders sell food, clothing, household goods, and many other items. Most bus routes terminate near here, and it is the main sales point for fresh produce from the country districts. There are now plans to modernise the markets, and build new ones for fish and meat; improve the roads and sewers; construct parking areas for cars, trucks, and hand-carts; and improve the bus terminal.

24 Explain how these projects can between them:
  (a) Improve the appearance of the downtown area.
  (b) Create employment.
  (c) Improve living conditions for people in the area.
  (d) Encourage people from the rest of Kingston to use the downtown area.

Land use in Kingston: a mapwork exercise

25 Look at Figure 2.10. Each of these sentences fits one of the grid squares listed below. Match each sentence with one of the 4-figure grid references.
  (a) The original city of Kingston had an area of less than 100 ha. It was laid out on a rectangular grid plan, with blocks 97.5 m across. A large open square was used as a military parade-ground.
  (b) This suburban area was developed in sections, each of which has a planned layout; but there is no regular grid, and many of the roads are curved.
  (c) This is an upper-income suburban area built on a hilly site. Many of the roads follow the contours to make driving easier. The density of housing development is much lower.
  (d) The city has not expanded in this direction, because the land slopes too steeply. The built-up area stops suddenly at the foot of the mountain.
  (e) Many main roads meet here. This district is now near the middle of the built-up area. It has become an important office and commercial centre.
  (f) This area is too marshy for development.
  (g) This is part of an area where land has been reclaimed to make a deep-water harbour and provide sites for industrial development.

65 49, 74 50, 71 46, 75 48, 67 51, 67 48, 71 50.

Housing problems

Any city which has grown as rapidly as Kingston will usually have a shortage of good-quality housing. There is some very good-quality housing in Kingston, but there are also some very bad slums. The worst areas are *tenement yards*, where many cramped and badly built houses are squeezed onto a strip of privately owned land, and *squatter settlements*, where houses are hurriedly put up on unoccupied land without the permission of the landowner. People

15.29 A squatter settlement in western Kingston.

15.30 Upgraded housing in Kingston. The watercourse has been canalized to prevent flooding. Roads, electricity and water mains have been provided.

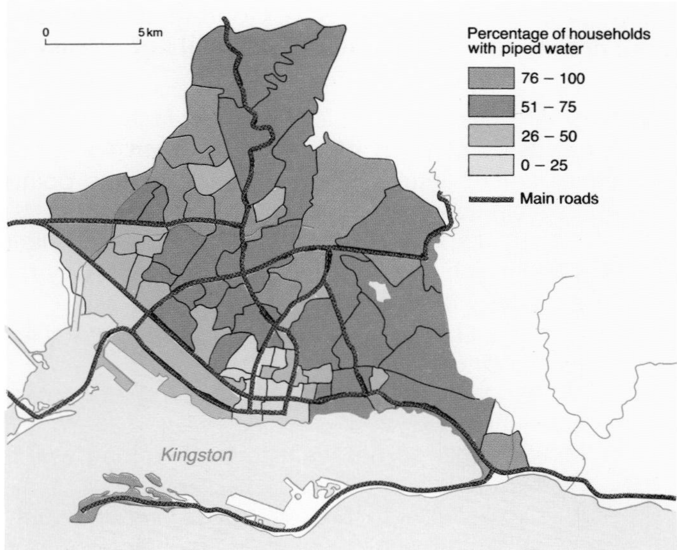

15.31 Kingston: housing quality.

who live in tenement yards or squatter settlements do not usually have electricity or a proper bathroom; and they can be asked to move at short notice, so it is not worth their while to make many improvements, even if they can afford to.

It has been estimated that 8,000 new houses will be needed in Kingston every year if all the unacceptable and overcrowded dwellings are to be replaced, and if the needs of a rising population are to be met.

There are many ways in which new housing can be provided:

- Private developers build houses for sale. Unfortunately, these houses are too expensive for most families to afford.
- Government has also built houses for sale. These are sold at a low price; but even if the design is kept simple, this is an expensive way to house people. It is not possible to build enough of these units.
- In some experimental schemes, a small *core unit* is built by a government agency. Families can borrow money on easy terms to pay for the core unit. Later on, it can be expanded, to make a three-bedroom house. It costs government much less to house a family in this way, so more people can benefit than with a more expensive scheme.
- Families who live in tenement yards and squatter settlements often want to improve their homes. They can do this once they have security of tenure, so that they cannot be asked to move; and once they have access to a proper water and electricity supply. In some areas, government agencies have bought land from private owners, put in roads, footpaths, water supply, and improved drainage, and then sold lots to the families who live there. When this happens, people often improve their houses very quickly.

26 List one *advantage* and one *disadvantage* of each of these ways of improving housing conditions.

27 Look at Figure 15.31:
(a) Explain why it is important for every household to have a piped water supply.
(b) Write a few sentences describing the location of the areas of Kingston where housing conditions are worst.

Urban expansion

Kingston has grown so much that land for development has become a real problem. There is still some vacant land in the Metropolitan Area, but not nearly

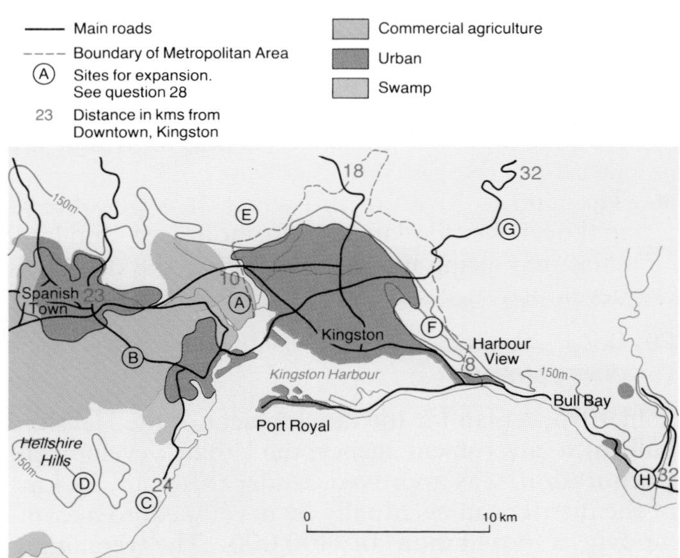

15.32 Kingston: some possible sites for expansion.

enough for future housing needs. Good-quality building land near to the Metropolitan Area will not be easy to find.

28 Look at Figure 15.32. List the *advantages* and *disadvantages* of each of the sites shown for urban development (letters A to H). These are the points you should consider:
- It is very expensive to build on steeply sloping land.
- Land which is *very* flat may flood after heavy rain, especially if there are large rivers nearby.
- It may not be sensible to use good agricultural land for building.
- Many people do not want to move too far from the area where they now live.
- Most people do not want to travel a long way to their workplace every day.
- It is expensive to provide roads, water supply, schools, and public services for completely new areas.
- Some areas near to Kingston would be very pleasant places to live if they were developed.

Look back to Figure 4.18. Large areas of land in the Yallahs River delta have been laid out with roads and services for housing development. But few houses have been built there as yet, because the distance to Kingston is too great.

The Hellshire Hills

The Hellshire Hills, to the south-west of Kingston, are in many ways very suitable for urban development:

- There is a large area of vacant land, almost 110 km^2.
- It is a dry area, with thin soil and no agricultural potential.
- The land is well drained.
- There are slopes, but they are not steep enough to make development difficult.
- There is plenty of open space for parks and recreation, and many beaches, some of which are safe for bathing.
- The land is government-owned. It is possible to make an overall plan for the whole area, and land sales may bring in extra revenue if the district is developed successfully.

29 Does this area have any disadvantages for urban development?

In 1975, a plan for the development of the Hellshire Hills by a government agency, the Urban Development Corporation, was approved. Under this plan, 32 km^2 of the district can eventually be developed, to accommodate a population of 400,000. The remaining 76 km^2 will be open space; it will be used for parks,

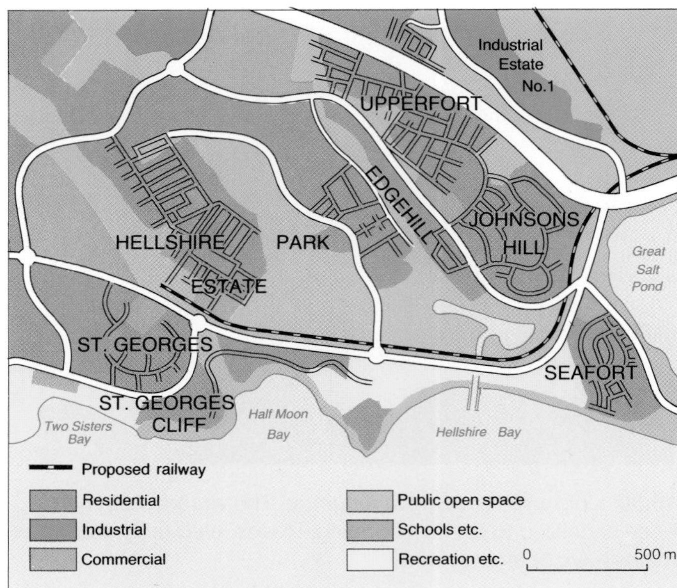

15.33 Part of the Hellshire Bay development.

forest reserves, and recreation. There will be three urban 'growth points'. Figure 15.33 is the plan for part of the first of these, Hellshire Bay. Phase 1 of the Hellshire Bay development will provide housing for 25,000 people.

Study the plan carefully. There are several housing neighbourhoods.

30 What provision has been made for:
(a) Transportation?
(b) Recreation?
(c) Education?

31 What employment opportunities will there be when the development has been completed?

32 Compare the layout of one of the housing neighbourhoods with an area which you know well.

At present, the Phase 1 development is still a long way from completion. About 40 km of roads have been completed, and services like water mains, electricity, and sewers have been installed. Over 400 housing units have been built, and many other lots have been sold for development. There is a beach park with a restaurant and bar, a few shops, a small factory, a 'basic school', a minibus service to Kingston, and a few other community services.

33 Hellshire Bay will eventually have a full range of services for people who live there. Which services are still not provided?

34 Why is it difficult to provide a full range of services for a small population?

35 For a family in Kingston, what would be the *advantages* and *disadvantages* of a move to Hellshire Bay?

15.6 Tokyo and New York: two world cities

Tokyo has a population of 11.6 million, and there are another 14 million in the urbanised industrial region around the city.

The city was founded in 1457, when a castle was built at a place called Edo, on the shore of what is now Tokyo Bay. This was an important location because it is:

- In the Kanto Plain, the largest area of agricultural land in Japan.
- On the southern side of the plain, on the main road to Kyoto, which was then the capital of Japan.
- At the mouth of the Arakawa river, which could be used as a waterway by small boats.
- On a bay which is sheltered from storms, and contained good fishing-grounds.

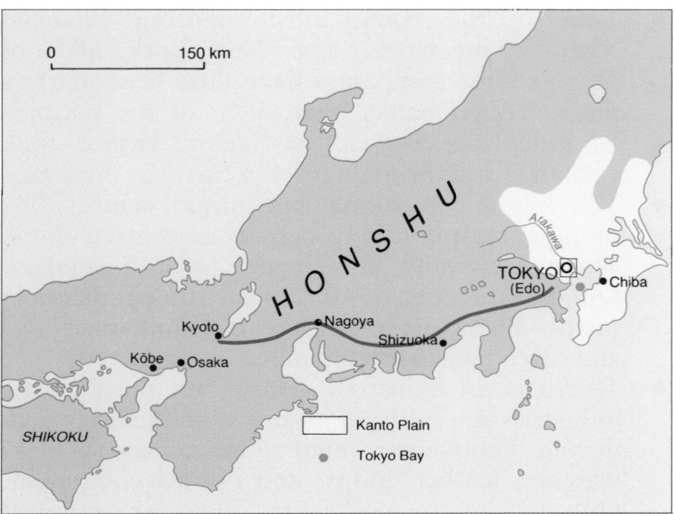

15.34 The location of Tokyo.

In 1603, the lord of the castle became the effective ruler of Japan, although the emperor still lived in Kyoto. The city grew very rapidly, and by the early eighteenth century it had more than a million people, making it the largest city in the world. Samurai, or feudal lords, came to Edo with their households because it was an important political centre; they spent money there, and this attracted a huge population of merchants and craftsmen. In1868, when Japan was just beginning to develop into a modern society, Edo became the capital and was renamed Tokyo.

Tokyo has been devastated twice this century; by a major earthquake in 1923, and by heavy bombing in the Second World War.

In spite of this, the city has grown rapidly. This is because Japan has developed from an agricultural to an urban economy, and many people have moved from the rural areas to the city to seek work.

The proportion of Japanese workers employed in agriculture was:

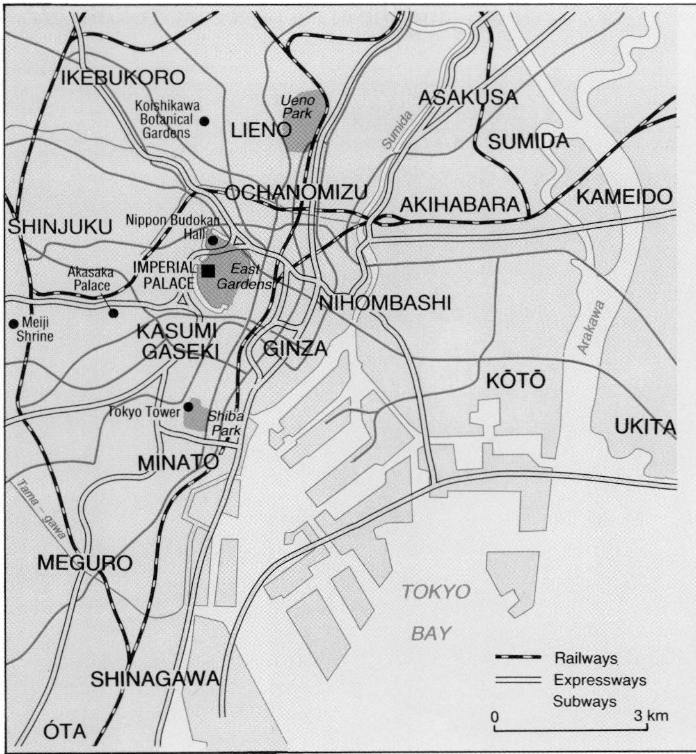

1 The Imperial Palace, which used to be Edo castle, is in the centre of the modern city.

2 Parliament and the main government offices are in Kasumigaseki, just outside the palace.

3 Ginza is the main shopping and entertainment district. It was laid out in the last century on a grid plan. Land in the Ginza can sell for \$200,000 per m^2.

4 Most of the land along the shore of Tokyo Bay has been reclaimed from the sea.

5 There are new commercial, shopping, and entertainment centres at Shibuya, Ikebukoro, and Shinjuku.

6 Nihombashi is the main financial centre. It contains the Bank of Tokyo, the Bank of Japan, and the Stock Exchange.

7 There are many museums in Ueno, and also the main part of Tokyo University.

8 There are many small-scale industries in Asakusa.

9 In the older residential districts, the roads are narrow. It is very easy to lose your way.

10 There are a large number of railways and expressways. Most of them converge near the city centre.

15.35 Tokyo.

15.36 Skyscrapers at Shinjiku.

- 50% before the Second World War.
- 22% in 1954.
- 8% in 1985.

35% of all jobs are now in manufacturing and construction, and 56% are in the service sector. Tokyo has grown because it is a centre for manufacturing and service employment.

Like all major cities, the functions of Tokyo are very varied:

- Tokyo is the national capital. All the government ministries and many other departments have their headquarters there.
- Tokyo is the second most important financial centre in the world, after New York. 60% of Japan's large companies have their headquarters there. Tokyo banks have 45% of the nation's bank deposits. The city has Japan's largest stock exchange and the main foreign currency market.
- Tokyo is an educational and cultural centre. 80% of Japanese publishing activity is centred there. There are many universities, with a total of 660,000 students, or 40% of the student places in Japan. There are many theatres and museums, and seven television channels.
- Tokyo is an industrial centre; but most of the industries are fairly small firms, or factories producing lightweight, high-value goods such as watches, leather goods, and optical equipment. Only 15% of the workers in Tokyo are employed by firms with more than 100 employees. Most of the heavy industry on Tokyo Bay is at Kawasaki, or elsewhere; and the main port is at Yokohama.

15.37 Central Tokyo.

15.38 Travelling to work may take several hours a day.

Urban problems

Density There is very little public open space in Tokyo, although some streets are closed to traffic on Sundays. Most people live in wooden houses measuring 30–50 m^2. It is very unusual to have even a small garden.

Transport Traffic congestion is always a problem, in spite of the expressways. Trains are packed tight with passengers in busy periods. 1.7 million people from the surrounding region travel into Tokyo to work every day; on average, their journey takes 1½ hours each way.

Pollution Air pollution is always a problem in Japanese cities, and Tokyo Bay was so badly polluted in the 1950s that there was almost no marine life. The city produces 15,000 tonnes of garbage every day, which has to be dumped somewhere. But the situation has now improved a little. It is still not safe to swim in the Bay, but there are beaches were children can play and people can collect shellfish.

Crime Crime is a problem in every major city, but Tokyo has a surprisingly low crime rate. Only 36 cases of heroin addition were recorded in 1982; Washington DC, which is a much smaller city, had 1,700.

1 Why are Shinjuku and Ikebukoro good locations for shopping and entertainment centres?

Earthquakes

Tokyo lies close to the boundary between the Philippine and Eurasian plates. Earthquakes are very frequent; on average, there are three noticeable earthquakes every month; but most of them are not too serious.

On 1 September 1923, Tokyo was devastated by a major earthquake, measuring 8.3 on the Richter scale. It caused the collapse of 5,000 buildings. Many small fires were started when charcoal-burning cooking-stoves collapsed; and these spread rapidly through the wooden houses of the old city. Two-thirds of the city was destroyed by the fire; and almost 100,000 people were killed.

There could be another major earthquake at any time. The Tokyo Metropolitan Plan aims to make sure that next time there is a powerful earthquake, the effects will not be so damaging:

- Older housing is to be strengthened and fireproofed over an area of 5.45 km^2.
- Old gas pipes are to be renewed to reduce the danger of gas leaks and explosions.
- Slopes will be protected to prevent landslides.
- Eastern Tokyo will be protected against tsunamis with 35 km of new embankment.
- Emergency water tanks hold enough drinking-water to keep the city supplied for ten days.
- There are 307 km of official evacuation route, which will be kept clear for people leaving the city.
- Parks and open spaces will be 'refuges' where people can go to escape the danger of falling buildings.
- Tall buildings must be built on solid rock, with a deep pile foundation. They have strong concrete walls. Some modern buildings have computer-controlled cable-tensioning systems to protect them against earthquake stress.
- Householders are encouraged to keep earthquake kits, with bottled water, rice, a radio, a fire extinguisher, and blankets for emergency use.

2 Which of these precautions would be appropriate in Caribbean cities?

3 Compare Tokyo with Kingston, Jamaica. Use these headings:
(a) Site.
(b) Functions.
(c) Growth.
(d) Pollution.
(e) Urban landscape.
(f) Natural hazards.
(g) Commercial centres.
(h) Transport system.

15.7 New York

Figure 15.41 shows the position of New York City. An important city has developed on this site, because:

- It is on the eastern seaboard of the United States. Sea communications with Europe are good. This was particularly important when North America was being settled by Europeans.
- There is a good natural harbour: a stretch of calm water which is deep enough for large ships to dock.
- The Hudson River provides an excellent communications route with the interior. Ships can sail up the river as far as Albany, more than 200 km upstream.
- A site on Manhattan Island was relatively easy to defend against attack from the land.

In 1626, the Dutch 'bought' Manhattan Island from the local Amerindian population for goods worth $24. A small trading centre grew up at the southern tip of the island. Its northern boundary ran along the line of what is now Wall Street. The settlement was known as New Amsterdam, until it was taken by the British in 1664 and renamed New York.

New York grew rapidly during the rest of the colonial period. It became the largest city and most important port in North America.

Population growth

Figure 15.39 shows the growth of the population of New York since the late eighteenth century.

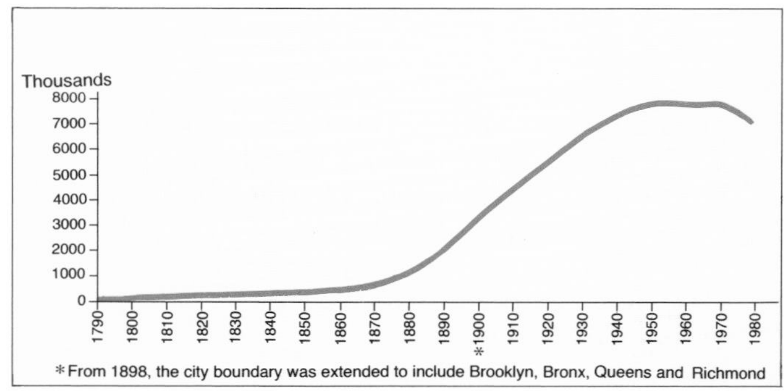

15.39 The population of New York City.

4 In which 10-year period did the population of New York reach:
  (a) 100,000?
  (b) 1 million?
  (c) 5 million?
5 In which 40-year period did the city grow most rapidly?
6 In what year was the highest population recorded?
7 What happened to the population of New York City in the period 1970–80?

15.40 New York: Manhattan from the air.

The New York region

- At the centre of New York is the southern part of Manhattan Island. Most of the tall office buildings are in two districts of southern Manhattan. The

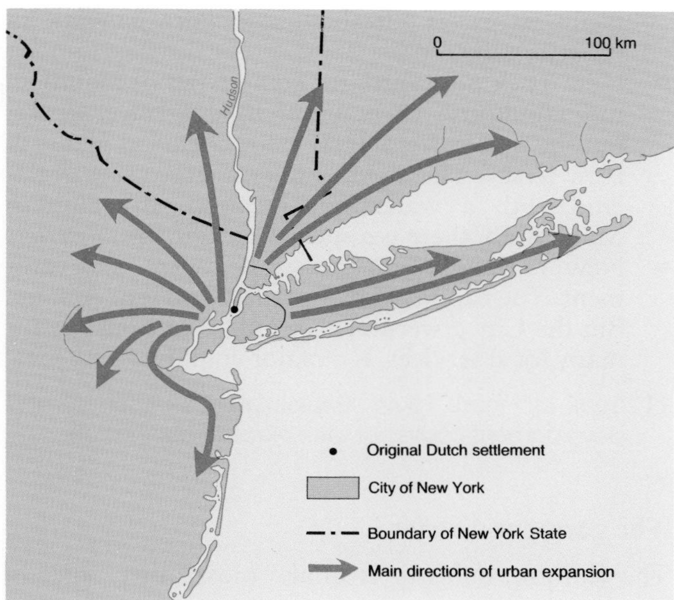

15.41 The New York region.

main department stores, theatres, and museums are in the midtown area, and the main financial district is around Wall Street in the downtown area, near to the original Dutch settlement. Few people actually live in this part of Manhattan.

- The northern part of Manhattan is very densely populated. There are 1.4 million people living in the 59 km^2 of Manhattan Island. Much of the housing in Manhattan is in very poor condition; but there are also many luxury apartments. Manhattan Island is about $\frac{2}{3}$ the size of Montserrat.

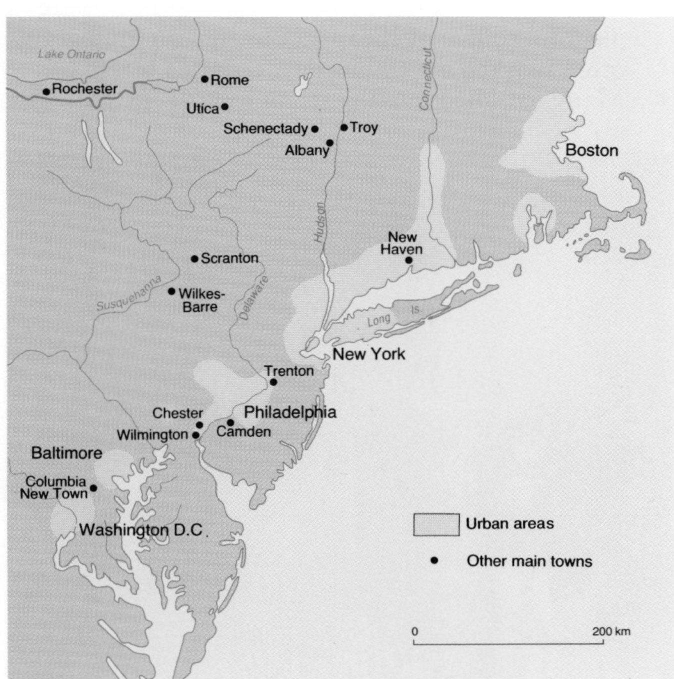

15.42 The main urbanised areas of the Megalopolis.

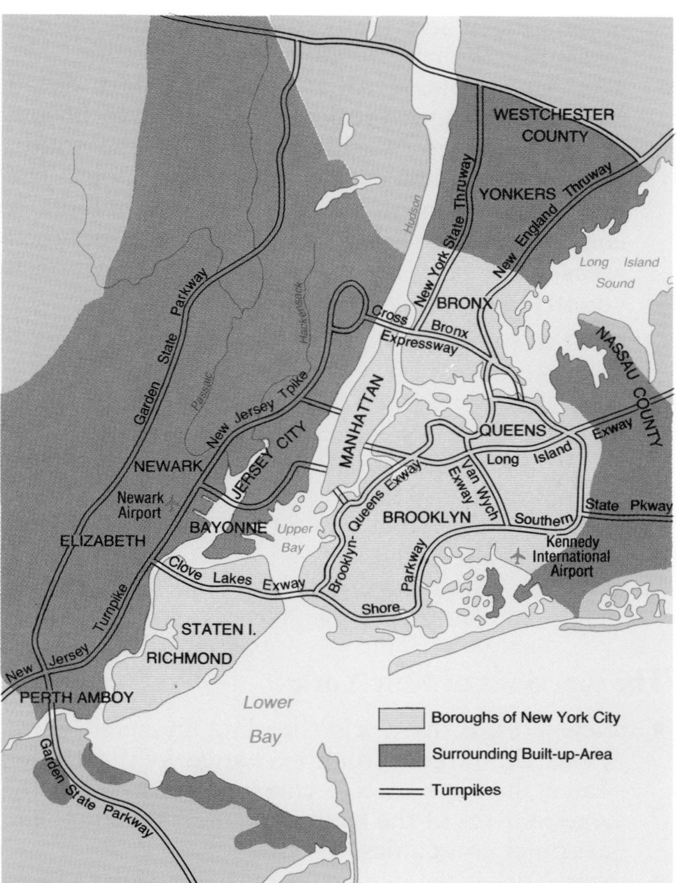

15.43 Metropolitan New York.

- New York City consists of five boroughs. Manhattan is one of them. The others are Brooklyn, Queens, Richmond, and the Bronx. Many people from these boroughs travel into Manhattan every day to work.
- In 1980, the City had a population of just over seven million. Population density in the other four boroughs is less than one-third as high as in Manhattan. The total area of New York City is 830 km^2; it is about twice the size of Barbados.
- The City boundaries were fixed in 1898. But the growth of New York did not stop at the City boundary. There is now a continuous urbanised area almost as large as Jamaica, with a population of over 15 million, which stretches over much of northern New Jersey, covers Long Island, and reaches across the southern part of New York State to the borders of Connecticut. In this Metropolitan Area, there are some communities which are large cities in their own right. Newark in New Jersey has a population of almost two million. There are areas like Jersey City, just across the Hudson River from Manhattan, which are very similar to Brooklyn or the Bronx. And there are newer suburban areas with a very low density of

population where many houses are built on lots measuring 0.5 ha.

- The Metropolitan Area is in turn part of an enormous urbanised region, stretching from Boston in the north to Washington DC in the south, which is sometimes known as Megalopolis. The total population of Megalopolis is 46 million. It contains large cities like New York, huge suburban areas, and also many wide stretches of open countryside.

8 Refer to Figure 15.43. Of the boroughs which make up New York City:
(a) Which two are on Long Island?
(b) Which is on the mainland?
(c) Which contains John F. Kennedy International Airport?

9 Refer to Figure 15.42. What is the distance from Boston to Washington DC?

10 List five cities outside the New York Metropolitan Area which are part of Megalopolis.

The functions of New York

- New York is the world's leading financial centre. It has the largest stock exchange in the United States, the main foreign currency market, and the headquarters of the leading finance, banking, and insurance companies.
- New York is the main cultural focus of the United States. Books and magazine publishing, live theatre, and music are all centred in New York.
- Advertising is an important industry in the USA. Of the large advertising agencies, 70% have their headquarters in New York.
- New York is the most important port in the US; but the port is no longer in its old position on Manhattan Island. The main container-handling facilities are at Elizabeth and Port Newark in New Jersey.
- New York is a centre for some types of manufacturing industry. There are no iron and steel works; but there are several large petrochemical plants in New Jersey. These were built on large areas of flat land with a waterfront location. In southern Manhattan, there is a specialised *garment district*.
- New York is not an important centre of government. The capital of New York State is at Albany. But the City government, which is responsible for many local services, is a major employer.

11 Look at Figure 15.44. Explain why this sort of port development could not take place in Manhattan.

The garment district

The clothing industry is unlike most other types of manufacturing for two reasons:

- Small-scale businesses can still be very profitable.
- A city-centre location is still very common.

In a small area of 80 ha in southern Manhattan, there are more than 4,000 small factories and other businesses connected with the clothing industry. This is the main centre for fashion in the USA.

The garment district grew up here because:

- Fashions in clothing change very quickly. It is important for designers and manufacturers to be on the spot where new ideas are developed, so they can hear of the latest styles in time to catch the market.
- The clothing industry is labour-intensive. In the early part of this century, immigrants were a plentiful source of cheap labour. Jewish immigrants often worked a 12-hour day, 6 days a week.
- Many of the wealthiest and most fashionably

15.44 A container terminal, New York.

15.45 A street scene in a low-income neighbourhood.

dressed people in the USA live in New York. The New York department stores are a large part of the market for high-fashion clothing.

As recently as 1975, there were still 200,000 workers employed in the New York garment industry, in small workshops which specialise in cutting, stitching, finishing, or wholesaling. A rack of dresses being wheeled through the streets from one establishment to the next is still a common sight.

However, the garment district is no longer quite as important as it was.

- The days of very low wages and long hours have fortunately long since gone.
- Rents in Manhattan are very high. They may make up 20% of total manufacturing costs.
- Telecommunications make it far easier to operate a successful clothing business away from a big city. Designers and buyers can travel when they need to, and drawings and market information can be transmitted instantly.
- Automation means that fewer workers are needed by those clothing firms that are still in the city.

Increasingly, the routine jobs like cutting and stitching are completed away from Manhattan, in New Jersey, or the southern states of the USA, or in the Caribbean. Those who are likely to remain in Manhattan are the designers, the buyers, the organisers of the business, and the highly skilled workers in the high-fashion workshops who may take half a day to make one dress.

Immigration

Historically, New York has been the main point of entry for immigrants travelling to the United States. From the mid-nineteenth century, large numbers of immigrants came in, first mainly from Ireland and Germany, then mainly from Italy and eastern Europe, then from Puerto Rico and elsewhere. Today, there are also large immigrant communities from many Commonwealth Caribbean countries.

Many immigrants have always used New York simply as a point of entry to the USA. They moved straight on to agricultural communities and manufacturing centres in the midwest or elsewhere. But many others stayed in New York. At most points in the city's history, 40% of the residents have been either foreign-born, or born in the US of foreign parents. An even higher proportion of the population would still identify themselves as 'Irish-American' or 'Italian-American', even if in some cases none of their parents or grandparents were born overseas.

Many parts of New York have a distinctive cultural identity. One neighbourhood may be predominantly Puerto Rican or Haitian; another may be Jewish or Greek.

Today, the city's ethnic mix is probably one of the most positive features of life in New York. But it has also been a source of conflict, when one group has suffered from the effects of discrimination in housing and employment. This has been a particular problem for Puerto Ricans, and for black people from the southern states of the US, who were often treated as if they were 'immigrants' in their own country.

Urban problems

New York is in many ways a successful city; but it also has more than its share of urban problems.

Poverty Poor people in New York have a standard of living which would be considered quite high in many other countries. But basic living costs are very high in the city, and life is not easy for many people in New York. Over a million people in New York City alone are supported by the public welfare system. Unemployment is high, especially for the unskilled. Many people live in overcrowded and dilapidated housing.

Crime Many parts of New York are unsafe at night, and some are unsafe even by day. Middle-class apartments need to be built almost like fortresses to keep away intruders. Drug addiction and prostitution are major problems, to an extent which shocks many visitors from other countries, or from many parts of the United States.

Transportation Many people have long journeys to work every day. All the major routes into Manhattan are packed tight with office workers at the start and finish of the working day. Although thousands of millions of dollars have been spent on road construction, traffic congestion is still severe.

Public finances Most of the poor housing and most of the poor people are in the City of New York. But the majority of the wealthier people live in the suburban areas. Many large businesses have moved out of the city, too. This makes it hard for the city to raise money through local taxation. In 1975, the city faced bankruptcy, and was only rescued through outside help at the last minute. Since then there have been recurrent financial problems.

12 Compare Tokyo and New York under these headings:
- (a) Site.
- (b) Functions.
- (c) Urban landscape.
- (d) Urban problems.

15.8 Urban poverty: Port au Prince

Port au Prince is a *primate* city. It overshadows the rest of Haiti. Although it contains only 12% of the population:

- It is fourteen times the size of the second city, Cap Haitien.
- 25% of agricultural production is consumed there.
- 70% of housing construction takes place there.
- 70% of the money budgeted for government services is spent there.
- 80% of the industrial output is produced there.
- The average income is 1.4 times as high as in the smaller towns, and 4.5 times as high as in the country districts.

People from rural areas migrate to Port au Prince because they feel that there is a better chance of earning money there. The city is not rich, but there are more opportunities than in rural Haiti.

Social services are also concentrated in the city. In rural Haiti, there is one doctor for every 43,000 persons; in the capital, there is one for every 2,100 persons.

In the city, there is an enormous gap between rich and poor. Half of all the money earned in the city goes to 6% of the population. Some of the people in Port au Prince would be considered rich even in the more prosperous Caribbean islands; and at the top of the ladder are a handful of families with incomes that put them in the international millionaire category.

The other half of the total income is shared by the remaining 94% of the population. Almost all of these families would be considered very poor anywhere else in the Caribbean. For many people, the main aim is simply to find enough food for the next meal.

St Martin

St Martin is a district quite close to the main market area in the city centre. It contains 20,000 people, or about the same number as Kingstown, St Vincent, in an area of 0.13 km^2.

The district has recently been upgraded with an improvement scheme funded by overseas agencies, but living conditions are still poor.

Almost all the houses are single storey structures, built of wooden planks or concrete blocks. They are roofed with galvanised sheets, and the floor is often of bare earth. Some houses are subdivided by internal partitions into several rooms, each occupied by a single family. Toilet facilities consist of a pit latrine, shared by as many as thirty or forty people.

Most of the buildings do not have proper road access. There are ten major pedestrian walkways, and a huge number of tiny paths which zigzag between the houses. Many of these paths are less than a metre wide, and a stranger would get lost very quickly without a local guide.

15.46 Low income housing in St Martin.

A few years ago, a large gully in the middle of the district was still being used as a dump for refuse, and a feeding area for pigs. After heavy rain, water poured into the gully. Where rubbish had accumulated, a dam was formed; and the surrounding area might be flooded.

There were no public standpipes. A few families on the edge of the district had water connections. They sold water to 1,200 water vendors who retailed it for 0.55 $ US per litre. Most households spent ⅛ of their total income on water, the one commodity which was seen as more important than food.

As part of an improvement scheme:

- An electricity supply was provided for the first time. Relatively well off families can pay for a connection.
- A road suitable for motor vehicles has been built through the area.
- The gully has been lined with concrete, and retaining walls have been built. There is no longer a serious flood hazard.
- A basic water supply has been provided. There are nine sets of standpipes where people can wash or fill buckets. The water is not safe to drink, however; and it runs for only a few hours every day.
- Some new apartments have been built. Each apartment consists of one room only. There are shared latrines and space for an outdoor charcoal stove.

Further from the city centre, there are other low income neighbourhoods, such as Cité Soleil and La Saline. Conditions are much worse in these districts than in St Martin

- There are fewer concrete houses. Many dwellings are put together from waste materials such as old packing cases.

15.47 There is now a public water supply. For a few hours every day, water is available for washing and domestic use.

- In most parts of these districts, there are no roads and there is no electricity supply.
- Water still has to be bought from water sellers, by the bucket.
- There is no proper drainage or refuse disposal system. Stagnant water and rotting waste are a permanent problem.

1 Compare living conditions in St Martin with a low income area in an urban settlement in your country.
2 What would have to be done to bring living conditions in St Martin to a standard which you would consider acceptable?
3 Was the improvement scheme for St Martin appropriate for a low income area in a country like Haiti? Explain your answer carefully.

The informal sector

In less developed countries, the economy can be divided into a *formal* and *informal* sector.

The formal sector includes everyone who is in regular paid employment: factory workers, civil servants, secretaries, and supermarket managers. Not all formal-sector jobs are well paid, but they provide a regular source of income.

In the informal sector, there is much less security. People may earn quite a good living, but they are not employed by an organised business or by the government. There is usually very little reliable information about the informal sector of the economy.

Somewhere between one-half and three-quarters of the jobs in Port au Prince are in the informal sector:

- Prosperous households employ large numbers of maids, cooks, gardeners, yard boys, and guards. They are given meals, and sometimes a place to sleep. Usually, but not always, they get a small monthly payment, too – generally a fraction of the official minimum wage.
- Many factories employ people to work off the premises. A clothing firm may employ women to do beadwork or knitting at home, where they are not covered by wage legislation; there is no need to pay for factory space for them to work in.
- Civil servants may employ unofficial assistants to do much of their work. The official is free to spend most of the working week at home, or running a private business, while the assistant is in the office.
- In the city centre, many young men spend their time in the streets, looking out for the chance to earn a little money carrying parcels, watching a parked car, or showing a tourist around the city. There are shoe-cleaners, street vendors, and a crowd of other people looking for work.
- Scattered throughout the city, there are a huge number of craft industries, making clothes, bags, shoes, furniture and other items for sale. Most sell to local people, but other craft items are exported through a network of middlemen and small traders.
- Everywhere, there are people in the streets buying and selling. There are vendors with piles of fruits and vegetables, women wrapping and selling little packets of sugar and rice, traders selling leather sandals made in Port au Prince or imported plastic kitchenware. Even out-of-order digital watches have a small cash value, and can earn a street trader a tiny profit.

Every country has an informal sector of some sort, though it will be very small in rich countries with a well-developed social security system, like Sweden or West Germany. Some people in most Caribbean countries earn their living from jobs that are really part of the informal sector. They are not recorded in the employment statistics, and do not pay tax or social security contributions.

4 Which economic activities in your own country would form part of the informal sector?
5 Why is the informal sector less significant in your country than in Haiti?

15.48 Small scale traders. The wood will be used for construction.

16 · TRANSPORT AND TRADE

16.1 Transport

The importance of transport

1 Make a list of all the journeys made by people in your household on a typical day.
2 Classify the journeys like this:
   (a) By distance (e.g. less than 1 km, 2–14 km, over 15 km).
   (b) By purpose (e.g. to work, to school, leisure, shopping, etc.).
   (c) By mode of transport (e.g. on foot, by car, by bus, etc.).
3 Explain why a good transportation system is important for:
   (a) Your family.
   (b) A farmer (look at Figure 12.4).
   (c) A factory (look at Figure 13.1).
   (d) A hotel.
   (e) A shop.

Modes of transport

There are many different modes of transport. Each one has *advantages* and *disadvantages*.

4 Copy Figure 16.1 into your exercise book, and make a tick where a description fits for a particular mode of transport.
5 Explain why most journeys are still made by road.
6 What mode of transport is most important for international travel?
7 Road transport is usually too expensive for very bulky commodities. Look back to Sections 13.5 and 13.6, and list the modes of transport which are used for:
   (a) Natural gas.
   (b) Bauxite.

The development of a road network: Dominica

Figure 16.2 shows the main phases in the development of the road network in Dominica. Road construction was difficult in Dominica because:

- There are many steep slopes.
- Along much of the coastline, these steep slopes plunge straight into the sea, with no coastal plain.
- There are many rivers, so bridges have to be built.
- Rainfall is high. After heavy rain, the rivers may flood, and there are many landslides where steep slopes have been cut away for road construction.

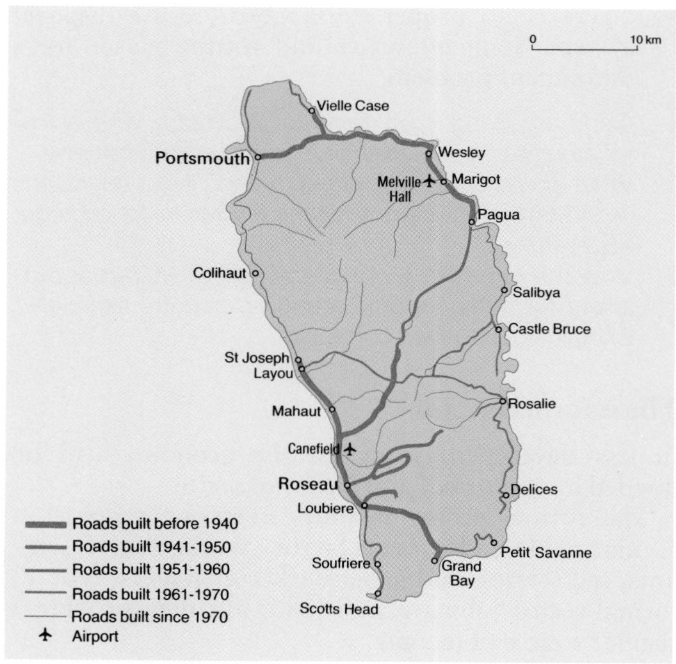

16.2 The development of the road network in Dominica.

	Road	Rail	Air	Ship/Boat	Walking
Quick					
Cheap					
Flexible – door-to-door transport					
Only possible on certain routes					
Suitable for passengers					
Suitable for goods					
Suitable for travelling between islands					
Suitable for very short journeys					
Suitable for long journeys					

16.1 Modes of transport.

- The island has a small population. Many people have low incomes. This has made it difficult to raise money for road construction.

8 Name two settlements which could not be reached by road from Roseau in:
   (a) 1950.
   (b) 1970.
9 What modes of transport would people from these settlements have used before there was a road link to Roseau?
10 Explain why the lack of roads makes it difficult to:
   (a) Provide education and health care for rural areas.
   (b) Increase exports of agricultural products like bananas.

Since the 1950s, many new roads have been constructed. The government has borrowed money to pay for some of them from agencies like the European Development Fund; road construction can help the country earn money to repay the debt once the roads are completed. There are two types of road:

- Main roads which connect the main towns and villages with each other.
- Feeder roads which run through the farming areas.

11 Look at Figure 15.9. Make a sketch map to show the main roads and the feeder roads in this small area.
12 How has the road pattern of Dominica been influenced by relief?
13 Explain why feeder roads are important for the operation of a successful farming system.
14 Is the road network complete?

Barbados

Figure 16.3 shows the road network of Barbados. Only the main roads are shown on this map. There are more roads than in Dominica, because:

- Most of the island is relatively flat.
- Although there are some deep gullies, there are very few rivers and streams.
- Over most of the island, the surface rock is limestone, which provides a good foundation for road construction.
- The island has about three times the population of Dominica.
- The Government has made funds available for road construction over a long period.
- A high proportion of households own cars. There are about ten times as many cars as in Dominica. Roads have to be built to control the traffic congestion problem.

The road network covers the whole island. There is no large uninhabited area in the interior, as there is in Dominica, where no roads are needed.

Most of the main roads radiate out from Bridgetown.

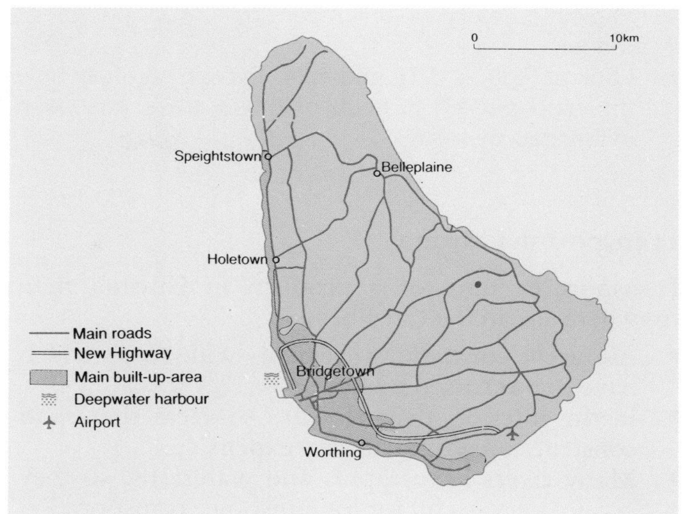

16.3 The Barbados road network.

They were built so that sugar could be transported from the factories to the port, and so that people from the country districts could travel to the city.

Traffic congestion in Barbados is sometimes a very serious problem. To ease the situation, a new highway has been built.

15 Explain why the traditional road pattern caused serious traffic congestion in Bridgetown.
16 Explain why the new highway reduces traffic congestion in Bridgetown.
17 Comment on the route of the highway.

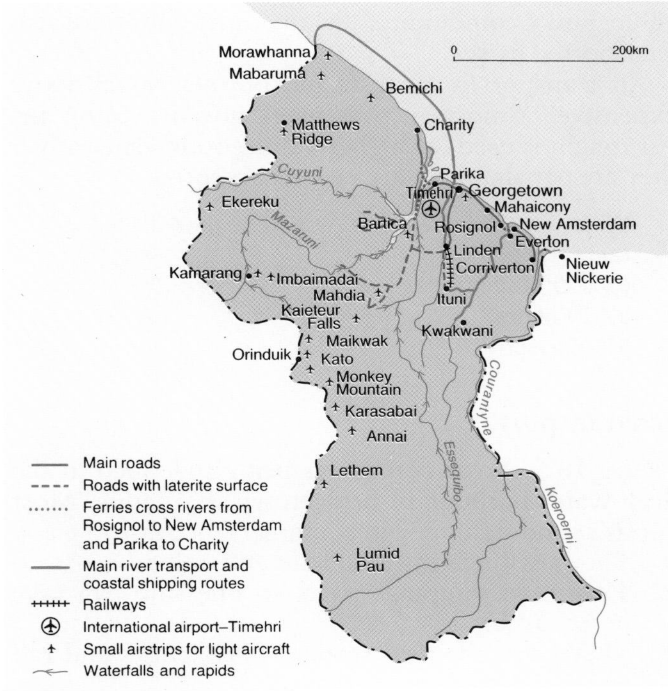

16.4 Transport in Guyana.

18 Explain carefully what is meant by a radial pattern of roads.

19 Look at Figures 3.16 and 4.24. Explain carefully how the road pattern in each of these areas has been influenced by relief.

Transport in Guyana

Transport is more of a problem in Guyana than anywhere else in the Caribbean:

- Along the coast, there are many wide rivers which have to be crossed by ferry.
- In the interior, distances are so great that road construction would be very expensive.
- Many rivers have rapids and waterfalls, so they are not very useful for long-distance transport.
- Water transport is generally quite slow.
- Air travel is expensive, especially for bulky goods.

There is a good road with a hard surface along the coast, and another running from Georgetown to Linden. These two roads serve the bulk of the population. But in the interior, many different modes of transport are used:

- There are some roads which are surfaced with laterite. They are suitable for four-wheel-drive vehicles.
- There are regular ferry services on some rivers.
- There is a railway from Linden to Ituni.
- Ocean-going ships can travel up the Demerara river to Linden for bauxite. Bauxite is also transported down the Berbice river by barge.
- Light aircraft fly to many parts of the interior. Guyana Airways serves the gold- and diamond-mining areas in the west of the country, the cattle-raising area in the Rupununi savanna, and some other places. Most of the smaller airstrips are surfaced with laterite.

20 Read Section 9.4 again. Explain what laterite is, and why it is a good material for surfacing roads and runways.

21 What is the distance from Lethem to the nearest all-weather road?

22 List five settlements which cannot be reached from Georgetown by road.

23 How many ferries have to be used on a journey from Charity to Nieuw Nickerie in Surinam?

24 Read Section 15.3 again. Explain why the settlement pattern makes it easy to provide road transport for the coastal areas of Guyana.

16.2 International transport

International transport is by sea or by air.

Sea transport is comparatively slow, but it is cheap. It is the only economic mode of transport for low-value, bulky commodities. Many other goods are also transported by sea.

Air transport is much faster, but also much more expensive. Almost all passengers now travel by air. Air freight is used for higher-value goods, especially if they are perishable or are needed urgently.

1 Which mode of transport would be used for:
   (a) Iron ore?
   (b) Computer parts?
   (c) Flowers?
   (d) Sugar?

Sea transport

Figure 16.5 shows *containers* being unloaded in the deep-water harbour in Bridgetown, Barbados. Most goods are now shipped in containers, because:

- They are much easier to load and unload.
- They save shipping space, so one ship can take more cargo.
- They can be loaded straight onto trucks and rail wagons for transport on land.
- Containers are sealed. When items like videos are

16.5 Unloading a container from a ship in Bridgetown port.

16.6 Bulk handling facilities for loading sugar.

being transported, there are fewer breakages and other losses.

Some ports do not have mechanical equipment for handling containers. They can still unload containers, but the cost is much higher.

Ports on very small islands do not have a deep-water harbour. Large container ships cannot dock there. These ports are only suitable for small schooners.

Cargoes like sugar, bauxite, iron ore, and oil are not tranported in container ships; it is much cheaper to use specially designed bulk carriers. Ports which handle these commodities need specialised bulk-handling facilities.

Figure 16.6 shows bulk-handling equipment used for loading sugar at Bridgetown. Sugar is taken from the factories to a bulk store by truck. When a ship needs to load, the sugar is taken from the store by conveyor belt, and poured into the hold of the ship through a chute. A thrower makes sure that the sugar is evenly distributed in the hold of the ship.

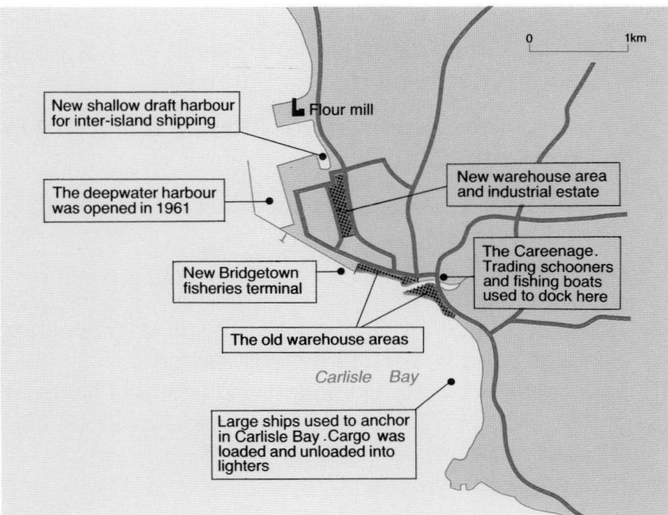

16.7 Port development in Bridgetown.

Until 1961, sugar at Bridgetown was loaded by hand. There was no deep-water harbour and no bulk-handling facility. Barrels of sugar were taken from the factories to the Careenage in the middle of the city. Then they were loaded onto lighters which were rowed out to Carlisle Bay where the large ocean-going ships could moor. Then the bags of sugar, which weighed over 100 kg, were loaded onto the ships by hand.

As many as 50 men were employed to load a ship with sugar in the crop season. Today, ten men can load a much larger ship at a rate of 500 tonnes per hour. Many jobs have been 'lost'. But if the port had not been modernised in this way, the cost of exporting sugar would be so high that the industry could not survive.

2 Name a Caribbean port with specialised bulk-handling facilities for:
   (a) Oil.
   (b) Bauxite.
   (c) Methanol and ammonia.
3 Look at Figure 16.7.
   (a) Write a few sentences to describe the main changes in the port area of Bridgetown.
   (b) Explain why these changes made the port more efficient.

Air transport

Figure 16.8 shows the airports in the eastern Caribbean. There are:

- Large airports with long runways which can take intercontinental jets.

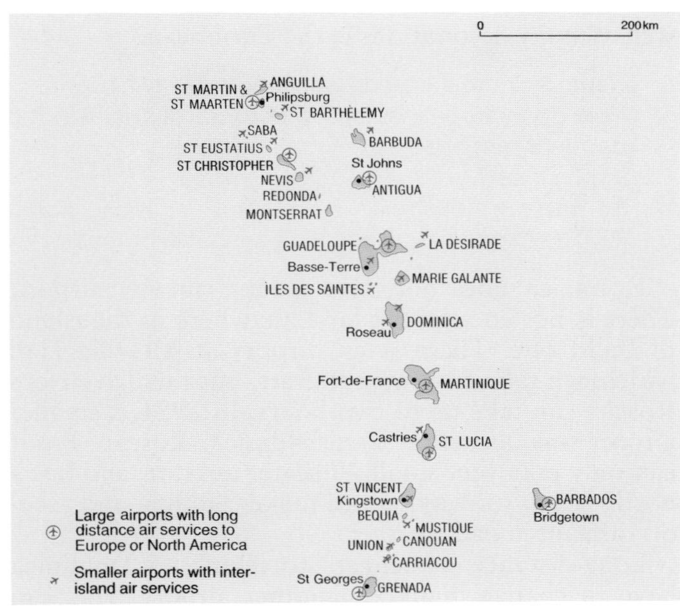

16.8 The eastern Caribbean: air travel.

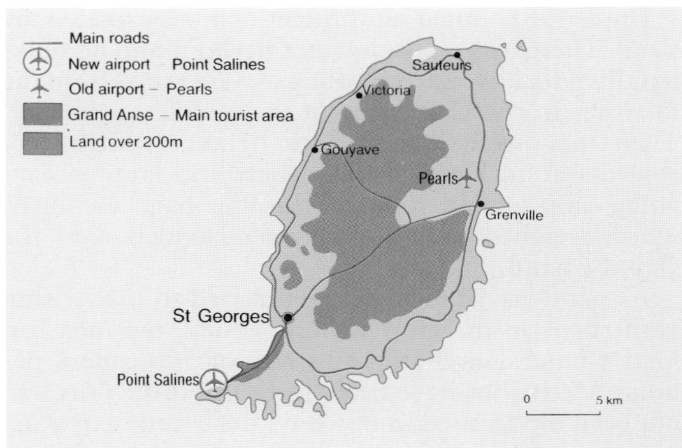

16.9 Grenada airport development.

- Airports with short runways which can only take small planes.

Some very small islands may have long-runway airports; but on many islands, they are very hard to build. An airport needs:

- Flat land for the runway.
- A clear flight path, with no dangerous hills which could cause crashes.
- A runway which lies approximately east–west, so that aircraft can take advantage of the prevailing winds they they are landing and taking off.
- Good communictions with the rest of the island.

Barbados has a long-runway airport. The airport was relatively easy to construct, because there are large areas of flat land. The island has a population of over 250,000, and a well-developed tourist industry, so many international airlines find it profitable to use this airport. There are flights to the USA, Canada, the UK, Brussels, Frankfurt, Caracas, and Manaus, as well as many destinations in the Caribbean.

4 Name four other islands with long-runway airports.
5 How do intercontinental flights to Barbados help the development of:
(a) Tourism?
(b) Enclave industries?
(c) The export of flowers and perishable crops?

Dominica does not have a long-runway airport. There is not enough flat land anywhere in the island to build one. There is an airport at Melville Hall which can take 56-seater aircraft, but the drive from Roseau can take up to two hours. In 1981, a smaller airport was opened at Canefield, near Roseau. But it can only take very small 20-seater aircraft, and has a north–south runway, which makes landing and take-off difficult in bad weather.

Long-distance passengers travelling to Dominica have to change flights at another airport. This can cause a long delay on some journeys.

16.10 The airport on Les Saintes, near Guadeloupe.

6 Name four other islands which do not have long-runway airports.

Grenada has recently built a long-runway airport. Figure 16.9 shows the new airport at Port Salines, and the old airport at Pearls, which could only take small aircraft and was not suitable for night flying. Part of the new airport runway is shown in Figure 6.16.

7 Give three reasons why Point Salines was a good site for the new airport.

Air transport is important for internal travel within some Caribbean countries.

8 Explain why air transport is important for travel within:
(a) the Bahamas.
(b) Guyana.
(c) Trinidad and Tobago.
9 Look at Figure 14.5. Explain why it is useful for Jamaica to have *two* international airports.
10 Look at Figure 2.10. Comment on the site of Norman Manley Airport (73 42) and Tinson Pen Airport (68 48). Which is more suitable for:
(a) Long-distance travel?
(b) Short flights within Jamaica?
Give reasons fo your answers.

16.3 International trade

1 Read through Section 1.2 again. Explain why modern communities depend on national, regional, and international trade.

Caribbean countries depend even more on international trade than many other nations. There are two reasons for this:

- There are many resources which are not found in the Caribbean. Some commodities will always have to be imported.
- Some industries are only profitable when they are organised on a large scale. Even the largest Caribbean countries are too small to support the full range of modern manufacturing industries.

2 Which of these commodities can be produced commercially in your country?

Iron ore	Bauxite	Oil
Wheat	Beef	Sugar

3 Which of these items could be manufactured profitably in your country for the local market alone?

Clothing	Beer	Aircraft
Computers	Oil tankers	Furniture

All countries have to *specialise* in the production of certain commodities and manufactured goods, although larger countries can supply quite a high proportion of their own requirements.

4 Look at Figure 16.11. Which countries are most dependent on international trade? What pattern do you notice?

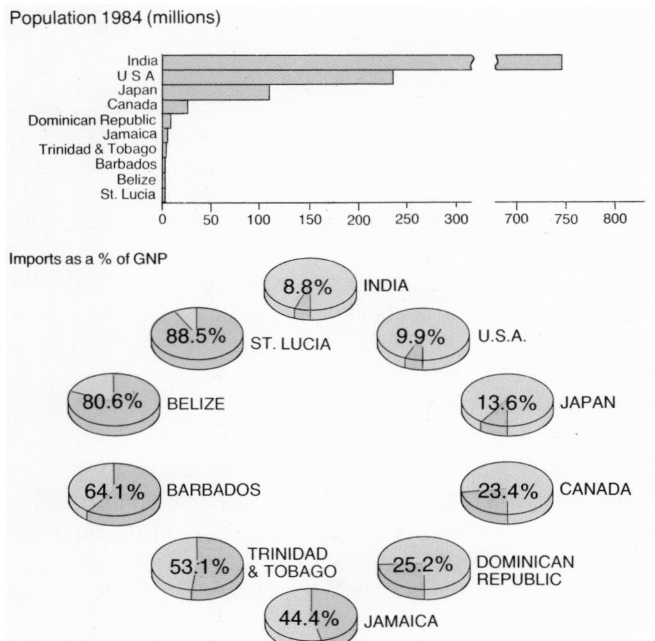

16.11 Dependence on international trade.

These countries were very dependent on one trading partner.

Country	Main trading partner	% of exports going to main partner
Dominican Republic	USA	66
Trinidad and Tobago	USA	60
Belize	USA	48

These countries were very dependent on one export commodity

Country	Commodity	% of exports
Dominican Republic	Sugar and molasses	43
Trinidad and Tobago	Oil and petroleum products	80
Jamaica	Bauxite and alumina	54
St Christoper & Nevis	Sugar and molasses	67

Source: UN International Trade Statistics Yearbook, 1983, and other sources.

16.12 Specialized patterns of trade.

All countries specialise to a certain extent. They earn foreign exchange by exporting what they can produce well, and spend the money on imports from abroad.

But if a country depends too much on one commodity, or on selling to one trading partner, then there may be problems. When prices are high, it will be prosperous. But there will be serious problems if the price of the main export commodity falls. When prices are low, it is difficult to pay for imports from overseas.

5 Look at Figure 16.12.
 (a) Which Caribbean countries are dependent on one or two main export commodities?
 (b) Which are most dependent on a single trading partner?

6 Read through Sections 12.4 and 13.6 again:
 (a) Explain why it is difficult for Caribbean countries to influence world prices of goods like sugar and bauxite.
 (b) Which countries have had economic problems because of low prices or falling sales for their exports?

Most Caribbean countries are trying to *diversify* their trading pattern, so that they do not depend so much on one commodity and one trading partner. This means:

- Developing new 'non-traditional' exports like manufactured goods or new crops.
- Maintaining traditional exports like sugar, bananas, bauxite, and oil where they are still profitable.
- Developing new markets in Europe, Latin America, Africa and elsewhere.
- Maintaining sales in traditional markets like the USA, Canada, and the UK.

Jamaica's trading pattern

Look at Figures 16.13 and 16.14.

7 What was Jamaica's main trading partner in:
(a) 1960?
(b) 1985?

8 What proportion of Jamaica's exports went to its three main markets in:
(a) 1960?
(b) 1985?

9 How successful has Jamaica been in:
(a) Finding new sources of supply for imported goods?
(b) Finding new markets for exports?

10 How important are the other Caricom countries as trading partners for Jamaica?

11 How dependent was Jamaica on its most important export commodity in:
(a) 1960?
(b) 1970?
(c) 1985?

12 How important were non-traditional exports like manufactured goods in:
(a) 1970?
(b) 1985?

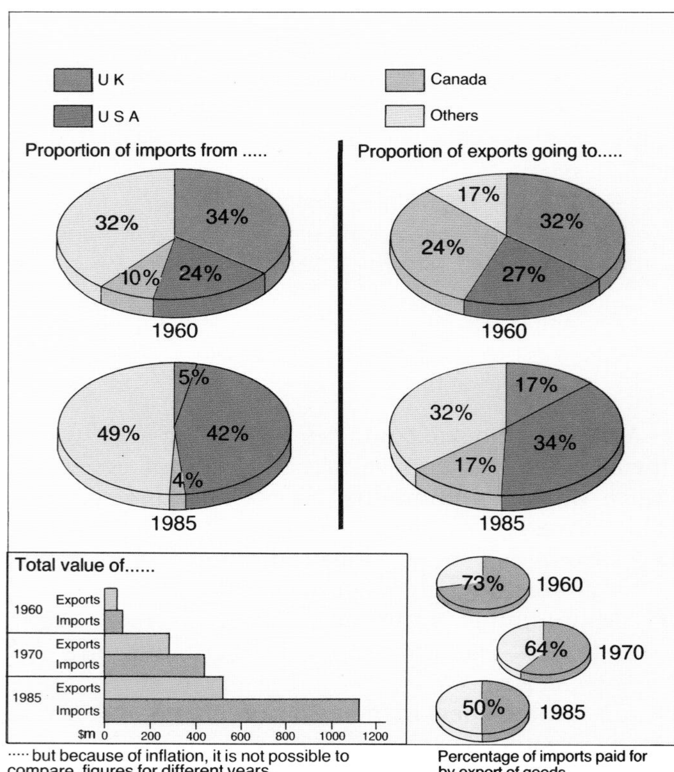

16.13 Jamaica's overseas trade.

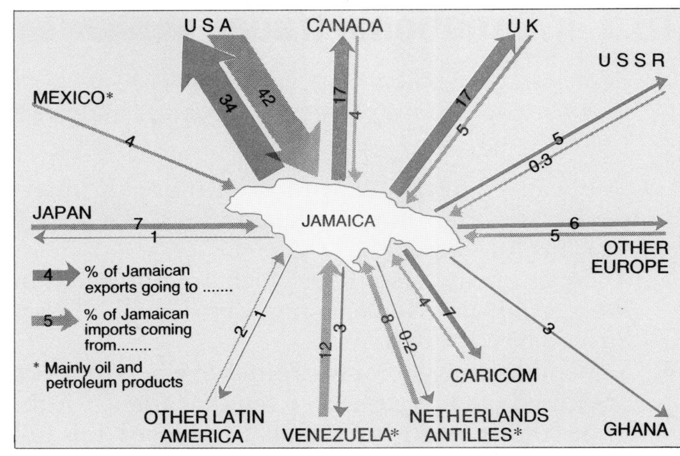

16.14 Jamaica's trading partners, 1985.

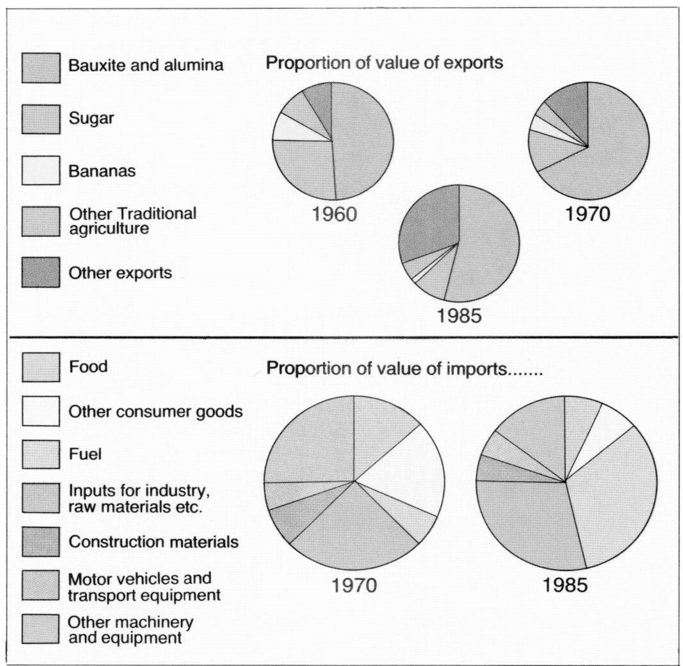

16.15 Jamaica's overseas trade.

13 How successful has Jamaica been in maintaining its traditional exports?

14 What proportion of the import bill could be paid with earnings from exports in:
(a) 1960?
(b) 1970?
(c) 1985?

15 Which trading partners:
(a) Buy a high proportion of Jamaica's exports?
(b) Supply a high proportion of Jamaica's imports?

16 If it was necessary to cut back on imports, how would this affect:
(a) The choice of gcods in the shops?
(b) Manufacturing industry?
(c) Agriculture?
(d) The transport system?

17 How much of Jamaica's trade is with:
   (a) Developed countries?
   (b) Less developed countries?
18 Has Jamaica succeeded in diversifying its trading pattern?
19 Explain how enclave industries increase:
   (a) Earnings from exports of manufactured goods.
   (b) Expenditure on imports of materials and equipment.

Invisible trade

Most Caribbean countries do not export enough to pay for the goods they buy from abroad. Some of the difference is made up by *invisible exports*, money which comes into the country to pay for *services* without any *goods* actually leaving the country.

- Tourism is an important invisible export. Tourists spend money on hotel bills, taxi fares, and restaurant meals. This money is just as useful as foreign exchange earned by exporting bauxite or sugar.
- Financial services are also invisible exports. If someone from overseas opens a bank account or registers a company in the Caribbean, they will pay a fee for this service. Some countries have laws which make it easy for foreigners to use their financial services. They may have a very low rate of tax to attract this sort of business.

The Cayman Islands have almost no mineral or agricultural resources; but they have a very high standard of living because of their invisible exports. There are over 200,000 cruise ship passengers and 150,000 other tourists per year. With a population of over 19,000, the islands have 460 banks and there are almost 18,000 companies registered. The owners of these companies may never have been anywhere near the Caymans. The islands' financial institutions deal with \$350 million every day. 95% of the goods sold on the island are imported, but under these conditions that poses no problem.

Small-scale trade

Small-scale trade is very important for some Caribbean countries.

- In many areas, there are small farmers who grow fresh fruit and vegetables and other goods. But they do not produce enough to interest a big international wholesaler, and do not have time to travel far from their home area to sell what they grow.
- Some islands cannot grow enough fresh produce, because they have a dense population, or because the climate is too dry, or because there are not enough peasant farmers. These islands need to import fruit and vegetables.

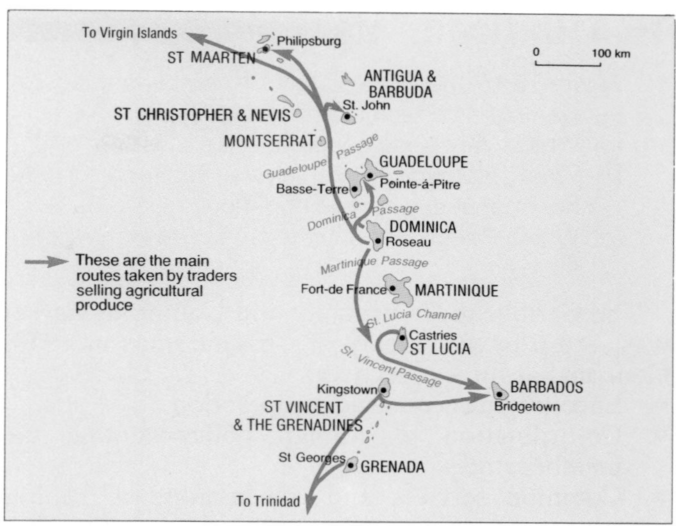

16.16 The eastern Caribbean: small-scale trade.

- Small traders, who are also called higglers or hucksters, buy produce from small farmers, transport it to a large city or to an island where it is in demand, and sell it. They usually buy clothing or household goods with the proceeds, which they can sell when they reach home.

20 Figure 16.16 shows some of the routes taken by small traders in the eastern Caribbean:
   (a) Which countries export agricultural produce through this system?
   (b) Which countries do the traders sell to?

Many of these small business people are now involved in long-distance trade. Jamaican higglers often travel to Haiti, Puerto Rico, or the United States to buy low-priced goods which they can sell when they return. Most long-distance traders do not take agricultural produce with them to sell.

Much of this activity is not recorded in the official statistics. But it is still an important part of the economy.

16.17 Small-scale trade at St Marc, Haiti. Sisal and other goods are still transported on small sailing ships.

16.4 Caricom

1 Figure 16.18 shows the Caricom member states:
   (a) Name the thirteen member states.
   (b) Which Caribbean countries are not in Caricom?
   (c) What historical and cultural features do the member states have in common?
   (d) Which Caricom country is not yet an independent state?

The Caribbean Community and Common Market was set up by the Treaty of Chaguaramas in 1973. Caricom has three objectives:

- Encouraging economic co-operation.
- Co-ordination of foreign policy among the member states.
- Common services and co-operation in health, education, culture, communications, and other fields.

Economic co-operation

Economic development is difficult for small countries because:

- They cannot produce very many of the goods they need.
- Factories producing for the home market have to work on a very small scale. This makes it hard for them to use the most efficient production methods.
- Small countries are always at the mercy of outside economic forces. They can do little to influence world commodity prices or the actions of larger nations.

On their own, even the largest Caricom countries are very small by world standards. But together, they have a population of over five million. This is a reasonably large market for industrial and agricultural goods.

The aims of Caricom include:

- Abolishing customs duties between member states, so that producers in even the smallest countries have access to a regional market of over five million people.
- A common level of customs duties for goods coming into the region, so that people in all the member states are encouraged to buy Caricom-produced goods.
- Making better use of Caricom raw materials, and encouraging producers to buy their inputs from within Caricom.
- Spreading the benefits of industrialisation, and encouraging industries to locate in the smaller countries.
- Encouraging regional trade in agricultural products, and fixing the price of commodities like coconut oil so that producers can plan ahead.
- Negotiating with countries outside the region who buy commodities like sugar, bananas, and rum from Caricom producers.

Working together

Caricom is not just an economic organisation. There are many other areas in which small countries need to work together. *Associate Institutions* of Caricom include:

- The Caribbean Development Bank, which promotes development projects and provides funding

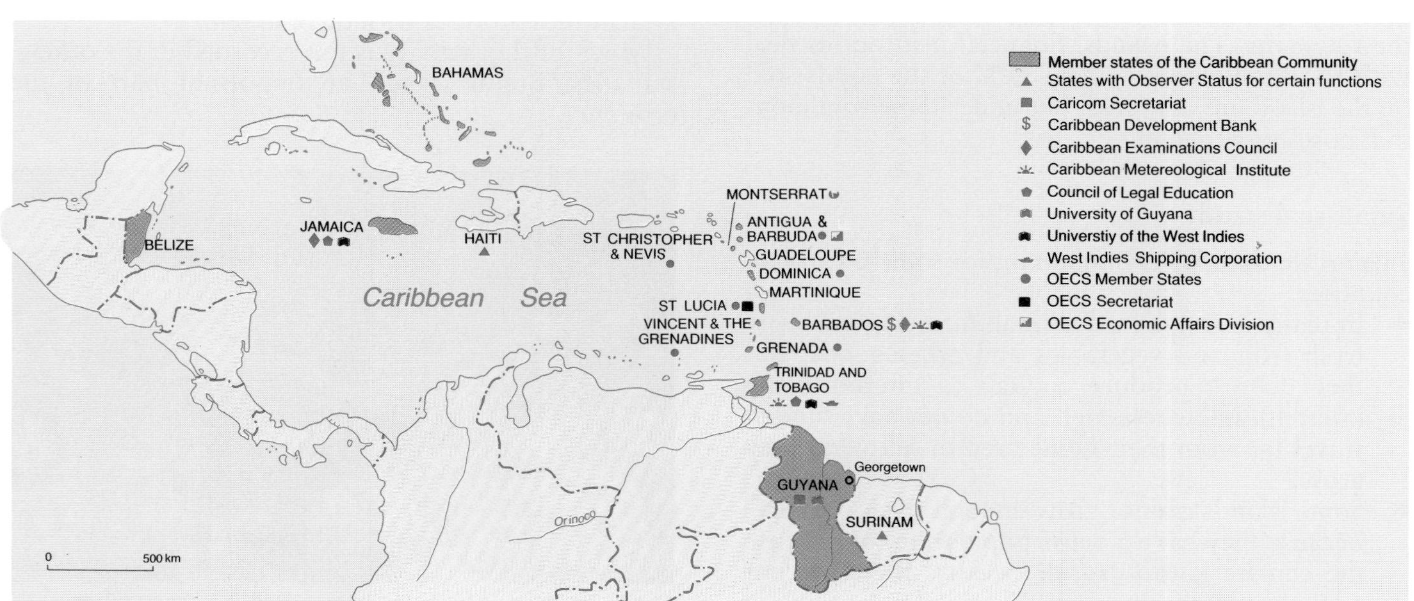

16.18 The Caribbean Community.

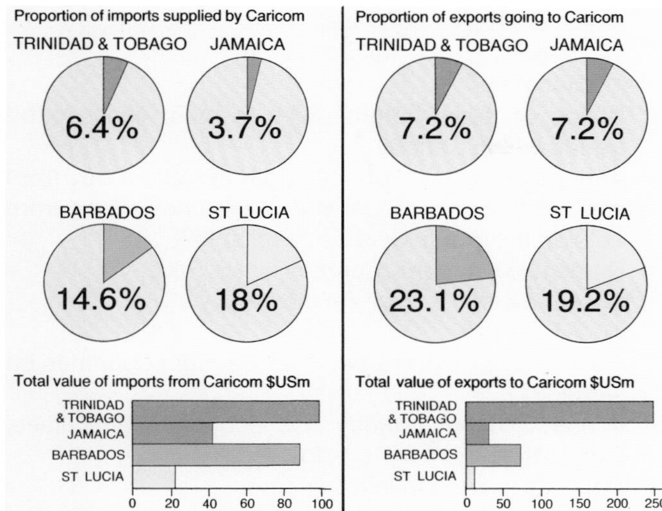

16.19 Trade within Caricom for four selected countries.

for them. Canada, the UK, Venezuela, Colombia and Mexico are also members of the CDB and help to finance it.

- The Caribbean Examinations Council, which organises school-leaving examinations for the Caribbean and ensures that they are recognised internationally.
- The Caribbean Meteorological Organisation, which provides training and carries out research in meteorology, and helps the different national, regional, and international organisations which deal with weather and climate to work together.
- The Council of Legal Education.
- The University of Guyana.
- The University of the West Indies.
- The Organisation of Eastern Caribbean States.
- The West Indies Shipping Corporation.

There are also other regional bodies linked to the community, like the Caribbean Agricultural Research and Development Institute, and the airline LIAT, which is jointly owned by the governments of eleven Caricom countries (the Bahamas and Belize do not participate in LIAT).

These are all fields where it is essential for all the regional governments to work together. It would be very difficult for every national Ministry of Education to organise its own school-leaving examinations, and get them recognised internationally; and it would not be a good idea to leave such an important area of activity to be run by an outside body. Again, it would not be sensible for every separate island in the eastern Caribbean to organise its own regional carrier, and to run a service in competition with its neighbours. And in sports like cricket, a West Indies team can make a much greater international impact than a whole series of national teams, each with only a few of the world-class players.

Many of the Associate Institutions and other regional bodies include other Caribbean territories, like the Cayman Islands, which are not members of Caricom.

How Caricom is organised

Caricom is run by:

- The Conference of Heads of Government, which meets from time to time. The Conference is the supreme authority for Caricom, and decides the general policies of the organisation.
- The Common Market Council, which meets more frequently. It consists of government ministers from each of the member states. The Council is responsible for the smooth running of the economic aspects of the community, and for ironing out any problems which may arise.
- Standing committees, where ministers responsible for other areas of activity meet. For example, there is a Standing Committee of Ministers for Agriculture. The Committee of Ministers for Foreign Affairs deals with the co-ordination of foreign policy.
- The Secretariat, which is the 'civil service' of the organisation. The officials in the Secretariat do not make policy decisions; but they are responsible for taking follow-up action when a decision has been made, and for carrying out studies on regional co-operation.

Some problems with Caricom

Everyone would agree that trade between Caricom countries should be increased; but this is not always easy to achieve:

- All the Caricom countries have tropical climates. They often produce a similar range of agricultural products. There is no need for Trinidad to buy sugar from Guyana, or for Jamaica to buy bananas from St Vincent.
- No Caribbean country can grow wheat, or English apples, or produce commercial quantities of butter and cheese.
- There is no market for some Caricom products within the region. Unless a smelter is built, alumina from the Caribbean will have to be sold outside Caricom.
- Caricom countries often have a similar range of manufacturing industries. There would be no reason for Jamaica to buy cement from Barbados, for example, because both countries have a cement plant. Governments may want to protect their own industries, by keeping out goods from elsewhere in the region.

- Manufactured goods from outside the region may be less expensive, or better designed, or just be better known because they have established brand names. It may be hard to persuade other regional governments to put a high rate of duty on imports so as to help an industry in another Caricom country to get started.

2 Where was the most recent Heads of Government Conference held?

3 Figure 16.18 gives some information about the trade of four Caricom member states:
   (a) Which country sends the biggest *proportion* of its exports to other Caricom countries?
   (b) Which country buys the biggest *proportion* of its imports from Caricom?
   (c) What is the main commodity exported to other Caricom countries by Trinidad and Tobago?
   (d) Which of the four countries provides the biggest market for other Caricom countries?

4 Which Caricom countries produce:
   (a) Sugar? (c) Petroleum?
   (b) Bananas?

5 Which of these commodities is most likely to be traded within Caricom?

6 Antigua does not produce sugar. Should it buy from another Caricom country if lower-cost sugar from outside the grouping is also available?

7 Name two Caricom countries which have:
   (a) A brewery. (c) An oil refinery.
   (b) A flour mill.

8 How should disputes between Caricom countries be settled?

9 If one Caricom country has economic difficulties, should the others try to help it out?

10 Haiti has applied to join Caricom:
   (a) Would the organisation have to change in any way if Haiti joined?
   (b) Give one argument *for* allowing Haiti to join, and one argument *against*.

16.5 The Organisation of Eastern Caribbean States

The OECS is a grouping of the seven Caricom countries in the Windward and Leeward Islands. They are the smallest Caricom countries in population. These countries have agreed to co-operate more closely in foreign affairs, defence and security, and economic matters.

One of the most successful institutions set up by the OECS countries is the East Caribbean Central Bank. Running a central bank is a complex matter, and there would be considerable duplication of effort if each of these seven small countries attempted to set one up independently. Together, they can support a single institution, which can:

- Issue currency.
- Supervise the workings of the commercial banks and financial institutions.
- Centralise economic and financial information for the seven member countries.

The OECS countries have also set up an East Caribbean Common Market (ECCM), which aims to go further than Caricom in the field of economic integration.

The ECCM aims to:

- Abolish customs duties between member states.
- Introduce a common level of duties for goods from outside the OECS countries.
- Harmonise industrial development policies. There should be a common policy on tax incentives for outside investors, so that the islands do not try to outbid each other in this field.
- Co-operate in the field of transport and communications.
- Develop a common agricultural policy.
- Remove controls on the movement of labour and capital, so that OECS nationals can live, work, and invest in any of the member states.

Some of these aims are easy to state on paper, but difficult to achieve in practice. Significant progress has been made, but it will be some years before the ECCM is fully operational.

1 List the seven member states of the OECS.

2 Compare the aims of the ECCM and Caricom. List two similarities and one difference between the two organisations.

3 For one of the aims of the OECS or the ECCM:
   (a) Explain the objective carefully in your own words.
   (b) Explain why the objective is a desirable one.
   (c) Outline some of the steps needed to achieve the objective.

16.6 The European Community

Figure 16.20 shows the twelve member states of the European Community.

1 Name the twelve countries.
2 Find out the capital of each country.
3 What is the total population of the Community?
4 Which European countries are *not* in the Community?

In some ways, the European Community is similar to Caricom:

- There are no customs duties within the Community.
- There is a common level of customs duty for imports from outside countries.
- The Community is not merely an economic organisation. The member states work together in many other areas, too.
- The member states try to co-ordinate their foreign policy.

But there are also big differences between the two organisations:

- Most of the countries in the Community have a larger population than all the Caricom countries put together. Even countries as big as this do not have a big enough internal market to be independent car or aircraft producers without joining together.
- All the countries in the European Community are developed industrial economies. But it is also true that many parts of Portugal, Spain, Italy, and Greece were desperately poor at the time when the Community was formed; and the richest countries in Caricom have a higher average income than the poorest countries in the Community.
- The European countries do not have a common language, history, and culture. Every document and report has to be translated into nine different languages. Less than fifty years ago, most of the Community countries were at war with each other.
- In spite of this, the Community countries have given up more of their independence. There is a Council, where important decisions are made by ministers of member countries. But the affairs of the Community are managed by a Commission based in Brussels. The Commission can raise money through taxation, and can make regulations. If there is a dispute on Community matters, it is settled by the European Court in Luxembourg. Community regulations and decisions by the Court are binding for all the member states.
- There is a European Parliament in Strasbourg, in France, which is elected every five years. Parliament can dismiss the Commission, and alter or reject the Community budget.
- People who are citizens of a member state can live and work anywhere in the Community without a special permit.

The European Community is important for the Caribbean because:

- Three Caribbean territories, Martinique, Guadeloupe, and Guyane Francaise (French Guiana) are part of the Community because they are French overseas departments.
- The Community is an important trading partner for all the Caricom countries.
- The European Development Fund has financed several important projects in the Caribbean.
- All the Caricom countries, as well as Surinam, the Netherlands Antilles, and the British colonies in the region, are members of the Africa–Caribbean–Pacific group of countries which is linked to the European Community through the Lomé Convention.

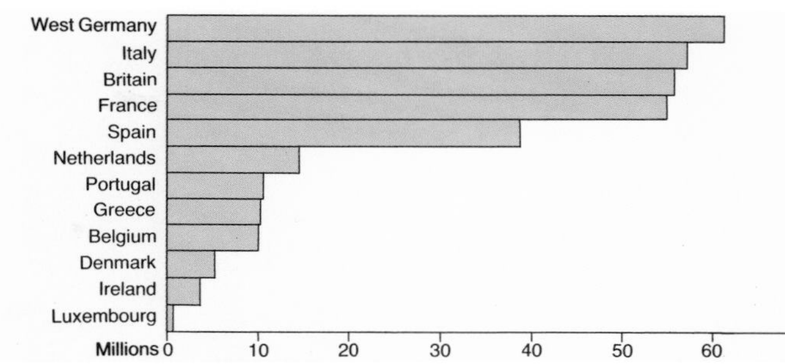

16.21 The population of the twelve EC countries.

16.20 The twelve member states of the European Community.

16.7 Some other international groupings

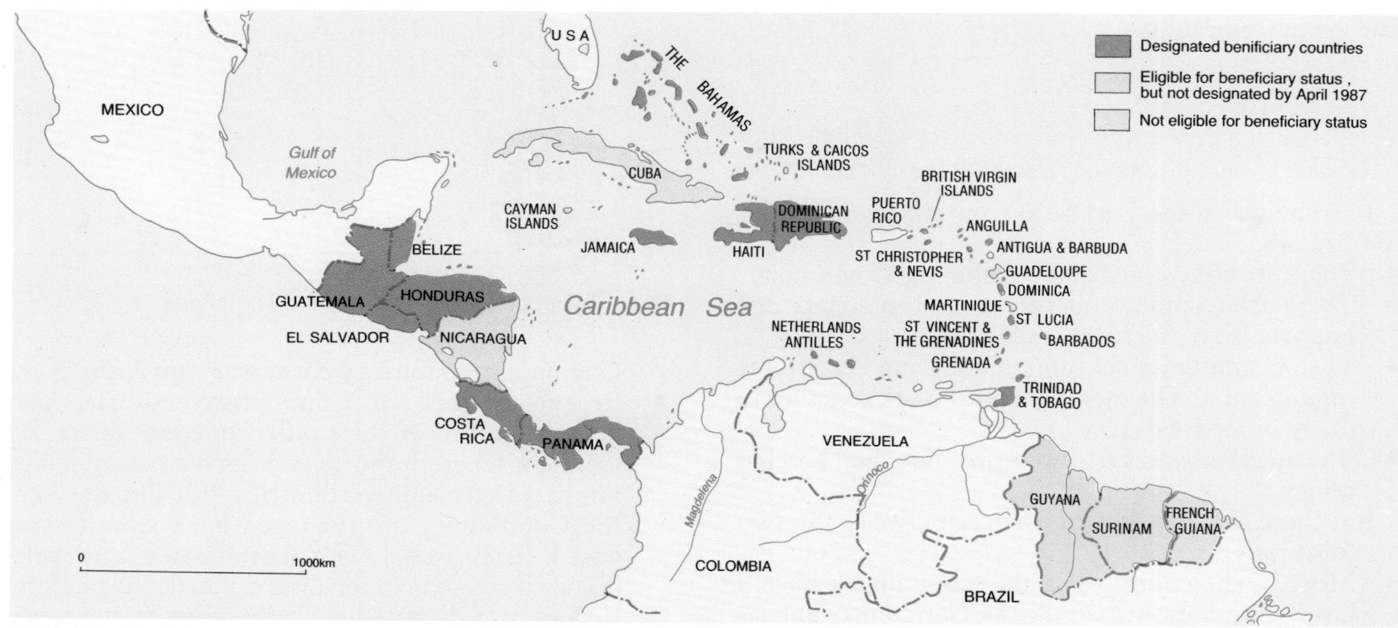

16.22 The Caribbean Basin Initiative: beneficiary countries.

The Caribbean Basin Initiative

The Caribbean Basin Initiative is not an international organisation set up by a treaty, like Caricom, the ACP grouping, or the European Community. It is a policy initiative by a major industrialised country, the USA, which aims to strengthen its links with the Caribbean.

Under the legislation governing the CBI, goods from certain countries can be imported duty-free into the US. However :

- Some manufactured goods, including clothing, textiles, and leather goods, are excluded from the provisions of the CBI. Oil is also excluded.
- Other goods are subject to *quotas* which restrict the *quantity* of exports to the US. There are quotas on items like sugar and steel.

There is no treaty governing sugar imported by the USA. The USA produces both beet sugar and cane sugar, but every year a small proportion of the sugar consumed in the USA is imported. This sugar is purchased at the USA price, which, like the EC price, is well above the level of the world market. Every year, the Caricom sugar producers and the Dominican Republic are allocated a quota, which can be sold to the USA. In 1986, the USA needed less imported sugar than before, so sugar quotas were cut by 40%. For the Dominican Republic, where sugar exports to the USA are of vital economic importance, this was a major problem.

Like the EC countries, the USA is an important source of overseas aid for the Caribbean.

5 Look at Figure 16.22:
   (a) List five designated beneficiary countries in the Caribbean and five in Central America.
   (b) List two Caribbean countries which are not eligible for beneficiary status or have not been designated.

6 List two similarities and two differences between the Caribbean Basin Initiative and the Lomé Convention.

7 Look at Figure 16.23. How successful has the CBI been in increasing exports from the beneficiary countries to the USA?

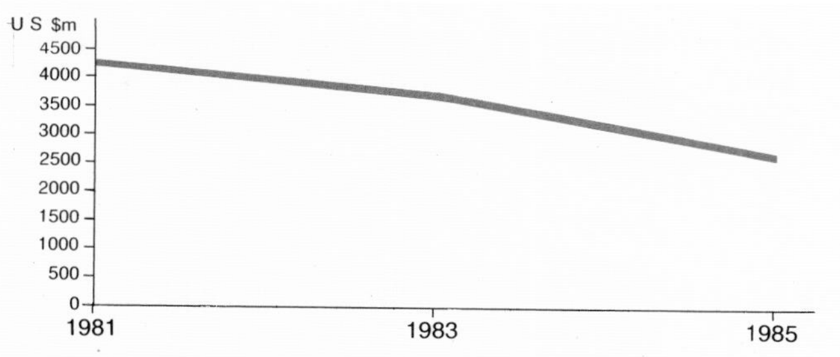

16.23 US imports from Caricom countries with beneficiary status under the CBI.

Comecon

The Council for Mutual Economic Aid (Comecon) is a grouping which includes the USSR, its east European allies, some Asian countries, and one Caribbean country, Cuba. All the members of Comecon are communist countries with centrally planned economies.

The most important economic decisions in each of these countries are taken by the Government.

Through Comecon:

- The USSR buys Cuban sugar at above the world market price.
- The USSR sells oil to Cuba for less than the world market price. Cuba can sell some of this oil to other countries at a profit.
- Cuba buys manufactured goods and raw materials, from other Comecon countries.

The ACP countries

The Lomé Convention is a treaty between the countries of the European Community and 66 African, Caribbean, and Pacific countries, most of which were once colonies of EC countries. These countries are known collectively as the ACP grouping.

Under the Lomé Convention, manufactured products from the ACP countries have duty-free access to the European market. The main exception is steel. There is too much steel-making capacity in the EC, and a quota system is in force to protect domestic producers.

There are also protocols covering trade in sugar, rum, and bananas:

- Under the sugar protocol, the EC countries buy a fixed quantity of sugar from 16 ACP countries. They pay substantially more than the world market price for this sugar. The ACP producers are paid at the same rate as the European beet sugar producers.
- Under the rum protocol, the EC countries agree to buy at least 170,000 hectolitres of rum per year. This rum is given duty-free access to the European market.
- Under the banana protocol, Caribbean countries are guaranteed access to their traditional market in the UK; at the same time, other producers are guaranteed access to traditional markets in other European countries.

The Stabex scheme is an attempt to stabilise the export earnings of ACP countries from commodities like bananas, coffee, and cocoa. When export earnings from these commodities fall, payments are made from the Stabex fund. This makes it easier for the exporters to plan ahead. However, the Stabex fund is not enough to provide complete protection for export earnings in a year when the price of many commodities is very low.

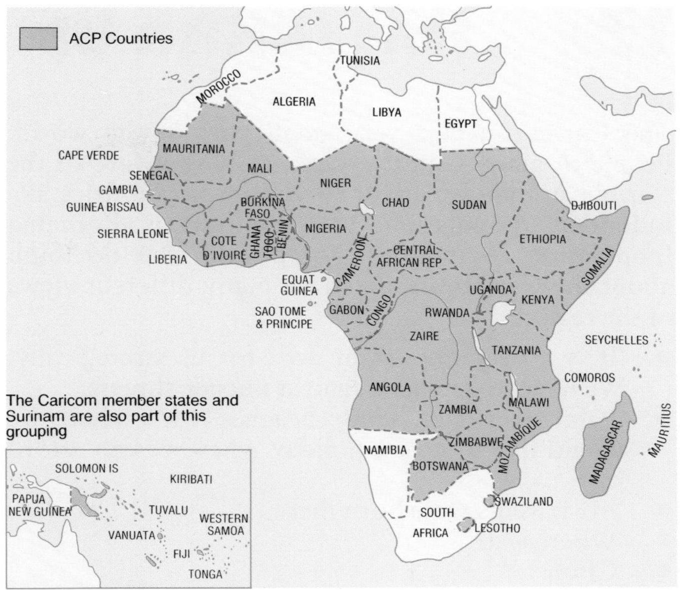

16.24 The ACP countries.

The EC countries are the main source of overseas aid to developing nations. Much of this aid is channelled through the European Development Fund. EC aid has contributed to forestry development in Guyana, banana production in Jamaica, road construction in Dominica, and the Oistins fisheries project in Barbados.

1 Look at Figure 16.24:
   (a) List four ACP members in the Caribbean.
   (b) List two Caribbean states which are *not* in the ACP grouping.
   (c) List four ACP countries in Africa and the Pacific.

17 PATTERNS OF DEVELOPMENT

The Caribbean is a very small part of the world. People in many countries are no more aware of the Caribbean than we are of conditions in countries like Indonesia (population 156 million) or Romania (population 23 million). For people who do think about the Caribbean, there are many different views of the region:

- 'It is a very important area for us strategically. We have to defend it against outside threats.'
- 'Palm trees, sun, sandy beaches – it's where we would like to go on holiday when we can afford it.'
- 'My parents were born there.'
- 'Where is it?'
- 'Cricket.'
- 'Some of the alumina we use in our smelter comes from Jamaica.'
- 'We live here.'

Within the Caribbean, people's image of the region can vary according to where they live. Figure 17.1 is a postcard from Guadeloupe.

1 Which islands have been left out?
2 Do we 'leave out' certain countries when we think about the Caribbean?
3 Mainland countries like Venezuela and Costa Rica are members of organisations like the Caribbean Conservation Association and the Caribbean Tourism Research Centre. They are on the Caribbean Sea. Are they part of the Caribbean?

17.1 The eastern Caribbean – a view from Guadeloupe.

There are also many different views about the future of the Caribbean:

- 'Worrying about wildlife and the natural environment is a luxury which rich countries can afford. For developing countries, the priority is to increase production, so that everyone can enjoy a high standard of living.'
- 'If we do not act to preserve the natural environment, it will be wrecked before we realise what is happening. Then it will be too late to put the damage right. Even if we have new cars and large houses, the *quality* of life will suffer.'
- 'Conservation is common sense, because if we do not protect our natural resources, then agriculture, tourism, and manufacturing industry will be in trouble.'
- 'The Caribbean is a group of small countries with few natural resources.'
- 'Taken as a whole, the Caribbean has a rich variety of natural resources of all types.'
- 'Traditional industries like sugar, bananas, and bauxite have run into trouble. The future for the Caribbean is in providing services like banking and tourism.'
- 'Industries based on Caribbean agricultural and mineral resources are still big foreign-exchange earners. They will continue to be important in the future.'
- 'Today's technology works best in large/scale projects. It is most suited to large factories, agricultural estates of several hundred ha, and multinational companies.'
- 'Craft industry, small-scale family farms, and small factories are vital for the Caribbean. Microcomputers and small machinery mean that they can benefit from modern technology, too.'
- 'The countries of the Caribbean are too small to be self-sufficient. They should develop very close trading links with Europe and North America, and specialise in producing goods which these countries need.'

- 'The Caribbean nations should develop closer links with the Spanish and Portuguese-speaking countries which are in many cases our nearest neighbours; and with countries in Africa and the Indian subcontinent, with which the Caribbean has a strong cultural affinity. These countries can also provide important markets for Caribbean goods.'
- 'Each Caribbean country should try to develop a wide range of manufacturing industries, and import as little food as possible. This is the only way of ensuring that independence is a reality.'
- 'The countries of the Caribbean should work together as closely as possible, even if it means giving up something in the short term. When one country is in difficulties, the others should help out.'

You should be in a better position to develop your own ideas on some of these questions than when you started your CXC geography course. But remember, these are difficult issues, and there are no simple answers. What is important is that you should:

- Be aware of the issues.
- Base your views on the *evidence* available to you.
- Keep your mind open to new evidence and fresh thinking.

4 What forms of evidence are relevant to issues like these? Make a list under the headings:
(a) First-hand evidence, from your own experience.
(b) Second-hand evidence, from other sources.

Indexes

An attempt has been made to ensure that all the skills and concepts included in the CXC General and Basic Geography syllabus have been covered in this book. These concepts are listed in abbreviated form below, together with page references to the relevant sections of text. For a full description of the syllabus content, the syllabus document published by CXC should of course be consulted.

Index to Syllabus Content

Index of Place Names

Page references in italics are to illustrations only

Oxford University Press, Walton Street, Oxford OX2 6DP

Oxford New York Toronto
Delhi Bombay Calcutta Madras Karachi
Petaling Jaya Singapore Hong Kong Tokyo
Nairobi Dar es Salaam Cape Town
Melbourne Auckland

and associated companies in
Berlin Ibadan

Oxford is a trademark of Oxford University Press

Reprinted 1990, 1991

ISBN 0 19 833445 1

The front cover photograph of the Kaieteur Falls in Guyana was supplied by the Hutchison Library.

All other photographs in this book are by the author, except for the following, for which permission to reproduce is gratefully acknowledged. Aspect Picture Library 8.7, 15.45; Peter Baker, International Photobank 10.24; Barnaby's Picture Library 12.3; Boccon & Gibod (Black Star) 4.21; Anne Bolt 13.23; British Museum of Natural History 3.10; Camera Press 12.2; Casella London 7.21; J. Allen Cash, Ltd. 3.9, 8.10, 10.23, 12.15, 13.38, 13.42, 15.45; Club Méditerranée 14.10; Sarah Errington 14.9; Frank Fournier Contact Press 3.1; Sally and Richard Greenhill 12.1; Susan Griggs Agency 13.55, 15.44; G.S.F. Picture Library 9.3; John Hillelson Agency 8.5, 15.40; Hutchison Library 8.8, 11.9, 13.40, 13.41, 14.9; ISCOTT Iron & Steel Co. Ltd. 13.30; Japan Information Centre 15.36, 15.37, 15.38; Malals, Ottawa 12.36; McIntyre Educational Media Ltd. 12.39, 12.54, 12.55; Ministry of Communications, Guyana 10.1, 10.3; Michael Mordecai 7.40; Munro (Kenneth Prater) 7.24; Nasa/ Science Photo Library 2.1; National Weather Service 7.11, 7.38; Picture Point Ltd. 13.43, 13.46; Survey Department, Jamaica 2.20; Swiss National Tourist Office 14.12; Tropix Photo Library 3.7, 4.4, 10.18, 13.52; J. S. Tynedale-Biscoe 14.6, 14.7

Editorial and design by Hart McLeod, Cambridge

Maps and diagrams by Thames Cartographic

Printed and bound in Hong Kong